1789
THE
CONSTITUTION
OF THE
UNITED STATES
OF
AMERICA
1853.

THE CONSTITUTION OF THE UNITED STATES OF AMERICA,

WITH AN ALPHABETICAL ANALYSIS;

THE DECLARATION OF INDEPENDENCE;

THE ARTICLES OF CONFEDERATION;

THE PROMINENT POLITICAL ACTS OF

GEORGE WASHINGTON;

ELECTORAL VOTES FOR ALL THE

PRESIDENTS AND VICE-PRESIDENTS;

THE HIGH AUTHORITIES AND CIVIL OFFICERS OF GOVERNMENT,

FROM MARCH 4, 1789, TO MARCH 3, 1847;

Chronological Narrative of the Several States;

AND OTHER INTERESTING MATTER;

WITH A DESCRIPTIVE ACCOUNT OF THE

STATE PAPERS, PUBLIC DOCUMENTS,

AND OTHER SOURCES OF

POLITICAL AND STATISTICAL INFORMATION

AT THE SEAT OF GOVERNMENT.

BY

W. HICKEY.

SEVENTH EDITION.

PHILADELPHIA:

1854.

STEREOTYPED BY L. JOHNSON & CO.
PHILADELPHIA.
PRINTED BY T. K. & P. G. COLLINS.

TO

THE PEOPLE,

THE CONGRESS,

THE PRESIDENT,

AND THE

Supreme Court of the United States,

THIS SIXTH EDITION OF THE CONSTITUTION

IS DEDICATED BY

W. HICKEY.

"The Constitution in its words is plain and intelligible, and it is meant for the homebred, unsophisticated understandings of our fellow-citizens."

"The people alone are the absolute owners and uncontrollable movers of such sovereignty as human beings can claim to exercise; subject to the eternal and unchangeable rules of justice, of truth, and of good Faith. The moral law is out of its reach; sovereignty cannot violate that, and be more justified than the humblest individual."

"Yield away the Constitution and the Union, and where are we? Frittered into fragments, and not able to claim one portion of the past as peculiarly our own! Our Union is not merely a blessing; it is a political necessity. We can not exist without it. I mean, that all of existence which is worth having must depart with it. Our liberties could not endure the incessant conflicts of civil and conterminous strife; our independence would be an unreal mockery, our very memories would turn to bitterness."

(*Mr. Dallas in defence of the Constitution.*)

The provision under which THIS BOOK MAY BE TRANSMITTED BY MAIL FREE OF POSTAGE, by persons having the privilege of franking public documents, is contained in "*An act to establish certain post-routes, and for other purposes*," approved 3d March, 1847, in the following words:—

"Such publications or books as have been or may be published, procured, or purchased by order of either House of Congress, or a joint resolution of the two Houses, shall be considered as public documents, and entitled to be franked as such."

In Senate of the United States.

Thursday, February 18, 1847.

Resolved, That the secretary be directed to procure for the use of the Senate two thousand copies of the authentic copy of the Constitution, with an analytical index, and compilation of other public documents, recently printed and placed in the hands of the members, provided the price shall not exceed the sum of one dollar and twenty-five cents per copy.

Resolved, That ten thousand additional copies of the authentic copy of the Constitution, with an analytical index, etc., be procured for the use of the Senate, provided they will be furnished at a deduction of twenty per cent. on the price above stated.

Friday, April 14, 1848.

Resolved, That the secretary of the Senate purchase for the use of the Senate two thousand copies of the Constitution of the United States of America, with an alphabetical analysis, prepared and published by W. Hickey, provided the same can be purchased at a price per copy not exceeding that paid for ten thousand copies ordered to be purchased by a resolution of the Senate, adopted on the 18th day of February, 1847.

Thursday, April 27, 1848.

Resolved, That the secretary of the Senate be authorized and directed to purchase one hundred copies of Hickey's edition of the Constitution of the United States, and to deliver the same, in the name of the Senate of the United States, to Mr. Alexander Vattemare, of Paris, to be distributed by him in France, according to his system of national exchanges of books.

Friday, March 2, 1849.

Resolved, That the secretary be directed to furnish each member of the present Senate, who has not already received them, one copy of the Constitution and other books ordered to be furnished to the Senators by the resolutions of February 18th, 1847, and to the Senators from Iowa, and Wisconsin, the same number of the Constitution as have been already given to other members of the Senate.

Monday, September 23, 1850.

* *Resolved*, That the secretary be directed to procure from the proprietor, for the use of the Senate, ten thousand copies of Hickey's edition of the Constitution, with an alphabetical analysis, Washington's inaugural and farewell addresses, and other important statistical matter illustrative of the genius of the American government and the developement of its principles: *Provided*, That they be furnished at the same price as those last procured for the use of the Senate.

Thursday, January 22, 1852.

Resolved, That each of the new members of the Senate be supplied with the same number and description of books as were furnished to each of the members of the Senate of the last Congress.

* N. B.—A resolution similar to this was passed by the Senate the 5th January, 1853.

PREFACE.

The Constitution, as the fireside companion of the American citizen, preserves in full freshness and vigor the recollection of the patriotic virtues and persevering courage of those gallant spirits of the Revolution who achieved the national independence, and the intelligence and fidelity of those fathers of the republic who secured, by this noble charter, the fruits and the blessings of independence. The judgment of the Senate of the United States has declared the importance of familiarizing American citizens, more extensively, with this fundamental law of their country, and has approved its association with the examples of republican virtue and the paternal advice of the "Father of his country," joined to other kindred matter, constituting the body of this work. To this honorable body is due the credit of having provided for the first general promulgation of the Constitution, the continued dissemination of whose wise injunctions and conservative principles among the people, can alone preserve their fraternal union and the precious inheritance of freedom.

That branch of the government which is clothed by the Constitution with legislative, executive and judicial powers, and thus invested with three separate authorities to preserve, protect, and defend this venerated instrument, has been pleased to take the initiative in a measure calculated so powerfully to support the Constitution, as that of *giving it,* in its simplicity and purity, to the people, who possess, themselves, the sovereign power to judge of the manner in which it may be executed, to rebuke its infraction, and to defend its integrity, and who therefore require every legitimate aid to enable them to perform this vitally important duty in justice, truth, and good faith, for "The Constitution in its words is plain and intelligible, and *it is meant* for the homebred, unsophisticated understandings of our fellow-citizens." "It is addressed to the common sense of the people."

Several distinguished authorities and individuals having, in the plenitude of their liberality, honored the author and compiler with their sentiments on the subject-matter of the work, he claims the indulgence of the friends of the Constitution in giving them place in this edition, believing, that a salutary effect may be produced by the sanction of their special approbation, and the expression of their several views of the importance of an extended dissemination of that instrument. These may impress, in terms more unexceptionable, the obligation incumbent on every intelligent citizen to make himself acquainted with its provisions, restrictions, and limitations, and of imparting, so far as the ability may extend, a knowledge of this paramount law of our country to the minds of the rising generation.

The length of time required in the ordinary course of business, for obtaining a practical knowledge of the operations of government, by persons entering into public life, and their embarrassments for the want of a convenient mode of reference to the various sources of information, have suggested the utility of preparing, as a part of this work, and as germain to its design, a means of collecting and rendering available to the public interest the experience and information acquired in this respect, in the progress of time, by attention to the business of legislation in the public service. The five new chapters in this edition may therefore be considered an essay, to be improved and extended hereafter, with a view, not only to add to the intrinsic matter proper to be read and studied by the great body of American citizens, but to render it peculiarly a *vade mecum* to the statesman and legislator, the ministering to whose individual convenience must, necessarily, result in facilitating the performance of arduous public duty, and in promoting, in no inconsiderable degree, the public interests.

COMMUNICATIONS.

FROM THE VICE PRESIDENT OF THE UNITED STATES AND PRESIDENT OF THE SENATE.

Washington, 18 Feb. 1847.

My Dear Sir,

The volume on "The Constitution of the United States," which you were kind enough to send me, I have carefully examined, and must now beg you to accept my warm thanks for the compliment of its dedication* and for the admirable character of its contents. It is, without exception, the best designed, fullest, neatest, and most accurate manual and guide in relation to the great instrument of which it exclusively treats, that I have yet seen. It deserves, and I hope it will receive, universal circulation.

The Constitution is an object to which no American mind can be too attentive, and no American heart too devoted. On parts, provisions, or phrases, it is still and always will be possible for ingenuity to raise constructive doubts: but, on the whole, as the organic chart of a limited confederated government, a practical trial of nearly sixty years would seem to place its wisdom and efficiency beyond dispute or rivalry. And, although it is not unusual to hear it said, at moments of heat and disappointment, that, in the enactment or administration of our federal laws, the obligations of the Constitution are disregarded, an observation and experience of more than thirty years convince me of the reverse; and I am satisfied that its hold upon the conscience and the opinion of the country at large is constantly

* The first and second editions.

strengthening. This is, indeed, the natural result of its perfect fitness to produce the purposes for which it was designed—union, justice, tranquillity, defence, welfare, and liberty!—and proves how well its practical operations harmonize with the business, sentiments, relations, and progress of the American people. Restless and innovating as we are in most things, we have not invaded, and I do not think we shall invade for centuries to come, the sacred stability of the Constitution.

Such a fundamental and paramount law, in the picture of its origin and in the purity of its text, should be placed within the reach of every freeman. It should be found wherever there is a capacity to read: not alone in legislative halls, judicial councils, libraries, and colleges, but also in the cabins and steerages of our mariners, at every common-school, log-hut, factory, or fireside. It should form the rudimental basis of American thought, by being made a perpetually recurring object of memory. Your book enters upon the attainment of these aims more promisingly than any of whose existence I am aware. Its "Analysis" is singularly interesting and useful; while its tabular statements and historical records constitute most valuable examples of compression and precision. The Senate of the United States, forcibly struck by its merits, gave their cordial sanction to its extensive dissemination; and, indeed, it would be hard, if not impossible, to devise a better mode of enlightening and purifying public opinion as to the necessary powers, duties, and responsibilities of all the functionaries of the General Government, the limits of their agency, and the conciliatory spirit of the vast system to which they belong.

I am, dear Sir, very truly,

Your friend and servant,

G. M. Dallas.

Wm. Hickey, Esq.

FROM THE SPEAKER OF THE HOUSE OF REPRESENTATIVES OF THE UNITED STATES.

Washington City, Feb'y 19, 1847.

Dear Sir,

I have to thank you for a very neatly published copy of the Constitution of the United States. So far as I have examined the form in which the publication is made, it is decidedly the most perfect of any I have ever seen. The various and valuable information contained in your book—other than the Constitution—is of great value. The whole work is just such an one as ought to be found in the library of every citizen in the country.

Very respectfully, your ob't serv't,

Jno. W. Davis.

Wm. Hickey, Esq.

FROM THE CHIEF JUSTICE OF THE SUPREME COURT OF THE UNITED STATES.

Washington, March 3, 1847.

Sir,

I am directed by the Justices of the Supreme Court to thank you for your edition of the Constitution of the United States, which you have been good enough to send them, and to express their approbation of the manner in which the work has been executed. The care with which it has been compared with the original, and the evidence you have furnished of its perfect accuracy, will make it very valuable in the discussion of questions arising upon the construction of the Constitution; and, in order that, on such occasions, it may always be within the reach of the members of the court, and of the bar engaged in the argument, I shall direct the Librarian to purchase twenty-four copies for the Law Library.

With great respect, I am, Sir, your obed't s't,

R. B. Taney

W. Hickey, Esq., Washington.

FROM JUDGE WAYNE, ASSOCIATE JUSTICE OF THE SUPREME COURT OF THE UNITED STATES.

Supreme Court-room, March 3, 1847.

Dear Sir,

I am very much obliged to you for your edition of the Constitution, and will not, hereafter, use any other. All of us are much indebted to you.

Permit me to make a suggestion.* It is, that you would add to the edition, intended for distribution by the Senate, a statement of the times when the Constitution was adopted by the states, and when new states have been admitted; particularly designating, in the last, such of them as have been admitted upon constitutions formed before there had been any original action by Congress for admitting them. For reference it would be useful in many discussions, and has not been made, so far as I can find, by any one.

I am, dear Sir, with great regard,

Your obed't serv't,

James M. Wayne.

W. Hickey, Esq., Washington.

FROM THE CHIEF JUSTICE OF THE SUPREME COURT OF PENNSYLVANIA.

Philadelphia, 3d March, 1847.

Sir,

I have attentively perused a recent edition of the Federal Constitution, with a well-digested analysis and other matter appended, "by a citizen;"† and, it gives me pleasure to say, the compilation is, not only a convenient book of reference, but an

* In compliance with this friendly suggestion of Judge Wayne, the author has derived much satisfaction in devoting to it the entire 10th chapter of this edition.

† The first edition of this book.

invaluable compendium of political statistics for every day's use. The arrangement is an excellent one. In the United States, it is the duty of every man to take a part in the political movements of the day, and the book ought therefore to be in the hands of the masses: in Pennsylvania, it ought to be a text-book in the common schools. The compiler is personally unknown to me, but I am happy to give my testimony in favour of the merits of his production.

With great respect, Sir,

Your obedient servant,

Col. Hickey. *John B. Gibson.*

FROM THE JUDGE OF THE DISTRICT COURT OF THE UNITED STATES FOR THE EASTERN DISTRICT OF PENNSYLVANIA.

Dear Sir,

I have looked through the little volume which has been prepared, as I understand, under your charge, and I have really been surprised to find, in so compact a form, so many important subjects of constant reference.

The analytical index of topics embraced in the Federal Constitution is well devised, and, so far as I have tested its accuracy, bears proofs of care and skill. The several documents and tables, which form the rest of the book, are judiciously selected from numerous volumes, which are not generally accessible, and they present a series of annals of the Constitution, from the first movement towards its formation, in 1786.

I am obliged to you for the copy which has been sent to me, and shall, no doubt, have frequent use for it.

Very respectfully, yours,

J. K. Kane

Col. Hickey.

Philad. 3 Mar. 1847.

FROM THE HONORABLE SIDNEY BREESE, SENATOR OF THE UNITED STATES.

Washington, March 6, 1847.

My dear Sir,

I have examined, with great care, your edition of the Constitution of the United States, and I must be permitted to express my approval of the plan and of the merits of the work. I do hope it will have a very extensive demand—that the state legislatures will patronize it, and that its circulation may be co-extensive with the limits of our Union. It is a lamentable fact, that the Constitution of the United States—that most honored work of the patriots and sages of the Revolution—has not yet had a general circulation. I hope it may be introduced into our schools, academies, and all our seminaries of learning, and studied to be understood. You, sir, are entitled to great credit for the care and ability you have shown in preparing the present edition. I hope you and the country will profit by it.

Y'rs, very truly,

Col. W. Hickey. Sidney Breese.

FROM THE CHIEF JUSTICE OF THE CIRCUIT COURT OF THE UNITED STATES FOR THE DISTRICT OF COLUMBIA.

Washington, D. C., Ap. 8, 1847.

Wm. Hickey, Esq.

Dear Sir,

I am requested by my brethren on the bench of the Circuit Court of the District of Columbia to thank you for your new and corrected edition of the Constitution of the United States, which you have kindly sent to them, and for the valuable statistic information annexed to it; and especially for the laborious and very particular analysis which you have made of the Constitution, and for the correction of the errors in punctuation, as well as in the text, which you have discovered in the former editions.

The Judges have not had time to examine the text very carefully; but, from the partial examination they have had time to make, and the great care with which your copy has been compared with the original in the Department of State, they believe it to be the most correct copy extant, and they have no doubt it will be useful to all classes of society.

With great respect, I am, D'r Sir,

Your obed't serv't,

W. Cranch.

FROM THE HONORABLE SILAS WRIGHT, LATE GOVERNOR OF NEW YORK—FORMERLY SENATOR IN CONGRESS.

Canton, 9 April, 1847.

My dear Sir,

I thank you for the copy of your edition of the Constitution of the United States, with your copious index. The design, and the manner of its execution, are alike creditable to you, and I anticipate a wide circulation of the little volume, and great usefulness to our free institutions from it.

Many of the editions of the Constitution of the United States, in most common circulation, are very carelessly printed, with frequent erroneous punctuation, often increasing the doubts as to the true construction of the paragraphs. An edition, therefore, known to be correctly published, is of great value.

Your copious analytical index, however, constitutes the real value of your book. If studied faithfully, and by an unbiassed mind, it will lead it to read the Constitution practically, and to understand it as it is. Referring, as the analysis does, every provision and clause to its practical application in the affairs of the government, it cannot fail to have a natural and powerful tendency towards a strict construction of the instrument in the mind of the scholar,—the only construction of the Constitution safe to our free institutions and to the Constitution itself.

No one, familiar with the affairs of our government, can have failed to notice how large a proportion of our statesmen appear never to have read the Constitution of the United States with a careful reference to its precise language and exact provisions, but rather, as occasion presents, seem to exercise their ingenuity, unfortunately too often powerful and powerfully exerted, to stretch both to the line of what they, at the moment, consider expedient. A reference to a careful, perfect, and full analysis of that instrument, and of the grants of power really found in it, cannot fail to exert a strong and salutary influence upon such minds.

It is, however, upon the mind of the student and the rising generation of our country that I anticipate the widely extended useful influence of your book. If it shall be, as I hope it may, introduced as a class-book in our schools, it cannot fail soon to produce a more sound and correct and uniform understanding of the Constitution as it is, than has hitherto prevailed in our country.

It has long been a favorite wish of mine, as to this state, that our public laws of universal interest may be, by our Legislature, distributed to our common schools in a form to be made a class-book for the more advanced scholars, that the current legislation of the state may be early and thoroughly understood by those who are to be the voters of the state.

Your book suggests the addition of the Constitution of the State, with a full index, such as that you have prepared for the Federal Constitution, as a permanent class-book to precede the study of the current laws; and, if your Constitution and the laws of Congress of a general character and universal public interest could be connected with the course of study, I do not know any thing that would go so far soundly to qualify our young men to become freemen, and to discharge the duties of freemen at the polls of our elections so safely to their country and creditably to themselves.

I sincerely hope the publication of your book may lead the way to some such valuable addition to the education of the young men of the republic.

My leisure has not permitted me to examine your index in all its parts as carefully as the subject demands, but the examinations I have made, together with my knowledge of your accustomed accuracy, and invariable fidelity of intention, induce me to speak with the confidence I do of the whole work. The matter you have connected with the publication of the Constitution is pertinent, and such as the young student of the instrument ought to be made familiar with, while the lessons of wisdom from the Father of his Country will consecrate the whole to his memory and his heart.

With the repetition of my thanks for the copy of this work, believe me, Very respectfully, and truly, yours,

William Hickey, Esq. Silas Wright.

FROM THE HONORABLE JOHN MACPHERSON BERRIEN, SENATOR OF THE UNITED STATES.

Rockingham, 28th Sept., 1847.

Dear Sir,

I examined the copy of "The Constitution" which you sent to me on its first publication, and then expressed to you the favorable opinion which I entertained of the work, from its neatness, its accuracy, and its comprehensiveness. Of the importance of its distribution among all classes of our citizens, I think no one can doubt. It is the fundamental law, that which controls all others—the charter of our liberties, which every citizen has a personal interest in understanding thoroughly. I would be gratified, therefore, to know that every citizen was possessed of a copy of it, and had made himself familiar with its contents, by frequent and careful perusals of it. This would make him more perfectly comprehend his own position as a citizen of this great Republic; it would enable him to realize more cordially the intimate relation in which he stands to every other citizen; and thus its tendency would be to draw closer the fraternal bond which unites us as one people. He would become sensible how much the intelligence and virtue of each individual may promote the happiness of his fellows, and of the corresponding and unhappy influence of ignorance and vice; and this conviction would render him the advocate of all proper measures to enlarge the intelligence, and improve the morals, of those with whom he is politically associated. A knowledge of the Constitution, which is for the most part plain and simple in its provisions, would often enable him to spurn indignantly the efforts of demagogues to mislead him, and awaken him to a deeper sense of gratitude for the privileges which he is permitted to enjoy.

It would, in my opinion, be desirable that such a copy of the Constitution as that which you have prepared, should be in possession of each judicial tribunal throughout the land, as a standard to which reference may be had with undoubting confidence, in cases which involve questions of Constitutional law. But I would especially desire to see it introduced as a text-book in our schools and colleges, that our young men may be taught to know their rights, and to become acquainted with their duties, as citizens, before they engage in the employments of active life.

As a citizen of the United States, I thank you for the benefit which you have conferred upon the community by this compilation, and you have my best wishes that your labors may be amply remunerated. I am, dear sir, very resp'y, &c.

Col. Hickey. *Jno. Macpherson Berrien.*

FROM THE HON. HENRY CLAY, SENATOR OF THE UNITED STATES.

Washington, September, 1850.

Dear Sir,

Understanding that you intend to publish a fourth edition of the volume, compiled and prepared by you, containing the Constitution of the United States, and other highly useful and interesting matter, I take pleasure in expressing the satisfaction I have derived from an examination of the work. You have displayed judgment in the materials which it embodies, and in the order with which they have been arranged. Your residence at the city of Washington, and in one of the public offices, has afforded you an opportunity of access to the original text of the Constitution, and to the other documents and records contained in your volume, of which you appear to have assiduously availed yourself. Your work, therefore, deserves perfect confidence in its entire authenticity.

There are so many and such obvious reasons in favor of this book being extensively circulated, and in the hands of every citizen who can conveniently afford to purchase it, that I cannot doubt the existence of a constant and large demand for it. And citizens who are going abroad, and foreigners who are coming among us, would all do well to obtain possession of a book which comprises, within a small compass, the record of so many important National events and National transactions.

It is scarcely necessary to add an expression of my wishes that you may obtain a liberal patronage from the public, so richly merited for your labors.

I am respectfully,

Your obed't. servant,

H. Clay.

Col. W. Hickey.

FROM THE HON. LEWIS CASS, SENATOR OF THE UNITED STATES.

Detroit, November 15, 1850.

Dear Sir,

At your request I have carefully examined, and do not hesitate to give my opinion of the value of, your edition of the Constitution, though it is a work which does not need any testimonial of mine to its merits, nor will the expression of my judgment commend it the more to public favor. It is a monument of care, and labor, and accuracy, and may safely depend upon its own intrinsic claims, without calling to its aid any adventitious circumstances whatever. The voice of the country and the repeated orders of the Senate for its publication and distribution, are equally honorable to the character of the work, and to the ability and fidelity of the author. Its scrupulous accuracy, its analytical investigations, and the compression of the important historical facts which preceded and attended the proceedings of the Convention, and which marked the progress of the adoption of the Constitution, through all the stages of doubt and anxiety, till the final and happy consummation, have already received the approbation of several eminent men, whose letters are contained in the former edition. But if ever there was a period in the history of our country, which called upon us to look back upon the blessings which the Constitution has brought, and upon the difficulties it encountered before it received the sanction of the American States and people, that period is upon us. If we were now separated, as we were in 1787, no mortal power could bring us together. Whether, with all the experience of our dangers and our blessings, we can be kept together, must depend upon the spirit with which we come up to the work. Whether the feelings of concession and compromise which animated our fathers will continue to animate their sons, or enough of them, to preserve and perpetuate this precious heritage, acquired by services and sufferings which are written in our past history, and may find equal examples of national calamity in the future, should this confederation be broken up, is the great question of the day, which events are fast hastening to a solution, under circumstances as imposing as they are portentous.

Your reference to the practice of Rome and to that of the mediaeval ages in England, where the diffusion of the knowledge of their respective Constitutions, especially among the youth, was one of the cares of the government, furnishes an important lesson, which cannot be too strongly commended to the public attention. The Constitution should be a school-book, made familiar to us from our earliest years. Its principles, its provisions, its limitations, should be studied and understood, and the more they are studied the better will they be appreciated and the dearer they will become. I should be glad to see your edition of the Constitution in every school-house in the Union, and my colleague and myself are so impressed with the importance of this suggestion, that we intend to distribute all the copies we receive, among the school libraries of Michigan.

I am, dear sir,

Respectfully, your obed't serv't,

Lewis Cass

William Hickey, Esq.
Washington.

FROM THE HON. DANIEL WEBSTER, SECRETARY OF STATE OF THE UNITED STATES.

Washington, December 11th, 1850.

Dear Sir,

Understanding that you are about to publish a fourth Edition of the Book of the Constitution, I take pleasure in expressing my belief that the extensive distribution of that volume is of public and general importance.

The Constitution of the United States is a written Instrument; a recorded fundamental Law; it is the *Bond*, and the only *Bond*, of the *Union* of these States; it is all that gives us *a National* character.

Almost every man in the country is capable of reading it; and that which so deeply concerns all, should be made easily accessible to all. Your publication, I think, is better calculated to accomplish this end, than any which has preceded it.

Yours with very true regard,

Daniel Webster

William Hickey, Esq.

INTRODUCTORY REMARKS.

JAMES MADISON, President of the United States, on entering upon the duties of the office, declared, that "to support the Constitution, which is the cement of the Union, as well in its limitations as in its authorities, and *to favor the advancement of science and the diffusion of information*, as the best aliment to true liberty," with other salutary sentiments and intentions, would be a resource which could not fail him; and added, "but the source to which I look for the aid which alone can supply my deficiencies, is the well-tried *intelligence* and virtue of my fellow-citizens, and in the counsels of those representing them in the other departments associated in the care of the national interests."

"To *support* the Constitution" by his talents, by his best services, and with his life, if required, is the firm and irrevocable determination of every true patriot; but the "support" presupposes a *knowledge* of that valued instrument; and the knowledge can alone be expected to follow a careful reading and study of its letter and its spirit. To afford an opportunity to every American citizen to do this, is the object in the publication of the present edition.

If, as Cicero informs us, in ancient Rome the very boys were obliged to learn the twelve tables by heart, as a *carmen necessarium*, or indispensable lesson, to imprint on their tender minds an early knowledge of the laws and constitution of their country,

"Nocturna versate manu, versate diurna."

If it was deemed important to the preservation of British liberty, in the earlier and better days of that country, that *Magna Charta* should be authoritatively promulgated and read to the people—it is no less important to the preservation of American liberty, that every intelligent citizen should, *by his own will and authority*, aided by the liberality of the Government, possess a copy of this *great charter of American liberty.*

There appears to have been no formal provision made by the Government of the United States for the promulgation of the Constitution, except by a concurrent resolution of the two Houses of Congress, made during the first Congress, (6th July, 1789,) whereby it was "Resolved, that there be prefixed to the publication of the acts of the present session of Congress a correct copy of the Constitution of Government for the United States." This, however, was sufficient to show the intention and the judgment of the *Patres Patriæ* upon the subject.

Every good citizen, capable of reading and understanding its meaning, is bound by duty to his country, if in his power, to possess a copy of the Constitution. The compiler of this publication has added the Declaration of Independence, with invaluable matter claiming paternity of the "Father of his country," and other interesting information, and has so limited the cost of this *Constitutional bouquet*, as to enable the Government, should such be its pleasure, by a judicious and liberal investment in this provident stock—to lay up, for a time of need, a vast fund of available treasure in the minds and the hearts of the people, for the defence of their liberties and the perpetuity of their institutions—to sow the good seed in virgin soil, which might otherwise be occupied by noxious weeds. With diffidence it is submitted, that this *national object* may be practically effected by the distribution of barely so many copies as may place one in each village or neighborhood, which would introduce it to the knowledge of the people, who would then seek by their own means to possess it; and thus as a mustard seed would it multiply, and its salutary principles be extended. Nor could any means more convenient be proposed, than to intrust to the hands of the guardians of the Constitution in Congress the distribution, or the sowing of this good seed. It would appear from the tables of the last census, that there are, in the

United States, upwards of three and a half millions of men, over twenty years of age, capable of reading; and should there be only one copy furnished by the Government to every hundred men, a large portion of the other ninety-nine would, probably, by their own means, obtain it.

Viewing the immense diffusion of printed political matter through all the villages and hamlets of the Republic, as the abundance of material provided by the generosity of the Government and zeal of private enterprise, as political food for the mind, this compilation may be considered as *salt* for the preservation of such as may be wholesome, or as *lime* to neutralize and destroy such as may be carious. It would be a test by which to separate the wheat from the tares and cockle—a crucible by which to separate the gold from the dross and base metal, or the cupel by which to try the current coin of politics, and *a text book by which to judge of the orthodoxy of political disquisitions.*

By the British statute, "*confirmatio cartarum,*" the great charter was directed "to be allowed as the common law; all judgments contrary to it are declared void: *copies of it are ordered to be sent to all cathedral churches, and read twice a year to the people;*" whereby it was intended that the sanctity of the place should inspire a peculiar veneration for that noble structure of fundamental law—sacred to human liberty, civil and religious.

According to Plato and Aristotle, "*Lex est mens sine affectu, et quasi Deus,*"—*the law is mind without passion, and therefore like God.* Or, according to Grotius, "God approved and ratified the salutary constitutions of government made by men;" while Demosthenes declares, that "the design and object of laws is to ascertain what is just, honorable, and expedient; and when that is discovered, it is proclaimed as a general ordinance, equal and impartial to all. This is the origin of law, which, for various reasons, all are under an obligation to obey, but especially because all law is the invention and gift of *Heaven*, the resolution of wise men, the correction of every offence, and the general compact of the State, to live in conformity with which is the duty of every individual in society."

Bossuet remarks, that "If the Roman laws have appeared so sacred, that their majesty still subsists, notwithstanding the ruin of the empire, it is because good sense, which controls human life, reigns throughout the whole, and that there is nowhere to be found a finer application of the principles of natural equity."

Algernon Sidney adds, that "The Israelites, Spartans, Romans, and others, who framed their governments according to their own will, did it not by any peculiar privilege, but by a universal right conferred upon them by God and nature. They were made of no better clay than others; they had no right that does not as well belong to other nations; that is to say, the Constitution of every government is referred to those who are concerned in it, and no other has any thing to do with it."—

"Salus populi est lex suprema."

Judge Blackstone remarks, that "every man, when he enters into society, gives up a part of his natural liberty, as the price of so valuable a purchase; and, in consideration of receiving the advantages of mutual commerce, obliges himself to conform to those laws which the community has thought proper to establish. And this species of legal obedience and conformity is infinitely more desirable than that wild and savage liberty which is sacrificed to obtain it. For no man, that considers a moment, would wish to retain the absolute and uncontrolled power of doing whatever he pleases; the consequence of which is, that every other man would also have the same power, and then there would be no security to individuals in any of the enjoyments of life. Political, therefore, or civil liberty, which is that of a member of society, is no other than natural liberty, so far restrained by human laws (and no farther) as is necessary and expedient for the general advantage of the public. Hence, we may collect that the law, which restrains a man from doing mischief to his fellow-citizens, though it diminishes the natural, increases the civil liberty of mankind. And Locke has well observed, "*where there is no law there is no freedom.*"

Socrates made a promise, with himself, to observe the laws of his country; but this is nothing more than what every good man ought both to promise and to perform: and he ought to promise still further, that he will exert all his power, when constitutionally called upon, to compel others to obey them.

The compiler of this edition of *our own* venerated Constitution, to which he has with anxious labor prefixed a copious, and, he trusts, a faithful analytical index, believes that there are among his fellow-citizens many thousands of intelligent men capable of reading and understanding the great American charter of liberty, but who, without seeing and judging for themselves of "its limitations and its authorities," have, with a passive credulity, (which in other matters of comparative insignificance, would have been indignantly spurned,) reposed their faith, their birthright, and their safety, on the opinions of others, whose impassioned, and sometimes vituperative tones have appealed rather to the prejudices of the heart than to the integrity of the understanding.

Mr. Dallas has well said, that "*the Constitution in its words is plain and intelligible, and it is meant for the homebred, unsophisticated understandings of our fellow-citizens.*" To this sentiment, the compiler is indebted for suggesting to his mind the idea of publishing this edition of the Constitution, with its accompaniments; and he therefore believed that there would be propriety and justice in the dedication of it to this distinguished statesman, and through him to the American people.*

The compiler, diffident of his own ability to do adequate justice to the subject, has called to his aid some of the most eminent authorities to sustain the inviolable sanctity of the law, and to impress upon Americans a reverential attachment to the Constitution, as in the highest sense the palladium of American liberty; so that their judgment, as well as their affections, may be enlisted on the side of the Constitution, as the truest security of the Union, and the only solid basis on which to rest the private rights, the public liberties, and the substantial prosperity of the people composing the American Republic.

He will next have recourse to the authority of the universally esteemed and lamented Justice Story, as to the high responsibilities of the people, and the proper means of guarding the inestimable

* The 1st and 2d editions were dedicated to Mr. Dallas, and the 3d and subsequent editions, with his permission, to the people, &c.

rights they now enjoy. In reference to the Constitution of government he says: "It must perish, if there be not that vital spirit in the people, which alone can nourish, sustain, and direct all its movements. It is in vain that statesmen shall form plans of government, in which the beauty and harmony of a republic shall be embodied in visible order, shall be built up on solid substructions, and adorned by every useful ornament, if the inhabitants suffer the silent power of time to dilapidate its walls, or crumble its massy supporters into dust; if the assaults from without are never resisted, and the rottenness and mining from within are never guarded against. Who can preserve the rights and liberties of the people, when they shall be abandoned by themselves? Who shall keep watch in the temple, when the watchmen sleep at their posts? Who shall call upon the people to redeem their possessions, and revive the republic, when their own hands have deliberately and corruptly surrendered them to the oppressor, and have built the prisons or dug the graves of their own friends? This dark picture, it is to be hoped, will never be applicable to the Republic of America. And yet it affords a warning, which, like all the lessons of past experience, we are not permitted to disregard. America, free, happy, and enlightened as she is, must rest the preservation of her rights and liberties upon the virtue, independence, justice, and sagacity of the people. If either fail, the republic is gone. Its shadow may remain with all the pomp, and circumstance, and trickery of government, but its vital power will have departed. In America, the demagogue may arise as well as elsewhere. He is the natural, though spurious growth of republics; and, like the courtier, he may, by his blandishments, delude the ears and blind the eyes of the people to their own destruction. If ever the day shall arrive, in which the best talents and the best virtues shall be driven from office by intrigue or corruption, by the ostracism of the press, or the still more unrelenting persecution of party, legislation will cease to be national. It will be wise by accident, and bad by system."

"In every human society," says the celebrated *Beccaria*, "there is an effort continually tending to confer on one part the height of power and happiness, and to reduce the other to the extreme of weakness and misery. The intent of good laws is to oppose this effort, and to diffuse their influence universally and equally;" and Montesquieu declares that, "In a free state, every man, who is supposed a free agent, ought to be concerned in his own government; therefore *the legislative power* should reside in the whole body of the people, or their representatives. The political liberty of the citizen is a tranquillity of mind, arising from the opinion each person has of his safety. In order to have this liberty, it is requisite the government be so constituted, as that one man need not be afraid of another. *The enjoyment of liberty, and even its support and preservation, consists in every man's being allowed to speak his thoughts, and lay open his sentiments.*"

The compiler will next propose to his fellow-citizens the advice of a profound philosopher, as to the proper mode of preserving the independence of the mind, which is alike applicable to every free-born American citizen, and points out the means by which the native talent, the integrity of heart, and the indomitable spirit of the people, guided by patriotism, will be rendered available in the preservation of the purity of the government, and of their own liberties. It is submitted, that a copy of this edition of the Constitution be in the possession of every citizen capable of reading and understanding the meaning of language, before whom the following instructions of Locke would then be placed:

"Reading is for the improvement of the understanding."

"The improvement of the understanding is for two ends: first, for our own increase of knowledge; secondly, to enable us to deliver and make out that knowledge to others."

"I hope it will not be thought arrogance to say, that perhaps we should make greater progress in the discovery of rational and contemplative knowledge, if we sought it in the fountain—in the consideration of things themselves—and made use rather of our own thoughts than other men's to find it; for I think we may as rationally hope to see with other men's eyes, as to know by other men's understandings. So much as we ourselves consider and comprehend of truth and reason, so much we possess of real and true knowledge. The floating of other men's opinions in our brains makes us not one jot the more knowing, though they happen to be true. What in them was science, is in us but opiniatrety; whilst we give up our assent only to reverend names, and do not, as they did, employ our own reason to understand those truths which gave them reputation. Aristotle was certainly a knowing man, but nobody ever thought him so, because he blindly embraced, or confidently vented, the opinions of another. And if the taking up another's principles, without examining them, made not him a philosopher, I suppose it will hardly make anybody else so. In the sciences, every one has so much as he really knows and comprehends; what he believes only, and takes upon trust, are but shreds, which, however well in the whole piece, make no considerable addition to his stock who gathers them. Such borrowed wealth, like fairy money, though it were gold in the hand from which he received it, will be but leaves and dust when it comes to use."

"How many men have no other ground for their tenets than the supposed honesty, or learning, or number, of those of the same profession. As if honest or bookish men could not err, or truth were to be established by the vote of the multitude; yet this, with most men, serves the turn."

"All men are liable to error, and most men are, in many points, by passion or interest, under temptation to it. If we could but see the secret motives that influenced the men of name and learning in the world, and the leaders of parties, we should not always find that it was the embracing of truth, for its own sake, that made them espouse the doctrines they owned and maintained. This at least is certain, there is not an opinion so absurd which a man may not receive upon this ground. There is no error to be named, which has not had its professors; and a man shall never want crooked paths to walk in, if he thinks that he is in the right way wherever he has the footsteps of others to follow."

It is not hence to be inferred, however, that the opinions and the judgment of the wise and the good are to be disregarded, and more especially are we not permitted to treat with irreverence the political doctrines and maxims of the fathers of the republic, whose wisdom and counsel, and devoted patriotism, gave being to the Declaration of our independence and the Constitution of our country. In the fundamental principles of our Government, on what can the

American mind and faith repose with as much confidence and safety as the expositions contained in the "Federalist, an incomparable commentary of three of the greatest statesmen of their age," in the extraordinary judgments of the supreme judicial tribunal, and the solid wisdom embodied in the constitutional commentaries of those who have imparted dignity and purity to the moral ermine which ornaments that august tribunal?

Nor can the American people look to any source more entitled to their confidence, for an exposition of the essential principles of our Government, and, consequently, those which ought to shape its administration, than to the farewell address of the "Father of his country," (contained in this compilation,) and to the principles proclaimed by the "Fathers" of the memorable Declaration and of the immortal Constitution, when respectively "called upon to undertake the duties of the first executive office of our country."

Thomas Jefferson declared those principles to be—"Equal and exact justice to all men, of whatever state or persuasion, religious or political; for having banished from our land that religious intolerance under which mankind so long bled and suffered, we have yet gained little, if we countenance a political intolerance, as despotic, as wicked, and capable of as bitter and bloody persecutions; peace, commerce, and honest friendship with all nations, entangling alliances with none; the support of the State governments in all their rights, as the most competent administrations for our domestic concerns, and the surest bulwarks against anti-republican tendencies; the preservation of the General Government in its whole constitutional vigor, as the sheet-anchor of our peace at home and safety abroad; a jealous care of the right of election by the people; a mild and safe corrective of abuses which are lopped by the sword of revolution, where peaceful remedies are unprovided; absolute acquiescence in the decisions of the majority, the vital principle of republics, from which is no appeal but to force, the vital principle and immediate parent of despotism; a well-disciplined militia, our best reliance in peace and for the first moments of war, till regulars may relieve them; the supremacy of the civil over the military authority; economy in the public expense, that labor may be lightly burthened; the honest payment of our debts, and sacred preservation of the public faith; encouragement of agriculture, and of commerce as its handmaid; the diffusion of information, and arraignment of all abuses at the bar of the public reason; freedom of religion; freedom of the press; and freedom of person under the protection of the habeas corpus; and trial by juries impartially selected. These principles form the bright constellation which has gone before us, and guided our steps through an age of revolution and reformation. The wisdom of our sages, and blood of our heroes, have been devoted to their attainment: they should be the creed of our political faith; the text of civic instruction; the touchstone by which to try the services of those we trust; and should we wander from them in moments of error or of alarm, let us hasten to retrace our steps, and to regain the road which alone leads to peace, liberty, and safety."

James Madison, equally pursuing the principles of the Constitution, declared the purposes of Government to be:

"To cherish peace and friendly intercourse with all nations having correspondent dispositions; to maintain sincere neutrality towards belligerent nations; to prefer, in all cases, amicable discussion and reasonable accommodation of differences, to a decision of them by an appeal to arms; to exclude foreign intrigues, and foreign partialities, so degrading to all countries, and so baneful to free ones; to foster a spirit of independence, too just to invade the rights of others, too proud to surrender our own, too liberal to indulge unworthy prejudices ourselves, and too elevated not to look down upon them in others; to hold the union of the States as the basis of their peace and happiness; to support the Constitution, which is the cement of the Union, as well in its limitations as in its authorities; to respect the rights and authorities reserved to the States, and to the people, as equally incorporated with, and essential to the success of, the general system; to avoid the slightest interference with the rights of conscience, or the functions of religion, so wisely exempted from civil jurisdiction; to preserve, in their full energy, the other salutary provisions in behalf of private and personal rights, and of the freedom of the press; to observe economy in public expenditures; to liberate the public resources by an honorable discharge of the public debts; to keep within the requisite limits a standing military force, always remembering that an armed and trained militia is the firmest bulwark of republics—that without standing armies their liberty can never be in danger, nor with large ones safe; to promote, by authorized means, improvements friendly to agriculture, to manufactures, and to external as well as internal commerce; to favor, in like manner, the advancement of science and the diffusion of information, as the best aliment to true liberty; to carry on the benevolent plans which have been so meritoriously applied to the conversion of our aboriginal neighbors from the degradation and wretchedness of savage life, to a participation of the improvements of which the human mind and manners are susceptible in a civilized state. As far as sentiments and intentions such as these can aid the fulfilment of my duty, they will be a resource which cannot fail me. But the source to which I look for the aids which alone can supply my deficiencies, is in the well-tried intelligence and virtue of my fellow-citizens, and in the counsels of those representing them in the other departments associated in the care of the national interests. In these, my confidence will, under every difficulty, be best placed, next to that which we have all been encouraged to feel in the guardianship and guidance of that Almighty Being whose power regulates the destiny of nations, whose blessings have been so conspicuously dispensed to this rising republic, and to whom we are bound to address our devout gratitude for the past, as well as our fervent supplications and best hopes for the future."

The citizens of these United States were blessed with the virtue, the fortitude, and the perseverance to achieve their independence as a nation; their patriotism and valor, both by sea and on land, brought them, with increased honor, through the "second war of independence," and through all the trials and difficulties by which they have, from time to time, been environed, both as respects their foreign and domestic relations; and it is only necessary for them to have "*light*" as regards the fundamental law, and the operations of the Government, to enable them to judge of the fidelity of those whom they periodically intrust with the power which alone belongs to themselves as a nation of freemen, the proper use and application of which power is so vitally necessary to the preservation of their

3*

own liberties and best interests, and the perpetuity of our institutions.

"Light, true light in the mind," says Locke, "is or can be nothing else but the evidence of the truth of any proposition; and if it be not a self-evident proposition, all the light it has, or can have, is from the clearness and validity of those *proofs* upon which it is received. To talk of any other *light* in the understanding, is to put ourselves in the *dark*, or in the power of the Prince of Darkness, and by our own consent, to give ourselves up to delusion; for, if strength of persuasion be the light which must guide us, I ask how shall any one distinguish between the delusions of Satan and the inspirations of the Holy Ghost?"

Subtleties and authoritative corruscations have been repudiated by pure and true-hearted sages and statesmen; the advice of some of the most profound of whom, has been characterized by the simplicity of manner and of language in which they have borne witness to truth. Judge Story has remarked, that "upon subjects of Government it has always appeared to me, that metaphysical refinements are out of place. A constitution of government is addressed to the common sense of the people, and never was designed for trials of logical skill, or visionary speculation."

Of a constitution so wisely contrived, so strongly raised, and so highly finished, it is hard to speak with that praise which is justly and severely its due: the thorough and attentive contemplation of it will furnish its best panegyric. To sustain, to repair, to beautify this noble pile, is a charge intrusted principally to the people and their constitutional representatives, in all the branches of the Government.

If honor and confidence, in a pre-eminent degree, are, with a portion of their power, conferred by the people upon the Chief Executive Magistrate, the guardianship of the national honor is in no less a degree conferred upon their representatives in the two Houses of Congress, the intrinsic dignity of whose official character, in every moral point of view, transcends that of every other legislative assembly, in so much as our Constitution excels that of every other human government; and while the Constitution, practically animated by the people, thus confers honor and dignity upon Congress, to them it is given to stand by the Constitution, in spirit and in truth, inflexibly maintaining its principles—the principles of union, of liberty, of justice, of domestic tranquillity, of common defence, and of the general welfare. The Constitution and the Government, thus reciprocally animating and being animated, illustrates the beau ideal of good government—one of the choicest gifts of God to man.

The protection of the liberty of the United States of America is a duty which they owe to themselves, who enjoy it; to their ancestors, who transmitted it down; and to their posterity, who will claim at their hands this, the best birthright, the noblest inheritance of mankind.

To conclude, in the language of Judge Story—

"If, upon a closer survey of all the powers given by the Constitution, and all the guards upon their exercise, we shall perceive still stronger inducements to fortify this conclusion, and to increase our confidence in the Constitution, may we not justly hope, that every honest American will concur in the dying expression of Father Paul, 'may it be perpetual!'"

ESTO PERPETUA!!!

CONTENTS.

AN ANALYTICAL INDEX OF THE CONSTITUTION AND AMENDMENTS WILL BE SEEN AT PAGE 38, AND AN INDEX TO THE RESIDUE OF THE MATTER CONTAINED IN THIS VOLUME WILL BE FOUND AT THE CONCLUSION OF THE BOOK.

CHAPTER 1.

1. THE CONSTITUTION OF THE UNITED STATES 1
2. The dates of ratification of the Constitution by the Thirteen original States 24
3. THE ARTICLES OF AMENDMENT TO THE CONSTITUTION.... 25
4. The verification of the Constitution and amendments by the Secretary of State 31
5. The Headings and dates of ratification of the amendments of the Constitution 33
6. AN ANALYTICAL INDEX OF THE CONSTITUTION as amended 38

CHAPTER 2.

Introductory remarks to this Chapter 129

OFFICIAL PROCEEDINGS, AND THE CAUSES WHICH LED TO THE ADOPTION AND RATIFICATION OF THE CONSTITUTION OF THE UNITED STATES, viz: 130

1. REPORT OF A COMMITTEE OF THE CONGRESS OF THE CONFEDERATION, on the objections of one of the States to confer certain powers on Congress with regard to revenue and commerce. 16th December, 1782 131
2. ADDRESS OF CONGRESS TO THE STATES, calling upon their justice and plighted faith, and representing the consequences of a failure on their part to sustain the Government and provide for its wants. 26th April, 1783 139
3. PREAMBLE AND RESOLUTIONS OF CONGRESS, presenting the exposed condition of the trade and commerce with foreign countries, and the destructive effect of foreign policy, and recommending that power for their protection be vested in Congress. 30th April, 1784.... 140
4. REPORT OF A COMMITTEE OF CONGRESS, with a statement of the reasons why the States should confer upon Congress the powers therein enumerated. 13th July, 1785 142
5. REPORT OF A COMMITTEE OF CONGRESS, showing the failure of the States to comply with the requisitions of Congress, and the necessity for a complete accession of all the States to the Revenue System. 15th February, 1786 146

6. REPORT OF A COMMITTEE OF CONGRESS, relating to the continued non-compliance of some of the States with the requisitions of Congress, and recommending the subject again to their consideration. 3d March, 1786 ... 150

7. REPORT OF A COMMITTEE OF CONGRESS again earnestly recommending the subject to the consideration of the States. 23d October, 1786 ... 151

8. BRIEF HISTORICAL VIEW OF THE ACTS OF THE STATES which led to the formation and adoption of the Constitution of the United States ... 153

9. RESOLUTION OF CONGRESS appointing committees to repair to the States, to make such representations as might induce them to carry the requisitions of Congress into effect with the greatest despatch. 22d May, 1782 ... 155

10. RESOLUTIONS OF THE LEGISLATURE OF NEW YORK, on the critical condition of affairs,—that the existing system exposed the common cause to a precarious issue,—that the defects of the Confederation should be speedily repaired, and recommending a General Convention of the States for that purpose. 21st July, 1782 ... 155

11. RESOLUTIONS OF THE LEGISLATURE OF VIRGINIA, recommending to the States to empower Congress to regulate the trade and commerce of the country. 30th November, 1785 ... 158

12. RESOLUTION OF THE LEGISLATURE OF VIRGINIA, appointing commissioners to meet others to be appointed by the several States, to take into consideration the trade and commerce, and to empower Congress effectually to provide for the same. 21st January, 1786 ... 160

13. PROCEEDINGS AND REPORT OF THE COMMISSIONERS FROM SEVERAL OF THE STATES, AT ANNAPOLIS, recommending a Convention to meet at Philadelphia, with ample powers to adopt a Constitution adequate to the exigencies of the Union. 11–14th September, 1786 ... 161

14. PROCEEDINGS AND RESOLUTION OF CONGRESS OF THE CONFEDERATION, calling a Convention at Philadelphia, to render the Constitution adequate to the exigencies of the Government and the preservation of the Union. 21st February, 1787 ... 164

15. ACTS OF THE SEVERAL STATES FOR THE APPOINTMENT OF DEPUTIES TO MEET IN CONVENTION WITH POWER TO FORM A CONSTITUTION OF GOVERNMENT, viz.:

- VIRGINIA. 16th October, 1786 ... 167
- NEW JERSEY. 23d November, 1786 ... 170
- PENNSYLVANIA. 30th December, 1786 ... 172
- NORTH CAROLINA. 6th January, 1787 ... 174
- DELAWARE. 3d February, 1787 ... 177
- GEORGIA. 10th February, 1787 ... 179
- NEW YORK. 28th February, 1787 ... 181
- SOUTH CAROLINA. 8th March, 1787 ... 182
- MASSACHUSETTS. 10th March, 1787 ... 183

CONNECTICUT. 10th May, 1787 184
MARYLAND. 26th May, 1787 185
NEW HAMPSHIRE. 27th June, 1787 186
16. LETTER OF GEORGE WASHINGTON, the President, with Resolutions of the Convention, laying the Constitution before Congress, to be transmitted to the several States to be submitted to Conventions thereof for ratification. 17th September, 1787 187
17. RESOLUTION OF CONGRESS, transmitting the same to the States accordingly. 28th September, 1787 189
18. PREAMBLE AND RESOLUTION OF THE CONGRESS OF THE CONFEDERATION, in pursuance of the resolution of the Convention, fixing a day for the appointment of electors, a day for them to vote for President and Vice President, and the time and place for commencing proceedings under the Constitution 190
19. BRIEF HISTORICAL VIEW OF THE MANNER IN WHICH THE GOVERNMENT COMMENCED ITS PROCEEDINGS UNDER THE CONSTITUTION 191

CHAPTER 3.

1. PROCEEDINGS IN THE CONGRESS OF THE UNITED COLONIES respecting Independence 193
2. RESOLUTION OF CONGRESS DECLARING THE UNITED COLONIES FREE AND INDEPENDENT STATES. 2d July, 1776 195
3. A DECLARATION BY THE REPRESENTATIVES OF THE UNITED STATES OF AMERICA, IN CONGRESS ASSEMBLED. July 4, 1776 195

CHAPTER 4.

1. APPOINTMENT OF GEORGE WASHINGTON TO BE GENERAL AND COMMANDER-IN-CHIEF OF THE ARMY, BY THE CONGRESS OF THE UNITED COLONIES, on the 15th June, 1775 201
2. ADDRESS OF GEORGE WASHINGTON, accepting the appointment 16th June, 1775 201
3. COMMISSION OF GEORGE WASHINGTON for the same. 17th June, 1775 202
4. RESOLUTION OF CONGRESS that they would maintain and assist George Washington, and adhere to him in the maintenance and preservation of American liberty, with their lives and fortunes. 17th June, 1775 203
5. ADDRESS OF THE PRESIDENT OF CONGRESS of the Confederation to George Washington, on the termination of the war. 26th August, 1783 203
6. REPLY OF GEORGE WASHINGTON to the same. 26th August, 1783 204
7. INSCRIPTION AND REMARKS CONCERNING HOUDON'S STATUE OF WASHINGTON 205

8. RESIGNATION BY GEORGE WASHINGTON of the office of commander-in-chief of the army to Congress. 23d December, 1783 208
9. ANSWER OF THOMAS MIFFLIN, President of Congress, to the same. 23d December, 1783 209
10. ELECTION OF GEORGE WASHINGTON, as President of the United States, and his inaugural address. 30th April, 1789 210
11. FAREWELL ADDRESS OF GEORGE WASHINGTON, President, to the people of the United States. 17th September, 1796 215
12. APPOINTMENT OF GEORGE WASHINGTON TO BE LIEUTENANT-GENERAL AND COMMANDER-IN-CHIEF OF ALL THE ARMIES RAISED OR TO BE RAISED IN THE UNITED STATES. 3d July, 1798 231
13. TO THE MEMORY OF GEORGE WASHINGTON. Proceedings of the national authorities on the death of George Washington. 14th December, 1799 240

CHAPTER 5.

1 INTRODUCTORY REMARKS TO THIS CHAPTER 269
2 Inaugural address of GEORGE WASHINGTON. (Vide Chapter 4, Article 9.) 30th April, 1789 211
3. Inaugural address of JOHN ADAMS. 4th March, 1797 270
4 Inaugural address, first term of THOMAS JEFFERSON. 4th March, 1801 275
5. Inaugural address, second term of THOMAS JEFFERSON. 4th March, 1805 279
6. Inaugural address, first term of JAMES MADISON. 4th March, 1809 283

CHAPTER 6.

GENERAL LAWS relating to the continued organization of the Government, and providing the authorities and means of executing the Constitution in certain contingencies, and for other purposes 287
1. AN ACT to regulate the time and manner of administering certain oaths. This act prescribes the form of the oath to support the Constitution, and the officers and persons by whom it shall be taken. 1st June, 1789 287
2. AN ACT for the punishment of certain crimes. Sections 25, 26, 27, and 28, provide for the protection of foreign Ambassadors and other public Ministers and domestics. 30th April, 1790 289
3. AN ACT to prescribe the mode in which the public acts, records, and judicial proceedings, in each State, shall be authenticated so as to take effect in every other State. 26th May, 1790 290
4. AN ACT supplemental to the act establishing the Treasury Department, and for a farther compensation to certain officers. Sec. 2 requires every officer and clerk in the several Departments of the United States to take an oath to support the Constitution. 3d March, 1791 290

5. AN ACT relative to the election of a President and Vice President of the United States, and declaring the officer who shall act as President in case of vacancies in the offices both of President and Vice President. 1st March, 1792 291

6. AN ACT providing compensation to the President and Vice President of the United States. 18th February, 1793.

7. AN ACT to authorize certain officers and other persons to administer oaths. 3d May, 1798 294

8. AN ACT supplementary to the act, entitled An act to prescribe the mode in which the public acts, records, and judicial proceedings in each State shall be authenticated so as to take effect in every other State. 27th March, 1804 294

9. AN ACT to extend the provisions of the act to authorize certain officers and other persons to administer oaths, approved May 3, 1798. 8th February, 1817 295

10. AN ACT to provide for the publication of the laws of the United States, and for other purposes. 20th April, 1818 295

11. AN ACT in addition to the "Act for the punishment of certain crimes against the United States," and to repeal the acts therein mentioned. 20th April, 1818 296

12. AN ACT making compensation to the persons appointed by the electors to deliver the votes for President and Vice President. 11th February, 1825 300

13. AN ACT for the apportionment of Representatives among the several States according to the sixth census. Sec. 2 provides for the election of Representatives by Districts. 25th June, 1842 300

14. AN ACT to provide further remedial justice in the courts of the United States. 29th August, 1842 301

15. AN ACT to establish a uniform time for holding elections for electors of President and Vice President in all the States of the Union. 23d January, 1845 302

16. AN ACT to provide for the distribution of the edition of the Laws and Treaties of the United States, published by Little & Brown, under the provisions of the resolutions of Congress, approved March 3, 1845, and for other purposes. 8th August, 1846 302

17. AN ACT for giving effect to certain treaty stipulations between this and foreign governments, for the apprehension and delivering up of certain offenders. 12 August, 1848. 305

18. AN ACT providing for the taking of the seventh and subsequent censuses of the United States, and to fix the number of members of the House of Representatives, and to provide for their future apportionment among the several States. 23d May, 1850 305

19. An act to authorize Notaries Public to take and certify oaths, affirmations, and acknowledgments in certain cases. 16th September, 1850 306

20. A RESOLUTION relating to the publication of the Laws of the United States. 26th September, 1850 307

CHAPTER 7.

EXPLANATORY NOTES OF THE FOLLOWING TABLES 309

1. TABLES OF ELECTORAL VOTES FOR PRESIDENT AND VICE PRESIDENT of the United States, from March 4, 1789, to March 3, 1849 315

2. TABLE OF TERMS OF OFFICE, AND LENGTH OF SERVICE, IN THE SENATE, OF THE VICE PRESIDENTS AND PRESIDENTS PRO TEMPORE; and of the commencement, termination, and number of days in each session of Congress, and special session of the Senate, from March 4, 1789, to March 3, 1851 336

3. TABLES OF THE NAMES OF THE SENATORS OF THE UNITED STATES, from March 4, 1789, to March 3, 1851, with the commencement and termination of their service, respectively, and the classes into which they are divided under the Constitution 346

4. TABLE OF THE NAMES OF THE SECRETARIES OF THE SENATE OF THE UNITED STATES, from March 4, 1789, with the length of their service respectively 385

5. TABLE OF THE NAMES OF REPRESENTATIVES IN CONGRESS WHO HAVE BEEN ELECTED SPEAKERS OF THE HOUSE OF REPRESENTATIVES, from March 4, 1789, to March 3, 1851, with the commencement and termination of their service as such, and the States of which they were Representatives 386

6. TABLE OF THE NAMES OF THE CLERKS OF THE HOUSE OF REPRESENTATIVES OF THE UNITED STATES, from March 4, 1789, with the length of their service, respectively 388

CHAPTER 8.

THE NAMES, APPOINTMENT, AND SERVICE OF THE JUDGES AND OFFICERS OF THE SUPREME COURT OF THE UNITED STATES, from March 4, 1789, viz. 389

1. THE CHIEF JUSTICES OF THE SUPREME COURT OF THE UNITED STATES 389

2. THE ASSOCIATE JUSTICES OF THE SUPREME COURT OF THE UNITED STATES 390

3. THE CLERKS, REPORTERS OF DECISIONS, AND MARSHALS OF THE SUPREME COURT OF THE UNITED STATES 393

CHAPTER 9.

THE NAMES, APPOINTMENT, AND SERVICE OF THE SEVERAL HIGH EXECUTIVE OFFICERS OF THE GOVERNMENT, from March 4, 1789, viz. 395

1. SECRETARIES OF STATE 395
2. SECRETARIES OF THE TREASURY 396
3. SECRETARIES OF WAR 398

4. SECRETARIES OF THE NAVY 399
5. POSTMASTER GENERALS 401
6. ATTORNEY GENERALS 402

CHAPTER 10.

BRIEF CHRONOLOGICAL STATEMENT OF THE FORMATION OF THE GOVERNMENTS OF THE SEVERAL STATES AND TERRITORIES OF THE UNITED STATES 405

1. NEW HAMPSHIRE 407
2. MASSACHUSETTS 407
3. RHODE ISLAND 407
4. CONNECTICUT 407
5. NEW YORK 407
6. NEW JERSEY 407
7. PENNSYLVANIA 408
8. DELAWARE 408
9. MARYLAND 408
10. VIRGINIA 408
11. NORTH CAROLINA 408
12. SOUTH CAROLINA 408
13. GEORGIA 408
14. VERMONT 412
15. KENTUCKY 412
16. TENNESSEE 413
17. OHIO 413
18. LOUISIANA 429
19. INDIANA 430
20. MISSISSIPPI 430
21. ILLINOIS 431
22. ALABAMA 431
23. MAINE 432
24. MISSOURI 433
25. ARKANSAS 434
26. MICHIGAN 436
27. FLORIDA 436
28. TEXAS 439
29. WISCONSIN 441
30. IOWA 443
31. CALIFORNIA 445
32. OREGON TERRITORY 447
33. MINESOTA TERRITORY 447
34. NEW MEXICO TERRITORY 448
35. UTAH TERRITORY 448
36. NEBRASKA TERRITORY 448
37. DISTRICT OF COLUMBIA 449

CHAPTER 11.

SOURCES OF HISTORICAL, POLITICAL, STATISTICAL, AND OTHER INFORMATION REGARDING THE LEGISLATIVE, EXECUTIVE, AND JUDICIAL ACTION OF THE GOVERNMENT OF THE UNITED STATES OF AMERICA, IN POSSESSION OF THE PUBLIC OFFICES AT THE SEAT OF GOVERNMENT 451

CLASS No 1. THE COLONIAL HISTORY of the United States, and documentary History of the Revolution 452

CLASS No. 2. LEGISLATIVE PROCEEDINGS and acts of the Congress of the Confederation from the commencement of the Revolution to the commencement of the Government under the Constitution 453

CLASS No. 3. THE JOURNAL, Acts, and Proceedings of the Convention which formed the Constitution of the United States, from May 14 to September 17, 1787 453

CLASS No. 4. THE JOURNAL of the House of Representatives of the United States, from March 4, 1789, to March 3, 1851 454

CLASS No. 5. THE LEGISLATIVE JOURNAL of the Senate of the United States, from March 4, 1789, to March 3, 1851 455

CLASS No. 6. THE EXECUTIVE JOURNAL of the Senate of the United States, from March 4, 1789, to March 3, 1851. (A part only of which, as explained, has been made public.) 455
CLASS No. 7. THE JOURNAL or Record of the Senate on trials of impeachment, from March 4, 1789, to March 3, 1851 456
DESCRIPTION of the Legislative Journals of the Senate and House of Representatives of the United States 456
CLASS No. 8. DOCUMENTS ordered to be printed by the two Houses of Congress since March 4, 1789, embraced in 21 volumes folio State Papers, printed by Gales and Seaton 457
CLASS No. 9. DOCUMENTS printed in octavo form by order of the Senate, during each Session, from March 4, 1789, to March 3, 1851 458
CLASS No. 10. DOCUMENTS printed in octavo form by order of the House of Representatives, during each session, from March 4, 1789, to March 3, 1851 458
CLASS No. 11. SPEECHES AND DEBATES in the two Houses of the Congress of the United States, from March 4, 1789, to March 3, 1851 459
CLASS No. 12. THE LAWS of the United States, including the Treaties, &c., as embraced in the several editions heretofore published, up to March 3, 1851 461
CLASS No. 13. ABRIDGMENTS and Digests of the Laws of the United States, to March, 1851 465
CLASS No. 14. INDEXES prepared in conformity with orders or resolutions of the Senate and House of Representatives of the United States, to March 3, 1851 465
CLASS No. 15. REPORTS of the Decisions of the Supreme Court of the United States, to the January term, 1851 466
CLASS No. 16. PUBLICATIONS on the subject of the Public Lands and Private Land Claims, under the authority of the United States, to March 3, 1851 . 466
CLASS No. 17. REVENUE LAWS, Commercial Regulations, Digests of Tariff Laws, &c., to March 3, 1851 467
CLASS No. 18. MISCELLANEOUS BOOKS printed or published under the authority or patronage of the United States and not noticed under particular heads, to March 3, 1851 468
CLASS No. 19. MISCELLANEOUS PUBLICATIONS containing useful political, statistical, and other information, to March 3, 1851 471
CLASS No. 20. THE BOOKS contained in the Congress or National Library, to March 3, 1851 472
CLASS No. 21. THE BOOKS contained in the Library of the Department of State, to March 3, 1851 479

CHAPTER 12.

THE ARTICLES OF CONFEDERATION 483
THE MEMBERS OF THE THIRTY-FIRST CONGRESS 490

CHAPTER I.

THE CONSTITUTION,

As here presented and authenticated by the certificate of the Secretary of State, after a continued correction of proof copies until every deviation from the original Constitution, however small, was completely removed, *may with confidence be used as a true copy.* The necessity for a close and continued attention to the execution of a copy of this important instrument, became manifest by the use of a printed copy (considered as correct) to print from, which, on being compared with the original, was found to contain several errors in the words, and sixty-five in the punctuation. This circumstance led to a further comparison of copies, in several editions of the laws, printed by different individuals, and it was found, that one edition contained 204 and another 176 errors in the punctuation of the Constitution! Many of these are material in the construction of the sentences in which they occur.

It was also discovered, that, in the original manuscript, capital letters were used at the beginning of substantives, or nouns, as is understood to have been the practice generally in writing and printing at the time the Constitution was written. These appear to have been altogether disregarded in the editions above referred to, except in words at the beginning of sentences.

As the construction of important clauses may, sometimes, turn upon the punctuation, or the nature of a word, it is important that the former be of the right measure, and that the proper value of the latter be manifest, before the mind can decide upon the true meaning, as intended by the wise and learned framers of that masterpiece of composition, which bears the impress of the most minute and laborious attention to the construction of every particle of matter constituting this noble fabric, the preservation of whose simplicity is the only safeguard to its integrity.

These facts induced the determination to produce *a true copy of the Constitution* in text, orthography, letter, and punctuation, and the rigid examination, and subsequent verification of the Department having the care and custody of the venerated original, attest the success of the undertaking in the production of the following authentic Constitution.

THE
CONSTITUTION
ESTO PERPETUA
1789
1776
P. S. Duval & Co. Lith. Philad.

CONSTITUTION

OF THE

UNITED STATES OF AMERICA.

We the People of the United States, in order to form a more perfect Union, establish Justice, insure domestic Tranquillity, provide for the common defence, promote the general Welfare, and secure the Blessings of Liberty to ourselves and our Posterity, do ordain and establish this Constitution for the United States of America.

ARTICLE. I.

Section. 1. All legislative Powers herein granted shall be vested in a Congress of the United States, which shall consist of a Senate and House of Representatives.

Section. 2. [1]The House of Representatives shall be composed of Members chosen every second Year by the People of the several States, and the Electors in each State shall have the Qualifications requisite for Electors of the most numerous Branch of the State Legislature.

[2]No Person shall be a Representative who shall not have attained to the Age of twenty five Years, and been seven Years a Citizen of the United States, and who shall not, when elected, be an Inhabitant of that State in which he shall be chosen.

[3]Representatives and direct Taxes shall be apportioned among the several States which may be included within this Union, according to their respective Numbers, which shall be determined by adding to the whole Number of free Persons, including those bound to Service for a Term of Years, and excluding Indians not taxed, three fifths of all other Persons. The actual Enumeration shall be made within three Years after the first Meeting of the Congress of the United States, and within every subsequent Term of ten Years, in such Manner as they shall by Law direct. The Number of Representatives shall not exceed one for every thirty Thousand, but each State shall have at Least one Representative; and until such enumeration shall be made, the State of New Hampshire shall be entitled to chuse three, Massachusetts eight, Rhode-Island and Providence Plantations one, Connecticut five, New-York six, New Jersey four, Pennsylvania eight, Delaware one, Maryland six,

Virginia ten, North Carolina five, South Carolina five, and Georgia three.

[4]When vacancies happen in the Representation from any State, the Executive Authority thereof shall issue Writs of Election to fill such Vacancies.

[5]The House of Representatives shall chuse their Speaker and other Officers; and shall have the sole Power of Impeachment.

SECTION. 3. [1]The Senate of the United States shall be composed of two Senators from each State, chosen by the Legislature thereof, for six Years; and each Senator shall have one Vote.

[2]Immediately after they shall be assembled in Consequence of the first Election, they shall be divided as equally as may be into three Classes. The Seats of the Senators of the first Class shall be vacated at the Expiration of the second Year, of the second Class at the Expiration of the fourth Year, and of the third Class at the Expiration of the sixth Year, so that one-third may be chosen every second Year; and if Vacancies happen by Resignation, or otherwise, during the Recess of the Legislature of any State, the Executive thereof may make temporary Appointments until the next Meeting of the Legislature, which shall then fill such Vacancies.

[3]No Person shall be a Senator who shall not have attained to the Age of thirty Years, and been nine Years a Citizen of the United States, and who shall not, when elected, be an Inhabitant of that State for which he shall be chosen.

[4]The Vice President of the United States shall be President of the Senate, but shall have no Vote, unless they be equally divided.

[5]The Senate shall chuse their other Officers, and also a President pro tempore, in the Absence of the Vice President, or when he shall exercise the Office of President of the United States.

[6]The Senate shall have the sole Power to try all Impeachments. When sitting for that Purpose, they shall be on Oath or Affirmation. When the President of the United States is tried, the Chief Justice shall preside: And no Person shall be convicted without the Concurrence of two thirds of the Members present.

[7]Judgment in Cases of Impeachment shall not extend further than to removal from Office, and Disqualification to hold and enjoy any Office of honour, Trust or Profit under the United States: but the Party convicted shall nevertheless be liable and subject to Indictment, Trial, Judgment and Punishment, according to Law.

SECTION. 4. [1]The Times, Places and Manner of holding Elections for Senators and Representatives, shall be prescribed in each State by the Legislature thereof; but the Congress may at any time by Law make or alter such Regulations, except as to the places of chusing Senators.

[2]The Congress shall assemble at least once in every Year, and such Meeting shall be on the first Monday in December, unless they shall by Law appoint a different Day.

SECTION. 5. [1]Each House shall be the Judge of the Elections, Returns and Qualifications of its own Members, and a Majority of each shall constitute a Quorum to do Business; but a smaller Number may adjourn from day to day, and may be authorized to compel the Attendance of absent Members, in such Manner, and under such Penalties as each House may provide.

[2]Each House may determine the Rules of its Proceedings, punish its Members for disorderly Behaviour, and, with the Concurrence of two thirds, expel a Member.

[3]Each House shall keep a Journal of its Proceedings, and from time to time publish the same, excepting such Parts as may in their Judgment require Secrecy; and the Yeas and Nays of the Members of either House

on any question shall, at the Desire of one fifth of those Present, be entered on the Journal.

[4]Neither House, during the Session of Congress, shall, without the Consent of the other, adjourn for more than three days, nor to any other Place than that in which the two Houses shall be sitting.

SECTION. 6. [1]The Senators and Representatives shall receive a Compensation for their Services, to be ascertained by Law, and paid out of the Treasury of the United States. They shall in all Cases, except Treason, Felony and Breach of the Peace, be privileged from Arrest during their Attendance at the Session of their respective Houses, and in going to and returning from the same; and for any Speech or Debate in either House, they shall not be questioned in any other Place.

[2]No Senator or Representative shall, during the Time for which he was elected, be appointed to any civil Office under the Authority of the United States, which shall have been created, or the Emoluments whereof shall have been encreased during such time; and no Person holding any Office under the United States, shall be a Member of either House during his Continuance in Office.

SECTION. 7. [1]All Bills for raising Revenue shall originate in the House of Representatives; but the Senate may propose or concur with Amendments as on other Bills.

[2]Every Bill which shall have passed the House of Representatives and the Senate, shall, before it become a Law, be presented to the President of the United States; If he approve he shall sign it, but if not he shall return it, with his Objections to that House in which it shall have originated, who shall enter the Objections at large on their Journal, and proceed to reconsider it. If after such Reconsideration two thirds of that House shall agree to pass the Bill, it shall be sent, together with the Objections, to the other House, by which it shall likewise be reconsidered, and if approved by two thirds of that House, it shall become a Law. But in all such Cases the Votes of both Houses shall be determined by yeas and Nays, and the Names of the Persons voting for and against the Bill shall be entered on the Journal of each House respectively. If any Bill shall not be returned by the President within ten Days (Sundays excepted) after it shall have been presented to him, the Same shall be a law, in like Manner as if he had signed it, unless the Congress by their Adjournment prevent its Return, in which Case it shall not be a Law

3 Every Order, Resolution, or Vote to which the Concurrence of the Senate and House of Representatives may be necessary (except on a question of Adjournment) shall be presented to the President of the United States; and before the Same shall take Effect, shall be approved by him, or being disapproved by him, shall be repassed by two thirds of the Senate and House of Representatives, according to the Rules and Limitations prescribed in the Case of a Bill.

SECTION. 8. The Congress shall have Power

1 To lay and collect Taxes, Duties, Imposts and Excises, to pay the Debts and provide for the common Defence and general Welfare of the United States; but all Duties, Imposts and Excises shall be uniform throughout the United States;

2 To borrow Money on the credit of the United States;

3 To regulate Commerce with foreign Nations, and among the several States, and with the Indian Tribes;

4 To establish an uniform Rule of Naturalization, and uniform Laws on the subject of Bankruptcies throughout the United States;

5 To coin Money, regulate the Value thereof, and of foreign Coin, and fix the Standard of Weights and Measures;

[6] To provide for the Punishment of counterfeiting the Securities and current Coin of the United States;

[7] To establish Post Offices and post Roads;

[8] To promote the progress of Science and useful Arts, by securing for limited Times to Authors and Inventors the exclusive Right to their respective Writings and Discoveries;

[9] To constitute Tribunals inferior to the supreme Court;

[10] To define and punish Piracies and Felonies committed on the high Seas, and Offences against the Law of Nations;

[11] To declare War, grant Letters of Marque and Reprisal, and make Rules concerning Captures on Land and Water;

[12] To raise and support Armies, but no Appropriation of Money to that Use shall be for a longer Term than two Years;

[13] To provide and maintain a Navy;

[14] To make Rules for the Government and Regulation of the land and naval Forces;

[15] To provide for calling forth the Militia to execute the Laws of the Union, suppress Insurrections and repel Invasions;

[16] To provide for organizing, arming, and disciplining, the Militia, and for governing such Part of

them as may be employed in the Service of the United States, reserving to the States respectively, the Appointment of the Officers, and the Authority of training the Militia according to the Discipline prescribed by Congress;

17 To exercise exclusive Legislation in all Cases whatsoever, over such District (not exceeding ten Miles square) as may, by Cession of particular States, and the Acceptance of Congress, become the Seat of the Government of the United States, and to exercise like Authority over all Places purchased by the Consent of the Legislature of the State in which the Same shall be, for the Erection of Forts, Magazines, Arsenals, Dock-Yards, and other needful Buildings;—And

18 To make all Laws which shall be necessary and proper for carrying into Execution the foregoing Powers, and all other Powers vested by this Constitution in the Government of the United States, or in any Department or Officer thereof.

SECTION. 9. 1 The Migration or Importation of such Persons as any of the States now existing shall think proper to admit, shall not be prohibited by the Congress prior to the Year one thousand eight hundred and eight, but a Tax or Duty may be imposed on such Importation, not exceeding ten dollars for each Person.

[2] The Privilege of the Writ of Habeas Corpus shall not be suspended, unless when in Cases of Rebellion or Invasion the public Safety may require it.

[3] No Bill of Attainder or ex post facto Law shall be passed.

No Capitation, or other direct, Tax shall be laid, unless in Proportion to the Census or Enumeration herein before directed to be taken.

[5] No Tax or Duty shall be laid on Articles exported from any State.

[6] No Preference shall be given by any Regulation of Commerce or Revenue to the Ports of one State over those of another: nor shall Vessels bound to, or from, one State, be obliged to enter, clear, or pay Duties in another.

[7] No Money shall be drawn from the Treasury, but in Consequence of Appropriations made by Law; and a regular Statement and Account of the Receipts and Expenditures of all public Money shall be published from time to time.

[8] No Title of Nobility shall be granted by the United States: And no Person holding any Office of Profit or Trust under them, shall, without the Consent of the Congress, accept of any present, Emolument, Office,

or Title, of any kind whatever, from any King, Prince, or foreign State.

SECTION. 10. [1]No State shall enter into any Treaty, Alliance, or Confederation; grant Letters of Marque and Reprisal; coin Money; emit Bills of Credit; make any Thing but gold and silver Coin a Tender in Payment of Debts; pass any Bill of Attainder, ex post facto Law, or Law impairing the Obligation of Contracts, or grant any Title of Nobility.

[2]No State shall, without the consent of the Congress, lay any Imposts or Duties on Imports or Exports, except what may be absolutely necessary for executing it's inspection Laws: and the net Produce of all Duties and Imposts, laid by any State on Imports or Exports, shall be for the Use of the Treasury of the United States; and all such Laws shall be subject to the Revision and Controul of the Congress.

[3]No State shall, without the Consent of Congress, lay any Duty of Tonnage, keep Troops, or Ships of War in time of Peace, enter into any Agreement or Compact with another State, or with a foreign Power, or engage in War, unless actually invaded, or in such imminent Danger as will not admit of Delay.

ARTICLE. II.

SECTION. 1. [1]The executive Power shall be vested in a President of the United States of America. He shall hold his Office during the Term of four Years, and, together with the Vice President, chosen for the same Term, be elected, as follows

[2]Each State shall appoint, in such Manner as the Legislature thereof may direct, a Number of Electors, equal to the whole Number of Senators and Representatives to which the State may be entitled in the Congress: but no Senator or Representative, or Person holding an Office of Trust or Profit under the United States, shall be appointed an Elector.

[* The Electors shall meet in their respective States, and vote by Ballot for two Persons, of whom one at least shall not be an Inhabitant of the same State with themselves. And they shall make a List of all the Persons voted for, and of the Number of Votes for each; which List they shall sign and certify, and transmit sealed to the Seat of the Government of the United States, directed to the President of the Senate. The President of the Senate shall, in the Presence of the Senate and House of Representatives, open all the Certificates, and the Votes shall then be counted. The Person having the greatest Number of Votes shall be the President, if such Number be a Majority of the whole Number of Electors appointed; and if there be more than one who have such Majority, and have an equal Number of Votes, then the House of Representatives shall immediately chuse by Ballot one of them for President; and if no

---

* This clause within brackets has been superceded and annulled by the 12th amendment, on page 28.

Person have a Majority, then from the five highest on the List the said House shall in like Manner chuse the President. But in chusing the President, the Votes shall be taken by States, the Representation from each State having one Vote; A Quorum for this Purpose shall consist of a Member or Members from twothirds of the States, and a Majority of all the States shall be necessary to a Choice. In every Case, after the Choice of the President, the Person having the greatest Number of Votes of the Electors shall be the Vice President. But if there should remain two or more who have equal Votes, the Senate shall chuse from them by Ballot the Vice President.]

[3]The Congress may determine the Time of chusing the Electors, and the Day on which they shall give their Votes; which Day shall be the same throughout the United States.

[4]No Person except a natural born Citizen, or a Citizen of the United States, at the time of the Adoption of this Constitution, shall be eligible to the Office of President; neither shall any Person be eligible to that Office who shall not have attained to the Age of thirty five Years, and been fourteen Years a Resident within the United States.

[5]In Case of the Removal of the President from Office, or of his Death, Resignation, or Inability to discharge the Powers and Duties of the said Office, the same shall devolve on the Vice President, and the Congress may by Law provide for the Case of Re-

moval, Death, Resignation, or Inability, both of the President and Vice President, declaring what Officer shall then act as President, and such Officer shall act accordingly, until the Disability be removed, or a Preident shall be elected.

[6]The President shall, at stated Times, receive for his Services, a Compensation, which shall neither be encreased nor diminished during the Period for which he shall have been elected, and he shall not receive within that Period any other Emolument from the United States, or any of them.

[7]Before he enter on the Execution of his Office, he shall take the following Oath or Affirmation :—

"I do solemnly swear (or affirm) that I will faithfully " execute the Office of President of the United States, and " will to the best of my Ability, preserve, protect and " defend the Constitution of the United States.

SECTION. 2. [1]The President shall be Commander in Chief of the Army and Navy of the United States, and of the Militia of the several States, when called into the actual Service of the United States; he may require the Opinion, in writing, of the principal Of ficer in each of the executive Departments, upon any Subject relating to the Duties of their respective Offices, and he shall have Power to grant Reprieves and Pardons for Offences against the United States, except in Cases of Impeachment.

[2]He shall have Power, by and with the Advice and Consent of the Senate, to make Treaties, provided two thirds of the Senators present concur; and he shall nominate, and by and with the Advice and Consent of the Senate, shall appoint Ambassadors, other public Ministers and Consuls, Judges of the supreme Court, and all other Officers of the United States, whose Appointments are not herein otherwise provided for, and which shall be established by Law: but the Congress may by Law vest the Appointment of such inferior Officers, as they think proper, in the President alone, in the Courts of Law, or in the Heads of Departments.

[3]The President shall have Power to fill up all Vacancies that may happen during the Recess of the Senate, by granting Commissions which shall expire at the End of their next Session.

SECTION. 3. He shall from time to time give to the Congress Information of the State of the Union, and recommend to their Consideration such Measures as he shall judge necessary and expedient; he may, on extraordinary Occasions, convene both Houses, or either of them, and in Case of Disagreement between them, with Respect to the Time of Adjournment, he may adjourn them to such Time as he shall think proper; he shall receive Ambassadors and other public Ministers; he shall take Care that the Laws be faithfully executed, and shall Commission all the officers of the United States.

SECTION. 4. The President, Vice President and all civil Officers of the United States, shall be removed from Office on Impeachment for, and Conviction of, Treason, Bribery, or other high Crimes and Misdemeanors.

ARTICLE III.

SECTION. 1. The judicial Power of the United States, shall be vested in one supreme Court, and in such inferior Courts as the Congress may from time to time ordain and establish. The Judges, both of the supreme and inferior Courts, shall hold their Offices during good Behavior, and shall, at stated Times, receive for their Services, a Compensation, which shall not be diminished during their Continuance in Office.

SECTION. 2. [1]The judicial Power shall extend to all Cases, in Law and Equity, arising under this Constitution, the Laws of the United States, and Treaties made, or which shall be made, under their Authority;—to all Cases affecting Ambassadors, other public Ministers, and Consuls;—to all Cases of admiralty and maritime Jurisdiction;—to Controversies to which the United States shall be a Party;—to Controversies between two or more States;—between a State and Citizens of another State;—between Citizens of different States,—between Citizens of the same State claiming Lands under Grants of different States, and between a State, or the Citizens thereof, and foreign States, Citizens or Subjects.

[2]In all Cases affecting Ambassadors, other public Ministers and Consuls, and those in which a State shall be Party, the supreme Court shall have original Jurisdiction. In all the other Cases before mentioned, the supreme Court shall have appellate Jurisdiction, both as to Law and Fact, with such Exceptions, and under such Regulations as the Congress shall make.

[3]The Trial of all Crimes, except in Cases of Impeachment, shall be by Jury; and such Trial shall be held in the State where the said Crimes shall have been committed; but when not committed within any State, the Trial shall be at such Place or Places as the Congress may by Law have directed.

SECTION. 3. [1]Treason against the United States, shall consist only in levying War against them, or in adhering to their Enemies, giving them Aid and Comfort. No Person shall be convicted of Treason unless on the Testimony of two Witnesses to the same overt Act, or on Confession in open Court.

[2]The Congress shall have Power to declare the Punishment of Treason, but no Attainder of Treason shall work Corruption of Blood, or Forfeiture except during the Life of the Person attainted.

ARTICLE. IV.

SECTION. 1. Full Faith and Credit shall be given in each State to the public Acts, Records, and judicial Proceedings of every other State. And the Congress may by general Laws prescribe the Manner in which such Acts, Records and Proceedings shall be proved, and the Effect thereof.

SECTION. 2. [1]The Citizens of each State shall be entitled to all Privileges and Immunities of Citizens in the several States.

[2]A Person charged in any State with Treason, Felony, or other Crime, who shall flee from Justice, and be found in another State, shall on Demand of the executive Authority of the State from which he fled, be delivered up, to be removed to the State having Jurisdiction of the Crime.

[3]No Person held to Service or Labour in one State, under the Laws thereof, escaping into another, shall, in Consequence of any Law or Regulation therein, be discharged from such Service or Labour, but shall be delivered up on Claim of the Party to whom such Service or Labour may be due.

SECTION. 3. [1]New States may be admitted by the Congress into this Union; but no new State shall be formed or erected within the Jurisdiction of any other State; nor any State be formed by the Junction of two or more States, or Parts of States, without the Consent of the Legislatures of the States concerned as well as of the Congress.

[2]The Congress shall have Power to dispose of and make all needful Rules and Regulations respecting the Territory or other Property belonging to the United States; and nothing in this Constitution shall be so construed as to Prejudice any Claims of the United States, or of any particular State.

SECTION. 4. The United States shall guarantee to every State in this Union a Republican Form of Government, and shall protect each of them against Invasion, and on Application of the Legislature, or of the Executive (when the Legislature cannot be convened) against domestic Violence.

ARTICLE. V.

The Congress, whenever two thirds of both Houses shall deem it necessary, shall propose Amendments to this Constitution, or, on the Application of the Legislatures of two thirds of the several States, shall call a Convention for proposing Amendments, which, in either Case, shall be valid to all Intents and Purposes, as Part of this Constitution, when ratified by the Legislatures of three fourths of the several States, or by Conventions in three fourths thereof, as the one or the other Mode of Ratification may be proposed by the Congress; Provided that no Amendment which may be made prior to the Year one thousand eight hundred and eight shall in any Manner affect the first and fourth Clauses in the Ninth Section of the first Article; and that no State, without its Consent, shall be deprived of its equal Suffrage in the Senate.

ARTICLE. VI.

[1] All Debts contracted and Engagements entered into, before the Adoption of this Constitution, shall be as valid against the United States under this Constitution, as under the Confederation.

[2] This Constitution, and the Laws of the United States which shall be made in Pursuance thereof; and all Treaties made, or which shall be made, under the

authority of the United States, shall be the supreme Law of the Land; and the Judges in every State shall be bound thereby, any Thing in the Constitution or Laws of any State to the Contrary notwithstanding.

[3] The Senators and Representatives before mentioned, and the Members of the several State Legislatures, and all executive and judicial Officers, both of the United States and of the several States, shall be bound by Oath or Affirmation, to support this Constitution; but no religious Test shall ever be required as a Qualification to any Office or public Trust under the United States.

ARTICLE. VII.

The Ratification of the Conventions of nine States, shall be sufficient for the Establishment of this Constitution between the States so ratifying the Same.

Done in Convention by the Unanimous Consent of the States present the Seventeenth Day of September in the Year of our Lord one thousand seven hundred and Eighty seven and of the Independance of the United States of America the Twelfth **In Witness** whereof We have hereunto subscribed our Names,

GEO WASHINGTON—

Presidt and deputy from Virginia

NEW HAMPSHIRE.

John Langdon, Nicholas Gilman.

MASSACHUSETTS.

Nathaniel Gorham, Rufus King.

CONNECTICUT.

Wm. Saml. Johnson, Roger Sherman.

NEW YORK.

Alexander Hamilton.

NEW JERSEY.

Wil: Livingston, David Brearley,
Wm. Paterson, Jona. Dayton.

PENNSYLVANIA.

B. Franklin, Thomas Mifflin,
Robt. Morris, Geo: Clymer,
Tho: Fitzsimons, Jared Ingersoll,
James Wilson, Gouv: Morris.

DELAWARE.

Geo: Read, Gunning Bedford, Jun'r,
John Dickinson, Richard Bassett,
Jaco: Broom.

MARYLAND.

James M'Henry Dan: of St. Thos. Jenifer,
Danl. Carroll.

VIRGINIA.

John Blair, James Madison, Jr.,

NORTH CAROLINA.

Wm. Blount, Rich'd Dobbs Spaight,
Hu. Williamson.

SOUTH CAROLINA.

J. Rutledge, Charles Cotesworth Pinckney
Charles Pinckney, Pierce Butler.

GEORGIA.

William Few, Abr. Baldwin.

Attest: WILLIAM JACKSON, *Secretary.*

The Constitution was adopted on the 17th September, 1787, by the Convention appointed in pursuance of the resolution of the Congress of the Confederation, of the 21st February, 1787, and was ratified by the Conventions of the several States, as follows, viz.:

By Convention	of	Delaware,	on the	7th December,	1787.
"	"	Pennsylvania,	"	12th December,	1787.
"	"	New Jersey,	"	18th December,	1787.
"	"	Georgia,	"	2d January,	1788.
"	"	Connecticut,	"	9th January,	1788.
"	"	Massachusetts,	"	6th February,	1788.
"	"	Maryland,	"	28th April,	1788.
"	"	South Carolina,	"	23d May,	1788.
"	"	New Hampshire,	"	21st June,	1788.
"	"	Virginia,	"	26th June,	1788.
"	"	New York,	"	26th July,	1788.
"	"	North Carolina,	"	21st November,	1789.
"	"	Rhode Island,	"	29th May,	1790.

ARTICLES

IN ADDITION TO, AND AMENDMENT OF,

THE CONSTITUTION

OF THE

UNITED STATES OF AMERICA,

Proposed by Congress, and ratified by the Legislatures of the several States, pursuant to the fifth article of the original Constitution.

(ARTICLE 1.)

Congress shall make no law respecting an establishment of religion, or prohibiting the free exercise thereof; or abridging the freedom of speech, or of the press; or the right of the people peaceably to assemble, and to petition the Government for a redress of grievances.

(ARTICLE 2.)

A well regulated Militia, being necessary to the security of a free State, the right of the people to keep and bear Arms, shall not be infringed.

(ARTICLE III.)

No Soldier shall, in time of peace be quartered in any house, without the consent of the Owner, nor in time of war, but in a manner to be prescribed by law.

(ARTICLE IV.)

The right of the people to be secure in their persons, houses, papers, and effects, against unreasonable searches and seizures, shall not be violated, and no Warrants shall issue, but upon probable cause, supported by Oath or affirmation, and particularly describing the place to be searched, and the persons or things to be seized.

(ARTICLE V.)

No person shall be held to answer for a capital, or otherwise infamous crime, unless on a presentment or indictment of a Grand Jury, except in cases arising in the land or naval forces, or in the Militia, when in actual service in time of War or public danger; nor shall any person be subject for the same offence to be twice put in jeopardy of life or limb; nor shall be compelled in any Criminal Case to be a witness against himself, nor be deprived of life, liberty, or property, without due process of law; nor shall private property be taken for public use, without just compensation.

(ARTICLE VI.)

In all criminal prosecutions, the accused shall enjoy the right to a speedy and public trial, by an impartial jury of the State and district wherein the crime shall have been committed, which district shall have been previously ascertained by law, and to be informed of the nature and cause of the accusation; to be confronted with the witnesses against him; to have Compulsory process for obtaining Witnesses in his favour, and to have the Assistance of Counsel for his defence.

(ARTICLE VII.)

In Suits at common law, where the value in controversy shall exceed twenty dollars, the right of trial by jury shall be preserved, and no fact tried by a jury shall be otherwise re-examined in any Court of the United States, than according to the rules of the common law.

(ARTICLE VIII.)

Excessive bail shall not be required, nor excessive fines imposed, nor cruel and unusual punishments inflicted.

(ARTICLE IX.)

The enumeration in the Constitution, of certain rights, shall not be construed to deny or disparage others retained by the people.

(ARTICLE X.)

The powers not delegated to the United States by the Constitution, nor prohibited by it to the States, are reserved to the States respectively, or to the people.

ARTICLE XI.

The Judicial power of the United States shall not be construed to extend to any suit in law or equity, commenced or prosecuted against one of the United States by Citizens of another State, or by Citizens or Subjects of any Foreign State.

ARTICLE XII.

The Electors shall meet in their respective states, and vote by ballot for President and Vice President, one of whom, at least, shall not be an inhabitant of the same state with themselves; they shall name in their ballots the person voted for as President, and in distinct ballots the person voted for as Vice-President, and they shall make distinct lists of all persons voted for as President, and of all persons voted for as Vice-President, and of the number of votes for each, which lists they shall sign and certify, and transmit sealed to the seat of the government of the United States, directed to the President of the Senate;—The President of the Senate shall, in presence of the Senate and House of Representatives, open all the certificates and the votes shall then be counted;—The person having the greatest number of votes for President, shall be the President, if such number be a majority of the whole number of Electors appointed; and if no person have such majority, then from the persons having the highest numbers not exceeding three on the list of those voted for as President, the House of Representatives shall choose immediately, by ballot, the President. But in choosing the President, the votes shall be taken by states, the representation from each state having one vote; a quorum for this purpose shall consist of a member or members from two-thirds of the states, and a majority of all the states shall be necessary to a choice. And if the House of Representatives shall not choose a President whenever the right of choice shall devolve upon them, before the fourth day of March next following, then the Vice-President shall act as President, as in the case of the death or other constitutional disability of the President. The person having the greatest number of votes as Vice-President, shall be the Vice-President, if such number be a majority of the whole number of Electors appointed, and if no person have a majority, then from the two highest numbers on the list, the Senate shall choose the Vice-President; a quorum for the purpose shall consist of two-thirds of the whole number of Senators, and a majority of the whole number shall be necessary to a choice. But no person constitutionally ineligible to the office of President shall be eligible to that of Vice-President of the United States.

Department of State
July 20th 1846

This edition of the Constitution & amendments has been critically compared with the originals in this Department & found to be correct, in text, letter & punctuation. It may, therefore, be relied upon as a standard edition. (The small figures designating the clauses are not in the original & are added merely for convenience of reference.)

James Buchanan
Secretary of State.

By the Secretary
N. P. Trist, Chief Clerk.

The following is prefixed to the first ten of the preceding amendments.*

CONGRESS OF THE UNITED STATES,

Begun and held at the City of New York, on Wednesday, the fourth of March, one thousand seven hundred and eighty-nine.

The Conventions of a number of the States, having at the time of their adopting the Constitution, expressed a desire, in order to prevent misconstruction or abuse of its powers, that further declaratory and restrictive clauses should be added: And as extending the ground of public confidence in the Government, will best insure the beneficent ends of its institution;

Resolved by the Senate and House of Representatives

---

* It may be proper here to state that 12 articles of amendment were proposed by the first Congress, of which but 10 were ratified by the States—the first and second in order not having been ratified by the requisite number of States.

These two were as follows:

Article the first....After the first enumeration required by the first Article of the Constitution, there shall be one Representative for every thirty thousand, until the number shall amount to one hundred, after which, the proportion shall be so regulated by Congress, that there shall not be less than one hundred Representatives, nor less than one Representative for every forty thousand persons, until the number of Representatives shall amount to two hundred, after which the proportion shall be so regulated by Congress, that there shall not be less than two hundred Representatives, nor more than one Representative for every fifty thousand persons.

Article second....No law, varying the compensation for the services of the Senators and Representatives, shall take effect, until an election of Representatives shall have intervened.

of the United States of America, in Congress assembled, two thirds of both Houses concurring, That the following Articles be proposed to the Legislatures of the several States, as amendments to the Constitution of the United States, all, or any of which articles, when ratified by three-fourths of the said Legislatures, to be valid to all intents and purposes, as part of the said Constitution; viz.

Articles in addition to, and Amendment of the Constitution of the United States of America, proposed by Congress, and ratified by the Legislatures of the several States pursuant to the fifth article of the original Constitution.

The first ten amendments of the Constitution were ratified by the States as follows, viz.:

By New Jersey, 20th November, 1789.

By Maryland, 19th December, 1789.

By North Carolina, 22d December, 1789.

By South Carolina, 19th January, 1790.

By New Hampshire, 25th January, 1790.

By Delaware, 28th January, 1790.

By Pennsylvania, 10th March, 1790.

By New York, 27th March, 1790.

By Rhode Island, 15th June, 1790.

By Vermont, 3 November, 1791.

By Virginia, 15 December, 1791.

The following is prefixed to the eleventh of the preceding amendments:

THIRD CONGRESS OF THE UNITED STATES:

At the first session, begun and held at the city of Philadelphia, in the State of Pennsylvania, on Monday the second of December, one thousand seven hundred and ninety-three.

Resolved by the Senate and House of Representatives of the United States of America, in Congress assembled, two thirds of both Houses concurring, That the following Article be proposed to the Legislatures of the several States, as an amendment to the Constitution of the United States; which when ratified by three-fourths of the said Legislatures shall be valid as part of the said Constitution, viz:

The following is prefixed to the twelfth of the preceding amendments:

EIGHTH CONGRESS OF THE UNITED STATES:

At the first session, begun and held at the city of Washington, in the Territory of Columbia, on Monday the seventeenth of October, one thousand eight hundred and three.

Resolved by the Senate and House of Representatives of the United States of America, in Congress assembled, Two thirds of both Houses concurring, that in lieu of the third paragraph of the first section of the second article of the Constitution of the United States, the following be proposed as an amendment to the Constitution of the United States, which, when ratified by three-fourths of the legislatures of the several states, shall be valid to all intents and purposes, as part of the said Constitution, to wit:

The ten first of the preceding amendments were proposed at the first session of the first Congress, of the United States, 25 September, 1789, and were finally ratified by the constitutional number of States, on the 15th day of December, 1791. The eleventh amendment was proposed at the first session of the third Congress, 5 March, 1794, and was declared in a message from the President of the United States to both houses of Congress, dated 8th January, 1798, to have been adopted by the constitutional number of States. The twelfth amendment was proposed at the first session of the eighth Congress, 12 December, 1803, and was adopted by the constitutional number of States in 1804, according to a public notice thereof by the Secretary of State, dated 25th September, of the same year.

DESIGN OF THE ANALYSIS.

1. Every substantive matter, or point, contained in each article, section, or clause, embracing every subject, name and definition in the Constitution, has been arranged in alphabetical order. The entire clause in which each word so arranged occurs, being given.

2. All similar words, names, or terms used in the Constitution being thus brought together, saves the time and trouble of reading over that instrument in search of supposed terms or provisions, which, if they cannot be found in this Alphabetical Analysis, will not be found in the Constitution. Under the head of each branch of the Government, as Congress, Senate, House of Representatives, Executive or President, Judiciary, &c., will be found every power, duty, privilege, and restriction belonging to each, and joint or concurrent power with the other branches. In like manner, all provisions, regarding States, legislatures, persons, people, citizens, powers, offices, laws, elections, army, militia, navy, and every other subject contained in the Constitution, will all respectively, be found under one head.

3. By this arrangement the entire instrument is resolved into its elements, while all clauses containing like terms or provisions are drawn together in close contact, by the strictly alphabetical position of the similar terms or words in each, which proximity brings the whole into one view, to be seen at a glance, and being thus presented to the mind at once, the connection is more easily impressed upon and retained in the memory.

AN ALPHABETICAL ANALYSIS OF THE CONSTITUTION OF THE UNITED STATES, AND OF THE AMENDMENTS THERETO.

	Art.	sec.	cl.	page.
ABSENCE. In the absence of the Vice President the Senate shall choose a President pro tem.	1	3	5	4
ABSENT members. A smaller number than a majority of either House of Congress may compel the attendance of absent members, in such manner, and under such penalties, as each House may provide	1	5	1	5
ACCEPT. No person holding any office of profit or trust under the United States, shall, without the consent of Congress, accept of any present, emolument, office, or title, of any kind whatever, from any king, prince, or foreign states	1	9	8	11
ACCOUNT. A regular statement and account of the receipts and expenditures of all public money shall be published from time to time	1	9	7	11
ACCUSATION. In all criminal prosecutions, the accused to be informed of the nature and cause of the accusation	6th amend.			27
ACTS, records, and judicial proceedings. Full faith and credit shall be given in each State to the public acts, records, and judicial proceedings of every other State. And the Congress may, by general laws, prescribe the manner in which such acts, records, and judicial proceedings shall be proved, and the effect thereof	4	1	1	19
ACT as President. In case of the removal, death, resignation, or inability, of both the President and Vice President, the Congress shall, by law, declare what officer shall then act as President, and such officer shall act accordingly until the disability be removed, or a President shall be elected	2	1	5	14
ADJOURN from day to day. A smaller number than a majority of each House of Congress may adjourn from day to day	1	5	1	5
ADJOURN. Neither House, during the session of Congress, shall, without the consent of the other, adjourn for more than three days, nor to any other place than that in which the two Houses may be sitting	1	5	4	6
ADJOURNMENT. If any bill shall not be returned by the President within ten days (Sundays excepted) after it shall have been presented to him, the same shall be a law, in like man-				

ner as if he had signed it, unless the Congress by their adjournment prevent its return, in which case it shall not be a law	1	7	2	7
ADJOURNMENT. Every order, resolution, or vote, to which the concurrence of the Senate and House of Representatives may be necessary, (except on a question of adjournment,) shall be presented to the President of the United States. (For proceedings, see resolution.)	1	7	3	8
ADJOURNMENT. In case of disagreement between the two Houses of Congress with respect to the time of adjournment, the President may adjourn them to such time as he shall think proper	2	3	1	16
ADMIRALTY and maritime jurisdiction. The judicial power shall extend to all cases of admiralty and maritime jurisdiction	3	2	1	18
ADMITTED. New States may be admitted by the Congress into this Union	4	3	1	20
ADOPTION of this Constitution. All debts contracted or engagements entered into before the adoption of this Constitution, shall be as valid against the United States under this Constitution as under the Confederation	6	1	1	21
ADVICE and consent of the Senate. (See Senate.)				
AFFIRMATION. (See Oath or affirmation.)				
AGE of qualification for a Representative in Congress, 25 years	1	2	2	2
AGE of qualification for a Senator in Congress, 30 years	1	3	3	4
AGE of qualification for President of the United States, 35 years	2	1	4	14
AGE of qualification for Vice President of the United States, 35 years	12th amend.			30
AGREEMENT or compact. No State shall, without the consent of Congress, enter into any agreement or compact with another State or a foreign power	1	10	3	12
ALLIANCE. No State shall enter into any alliance	1	10	1	12
ALIENS, or persons of foreign birth, not eligible as President or Vice President of the United States	2	1	4	14
	12th amend.			30
AMBASSADORS. The President shall nominate, and by and with the advice and consent of the Senate, appoint ambassadors, &c.	2	2	2	16
AMBASSADORS. The President shall receive ambassadors and other public ministers	2	3	1	17
AMBASSADORS. The judicial power shall extend to all cases affecting ambassadors, other public ministers, and consuls	3	2	1	18
AMBASSADORS. In all cases affecting ambassadors, other public ministers, and consuls, the Supreme Court shall have original jurisdiction	3	2	2	18
AMENDMENTS, as on other bills. All bills for raising revenue shall originate in the House of				

ALPHABETICAL ANALYSIS—Continued.

	Art.	sec.	cl.	page.
Representatives; but the Senate may propose, or concur with, amendments as on other bills	1	7	1	7
AMENDMENTS to the Constitution. The Congress, whenever two-thirds of both Houses shall deem it necessary, shall propose amendments to this Constitution, or, on the application of the legislatures of two-thirds of the several States, shall call a convention for proposing amendments, which, in either case, shall be valid, to all intents and purposes, as part of this Constitution, when ratified by the legislatures of three-fourths of the several States, or by conventions in three-fourths thereof, as the one or the other mode of ratification may be proposed by the Congress; provided that no amendment, which may be made prior to the year 1808, shall, in any manner, affect the first and fourth clauses in the ninth section of the first article; and that no State, without its consent, shall be deprived of its equal suffrage in the Senate	5	1	1	21
APPELLATE jurisdiction. (See Supreme Court.)	3	2	2	18
APPOINTED. No Senator or Representative shall, during the time for which he was elected, be appointed to any civil office under the authority of the United States, which shall have been created, or the emoluments of which shall have been increased during such time	1	6	2	6
APPOINTED. No Senator or Representative, or person holding an office of trust or profit under the United States, shall be appointed an Elector	2	1	2	13
APPOINTMENTS. The Executives of States may make temporary appointments of Senators in the recess of the legislatures thereof to fill vacancies	1	3	2	3
APPOINTMENT of officers of the militia reserved to the States respectively	1	8	16	10
APPOINTMENT of Electors of President and Vice President of the United States. (See Electors.)	2	1	2	13
	12th amend.			8
APPOINTMENTS. The President shall nominate, and by and with the advice and consent of the Senate, shall appoint ambassadors, other public ministers, and consuls, judges of the Supreme Court, and all other officers of the United States whose appointments are not herein otherwise provided for, and which shall be established by law. But the Congress may by law vest the appointment of such inferior officers, as they think proper, in the President alone, in the courts of law, or in the heads of departments	2	2	2	16
APPOINTMENTS. The President shall have power to fill up all vacancies that may happen				

during the recess of the Senate, by granting commissions, (or appointments,) which shall expire at the end of their next session........ 2 2 3 16

APPORTIONED. Representatives and direct taxes to be apportioned among the several States according to their respective numbers, &c........ 1 2 3 2

APPROPRIATION of money to the use of armies shall not be for a longer period than two years........ 1 8 12 9

APPROPRIATIONS. No money shall be drawn from the Treasury but in consequence of appropriations made by law, and a regular statement and account of the receipts and expenditures of all public money shall be published from time to time........ 1 9 7 11

APPROVED. Every bill, resolution, or vote to which the concurrence of the Senate and House of Representatives may be necessary, (except on a question of adjournment,) shall be presented to the President of the United States to be approved or disapproved by him.... 1 7 2–3 7–8

APPROVED. Any bill returned by the President with objection, may become a law if approved by two-thirds of both Houses of Congress........ 1 7 2 7

ARMIES. Congress shall have power to raise and support armies, but no appropriation of money to that use shall be for a longer term than two years........ 1 8 12 9

ARMING. Congress shall have power to provide for organizing, arming, and disciplining the militia........ 1 8 16 9

ARMS. The right of the people to keep and bear arms shall not be infringed........ 2d amend. 25

ARMY. Congress shall have power to make rules for the government and regulation of the land and naval forces........ 1 8 14 9

ARMY. The President shall be Commander-in-Chief of the army........ 2 2 1 15

ARMY. No soldier shall, in time of peace, be quartered in any house without the consent of the owner, nor in time of war, but in a manner to be prescribed by law........ 3d amend. 26

ARMY or Navy. No person shall be held to answer for a capital or otherwise infamous crime, unless on a presentment or indictment of a grand jury, except in cases arising in the land or naval forces, or in the militia, when in actual service, in time of war or public danger.. 5th amend. 26

ARREST. Senators and Representatives shall, in all cases except treason, felony, and breach of the peace, be privileged from arrest during their attendance at the sessions of their respective Houses, and in going to and returning from the same........ 1 6 1 6

ARSENALS, &c. Congress shall have power to exercise exclusive legislation over arsenals, &c. 1 8 17 10

ARTS. Congress shall have power to promote the progress of science and useful arts, by se-

ALPHABETICAL ANALYSIS—Continued.

	Art.	sec.	cl.	page.
curing, for limited times, to authors and inventors, the exclusive right to their respective writings and discoveries	1	8	8	9
ASSEMBLE. Congress shall assemble at least once in every year, on the first Monday in December, unless they shall by law appoint a different day	1	4	2	5
ASSEMBLE. Congress shall make no law abridging the right of the people peaceably to assemble and to petition the Government for a redress of grievances	1st amend.			25
ATTAINDER. No bill of attainder or ex post facto law shall be passed	1	9	3	11
ATTAINDER. No State shall pass any bill of attainder	1	10	1	12
ATTAINDER of treason. The Congress shall have power to declare the punishment of treason, but no attainder of treason shall work corruption of blood or forfeiture, except during the life of the person attainted	3	3	2	19
ATTENDANCE. Less than a quorum of either House may compel the attendance of absent members	1	5	1	5
ATTENDANCE. Members of Congress privileged from arrest during their attendance at sessions, &c. (See Arrest.)	1	6	1	6
AUTHENTICATION of records, acts, and judicial proceedings of States	4	1	1	19
AUTHORS may secure exclusive rights to their writings for a limited time	1	8	8	9
BAIL. Excessive bail shall not be required, nor excessive fines imposed, nor cruel and unusual punishments inflicted	8th amend.			27
BALDWIN, deputy from Georgia, signed this Constitution. Abraham	–	–	–	23
BALLOT. The electors shall vote by ballot for President and Vice President of the United States. They shall name in their ballots the person voted for as President, and, in distinct ballots, the person voted for as Vice President	12th amend.			28
BALLOT. If no person have a majority of the electoral votes, the House of Representatives shall choose, immediately, by ballot, the President	12th amend.			29
BANKRUPTCIES. Congress shall have power to establish uniform laws on the subject of bankruptcies throughout the United States	1	8	4	8
BASSETT, deputy from Delaware, signed this Constitution. Richard				23
BEDFORD, jr., deputy from Delaware, signed this Constitution. Gunning				23
BILL of attainder. No bill of attainder or ex post facto law shall be passed	1	9	3	11

BILLS. All bills for raising revenue shall originate in the House of Representatives, but the Senate may propose or concur with amendments, as on other bills	1	7	1	7
BILL. Every bill which shall have passed the House of Representatives and the Senate shall, before it become a law, be presented to the President of the United States; if he approve, he shall sign it, but if not, he shall return it, with his objections, to that House in which it shall have originated, who shall enter the objections at large on their Journal, and proceed to reconsider it. If, after such reconsideration, two-thirds of that House shall agree to pass the bill, it shall be sent, together with the objections, to the other House, by which it shall likewise be reconsidered, and if approved by two-thirds of that House, it shall become a law. But in all such cases, the votes of both Houses shall be determined by yeas and nays, and the names of the persons voting for and against the bill shall be entered on the Journal of each House respectively	1	7	2	7
BILL. If any bill shall not be returned by the President within ten days (Sundays excepted) after it shall have been presented to him, the same shall be a law, in like manner as if he had signed it, unless the Congress, by their adjournment, prevent its return, in which case it shall not be a law	1	7	2	7
BILL. Every order, resolution, or vote to which the concurrence of the Senate and House of Representatives may be necessary, (except on a question of adjournment,) shall be presented to the President of the United States; and, before the same shall take effect, shall be approved by him, or, being disapproved by him, shall be re-passed by two-thirds of the Senate and House of Representatives, according to the rules and limitations prescribed in the case of a bill	1	7	3	8
BILLS of credit. No State shall emit bills of credit	1	10	1	12
BLAIR, deputy from Virginia, signed this Constitution. John	–	–	–	23
BLOOD. No attainder of treason shall work corruption of blood or forfeiture, except during the life of the person attainted	3	3	2	19
BLOUNT, deputy from North Carolina, signed this Constitution. William				23
BORROW money. Congress shall have power to borrow money on the credit of the United States	1	8	2	8
BOUND. Persons bound to service for a term of years, included in representative numbers	1	2	3	2
BREACH of the peace. For a breach of the peace, a Senator or Representative may be arrested.	1	6	1	6
BREARLEY, deputy from New Jersey, signed this Constitution. David				23

ALPHABETICAL ANALYSIS—Continued.

	Art.	sec.	cl.	page.
BRIBERY. All civil officers shall be removed from office on impeachment for, and conviction of, bribery, &c.	2	4	1	17
BROOM, deputy from Delaware, signed this Constitution. Jacob				23
BUILDINGS. Congress shall have power to exercise exclusive legislation over needful buildings in places purchased by the consent of the Legislatures of the States	1	8	17	10
BUSINESS. A majority of each House shall constitute a quorum to do business	1	5	1	5
BUTLER, deputy from South Carolina, signed this Constitution. Pierce				23
CAPITAL crime. No person shall be held to answer for a capital or otherwise infamous crime, unless on a presentment or indictment of a grand jury, except in cases arising in the land or naval forces, or in the militia, when in actual service in time of war or public danger	5th amend.			26
CAPITATION tax. No capitation, or other direct, tax shall be laid, unless in proportion to the census or enumeration hereinbefore directed to be taken	1	9	4	11
CAPITATION tax. No amendment shall be made prior to 1808 to affect the preceding clause	5	0	0	21
CAPTURES. Congress shall have power to declare war, to grant letters of marque and reprisal, and make rules concerning captures on land and water	1	8	11	9
CARE. The President shall take care that the laws be faithfully executed	2	3	1	17
CARROLL, deputy from Maryland, signed this Constitution. Daniel				23
CASES to which the judicial power shall extend. (See Judicial Power.)	3	2	1	17
CAUSE. No warrant shall issue but upon probable cause	4th amend.			26
CENSUS to be taken within three years after first meeting of Congress, and every ten years thereafter, in such manner as they shall by law direct	1	2	3	2
CENSUS. No capitation, or other direct, tax shall be laid, unless in proportion to the census or enumeration hereinbefore directed to be taken	1	9	4	11
CENSUS. No amendment shall be made prior to 1808 to affect the preceding clause	5	0	0	21
CESSION. On the cession by particular States of a district, (not exceeding ten miles square,) and the acceptance of Congress, it may become the seat of Government of the United States	1	8	17	10
CHARGE of treason. A person charged in any State with treason, &c., who may fly from justice, to be delivered up and removed to the State having jurisdiction of the crime	4	2	2	19

Entry				
CHIEF JUSTICE shall preside when the President of the United States is tried on an impeachment by the Senate. The	1	3	6	4
CHOSEN. (See Elected, &c.)				
CHUSE. (See Elect.)				
CITIZEN of United States. No person shall be a Representative in Congress who has not been seven years a *citizen of the United States*	1	2	2	2
CITIZEN of United States. No person shall be a Senator in Congress who has not been nine years a citizen of the United States	1	3	3	4
CITIZEN. No person except a natural born citizen, or a citizen of the United States at the time of the adoption of the Constitution, shall be eligible to the office of President	2	1	5	14
CITIZENS. The judicial power shall extend to controversies between a State and citizens of another State; between citizens of different States; between citizens of the same State claiming lands under grants of different States; and between a State, or the citizens thereof, and foreign States, citizens, or subjects	3	2	1	18
CITIZENS. The citizens of each State shall be entitled to all privileges and immunities of citizens in the several States	4	2	1	19
CITIZENS. The judicial power of the United States shall not be construed to extend to any suit in law or equity commenced or prosecuted against one of the United States by citizens of another State, or by citizens or subjects of any foreign State	11th amend.			28
CIVIL office. (See Office.)				
CIVIL officers. All civil officers of the United States shall be removed from office on impeachment for, and conviction of, treason, bribery, or other high crimes and misdemeanors	2	4	1	17
CLAIM. Fugitive slaves shall be delivered up on claim of the party to whom they belong, &c.	4	2	3	20
CLAIMS. The Congress shall have power to dispose of and make all needful rules and regulations respecting the territory or other property belonging to the United States; and nothing in this Constitution shall be so construed as to prejudice any claims of the United States, or of any particular State	4	3	2	20
CLASSES. The Senators shall be divided as equally as may be into three classes. (See Senators.)	1	3	2	3
CLEAR. Vessels bound to or from one State shall not be obliged to enter, clear, or pay duties in another	1	9	6	11
CLYMER, Deputy from Pennsylvania, signed this Constitution, George	–	–	–	23
COIN money. Congress shall have power to coin money, regulate the value thereof, and of foreign coin	1	8	5	8

ALPHABETICAL ANALYSIS—Continued.

	Art.	sec.	cl.	page.
COIN. (See Counterfeiting.)	1	8	6	9
COIN money. No State shall coin money	1	10	1	12
COIN. No State shall make any thing but gold and silver coin a tender in payment of debts	1	10	1	12
COLLECT duties. Congress shall have power to lay and collect duties, taxes, imposts, and excises	1	8	1	8
COMMANDER-IN-CHIEF. The President shall be Commander-in-Chief of the Army and Navy of the United States, and of the militia of the several States, when called into the actual service of the United States	2	2	1	15
COMMERCE. Congress shall have power to regulate commerce with foreign nations, and among the several States, and with the Indian tribes	1	8	3	8
COMMERCE. No preference shall be given by any regulations of commerce or revenue to the ports of one State over those of another; nor shall vessels, bound to or from one State, be obliged to enter, clear, or pay duties in another	1	9	6	11
COMMISSIONS. The President shall have power to fill up all vacancies that may happen during the recess of the Senate, by granting commissions which shall expire at the end of their next session	2	2	3	16
COMMISSIONS. The President shall commission all the officers of the United States	2	3	1	17
COMMON defence, &c. The Constitution established to provide for the common defence, &c.	Preamble.			1
COMMON defence. Congress shall have power to provide for the common defence	1	8	1	8
COMMON law. In suits at common law, where the value in controversy shall exceed twenty dollars, the right of trial by jury shall be preserved: and no fact tried by a jury shall be otherwise re-examined in any court of the United States, than according to the rules of the common law	7th amend.			27
COMPACT. No State shall, without the consent of Congress, enter into any agreement or compact with another State or a foreign power	1	10	3	12
COMPEL the attendance of absent members. A smaller number than a quorum of each House may compel the attendance of absent members, in such manner and under such penalties as each House may provide	1	5	1	5
COMPENSATION. The Senators and Representatives shall receive a compensation for their services to be ascertained by law and paid out of the Treasury of the United States	1	6	1	6
COMPENSATION of the President of the United States. The President shall, at stated times,				

Subject	Art.	Sec.	Cl.	Page
receive for his services a compensation which shall be neither increased nor diminished during the period for which he shall have been elected, and he shall not receive within that period any other emolument from the United States, or any of them	2	1	7	15
COMPENSATION. The judges both of the Supreme and Inferior courts shall hold their offices during good behaviour, and shall, at stated times, receive for their services a compensation which shall not be diminished during their continuance in office	3	1	1	17
COMPENSATION. Nor shall private property be taken for public use without just compensation	5th amend.			26
COMPULSORY process. In all criminal prosecutions the accused to have compulsory process for obtaining witnesses in his favour	6th amend.			27
CONCUR. The Senate may propose and concur in amendments to revenue bills, &c.	1	7	1	7
CONCURRENCE. No person shall be convicted on an impeachment without the concurrence of two-thirds of the Senators present	1	3	6	4
CONCURRENCE. Every order, resolution, or vote, to which the concurrence of the two Houses may be necessary, shall be presented to the President, except, &c.	1	7	3	8
CONFEDERATION. No State shall enter into any confederation	1	10	1	12
CONFEDERATION. All debts contracted or engagements entered into before the adoption of this Constitution, shall be as valid against the United States under this Constitution as under the Confederation	6	1	1	21
CONFESSION in open court. No person shall be convicted of treason unless on the testimony of two witnesses to the same overt act, or on confession in open court	3	3	1	19
CONFRONTED. In all criminal prosecutions, the accused shall enjoy the right to be confronted with the witnesses against him	6th amend.			27
CONGRESS United States. All legislative powers herein granted shall be vested in Congress	1	1	-	1
CONGRESS United States shall consist of a Senate and House of Representatives	1	1	-	1
CONGRESS, members of. (See Senators.) (See Representatives.)				
CONGRESS shall by law direct the manner in which the census or enumeration of the people shall be made	1	2	3	2
CONGRESS. The first Congress to consist of 65 members from the several States, as mentioned herein. (See Representatives.)	1	2	3	2
CONGRESS. The time, places, and manner of holding elections for Senators and Representatives, shall be prescribed in each State by the Legislature thereof; but the Congress may,				

ALPHABETICAL ANALYSIS—Continued.

	Art.	sec.	cl.	page.
at any time, by law, make or alter such regulations, except as to the places of choosing Senators	1	4	1	5
CONGRESS shall assemble at least once in every year, and such meeting shall be on the first Monday in December, unless they shall by law appoint a different day	1	4	2	5
CONGRESS of the United States:—				
Each House shall be the judge of the elections, returns, and qualifications of its own members, and a majority of each shall constitute a quorum to do business; but a smaller number may adjourn from day to day, and may be authorized to compel the attendance of absent members, in such manner and under such penalties as each House may provide	1	5	1	5
Each House may determine the rules of its proceedings, punish its members for disorderly behavior, and, with the concurrence of two-thirds, expel a member	1	5	2	5
Each House shall keep a Journal of its proceedings, and from time to time publish the same, excepting such parts as may, in their judgment, require secrecy; and the yeas and nays of the members of either House, on any question, shall, at the desire of one-fifth of those present, be entered on the Journal	1	5	3	5
Neither House, during the session of Congress, shall, without the consent of the other, adjourn for more than three days, nor to any other place than that in which the two Houses shall be sitting	1	5	4	6
All bills for raising revenue shall originate in the House of Representatives; but the Senate may propose, or concur with, amendments, as on other bills	1	7	1	7
Every bill which shall have passed the House of Representatives and the Senate, shall, before it become a law, be presented to the President of the United States; if he approve, he shall sign it, but if not, he shall return it, with his objections, to that House in which it shall have originated, who shall enter the objections at large on their Journal, and proceed to reconsider it	1	7	2	7
If, after such reconsideration, two-thirds of that House shall agree to pass the bill, it shall be sent, together with the objections, to the other House, by which it shall likewise be reconsidered, and if approved by two-thirds of that House, it shall become a law	1	7	2	7
But, in all such cases, the votes of both Houses shall be determined by yeas and nays,				

and the names of the persons voting for and against the bill, shall be entered on the Journal of each House respectively	1	7	2	7
If any bill shall not be returned by the President within ten days (Sundays excepted) after it shall have been presented to him, the same shall be a law, in like manner as if he had signed it, unless the Congress, by their adjournment, prevent its return, in which case it shall not be a law	1	7	2	7
Every order, resolution, or vote, to which the concurrence of the Senate and House of Representatives may be necessary, (except on a question of adjournment,) shall be presented to the President of the United States, and, before the same shall take effect, shall be approved by him, or, being disapproved by him, shall be repassed by two-thirds of the Senate and House of Representatives, according to the rules and limitations prescribed in the case of a bill	1	7	3	8
CONGRESS shall have power				
To lay and collect taxes, duties, imposts, and excises, to pay the debts and provide for the common defence and general welfare of the United States; but all duties, imposts and excises shall be uniform throughout the United States	1	8	1	8
To borrow money on the credit of the United States	1	8	2	8
To regulate commerce with foreign nations, and among the several States, and with the Indian tribes	1	8	3	8
To establish an uniform rule of naturalization, and uniform laws on the subject of bankruptcies throughout the United States	1	8	4	8
To coin money, regulate the value thereof, and of foreign coin; and fix the standard of weights and measures	1	8	5	8
To provide for the punishment of counterfeiting the securities and current coin of the United States	1	8	6	9
To establish post offices and post roads	1	8	7	9
To promote the progress of science and useful arts, by securing, for limited times, to authors and inventors, the exclusive right to their respective writings and discoveries	1	8	8	9
To constitute tribunals inferior to the Supreme Court	1	8	9	9
To define and punish piracies and felonies committed on the high seas, and offences against the law of nations	1	8	10	9
To declare war, grant letters of marque and reprisal, and make rules concerning captures on land and water	1	8	11	9

ALPHABETICAL ANALYSIS—Continued.

	Art.	sec.	cl.	page.
To raise and support armies; but no appropriation of money to that use shall be for a longer term than two years	1	8	12	9
To provide and maintain a navy	1	8	13	9
To make rules for the government a d regulation of the land and naval forces	1	8	14	9
To provide for calling forth the militia to execute the laws of the Union, suppress insurrections, and repel invasions	1	8	15	9
To provide for organizing, arming, and disciplining the militia, and for governing such part of them as may be employed in the service of the United States, reserving to the States, respectively, the appointment of the officers, and the authority of training the militia according to the discipline prescribed by Congress	1	8	16	9
To exercise exclusive legislation in all cases whatsoever, over such district (not exceeding ten miles square) as may, by cession of particular States, and the acceptance of Congress, become the seat of the Government of the United States, and to exercise like authority over all places purchased by the consent of the Legislature of the State in which the same shall be, for the erection of forts, magazines, arsenals, dock-yards, and other needful buildings; and	1	8	17	10
To make all laws which shall be necessary and proper for carrying into execution the foregoing powers, and all other powers vested by this Constitution in the Government of the United States, or in any department or office thereof	1	8	18	10
CONGRESS. The migration or importation of such persons as any of the States now existing shall think proper to admit, shall not be prohibited by the Congress prior to the year 1808, but a tax or duty may be imposed on such importation, not exceeding ten dollars for each person	1	9	1	10
CONGRESS. No title of nobility shall be granted by the United States; and no person holding any office of profit or trust under them shall, without the consent of Congress, accept of any present, emolument, office, or title of any kind whatever, from any king, prince, or foreign State	1	9	8	11
CONGRESS. No State shall, without the consent of Congress, lay any imposts or duties on imports or exports, except what may be absolutely necessary for executing its inspection laws: and the nett produce of all duties and imposts, laid by any State on imports or				

exports, shall be for the use of the Treasury of the United States; and all such laws shall be subject to the revision and control of the Congress..........	1	10	2	12
CONGRESS. No State shall, without the consent of Congress, lay any duty of tonnage, keep troops or ships of war, in time of peace—enter into any agreement or compact with another State, or with a foreign power, or engage in war, unless actually invaded, or in such imminent danger as will not admit of delay..........	1	10	3	12
CONGRESS. Each State shall appoint, in such manner as the Legislature thereof may direct, a number of electors, equal to the whole number of Senators and Representatives to which the State may be entitled in the Congress..........	2	1	2	13
CONGRESS. The Congress may determine the time of choosing the electors, and the day on which they shall give their votes; which day shall be the same throughout the United States..........	2	1	3	14
CONGRESS. The Congress may, by law, provide for the case of removal, death, resignation, or inability, both of the President and Vice President, declaring what officer shall then act as President, and such officer shall act accordingly, until the disability be removed, or a President shall be elected..........	2	1	5	14
CONGRESS. The Congress may by law vest the appointment of such inferior officers, as they think proper, in the President alone, in the courts of law, or in the heads of Departments..........	2	2	2	16
CONGRESS. The President shall, from time to time, give to the Congress information of the state of the Union, and recommend to their consideration such measures as he shall judge necessary and expedient; he may, on extraordinary occasions, convene both Houses, or either of them, and, in case of disagreement between them with respect to the time of adjournment, he may adjourn them to such time as he shall think proper..........	2	3	1	16
CONGRESS. The judicial power of the United States shall be vested in one Supreme Court, and in such inferior courts as the Congress may from time to time ordain and establish..	3	1	1	17
CONGRESS. In certain cases the Supreme Court shall have appellate jurisdiction, both as to law and fact, with such exceptions, and under such regulations, as the Congress shall make..........	3	2	2	18
CONGRESS. When crimes are not committed within any State, the trial shall be at such place or places as the Congress may by law have directed..........	3	2	3	18
CONGRESS shall have power to declare the punishment of treason; but no attainder of treason shall work corruption of blood or forfeiture, except during the life of the person attainted.	3	3	2	19

ALPHABETICAL ANALYSIS—Continued.

	Art.	sec.	cl.	page.
CONGRESS. Full faith and credit shall be given in each State, to the public acts, records, and judicial proceedings of every other State. And the Congress may, by general laws, prescribe the manner in which such acts, records, and proceedings shall be proved, and the effect thereof	4	1	1	19
CONGRESS. New States may be admitted by the Congress into this Union; but no new State shall be formed or erected within the jurisdiction of any other State; nor any State be formed by the junction of two or more States, or parts of States, without the consent of the Legislatures of the States concerned, as well as of the Congress	4	3	1	20
CONGRESS. The Congress shall have power to dispose of and make all needful rules and regulations respecting the territory or other property belonging to the United States; and nothing in this Constitution shall be so construed as to prejudice any claims of the United States, or of any particular State	4	3*	2	20
CONGRESS. The Congress, whenever two-thirds of both Houses shall deem it necessary, shall propose amendments to this Constitution; or, on the application of the Legislatures of two-thirds of the several States, shall call a convention for proposing amendments, which, in either case, shall be valid to all intents and purposes, as part of this Constitution, when ratified by the Legislatures of three-fourths of the several States, or by conventions in three-fourths thereof, as the one or the other mode of ratification may be proposed by the Congress: Provided, that no amendment which may be made prior to the year 1808, shall, in any manner, affect the first and fourth clauses in the ninth section of the first article; and that no State, without its consent, shall be deprived of its equal suffrage in the Senate	5	0	0	21
CONGRESS. The Senators and Representatives in Congress shall be bound by an oath or affirmation, to support this Constitution	6	0	3	22
CONGRESS shall make no law respecting an establishment of religion, or prohibiting the free exercise thereof; or abridging the freedom of speech or of the press; or the right of the people peaceably to assemble and to petition the Government for a redress of grievances.	1st amend.			25
CONGRESS. The certificates of the electoral votes for President and Vice President of the United States shall be opened by the President of the Senate, in the presence of the Senate and House of Representatives, and the votes shall then be counted	12th amend.			29
CONNECTICUT entitled to 5 Representatives in the first Congress	1	2	3	2

CONSENT of Congress. No person holding any office of profit or trust under the United States shall, without the consent of Congress, accept of any present, emolument, office, or title of any kind whatever, from any king, prince, or foreign State........ 1 9 8 11

CONSENT of either House. Neither House, during the session of Congress, shall, without the consent of the other, adjourn for more than three days, nor to any other place than that in which the two Houses shall be sitting........ 1 5 4 6

CONSENT of Congress. No State shall, without the consent of the Congress, lay any imposts or duties on imports or exports, except what may be absolutely necessary for executing its inspection laws........ 1 10 2 12

CONSENT of Congress. No State shall, without the consent of Congress, lay any duty of tonnage; keep troops or ships of war in time of peace; enter into any agreement or compact with another State, or with a foreign power, or engage in war, unless actually invaded, or in such imminent danger as will not admit of delay........ 1 10 3 12

CONSENT of the Legislatures. No State shall be formed by the junction of two or more States, or parts of States, without the consent of the Legislatures of the States concerned, as well as of the Congress........ 4 3 1 20

CONSENT. No State, without its consent, shall be deprived of its equal suffrage in the Senate 5 – – 21

CONSENT. This Constitution adopted or done in convention by the unanimous consent of the States present........ 7 – – 22

CONSENT. No soldier shall, in time of peace, be quartered in any house without the consent of the owner, nor in time of war, but in a manner to be prescribed by law........ 3d amend. 26

CONSTITUTION ordained and established in order to form a more perfect Union; establish justice; ensure domestic tranquillity; provide for the common defence; promote the general welfare, and to secure the blessings of liberty........ Preamble. 1

CONSTITUTION. Congress shall have power to make all laws which shall be necessary and proper for carrying into execution the foregoing powers, and all other powers vested by this Constitution in the Government of the United States, or in any department or office thereof........ 1 8 18 10

CONSTITUTION. No person except a natural born citizen, or a citizen at the time of the adoption of this Constitution, shall be eligible to the office of President of the United States........ 2 1 4 14

CONSTITUTION of the United States. The President shall, before he enter on the execution

ALPHABETICAL ANALYSIS—Continued.

	Art.	sec.	cl.	page.
of his office, take an oath that he will, to the best of his ability, "preserve, protect, and defend the Constitution of the United States"	2	1	7	15
CONSTITUTION. The Judicial power shall extend to all cases, in law and equity, arising under the Constitution	3	2	1	17
CONSTITUTION. Nothing in this Constitution shall be so construed as to prejudice any claims of the United States, or of any particular State, respecting the territory or other property thereof	4	3	2	20
CONSTITUTION. The Congress, whenever two-thirds of both Houses shall deem it necessary, shall propose amendments to this Constitution, or, on the application of the Legislatures of two-thirds of the several States, shall call a convention for proposing amendments, which, in either case, shall be valid, to all intents and purposes, as part of this Constitution, when ratified by the Legislatures of three-fourths of the several States, or by conventions in three-fourths thereof, as the one or the other mode of ratification may be proposed by the Congress; provided that no amendment which may be made prior to the year 1808, shall, in any manner, affect the first and fourth clauses in the ninth section of the first article; and that no State, without its consent, shall be deprived of its equal suffrage in the Senate	5	0	0	21
CONSTITUTION. All debts contracted, and engagements entered into, before the adoption of this Constitution, shall be as valid against the United States under this Constitution, as under the Confederation	6	0	1	21
CONSTITUTION. This Constitution, and the laws of the United States which shall be made in pursuance thereof, and all treaties made, or which shall be made, under the authority of the United States, shall be the supreme law of the land; and the judges in every State shall be bound thereby, any thing in the Constitution or laws of any State to the contrary notwithstanding	6	0	2	22
CONSTITUTION or laws of any State. The judges in every State shall be bound by the Constitution, laws, and treaties of the United States, any thing in the Constitution or laws of any State to the contrary notwithstanding	6	0	2	22
CONSTITUTION. The Senators and Representatives before mentioned, and the members of the several State Legislatures, and all executive and judicial officers, both of the United States and of the several States, shall be bound by oath or affirmation to support this Con-				

stitution; but no religious test shall ever be required as a qualification to any office of public trust under the United States........ 6 0 3 22

CONSTITUTION. The ratification of the conventions of nine States shall be sufficient for the establishment of this Constitution between the States so ratifying the same........ 7 0 1 22

CONSTITUTION. The adoption of the Constitution, done in convention by the unanimous consent of the States present, the 17th day of September, A. D. 1787. and of the independence of the United States the twelfth........ 7 0 1 22

CONSTITUTION. The enumeration in the Constitution of certain rights shall not be construed to deny or disparage others retained by the people........ 9th amend. 28

CONSTITUTION. The powers not delegated to the United States by the Constitution, nor prohibited by it to the States, are reserved to the States, respectively, or to the people.. 10th amend. 28

CONSTRUCTION. Nothing in this Constitution shall be so construed as to prejudice any claims of the United States, or of any particular State........ 4 3 2 20

CONSTRUED. The enumeration in the Constitution of certain rights shall not be construed to deny or disparage others retained by the people........ 9th amend. 28

CONSTRUED. The judicial power of the United States shall not be construed to extend to any suit in law or equity, commenced or prosecuted against one of the United States by citizens of another State, or by citizens or subjects of any foreign State........ 11th amend. 28

CONSULS. (See Appointments.)

CONSULS. The judicial power shall extend to all cases affecting ambassadors, other public ministers, and consuls, in which the Supreme Court shall have original jurisdiction...... 3 2 1–2 18

CONTRACTS. No State shall pass any law impairing the obligation of contracts........ 1 10 1 12

CONTRACTED. All debts contracted, and engagements entered into before the adoption of this Constitution, shall be as valid against the United States under this Constitution as under the Confederation........ 6 1 1 21

CONTROVERSIES. The judicial power shall extend to controversies to which the United States shall be a party; to controversies between two or more States; between a State and citizens of another State; between citizens of different States; between citizens of the same State claiming lands under grants of different States, and between a State or the citizens thereof and foreign States, citizens, or subjects........ 3 2 1 18

CONTROVERSY. In suits at common law, where the value in controversy shall exceed twenty dollars, the right of trial by jury shall be preserved........ 7th amend. 27

ALPHABETICAL ANALYSIS—Continued.

	Art.	sec.	cl.	page.
CONVENE CONGRESS. The President may, on extraordinary occasions, convene both Houses, or either of them	2	3	1	16
CONVENED. The United States shall, on application of the Executive of a State, when the legislature cannot be convened, protect such State from domestic violence	4	4	1	20
CONVENTION. The adoption of the Constitution, done in convention by the unanimous consent of the States present, the 17th September, A. D. 1787	7	0	1	22
CONVENTIONS for proposing and ratifying amendments of the Constitution. (See Constitution.)	5	0	0	21
CONVENTIONS of States. The ratification of the conventions of nine States shall be sufficient for the establishment of this Constitution between the States so ratifying the same	7	0	1	22
CONVICTED. No person shall be convicted on an impeachment, without the concurrence of two-thirds of the Senators present	1	3	6	4
CONVICTED. No person shall be convicted of treason, unless on the testimony of two witnesses to the same overt act, or on confession in open court	3	3	1	19
CORRUPTION of blood. No attainder of treason shall work corruption of blood or forfeiture, except during the life of the person attainted	3	3	2	19
COUNSEL. In all criminal prosecutions the accused to have the assistance of counsel for his defence	6th amend.			27
COUNTERFEITING. Congress shall have power to provide for the punishment of counterfeiting the securities and current coin of the United States	1	8	6	9
COURT of impeachment. (See Impeachment.)				
COURT. (See Appointment of Judges of the Supreme Court.)	2	2	2	16
COURT. No person shall be convicted of treason, unless on the testimony of two witnesses to the same overt act, or on confession in open court	3	3	1	19
COURT of the United States. In suits at common law, where the value in controversy shall exceed twenty dollars, the right of trial by jury shall be preserved; and no fact tried by a jury shall be otherwise re-examined in any court of the United States, than according tc the rules of the common law	7th amend.			27
COURTS. Congress shall have power to constitute tribunals inferior to the Supreme Court	1	8	9	9
COURTS of law. The Congress may, by law, vest the appointment of such inferior officers as				

they think proper in the President alone, in the courts of law, or in the heads of departments... 2 2 2 16

COURTS. The judicial power of the United States shall be vested in one Supreme Court, and in such inferior courts as the Congress may, from time to time, ordain and establish. (See Judicial power.)... 3 1-2 0 17

CREDIT of the United States. Congress shall have power to borrow money on the credit of the United States... 1 8 2 8

CREDIT. No State shall emit bills of credit... 1 10 1 12

CREDIT. Full faith and credit shall be given in each State to the public acts, records, and judicial proceedings of every other State... 4 1 1 19

CRIME. A person charged with treason, felony, or other crime, and fleeing from justice, to be delivered up to the State having jurisdiction of the crime... 4 2 2 19

CRIME. No person shall be held to answer for a capital, or otherwise infamous crime, unless on a presentment or indictment of a grand jury... 5th amend. 26

CRIMES. (See Removal of Civil Officers.)... 2 4 1 17

CRIMES. The trial of all crimes, except in cases of impeachment, shall be by jury... 3 2 3 18

CRIMINAL case. Nor shall any person be compelled in any criminal case to be a witness against himself... 5th amend. 26

CRIMINAL prosecutions. In all criminal prosecutions the accused shall enjoy the right to a speedy and public trial, by an impartial jury of the State and district wherein the crime shall have been committed; which district shall have been previously ascertained by law, and to be informed of the nature and cause of the accusation; to be confronted with the witnesses against him; to have compulsory process for obtaining witnesses in his favor; and to have the assistance of counsel for his defence... 6th amend. 27

CRUEL and unusual punishment. Excessive bail shall not be required, nor excessive fines imposed, nor cruel and unusual punishments inflicted... 8th amend. 27

DANGER. (See Public Danger.)

DAYTON, deputy from New Jersey, signed this Constitution. Jonathan... 23

DEATH. In case of the death of the President, the duties of that office shall devolve on the Vice President, and in case of the death of both President and Vice President, Congress shall by law declare what officer shall then act as President... 2 1 5 14

ALPHABETICAL ANALYSIS—Continued.

	Art.	sec.	cl.	page.
DEBATE. Senators and Representatives, for any speech or debate in either House, shall not be questioned in any other place	1	6	1	6
DEBTS of the United States. Congress shall have power to pay the debts of the United States	1	8	1	8
DEBTS. No State shall make any thing but gold and silver coin a tender in payment of debts	1	10	1	12
DEBTS. All debts contracted and engagements entered into before the adoption of this Constitution, shall be as valid against the United States under this Constitution as under the Confederation	6	0	1	21
DEFENCE. Constitution established to provide for the common defence	Preamble.			1
DEFENCE. Congress shall have power to provide for the common defence	1	8	1	8
DEFENCE. In all criminal prosecutions the accused shall enjoy the right to have the assistance of counsel for his defence	6th amend.			27
DEFEND the Constitution. The President of the United States shall swear or affirm to preserve, protect, and defend the Constitution of the United States	2	1	7	15
DELAWARE entitled to one Representative in first Congress	1	2	3	2
DELEGATED. The powers not delegated to the United States by the Constitution nor prohibited by it to the States, are reserved to the States respectively or to the people	10th amend.			28
DELEGATES or members of State Legislatures shall be bound by oath or affirmation to support this Constitution	6	0	3	22
DELIVERED up. Fugitives from justice to be delivered up to be removed to the State having jurisdiction of the crime	4	2	2	19
DELIVERED up. Persons held to service or labor (or slaves) escaping into another State shall be delivered up on claim of the party to whom such service or labor may be due	4	2	3	20
DEMAND. A fugitive from justice shall, on demand of the Executive authority of the State from which he fled, be delivered up to be removed to the State having jurisdiction of the crime	4	2	2	19
DEPARTMENT of the Government. Congress shall have power to make all laws which shall be necessary and proper for carrying into execution the foregoing powers, and all other powers vested by this Constitution in the Government of the United States, or in any department or office thereof	1	8	18	10
DEPARTMENTS. The President may require the opinion in writing of the principal officer in each of the Executive departments	2	2	1	15

DEPARTMENTS. The Congress may by law vest the appointment of such inferior officers as they think proper in the President alone, in the courts of law or in the heads of departments	2	2	2	16
DEPRIVED. No State without its consent shall be deprived of its equal suffrage in the Senate.	5	-	-	21
DEVOLVE. In case of the removal of the President from office, or of his death, resignation, or inability to discharge the powers and duties of the said office, the same shall devolve on the Vice President	2	1	5	14
DICKINSON, deputy from Delaware, signed this Constitution. John	-	-	-	23
DIRECT tax. Representatives and direct taxes to be apportioned among the States according to their respective numbers, &c. (See Representatives.)	1	2	3	2
DIRECT tax. No capitation or other direct tax shall be laid, unless in proportion to the census or enumeration hereinbefore directed to be taken	1	9	4	11
DISCHARGED from service or labor. No person held to service or labor in one State shall be discharged from such service or labor in another	4	2	3	20
DISCIPLINING the militia. Congress shall have power to provide for organizing, arming, and disciplining the militia, and for governing such part of them as may be employed in the service of the United States, reserving to the States respectively the appointment of the officers, and the authority of training the militia according to the discipline prescribed by Congress	1	8	16	9
DISCOVERIES. Exclusive right to discoveries may be secured by inventors for a limited time.	1	8	8	9
DISORDERLY behavior. Each House may punish its members for disorderly behavior	1	5	2	5
DISTRICT not exceeding ten miles square. Congress shall have power to exercise exclusive legislation in all cases whatsoever over such district (not exceeding ten miles square) as may, by cession of particular States and the acceptance of Congress, become the seat of the Government of the United States	1	8	17	10
DISTRICT. In all criminal prosecutions the accused shall enjoy the right to a speedy and public trial by an impartial jury of the State and District wherein the crime shall have been committed, which district shall have been previously ascertained by law	6th amend.			27
DISQUALIFICATION. Judgment on impeachment a disqualification to hold and enjoy any office, &c., under the United States	1	3	7	4
DIVIDED. The Vice President shall have no vote unless the Senate be equally divided	1	3	4	4
DOCK yards, &c. Congress shall have power to exercise exclusive legislation over dock yards, &c.	1	8	17	10

ALPHABETICAL ANALYSIS—Continued.

	Art.	sec.	cl.	page.
DOMESTIC tranquillity. The Constitution established to ensure domestic tranquillity	Preamble.			1
DOMESTIC violence. The United States shall, on application of the Legislature, or of the Executive, (when the Legislature cannot be convened,) protect each State against domestic violence	4	4	1	20
DURING good behavior. The Judges, both of the Supreme and Inferior courts, shall hold their offices during good behavior	3	1	1	17
DUTIES. Congress shall have power to lay duties	1	8	1	8
DUTIES. All duties, imposts, and excises shall be uniform throughout the United States	1	8	1	8
DUTIES. No preference shall be given by any regulation of commerce or revenue to the ports of one State over those of another; nor shall vessels bound to or from one State be obliged to enter, clear, or pay duties in another	1	9	6	11
DUTIES on imports. No State shall, without the consent of the Congress, lay any imposts or duties on imports or exports, except what may be absolutely necessary for executing its inspection laws: and the nett produce of all duties and imposts laid by any State on imports or exports shall be for the use of the Treasury of the United States, and all such laws shall be subject to the revision and control of the Congress	1	10	2	12
DUTIES. In case of the death, removal, resignation, or inability of the President to discharge the powers and duties of that office, the same shall devolve on the Vice President, &c.	2	1	5	14
DUTIES. The President may require the opinion in writing of the principal officer in each of the Executive departments, upon any subject relating to the duties of their respective offices	2	2	1	15
DUTY or tax might have been imposed on imported persons (or slaves) up to 1808	1	9	1	10
DUTY. No tax or duty shall be laid on articles exported from any State	1	9	5	11
DUTY of tonnage. No State shall, without the consent of Congress, lay any duty of tonnage	1	10	3	12
EFFECT of proceedings of States. Congress may, by general laws, prescribe the effect of the public acts, records, and proceedings of States	4	1	1	19
EFFECTS. The right of the people to be secure in their effects against unreasonable searches and seizures shall not be violated	4th amend.			26
ELECTED. Representatives in Congress shall be chosen or elected every second year by the people of the several States	1	2	1	1

ELECTED. Two Senators from each State shall be chosen or elected by the Legislature thereof for six years........ 1 3 1 3

ELECT. The Senate shall elect or choose their other officers, and also a President pro tempore, in the absence of the Vice President, or when he shall exercise the office of President of the United States........ 1 3 5 4

ELECTION. When vacancies happen in the representation from a State, the Executive thereof shall issue writs of election to fill them........ 1 2 4 3

ELECTION of President and Vice President United States. The President shall hold his office during the term of four years, and, together with the Vice President, chosen for the same term, be *elected* as follows:........ 2 1 1 13

ELECTION. President and Vice President United States—

Each State shall appoint, in such manner as the Legislature thereof may direct, a number of electors, equal to the whole number of Senators and Representatives to which the State may be entitled in the Congress; but no Senator or Representative, or person holding an office of trust or profit under the United States, shall be appointed an elector..... 2 1 2 13

The electors shall meet in their respective States, and vote by ballot for President and Vice President, one of whom, at least, shall not be an inhabitant of the same State with themselves. They shall name in their ballots the person voted for as President, and, in distinct ballots, the person voted for as Vice President; and they shall make distinct lists of all persons voted for as President, and of all persons voted for as Vice President, and of the number of votes for each; which lists they shall sign and certify, and transmit sealed to the seat of Government of the United States, directed to the President of the Senate. The President of the Senate shall, in presence of the Senate and House of Representatives, open all the certificates, and the votes shall then be counted: the person having the greatest number of votes for President shall be the President, if such number be a majority of the whole number of electors appointed; and if no person have such majority, then, from the persons having the highest numbers, not exceeding three, on the list of those voted for as President, the House of Representatives shall choose, immediately, by ballot, the President. But, in choosing the President, the votes shall be taken by States, the representation from each State having one vote: a quorum for this purpose shall consist of a member or members from two-thirds of the States, and a majority of all the States shall be necessary to a choice. And if the House of Representatives shall not choose a President whenever the right of choice shall devolve upon them, before the fourth

ALPHABETICAL ANALYSIS—Continued.

	Art.	sec.	cl.	page.
day of March next following, then the Vice President shall act as President, as in the case of the death, or other constitutional disability of the President	12th amend.			28
The person having the greatest number of votes as Vice President shall be the Vice President, if such number be a majority of the whole number of electors appointed; and if no person have a majority, then from the two highest numbers on the list the Senate shall choose the Vice President: a quorum for the purpose shall consist of two-thirds of the whole number of Senators, and a majority of the whole number shall be necessary to a choice	12th amend.			30
But no person constitutionally ineligible to the office of President, shall be eligible to that of Vice President of the United States	12th amend.			30
Congress may determine the time of choosing the electors, and the day on which they shall give their votes; which day shall be the same throughout the United States	2	1	4	14
In case of the removal of the President from office, or of his death, resignation, or inability to discharge the powers and duties of the said office, the same shall devolve on the Vice President, and the Congress may by law provide for the case of removal, death, resignation, or inability, both of the President and Vice President, declaring what officer shall then act as President, and such officer shall act accordingly, until the disability be removed, or a President shall be elected	2	1	5	14
ELECTIONS. The times, places, and manner of holding elections for Senators and Representatives shall be prescribed in each State by the Legislature thereof, but the Congress may, at any time, by law make or alter such regulations, except as to the places of choosing Senators	1	4	1	5
ELECTIONS. Each House shall be the judge of the elections, returns, and qualifications of its own members	1	5	1	5
ELECTOR. No Senator or Representative, or person holding an office of trust or profit under the United States, shall be appointed an elector of President or Vice President of the United States	2	1	2	13
ELECTORS. The qualifications of electors of Representatives in Congress to be the same as for electors of the most numerous branch of the State Legislature	1	2	0	1
ELECTORS of President and Vice President of the United States. Appointment, qualification, time of choosing, and duties of electors. (See Election.)	2	1	2	13
	12th amend.			28

Entry				
ELIGIBILITY of a Representative in Congress. No person shall be a Representative who shall not have attained to the age of twenty-five years, and been seven years a citizen of the United States, and who shall not when elected be an inhabitant of that State in which he shall be chosen	1	2	2	2
ELIGIBILITY of a Senator in Congress. No person shall be a Senator who shall not have attained to the age of thirty years, and been nine years a citizen of the United States, and who shall not, when elected, be an inhabitant of that State for which he shall be chosen	1	3	3	4
ELIGIBILITY of electors of President and Vice President of the United States. No Senator or Representative, or person holding an office of trust or profit under the United States, shall be appointed an elector	2	1	4	13
ELIGIBILITY of the President of the United States. No person, except a natural born citizen, or a citizen of the United States at the time of the adoption of this Constitution, shall be eligible to the office of President; neither shall any person be eligible to that office who shall not have attained to the age of thirty-five years, and been fourteen years a resident within the United States	2	1	4	14
ELIGIBILITY of the Vice President of the United States. No person constitutionally ineligible to the office of President shall be eligible to that of Vice President of the United States	12th amend.			30
EMOLUMENTS. No Senator or Representative shall, during the time for which he was elected, be appointed to any civil office under the authority of the United States, which shall have been created, or the emoluments whereof shall have been increased, during such time	1	6	2	6
EMOLUMENT. No person holding any office of profit or trust under the United States, shall, without the consent of Congress, accept of any present, emolument, office, or title of any kind whatever from any King, Prince, or foreign State	1	9	8	11
EMOLUMENT of the President of the United States. The President shall receive a stated compensation, but no other emolument from the United States, or either of them	2	1	6	15
ENEMIES. Treason against the United States shall consist only in levying war against them, or in adhering to their enemies, giving them aid and comfort	3	3	1	18
ENGAGEMENTS entered into. All debts contracted or engagements entered into before the adoption of this Constitution, shall be as valid against the United States under this Constitution as under the Confederation	6	0	1	21

ALPHABETICAL ANALYSIS—Continued.

	Art.	sec.	cl.	page.
ENSURE domestic tranquillity. The Constitution established in order to ensure domestic tranquillity, &c.	Preamble.			1
ENTER. Vessels bound to or from one State shall not be obliged to enter, clear, or pay duties in another	1	9	6	11
ENTITLED. The citizens of each State shall be entitled to all the privileges and immunities of citizens in the several States	4	2	1	19
ENUMERATION of the people to be made within three years after first meeting of Congress, and every ten years thereafter, in such manner as they shall by law direct. The	1	2	3	2
ENUMERATION. No capitation or other direct tax shall be laid, unless in proportion to the census or enumeration hereinbefore directed to be taken	1	9	4	11
ENUMERATION of rights. The enumeration in the Constitution of certain rights shall not be construed to deny or disparage others retained by the people	9th amend.			28
EQUAL suffrage. No State without its consent shall be deprived of its equal suffrage in the Senate	5	–	–	21
EQUITY. The Judicial power shall extend to all cases in law and equity arising under this Constitution, the laws of the United States, and treaties made or which shall be made under their authority	3	2	1	17
EQUITY. The Judicial power of the United States shall not be construed to extend to any suit in law or equity commenced or prosecuted against one of the United States by citizens of another State, or by citizens or subjects of any foreign State	11th amend.			28
ESCAPING. Persons held to service or labor (or slaves) escaping into another State shall be delivered up on claim of the party to whom such service or labor may be due	4	2	3	20
ESTABLISH justice. The Constitution formed in order to establish justice, &c.	Preamble.			1
ESTABLISH. The Judicial power of the United States shall be vested in one Supreme Court and in such Inferior courts as the Congress may from time to time ordain and establish	3	1	1	17
ESTABLISHMENT of the Constitution. We, the people of the United States, in order to form a more perfect union, establish justice, ensure domestic tranquillity, provide for the common defence, promote the general welfare, and secure the blessings of liberty to ourselves and our posterity, do ordain and establish this Constitution for the United States of America	Preamble.			1
ESTABLISHMENT of this Constitution. The ratification of the conventions of nine States				

shall be sufficient for the establishment of this Constitution between the States so ratifying the same	7	0	1	22
ESTABLISHMENT of religion. Congress shall make no law respecting an establishment of religion	1st amend.			25
EXCESSIVE bail shall not be required, nor excessive fines imposed, nor cruel and unusual punishments inflicted	8th amend.			27
EXCISES. Congress shall have power to lay excises	1	8	1	8
EXCISES. All duties, imposts, and excises shall be uniform throughout the United States	1	8	1	8
EXCLUSIVE rights to writings and discoveries in science and the useful arts may be secured to authors and inventors for a limited time	1	8	8	9
EXCLUSIVE legislation in all cases whatsoever shall be exercised by Congress over such district (not exceeding ten miles square) as may, by cession of particular States and the acceptance of Congress, become the seat of the Government of the United States	1	8	17	10
EXECUTE. The militia may be called forth to execute the laws of the Union	1	8	15	9
EXECUTE. The President is required to take an oath faithfully to execute the office of President of the United States	2	1	8	15
EXECUTED. The President shall take care that the laws be faithfully executed	2	3	1	17
EXECUTION of the powers of the Government. Congress shall have power to make all laws which shall be necessary and proper for carrying into execution the foregoing powers and all other powers vested by this Constitution in the Government of the United States, or any department or office thereof	1	8	18	10
EXECUTION. Before the President enters upon the execution of his office, he shall take the following oath or affirmation. (See Oath.)	2	1	7	15
EXECUTIVE authority of any State shall issue writs of election to fill vacancies that may happen in the representation of such State. The	1	2	4	3
EXECUTIVE of any State may make temporary appointments to fill vacancies in seats of Senators until the next meeting of the Legislature of such State, which shall then fill such vacancies. The	1	3	2	3
EXECUTIVE power. The Executive power shall be vested in a President of the United States of America	2	1	1	13
EXECUTIVE departments. The President may require the opinion in writing of the principal officer in each of the Executive departments upon any subject relating to the duties of their respective offices	2	2	1	15

ALPHABETICAL ANALYSIS—Continued.

	Art.	sec.	cl.	page.
EXECUTIVE authority of a State. On demand of the Executive authority of a State, fugitives from justice shall be delivered up, &c.	4	2	2	19
EXECUTIVE of a State. The United States shall, on application of the Legislature, or of the Executive of any State when the Legislature cannot be convened, protect each of them against domestic violence	4	4	1	20
EXECUTIVE officers, both of the United States and of the several States, shall be bound by oath or affirmation to support this Constitution	6	0	3	22
EXPEDIENT. The President shall, from time to time, recommend to Congress such measures as he shall judge necessary and expedient	2	3	1	16
EXPEL a member. Either House of Congress may, with the concurrence of two-thirds, expel a member	1	5	2	5
EXPENDITURES. A regular statement and account of the receipts and expenditures of all public money shall be published from time to time	1	9	7	11
EXPORTS. No tax or duty shall be laid on articles exported from any State	1	9	5	11
EXPORTS, &c. No State shall, without the consent of Congress, lay any duty on imports or exports	1	10	2	12
EX POST facto law. No bill of attainder or ex post facto law shall be passed	1	9	3	11
EX POST facto law. No State shall pass any ex post facto law	1	10	1	12
EXTRAORDINARY occasions. The President may, on extraordinary occasions, convene both Houses of Congress, or either of them	2	3	1	16
FACT and law. The Supreme Court shall have appellate jurisdiction both as to law and fact, &c.	3	2	2	18
FAITH and credit to be given to public acts, records, and proceedings of States, &c.	4	1	1	19
FELONIES. Congress shall have power to define and punish piracies and felonies committed on the high seas, and offences against the law of nations	1	8	10	9
FELONY. For felony a Senator or Representative may be arrested	1	6	1	6
FELONY. A person charged with felony, and fleeing from one State to another, to be delivered up on demand of the State having jurisdiction	4	2	2	19
FEW, deputy from Georgia, signed this Constitution. William	–	–	–	23
FINES. Excessive bail shall not be required, nor excessive fines imposed, nor cruel and unusual punishments inflicted	8th amend.			27

FITZSIMONS, deputy from Pennsylvania, signed this Constitution. Thomas	–	–	–	23
FOREIGN nations. Congress shall have power to regulate commerce with foreign nations	1	8	3	8
FOREIGN coin. Congress shall have power to coin money, regulate the value thereof, and of foreign coin	1	8	5	8
FOREIGN State. No title of nobility shall be granted by the United States, and no person holding any office of profit or trust under them, shall, without the consent of the Congress, accept of any present, emolument, office, or title, of any kind whatever, from any king, prince, or foreign State	1	9	8	11
FOREIGN power. No State shall, without the consent of Congress, enter into any agreement or compact with another State, or with any foreign power	1	10	3	12
FOREIGN States, citizens, or subjects. The Judicial power shall extend to controversies between a State, or the citizens thereof, and foreign States, citizens or subjects	3	2	1	18
FOREIGN State. The Judicial power of the United States shall not be construed to extend to any suit, in law or equity, commenced or prosecuted against one of the United States by citizens of another State, or by citizens or subjects of any foreign State	11th amend.			28
FORFEITURE. No attainder of treason shall work corruption of blood or forfeiture, except during the life of the person attainted	3	3	2	19
FORM a more perfect union. The Constitution established in order to form a more perfect union.	Preamble.			1
FORTS, &c. Congress shall have power to exercise exclusive legislation over forts, &c.	1	8	17	10
FRANKLIN, deputy from Pennsylvania, signed this Constitution. Benjamin	–	–	–	23
FREE State. A well-regulated militia being necessary to the security of a free State, the right of the people to keep and bear arms shall not be infringed	2d amend.			25
FREEDOM of speech and of the press. Congress shall make no law respecting an establishment of religion, or prohibiting the free exercise thereof; or abridging the freedom of speech or of the press	1st amend.			25
FUGITIVES from justice. A person charged in any State with treason, felony, or other crime, who shall flee from justice, and be found in another State, shall, on demand of the Executive authority of the State from which he fled, be delivered up, to be removed to the State having jurisdiction of the crime	4	2	2	19
FUGITIVE slaves. No person held to service or labor in one State, under the laws thereof, escaping into another, shall, in consequence of any law or regulation therein, be discharged from such service or labor, but shall be delivered up on claim of the party to whom such service or labor may be due	4	2	3	20

ALPHABETICAL ANALYSIS—Continued.

Entry	Art.	sec.	cl.	page.
GENERAL welfare. The Constitution established to promote the general welfare	Preamble.			1
GENERAL welfare. Congress shall have power to provide for the general welfare	1	8	1	8
GENERAL laws. Congress may, by general laws, prescribe the manner in which the public acts, records, and judicial proceedings of States shall be proved, and the effect thereof	4	1	1	19
GEORGIA entitled to three Representatives in the first Congress	1	2	3	3
GILMAN, deputy from New Hampshire, signed this Constitution. Nicholas	–	–	–	23
GOLD and silver coin. No State shall make any thing but gold and silver coin a tender in payment of debts	1	10	1	12
GOOD behavior. The Judges, both of the Supreme and Inferior courts, shall hold their offices during good behavior	3	1	1	17
GORHAM, deputy from Massachusetts, signed this Constitution. Nathaniel	–	–	–	23
GOVERNING the militia. Congress shall have power to provide for governing such part of the militia as may be employed in the service of the United States	1	8	16	9
GOVERNMENT. Congress shall have power to make rules for the government and regulation of the land and naval forces	1	8	14	9
GOVERNMENT. Seat of Government established	1	8	17	10
GOVERNMENT of the United States. Congress shall have power to make all laws which shall be necessary and proper for carrying into execution the foregoing powers, and all other powers vested by this Constitution in the Government of this United States, or in any department or office thereof	1	8	18	10
GOVERNMENT. The United States shall guaranty to every State in the Union a Republican form of government	4	4	1	20
GOVERNMENT. Congress shall make no law abridging the right of the people peaceably to assemble and to petition the Government for a redress of grievances	1st amend.			25
GRAND jury. No person shall be held to answer for a capital or otherwise infamous crime, unless on a presentment or indictment of a grand jury, &c.	5th amend.			26
GRANT. No State shall grant any title of nobility	1	10	1	12
GRANT. The President shall have power to grant reprieves and pardons for offences against the United States, except in cases of impeachment	2	2	1	16
GRANTED powers. All legislative powers granted shall be vested in a Congress of the United States	1	1	1	1

GRANTING commissions. The President shall have power to fill up all vacancies that may happen during the recess of the Senate, by granting commissions which shall expire at the end of their next session 2 2 3 16
GRANTS of States. The Judicial power shall extend to cases between citizens of the same State claiming lands under grants of different States 3 2 1 18
GRIEVANCES. Congress shall make no law abridging the right of the people peaceably to assemble and to petition the Government for a redress of grievances .... 1st amend. 25
GUARANTY. The United States shall guaranty to every State in this Union a Republican form of government 4 4 1 20

HABEAS corpus. The privilege of the writ of habeas corpus shall not be suspended, unless when, in cases of rebellion or invasion, the public safety may require it 1 9 2 11
HAMILTON, deputy from New York, signed this Constitution. Alexander .... – – – 23
HAPPEN. When vacancies happen in the representation from any State, the Executive authority thereof shall issue writs of election to fill such vacancies 1 2 4 3
HAPPEN. When vacancies happen, by resignation or otherwise, during the recess of the Legislature of any State, the Executive thereof may make temporary appointments, &c. 1 3 2 3
HAPPEN. The President shall have power to fill up all vacancies that may happen during the recess of the Senate, &c. 2 2 3 16
HEADS of Departments. The President may require the opinion, in writing, of the principal officer in each of the Executive departments, upon any subject relating to the duties of their respective offices 2 2 1 15
HEADS of Departments. The Congress may, by law, vest the appointment of such inferior officers as they think proper, in the President alone, in the courts of law, or in the heads of departments 2 2 2 16
HIGH crimes and misdemeanors. The President, Vice President, and all civil officers of the United States, shall be removed from office on impeachment for, and conviction of, treason, bribery, or other high crimes and misdemeanors 2 4 1 17
HONOR. Judgment in cases of impeachment shall not extend further than to removal from office, and disqualification to hold and enjoy any office of honor, trust, or profit, under the United States 1 3 7 4
HOUSE of Reps. Congress shall consist of a Senate and House of Representatives .... 1 1 - 1

ALPHABETICAL ANALYSIS—Continued.

	Art.	sec.	cl.	page.
HOUSE of Reps. Members of the House of Representatives chosen every second year by the people	1	2	–	1
HOUSE of Reps., members of the. (See Representatives.)				
HOUSE of Reps. Qualifications of electors of members of the House of Reps., the same as for electors of the most numerous branch of the State Legislature	1	2	–	1
HOUSE of Reps. shall choose their Speaker and other officers. The	1	2	5	3
HOUSE of Reps. shall have the sole power of impeachment. The	1	2	5	3
HOUSE of Representatives. The—				
Shall be the judge of the elections, returns, and qualifications of its own members, and a majority shall constitute a quorum to do business; but a smaller number may adjourn from day to day, and may be authorized to compel the attendance of absent members in such manner and under such penalties as that House may provide	1	5	1	5
May determine the rules of its proceedings, punish its members for disorderly behavior, and, with the concurrence of two-thirds, expel a member	1	5	2	5
Shall keep a Journal of its proceedings, and from time to time publish the same, excepting such parts as may, in their judgment, require secrecy; and the yeas and nays of the members of either House, on any question, shall, at the desire of one-fifth of those present, be entered on the Journal	1	5	3	5
Shall not, during the session of Congress, without the consent of the Senate, adjourn for more than three days, nor to any other place than that in which the two Houses shall be sitting	1	5	4	6
HOUSE of Reps. All bills for raising revenue shall originate in the House of Representatives, but the Senate may propose, or concur with, amendments, as on other bills	1	7	1	7
HOUSE of Reps. and Senate. Every bill which shall have passed the House of Representatives and the Senate shall, before it become a law, be presented to the President of the United States; if he approve, he shall sign it, but if not, he shall return it, with his objections, to that House in which it shall have originated, who shall enter the objections at large on their journal, and proceed to reconsider it. If, after such reconsideration, two-thirds of that House shall agree to pass the bill, it shall be sent, together with the objections, to the other House, by which it shall likewise be reconsidered, and if approved by two-thirds of that House, it shall become a law. But in all such cases the votes of both Houses shall				

be determined by yeas and nays, and the names of the persons voting for and against the bill shall be entered on the Journal of each House respectively. If any bill shall not be returned by the President within ten days (Sundays excepted) after it shall have been presented to him, the same shall be a law, in like manner as if he had signed it, unless the Congress, by their adjournment, prevent its return; in which case it shall not be a law.. 1 7 2 7

HOUSE of Reps. and Senate. Every order, resolution, or vote to which the concurrence of the Senate and House of Representatives may be necessary, (except on a question of adjournment,) shall be presented to the President of the United States, and, before the same shall take effect, shall be approved by him; or, being disapproved by him, shall be repassed by two-thirds of the Senate and House of Representatives, according to the rules and limitations prescribed in the case of a bill 1 7 3 8

HOUSE of Representatives and Senate. (See Congress.)

HOUSES of Congress. The President may, on extraordinary occasions, convene both Houses of Congress, or either of them.......... 2 3 1 16

HOUSES of Congress. The Congress, whenever two-thirds of both Houses shall deem it necessary, shall propose amendments to this Constitution.......... 5 – – 21

HOUSE. No soldier shall, in time of peace, be quartered in any house without the consent of the owner, nor in time of war, but in a manner to be prescribed by law.......... 3d amend. 26

HOUSES. The right of the people to be secure in their houses against unreasonable searches and seizures, shall not be violated.......... 4th amend. 26

HOUSE of Reps. If no person have a majority, (of the electoral votes as President of the United States,) then, from the persons having the highest numbers, not exceeding three, on the list of those voted for as President, the House of Representatives shall choose, immediately, by ballot, the President. But, in choosing the President, the votes shall be taken by States, the representatives from each State having one vote: a quorum for this purpose shall consist of a member or members from two-thirds of the States, and a majority of all the States shall be necessary to a choice. And if the House of Reps. shall not choose a President whenever the right of choice shall devolve upon them, before the 4th day of March next following, then the Vice President shall act as President, as in the case of the death or other constitutional disability of the President.......... 12th amend. 29

IMMUNITIES. The citizens of each State shall be entitled to all privileges and immunities of citizens in the several States.......... 4 2 1 19

ALPHABETICAL ANALYSIS—Continued.

	Art.	sec.	cl.	page.
IMPEACHMENT. The House of Reps. shall have the sole power of impeachment	1	2	5	3
IMPEACHMENTS. The Senate of the United States shall have the sole power to try all impeachments	1	3	6	4
IMPEACHMENT. When sitting to try an impeachment, the Senate shall be on oath or affirmation	1	3	6	4
When the President is tried, the Chief Justice shall preside	1	3	6	4
No person shall be convicted without the concurrence of two-thirds of the members present	1	3	6	4
Judgment in cases of impeachment shall not extend further than removal from office, and disqualification to hold and enjoy any office of honor, trust, or profit under the United States	1	3	6	4
But the party convicted shall, nevertheless, be liable and subject to indictment, trial, judgment, and punishment, according to law	1	3	6	4
IMPEACHMENT. The President shall have power to grant reprieves and pardons for offences against the United States, except in cases of impeachment	2	2	1	16
IMPEACHMENT. All civil officers of the United States shall be removed from office on impeachment for, and conviction of, treason, bribery, or other high crimes and misdemeanors	2	4	1	17
IMPEACHMENT. The trial of all crimes, except in cases of impeachment, shall be by jury	3	2	3	18
IMPORTATION of persons. (Slaves.) The migration or importation of such persons as any of the States now existing shall think proper to admit, shall not be prohibited by Congress prior to the year eighteen hundred and eight, but a tax or duty may be imposed on such importation, not exceeding ten dollars for each person	1	9	1	10
IMPORTATION. No amendment made prior to 1808 shall affect the preceding clause	5	–	–	21
IMPOSTS. Congress shall have power to lay imposts	1	8	1	8
IMPOSTS. All duties, imposts, and excises shall be uniform throughout the United States	1	8	1	8
IMPOSTS. No State shall, without the consent of Congress, lay any imposts or duties on imports or exports, &c. (See Duties.)	1	10	2	12
INABILITY. In case of the inability of the President to discharge the powers and duties of that office, the same shall devolve on the Vice President; and in case of the inability of both				

President and Vice President, Congress shall by law declare what officer shall then act as President	2	1	5	14
INDIANS not taxed, excluded from representative numbers	1	2	3	2
INDIAN tribes. Congress shall have power to regulate commerce among the several States, and with the Indian tribes	1	8	3	8
INDICTMENT. Persons convicted on an impeachment, shall nevertheless be subject to indictment, trial, judgment, and punishment, according to law	1	3	7	4
INDICTMENT. No person shall be held to answer for a capital or otherwise infamous crime, unless on a presentment or indictment of a grand jury, &c.	5th amend.			26
INFERIOR officers. (See Appointment.)	2	2	2	16
INFERIOR courts. The judicial power of the United States shall be vested in one Supreme Court, and in such Inferior courts as Congress may from time to time ordain and establish. The judges, both of the Supreme and Inferior courts, shall hold their offices during good behavior	3	1	1	17
INFERIOR courts. (See Judicial power.)	3	1&2		17
INGERSOLL, deputy from Pennsylvania, signed this Constitution. Jared	–	–	–	23
INHABITANT. A Representative in Congress shall be an inhabitant of the State in which he shall be chosen	1	2	2	2
INHABITANT. A Senator in Congress shall be an inhabitant of the State in which he shall be chosen	1	3	3	4
INHABITANT. The electors shall meet in their respective States, and vote by ballot for President and Vice President, one of whom, at least, shall not be an inhabitant of the same State with themselves	12th amend.			28
INSPECTION laws. No State shall, without the consent of Congress, lay any imposts or duties on imports or exports, except what may be absolutely necessary for executing its inspection laws	1	10	2	12
INSURRECTIONS. Congress shall have power to provide for calling forth the militia to execute the laws of the Union, suppress insurrections, and repel invasions	1	8	15	9
INSURRECTION. The United States shall, on application of the Legislature, or of the Executive, (when the Legislature cannot be convened,) protect each State against domestic violence or insurrection	4	4	1	20
INVADED. No State shall, without the consent of Congress, engage in war unless actually invaded, or in such imminent danger as will not admit of delay	1	10	3	12

ALPHABETICAL ANALYSIS—Continued.

	Art.	sec.	cl.	page.
INVASIONS. Congress shall have power to provide for calling forth the militia to execute the laws of the Union, suppress insurrections, and repel invasions	1	8	15	9
INVASION. The privilege of the writ of habeas corpus shall not be suspended, unless when, in cases of rebellion or invasion, the public safety may require it	1	9	2	11
INVASION. The United States shall protect each State against invasion	4	4	1	20
INVENTORS may secure exclusive rights to their discoveries for a limited time	1	8	8	9
JENIFER, deputy from Maryland, signed this Constitution. Daniel of St. Thomas	–	–	–	23
JEOPARDY. Nor shall any person be subject, for the same offence, to be twice put in jeopardy of life or limb	5th amend.			25
JOHNSON, deputy from Connecticut, signed this Constitution. William Samuel	–	–	–	23
JOURNAL. Each House of Congress shall keep a Journal of its proceedings, and from time to time publish the same, excepting such parts as may, in their judgment, require secrecy; and the yeas and nays of the members of either House, on any question, shall, at the desire of one-fifth of those present, be entered on the Journal	1	5	3	5
JOURNAL. When the President shall return a bill, with his objections, to the House in which it originated, those objections shall be entered at large on their Journal, and the votes, by yeas and nays, on the reconsideration of such bill, shall be entered on the Journal of each House respectively. (See Bill.)	1	7	2	7
JUDGES of the Supreme Court. The President shall nominate, and by and with the advice and consent of the Senate, appoint the judges of the Supreme Court of the United States	2	2	2	16
JUDGES of the Supreme and Inferior courts shall hold their offices during good behavior, and shall, at stated times, receive for their services a compensation which shall not be diminished during their continuance in office	3	1	1	17
JUDGES. The judges in every State shall be bound by the Constitution, laws, and treaties—any thing in the constitution or laws of any State to the contrary notwithstanding	6	–	2	23
JUDGMENT, in cases of impeachment, shall not extend farther than to removal from office, and disqualification to hold and enjoy any office of honor, trust, or profit under the United States; but the party convicted shall, nevertheless, be liable and subject to indictment, trial, judgment, and punishment, according to law	1	3	7	4
JUDICIAL power. The judicial power of the United States shall be vested in one Supreme				

Court, and in such Inferior courts as the Congress may from time to time ordain and establish. The judges, both of the Supreme and Inferior courts, shall hold their offices during good behavior, and shall, at stated times, receive for their services a compensation which shall not be diminished during their continuance in office 3 1 1 17

JUDICIAL power. The judicial power shall extend to all cases in law and equity arising under this Constitution, the laws of the United States, and the treaties made, or which shall be made, under their authority; to all cases affecting ambassadors, other public ministers, and consuls; to all cases of admiralty and maritime jurisdiction; to controversies to which the United States shall be a party; to controversies between two or more States; between a State and the citizens of another State; between citizens of different States; between citizens of the same State, claiming lands under grants of different States; and between a State, or the citizens thereof, and foreign States, citizens, or subjects 3 2 1 17

In all cases affecting ambassadors, other public ministers, and consuls, and those in which a State shall be a party, the Supreme Court shall have original jurisdiction. In all the other cases before mentioned, the Supreme Court shall have appellate jurisdiction, both as to law and fact, with such exceptions, and under such regulations, as the Congress shall make 3 2 2 18

The trial of all crimes, except in cases of impeachment, shall be by jury, and such trial shall be held in the State where the said crimes shall have been committed; but when not committed within any State, the trial shall be at such place or places as the Congress may by law have directed 3 2 3 18

JUDICIAL proceedings. Full faith, credit, proof, and effect to be given in each State to the acts, records, and judicial proceedings of every other State 4 1 1 19

JUDICIAL officers, both of the United States, and of the several States, shall be bound by oath or affirmation to support this Constitution 6 0 3 22

JUDICIAL power. The judicial power of the United States shall not be construed to extend to any suit, in law or equity, commenced or prosecuted against one of the United States, by citizens of another State, or by citizens or subjects of any foreign State .... 11th amend. 28

JURISDICTION. The judicial power shall extend to all cases of admiralty and maritime jurisdiction 3 2 1 18

JURISDICTION. Original and appellate jurisdiction in the Supreme Court 3 2 2 18

JURISDICTION. A person charged in any State with treason, felony, or other crime, and

ALPHABETICAL ANALYSIS—*Continued.*

	Art.	sec.	cl.	page.
fleeing from justice, to be delivered up and removed to the State having jurisdiction of the crime	4	2	2	19
JURISDICTION. No new State shall be erected within the jurisdiction of any other State	4	3	1	20
JURY. The trial of all crimes, except in cases of impeachment, shall be by jury	3	2	3	18
JURY. No person shall be held to answer for a capital or otherwise infamous crime, unless on a presentment or indictment of a grand jury, &c.	5th amend.			26
JURY. In all criminal prosecutions, the accused shall enjoy the right to a speedy and public trial, by an impartial jury of the State and district wherein the crime shall have been committed, which district shall have been previously ascertained by law	6th amend.			27
JURY. In suits at common law, where the value in controversy shall exceed twenty dollars, the right of trial by jury shall be preserved; and no fact tried by a jury shall be otherwise re-examined in any court of the United States, than according to the rules of the common law	7th amend.			27
JUSTICE. Constitution ordained in order to establish justice	Preamble.			1
JUSTICE. The Chief Justice shall preside when the President is tried on an impeachment	1	3	6	4
JUSTICE. Fugitives from justice to be delivered up and removed to the State having jurisdiction of the crime	4	2	2	19
KING, prince, or foreign State. No title of nobility shall be granted by the United States, and no person holding any office of profit or trust under them, shall, without the consent of the Congress, accept of any present, emoluments, office, or title, of any kind whatever, from any king, prince, or foreign State	1	9	8	11
KING, deputy from Massachusetts, signed this Constitution. Rufus	–	–	–	23
LABOR. No person held to service or labor in one State, shall be discharged from such service or labor in another State	4	2	3	20
LAND and naval forces. Congress shall have power to make rules for the government and regulation of the land and naval forces	1	8	14	9
LAND ceded to or purchased by the United States. Congress shall have power to exercise exclusive legislation, in all cases whatsoever, over all places purchased by the consent of the				

Legislature of the State in which the same shall be, for the erection of forts, magazines, arsenals, dock yards, and other needful buildings........ 1 8 17 10

LAND forces. (See Army—Militia.)

LANDS. The judicial power shall extend to controversies between citizens of the same State, claiming lands under grants of different States........ 3 2 1 18

LANGDON, deputy from New Hampshire, signed this Constitution. John........ - - - 23

LAW. The actual enumeration of the people, or census, shall be made within three years after the first meeting of the Congress of the United States, and within every subsequent term of ten years, in such manner as they shall by law direct........ 1 2 3 2

LAW. A person convicted on an impeachment, shall nevertheless be liable to indictment, trial, judgment, and punishment, according to law........ 1 3 7 4

LAW. The times, places, and manner, of holding elections for Senators and Representatives shall be prescribed in each State by the Legislature thereof; but the Congress may, at any time, by law, make or alter such regulations, except as to the places of choosing Senators........ 1 4 1 5

LAW. The Congress shall assemble at least once in every year, and such meeting shall be on the first Monday in December, unless they shall by law appoint a different day........ 1 4 2 5

LAW. The Senators and Representatives shall receive a compensation for their services, to be ascertained by law, and paid out of the Treasury of the United States........ 1 6 1 6

LAW. Every bill which shall have passed the House of Representatives and the Senate, shall, before it become a law, be presented to the President of the United States; if he approve he shall sign it, but if not, he shall return it with his objections to that House in which it shall have originated, who shall enter the objections at large on their Journal, and proceed to reconsider it. If, after such reconsideration, two-thirds of that House shall agree to pass the bill, it shall be sent, together with the objections, to the other House, by which it shall likewise be reconsidered, and if approved by two-thirds of that House, it shall become a law........ 1 7 2 7

LAW. If any bill shall not be returned by the President within ten days (Sundays excepted) after it shall have been presented to him, the same shall be a law, in like manner as if he had signed it, unless the Congress, by their adjournment, prevent its return; in which case it shall not be a law........ 1 7 2 7

LAW. Every order, resolution, or vote, to which the concurrence of the Senate and House of Representatives may be necessary, (except on a question of adjournment,) shall be pre-

ALPHABETICAL ANALYSIS—Continued.

	Art.	sec.	cl.	page.
sented to the President of the United States; and before the same shall take effect shall be approved by him, or being disapproved by him, shall be repassed by two-thirds of the Senate and House of Representatives, according to the rules and limitations prescribed in the case of a bill	1	7	3	8
LAW of nations. Congress shall have power to define and punish piracies and felonies committed on the high seas, and offences against the law of nations	1	8	10	9
LAW. No bill of attainder or ex post facto law shall be passed	1	9	3	11
LAW. No money shall be drawn from the Treasury, but in consequence of appropriations made by law	1	9	7	11
LAW. No State shall pass any ex post facto law	1	10	1	12
LAW. No State shall pass any law impairing the obligation of contracts	1	10	1	12
LAW. In case of the removal, death, resignation, or inability, of both President and Vice President, Congress shall, by law, declare what officer shall then act as President	2	1	5	14
LAW. The President shall have power, by and with the advice and consent of the Senate, to appoint officers not provided for in the Constitution, and whose offices shall be established by law; but the Congress may, by law, vest the appointment of such inferior officers as they think proper in the President alone, in the courts of law, or in the heads of departments	2	2	2	16
LAW and equity. The judicial power shall extend to all cases in law and equity arising under this Constitution, the laws of the United States, and the treaties made, or which shall be made, under their authority, &c. (See Judicial power.)	3	2	1,2,3	17
LAW and fact. The Supreme Court shall have appellate jurisdiction, both as to law and fact, with such exceptions, and under such regulations, as the Congress shall make	3	2	2	18
LAW. When crimes shall not have been committed within any State, the trial shall be at such place or places as the Congress may by law have directed	3	2	3	18
LAW. No person held to service or labor in one State, under the laws thereof, escaping into another, shall, in consequence of any law or regulation therein, be discharged from such service or labor, but shall be delivered up on claim of the party to whom such service or labor may be due	4	2	3	20
LAW. This Constitution, and the laws of the United States which shall be made in pursuance thereof, and all treaties made, or which shall be made, under the authority of the United				

States, shall be the supreme law of the land; and the judges in every State shall be bound thereby, any thing in the Constitution or laws of any State to the contrary notwithstanding 6 0 2 21

LAW. Congress shall make no law respecting an establishment of religion, or prohibiting the free exercise thereof; or abridging the freedom of speech or of the press; or the right of the people peaceably to assemble, and to petition the government for a redress of grievances .... 1st amend. 25

LAW. No soldier shall, in time of peace, be quartered in any house without the consent of the owner, nor in time of war, but in a manner to be prescribed by law .... 3d amend. 26

LAW. Nor shall any person be deprived of life, liberty, or property, without due process of law. 5th amend. 26

LAW. In all criminal prosecutions the accused shall enjoy the right to a speedy and public trial, by an impartial jury of the State and district wherein the crime shall have been committed; which district shall have been previously ascertained by law .... 6th amend. 27

LAW. In suits at common law, where the value in controversy shall exceed twenty dollars, the right of trial by jury shall be preserved; and no fact tried by a jury shall be otherwise re-examined in any court of the United States than according to the rules of the common law .... 7th amend. 27

LAW or equity. The Judicial power of the United States shall not be construed to extend to any suit in law or equity, commenced or prosecuted against one of the United States by citizens of another State, or by citizens or subjects of any foreign State .... 11th amend. 28

LAWS. Congress shall have power to establish an uniform rule of naturalization, and uniform laws on the subject of bankruptcies, throughout the United States 1 8 4 8

LAWS of the Union. Congress shall have power to provide for calling forth the militia to execute the laws of the Union, suppress insurrections, and repel invasions 1 8 15 9

LAWS. Congress shall have power to make all laws which shall be necessary and proper for carrying into execution the foregoing powers, and all other powers vested by this Constitution in the Government of the United States, or in any department or office thereof 1 8 18 10

LAWS. No State shall, without the consent of the Congress, lay any imposts or duties on imports or exports, except what may be absolutely necessary for executing its inspection laws 1 10 2 12

LAWS. All such State laws shall be subject to the revision and control of the Congress 1 10 2 12

LAWS. The President shall take care that the laws be faithfully executed 2 3 1 17

LAWS of the United States. The Judicial power shall extend to all cases in law and equity arising under the laws of the United States, &c. 3 2 1 17

ALPHABETICAL ANALYSIS—Continued.

	Art.	sec.	cl.	page.
LAWS. Congress may, by general laws, prescribe the manner in which the public acts, records, and judicial proceedings of States shall be proved, and the effect thereof	4	1	1	19
LAWS of any State subordinate to the Constitution, laws, and treaties of the United States	6	0	2	21
LAY and collect duties. Congress shall have power to lay and collect duties, taxes, imposts, and excises	1	8	1	8
LEGISLATION, exclusive. Congress shall have power to exercise exclusive legislation in all cases whatsoever, over such district (not exceeding ten miles square) as may, by cession of particular States and the acceptance of Congress, become the seat of Government of the United States, and to exercise like authority over all places purchased by the consent of the Legislature of the State in which the same shall be, for the erection of forts, magazines, arsenals, dock yards, and other needful buildings	1	8	17	10
LEGISLATIVE powers vested in Congress. All	1	1	–	1
LEGISLATURE. Electors of Representatives in Congress shall have qualifications same as for electors of most numerous branch of the State Legislature	1	2	1	1
LEGISLATURE of each State shall choose two Senators for six years. The	1	3	1	3
LEGISLATURE. If vacancies happen by resignation or otherwise in the seats of Senators, during the recess of the Legislature of any State, the Executive thereof may make temporary appointments to fill such vacancies, until the next meeting of the Legislature, which shall then fill such vacancies	1	3	2	3
LEGISLATURE. The times, places, and manner of holding elections for Senators and Representatives shall be prescribed in each State by the Legislature thereof; but the Congress may, at any time, by law make or alter such regulations, except as to the places of choosing Senators	1	4	1	5
LEGISLATURE. The United States shall, on the application of the Legislature, or of the Executive, (when the Legislature cannot be convened,) protect each State against domestic violence	4	4	1	20
LEGISLATURES of States. Congress shall exercise exclusive legislation over all places purchased by the consent of the Legislature of the State in which the same shall be, for the erection of forts, magazines, arsenals, dock yards, and other needful buildings	1	8	17	10
LEGISLATURES of States may direct the manner of appointing electors of President and Vice President of the United States	2	1	2	13

LEGISLATURES of States. No new State shall be formed within another State, nor any State be formed by the junction of two or more States, without the consent of the Legislatures of the States concerned and of Congress	4	3	1	20
LEGISLATURES. The Congress, whenever two-thirds of both Houses shall deem it necessary, shall propose amendments to this Constitution, or, on the application of the Legislatures of two-thirds of the several States, shall call a convention for proposing amendments, which, in either case, shall be valid to all intents and purposes, as part of this Constitution, when ratified by the Legislatures of three-fourths of the several States, or by conventions in three-fourths thereof, as one or the other mode of ratification may be proposed by Congress	5	–	–	21
LEGISLATURES. The members of the several State Legislatures shall be bound by oath or affirmation to support this Constitution	6	–	3	22
LETTERS of marque and reprisal. Congress shall have power to grant letters of marque and reprisal	1	8	11	9
LETTERS of marque and reprisal. No State shall grant letters of marque and reprisal	1	10	1	12
LIBERTY. The Constitution established to secure the blessings of liberty, &c.	Preamble.			1
LIBERTY. Nor shall any person be deprived of life, liberty, or property without due process of law	5th amend.			26
LIFE. No attainder of treason shall work corruption of blood or forfeiture, except during the life of the person attainted	3	3	2	19
LIFE or limb. Nor shall any person be subject, for the same offence, to be twice put in jeopardy of life or limb	5th amend.			26
LIFE, liberty, or property. Nor shall any person be deprived of life, liberty, or property without due process of law	5th amend.			26
LISTS of electoral votes for President and Vice President of the United States to be made	12th amend.			29
LIVINGSTON, deputy from New Jersey, signed this Constitution. William	–	–	–	23
MADISON, jr., deputy from Virginia, signed this Constitution. James	–	–	–	23
MAGAZINES, &c. Congress shall have power to exercise exclusive legislation over forts, magazines, &c.	1	8	17	10
MAJORITY of each House of Congress shall constitute a quorum to do business. A	1	5	1	5
MAJORITY of the whole number of electors necessary to elect the President and Vice President of the United States. A	12th amend.			29

ALPHABETICAL ANALYSIS—Continued.

	Art.	sec.	cl.	page.
MAJORITY of all the States shall be necessary to a choice of President when the election shall devolve on the House of Representatives. A	12th amend.			29
MAJORITY of the whole number of Senators shall be necessary to a choice of Vice President, when the election of that officer devolves upon the Senate. A	12th amend.			30
MARITIME jurisdiction. The judicial power shall extend to all cases of admiralty and maritime jurisdiction	3	2	1	18
MARQUE and reprisal. Congress shall have power to grant letters of marque and reprisal	1	8	11	9
MARQUE and reprisal. No State shall grant letters of marque and reprisal	1	10	1	12
MARYLAND entitled to six Representatives in the first Congress	1	2	3	2
MASSACHUSETTS entitled to eight Representatives in the first Congress	1	2	3	2
McHENRY, deputy from Maryland, signed this Constitution. James	–	–	–	23
MEASURES. Congress shall have power to fix the standard of weights and measures	1	8	5	8
MEASURES. The President shall, from time to time, recommend to the consideration of Congress such measures as he shall judge necessary and expedient	2	3	1	16
MEETING of Congress. The census to be taken within three years of the first meeting of Congress	1	2	3	2
MEETING. The Congress shall assemble at least once in every year, and such meeting shall be on the first Monday in December, unless they shall by law appoint a different day	1	4	2	5
MEMBERS of House of Representatives. (See Representatives.)				
MEMBERS of the Senate. (See Senators.)				
MIFFLIN, deputy from Pennsylvania, signed this Constitution. Thomas	–	–	–	23
MIGRATION of persons. (See Importation.)	1	9	1	10
MILITIA. Congress shall have power to provide for calling forth the militia to execute the laws of the Union, suppress insurrections, and repel invasions	1	8	15	9
MILITIA. Congress shall have power to provide for organizing, arming, and disciplining the militia, and for governing such part of them as may be employed in the service of the United States, reserving to the States, respectively, the appointment of the officers, and the authority of training the militia according to the discipline prescribed by Congress	1	8	16	9
MILITIA. The President shall be commander-in-chief of the army and navy of the United States, and of the militia of the several States, when called into the actual service of the United States	2	2	1	15

MILITIA. A well-regulated militia being necessary to the security of a free State, the right of the people to keep and bear arms shall not be infringed.............. 2d amend. 25

MILITIA. No person shall be held to answer for a capital or otherwise infamous crime, unless on a presentment or indictment of a grand jury, except in cases arising in the land or naval forces, or in the militia when in actual service, in time of war or public danger .... 5th amend. 26

MINISTERS, public. (See Appointments—Ambassadors.).............. 2 2 2 16

MINISTERS, public. The President shall receive ambassadors and other public ministers..... 2 3 1 17

MISDEMEANORS. All civil officers shall be removed from office on impeachment for, and conviction of, misdemeanors, &c.............. 2 4 1 17

MONEY. Congress shall have power to borrow money on the credit of the United States...... 1 8 2 8

MONEY. Congress shall have power to coin money, regulate the value thereof, and of foreign coin.............. 1 8 5 8

MONEY. Congress shall have power to raise and support armies, but no appropriation of money to that use shall be for a longer term than two years.............. 1 8 12 9

MONEY. No money shall be drawn from the Treasury, but in consequence of appropriations made by law; and a regular statement and account of the receipts and expenditures of all public money shall be published from time to time.............. 1 9 7 11

MONEY. No State shall coin money.............. 1 10 1 12

MORRIS, deputy from Pennsylvania, signed this Constitution. Robert.............. – – – 23

MORRIS, deputy from Pennsylvania, signed this Constitution. Gouverneur.............. – – – 23

NAMES of the members. The yeas and nays of the members of either House, on any question, shall, at the desire of one-fifth of those present, be entered on the Journal.............. 1 5 3 5

NATURAL born citizen. No person, except a natural born citizen, or a citizen of the United States at the time of the adoption of this Constitution, shall be eligible to the office of President.............. 2 1 4 14

NATURALIZATION. Congress shall have power to establish a uniform rule of naturalization.............. 1 8 4 8

NAVAL forces. Congress shall have power to make rules for the government and regulation of the land and naval forces.............. 1 8 14 9

NAVAL forces. No person shall be held to answer for a capital or otherwise infamous crime, unless on a presentment of a grand jury, except in cases arising in the land or naval forces, &c.............. 5th amend. 26

ALPHABETICAL ANALYSIS—Continued.

	Art.	sec.	cl.	page.
NAVY. Congress shall have power to provide and maintain a navy	1	8	13	9
NAVY. The President shall be commander-in-chief of the navy	2	2	1	15
NECESSARY. The President shall, from time to time, recommend to Congress such measures as he shall judge necessary and expedient	2	3	1	16
NECESSARY. The Congress, whenever two-thirds of both Houses shall deem it necessary, shall propose amendments to this Constitution, &c.	5	1	1	21
NECESSARY. A well-regulated militia being necessary to the security of a free State, the right of the people to keep and bear arms shall not be infringed	2d amend.			25
NEW Hampshire entitled to three Representatives in the first Congress	1	2	3	2
NEW Jersey entitled to four Representatives in first Congress	1	2	3	2
NEW States may be admitted by the Congress into this Union	4	3	1	20
NEW York entitled to six Representatives in first Congress	1	2	3	2
NOBILITY. No title of nobility shall be granted by the United States	1	9	8	11
NOBILITY. No State shall grant any title of nobility	1	10	1	12
NOMINATE. The President shall nominate, and, by and with the advice and consent of the Senate, shall appoint ambassadors, other public ministers and consuls, judges of the Supreme Court, and all other officers of the United States, whose appointments are not herein otherwise provided for, and which shall be established by law	2	2	2	16
NORTH Carolina entitled to five Representatives in first Congress	1	2	3	3
OATH or affirmation. Senators when sitting to try impeachments shall be on oath or affirmation	1	3	6	4
OATH of the President United States. Before he enter on the execution of his office, he shall take the following oath or affirmation: "I do solemnly swear or affirm, that I will faithfully execute the office of President of the United States, and will, to the best of my ability, preserve, protect, and defend the Constitution of the United States"	2	1	7	15
OATH or affirmation. The Senators and Representatives before mentioned, and the members of the several State Legislatures, and all executive and judicial officers, both of the United States and of the several States, shall be bound by oath or affirmation to support this Constitution, but no religious test shall ever be required as a qualification to any office or public trust under the United States	6	-	3	22

Entry				
OATH or affirmation. No warrants shall issue but upon probable cause, supported by oath or affirmation	4th amend.			26
OBJECTIONS of the President to bills. (See Bills.)	1	7	2	7
OBLIGATION of contracts. No State shall pass any bill impairing the obligation of contracts	1	10	1	12
OCCASIONS. The President may, on extraordinary occasions, convene both Houses of Congress, or either of them	2	3	1	16
OFFENCES against the law of nations may be defined and punished by Congress	1	8	10	9
OFFENCES. The President shall have power to grant reprieves and pardons for offences against the United States	2	2	1	16
OFFENCE. Nor shall any person be subject for the same offence to be twice put in jeopardy of life or limb	5th amend.			26
OFFICE. Judgment in cases of impeachment shall not extend further than to removal from office, and disqualification to hold and enjoy any office of honor, trust, or profit, under the United States	1	3	7	4
OFFICE. No Senator or Representative shall, during the time for which he was elected, be appointed to any civil office under the authority of the United States which shall have been created, or the emoluments whereof shall have been increased during such time	1	6	2	6
OFFICE. No person holding any office under the United States shall be a member of either House of Congress during his continuance in office	1	6	2	6
OFFICE of the Government. Congress shall have power to make all laws which shall be necessary and proper for carrying into execution the foregoing powers, and all other powers vested by this Constitution in the Government of the United States, or in any department or officer thereof	1	8	18	10
OFFICE. No person holding any office of profit or trust under the United States, shall, without the consent of the Congress, accept of any present, emolument, office, or title, of any kind whatever, from any king, prince, or foreign State	1	9	8	11
OFFICE. The President shall hold his office during the term of four years, and the Vice President chosen for the same time	2	1	1	13
OFFICE. No person holding an office of trust or profit under the United States shall be appointed an elector of President or Vice President of the United States	2	1	2	13
OFFICE of President United States. Eligibility of a person to the office of President of the United States. (See Eligibility.)	2	1	4	14
OFFICE. In case of the removal of the President from office, or of his death, resignation, or in-				

ALPHABETICAL ANALYSIS—Continued.

	Art.	sec.	cl.	page.
ability to discharge the powers and duties of the said office, the same shall devolve on the Vice President, and the Congress may, by law, provide for the case of removal, death, resignation, or inability, both of the President and Vice President, declaring what officer shall then act as President; and such officer shall act accordingly until the disability be removed or a President shall be elected	2	1	5	14
OFFICE. Oath of office of the President of the United States	2	1	7	15
OFFICERS. The House of Representatives shall choose their Speaker and other officers	1	2	5	3
OFFICERS. The Senate shall choose their other officers, and also a president pro tempore, in the absence of the Vice President	1	3	5	4
OFFICERS of militia. The appointment of officers of the militia reserved to the States respectively	1	8	16	10
OFFICERS of the United States. (See Appointments of.)	2	2	2–3	16
OFFICERS. The President shall commission all the officers of the United States	2	3	1	17
OFFICERS. All civil officers of the United States shall be removed from office on impeachment for, and conviction of, treason, bribery, or other high crimes and misdemeanors	2	4	1	17
OFFICERS. All the executive and judicial officers, both of the United States and of the several States, shall be bound by oath or affirmation to support this Constitution	6	–	3	22
OFFICES. The President may require the opinion, in writing, of the principal officer in each of the executive departments, upon any subject relating to the duties of their respective offices	2	2	1	15
OFFICES. The judges, both of the Supreme and Inferior courts, shall hold their offices during good behavior, and shall, at stated times, receive for their services a compensation, which shall not be diminished during their continuance in office	3	1	1	17
ONE-FIFTH of the members present. The yeas and nays of the members of either House, on any question, shall, at the desire of one-fifth of those present, be entered on the Journal	1	5	3	5
OPINION. The President may require the opinion, in writing, of the principal officer in each of the executive departments	2	2	1	15
ORDAIN and establish this Constitution for the United States of America, &c. We the people do	Preamble.			1
ORDAIN and establish. The judicial power of the United States shall be vested in one Supreme				

Court, and in such Inferior courts as the Congress may, from time to time, ordain and establish	3	1	1	17
ORDER, resolution, or vote, to which the concurrence of the Senate and House of Representatives may be necessary, except on questions of adjournment, shall be presented to the President. (See Resolution.)	1	7	3	8
ORGANIZING the militia. Congress shall have power to provide for organizing, arming, and disciplining the militia	1	8	16	9
ORIGINAL jurisdiction. In all cases affecting ambassadors, other public ministers, and consuls, and those in which a State shall be a party, the Supreme Court shall have original jurisdiction	3	2	2	18
ORIGINATE. All bills for raising revenue shall originate in the House of Representatives	1	7	1	7
ORIGINATED. Every bill, resolution, order, or vote, not approved, shall be returned by the President, with his objections, to that House in which it shall have originated	1	7	2	7
OVERT act. No person shall be convicted of treason, unless on the testimony of two witnesses to the same overt act	3	3	1	19
OWNER. No soldier shall, in time of peace, be quartered in any house without the consent of the owner	3d amend.			26
OWNERS of slaves. No person held to service or labor in one State, under the laws thereof, escaping into another, shall, in consequence of any law or regulation therein, be discharged from such service or labor, but shall be delivered up on claim of the party to whom such service or labor may be due	4	2	3	20
PAPERS. The right of the people to be secure in their effects against unreasonable searches or seizures shall not be violated	4th amend.			26
PARDONS. The President shall have power to grant pardons	2	2	1	16
PASSED the House of Representatives and Senate. Every bill, resolution, &c., passed by the House of Representatives and Senate, shall be presented to the President, &c.	1	7	2	7
PASSED. Bills, resolutions, &c., returned by the President, may be passed by two-thirds of both Houses	1	7	2	8
PASS any bills. No State shall pass any bill of attainder, ex post facto law, or law impairing the obligation of contracts	1	10	1	12
PATENT rights. Congress shall have power to promote the progress of science and useful arts,				

ALPHABETICAL ANALYSIS—Continued.

	Art.	sec.	cl.	page.
by securing for limited times to authors and inventors the exclusive right to their respective writings and discoveries	1	8	8	9
PATERSON, deputy from New Jersey, signed this Constitution. William	–	–	–	23
PAY the debts United States. Congress shall have power to pay the debts of the United States	1	8	1	8
PAYMENTS of debts. No State shall make any thing but gold and silver coin a tender in payment of debts	1	10	1	12
PEACE. For a breach of the peace a Senator or Representative may be arrested	1	6	1	6
PEACE. No State shall, without the consent of Congress, keep troops or ships of war in time of peace	1	10	3	12
PEACE. No soldier shall, in time of peace, be quartered in any house without the consent of the owner	3d amend.			26
PENALTIES. Each House may be authorized to compel the attendance of absent members, in such manner and under such penalties as each House may provide	1	5	1	5
PENNSYLVANIA entitled to eight Representatives in first Congress	1	2	3	2
PEOPLE United States ordain and establish this Constitution	Preamble.			1
PEOPLE. Members of House Representatives to be chosen every second year by the people of the several States	1	2	1	1
PEOPLE represented are—all free persons, those bound for a term of years, Indians taxed, and three-fifths of all other persons. The	1	2	3	2
PEOPLE. The enumeration of the people to be made within three years after first meeting of Congress, and every ten years thereafter, in such manner as they may by law direct	1	2	3	2
PEOPLE. Congress shall make no law abridging the rights of the people peaceably to assemble and to petition the government for a redress of grievances	1st amend.			25
PEOPLE. The right of the people to keep and bear arms shall not be infringed	2d amend.			25
PEOPLE. The right of the people to be secure in their persons, houses, papers, and effects, against unreasonable searches and seizures, shall not be violated; and no warrants shall issue but upon probable cause, supported by oath or affirmation, and particularly describing the place to be searched, and the persons or things to be seized	4th amend.			26
PEOPLE. The enumeration in the Constitution of certain rights, shall not be construed to deny or disparage others retained by the people	9th amend.			28

PEOPLE. The powers not delegated to the United States by the Constitution, nor prohibited by it to the States, are reserved to the States respectively, or to the people .... 10th amend. 28

PERSON. Qualification of a person to be a Representative in Congress 1 2 2 1

PERSON. Qualification of a person to be a Senator in Congress 1 3 3 4

PERSON. No person shall be convicted on an impeachment without the concurrence of two-thirds of the Senators present 1 3 6 4

PERSON. No person holding any office under the United States shall be a member of either House during his continuance in office 1 6 2 6

PERSON. No person holding any office of profit or trust under the United States, shall, without the consent of the Congress, accept of any present, emolument, office, or title, of any kind whatever, from any king, prince, or foreign State 1 9 8 11

PERSON. No person, holding an office of trust or profit under the United States, shall be appointed an elector of President and Vice President 2 1 2 13

PERSON. Eligibility of a person to be President or Vice President of the United States. (See Eligibility.) .... 2 1 4 14; 12th amend. 30

PERSON. No person shall be convicted of treason unless on the testimony of two witnesses to the same overt act, or on confession in open court 3 3 1 19

PERSON. No attainder of treason shall work corruption of blood or forfeiture except during the life of the person attainted 3 3 2 10

PERSON. A person charged in any State with treason, felony, or other crime, who shall flee from justice and be found in another State, shall, on demand of the executive authority of the State from which he fled, be delivered up, to be removed to the State having jurisdiction of the crime 4 2 2 19

PERSON. No person held to service or labor in one State under the laws thereof, escaping into another, shall, in consequence of any law or regulation therein, be discharged from such service or labor, but shall be delivered up on claim of the party to whom such service or labor may be due 4 2 3 20

PERSON. No person shall be held to answer for a capital or otherwise infamous crime, unless on a presentment or indictment of a grand jury, except in cases arising in the land or naval forces, or in the militia when in actual service, in time of war or public danger; nor shall any person be subject, for the same offence, to be twice put in jeopardy of life or limb; nor shall be compelled, in any criminal case, to be a witness against himself; nor be de-

ALPHABETICAL ANALYSIS—Continued.

	Art.	sec.	cl.	page.
prived of life, liberty, or property, without due process of law; nor shall private property be taken for public use without just compensation	5th amend.			26
PERSONAL privilege. The privilege of the writ of habeas corpus shall not be suspended, unless when, in cases of rebellion or invasion, the public safety may require it	1	9	2	11
PERSONS or people of the United States ordain and establish this Constitution. The	Preamble.			1
PERSONS or people of the several States choose members of House of Representatives every second year	1	2	1	1
PERSONS or people to be enumerated every ten years, in such manner as Congress may by law direct	1	2	3	2
PERSONS constituting representative numbers to be embraced in census are, all free persons, those bound for a term of years, Indians taxed, and three-fifths of all other persons, (slaves.)	1	2	3	2
PERSONS convicted on an impeachment shall, nevertheless, be liable and subject to indictment, trial, judgment, and punishment	1	3	7	4
PERSONS. When the yeas and nays are ordered the names of persons (members) voting shall be entered on the Journal	1	7	2	6
PERSONS. The migration or importation of persons (slaves) shall not be prohibited prior to 1808, but a tax or duty may be imposed on such importation not exceeding ten dollars for each person	1	9	1	10
PERSONS or citizens. To what citizens or persons the judicial power shall extend	3	2	1	18
PERSONS. The citizens of each State shall be entitled to all privileges and immunities of citizens in the several States	4	2	1	19
PERSONS or people. Congress shall make no law abridging the right of the people peaceably to assemble, and to petition the government for a redress of grievances	1st amend.			25
PERSONS or people. The right of the people to keep and bear arms shall not be infringed	2d amend.			25
PERSONS or people. The right of the people to be secure in their persons, houses, papers and effects, against unreasonable searches and seizures, shall not be violated; and no warrants shall issue but upon probable cause, supported by oath or affirmation, and particularly describing the place to be searched, and the persons or things to be seized	4th amend.			26
PERSONS. In all criminal prosecutions, the accused shall enjoy the right to a speedy and public trial, by an impartial jury of the State and district wherein the crime shall have been com-				

mitted, which district shall have been previously ascertained by law; and to be informed of the nature and cause of the accusation; to be confronted with the witnesses against him; to have compulsory process for obtaining witnesses in his favor; and to have the assistance of counsel for his defence	6th amend.			27
PERSONS voted for as President and Vice President to be named in the ballots	12th amend.			28
PETITION. Congress shall make no law abridging the right of the people to petition the government for a redress of grievances	1st amend.			25
PINCKNEY, deputy from South Carolina, signed this Constitution. Charles C.	–	–	–	23
PINCKNEY, deputy from South Carolina, signed this Constitution. Charles	–	–	–	23
PIRACIES. Congress shall have power to define and punish piracies and felonies committed on the high seas, and offences against the law of nations	1	8	10	9
PORTS. No preference shall be given by any regulation of commerce or revenue, to the ports of one State over those of another: nor shall vessels bound to, or from, one State, be obliged to enter, clear, or pay duties in another	1	9	6	11
POSTERITY. The Constitution established in order to secure the blessings of liberty to ourselves and to our posterity	Preamble.			1
POST Offices and Post Roads. Congress shall have power to establish post offices and post roads	1	8	7	9
POWER of impeachment. The House of Representatives shall have the sole power of impeachment	1	2	5	3
POWER. Congress shall have power. (See Congress.)	1	8	–	8
POWER. The Senate shall have the sole power to try all impeachments	1	3	6	4
POWER. The Executive power shall be vested in a President of the United States of America	2	1	1	13
POWER. The President shall have power to grant reprieves and pardons for offences against the United States, except in cases of impeachment	2	2	1	16
POWER. The power of the President in making treaties, appointments, &c. (See President.)	2	2	2&3	16
POWER. (See Judicial power.)	3	1–2	–	17
POWER. The judicial power of the United States shall not be construed to extend to any suit, in law or equity, commenced or prosecuted against one of the United States by citizens of another State, or by citizens or subjects of any foreign State	11th amend.			28
POWERS herein granted vested in Congress. All legislative	1	1	–	1
POWERS. Congress shall have power to make all laws which shall be necessary and proper for carrying into execution the foregoing powers, and all other powers vested by this Consti-				

ALPHABETICAL ANALYSIS—Continued.

	Art.	sec.	cl.	page.
tution in the Government of the United States, or any department or officer thereof. (See Congress.)	1	8	18	10
POWERS. In case of the inability of the President to discharge the powers and duties of the office, the same shall devolve on the Vice President	2	1	6	14
POWERS. The powers not delegated to the United States by the Constitution, nor prohibited by it to the States, are reserved to the States respectively, or to the people	10th amend.			28
PREFERENCE regarding ports of States. No preference shall be given by any regulation of commerce or revenue to the ports of one State over those of another; nor shall vessels bound to or from one State be obliged to enter, clear, or pay duties in another	1	9	6	11
PREJUDICE of Claims. Nothing in this Constitution shall be so construed as to prejudice any claims of the United States, or of any particular State	4	3	2	20
PRESENT. No person shall be convicted on an impeachment without the concurrence of two-thirds of the Senators present	1	3	6	4
PRESENT. The yeas and nays of the members of either House on any question shall, at the desire of one-fifth of those present, be entered on the Journal	1	5	3	6
PRESENT. No title of nobility shall be granted by the United States; and no person holding any office of profit or trust under them, shall, without the consent of the Congress, accept of any present, emolument, office, or title, of any kind whatever, from any king, prince, or foreign State	1	9	8	11
PRESENTED. Every bill, order, resolution, or vote, to which the concurrence of the Senate and House of Representatives may be necessary, &c., shall be presented to the President	1	7	2–3	7
PRESENTMENT of a grand jury. No person shall be held to answer for a capital or otherwise infamous crime, unless on a presentment or indictment of a grand jury, except in cases arising in the land or naval forces, or in the militia when in actual service in time of war or public danger	5th amend.			26
PRESERVE the Constitution. The President of the United States shall take an oath, or affirmation, to preserve, protect, and defend the Constitution	2	1	7	15
PRESIDENT of the Senate. (See Senate of the United States.)				
PRESIDENT pro tempore. (See Senate of the United States.)				
PRESIDENT of the United States. The Senate shall choose a President pro tempore when the Vice President shall act as	1	3	5	4

Entry				
PRESIDENT of the United States is tried by the Senate on an impeachment, the Chief Justice shall preside. When the	1	3	6	4
PRESIDENT of the United States. Every bill which shall have passed the House of Representatives and the Senate, shall, before it become a law, be presented to the President of the United States; if he approve he shall sign it, but if not, he shall return it, with his objections, to that House in which it shall have originated, who shall enter the objections at large on their Journal, and proceed to reconsider it. (See Bill.)	1	7	2	7
PRESIDENT of the United States. If any bill shall not be returned by the President within ten days (Sundays excepted) after it shall have been presented to him, the same shall be a law, in like manner as if he had signed it, unless the Congress, by their adjournment, prevent its return; in which case it shall not be a law. (See Bill.)	1	7	2	7
PRESIDENT of the United States. Every order, resolution, or vote, to which the concurrence of the Senate and House of Representatives may be necessary, (except on a question of adjournment,) shall be presented to the *President* of the United States, and, before the same shall take effect, shall be approved by him; or, being disapproved by him, shall be repassed by two-thirds of the Senate and House of Representatives. (See Resolution.)	1	7	3	8
PRESIDENT of the United States. The Executive power shall be vested in a President of the United States of America. He shall hold his office during the term of four years, and together with the Vice President, chosen for the same term, be elected as follows:	2	1	1	13
Electors appointed. Each State shall appoint, in such manner as the Legislature thereof may direct, a number of electors equal to the whole number of Senators and Representatives to which the State may be entitled in the Congress; but no Senator or Representative, or person holding an office of trust or profit under the United States, shall be appointed an elector	2	1	2	13
Electors' proceedings. The electors shall meet in their respective States and vote by ballot for President and Vice President, one of whom, at least, shall not be an inhabitant of the same State with themselves. They shall name in their ballots the person voted for as President, and, in distinct ballots, the person voted for as Vice President; and they shall make distinct lists of all persons voted for as President, and of all persons voted for as Vice President, and of the number of votes for each, which lists they shall sign and certify, and transmit sealed to the seat of the Government of the United States, directed to the President of the Senate	12th amend.			28
Electoral votes opened and counted. The President of the Senate shall, in presence of				

ALPHABETICAL ANALYSIS—Continued.

Art. sec. cl. page.

the Senate and House of Representatives, open all the certificates, and the votes shall then be counted; the person having the greatest number of votes for President, shall be the President, if such number be a majority of the whole number of electors appointed...... 12th amend. 29

Election by House of Representatives. And if no person have such majority, then from the persons having the highest numbers, not exceeding three, on the list of those voted for as President, the House of Representatives shall choose, immediately, by ballot, the President. But, in choosing the President, the votes shall be taken by States, the representation from each State having one vote: a quorum for this purpose shall consist of a member or members from two-thirds of the States, and a majority of all the States shall be necessary to a choice........ 12th amend. 29

Election failing the Vice President shall act. And if the House of Representatives shall not choose a President whenever the right of choice shall devolve upon them, before the fourth of March next following, then the Vice President shall act as President, as in the case of the death or other constitutional disability of the President........ 12th amend. 29

PRESIDENT of the United States. No person except a natural born citizen, or a citizen of the United States at the time of the adoption of this Constitution, shall be eligible to the office of President; neither shall any person be eligible to the office who shall not have attained to the age of 35 years, and been 14 years a resident within the United States........ 2 1 4 14

PRESIDENT of the United States. In case of the removal of the President from office, or of his death, resignation, or inability to discharge the powers and duties of the said office, the same shall devolve on the Vice President; and the Congress may, by law, provide for the case of removal, death, resignation, or inability, both of the President and Vice President, declaring what officer shall then act as President, and such officer shall act accordingly, until the disability be removed, or a President shall be elected........ 2 1 5 14

PRESIDENT of the United States. The President shall, at stated times, receive for his services a compensation, which shall neither be increased nor diminished during the period for which he shall have been elected, and he shall not receive within that period any other emolument from the United States, or any of them........ 2 1 6 15

PRESIDENT of the United States. Before he enter on the execution of his office, he shall take the following oath or affirmation: "I do solemnly swear, (or affirm,) that I will faithfully

execute the office of President of the United States, and will, to the best of my ability, preserve, protect, and defend the Constitution of the United States''	2	1	7	15
PRESIDENT of the United States. The President shall be commander-in-chief of the army and navy of the United States, and of the militia of the several States; when called into the actual service of the United States; he may require the opinion in writing of the principal officer in each of the executive departments, upon any subject relating to the duties of their respective offices; and he shall have power to grant reprieves aud pardons for offences against the United States, except in cases of impeachment	2	2	1	15
PRESIDENT of the United States. He shall have power, by and with the advice and consent of the Senate, to make treaties, provided two-thirds of the Senators present concur; and he shall nominate, and, by and with the advice and consent of the Senate, shall appoint ambassadors, other public ministers, and consuls, judges of the Supreme Court, and all other officers of the United States, whose appointments are not herein otherwise provided for, and which shall be established by law: but the Congress may by law vest the appointment of such inferior officers, as they think proper, in the President alone, in the courts of law, or in the heads of departments	2	2	2	16
PRESIDENT of the United States. The President shall have power to fill up all vacancies that may happen during the recess of the Senate, by granting commissions which shall expire at the end of their next session	2	2	3	16
PRESIDENT of the United States. He shall, from time to time, give to the Congress information of the state of the Union, and recommend to their consideration such measures as he shall judge necessary and expedient; he may, on extraordinary occasions, convene both Houses, or either of them, and, in case of disagreement between them, with respect to the time of adjournment, he may adjourn them to such time as he shall think proper; he shall receive ambassadors and other public ministers; he shall take care that the laws be faithfully executed, and shall commission all the officers of the United States	2	3	1	16
PRESIDENT of the United States. The President, Vice President, and all civil officers of the United States, shall be removed from office on impeachment for, and conviction of, treason, bribery, or other high crimes and misdemeanors	2	4	1	17
PRESS. Congress shall make no law abridging the freedom of speech and of the press	1st amend.			25
PRINCE. No person holding any office of profit or trust under the United States, shall, without the consent of the Congress, accept of any present, emolument, office, or title, of any kind whatever, from any king, prince, or foreign State	1	9	8	11

ALPHABETICAL ANALYSIS—Continued.

	Art.	sec.	cl.	page.
PRINCIPAL officer. The President may require the opinion, in writing, of the principal officer in each of the executive departments	2	2	1	15
PRIVATE property. Nor shall private property be taken for public use, without just compensation	5th amend.			26
PRIVILEGE of the writ of habeas corpus shall not be suspended, unless when, in cases of rebellion or invasion, the public safety may require it	1	9	2	11
PRIVILEGED. Senators and Representatives shall, in all cases, except treason, felony, and breach of the peace, be privileged from arrest during their attendance at the session of their respective Houses, and in going to and returning from the same	1	6	1	6
PRIVILEGES and immunities. The citizens of each State shall be entitled to all the privileges and immunities of citizens in the several States	4	2	1	19
PROCEEDINGS. Each House may determine the rules of its proceedings	1	5	2	5
PROCEEDINGS. Each House shall keep a Journal of its proceedings	1	5	3	5
PROCEEDINGS. Credit, proof, and effect of judicial proceedings of States	4	1	1	19
PROCESS of law. Nor shall any person be deprived of life, liberty, or property, without due process of law	5th amend.			26
PROCESS. In all criminal prosecutions the accused to have compulsory process for obtaining witnesses in his favor	6th amend.			27
PROFIT. Judgment, in cases of impeachment, shall not extend farther than to removal from office, and disqualification to hold and enjoy any office of honor, trust, or profit under the United States	1	3	7	4
PROFIT. No person holding an office of trust or profit under the United States shall be appointed an elector	2	1	2	13
PROHIBITED powers. The powers not delegated to the United States by the Constitution, nor prohibited by it to the States, are reserved to the States respectively, or to the people	10th amend.			28
PROMOTE the general welfare. The Constitution established in order to promote the general welfare, &c.	Preamble.			1
PROOF. Congress may, by general laws, prescribe the manner in which the acts, records, and judicial proceedings of States shall be proved, and the effect thereof	4	1	1	19
PROPERTY of the United States. The Congress shall have power to dispose of and make all				

Entry				
needful rules and regulations respecting the territory, or other property belonging to the United States	4	3	2	20
PROPERTY or effects. The right of the people to be secure in their effects against unreasonable searches or seizures shall not be violated	4th amend.			26
PROPERTY. Nor shall any person be deprived of life, liberty, or property, without due process of law	5th amend.			26
PROPERTY. Nor shall private property be taken for public use, without just compensation	5th amend.			26
PROPOSE amendments. The Congress, whenever two-thirds of both Houses shall deem it necessary, shall propose amendments to this Constitution, or, on the application of the Legislatures of two-thirds of the several States, shall call a convention for proposing amendments, &c.	5	1	1	21
PROSECUTIONS. Criminal prosecutions against persons. (See Criminal.)	6th amend.			27
PROSECUTED. The judicial power of the United States shall not be construed to extend to any suit in law or equity, commenced or prosecuted against one of the United States by citizens of another State, or by citizens or subjects of any foreign State	11th amend.			28
PROTECT the Constitution. The President of the United States shall take an oath or affirmation to preserve, protect, and defend, the Constitution	2	1	7	15
PROTECT. The United States shall protect each State against invasion	4	4	1	20
PROVIDE for the common defence. The Constitution established in order to provide for the common defence, &c.	Preamble.			1
PUBLIC acts, records, and judicial proceedings of States, to have full faith and credit, &c.	4	1	1	19
PUBLIC danger. No State shall, without the consent of Congress, engage in war, unless actually invaded. or in such imminent danger as will not admit of delay	1	10	3	12
PUBLIC danger. (See War.)	5th amend.			26
PUBLIC ministers. (See Appointments—Ambassadors.)	2	2	2	16
PUBLIC ministers. The President shall receive ambassadors and other public ministers	2	3	1	17
PUBLIC money. (See Money.)	1	9	7	11
PUBLIC safety. The privilege of the writ of habeas corpus shall not be suspended, unless when in cases of rebellion or invasion the public safety may require it	1	9	2	11
PUBLIC trust. No religious test shall ever be required as a qualification to any office or public trust under the United States	6	–	3	22
PUBLIC use. Nor shall private property be taken for public use without just compensation	5th amend.			26

ALPHABETICAL ANALYSIS—Continued

	Art.	sec.	cl.	page.
PUBLISH. The Journal of each House shall be published from time to time, except such parts as may in their judgment require secrecy	1	5	3	5
PUBLISHED. A regular statement and account of the receipts and expenditures of all public money shall be published from time to time	1	9	7	11
PUNISH. Each House of Congress may punish its members for disorderly behavior	1	5	2	5
PUNISHMENT. Persons convicted on an impeachment shall, nevertheless, be liable and subject to indictment, trial, judgment, and punishment, according to law	1	3	7	4
PUNISHMENT. Congress shall have power to provide for the punishment of counterfeiting the securities and current coin of the United States	1	8	6	9
PUNISHMENT. The Congress shall have power to declare the punishment of treason	3	3	2	19
PUNISHMENTS. Excessive bail shall not be required, nor excessive fines imposed, nor cruel and unusual punishments inflicted	8th amend.			27
QUALIFICATION of a Representative in Congress shall be 25 years of age, seven years a citizen of the United States, and when elected an inhabitant of same State	1	2	2	2
QUALIFICATION of a Senator in Congress shall be 30 years of age, nine years a citizen of the United States, and when elected an inhabitant of same State	1	3	3	4
QUALIFICATION to office. The Senators and Representatives before mentioned, and the members of the several State Legislatures, and all executive and judicial officers, both of the United States and of the several States, shall be bound by oath or affirmation to support this Constitution; but no religious test shall ever be required as a qualification to any office or public trust under the United States	6	–	3	22
QUALIFICATIONS for electors of Representatives in Congress the same as for electors of the most numerous branch of the State Legislature	1	2	1	1
QUALIFICATIONS of its own members. Each House of Congress shall be the judge of the elections, returns, and qualifications of its own members	1	5	1	5
QUALIFICATIONS of President United States. No person except a natural born citizen, or a citizen of the United States at the time of the adoption of this Constitution, shall be eligible to the office of President; neither shall any person be eligible to that office who shall not have attained to the age of 35 years, and been 14 years a resident within the United States	2	1	4	14

QUALIFICATIONS of Vice President the same as that of President of the United States	12th amend.			30
QUARTERED. No soldier shall, in time of peace, be quartered in any house without the consent of the owner; nor in time of war, but in a manner to be prescribed by law	3d amend.			26
QUESTION. The yeas and nays of the members of either House on any question shall, at the desire of one-fifth of those present, be entered on the Journal	1	5	3	5
QUESTION. On question of adjournment of the two Houses, the approbation of the President is not necessary	1	7	3	8
QUESTIONED. For any speech or debate in either House, they shall not be questioned in any other place	1	6	1	6
QUORUM. A majority of each House shall constitute a quorum to do business, but a smaller number may adjourn from day to day, and may be authorized to compel the attendance of absent members, in such manner, and under such penalties as each House may provide	1	5	1	5
QUORUM of the House of Representatives. A quorum (for the election of President by the House of Representatives) shall consist of a member or members from two-thirds of the States, and a majority of all the States shall be necessary to a choice	12th amend.			29
QUORUM of the Senate. A quorum (for the election of Vice President by the Senate) shall consist of two-thirds of the whole number of Senators, and a majority of the whole number shall be necessary to a choice	12th amend.			30
RATIFICATION. The ratifications of the conventions of nine States shall be sufficient for the establishment of this Constitution between the States so ratifying the same	7	0	1	22
RATIFICATION of amendments to the Constitution. (See Constitution.)	5	0	0	21
REBELLION. The privilege of the writ of habeas corpus shall not be suspended, unless when, in cases of rebellion or invasion, the public safety may require it	1	9	2	11
RECEIPTS and expenditures. A regular statement and account of the receipts and expenditures of all public money shall be published from time to time	1	9	7	11
RECESS of the Senate. The President shall have power to fill up all vacancies that may happen during the recess of the Senate, by granting commissions, which shall expire at the end of their next session	2	2	3	16
RECOMMEND to Congress. The President shall from time to time recommend to the consideration of Congress such measures as he shall judge necessary and expedient	2	3	1	16
RECONSIDERED. Bills returned with objections by the President of the United States to be				

ALPHABETICAL ANALYSIS—Continued.

	Art.	sec.	cl	page.
reconsidered by the two Houses of Congress, and if approved by two-thirds of both Houses, shall become a law	1	7	2	7
RECONSIDERED. Any order, resolution, or vote, returned with objections by the President, may be reconsidered, and repassed by two-thirds of both Houses	1	7	3	8
RECORDS. Full faith and credit shall be given in each State to the public acts, records, and judicial proceedings, of every other State; and the Congress may, by general laws, prescribe the manner in which such acts, records, and proceedings, shall be proved, and the effect thereof	4	1	1	19
REDRESS of grievances. Congress shall make no law abridging the right of the people peaceably to assemble, and to petition the Government for a redress of grievances	1st amend.			25
READ, deputy from Delaware, signed this Constitution. George	–	–	–	23
REGULATION. No person held to service or labor, escaping into another State, shall, in consequence of any law or regulation of such State, be discharged from such service or labor	4	2	3	20
REGULATIONS for the election of Senators and Representatives. (See Senators.)	1	4	1	5
REGULATIONS. The Supreme Court shall have appellate jurisdiction in certain cases, both as to law and fact, with such exceptions, and under such regulations, as the Congress shall make	3	2	2	18
REGULATIONS. The Congress shall have power to dispose of, and make, all needful rules and regulations respecting the territory and other property belonging to the United States	4	3	2	20
RELIGION. Congress shall make no law respecting an establishment of religion, or prohibiting the free exercise thereof	1st amend.			25
RELIGIOUS test. No religious test shall ever be required as a qualification to any office or public trust under the United States	6	0	3	22
REMOVAL. Judgment, in cases of impeachment, shall not extend further than to removal from office, and disqualification to hold and enjoy any office of honor, trust, or profit, under the United States	1	3	7	4
REMOVAL. In case of the removal of the President from office, it shall devolve on the Vice President	2	1	5	14
REMOVAL. In case of removal, both of the President and Vice President, the Congress may by law provide, declaring what officer shall then act as President	2	1	5	15
REMOVED from office. All civil officers of the United States shall be removed from office on				

impeachment for, and conviction of, treason, bribery, or other high crimes and misdemeanors	2	4	1	17
REPRESENTATION. When vacancies happen in the representation from any State, the Executive thereof shall issue writs of election to fill them	1	2	4	3
REPRESENTATIVE. No person shall be a Representative unless 25 years old, been 7 years a citizen of the United States, and, when elected, an inhabitant of the same State	1	2	2	2
REPRESENTATIVE numbers include all free persons; those bound to service for a term of years, Indians taxed, and three-fifths of all other persons, (slaves,) all to be enumerated every ten years, &c.	1	2	3	2
REPRESENTATIVE. No Senator or—shall, during the time for which he was elected, be appointed to any civil office under the authority of the United States, which shall have been created, or the emoluments whereof shall have been increased during such time: and no person holding any office under the United States shall be a member of either House during his continuance in office	1	6	2	6
REPRESENTATIVE. No Representative shall be appointed an elector of President or Vice President of the United States	2	1	2	13
REPRESENTATIVES. Congress shall consist of a Senate and House of Representatives	1	1	0	1
REPRESENTATIVES. Members of the House of Representatives to be chosen every second year by the people	1	2	1	1
REPRESENTATIVES in Congress. Qualifications of electors of Representatives in Congress the same as for electors of the most numerous branch of the State Legislature	1	2	1	1
REPRESENTATIVES and direct taxes to be apportioned among the States according to their respective numbers	1	2	3	2
REPRESENTATIVES shall not exceed one for every 30,000, but each State shall have at least one Representative. The	1	2	3	2
REPRESENTATIVES allowed in first Congress were—				
To New Hampshire 3	1	2	3	2
Massachusetts 8	1	2	3	2
Rhode Island and Providence Plantations 1	1	2	3	2
Connecticut 5	1	2	3	2
New York 6	1	2	3	2
New Jersey 4	1	2	3	2

ALPHABETICAL ANALYSIS—Continued.

	Art.	sec.	cl.	page.
Pennsylvania 8	1	2	3	2
Delaware 1	1	2	3	2
Maryland 6	1	2	3	2
Virginia 10	1	2	3	2
North Carolina 5	1	2	3	3
South Carolina 5	1	2	3	3
Georgia 3	1	2	3	3
—65.				
REPRESENTATIVES. The House of Representatives shall choose their Speaker and other officers	1	2	5	3
REPRESENTATIVES. The House of Representatives shall have the sole power of impeachment	1	2	5	3
REPRESENTATIVES. The times, places, and manner of holding elections for Senators and Representatives shall be prescribed in each State by the Legislature thereof; but the Congress may, at any time, by law, make or alter such regulations, except as to the places of choosing Senators	1	4	1	5
REPRESENTATIVES. The House of—				
Shall be the judge of the elections, returns, and qualifications of its own members	1	5	1	5
A majority thereof shall constitute a quorum to do business; but a smaller number may adjourn from day to day, and may be authorized to compel the attendance of absent members, in such manner, and under such penalties, as that House may provide	1	5	1	5
May determine the rules of its proceedings, punish its members for disorderly behavior, and, with the concurrence of two-thirds, expel a member	1	5	2	5
Shall keep a Journal of its proceedings, and from time to time publish the same, excepting such parts as may, in their judgment, require secrecy; and the yeas and nays of the members on any question, shall, at the desire of one-fifth of those present, be entered on the Journal	1	5	3	5
Shall not, during the session of Congress, without the consent of the Senate, adjourn for more than three days, nor to any other place than that in which the two Houses shall be sitting	1	5	4	6

Entry				
REPRESENTATIVES. The Senators and—				
Shall receive a compensation for their services, to be ascertained by law, and paid out of the Treasury of the United States	1	6	1	6
They shall, in all cases except treason, felony, and breach of the peace, be privileged from arrest during their attendance at the session of their respective Houses, and in going to and returning from the same; and for any speech or debate in either House, they shall not be questioned in any other place	1	6	1	6
REPRESENTATIVES. All bills for raising revenue shall originate in the House of Representatives; but the Senate may propose, or concur with, amendments, as on other bills	1	7	1	7
REPRESENTATIVES. Every bill, order, resolution, or vote, (except on a question of adjournment,) originating in either House of Congress, shall be presented to the President of the United States. (For proceedings see Bill—Resolution.)	1	7	2—3	7
REPRESENTATIVES in Congress, and members of State Legislatures, shall be bound by oath or affirmation, to support this Constitution	6	0	3	22
REPRIEVES. The President shall have power to grant reprieves	2	2	1	16
REPRISAL. Congress shall have power to grant letters of marque and reprisal	1	8	11	9
REPRISAL. No State shall grant letters of marque and reprisal	1	10	1	12
REPUBLICAN. The United States shall guaranty to every State in this Union a republican form of government	4	4	1	24
RESERVED rights. (See Retained rights.)	9th amend.			28
RESERVED powers. The powers not delegated to the United States by the Constitution, nor prohibited by it to the States, are reserved to the States respectively, or to the people	10th amend.			28
RESERVING to the States. Congress shall have power to provide for organizing, arming, and disciplining the militia, and governing such part as may be in the service of the United States, reserving to the States the appointment of the officers, and the authority of training the militia according to the discipline prescribed by Congress	1	8	16	9
RESIDENCE of 14 years within the United States requisite in eligibility of a person to the office of President or Vice President of the United States	2	1	4	14
RESIGNATION. Vacancies by resignation of Senators may be filled by the Executive of a State in recess of Legislature	1	3	2	3
RESIGNATION. In case of the resignation of the President, the office shall devolve on the Vice President, &c.	2	1	5	14
RESOLUTION. Every order, resolution, or vote, to which the concurrence of the Senate and				

ALPHABETICAL ANALYSIS—Continued.

	Art.	sec.	cl.	page.
House of Representatives may be necessary, (except on a question of adjournment,) shall be presented to the President of the United States, and, before the same shall take effect, shall be approved by him; or, being disapproved by him, shall be repassed by two-thirds of the Senate and House of Representatives, according to the rules and limitations prescribed in the case of a bill. (See Bills.)	1	7	3	8
RETAINED rights. The enumeration, in the Constitution, of certain rights, shall not be construed to deny or disparage others retained by the people	9th amend.			28
RETURNED. Bills, resolutions, &c., not approved, to be returned by the President to the House in which they originated	1	7	2	7
RETURNED. Bills, resolutions, &c., not returned within ten days, Sundays excepted, to become laws unless Congress adjourn	1	7	2	7
RETURNS. Each House shall be the judge of the elections, returns, and qualifications of its own members	1	5	1	5
REVENUE. All bills for raising revenue shall originate in the House of Representatives; but the Senate may propose, or concur with, amendments, as on other bills	1	7	1	7
REVENUE. No preference shall be given, by any regulation of commerce or revenue, to the ports of one State over those of another	1	9	6	11
RHODE Island and Providence Plantations entitled to one Representative in first Congress	1	2	3	2
RIGHT of conscience. (See Religion.)				
RIGHT of the people. Congress shall make no law abridging the right of the people peaceably to assemble and to petition the Government for a redress of grievances	1st amend.			25
RIGHT of the people. A well-regulated militia being necessary to the security of a free State, the right of the people to keep and bear arms shall not be infringed	2d amend.			26
RIGHT of the people. The right of the people to be secure in their persons, houses, papers, and effects, against unreasonable searches and seizures, shall not be violated; and no warrants shall issue but upon probable cause, supported by oath or affirmation, and particularly describing the place to be searched, and the persons or things to be seized	4th amend.			26
RIGHT of. (See Life—Liberty—Property.)				
RIGHT of evidence and defence in criminal prosecutions. (See Criminal.)				
RIGHT of trial by jury. In suits at common law, where the value in controversy shall exceed twenty dollars, the right of trial by jury shall be preserved, and no fact tried by a jury				

shall be otherwise re-examined in any court of the United States, than according to the rules of the common law........ 7th amend. 27
RIGHTS. Exclusive rights to writings and discoveries may be secured to their authors and inventors for a limited time........ 1 8 8 9
RIGHTS of domestic security. No soldier shall, in time of peace, be quartered in any house without the consent of the owner, nor in time of war, but in a manner to be prescribed by law 3d amend. 26
RIGHTS. The enumeration, in the Constitution, of certain rights, shall not be construed to deny or disparage others retained by the people........ 9th amend. 28
ROADS. Congress shall have power to establish post offices and post roads........ 1 8 7 9
RULES of proceedings. Each House of Congress may determine the rules of its proceedings.... 1 5 2 5
RULES concerning captures. Congress shall have power to make rules concerning captures on land and water........ 1 8 11 9
RULES and articles of war. Congress shall have power to make rules for the government and regulation of the land and naval forces........ 1 8 14 9
RULES of the common law. No fact tried by a jury shall be otherwise re-examined in any court of the United States, than according to the rules of the common law........ 7th amend. 26
RUNAWAY slaves, or persons held to service or labor, and fugitives from justice, shall be delivered up, &c........ 4 2 2to3 19
RUTLEDGE, deputy from South Carolina, signed this Constitution. John........ - - - 23

SCIENCE and useful arts. Congress shall have power to promote the progress of science and useful arts, by securing, for limited times, to authors and inventors, the exclusive right to their respective writings and discoveries........ 1 8 8 9
SEARCHES and seizures. The right of the people to be secure in their persons, houses, papers, and effects against unreasonable searches and seizures shall not be violated, and no warrant shall issue but upon probable cause, supported by oath or affirmation, and particularly describing the place to be searched, and the persons or things to be seized........ 4th amend. 26
SEAT of Government. Neither House, during the session of Congress, shall, without the consent of the other, adjourn for more than three days, nor to any other place than that in which the two Houses shall be sitting........ 1 5 4 6
SEAT of Government. Congress shall have power to exercise exclusive legislation in all cases whatsoever, over such district (not exceeding ten miles square) as may, by cession of particular States, and the acceptance of Congress, become the seat of the Government of the

13

ALPHABETICAL ANALYSIS—Continued.

	Art.	sec.	cl.	page.
United States, and to exercise like authority over all places purchased by consent of the Legislature of the State in which the same shall be, for the erection of forts, magazines, arsenals, dock-yards, and other needful buildings	1	8	17	10
SEAT of Government of the United States. The list of electoral votes for President and Vice President shall be transmitted, sealed, to the seat of the Government of the United States, directed to the President of the Senate	12th amend.			29
SEATS of Senators. Terms at which the seats of the several classes of Senators shall be vacated	1	3	2	3
SECRECY. Each House of Congress shall keep a Journal of its proceedings, and from time to time publish the same, excepting such parts as may in their judgment require secrecy	1	5	3	5
SECURE the blessings of liberty. The Constitution established to secure the blessings of liberty to ourselves and our posterity, &c.	Preamble.			1
SECURE. The right of the people to be secure in their persons, houses, papers, and effects, against unreasonable searches and seizures, shall not be violated	4th amend.			26
SECURITIES. Congress shall have power to provide for the punishment of counterfeiting the securities and current coin of the United States	1	8	6	9
SECURITY of a free State. A well regulated militia being necessary to the security of a free State, the right of the people to keep and bear arms shall not be infringed	2d amend.			25
SEIZURES. The right of the people to be secure against unreasonable seizures shall not be violated. (See Searches.)	4th amend.			26
SENATE and House of Representatives. The Congress of the United States shall consist of a Senate and House of Representatives	1	1	-	1
SENATE and House of Representatives. (See Congress.)				
SENATE. The Senate shall be composed of two Senators from each State, chosen by the Legislature for six years, and each Senator shall have one vote	1	3	1	3
SENATE. The Vice President of the United States shall be President of the Senate, but shall have no vote unless they be equally divided	1	3	4	4
SENATE. The Senate shall choose their other officers, and also a President pro tempore, in the absence of the Vice President, or when he shall exercise the office of President of the United States	1	3	5	4
SENATE. The Senate shall have the sole power to try all impeachments: when sitting for that purpose they shall be on oath or affirmation. When the President of the United States is				

tried, the Chief Justice shall preside; and no person shall be convicted without the concurrence of two-thirds of the members present 1 3 6 4

SENATE. The judgment of the Senate, in cases of impeachment, shall not extend further than to removal from office, and disqualification to hold and enjoy an office of honor, trust, or profit under the United States, but the party convicted shall, nevertheless, be liable and subject to indictment, trial, judgment and punishment, according to law 1 3 7 4

SENATE of the United States. The Senate shall be the judge of the elections, returns, and qualifications of its own members; a majority shall constitute a quorum to do business, but a smaller number may adjourn from day to day, and may be authorized to compel the attendance of absent members, in such manner, and under such penalties, as that House may provide........ 1 5 1 5

SENATE. The Senate may determine the rules of its proceedings, punish its members for disorderly behavior, and, with the concurrence of two thirds, expel a member 1 5 2 5

SENATE. The Senate shall keep a Journal of its proceedings, and from time to time publish the same, excepting such parts as may, in their judgment, require secrecy; and the yeas and nays of the members, on any question, shall, at the desire of one-fifth of those present, be entered on the Journal........ 1 5 3 5

SENATE. The Senate shall not, during the session of Congress, without the consent of the House of Representatives, adjourn for more than three days, nor to any other place than that in which the two Houses shall be sitting........ 1 5 4 6

SENATE. All bills for raising revenue shall originate in the House of Representatives; but the Senate may propose, or concur with, amendments, as on other bills. (See Bills.) 1 7 1 7

SENATE. Every bill, order, resolution, and vote, (except on a question of adjournment,) originating in either House of Congress, shall be presented to the President of the United States. (For proceedings, see Bill—Resolution.) .... 1 7 2—3 7

SENATE. Action of Senate on bills, resolutions, orders, and votes. (See Bills, &c.)

SENATE. The President shall have power, by and with the advice and consent of the Senate, to make treaties, provided two-thirds of the Senators present concur; and he shall nominate, and, by and with the advice and consent of the Senate, shall appoint ambassadors, other public ministers, and consuls, judges of the Supreme Court, and all other officers of the United States, whose appointments are not herein otherwise provided for, and which shall be established by law. But the Congress may, by law, vest the appointment of such

ALPHABETICAL ANALYSIS—Continued.

	Art.	sec.	cl.	page.
inferior officers, as they think proper, in the President alone, in the courts of law, or in the heads of departments	2	2	2	16
SENATE. The President shall have power to fill up all vacencies that may happen during the recess of the Senate, by granting commissions which shall expire at the end of their next session	2	2	3	16
SENATE. The President may, on extraordinary occasions, convene both Houses of Congress, or either of them	2	3	1	16
SENATE. No State, without its consent, shall be deprived of its equal suffrage in the Senate	5	–	–	21
SENATE. The lists of votes of electors of President and Vice President shall be directed to the President of the Senate	12th amend.			29
SENATE. The President of the Senate shall, in presence of the Senate and House of Representatives, open all the certificates of the electors of President and Vice President of the United States	12th amend.			29
SENATE. If no person have a majority of the electoral votes as Vice President, then, from the two highest numbers on the list the Senate shall choose the Vice President; a quorum for the purpose shall consist of two-thirds of the whole number of Senators, and a majority of the whole number shall be necessary to a choice	12th amend.			30
SENATOR. Each Senator shall have one vote	1	3	1	3
SENATOR. No person shall be a Senator who shall not have attained the age of 30 years—been 9 years a citizen of the United States, and, when elected, an inhabitant of the State for which he shall be chosen	1	3	3	4
SENATOR or Representative. No Senator or Representative shall, during the time for which he was elected, be appointed to any civil office under the authority of the United States which shall have been created, or the emoluments whereof shall have been increased during such time; and no person holding any office under the United States shall be a member of either House during his continuance in office	1	6	2	6
SENATOR. No Senator shall be appointed an elector of President or Vice President United States	2	1	2	13
SENATORS. The Senate of the United States shall be composed of two Senators from each State	1	3	1	3
SENATORS. Two Senators shall be chosen by the Legislature of each State for six years	1	3	1	3

SENATORS divided as nearly as may be into three classes after the first election: The seats of the first class vacated at expiration of the second year. The seats of the second class vacated at expiration of the fourth year. The seats of the third class vacated at expiration of the sixth year; so that one-third may be chosen every second year..............	1	3	2	3
SENATORS. If vacancies happen in seats of Senators, by resignation or otherwise, during the recess of the Legislature of any State, the Executive thereof may make temporary appointments until next meeting of the Legislature, which shall then fill such vacancies	1	3	2	3
SENATORS. The times, places, and manner of holding elections for Senators and Representatives, shall be prescribed in each State by the Legislature thereof; but the Congress may, at any time, by law, make or alter such regulations, except as to the places of choosing Senators	1	4	1	5
SENATORS and Representatives shall receive a compensation for their services, to be ascertained by law, and paid out of the Treasury of the United States......................	1	6	1	6
They shall, in all cases except treason, felony, and breach of the peace, be privileged from arrest during their attendance at the session of their respective Houses, and in going to and returning from the same; and for any speech or debate in either House, they shall not be questioned in any other place..	1	6	1	6
SENATORS of the United States shall be bound by oath or affirmation to support the Constitution of the United States..	6	–	3	22
SERVICE. Persons bound to service for a term of years included in representative numbers....	1	2	3	2
SERVICE of the United States. The Congress shall have power to provide for governing such parts of the militia as may be employed in the service of the United States.............	1	8	16	9
SERVICE of the United States. The President shall be commander-in-chief of the militia of the several States, when called into the actual service of the United States................	2	2	1	15
SERVICE or labor. (See Slaves.)..	4	2	3	20
SERVICE. No person shall be held to answer for a capital or otherwise infamous crime, unless on a presentment or indictment of a grand jury, except in cases arising in the land or naval forces, or in the militia when in actual service, in time of war or public danger.....	5th amend.			26
SERVICES. The Senators and Representatives shall receive a compensation for their services, to be ascertained by law, and paid out of the Treasury of the United States............	1	6	1	6
SERVICES. The President shall, at stated times, receive for his services a compensation, &c.	2	1	6	15
SERVICES. The judges, both of the Supreme and Inferior courts, shall hold their offices during				

ALPHABETICAL ANALYSIS—Continued.

	Art.	sec.	cl.	page.
good behavior, and shall, at stated times, receive for their services a compensation which shall not be diminished during their continuance in office	3	1	1	17
SESSION of Congress. (See Meeting.)				
SESSION. The Congress shall assemble at least once in every year, and such meeting or session shall be on the first Monday in December, unless they shall by law appoint a different day	1	4	2	5
SESSION. Neither House, during the session of Congress, shall, without the consent of the other, adjourn for more than three days, nor to any other place than that in which the two Houses shall be sitting	1	5	4	6
SESSION. Senators and Representatives shall, in all cases except treason, felony, and breach of the peace, be privileged from arrest during their attendance at the session of their respective Houses, and in going to and returning from the same	1	6	1	6
SESSION of the Senate. The President shall have power to fill up all vacancies that may happen during the recess of the Senate, by granting commissions which shall expire at the end of their next session	2	2	3	16
SHERMAN, deputy from Connecticut, signed this Constitution. Roger	–	–	–	23
SHIPS of war. No State shall, without the consent of Congress, keep ships of war in time of peace	1	10	3	12
SIGNED. Every bill, resolution, order, or vote, approved, shall be signed by the President	1	7	2	7
SIGNED. Any bill, resolution, &c., not returned within ten days, to become a law as if it had been signed by the President	1	7	2	7
SIGNERS of the Constitution	–	–	–	23
Geo. Washington, President and deputy from Virginia	–	–	–	23
John Langdon, Nicholas Gilman, New Hampshire	–	–	–	23
Nathaniel Gorham, Rufus King, Massachusetts	–	–	–	23
William Samuel Johnson, Roger Sherman, Connecticut	–	–	–	23
Alexander Hamilton, New York	–	–	–	23
William Livingston, David Brearley, William Paterson, Jonathan Dayton, New Jersey	–	–	–	23
Benjamin Franklin, Thomas Mifflin, Robert Morris, George Clymer, Thomas Fitzsimons, Jared Ingersoll, James Wilson, Gouverneur Morris, Pennsylvania	–	–	–	23

George Reed, Gunning Bedford, jun'r, John Dickinson, Richard Bassett, Jacob Broom, Delaware .... – – – 23
James McHenry, Daniel of St. Thomas Jenifer, Daniel Carroll, Maryland .... – – – 23
John Blair, James Madison, jun'r, Virginia .... – – – 23
William Blount, Richard Dobbs Spaight, Hugh Williamson, North Carolina .... – – – 23
John Rutledge, Charles C. Pinckney, Charles Pinckney, Pierce Butler, South Carolina – – – 23
William Few, Abraham Baldwin, Georgia .... – – – 23
Attest: William Jackson, Secretary .... – – – 23

SILVER. No State shall make any thing but gold and silver coin a tender in payment of debts.. 1 10 1 12

SLAVES. Three-fifths of all slaves included in representative numbers 1 2 3 2

SLAVES. The migration or importation of such persons as any of the States now existing shall think proper to admit, shall not be prohibited by the Congress prior to the year 1808, but a tax or duty may be imposed on such importation, not exceeding ten dollars for each person 1 9 1 10

SLAVES. No amendment of the Constitution, made prior to 1808, shall affect the preceding clause .... 5 – – 21

SLAVES. No person held to service or labor in one State, under the laws thereof, escaping into another, shall, in consequence of any law or regulation therein, be discharged from such service or labor, but shall be delivered up on claim of the party to whom such service or labor may be due 4 2 3 20

SLAVES. No amendment made prior to 1808 shall prohibit the importation of persons (or slaves) 5 – – 21

SOLDIER. No soldier shall, in time of peace, be quartered in any house without the consent of the owner, nor in time of war, but in a manner to be prescribed by law........ 3d amend. 26

SOUTH Carolina entitled to five Representatives in first Congress 1 2 3 3

SPAIGHT, deputy from North Carolina, signed this Constitution. Richard Dobbs .... – – – 23

SPEAKER and other officers. The House of Representatives shall choose their Speaker and other officers........ 1 2 5 3

SPEECH. Senators and Representatives, for any speech or debate in either House, shall not be questioned in any other place 1 6 1 6

SPEECH. Congress shall make no law abridging the freedom of speech .... 1st amend. 25

STANDARD. Congress shall have power to fix the standard of weights and measures........ 1 8 5 8

STATE of the Union. The President shall, from time to time, give to the Congress information

ALPHABETICAL ANALYSIS—Continued.

	Art.	sec.	cl.	page.
of the State of the Union, and recommend to their consideration such measures as he shall judge necessary and expedient	2	3	1	16
STATE. A Representative in Congress shall be an inhabitant of the State in which he shall be chosen	1	2	2	2
STATE. Each State shall have at least one Representative in Congress	1	2	3	2
STATE. When vacancies happen in the representation from a State, the Executive thereof shall issue writs of election to fill them	1	2	4	3
STATE. The Senate of the United States shall be composed of two Senators from each State, chosen by the Legislature thereof	1	3	1	3
STATE. If vacancies happen in seats of Senators, by resignation or otherwise, during the recess of the Legislature of any State, the Executive thereof may make temporary appointments, until the next meeting of the Legislature, which shall then fill such vacancies	1	3	2	3
STATE. A Senator in Congress shall be an inhabitant of the State for which he shall be chosen	1	3	3	4
STATE. The times, places, and manner of holding elections for Senators and Representatives shall be prescribed in each State by the Legislature thereof; but the Congress may, at any time, by law, make or alter such regulations, except as to the places of choosing Senators	1	4	1	5
STATE. No tax or duty shall be laid on articles exported from any State	1	9	5	11
STATE. No preference shall be given, by any regulation of commerce or revenue, to the ports of one State over those of another; nor shall vessels bound to or from one State be obliged to enter, clear, or pay duties in another	1	9	6	11
STATE. No State shall enter into any treaty, alliance, or confederation; grant letters of marque and reprisal; coin money; emit bills of credit; make any thing but gold and silver coin a tender in payment of debts: pass any bill of attainder, ex post facto law, or law impairing the obligation of contracts, or grant any title of nobility	1	10	1	12
STATE. No State shall, without the consent of the Congress, lay any imposts or duties on imports or exports, except what may be absolutely necessary for executing its inspection laws; and the nett produce of all duties and imposts, laid by any State on imports or exports, shall be for the use of the Treasury of the United States; and all such laws shall be subject to the revision and control of the Congress	1	10	2	12
STATE. No State shall, without the consent of Congress, lay any duty of tonnage, keep troops				

or ships of war in time of peace, enter into any agreement or compact with another State, or with a foreign power, or engage in war, unless actually invaded, or in such imminent danger as will not admit of delay	1	10	3	12
STATE. Each State shall appoint, in such manner as the Legislature thereof may direct, the electors of President and Vice President of the United States. (See Election.)	2	1	2	13
STATE. The judicial power shall extend to controversies to which the United States shall be a party; to controversies between two or more States; between a State and citizens of another State; between citizens of different States; between citizens of the same State claiming lands under grants of different States; and between a State, or the citizens thereof, and foreign States, citizens, or subjects	3	2	1	18
STATE. In all cases in which a State shall be a party, the Supreme Court shall have original jurisdiction	3	2	2	18
STATE. The trial of all crimes, except in cases of impeachment, shall be by jury; and such trial shall be held in the State where the said crimes shall have been committed; but when not committed within any State, the trial shall be at such place or places as the Congress may by law have directed	3	2	3	18
STATE. Full faith and credit shall be given in each State to the public acts, records, and judicial proceedings of every other State. And the Congress may, by general laws, prescribe the manner in which such acts, records, and proceedings shall be proved, and the effect thereof	4	1	1	19
STATE. The citizens of each State shall be entitled to all privileges and immunities of citizens in the several States	4	2	1	19
STATE. A person charged in any State with treason, felony, or other crime, who shall flee from justice, and be found in another State, shall, on demand of the Executive authority of the State from which he fled, be delivered up to be removed to the State having jurisdiction of the crime	4	2	2	19
STATE. No person held to service or labor in one State, under the laws thereof, escaping into another, shall, in consequence of any law or regulation therein, be discharged from such service or labor, but shall be delivered up on claim of the party to whom such service or labor may be due	4	2	3	20
STATE. The Congress shall have power to dispose of, and make all needful rules and regulations respecting the territory or other property belonging to the United States; and no-				

ALPHABETICAL ANALYSIS—Continued.

	Art.	sec.	cl.	page.
thing in this Constitution shall be so construed as to prejudice any claim of the United States, or of any particular State	4	3	2	20
STATE. The United States shall guaranty to every State in this Union a republican form of government, and shall protect each of them against invasion, and, on application of the Legislature or of the Executive, (when the Legislature cannot be convened,) against domestic violence	4	4	1	20
STATE. No State, without its consent, shall be deprived of its equal suffrage in the Senate	5	–	–	21
STATE. The judges in every State shall be bound by the Constitution, laws, and treaties of the United States, any thing in the constitution or laws of any State to the contrary notwithstanding	6	2	–	22
STATE Legislatures. The members of the several State Legislatures, and all executive and judicial officers, both of the United States and of the several States, shall be bound by oath or affirmation to support this Constitution	6	–	3	22
STATE. A well-regulated militia being necessary to the security of a free State, the right of the people to keep and bear arms shall not be infringed	2d amend.			25
STATE. In all criminal prosecutions, the accused shall enjoy the right to a speedy and public trial, by an impartial jury of the State and district wherein the crime shall have been committed; which district shall have been previously ascertained by law	6th amend.			27
STATE. In choosing the President, (by the House of Reps.,) the vote shall be taken by States, the Representatives from each State having one vote: a quorum for this purpose shall consist of a member or members from two-thirds of the States, and a majority of all the States shall be necessary to a choice	12th amend.			29
STATE. The electors shall meet in their respective States and vote, by ballot, for President and Vice President, one of whom at least shall not be an inhabitant of the same State with themselves	12th amend.			28
STATES. Representatives in Congress to be chosen every two years by the people of the States	1	2	1	1
STATES. Representatives and direct taxes to be apportioned among the several States according to their respective numbers	1	2	3	2
STATES entitled to representatives in the first Congress were. The	1	2	3	2
New Hampshire, 3; Massachusetts, 8; Rhode Island and Providence Plantations, 1; Connecticut, 5; New York, 6; New Jersey, 4; Pennsylvania, 8; Delaware, 1;				

Maryland, 6; Virginia, 10; North Carolina, 5; South Carolina, 5; Georgia, 3. Whole number, 65	1	2	3	2
STATES. Congress shall have power to regulate commerce among the several States and with the Indian tribes	1	8	3	8
STATES. Congress shall have power to provide for organizing, arming, and disciplining the militia, and for governing such part of them as may be employed in the service of the United States, reserving to the States respectively the appointment of the officers, and the authority of training the militia according to the discipline prescribed by Congress	1	8	16	9
STATES. Congress shall have power to exercise exclusive legislation in all cases whatsoever, over such district (not exceeding ten miles square) as may, by cession of particular States, and the acceptance of Congress, become the seat of the Government of the United States; and to exercise like authority over all places purchased by the consent of the Legislature of the State in which the same shall be, for the erection of forts, magazines, arsenals, dock-yards, and other needful buildings	1	8	17	10
STATES. The migration or importation of such persons as any of the States now existing shall think proper to admit, shall not be prohibited by Congress prior to the year 1808, but a tax or duty may be imposed on such importation not exceeding ten dollars for each person	1	9	1	10
STATES. The President shall not receive, during the time for which he shall have been elected, any emolument from any of the States	2	1	6	15
STATES. The President shall be Commander-in-Chief of the militia of the several States when called into the actual service of the United States	2	2	1	15
STATES. New States may be admitted by the Congress into this Union; but no new State shall be formed or erected within the jurisdiction of any other State; nor any State be formed by the junction of two or more States, or parts of States, without the consent of the Legislatures of the States concerned, as well as of the Congress	4	3	1	20
STATES. The Congress, whenever two-thirds of both Houses shall deem it necessary, shall propose amendments to this Constitution, or, on the application of the Legislatures of two-thirds of the several States, shall call a convention for proposing amendments, which, in either case, shall be valid to all intents and purposes as part of this Constitution, when ratified by the Legislatures of three-fourths of the several States, or by conventions in three-fourths thereof	5	-	-	21
STATES. The ratification of the conventions of nine States shall be sufficient for the establishment of this Constitution between the States so ratifying the same	7	-	1	22

ALPHABETICAL ANALYSIS—Continued.

	Art.	sec.	cl.	page.
STATES. The Constitution adopted in Convention by the unanimous consent of the deputies from all the States present, the 17th day of September, A. D. 1787, and of the Independence of the United States of America the twelfth. The following States being represented: New Hampshire, Massachusetts, Connecticut, New York, New Jersey, Pennsylvania, Delaware, Maryland, Virginia, North Carolina, South Carolina, Georgia	–	–	–	22
STATES. The powers not delegated to the United States by the Constitution, nor prohibited by it to the States, are reserved to the States respectively, or to the people	10th amend.			28
STATES. The judicial power of the United States shall not be construed to extend to any suit in law or equity, commenced or prosecuted against one of the United States by citizens of another State, or by citizens or subjects of any foreign State	11th amend.			28
SUBJECTS. The judicial power shall extend to all cases between a State, or the citizens thereof, and foreign States, citizens or subjects	3	2	1	18
SUBJECTS of any foreign State. The judicial power of the United States shall not be construed to extend to any suit in law or equity, commenced or prosecuted against one of the United States by citizens of another State, or by citizens or subjects of any foreign State	11th amend.			28
SUFFRAGE. No State, without its consent, shall be deprived of its equal suffrage in the Senate	5	–	–	21
SUITS. In suits at common law, where the value in controversy shall exceed twenty dollars, the right of trial by jury shall be preserved; and no fact tried by a jury shall be otherwise re-examined in any court of the United States than according to the rules of the common law	7th amend.			27
SUITS. The judicial power of the United States shall not be construed to extend to any suit in law or equity, commenced or prosecuted against one of the United States by citizens of another State, or by citizens or subjects of any foreign State	11th amend.			28
SUNDAYS excepted. Ten days allowed the President to return a bill, resolution, &c.	1	7	2	7
SUPPORT the Constitution. The Senators and Representatives before mentioned, and the members of the several State Legislatures, and all Executive and judicial officers, both of the United States and of the several States, shall be bound by oath or affirmation to support this Constitution, &c.	6	1	3	22
SUPREME Court. Congress shall have power to constitute tribunals inferior to the Supreme Court	1	8	9	9
SUPREME Court. (See appointment of Judges of. &c.)	2	2	2	16

SUPREME Court. The judicial power of the United States shall be vested in one Supreme Court, and in such Inferior courts as the Congress may from time to time ordain and establish. The judges, both of the Supreme and Inferior courts, shall hold their offices during good behavior, and shall, at stated times, receive for their services a compensation which shall not be diminished during their continuance in office	3	1	1	17
SUPREME Court. In all cases affecting ambassadors, other public ministers, and consuls, and those in which a State shall be party, the Supreme Court shall have original jurisdiction. In all the other cases before mentioned, the Supreme Court shall have appellate jurisdiction, both as to law and fact, with such exceptions, and under such regulations, as the Congress shall make	3	2	2	18
SUPREME law of the land. (See Constitution—Laws—Treaties.)	6	–	2	21
TAX. A tax or duty on imported persons (slaves) might have been imposed up to 1808	1	9	1	10
TAX. No capitation or other direct tax shall be laid, unless in proportion to the census or enumeration hereinbefore directed to be taken	1	9	4	11
TAX. No amendment made prior to 1808, shall in any manner affect the preceding clause	5	–	–	21
TAX. No tax or duty shall be laid on articles exported from any State	1	9	5	11
TAXED. Indians not taxed excluded from representative numbers	1	2	3	2
TAXES. Representatives and direct taxes to be apportioned among the States according to their respective numbers	1	2	3	2
TAXES. Congress shall have power to lay and collect taxes	1	8	1	8
TENDER. No State shall make any thing but gold and silver coin a tender in payment of debts	1	10	1	12
TERM of election of Representatives in Congress—to be chosen every two years	1	2	1	1
TERM of ten years. The census shall be taken within every term of ten years subsequent to the first	1	2	3	2
TERM of citizenship as qualification for a Representative in Congress—seven years	1	2	2	2
TERM of years. Representative numbers include those persons bound to service for a term of years	1	2	3	2
TERM of office of Senators in Congress—to be chosen for six years	1	3	1	3
TERM of citizenship as qualification for a Senator in Congress—nine years	1	3	3	4
TERM of office. The President shall hold his office during the term of four years, and the Vice President chosen for the same term	2	1	1	13

ALPHABETICAL ANALYSIS—Continued.

	Art.	sec.	cl.	page.
TERRITORY. Congress shall exercise exclusive legislation over all places (or territory) acquired for public purposes by cession of particular States	1	8	17	10
TERRITORY. The Congress shall have power to dispose of and make all needful rules and regulations respecting the territory or other property belonging to the United States	4	3	2	20
TEST. No religious test shall ever be required as a qualification to any office or public trust under the United States	6	–	3	22
TESTIMONY. No person shall be convicted of treason unless on the testimony of two witnesses to the same overt act, or on confession in open court	3	3	1	19
THINGS. No warrants shall issue but upon probable cause, supported by oath or affirmation, and particularly describing the place to be searched, and the persons or things to be seized	4th amend.			26
THREE-fifths of all other persons (slaves) included in representative numbers	1	2	3	2
THREE-fourths. Amendments to the Constitution must be ratified by the Legislatures or Conventions of three-fourths of the States	5	–	–	21
TIME of choosing electors may be determined by Congress	2	1	3	14
TITLE of nobility. No title of nobility shall be granted by the United States; and no person holding any office of profit or trust under them, shall, without the consent of the Congress, accept of any present, emolument, office, or title, of any kind whatever, from any king, prince, or foreign State	1	9	8	11
TITLE of nobility. No State shall grant any title of nobility	1	10	1	12
TONNAGE. No State shall, without the consent of Congress, lay any duty of tonnage	1	10	3	12
TRAINING the militia. The authority of training the militia reserved to the States	1	8	16	10
TRANQUILLITY. Constitution established to insure domestic tranquillity	Preamble.			1
TREASON. For treason a Senator or Representative may be arrested	1	6	1	6
TREASON. All civil officers shall be removed from office on impeachment for, and conviction of treason, &c.	2	4	1	17
TREASON against the United States shall consist only in levying war against them, or in adhering to their enemies, giving them aid and comfort. No person shall be convicted of treason unless on the testimony of two witnesses to the same overt act, or on confession in open court	3	3	1	15
The Congress shall have power to declare the punishment of treason, but no attainder				

of treason shall work corruption of blood or forfeiture, except during the life of the person attainted........ 3 3 2 19

TREASON. A person charged with treason and fleeing from one State to another, to be delivered up, on demand, to the State having jurisdiction........ 4 2 2 19

TREASURY. The Senators and Representatives shall receive a compensation for their services, to be ascertained by law, and paid out of the Treasury of the United States........ 1 6 1 6

TREASURY. No money shall be drawn from the Treasury but in consequence of appropriations made by law; and a regular statement and account of the receipts and expenditures of all public money shall be published from time to time........ 1 9 7 11

TREASURY of the United States. The nett produce of all duties and imposts, laid by any State on imports or exports, shall be for the use of the Treasury of the United States........ 1 10 2 12

TREATIES. The President shall have power, by and with the advice and consent of the Senate, to make treaties, provided two-thirds of the Senators present concur........ 2 2 2 16

TREATIES. The Judicial power shall extend to all cases in law and equity arising under this Constitution, the laws of the United States, and the treaties made, or which shall be made, under their authority........ 3 2 1 17

TREATIES. All treaties made, or which shall be made, under the authority of the United States, shall be the supreme law of the land........ 6 – 2 21

TREATY. No State shall enter into any treaty........ 1 10 1 12

TRIAL. A party convicted on an impeachment shall nevertheless be liable and subject to indictment, trial, judgment, and punishment, according to law........ 1 3 7 4

TRIAL by jury. The trial of all crimes, except in cases of impeachment, shall be by jury, and such trial shall be held in the State where the said crimes shall have been committed; but when not committed within any State, the trial shall be at such place or places as the Congress may by law direct........ 3 2 3 18

TRIAL. In all criminal prosecutions, the accused shall enjoy the right to a speedy and public trial, by an impartial jury of the State and district wherein the crime shall have been committed, which district shall have been previously ascertained by law........ 6th amend. 27

TRIAL by jury. In suits at common law, where the value in controversy shall exceed twenty dollars, the right of trial by jury shall be preserved; and no fact tried by a jury shall be otherwise re-examined in any court of the United States........ 7th amend. 27

TRIBUNALS. Congress shall have power to constitute tribunals inferior to the Supreme Court 1 8 9 9

ALPHABETICAL ANALYSIS—Continued.

	Art.	sec.	cl.	page.
TRIED. When the President of the United States is tried on an impeachment, the Chief Justice shall preside	1	3	6	4
TROOPS. No State shall, without the consent of Congress, lay any duty of tonnage, keep troops or ships of war, in time of peace	1	10	3	12
TRUST. Judgment, in cases of impeachment, shall not extend further than removal from office, and disqualification to hold and enjoy any office of honor, trust, or profit, under the United States	1	3	7	4
TRUST. No person holding an office of trust or profit under the United States shall be appointed an elector	2	1	2	13
TRUST. No religious test shall ever be required as a qualification to any office or public trust under the United States	6	-	3	22
TRY all impeachments. The Senate shall have the sole power to try all impeachments	1	3	6	4
TWENTY dollars. In suits at common law, when the value in controversy shall exceed twenty dollars, the right of trial by jury shall be preserved	7th amend.			27
TWO-thirds. No person shall be convicted by the Senate on an impeachment without the concurrence of two-thirds of the members present	1	3	6	4
TWO-thirds. Each House of Congress may, by the concurrence of two-thirds, expel a member.	1	5	2	5
TWO-thirds. Bills returned with objections by the President, may be passed by two-thirds of both Houses of Congress and become a law	1	7	2	7
TWO-thirds. Any order, resolution, or vote, to which the concurrence of the Senate and House of Representatives may be necessary, (except on a question of adjournment,) and returned with objections by the President, may be re-passed by two-thirds of both Houses of Congress	1	7	8	3
TWO-thirds. The President shall have power, by and with the advice and consent of the Senate, to make treaties, provided two thirds of the Senators present concur	2	2	2	16
TWO-thirds. The Congress, whenever two-thirds of both Houses shall deem it necessary, shall propose amendments to this Constitution	5	-	-	21
TWO-thirds. On the application of the Legislatures of two-thirds of the several States, Congress shall call a convention for proposing amendments to the Constitution	5	-	-	21
TWO-thirds. A quorum (of the House of Representatives for the election of President) shall con-				

sist of a member or members from two-thirds of the States, and a majority of all the States shall be necessary to a choice. 12th amend. 29

TWO-thirds. A quorum (for the election of Vice President by the Senate) shall consist of two-thirds of the whole number of Senators, and a majority of the whole number shall be necessary to a choice. 12th amend. 30

UNIFORM. All duties, imports, and excises, shall be uniform throughout the United States. 1 8 1 8

UNIFORM. Congress shall have power to establish a uniform rule of naturalization, and uniform laws on the subject of bankruptcies, throughout the United States. 1 8 4 8

UNION. The Constitution established in order to form a more perfect Union. Preamble. 1

UNION. Representatives and direct taxes shall be apportioned among the several States which may be included within this Union according to their respective numbers, &c. 1 2 3 2

UNION. The President shall, from time to time, give to the Congress information of the State of the Union, and recommend to their consideration such measures as he shall judge necessary and expedient. 2 3 1 16

UNION. New States may be admitted by the Congress into this Union. 4 3 1 20

UNION. The United States shall guaranty to every State in the Union a republican form of government. 4 4 1 20

UNITED States, or Government of the United States. We the people of the United States, &c., do ordain and establish this Constitution for the United States of America. Preamble. 1

UNITED States. All legislative powers herein granted shall be vested in à Congress of the United States. 1 1 1 1

UNITED States. No person shall be a Representative who shall not have attained to the age of 25 years, and been seven years a citizen of the United States. 1 2 2 2

UNITED States. The Senate of the United States shall be composed of two Senators from each State. 1 3 1 3

UNITED States. Judgment in cases of impeachment shall not extend further than to removal from office, and disqualification to hold and enjoy any office of honor, trust, or profit, under the United States. 1 3 7 4

UNITED States. The Senators and Representatives shall receive a compensation for their services, to be ascertained by law, and paid out of the Treasury of the United States. 1 6 1 6

UNITED States. No Senator or Representative shall, during the time for which he was elected, be appointed to any civil office under the authority of the United States, which shall have

ALPHABETICAL ANALYSIS—Continued.

	Art.	sec.	cl.	page.
been created. or the emoluments whereof shall have been increased, during such time: and no person holding any office under the United States shall be a member of either House during his continuance in office	1	6	2	6
UNITED States. Congress shall have power to provide for the common defence and general welfare of the United States	1	8	1	8
UNITED States. All duties, imposts, and excises shall be uniform throughout the United States	1	8	1	8
UNITED States. Congress shall have power to establish an uniform rule of naturalization, and uniform laws on the subject of bankruptcies throughout the United States	1	8	4	8
UNITED States. Congress shall have power to provide for the punishment of counterfeiting the securities and current coin of the United States	1	8	6	9
UNITED States. Establishment of the seat of Government of the United States	1	8	17	10
UNITED States. Congress shall have power to make all laws which shall be necessary and proper for carrying into execution the foregoing powers, and all other powers vested by this Constitution in the Government of the United States, or in any department or office thereof	1	8	18	10
UNITED STATES. No title of nobility shall be granted by the United States	1	9	8	11
UNITED States Treasury. (See Treasury.)				
UNITED States. No State shall, without the consent of Congress, lay any imposts or duties on imports or exports, except what may be absolutely necessary for executing its inspection laws, and the net produce of all duties and imposts laid by any State on imports or exports shall be for the use of the Treasury of the United States, and all such laws shall be subject to the revision and control of the Congress	1	10	2	12
UNITED States. The Executive power shall be vested in a President of the United States of America	2	1	1	13
UNITED States. No Senator or Representative, or person holding an office of trust or profit under the United States, shall be appointed an elector of President and Vice President	2	1	2	13
UNITED States. The time of choosing electors shall be the same throughout the United States	2	1	3	14
UNITED States. No person except a natural born citizen, or citizen of the United States at the time of the adoption of the Constitution, nor unless he shall have attained the age of 35 years, and been 14 years a resident of the United States, shall be President of the United States	2	1	4	14

Entry				
UNITED States. The President shall be Commander-in-Chief of the army and navy of the United States, and of the militia of the several States, when called into actual service of the United States	2	2	1	15
UNITED States. The President shall have power to grant reprieves and pardons for offences against the United States, except in cases of impeachment	2	2	1	16
UNITED States. The President shall nominate, and, by and with the advice and consent of the Senate, appoint officers of the United States, whose appointments are not herein otherwise provided for, and which shall be established by law	2	2	2	16
UNITED States. The President shall commission all officers of the United States	2	3	1	17
UNITED STATES. The President, Vice President, and all civil officers of the United States, shall be removed from office on impeachment for, and conviction of, treason, bribery, or other high crimes and misdemeanors	2	4	1	17
UNITED States. The judicial power of the United States shall be vested in one Supreme Court, and in such Inferior courts as the Congress may from time to time ordain and establish	3	1	1	17
UNITED States. The judicial power shall extend to all controversies to which the United States shall be a party	3	2	1	18
UNITED States. The judicial power shall extend to all cases in law and equity arising under this Constitution, the laws of the United States, and treaties made or which shall be made under their authority	3	2	1	17
UNITED States. Treason against the United States shall consist only in levying war against them, or in adhering to their enemies, giving them aid and comfort	3	3	1	18
UNITED States. The Congress shall have power to dispose of and make all needful rules and regulations respecting the territory or other property belonging to the United States; and nothing in this Constitution shall be so construed as to prejudice any claims of the United States, or of any particular State	4	3	2	20
UNITED States. The United States shall guaranty to every State in this Union a republican form of government, and shall protect each of them against invasion; and on application of the Legislature, or of the Executive, (when the Legislature cannot be convened,) against domestic violence	4	4	1	20
UNITED States. No person shall be a Senator who shall not have attained to the age of thirty years, and been nine years a citizen of the United States	1	3	3	4
UNITED States. All debts contracted, and engagements entered into, before the adoption of				

ALPHABETICAL ANALYSIS—Continued.

	Art.	sec.	cl.	page.
this Constitution, shall be as valid against the United States under this Constitution as under the Confederation	6	–	1	21
UNITED States. This Constitution, and the Laws of the United States, which shall be made in pursuance thereof, and all treaties made, or which shall be made, under the authority of the United States, shall be the supreme law of the land	6	–	2	21
UNITED States. The Senators and Representatives before mentioned, and the members of the several State Legislatures, and all executive and judicial officers, both of the United States and of the several States, shall be bound by oath or affirmation, to support this Constitution; but no religious test shall ever be required as a qualification, to any office or public trust under the United States	6	–	3	22
UNITED States court. In suits at common law, where the value in controversy shall exceed twenty dollars, the right of trial by jury shall be preserved; and no fact tried by a jury shall be otherwise re-examined in any court of the United States, than according to the rules of the common law	7th amend.			27
UNITED States. The powers not delegated to the United States by the Constitution, nor prohibited by it to the States, are reserved to the States respectively, or to the people	10th amend.			28
UNITED States. The Judicial power of the United States shall not be construed to extend to any suit in law or equity commenced or prosecuted against one of the United States by citizens of another State, or by citizens or subjects of any foreign State	11th amend.			28
UNITED States. The lists of votes for President and Vice President shall be transmitted to the seat of the Government of the United States	12th amend.			29
UNUSUAL punishments. Excessive bail shall not be required, nor excessive fines imposed, nor cruel and unusual punishments inflicted	8th amend.			27
VACANCIES happen in the representation from any State, the Executive thereof shall issue writs of election to fill them. When	1	2	4	3
VACANCIES happen, by resignation or otherwise, in the seats of Senators, during the recess of the Legislature of any State, the Executive thereof may make temporary appointments, until the next meeting of the Legislature, which shall then fill such vacancies. If	1	3	2	3
VACANCIES. The President shall have power to fill up all vacancies that may happen during				

Entry	Art.	Sec.	Cl.	Page
the recess of the Senate, by granting commissions which shall expire at the end of their next session	2	2	3	16
VALIDITY of contracts or engagements. All debts contracted, and engagements entered into. before the adoption of this Constitution, shall be as valid against the United States under this Constitution, as under the Confederation	6	1	1	21
VALUE. Congress shall have power to coin money, regulate the value thereof, and of foreign coin	1	8	5	8
VALUE in controversy. In suits at common law, when the value in controversy shall exceed twenty dollars, the right of trial by jury shall be preserved, &c.	7th amend.			27
VESSELS. No preference shall be given by any regulation of commerce or revenue to the ports of one State over those of another; nor shall vessels bound to or from one State be obliged to enter, clear, or pay duties in another	1	9	6	11
VEST. Congress may by law vest the appointment of such inferior offices as they think proper in the President alone, in the courts of law, or in the heads of departments	2	22		16
VESTED in the Government. Congress shall have power to make all laws which shall be necessary and proper for carrying into execution the foregoing powers, and all other powers vested by this Constitution in the Government of the United States, or in any department or office thereof	1	8	18	10
VESTED in a President. The Executive power shall be vested in a President of the United States of America	2	1	1	13
VESTED in one Supreme Court. The judicial power of the United States shall be vested in one Supreme Court, and in such Inferior courts as the Congress may from time to time ordain and establish	3	1	1	17
VESTED in a Congress. All legislative powers herein granted shall be vested in a Congress of the United States, which shall consist of a Senate and House of Representatives	1	1	1	1
VETO power of the President. (See President.)	1	7	2	7
VICE President shall have no vote in the Senate unless they be equally divided. The	1	3	4	4
VICE President, or when he shall exercise the office of President of the United States. The Senate shall choose a President pro tempore in the absence of the	1	3	5	4
VICE President. The President shall hold his office during the term of four years, and, together with the Vice President, chosen for the same term, be elected as follows:	2	1	1	13
(See Election of President and Vice President of the United States.)	12th amend.			28

ALPHABETICAL ANALYSIS—Continued.

Entry	Art.	sec.	cl.	page.
VICE President of the United States. Qualification required as Vice President same as for President of the United States	12th amend.			30
VICE President. In case of the removal of the President from office, or of his death, resignation, or inability to discharge the powers and duties of the said office, the same shall devolve on the Vice President; and the Congress may by law provide for the case of removal, death, resignation, or inability, both of the President and Vice President, declaring what officer shall then act as President, and such officer shall act accordingly, until the disability be removed, or a President shall be elected	2	1	5	14
VICE President shall be removed from office on impeachment for, and conviction of, treason, bribery, or other high crimes and misdemeanors. The	2	4	1	17
VICE President of the United States. Election of Vice President of the United States. (See Election.)	12th amend.			28
VICE President. The lists of votes of electors of President and Vice President shall be directed to the President of the Senate	12th amend.			29
VICE President. The President of the Senate shall, in presence of the Senate and House of Representatives, open all the certificates of the electors of President and Vice President of the United States	12th amend.			29
VICE President. If the House of Representatives shall not choose a President whenever the right of choice shall devolve upon them, before the 4th day of March next following, then the Vice President shall act as President, as in the case of the death or other constitutional disability of the President	12th amend.			29
VICE President. The person having the greatest number of votes as Vice President shall be the Vice President, if such number be a majority of the whole number of electors appointed; and if no person have a majority, then, from the two highest numbers on the list, the Senate shall choose the Vice President: a quorum for the purpose shall consist of two-thirds of the whole number of Senators, and a majority of the whole number shall be necessary to a choice. But no person, constitutionally ineligible to the office of President, shall be eligible to that of Vice President of the United States	12th amend.			30
VIOLATED. The right of the people to be secure in their persons, houses, papers, and effects, against unreasonable searches and seizures, shall not be violated	4th amend.			26
VIRGINIA entitled to ten Representatives in the first Congress	1	2	3	2

VOTE. Each Senator shall have one	1	3	1	3
VOTE. The Vice President shall have no vote unless the Senate be equally divided	1	3	4	4
VOTE. Every vote to which the concurrence of the Senate and House of Representatives may be necessary, (except on a question of adjournment,) shall be presented to the President. (See Resolution.)	1	7	3	8
VOTES in the two Houses of Congress, on passage of any bill, order, resolution or vote, returned with objections by the President, shall be taken by yeas and nays	1	7	2–3	7
VOTES of electors of President and Vice President. Place and manner of giving the votes; lists of votes to be made, signed, certified, transmitted sealed to the seat of Government, directed to the President of the Senate, to be opened and counted by that officer in the presence of the Senate and House of Representatives; the number necessary to a choice; the day on which electoral votes shall be given throughout the United States. (See Election.)	12th amend.			29
VOTES taken by States. In choosing the President by the House of Representatives, the votes shall be taken by States, the representation from each State having one vote	12th amend.			29
WAR. Congress shall have power to declare war, grant letters of marque and reprisal, and make rules concerning captures on land and water	1	8	11	9
WAR. Congress shall have power to make rules ("rules and articles of war") for the government of the land and naval forces	1	8	14	9
WAR. No State shall, without the consent of Congress, engage in war unless actually invaded, or in such imminent danger as will not admit of delay	1	10	3	12
WAR. Treason against the United States shall consist only in levying war against them, or in adhering to their enemies, giving them aid and comfort	3	3	1	18
WAR. No soldier shall be quartered in any house in time of war, but in a manner to be prescribed by law	3d amend.			26
WAR. No person shall be held to answer for a capital or otherwise infamous crime, unless on a presentment or indictment of a grand jury, except in cases arising in the land or naval forces, or in the militia when in actual service, in time of war or public danger	5th amend.			26
WARRANTS. No warrants shall issue but upon probable cause, supported by oath or affirmation, and particularly describing the place to be searched, and the persons or things to be seized	4th amend.			26
WASHINGTON, President and deputy from Virginia, signed this Constitution. George	–	–	–	22

ALPHABETICAL ANALYSIS—Continued.

	Art.	sec.	cl.	page.
WE the people establish this Constitution	Preamble.			1
WEIGHTS and measures. Congress shall have power to fix the standard of weights and measures	1	8	5	8
WELFARE. Constitution established to promote the general welfare	Preamble.			1
WELFARE. Congress shall have power to promote the general welfare	1	8	1	8
WILLIAMSON, deputy from North Carolina, signed this Constitution. Hugh	–	–	–	23
WILSON, deputy from Pennsylvania, signed this Constitution. James	–	–	–	23
WITNESSES. No person shall be convicted of treason, unless on the testimony of two witnesses to the same overt act, or on confession in open court	3	3	1	19
WITNESS against himself. Nor shall any person be compelled, in any criminal case, to be a witness against himself	5th amend.			26
WITNESSES against him. In all criminal prosecutions, the accused to be confronted with the witnesses against him	6th amend.			27
WITNESSES in his favor. In all criminal prosecutions, the accused to have compulsory process for obtaining witnesses in his favor	6th amend.			27
WRITINGS. Exclusive right to writings may be secured by authors for a limited time	1	8	8	9
WRIT of habeas corpus. The privilege of the writ of habeas corpus shall not be suspended, unless when in cases of rebellion or invasion the public safety may require it	1	9	2	11
YEAS and nays of the members of either House of Congress, on any question, shall, at the desire of one-fifth of those present, be entered on the Journal. The	1	5	3	5
YEAS and nays. Votes in the two Houses of Congress, on passage of any bill, order, resolution, or vote, returned with objections by the President, shall be taken by yeas and nays	1	7	2-3	7

CHAPTER 2.

THE Confederation having given place to the American Union, under the Constitution of the United States, it was considered unnecessary to insert, in *the first and second editions of this book*, the Articles of Confederation, which were agreed to by the Delegates of the thirteen Original States, in Congress assembled, on the 15th November, 1777; ratified by eight States, on the 9th July, 1778; and finally ratified by all the States, on the 1st March, 1781; *but on further consideration, those articles have been inserted at page 471, merely as matter of history*, as it were out of place to mingle that inefficient form of government with the present approved and successful system, which has stood the test of more than half a century, and which is destined, under Divine Providence, not only to perpetuate the happiness and safety of the people of the United States, but to be the Great Exemplar of Nations, when governments shall, by the natural and just power of man, be brought to their legitimate purposes and uses—to establish justice, insure domestic tranquillity, provide for the common defence, promote the general welfare, and secure the blessings of liberty *to the people.*

The matter contained in this chapter exhibits the deplorable condition of the finances and credit of the government under the old form, and the incompetency of the Congress of the Confederation to raise a revenue, support the public credit, regulate trade or commerce, or to provide for the wants and safety of the country; and it is intended thereby to show the immediate and prominent causes that led to the abandonment of that inefficient form, and the adoption of the present system of government; and, also, to show the official proceedings by which the change was effected and the present Constitution established.

These facts and proceedings may prove a warning against the treasonable suggestions of the evil spirit, whose insidious and alluring temptations are, not unfrequently, directed towards the most ardent and honest citizens, whose zeal in the defence of the supposed interests of a part of the Union might induce them even to go so far as to calculate the value of the Union itself, and of the Constitution. By exhibiting the impotency of the measures adopted by the Old Confederation to provide for the wants and to secure the independence and safety of the people, the perusal of these proceedings will induce a due appreciation of the value of our inestimable Union, so firmly bound together by the conservative and protective principles of our noble Constitution, and will banish from the mind the least idea of a disorganizing tendency, or of relapsing into the enfeebled condition of the General Government before the adoption of the Constitution. The danger of extracting from the edifice one particle of the material which serves to support its magnificent superstructure, is here practically made manifest, and every true-hearted American citizen will firmly resolve, with heart and hand, and sleepless vigilance, to guard the Union, fortified by the Constitution, as the citadel of our liberties—the object of our greatest care, and the consummation of our earthly hope.

OFFICIAL PROCEEDINGS, AND THE CAUSES WHICH LED TO THE ADOPTION AND RATIFICATION OF THE CONSTITUTION OF THE UNITED STATES.

It was early discovered by the patriots and statesmen of the Revolution, that a bond of union, to connect the powers and means of the colonies for the common defence, was a measure of absolute necessity; and hence the assemblage of a number of delegates, chosen and appointed by the several colonies and provinces in North America, to meet and hold a Congress in Philadelphia, at the Carpenter's Hall, on Monday, the 5th September, 1774. This Congress continued to act under the powers separately conferred upon the delegates by the respective colonies, until the time arrived when, from their patriotic ardor, the delicacy of their position, and the force of circumstances, a total separation from the mother country became necessary, and they were obliged to assume a noble stand among the nations of the earth. Simultaneously with and consequent upon the Declaration of Independence, a provision for an adequate national government became so manifestly indispensable, that, on the 11th June, 1776, it was resolved that a committee be appointed to prepare and digest the form of a confederation to be entered into between the colonies. After due deliberation, the Articles of Confederation were agreed to, in Congress, on 15th November, 1777, subject to the ratification of the several States. The ratification by eight States was announced on the 9th July, 1778; but many objections were urged to these articles, and so reluctantly did some of the States part with a portion of their powers, that it was not until the 1st March, 1781, that these articles were fully ratified; and no sooner were they ratified than (indeed before their final ratification) it was found that the powers conferred by them upon Congress were totally inadequate to the indispensable purposes of a national government. The defects first became apparent in the want of the necessary means of raising a revenue, and next in the absence of power to regulate or control the foreign trade and commerce of the country; and on the 3d February, 1781, a member from New Jersey moved a recommendation to the States that Congress be vested with additional powers to provide means for paying the public debt, and prosecuting the existing war, by laying duties on imports and prize goods. One of the States having refused to comply with this recommendation, the subject was referred to a committee, by whom the following report was made:

1. IN THE CONGRESS OF THE CONFEDERATION.

MONDAY, DECEMBER 16, 1782.

The committee, consisting of Mr. Hamilton, Mr. Madison, and Mr. Fitzsimmons, to whom was referred the letter of 30th November, from the honorable William Bradford, speaker of the lower house of Assembly of the State of Rhode Island, containing, under three heads, the reasons of that State for refusing their compliance with the recommendation of Congress for a duty on imports and prize goods; report,

That they flatter themselves the State, on a reconsideration of the objections they have offered, with a candid attention to the arguments which stand in opposition to them, will be induced to retract their dissent, convinced that the measure is supported on the most solid grounds of equal justice, policy, and general utility. The following observations, contrasted with each head of the objections, successively, will furnish a satisfactory answer to the whole.

First objection. "That the proposed duty would be unequal in its operation, bearing hardest upon the most commercial States, and so would press peculiarly hard upon that State which draws its chief support from commerce."

The most common experience, joined to the concurrent opinions of the ablest commercial and political observers, have established beyond controversy this general principle, "that every duty on imports is incorporated with the price of the commodity, and ultimately paid by the consumer, with a profit on the duty itself, as a compensation to the merchant for the advance of his money."

The merchant considers the duty demanded by the State on the imported article, in the same light with freight, or any similar charge, and, adding it to the original cost, calculates his profit on the aggregate sum. It may happen that at particular conjunctures, where the markets are overstocked, and there is a competition among the sellers, this may not be practicable; but in the general course of trade the demand for consumption preponderates, and the merchant can with ease indemnify himself, and even obtain a profit on the advance. As a consumer, he pays his share of the duty; but it is no further a burden upon him. The consequence of the principle laid down is, that every class of the community bears its share of the duty in proportion to its consumption, which last is regulated by the comparative wealth of the respective classes, in conjunction with their habits of expense or frugality. The rich and luxurious pay in proportion to their riches and luxury; the poor and parsimonious, in proportion to their poverty and parsimony. A chief excellence of this mode of revenue is, that it preserves a just measure to the abilities of individuals, promotes frugality, and taxes extravagance. The same reasoning in our situation applies to the intercourse between two States; if one imports and the other does not, the latter must be supplied by the former. The duty, being transferred to the price of the commodity, is no more a charge on the importing State for what is consumed in the other, than it is a charge on the merchant for what is consumed by the farmer or artificer. Either State will only feel the burden in a ratio to its consumption, and this will be in a ratio to its population and wealth. What happens between the different classes of the same community, internally, happens between the two States; and as the merchant, in the first case, so far from losing the duty himself, has a profit on the money he advances for that purpose, so the importing State, which, in the second case, is the merchant with respect to the other, is not only reimbursed by the non-importing State, but has a like benefit on the duty advanced. It is, therefore, the reverse of a just position, that the duty proposed will bear hardest on the most commercial States: it will, if any thing, have a contrary effect, though not in a sufficient degree to justify an objection on the part of the non-importing States; for it is as reasonable they should allow an advance on the duty paid as on the first cost, freight, or any incidental charge. They have also other advantages in the measure fully equivalent to this disadvantage. Over-nice and minute calculations in matters of this nature are inconsistent with national measures, and, in the imperfect state of human affairs, would stagnate all the operations of government. Absolute equality is not to be obtained: to aim at it, is pursuing a shadow at the expense of the substance, and, in the event, we should find ourselves wider of the mark than if, in the first instance, we were content to approach it with moderation.

Second objection. "That the recommendation proposes to introduce into that and the other States officers unknown and unaccountable to them, and so is against the constitution of the State."

It is not to be presumed that the constitution of any State could mean to define and fix the precise numbers and descriptions of all officers to be permitted in the State, excluding the creation of any new ones, whatever might be the necessity derived from that variety of circumstances incident to all political institutions. The legislature must always have a discretionary power of appointing officers not expressly known to the constitution, and this power will include that of authorizing the federal government to make the appointments, in cases where the general welfare may require it. The denial of this would prove too much; to wit, that the power given by the Confederation to Congress to appoint all officers in the post-office was illegal and unconstitutional.

The doctrine advanced by Rhode Island would perhaps prove, also, that the Federal Government ought to have the appointment of no internal officers whatever—a position that would defeat all the provisions of the Confederation, and all the purposes of the Union. The truth is, that no federal constitution can exist without powers that in their exercise affect the internal police of the component members. It is equally true, that no government can exist without a right to appoint officers for those purposes which proceed from and concentre in itself; and therefore the Confederation has expressly declared that Congress shall have authority to appoint all such "civil officers as may be necessary for managing the general affairs of the United States under their direction." All that can be required is, that the Federal Government confine its appointments to such as it is empowered to make by the original act of union, or by the subsequent consent of the parties; unless there should be express words of exclusion in the constitution of a

State, there can be no reason to doubt that it is within the compass of legislative discretion to communicate that authority.

The propriety of doing it upon the present occasion is founded on substantial reasons.

The measure proposed is a measure of necessity. Repeated experiments have shown that the revenues to be raised within these States is altogether inadequate to the public wants. The deficiency can only be supplied by loans. Our applications to the foreign powers on whose friendship we depend have had a success far short of our necessities. The next resource is, to borrow from individuals. These will neither be actuated by generosity nor reasons of state. 'Tis to their interest alone we must appeal. To conciliate this, we must not only stipulate a proper compensation for what they lend, but we must give security for the performance. We must pledge an ascertained fund, simple and productive in its nature, general in its principle, and at the disposal of a single will. There can be little confidence in a security under the constant revisal of thirteen different deliberatives. It must, once for all, be defined and established on the faith of the States, solemnly pledged to each other, and not revocable by any without a breach of the general compact.

'Tis by such expedients that nations whose resources are understood, whose reputations and governments are erected on the foundation of ages, are enabled to obtain a solid and extensive credit. Would it be reasonable in us to hope for more easy terms, who have so recently assumed our rank among the nations? Is it not to be expected that individuals will be cautious in lending their money to a people in our circumstances, and that they will at least require the best security we can give?

We have an enemy vigilant, intriguing, well acquainted with our defects and embarrassments. We may expect that he will make every effort to instil diffidences into individuals; and, in the present posture of our internal affairs, he will have too plausible ground on which to tread. Our necessities have obliged us to embrace measures with respect to our public credit calculated to inspire distrust. The prepossessions on this article must naturally be against us, and it is therefore indispensable we should endeavor to remove them, by such means as will be the most obvious and striking.

It was with these views Congress determined on a general fund; and the one they have recommended must, upon a thorough examination, appear to have fewer inconveniences than any other.

It has been remarked, as an essential part of the plan, that the fund should depend on a single will. This will not be the case unless the collection, as well as the appropriation, is under the control of the United States; for it is evident that, after the duty is agreed upon, it may, in a great measure, be defeated by an ineffectual mode of levying it. The United States have a common interest in an uniform and equally energetic collection; and not only policy, but justice to all the parts of the Union, designates the utility of lodging the power of making it where the interest is common. Without this it might in reality operate as a very *unequal tax.*

Third objection. "That by granting to Congress a power to collect moneys from the commerce of these States, indefinitely as to time and quantity, and for the expenditure of which they would not be accountable to the States, they would become independent of their constituents, and so the proposed impost is repugnant to the liberty of the United States."

Admitting the principle of this objection to be true, still it ought to have no weight in the present case, because there is no analogy between the principle and the fact.

First. The fund proposed is sufficiently definite as to time, because it is only co-extensive with the existence of the debt contracted and to be contracted in the course of the war. Congress are persuaded that it is as remote from the intention of their constituents to perpetuate that debt, as to extinguish it at once by a faithless neglect of providing the means to fulfil the public engagements. Their ability to discharge it in a moderate time can as little be doubted as their inclination; and the moment that debt ceases, the duty, so far as respects the present provision, ceases with it.

The resolution recommending the duty specifies the object of it to be the discharge of the principal and interest of the debts already contracted, or which may be contracted, on the faith of the United States for supporting the present war.

Secondly. The rate per cent. is fixed, and it is not at the option of the United States to increase it. Though the product will vary according to the variations in trade, yet, as there is this limitation of the rate, it cannot be properly said to be indefinite as to quantity.

By the Confederation, Congress have an absolute discretion in determining the quantum of revenue requisite for the national expenditure. When this is done, nothing remains for the States, separately, but the mode of raising. No State can dispute the obligation to pay the sum demanded, without a breach of the Confederation; and when the money comes into the treasury, the appropriation is the exclusive province of the Federal Government. This provision of the Confederation (without which it would be an empty form) comprehends in it the principle, in its fullest latitude, which the objection under consideration treats as repugnant to the liberty of the United States—to wit, an indefinite power of prescribing the quantity of money to be raised, and of appropriating it when raised.

If it be said that the States, individually, having the collection in their own hands, may refuse a compliance with exorbitant demands, the Confederation will answer that this is a point of which they have no constitutional liberty to judge. Such a refusal would be an exertion of power, not of right; and the same power which could disregard a requisition made on the authority of the Confederation, might at any time arrest the collection of the duty.

The same kind of responsibility which exists with respect to the expenditure of the money furnished in the forms hitherto practised, would be equally applicable to the revenue from the imports.

The truth is, the security intended to the general liberty in the Confederation consists in the frequent election and in the rotation of the members of Congress, by which there is a constant and an effectual check upon them. This is the security which the people in every State enjoy against the usurpations of their internal governments, and it is the true source of security in a representative republic. The Government, so constituted, ought to have the means necessary to answer the end of its institution. By weakening its hands too much, it may be rendered incapable of providing for the interior harmony or the exterior defence of the State.

The measure in question, if not within the letter, is within the spirit, of the Confederation. Congress, by that, are empowered to borrow money for the use of the United States, and, by implication, to concert the means necessary to accomplish the end. But, without insisting upon this argument, if the Confederation has not made proper provision for the exigencies of the States, it will be at all times the duty of Congress to suggest further provisions; and, when their proposals are submitted to the unanimous consent of the States, they can never be charged with exceeding the bounds of their trust. Such a consent is the basis and sanction of the Confederation, which expressly, in the 13th article, empowers Congress to agree to and propose such additional provisions.

The remarks hitherto made have had reference principally to the future prosecution of the war. There still remains an interesting light in which the subject ought to be viewed.

The United States have already contracted a debt in Europe, and in this country, for which their faith is pledged. The capital of this debt can only be discharged by degrees; but a fund for this purpose, and for paying the interest annually, on every principle of policy and justice, ought to be provided. The omission will be the deepest ingratitude and cruelty to a large number of meritorious individuals, who, in the most critical periods of the war, have adventured their fortunes in support of our independence. It would stamp the national character with indelible disgrace.

An annual provision for the purpose will be too precarious. If its continuance and application were certain, it would not afford complete relief. With many, the regular payment of interest, by occasional grants, would suffice; but with many more it would not. These want the use of the principal itself, and they have a right to it; but, since it is not in our power to pay off the principal, the next expedient is to fund the debt and render the evidences of it negotiable.

Besides the advantage to individuals from this arrangement, the active stock of the nation would be increased by the whole amount of the domestic debt, and of course the abilities of the community to contribute to the public wants; the national credit would revive and stand hereafter on a secure basis.

This was another object of the proposed duty.

If it be conceded that a similar fund is necessary, it can hardly be disputed that the one recommended is the most eligible. It has been already shown that it affects all parts of the community in proportion to their consumption, and has therefore the best pretensions to equality. It is the most agreeable tax to the people that can be imposed, because it is paid insensibly, and seems to be voluntary.

It may perhaps be imagined that it is unfavorable to commerce; but the contrary can easily be demonstrated. It has been seen that it does not diminish the profit of the merchant, and, of course, can be no diminution of his inducements to trade. It is too moderate in its amount to discourage the consumption of imported goods, and cannot on that account abridge the extent of importations. If it even had this effect, it would be an advantage to commerce, by lessening the proportion of our imports to our exports, and inclining the balance in favor of this country.

The principal thing to be consulted for the advancement of commerce is to promote exports. All impediments to these, either by way of prohibition or by increasing the prices of native commodities, decreasing by that means their sale and consumption at foreign markets. are injurious Duties on exports have this operation. For the same reason, taxes on possessions and the articles of our own growth or manufacture, whether in the form of a land tax, excise, or any other, are more hurtful to trade than impost duties. The tendency of all such taxes is to increase the prices of those articles which are the objects of exportation, and to enable others to undersell us abroad. The farmer, if he pays a heavy land tax, must endeavor to get more for the products of his farm: the mechanic and laborer, if they find the necessaries of life grow dearer by an excise, must endeavor to exact higher wages; and these causes will produce an increase of prices within, and operate against foreign commerce.

It is not, however, to be inferred that the whole revenue ought to be drawn from imports: all extremes are to be rejected. The chief thing to be attended to is, that the weight of the taxes fall not too heavily, in the first instance, upon particular parts of the community. A judicious distribution to all kinds of taxable property is a first principle in taxation. The tendency of these observations is only to show that taxes on possessions—on articles of our own growth and manufacture—are more prejudicial to trade than duties on imports.

The observations which conclude the letter on which these remarks are made, naturally lead to reflections that deserve the serious attention of every member of the Union. There is a happy mean between too much confidence and excessive jealousy, in which the health and prosperity of a State consist. Either extreme is a dangerous vice: the first is a temptation to men in power to arrogate more than they have a right to; the latter enervates government, prevents system in the administration, defeats the most salutary measures, breeds confusion in the State, disgusts and discontents among the people, and may eventually prove as fatal to liberty as the opposite temper.

It is certainly pernicious to leave any government in a situation of responsibility disproportioned to its power.

The conduct of the war is intrusted to Congress, and the public expectation turned upon them, without any competent means at their command to satisfy the important trust. After the most full and solemn deliberation, under a collective view of all the public difficulties, they recommend a measure which appears to them the corner-stone of the public safety: they see this measure suspended for near two years; partially complied with by some of the States; rejected by one of them, and in danger on that account to be frustrated; the public embarrassments every day increasing; the dissatisfaction of the army growing more serious; the other creditors of the public clamoring for justice; both irritated by the delay of measures for their present relief or future security; the hopes of our enemies encouraged to protract the war; the zeal of our friends depressed by an appearance of remissness and want of exertion on our part; Congress harassed; the national character suffering, and the national safety at the mercy of events.

This state of things cannot but be extremely painful to Congress, and appear to your committee to make it their duty to be urgent to obviate the evils with which it is pregnant.

Resolved, That Congress agree to the said report.

2. IN THE CONGRESS OF THE CONFEDERATION.

FRIDAY, APRIL 18, 1783.

Resolutions were passed recommending to the several States to invest the Congress with certain specified powers for raising revenue to restore and maintain the public credit, &c. These resolutions were transmitted to the several States, with an address, prepared by a committee consisting of Mr. Madison, Mr. Ellsworth, and Mr. Hamilton, and adopted by Congress on the 26th April, 1783. The resolutions, as well as the address, consist, for the most part, of propositions and recommendations concerning the fiscal measures necessary to be adopted; from the latter, however, it is considered proper to make the following extracts:

"The plan thus communicated and explained by Congress must now receive its fate from their constituents. All the objects comprised in it are conceived to be of great importance to the happiness of this confederated republic, are necessary to render the fruits of the Revolution a full reward for the blood, the toils, the cares, and the calamities which have purchased it. But the object of which the necessity will be peculiarly felt, and which it is peculiarly the duty of Congress to inculcate, is the provision recommended for the national debt. Although this debt is greater than could have been wished, it is still less on the whole than could have been expected, and, when referred to the cause in which it has been incurred, and compared with the burdens which wars of ambition and of vain-glory have entailed on other nations, ought to be borne, not only with cheerfulness, but with pride. But the magnitude of the debt makes no part of the question. It is sufficient that the debt has been fairly contracted, and that justice and good faith demand that it should be fully discharged. Congress had no option but between different modes of discharging it. The same option is the only one that can exist with the States. The mode which has, after long and elaborate discussion, been preferred, is, we are persuaded, the least objectionable of any that would have been equal to the purpose. Under this persuasion, we call upon the justice and plighted faith of the several States, to give it its proper effect, to reflect on the consequences of rejecting it, and to remember that Congress will not be answerable for them.

"Let it be remembered, finally, that it has ever been the pride and boast of America that the rights for which she contended were the rights of human nature. By the blessings of the Author of these rights on the means exerted for their defence, they have prevailed against all opposition, and form the basis of thirteen independent States. No instance has heretofore occurred, nor can any instance be expected hereafter to occur, in which the unadulterated forms of republican government can pretend to so fair an opportunity of justifying themselves by their fruits. In this view, the citizens of the United States are responsible for the greatest trust ever confided to a political society. If justice, good faith, honor, gratitude, and all the other qualities which ennoble the character of a nation, and fulfil the ends of government, be the fruits of our establishments, the cause of liberty will acquire a dignity and lustre which it has never yet enjoyed, and an example will be set which cannot but have the most favorable influence on the rights of mankind. If, on the other side, our governments should be unfortunately blotted with the reverse of these cardinal and essential virtues, the great cause which we have engaged to vindicate will be dishonored and betrayed, the last and fairest experiment in favor of the rights of human nature will be turned against them, and their patrons and friends exposed to be insulted and silenced by the votaries of tyranny and usurpation.

"By order of the United States in Congress assembled."

3. IN THE CONGRESS OF THE CONFEDERATION

WEDNESDAY, APRIL 30. 1784

Congress assembled. Present: New Hampshire, Massachusetts, Rhode Island, Connecticut, New York, New Jersey, Pennsylvania, Maryland, Virginia, North Carolina, and South Carolina.

Congress took into consideration the report of a committee, consisting of Mr. Gerry, Mr. Reed, Mr. Williamson, Mr. Chase, and Mr. Jefferson, to whom were referred sundry letters and papers relative to commercial matters; and the same, being amended, was agreed to as follows:

"The trust reposed in Congress renders it their duty to be attentive to the conduct of foreign nations, and to prevent or restrain, as far as may be, all such proceedings as might prove injurious to the United States. The situation of commerce at this time claims the attention of the several States; and few objects of greater importance can present themselves to their notice. The fortune of every citizen is interested in the success thereof, for it is the constant source of wealth and incentive to industry; and the value of our produce and our land must ever rise or fall in proportion to the prosperous or adverse state of trade.

"Already has Great Britain adopted regulations destructive of our commerce with her West India Islands. There was reason to expect that measures so unequal and so little calculated to promote mercantile intercourse, would not be persevered in by an enlightened nation. But these measures are growing into system. It would be the duty of Congress, as it is their wish, to meet the attempts of Great Britain with similar restrictions on her commerce; but their powers on this head are not explicit, and the propositions made by the legislatures of the several States render it necessary to take the general sense of the Union on this subject.

"Unless the United States in Congress assembled shall be vested with powers competent to the protection of commerce, they can never command reciprocal advantages in trade; and, without these, our foreign commerce must decline, and eventually be annihilated. Hence it is necessary that the States should be explicit, and fix on some effectual mode by which foreign commerce not founded on principles of equality may be restrained.

"That the United States may be enabled to secure such terms they have

"*Resolved*, That it be, and it hereby is, recommended to the legislatures of the several States to vest the United States in Congress assembled, for the term of fifteen years, with power to prohibit any goods wares, or merchandise, from being imported into or exported from any of the States, in vessels belonging to or navigated by the subjects of any power with whom these States shall not have formed treaties of commerce.

"*Resolved*, That it be, and it hereby is, recommended to the legislatures of the several States to vest the United States in Congress assembled, for the term of fifteen years, with the power of prohibiting the subjects of any foreign state, kingdom, or empire, unless authorized by treaty, from importing into the United States any goods, wares, or merchandise, which are not the produce or manufacture of the dominions of the sovereign whose subjects they are.

"Provided, That to all acts of the United States in Congress assembled, in pursuance of the above powers, the assent of nine States shall be necessary."

4. IN THE CONGRESS OF THE CONFEDERATION.

WEDNESDAY, JULY 13, 1785.

Congress took into consideration the report of a committee, consisting of Mr. Monroe, Mr. Spaight, Mr. Houstoun, Mr. Johnson, and Mr. King, on a motion of Mr. Monroe, for vesting the United States in Congress assembled with the power of regulating trade; and, the same being read,

Ordered, That it be referred to a committee of the whole.

Congress was then resolved into a committee of the whole.

Mr. Holten was elected to the chair.

The President resumed the chair; and Mr. Holten reported that the committee of the whole have had under consideration the subject referred to them, but, not having come to a conclusion, desire leave to sit again to-morrow.

Resolved, That leave be granted.

[The following is the report referred to. It was afterwards farther considered; but Congress did not come to any final determination with respect to the constitutional alteration which it proposed. It was deemed most advisable, at the time, that any proposition for perfecting the act of confederation should originate with the State legislatures.]

The committee, consisting of Mr. Monroe, Mr. Spaight, Mr. Houstoun, Mr. Johnson, and Mr. King, to whom was referred the motion of Mr. Monroe, submit the following report:

That the first paragraph of the ninth of the Articles of Confederation be altered, so as to read thus, viz:

"The United States in Congress assembled shall have the sole and exclusive right and power of determining on peace and war, except in the cases mentioned in the sixth article—of sending and receiving embassadors—entering into treaties and alliances—of regulating the trade of the States, as well with foreign nations as with each other, and of laying such impost and duties upon imports and exports as may be necessary for the purpose; provided, that the citizens of the States shall in no case be subjected to pay higher imposts and duties than those imposed on the subjects of foreign powers; provided, also, that the legislative power of the several States shall not be restrained from prohibiting the importation or exportation of any species of goods or commodities whatsoever; provided, also, that all such duties as may be imposed shall be collected under the authority, and accrue to the use, of the State in which the same shall be payable; and provided, lastly, that every act of Congress for the above purpose shall have the assent of nine States in Congress assembled—of establishing rules for deciding in all cases what captures on land or water shall be legal, and in what manner prizes taken by land or naval forces in the service of the United States shall be divided or appropriated—of granting letters of marque and reprisal in time of peace—appointing courts for the trial of piracies and felonies committed on the high seas, and establishing courts for receiving and determining finally appeals in all cases of captures; providea that no member of Congress shall be appointed judge of any of the said courts."

That the following letter be addressed to the legislature of the several States, showing the principles on which the above alteration is proposed:

The United States having formed treaties of commerce with the most Christian king the King of Sweden, and the states-general of the United Netherlands; and having appointed ministers with full authority to enter into treaties with other powers, upon such principles of reciprocity as may promote their peace, harmony, and respective interests,—it becomes necessary that such internal arrangements should be made as may strictly comport with the faith of those treaties, and insure success to their future negotiations. But, in the pursuit of the means necessary for the attainment of these ends, considerable difficulties arise. If tne legislature of each State adopts its own measures, many and very eminent disadvantages must, in their opinion, necessarily result therefrom. They apprehend it will be difficult for thirteen different legislatures, acting separately and distinctly, to agree in the same interpretation of a treaty, to take the same measures for carrying it into effect, and to conduct their several operations upon such principles as to satisfy those powers, and at the same time preserve the harmony and interests of the Union, or to concur in those measures which may be necessary to counteract the policy of those powers with whom they shall not be able to form commercial treaties, and who avoid it merely from an opinion of their imbecility and indecision. And if the several States levy different duties upon their particular produce exported to the ports of those powers, or upon the produce and manufactures of those powers imported into each State, either in vessels navigated by and belonging to the citizens of these States or the subjects of those powers, it will, they apprehend, induce on their part similar discriminations in the duties upon the commercial intercourse with each State, and thereby defeat the object of those treaties, and promote the designs of those who wish to profit from their embarrassment. Unless the United States in Congress assembled are authorized to make those arrangements which become ne cessary under their treaties, and are enabled to carry them into effect, they cannot complain of a violation of them on the part of other powers. And unless they act in concert in the system of policy which may be necessary to frustrate the designs of those powers who lay injurious restraints on their trade, they must necessarily become the victims of their own indiscretion.

The common principle upon which a friendly commercial intercourse is conducted between independent nations, is that of reciprocal advantages; and if this is not obtained, it becomes the duty of the losing party to make such farther regulations, consistently with the faith of treaties, as will remedy the evil, and secure its interests. If, then, the commercial regulations of any foreign power contravene the interests of any particular State—if they refuse admittance to its produce into its ports upon the same terms that the State admits its manufactures here,—what course will it take to remedy the evil? If it makes similar regulations to counteract those of that power, by reciprocating the disadvantages which it feels, by impost or otherwise, will it produce the desired effect? What operation will it have upon the neighboring States? Will they enter into similar regulations, and make it a common cause? On the contrary, will they not, in pursuit of the same local policy, avail themselves of this circumstance to turn it to their particular advantage? Thus, then, we behold the several States taking separate measures in pursuit of their particular interests in opposition to the regulations of foreign powers, and separately aiding those powers to defeat the regulations of each other; for, unless the States act together, there is no plan of policy into which they can separately enter, which they will not be separately interested to defeat, and of course all their measures must prove vain and abortive.

The policy of each nation, in its commercial intercourse with other powers, is to obtain, if possible, the principal share of the carriage of the materials of either party; and this can only be effected by laying higher duties upon imports and exports in foreign vessels, navigated by the subjects of foreign powers, than in those which belong to and are navigated by those of its own dominions. This principle prevails, in a greater or less degree, in the regulations of the oldest and wisest commercial nations, with respect to each other, and will, of course, be extended to these States. Unless, therefore, they possess a reciprocal power, its operation must produce the most mischievous effects. Unable to counteract the restrictions of those powers by similar restrictions here, or to support the interests of their citizens by discriminations in their favor, their system will prevail. Possessing no advantages in the ports of his own country, and subjected to much higher duties and restrictions in those of other powers, it will necessarily become the interest of the American merchant to ship his produce in foreign bottoms: of course their prospects of national consequence must decline, their merchants become only the agents and retailers of those foreign powers, their extensive forests be hewn down and laid waste to add to their strength and national resources, and the American flag be rarely seen upon the face of the seas.

But if they act as a nation, the prospect is more favorable to them. The particular interests of every State will then be brought forward, and receive a federal support. Happily for them, no measures can be taken to promote the interests of either which will not equally promote that of the whole. If their commerce is laid under injurious restrictions in foreign ports, by going hand in hand in confidence together, by wise and equitable regulations, they will the more easily sustain the inconvenience or remedy the evil. If they wish to cement the Union by the strongest ties of interest and affection; if they wish to promote its strength and grandeur, founded upon that of each individual State,—every consideration of local as well as of federal policy urge them to adopt the following recommendation.*

The situation of the commercial affairs of the Union requires that the several legislatures should come to the earliest decision on the subject, which they now submit to their consideration. They have weighed it with that profound attention which is due to so important an object, and are fully convinced of its expedience. A further delay must be productive of inconvenience. The interests which will vest in every part of the Union must soon take root and have their influence. The produce raised upon the banks of those great rivers and lakes which have their sources high up in the interior parts of the continent will empty itself into the Atlantic in different directions; and, of course, as the States rearing to the westward attain maturity, and get admission into the Confederation, will their government become more complicated. Whether this will be a source of strength and wealth to the Union, must, therefore, in a great degree, depend upon the measures which may be now adopted.

A temporary power would not, in their opinion, enable the United States to establish the interests, nor attain the salutary object, which they propose: the expectation that it will revert to the States, and remain with them for the future, would lessen its weight with foreign

*Alluding to the alteration proposed. See p. 142.

powers; and, while the interests of each State and of the Federal Government continue to be the same, the same evils will always require the same correction, and of course the necessary powers should always be lodged in the same hands. They have therefore thought proper to propose an efficient and perpetual remedy.

[The subject was afterwards brought forward in the House of Delegates of the Commonwealth of Virginia, by Mr. Madison, whose proposed resolution and the proceedings thereon follow these proceedings in Congress.]

5. IN THE CONGRESS OF THE CONFEDERATION.

WEDNESDAY, FEBRUARY 15, 1786.

Congress assembled. Present: New Hampshire, Massachusetts, Connecticut, New Jersey, Pennsylvania, Virginia, Maryland, and South Carolina.

The committee, consisting of Mr. King, Mr. Pinckney, Mr. Kean, Mr. Monroe, and Mr. Pettit, to whom were referred several reports and documents concerning the system of general revenue, recommended by Congress on the 18th of April, 1783, report:

"That, in pursuance of the above reference, they have carefully examined the acts of the several States, relative to the general system of revenue recommended by Congress on the 18th of April, 1783, and find that the States of Delaware and North Carolina have passed acts in full conformity with the several parts thereof; the former of which States has inserted a proviso in their act, restraining the operation thereof until each of the other States shall have made a like and equally extensive grant; that the States of New Hampshire, Massachusetts, Connecticut, New Jersey, Virginia, and South Carolina, have each passed acts complying with that part of the system which recommends a general impost, but have come to no decision on the other part, which proposes the establishment of funds, supplementary to and in aid of the general impost; that the State of Pennsylvania has passed an act complying with the recommendation of the general impost, and in the same act has declared that their proportion or quota of the supplementary funds shall be raised and levied on the persons and estates of the inhabitants of that State, in such manner as the legislature thereof shall from time to time direct; with this proviso, that if any of the annual proportion of the supplementary funds shall be otherwise raised and paid to the United States, then such annual levy or tax shall be discontinued. The committee conceive that this clause is rather an engagement that Pennsylvania will provide adequate supplementary funds, than an actual establishment thereof; nevertheless, the act contains a proviso restraining its operation until each of the other States shall have passed laws in full conformity with the whole of the revenue system aforesaid. The committee further find, that the State of Rhode Island has passed an act on this subject, but so different from the plan recommended, and so wholly insufficient, that it cannot be considered as a compliance with any part of the system submitted for their adoption; that the State of Maryland passed an act in 1782, and a supplement thereto in 1784, complying with the recommendation of Congress of the 3d of February, 1781, which recommendation is not compatible with, and was relinquished by, the resolves of Congress of the 18th of April, 1783; but that neither the State of Maryland, New York, nor Georgia, has passed any act in pursuance of the system of the 18th of April, 1783.

"From this statement it appears that seven States—viz: New Hampshire, Massachusetts, Connecticut, New Jersey, Virginia, North Carolina, and South Carolina—have granted the impost in such manner that, if the other six States had made similar grants, the plan of the general impost might immediately begin to operate; that two other States—viz: Pennsylvania and Delaware—have also granted the impost, but have connected their grants with provisoes, which will suspend their operation until all the other States shall have passed laws in full conformity with the whole of the revenue system aforesaid; that two only of these nine States—viz: Delaware and North Carolina—have fully acceded to that system in all its parts; and that the four other States—viz: Rhode Island, New York, Maryland, and Georgia—have not decided in favor of any part of the system of revenue aforesaid, so long since and so repeatedly presented by Congress for their adoption.

"The committee have thought it their duty candidly to examine the principles of this system, and to discover, if possible, the reasons which have prevented its adoption. They cannot learn that any member of the Confederacy has stated or brought forward any objections against it; and the result of their impartial inquiries into the nature and operation of the plan, has been a clear and decided opinion that the system itself is more free from well-founded exceptions, and is better calculated to receive the approbation of the several States, than any other that the wisdom of Congress can devise.

"In the course of this inquiry, it most clearly appeared that the requisitions of Congress, for eight years past, have been so irregular in their operation, so uncertain in their collection, and so evidently unproductive, that a reliance on them in future, as a source from whence moneys are to be drawn to discharge the engagements of the Confederacy, definite as they are in time and amount, would be not less dishonorable to the understandings of those who entertain such confidence, than it would be dangerous to the welfare and peace of the Union. The committee are therefore seriously impressed with the indispensable obligation that Congress are under of representing to the immediate and impartial consideration of the several States the utter impossibility of maintaining and preserving the faith of the Federal Government by temporary requisitions on the States, and the consequent necessity of an early and complete accession of all the States to the revenue system of the 18th of April, 1783.

"Although, in a business of this magnitude and importance to the respective States, it was natural to expect a due degree of caution, and a thorough investigation of the system recommended, yet the committee cannot forbear to remark that this plan has been under reference for nearly three years; that, during that period, numerous changes have taken place in the delegations of every State, but that this system has received the repeated approbation of each successive Congress, and that the urgency of the public engagements at this time renders it the unquestionable duty of the several States to adopt, without further delay, those measures which alone, in the judgment of the committee, can preserve the sacred faith of the Confederacy."

"Thus it is evident that the sum of 2,457,987 25-90ths dollars only was received in the space of more than four years, when the requisitions, in the most forcible manner, pressed on the States the payment of much larger sums, and for purposes of the highest national importance. It should be here observed, that the receipts of the last fourteen months of the above period amount only to 432,897 81-90ths dollars, which is at the rate of 371,052 dollars per annum—a sum short of what is essentially necessary for the bare maintenance of the Federal Government on the most economical establishment, and in time of profound peace.

"The committee observe, with great concern, that the security of the navigation and commerce of the citizens of these States from the Barbary powers, the protection of the frontier inhabitants from the savages, the immediate establishment of military magazines in different parts of the Union, rendered indispensable by the principles of public safety, the maintenance of the Federal Government at home, and the support of the public servants abroad, each and all, depend upon the contributions of the States under the annual requisitions of Congress. The moneys essentially necessary for these important objects will so far exceed the sums formerly collected from the States by taxes, that no hope can be indulged of being able, from that source, to make any remittances for the discharge of foreign engagements.

"Thus circumstanced, after the most solemn deliberation, and under the fullest conviction that the public embarrassments are such as above represented, and that they are daily increasing, the committee are of the opinion that it has become the duty of Congress to declare, most explicitly, that the crisis has arrived when the people of these United States, by whose will and for whose benefit the Federal Government was instituted, must decide whether they will support their rank as a nation, by maintaining the public faith at home and abroad, or whether, for want of a timely exertion in establishing a general revenue, and thereby giving strength to the Confederacy, they will hazard not only the existence of the Union, but of those great and invaluable privileges for which they have so arduously and so honorably contended."

Resolved, That Congress agree to the said report.

And, to the end that Congress may remain wholly acquitted from every imputation of a want of attention to the interest and welfare of those whom they represent,

Resolved, That the requisitions of Congress of the 27th of April, 1784, and the 27th of September, 1785, cannot be considered as the establishment of a system of general revenue, in opposition to that recommended to the several States by the resolves of Congress of the 18th of April, 1783.

Resolved, That the resolves of Congress of the 18th of April, 1783, recommending a system of general revenue, be again presented to the consideration of the legislatures of the several States which have not fully complied with the same. That it be earnestly recommended to the Legislatures of New Hampshire, Massachusetts, Connecticut, New Jersey, Pennsylvania, Virginia, and South Carolina, which have complied only in part with the said system, completely to adopt the same, and to the Legislatures of the States of Rhode Island, New York, Maryland, and Georgia, which have not adopted the said system, either in whole or in part, to pass laws, without further delay, in full conformity with the same. But, as it is highly necessary that every possible aid should, in the most expeditious manner, be obtained to the revenue of the United States, it is therefore recommended to the several States, that, in adopting the said system, they enable the United States in Congress assembled, to carry into effect that part which relates to the impost, so soon as it shall be acceded to.

Resolved, That, whilst Congress are denied the means of satisfying those engagements which they have constitutionally entered into for the common benefit of the Union, they hold it their duty to warn their constituents that the most fatal evils will inevitably flow from a breach of public faith, pledged by solemn contract, and a violation of those principles of justice which are the only solid basis of the honor and prosperity of nations.

6. IN THE CONGRESS OF THE CONFEDERATION.

FRIDAY, MARCH 3, 1786.

The committee, consisting of Mr. Kean, Mr. Gorham, Mr. Pinckney, Mr. Smith, and Mr. Grayson, to whom were recommitted sundry papers and documents relative to commerce, and the acts passed by the States in consequence of the recommendations of Congress of the 30th April, 1784, report—

That, in examining the laws passed by the States in consequence of the act of 30th April, 1784, they find that four States—namely, Massachusetts, New York, New Jersey, and Virginia—have enacted laws conformable to the recommendations contained in the act, but have restrained their operation until the other States shall have substantially complied.

That three States—namely, Connecticut, Pennsylvania, and Maryland—have passed laws conforming to the same, but have determined the time from which they are to commence—the first from the time of passing their act, in May, 1785; and the two latter from the 30th April, 1784.

That New Hampshire, by an act passed the 23d June, 1785, has granted full powers to regulate their trade, by restrictions or duties, for fifteen years, with a proviso that the law shall be suspended until the other States have substantially done the same.

That Rhode Island, by acts passed in February and October, 1785, has granted power for the term of twenty-five years to regulate trade between the respective States, and of prohibiting, restraining, or regulating, the importation only of all foreign goods in any ships or vessels other than those owned by citizens of the United States, and navigated by a certain proportion of citizens; and also with a proviso restrictive of its operation until the other States shall have substantially complied.

That North Carolina, by an act passed the 2d June, 1784, has granted powers similar to those granted by Rhode Island, relative to foreign commerce, but unrestrained in duration, and clogged with a clause that when all the States shall have substantially complied therewith, it shall become an article of confederation and perpetual union.

That they cannot find that the three other States—namely, Delaware, South Carolina, and Georgia—have passed any laws in consequence of the recommendations.

The result is, that four States have fully complied; three others have also complied, but have determined the time of commencement, so that there will be a dissimilarity in the duration of the power granted; that three other States have passed laws in pursuance of the recommendations, but so inconsonant to them, both in letter and spirit, that they cannot be deemed compliances; and that three other States have passed no acts whatever.

That, although the powers to be vested by the recommendations do not embrace every object which may be necessary in a well-formed system, yet, as many beneficial effects may be expected from them, the committee think it the duty of Congress again to call the attention of the States to this subject, the longer delay of which must be attended with very great evils. Whereupon,

Resolved, That the recommendations of the 30th April, 1784, be again presented to the view of the States of Delaware, South Carolina, and Georgia, and that they be most earnestly called upon to grant powers conformable thereto.

Resolved, That the States of New Hampshire, Rhode Island, and North Carolina, be solicited to reconsider their acts, and to make them agreeable to the recommendations of the 30th April, 1784.

Resolved, That the time for which the power under the recommendations of the 30th April, 1784, is to continue, ought to commence on the day that Congress shall begin to exercise it; and that it be recommended to the States of Pennsylvania, Connecticut, and Maryland, to amend their acts accordingly.

7. IN THE CONGRESS OF THE CONFEDERATION.

MONDAY, OCTOBER 23, 1786.

The committee, consisting of Mr. Pinckney, Mr. Smith, and Mr. Henry, to whom was referred an act of the Legislature of the State of Georgia, passed in consequence of the resolutions of the 30th April, 1784, respecting commerce, and the subject of the said recommendation, having reported—

"That it appears, by the said resolutions, the United States in Congress assembled recommended to the legislatures of the several States to vest them, for the term of fifteen years, with powers to prohibit any goods, wares, or merchandise, from being imported into, or exported from, any of the States, in vessels belonging to, or navigated by, the subjects of any power with whom these States shall not have formed treaties of commerce; that they also recommended to the legislatures of the said States to vest the United States in Congress assembled, for the term of fifteen years, with the power of prohibiting the subjects of any foreign state, kingdom, or empire, unless authorized by treaty, from importing into the United States any goods, wares, or merchandise, which are not the produce or manufacture of the dominions of the sovereign whose subjects they are: provided, that to all acts of the United States in Congress assembled, in pursuance of the above powers, the assent of nine States shall be necessary. The committee have carefully examined the acts passed by the several States, in pursuance of the above recommendation, and find that the State of Delaware has passed an act in full compliance with the same; that the acts of the States of Massachusetts, Rhode Island, New York, New Jersey, Virginia, and Georgia, are in conformity to the said recommendation, but restrained in their operation until the other States should have granted powers equally extensive; that the States of Connecticut, Pennsylvania, and Maryland, have passed laws agreeable to the said resolution, but have fixed the time at which the powers thereby invested shall begin to operate, and not left the same to commence at the time at which Congress shall begin to exercise it, which your committee conceive to have been the intention of the same; that South Carolina, by an act passed the 11th March, 1786, has invested the United States in Congress assembled with the power of regulating the trade of the United States with the West Indies, and all other external or foreign trade of the said States, for the term of fifteen years from the passing of the said act; that New Hampshire, by their act of the 23d of June, 1785, invested the United States in Congress assembled with the full power of regulating trade for fifteen years, by restrictions or duties, with a proviso suspending its operation until all the other States shall have done the same; that North Carolina, by their act of the 2d of June, 1784, has authorized their delegates to agree to and ratify an article or articles by which Congress shall be empowered to prohibit the importation of all foreign goods, in any other than vessels owned by citizens of the United States, or navigated by such a proportion of seamen, citizens of the United States, as may be agreed to by Congress, which, when agreed to by all the States, shall be considered as a part of the Articles of Confederation and perpetual Union. From the above review of the acts passed by the several States in consequence of the said recommendation, it appears that, though, in order to make the duration of the powers equal, it will be necessary for the States of Connecticut, Pennsylvania, Maryland, and South Carolina, so far to amend their acts as to permit the authorities therein granted to commence their operation at the time Congress shall begin to exercise them; yet still the powers granted by them and by the States of Massachusetts, Rhode Island, New York, New Jersey, Delaware, Virginia, and Georgia, are otherwise in such compliance with the recommendation, that, if the States of New Hampshire and North Carolina had conformed their acts to the said resolution, agreeable to the urgent recommendation of Congress of the 3d of March last, the powers therein requested might immediately begin to operate. The committee, however, are of opinion that the acts of the States of New Hampshire and North Carolina manifest so liberal a disposition to grant the necessary powers upon this subject, that their not having complied with the recommendation of March last must be attributed to other reasons than a disinclination in them to adopt measures similar to those of their sister States. The committee, therefore, conceive it unnecessary to detail to them the situation of our commerce, languishing under the most ruinous restrictions in foreign ports, or the benefits which must arise from the due and equal use of powers competent to its protection and support, by that body which can alone beneficially, safely, and effectually exercise the same." Whereupon,

Resolved, That it be again earnestly recommended to the Legislatures of the States of New Hampshire and North Carolina, at their next session, to reconsider their acts, and pass them in such conformity with the resolutions of the 30th April, 1784, as to enable, on their part, the United States in Congress assembled to exercise the powers thereby invested, as soon as possible.

Resolved, That, as the extent and duration of the powers to be exercised by the United States in Congress assembled, under the recommendation above mentioned, ought to be equal, it be recommended to the Legislatures of Connecticut, Pennsylvania, Maryland, and South Carolina, so far to amend their acts as to vest the powers therein contained for the term of fifteen years from the day on which Congress shall begin to exercise the same.

8. REMARKS ON PROCEEDINGS WHICH IMMEDIATELY LED TO THE FORMATION OF THE CONSTITUTION OF THE UNITED STATES.

These extracts show the final efforts made by the Congress of the Confederation to obtain from the States an increase of power for the purposes apparent in these proceedings. These exertions of the friends of liberty and the Union having proved unsuccessful, and having completely disclosed the incompetency of the Confederation to provide for the credit and the wants of the country, or to fulfil the duties and obligations of a general government, manifested the necessity for that radical change in the system, under whose powerful and benign influence the United States have arrived at their present condition of strength, prosperity, and happiness.

The active measures which immediately led to the accomplishment of this momentous object, appear to have commenced under the lead of the Commonwealth of Virginia, and through the patriotic zeal and sagacity of her eminent statesmen: justice, however, to the great State of New York, and to the distinguished individuals who, at that day, guided her councils, demands the insertion of the proceedings, which, it will be perceived, took place more than three years before those in Virginia, and point more clearly and directly to the necessity for adopting the present form of government than the resolutions of Virginia. The ostensible object of the latter appearing to have been, to vest the Congress of the Confederation with the power of regulating the general trade and commerce of the country. The act of Virginia, however, led to the meeting of the commissioners of several States at Annapolis, who, being thus assembled, availed themselves of the idea adopted by the State of New Jersey, and incorporated in the commissions to her deputies inserted in this chapter, "extending the powers of their deputies to other objects than those of commerce," being "an improvement on the original plan, and will deserve to be incorporated into that of a future convention," &c.

These facts prove, that the credit of producing the vital change in the government, which gave being to our glorious Constitution, does not belong to any particular State or individual, but resulted from the widespread conviction of the wise and honest men, and true patriots with whom the country was blessed at that critical and eventful period in its history, which will, no doubt, become more apparent on the completion of the fifth and sixth series of Colonel Force's documentary history of the Revolution.

The proceedings in New York, appearing to have been consequent upon the condition of affairs as indicated in a previous resolution of Congress, and responsive to it, the insertion of that resolution previous to those proceedings, appears necessary to its proper understanding.

9. IN THE CONGRESS OF THE CONFEDERATION.

Wednesday, May 22, 1782.

On the report of a committee, consisting of Mr. Madison, Mr. Root, Mr. Lowell, Mr. Rutledge, and Mr. Clymer, to whom was referred a letter of the 17th, from the superintendent of finance, and who were instructed to confer with the said superintendent;

Resolved, That Mr. Rutledge and Mr. Clymer be appointed to repair forthwith to the several States southward of this, and Mr. Montgomery and Mr. Root to the States eastward; and that they be, and hereby are instructed to make such representations to the several States, as are best adapted to their respective circumstances and the present situation of public affairs, and as may induce them to carry the requisitions of Congress into effect with the greatest despatch: that they make the like representations to the State of Pennsylvania, before they leave this city, (Philadelphia:) that previous to their departure, they confer with the superintendent of finance, the secretary of war, and the secretary for foreign affairs, who are hereby directed to communicate to them such information from their respective departments as may be most conducive to the end proposed.

10. IN THE HOUSE OF ASSEMBLY OF THE STATE OF NEW YORK.

SUNDAY, JULY 21, 1782.

George Clinton, esq., Governor.

A copy of certain resolutions of the honorable the Senate, delivered by Mr. Paine, were read, and committed to a committee of the whole house, to be taken into consideration with the message of the honorable the Senate, of the 19th inst., on the state of the nation.

The house then resolved itself into a committee of the whole House, on the said resolutions, and the subject of the said message; and after some time spent thereon, Mr. Speaker resumed the chair, and Mr. Clark, from the said committee, reported, that the committee had gone through the said resolutions without amendment, which he was directed to report to the House; and he delivered the said resolutions in at the table, where the same were again read, and in the words following, to wit, viz:

Resolved, That it appears to this Legislature, after full and solemn consideration of the several matters communicated by the hon. the committee of Congress, relating to the present posture of our affairs, foreign and domestic, and contained in a letter from the secretary for foreign affairs respecting the former, as well as of the representations from time to time made by the superintendent of the finances of the United States, relative to his particular department—that the situation of these States is in a peculiar manner critical, and affords the strongest reason to apprehend, from a continuance of the present Constitution of the Continental Government, a subversion of public credit, and consequences highly dangerous to the safety and independence of these States.

Resolved, That while this Legislature are convinced by the before-mentioned communications, that notwithstanding the generous intentions of an ally from whom we have experienced, and doubtless shall still experience, all possible support, exigencies may arise to prevent our receiving pecuniary succours hereafter, in any degree proportioned to our necessities. They are also convinced, from facts within their own knowledge, that the provisions made by the respective States for carrying on the war, are not only inadequate to the end, but must continue to be so, while there is an adherence to the principles which now direct the operation of public measures.

Resolved, That it is also the opinion of this Legislature, that the present plan instituted by Congress for the administration of their finances, is founded in wisdom and sound policy. That the salutary effects of it have already been felt in an extensive degree; and that after so many violent shocks sustained by the public credit, a failure in this system, for want of the support which the States are able to give, would be productive of evils too pernicious to be hazarded.

Resolved, That it appears to this Legislature, that the present British ministry, with a disposition not less hostile than that of their predecessors, taught by experience to avoid their errors, and assuming the appearance of moderation, are pursuing a scheme calculated to conciliate in Europe, and seduce in America. That the economical arrangements they appear to be adopting, are adopted to enlarging the credit of their government, and multiplying its resources, at the same time that they serve to confirm the prepossessions and confidence of the people; and that the plan of a defensive war on this continent, while they direct all their attention and resources to the augmentation of their navy, is that which may be productive of consequences ultimately dangerous to the United States.

Resolved, That it is the opinion of this Legislature, that the present system of these States exposes the common cause to a precarious issue; and leaves us at the mercy of events over which we have no influence: a conduct extremely unwise in any nation, and at all times, and to a change of which we are impelled at this juncture, by reasons of peculiar and irresistible weight; and that it is the natural tendency of the weakness and disorders in our national measures, to spread diffidence and distrust among the people, and prepare their minds to receive the impressions the enemy wish to make.

Resolved, That the general state of European affairs, as far as they have come to the knowledge of this Legislature, affords, in their opinion, reasonable ground of confidence, and assures us, that with judicious and vigorous exertion on our part, we may rely on the final attainment of our object; but, far from justifying indifference and security, calls upon us by every motive of honor, good faith, and patriotism, without delay, to unite in some system more effectual, for producing energy, harmony, and consistency of measures, than that which now exists, and more capable of putting the common cause out of the reach of contingencies.

Resolved, That in the opinion of this Legislature, the radical source of most of our embarrassments, is the want of sufficient power in Congress, to effectuate that ready and perfect co-operation of the different States, on which their immediate safety and future happiness depend. That experience has demonstrated the Confederation to be defective in several essential points, particularly in not vesting the Federal Government either with a power of providing revenue for itself, or with ascertained and productive funds, secured by a sanction so solemn and general, as would inspire the fullest confidence in them, and make them a substantial basis of credit. That these defects ought to be without loss of time repaired; the powers of Congress extended, a solid security established for the payment of debts already incurred, and competent means provided for future credit, and for supplying the future demands of the war.

Resolved, That it appears evidently to this Legislature, that the annual income of these States, admitting the best means were adopted for drawing out their resources, would fall far short of the annual expenditure; and that there would be a large deficiency to be supplied on the credit of these States, which, if it should be inconvenient for those powers to afford, on whose friendship we justly rely, must be sought for from individuals, to engage whom to lend, satisfactory securities must be pledged for the punctual payment of interest, and the final redemption of the principal.

Resolved, That it appears to this Legislature, that the aforegoing important ends can never be attained by partial deliberations of the States separately; but that it is essential to the common welfare, that there should be, as soon as possible, a conference of the whole on the subject; and that it would be advisable for this purpose, to propose to Congress to recommend, and to each State to adopt the measure of assembling a general convention of the States, specially authorized to revise and amend the Confederation, reserving a right to the respective legislatures to ratify their determinations.

Resolved unanimously, That this House do concur with the honorable the Senate, in the said resolutions.

[Introduced and passed in Senate, on Saturday morning, July 20, 1782.]

State of New York, }
Secretary's Office. }

I certify the preceding to be true copies of certain concurrent resolutions of the Senate and Assembly of this State, copied from the printed journal of the assembly in this office.

ARCH'D. CAMPBELL, *Dep. Sec. of State.*

Albany, July 30, 1847.

11. IN THE HOUSE OF DELEGATES OF THE STATE OF VIRGINIA.

Wednesday, 30th November, 1785.

Mr. Alexander White reported, according to order, a resolution agreed to by the committee of the whole house on Monday last, respecting commerce; and he read the same in his place, and afterwards delivered it in at the clerk's table, where the same was again read, and is as followeth:

Whereas the relative situation of the United States has been found on trial to require uniformity in their commercial regulations, as the only effectual policy for obtaining in the ports of foreign nations a stipulation of privileges reciprocal to those enjoyed by the subjects of such nations in the ports of the United States, for preventing animosities which cannot fail to arise among the several States from the interference of partial and separate regulations; and whereas such uniformity can be best concerted and carried into effect by the federal councils, which, having been instituted for the purpose of managing the interests of the States in cases which cannot so well be provided for by measures individually pursued, ought to be invested with authority in this case, as being within the reason and policy of their institution:

Resolved, That it is the opinion of this committee, that the delegates representing this Commonwealth in Congress be instructed to propose in Congress a recommendation to the States in union to authorize that assembly to regulate their trade, on the following principles, and undeı the following qualifications:

1st. That the United States in Congress assembled be authorized to prohibit vessels belonging to any foreign nation from entering any of the ports thereof, or to impose any duties on such vessels and their cargoes which may be judged necessary; all such prohibitions and duties to be uniform throughout the United States, and the proceeds of the latter to be carried into the treasury of the State within which they shall accrue.

2d. That no State be at liberty to impose duties on any goods, wares, or merchandise, imported by land or by water from any other State, but may altogether prohibit the importation from any State of any particular species or description of goods, wares, or merchandise, of which the importation is at the same time prohibited from all other places whatsoever.

3d. That no act of Congress that may be authorized, as hereby proposed, shall be entered into by less than two-thirds of the confederated States, nor be in force longer than thirteen years.

A motion was made, and, the question being put to amend the resolution, by adding to the end thereof the following words, to wit: "unless continued by a like proportion of votes within one year immediately preceding the expiration of the said period, or be revived in like manner after the expiration thereof," it passed in the negative: ayes, 28; noes, 79.

On a motion made by Mr. Turberville, and seconded by Mr. Watkins,

Ordered, That the names of the ayes and noes, on the question to agree to the said amendment, be inserted in the journal.

And then the said resolution, being again read, was, on the question put thereupon, agreed to by the House.

Ordered, That Mr. Alexander White do carry the resolution to the Senate, and desire their concurrence.

THURSDAY, 1ST DECEMBER, 1785.

On a motion made to the following effect: that the resolutions reported from a committee of the whole house, and agreed to by the House on yesterday, containing instructions to the delegates of this Commonwealth in Congress, respecting commerce, does not, from a mistake, contain the sense of the majority of this House that voted for the said resolutions;

Ordered, therefore, That the direction to send the said resolution to the Senate for their concurrence be rescinded, and that this House do immediately resolve itself into a committee of the whole house, to reconsider the said resolution.

It was resolved in the affirmative: ayes, 60; noes, 33.

The House then accordingly resolved itself into a committee of the whole house on the said resolution; and, after some time spent therein, Mr. Speaker resumed the chair, and Mr. Matthews reported that the said committee had, according to order, had the said resolution under their consideration, and had made several amendments thereto, which they had directed him to report when the House should think proper to receive the same.

Ordered, That the said report do lie on the table.

[With the same object in view, the General Assembly of Virginia eventually pursued a different course to attain it, as will be seen by the subjoined resolution.]

12. IN THE HOUSE OF DELEGATES OF THE STATE OF VIRGINIA.

21ST JANUARY, 1786.

Resolved, That Edmund Randolph, James Madison, junior, Walter Jones, Saint George Tucker, Meriwether Smith, David Ross, William Ronald, and George Mason, esquires, be appointed commissioners, who, or any five of whom, shall meet such commissioners as may be appointed by the other States in the Union, at a time and place to be agreed on, to take into consideration the trade of the United States; to examine the relative situations and trade of the said States; to consider how far an uniform system in their commercial regulations may be necessary to their common interest and their permanent harmony; and to report to the several States such an act relative to this great object, as, when unanimously ratified by them, will enable the United States in Congress assembled effectually to provide for the same: that the said commissioners shall immediately transmit to the several States copies of the preceding resolution, with a circular letter requesting their concurrence therein, and proposing a time and place for the meeting aforesaid.

Test: JOHN BECKLEY, *C. H. D.*

1786, *January* 21*st*.

Agreed to by the Senate.

H. BROOKE, *C. S.*

By his excellency, Patrick Henry, esquire, Governor of the Commonwealth of Virginia, it is hereby certified that John Beckley, the person subscribing the above resolve, is clerk of the House of [L. S.] Delegates, and that due faith and credit is, and ought to be, paid to all things done by him by virtue of his office. Given under my hand as Governor, and under the seal of the Commonwealth, at Richmond, the 6th day of July, 1786.

P. HENRY.

[Certain other of the States came readily into the measure proposed, and a meeting of commissioners took place at Annapolis, whose proceedings are stated in the following report.]

13. ANNAPOLIS, IN THE STATE OF MARYLAND.

SEPTEMBER 11, 1786.

At a meeting of commissioners from the States of New York, New Jersey, Pennsylvania, Delaware, and Virginia:

PRESENT:

NEW YORK.
Alexander Hamilton,
Egbert Benson.

NEW JERSEY.
Abraham Clarke,
William C. Houston,
James Schureman.

PENNSYLVANIA.
Tench Coxe.

DELAWARE.
George Read,
John Dickinson,
Richard Bassett.

VIRGINIA.
Edmund Randolph,
James Madison, jun.,
St. George Tucker.

Mr. Dickinson was unanimously elected chairman.

The commissioners produced their credentials from their respective States, which were read.

After a full communication of sentiments, and deliberate consideration of what would be proper to be done by the commissioners now assembled, it was unanimously agreed that a committee be appointed to prepare a draught of a report to be made to the States having commissioners attending at this meeting.

Adjourned till Wednesday morning.

WEDNESDAY, SEPTEMBER 13, 1786.

Met agreeable to adjournment.

The committee appointed for that purpose reported the draught of the report; which being read, the meeting proceeded to the consideration thereof, and, after some time spent therein, adjourned till to-morrow morning.

THURSDAY, SEPTEMBER 14, 1786.

Met agreeable to adjournment.

The meeting resumed the consideration of the draught of the report, and, after some time spent therein, and amendments made, the same was unanimously agreed to, and is as follows, to wit:

To the honorable the Legislatures of Virginia, Delaware, Pennsylvania, New Jersey, and New York, the commissioners from the said States, respectively, assembled at Annapolis, humbly beg leave to report:

That, pursuant to their several appointments, they met at Annapolis, in the State of Maryland, on the 11th day of September instant, and having proceeded to a communication of their powers, they found that the States of New York, Pennsylvania, and Virginia, had, in substance, and nearly in the same terms, authorized their respective commissioners "to meet such commissioners as were or might be appointed by the other States in the Union, at such time and place as should be agreed upon by the said commissioners, to take into consideration the trade and commerce of the United States, to consider how far an uniform system in their commercial intercourse and regulations might be necessary to their common interest and permanent harmony, and to report to the several States such an act relative to this great object, as, when unanimously ratified by them, would enable the United States in Congress assembled effectually to provide for the same."

That the State of Delaware had given similar powers to their commissioners, with this difference only, that the act to be framed in virtue of these powers is required to be reported "to the United States in Congress assembled, to be agreed to by them, and confirmed by the legislatures of every State."

That the State of New Jersey had enlarged the object of their appointment, empowering their commissioners "to consider how far an uniform system in their commercial regulations and *other important matters* might be necessary to the common interest and permanent harmony of the several States;" and to report such an act on the subject as, when ratified by them, "would enable the United States in Congress assembled effectually to provide for the exigencies of the Union."

That appointments of commissioners have also been made by the States of New Hampshire, Massachusetts, Rhode Island, and North Carolina, none of whom, however, have attended; but that no information has been received by your commissioners of any appointment having been made by the States of Connecticut, Maryland, South Carolina, or Georgia.

That, the express terms of the powers to your commissioners supposing a deputation from all the States, and having for object the trade and commerce of the United States, your commissioners did not conceive it advisable to proceed on the business of their mission under the circumstance of so partial and defective a representation.

Deeply impressed, however, with the magnitude and importance of the object confided to them on this occasion, your commissioners cannot forbear to indulge an expression of their earnest and unanimous wish that speedy measures may be taken to effect a general meeting of the States, in a future convention for the same and such other purposes as the situation of public affairs may be found to require.

If, in expressing this wish, or in intimating any other sentiment, your commissioners should seem to exceed the strict bounds of their appointment, they entertain a full confidence that a conduct dictated by an anxiety for the welfare of the United States will not fail to receive an indulgent construction.

In this persuasion, your commissioners submit an opinion, that the idea of extending the powers of their deputies to other objects than ose of commerce, which has been adopted by the State of New Jersey, was an improvement on the original plan, and will deserve to be incorporated into that of a future convention. They are the more naturally led to this conclusion, as, in the course of their reflections on the subject, they have been induced to think that the power of regulating trade is of such comprehensive extent, and will enter so far into the genera. system of the Federal Government, that to give it efficacy, and to obviate questions and doubts concerning its precise nature and limits, may require a correspondent adjustment of other parts of the federal system.

That there are important defects in the system of the Federal Government, is acknowledged by the acts of all those States which have concurred in the present meeting; that the defects, upon a closer examination, may be found greater and more numerous than even these acts imply, is at least so far probable, from the embarrassments which characterize the present state of our national affairs, foreign and domestic, as may reasonably be supposed to merit a deliberate and candid discussion, in some mode which will unite the sentiments and councils of all the States. In the choice of the mode, your commissioners are of opinion that a convention of deputies from the different States, for the special and sole purpose of entering into this investigation, and digesting a plan for supplying such defects as may be discovered to exist, will be entitled to a preference, from considerations which will occur without being particularized.

Your commissioners decline an enumeration of those national circumstances on which their opinion respecting the propriety of a future convention, with more enlarged powers, is founded, as it would be an useless intrusion of facts and observations, most of which have been frequently the subject of public discussion, and none of which can have escaped the penetration of those to whom they would in this instance be addressed. They are, however, of a nature so serious, as, in the view of your commissioners, to render the situation of the United States delicate and critical, calling for an exertion of the united virtue and wisdom of all the members of the Confederacy.

Under this impression, your commissioners, with the most respectful deference, beg leave to suggest their unanimous conviction, that it may essentially tend to advance the interests of the Union, if the States, by whom they have been respectively delegated, would themselves concur, and use their endeavors to procure the concurrence of the other States in the appointment of commissioners, to meet at Philadelphia on the second Monday in May next, to take into consideration the situation of the United States, to devise such further provisions as shall appear to them necessary to render the Constitution of the Federal Government adequate to the exigencies of the Union; and to report such an act for that purpose to the United States in Congress assembled, as, when agreed to by them, and afterwards confirmed by the legislatures of every State, will effectually provide for the same.

Though your commissioners could not with propriety address these observations and sentiments to any but the States they have the honor to represent, they have nevertheless concluded, from motives of respect, to transmit copies of this report to the United States in Congress assembled, and to the executives of the other States.

By order of the commissioners.

Dated at Annapolis, September 14, 1786.

Resolved, That the chairman sign the aforegoing report in behalf of the commissioners.

Then adjourned without day.

NEW YORK.
Egbert Benson,
Alexander Hamilton.

NEW JERSEY.
Abra. Clark,
Wm. Ch. Houston,
James Schureman.

PENNSYLVANIA.
Tench Coxe.

DELAWARE.
George Read,
John Dickinson,
Richard Bassett.

VIRGINIA.
Edmund Randolph,
James Madison, jun.
St. George Tucker.

14. IN THE CONGRESS OF THE CONFEDERATION.

WEDNESDAY, FEBRUARY 21, 1787.

Congress assembled: Present, Massachusetts, Rhode Island, Connecticut, New York, New Jersey, Pennsylvania, Delaware, Virginia, Maryland, North Carolina, South Carolina, and Georgia.

The report of a Grand Committee, consisting of Mr. Dane, Mr. Varnum, Mr. S. M. Mitchell, Mr. Smith, Mr. Cadwallader, Mr. Irvine, Mr. N. Mitchell, Mr. Forrest, Mr. Grayson, Mr. Blount, Mr. Bull, and

Mr. Few, to whom was referred a letter of 14th September, 1786, from J. Dickinson, written at the request of commissioners from the States of Virginia, Delaware, Pennsylvania, New Jersey, and New York, assembled at the city of Annapolis, together with a copy of the report of the said commissioners to the legislatures of the States by whom they were appointed, being an order of the day, was called up, and which is contained in the following resolution, viz:

"Congress having had under consideration the letter of John Dickinson, esq., chairman of the commissioners who assembled at Annapolis during the last year; also the proceedings of the said commissioners; and entirely coinciding with them, as to the inefficiency of the Federal Government, and the necessity of devising such farther provisions as shall render the same adequate to the exigencies of the Union, do strongly recommend to the different legislatures to send forward delegates, to meet the proposed convention, on the second Monday in May next, at the city of Philadelphia."

The delegates for the State of New York thereupon laid before Congress instructions which they had received from their constituents, and, in pursuance of the said instructions, moved to postpone the further consideration of the report, in order to take up the following propositions, viz:

"That it be recommended to the States composing the Union that a convention of representatives from the said States respectively, be held at , on , for the purpose of revising the Articles of Confederation and perpetual union between the United States of America, and reporting to the United States in Congress assembled, and to the States respectively, such alterations and amendments of the said Articles of Confederation, as the representatives met in such convention shall judge proper and necessary to render them adequate to the preservation and support of the Union."

On the question to postpone, for the purpose above mentioned, the yeas and nays being required by the delegates for New York,

Massachusetts..........	Mr. King,	ay	ay
	Dane,	ay	
Connecticut............	Mr. Johnson,	ay	div.
	S. Mitchell,	no	
New York..............	Mr. Smith,	ay	ay
	Benson,	ay	
New Jersey............	Mr. Cadwallader,	ay	no
	Clarke,	no	
	Schureman,	no	
Pennsylvania..........	Mr. Irvine,	no	no
	Meredith,	ay	
	Bingham,	no	

Delaware	Mr. N. Mitchell,	no	*
Maryland	Mr. Forrest,	no	*
Virginia	Mr. Grayson,	ay	ay
	Madison,	ay	
N. Carolina............	Mr. Blount,	no	no
	Hawkins,	no	
S. Carolina	Mr. Bull,	no	no
	Kean,	no	
	Huger,	no	
	Parker,	no	
Georgia	Mr. Few,	ay	div.
	Pierce,	no	

So the question was lost.

A motion was then made by the delegates for Massachusetts, to postpone the further consideration of the report, in order to take into consideration a motion which they read in their place; this being agreed to, the motion of the delegates for Massachusetts was taken up, and, being amended, was agreed to, as follows:

Whereas there is provision in the Articles of Confederation and perpetual Union, for making alterations therein, by the assent of a Congress of the United States, and of the legislatures of the several States; and whereas experience hath evinced that there are defects in the present Confederation, as a mean to remedy which several of the States, and particularly the State of New York, by express instructions to their delegates in Congress, have suggested a convention for the purposes expressed in the following resolution; and such convention appearing to be the most probable mean of establishing in these States a firm National Government:

Resolved, That, in the opinion of Congress, it is expedient, that, on the second Monday in May next, a convention of delegates, who shall have been appointed by the several States, be held at Philadelphia, for the sole and express purpose of revising the Articles of Confederation, and reporting to Congress, and the several legislatures, such alterations and provisions therein as shall, when agreed to in Congress, and confirmed by the States, render the Federal Constitution adequate to the exigencies of Government, and the preservation of the Union.

15. *Acts of the several States for the appointment of Deputies to meet in Convention, for the purpose of forming a Constitution of Government, viz:*

COMMONWEALTH OF VIRGINIA.

General Assembly, begun and held at the public buildings in the city of Richmond, on Monday, the 16th day of October, in the year of our Lord 1786.

AN ACT for appointing Deputies from this Commonwealth to a Convention proposed to be held in the city of Philadelphia, in May next, for the purpose of revising the Federal Constitution.

Whereas the commissioners who assembled at Annapolis, on the 14th day of September last, for the purpose of devising and reporting the means of enabling Congress to provide effectually for the commercial interests of the United States, have represented the necessity of extending the revision of the Federal system to all its defects, and have recommended that deputies for that purpose be appointed by the several legislatures, to meet in convention, in the city of Philadelphia, on the second day of May next, a provision which was preferable to a discussion of the subject in Congress, where it might be too much interrupted by the ordinary business before them, and where it would, besides, be deprived of the valuable counsels of sundry individuals who are disqualified by the Constitution, or laws of particular States, or restrained by peculiar circumstances, from a seat in that assembly: And whereas the General Assembly of this Commonwealth, taking into view the actual situation of the Confederacy, as well as reflecting on the alarming representations made, from time to time, by the United States in Congress, particularly in their act of the 15th day of February last, can no longer doubt that the crisis is arrived at which the good people of America are to decide the solemn question, whether they will, by wise and magnanimous efforts, reap the just fruits of that independence which they have so gloriously acquired, and of that Union which they have cemented with so much of their common blood, or whether, by giving way to unmanly jealousies and prejudices, or to partial and transitory interests, they will renounce the auspicious blessings prepared for them by the Revolution, and furnish to its enemies an eventual triumph over those by whose virtue and valor it has been accomplished: And whereas the same noble and extended policy, and the same fraternal and affectionate sentiments which originally determined the citizens of this Commonwealth to unite with their brethren of the other States in establishing a Federal Government, cannot but be felt with equal force now as motives to lay aside every inferior consideration, and to concur in such farther concessions and provisions as may be necessary to secure the great objects for which that Government was instituted, and to render the United States as happy in peace as they have been glorious in war:

Be it therefore enacted by the General Assembly of the Commonwealth of Virginia, That seven commissioners be appointed by joint ballot of both Houses of Assembly, who, or any three of them, are hereby authorized, as deputies from this Commonwealth, to meet such deputies as may be appointed and authorized by other States, to assemble in convention at Philadelphia, as above recommended, and to join with them in devising and discussing all such alterations and farther provisions as may be necessary to render the Federal Constitution adequate to the exigencies of the Union, and, in reporting such an act for that purpose to the United States in Congress, as, when agreed to by them, and duly confirmed by the several States, will effectually provide for the same.

And be it further enacted, That, in case of the death of any of the said deputies, or of their declining their appointments, the executive are hereby authorized to supply such vacancies; and the Governor is requested to transmit forthwith a copy of this act to the United States in Congress, and to the executives of each of the States in the Union.

(Signed) JOHN JONES,
Specker of the Senate.
JOSEPH PRENTISS,
Speaker of the House of Delegates.

A true copy from the enrollment.
JOHN BECKLEY, *Clerk H. D.*

IN THE HOUSE OF DELEGATES.

MONDAY, THE 4TH OF DECEMBER, 1786.

The House, according to the order of the day, proceeded, by joint ballot with the Senate, to the appointment of seven deputies from this Commonwealth to a convention proposed to be held in the city of Philadelphia in May next, for the purpose of revising the Federal Constitution; and, the members having prepared tickets with the names of the persons to be appointed, and deposited the same in the ballot-boxes, Mr. Corbin, Mr. Matthews, Mr. David Stewart, Mr. George Nicholas, Mr. Richard Lee, Mr. Wills, Mr. Thomas Smith, Mr. Goodall, and Mr. Turberville, were nominated a committee to meet a committee from the Senate, in the conference chamber, and jointly with them to examine the ballot-boxes and report to the House on whom the majority of the votes should fall. The committee then withdrew, and after some time returned into the House, and reported that the committee had, according to order, met a committee from the Senate in the conference chamber, and jointly with them examined the ballot-boxes, and found a majority of votes in favor of George Washington, Patrick Henry, Edmund Randolph, John Blair, James Madison, George Mason, and George Wythe, esqrs. Extract from the journal.

JOHN BECKLEY,
Clerk House Delegates.

Attest: JOHN BECKLEY, *Clerk H. D.*

IN THE HOUSE OF SENATORS.

MONDAY, THE 4TH OF DECEMBER, 1786.

The Senate, according to the order of the day, proceeded, by joint ballot with the House of Delegates, to the appointment of seven deputies from this Commonwealth to a convention proposed to be held in the city of Philadelphia in May next, for the purpose of revising the Federal Constitution; and, the members having prepared tickets with the names of the persons to be appointed, and deposited the same in the ballot-boxes, Mr. Anderson, Mr. Nelson, and Mr. Lee, were nominated a committee to meet a committee from the House of Delegates, in the conference chamber, and jointly with them to examine the ballot-boxes, and report to the House on whom the majority of votes should fall. The committee then withdrew, and after some time returned into the House, and reported that the committee had, according to order, met a committee from the House of Delegates, in the conference chamber, and jointly with them examined the ballot-boxes, and found a majority of votes in favor of George Washington, Patrick Henry, Edmund Randolph, John Blair, James Madison, George Mason, and George Wythe, esqrs. Extract from the journal.

JOHN BECKLEY, *Clerk H. D.*

Attest: H. BROOK, *Clerk.*

[L. S.] VIRGINIA, *to wit:*

I do hereby certify and make known, to all whom it may concern, that John Beckley, esq., is clerk of the House of Delegates for this Commonwealth, and the proper officer for attesting the proceedings of the General Assembly of the said Commonwealth, and that full faith and credit ought to be given to all things attested by the said John Beckley, esq., by virtue of his office aforesaid.

Given under my hand, as Governor of the Commonwealth of Virginia, and under the seal thereof, at Richmond, this fourth day of May, 1787.

EDM. RANDOLPH.

[L. S.] VIRGINIA, *to wit:*

I do hereby certify, that Patrick Henry, esq., one of the seven commissioners appointed by joint ballot of both Houses of Assembly of the Commonwealth of Virginia, authorized as a deputy therefrom, to meet such deputies as might be appointed and authorized by other States, to assemble in Philadelphia, and to join with them in devising and discussing all such alterations and further provisions as might be necessary to render the Federal Constitution adequate to the exigencies of the Union, and in reporting such an act for that purpose to the United States in Congress, as, when agreed to by them, and duly confirmed by the several States, might effectually provide for the same, did decline his appointment aforesaid; and thereupon, in pursuance of an act of the General Assembly of the said Commonwealth, entitled "An act for appointing deputies from this Commonwealth to a convention proposed to be held in the city of Philadelphia in May next, for the purpose of revising the Federal Constitution," I do hereby, with the advice of the Council of State, supply the said vacancy by nominating James McClurg, esq., a deputy for the purposes aforesaid.

Given under my hand, as Governor of the said Commonwealth, and under the seal thereof, this second day of May, in the year of our Lord 1787.

EDM. RANDOLPH.

THE STATE OF NEW JERSEY.

To the honorable David Brearley, William Churchill Houston, William Paterson, and John Neilson, esqrs., greeting:

The Council and Assembly, reposing especial trust and confidence in your integrity, prudence, and ability, have, at a joint meeting, appointed you, the said David Brearley, William Churchill Houston, William Paterson, and John Neilson, esqrs., or any three of you, commissioners, to meet such commissioners as have been or may be appointed by the other States of the Union, at the city of Philadelphia, in the Commonwealth of Pennsylvania, on the second Monday in May next, for the purpose of taking into consideration the state of the Union, as to trade and other important objects, and of devising such other provisions as shall appear to be necessary to render the Constitution of the Federal Government adequate to the exigencies thereof.

In testimony whereof, the great seal of the State is hereunto affixed. Witness William Livingston, esq., Governor, captain general and commander-in-chief in and over the State of New Jersey, and territories thereunto belonging, chancellor and ordinary in the same, at Trenton, the 23d day of November, in the year of our Lord 1786, and of our sovereignty and independence the eleventh.

WILLIAM LIVINGSTON.

By his excellency's command.

BOWES REED, *Secretary.*

THE STATE OF NEW JERSEY.

To his excellency William Livingston, and the honorable Abraham
[L. S.] Clark, esqrs., greeting:

The Council and Assembly, reposing especial trust and confidence in your integrity, prudence, and ability, have, at a joint meeting, appointed you, the said William Livingston and Abraham Clark, esqrs., in conjunction with the honorable David Brearley, William Churchill Houston, and William Paterson, esqrs., or any three of you, commissioners, to meet such commissioners as have been appointed by the other States in the Union, at the city of Philadelphia, in the Commonwealth of Pennsylvania, on the second Monday of this present month, for the purpose of taking into consideration the state of the Union, as to trade and other important objects, and of devising such other provisions as shall appear to be necessary, to render the Constitution of the Federal Government adequate to the exigencies thereof.

In testimony whereof, the great seal of the State is hereunto affixed. Witness William Livingston, esq., Governor, captain general and commander-in-chief in and over the State of New Jersey, and territories thereunto belonging, chancellor and ordinary in the same, at Burlington, the 8th day of May, in the year of our Lord 1787, and of our sovereignty and independence the eleventh.

WILLIAM LIVINGSTON.

By his excellency's command.

BOWES REED, *Secretary.*

STATE OF NEW JERSEY.

To the honorable Jonathan Dayton, esq.

The Council and Assembly, reposing especial trust and confidence in your integrity, prudence, and ability, have, at a joint meeting, appointed you, the said Jonathan Dayton, esq., in conjunction with his excellency

William Livingston, the honorable David Brearley, William Churchill Houston, William Paterson, and Abraham Clark, esqrs., or any three of you, commissioners, to meet such commissioners as have been appointed by the other States in the Union, at the city of Philadelphia, in the Commonwealth of Pennsylvania, for the purpose of taking into consideration the state of the Union, as to trade and other important objects, and of devising such other provision as shall appear to be necessary to render the Constitution of the Federal Government adequate to the exigencies thereof.

In testimony whereof, the great seal of the State is hereunto affixed. Witness Robert Lettice Hooper, esq., vice president, captain general and commander-in-chief in and over the State of New Jersey, and territories thereunto belonging, chancellor and ordinary in the same, at Burlington, the fifth day of June, in the year of our Lord 1787, and of our sovereignty and independence the eleventh.

ROBERT L. HOOPER.

By his honor's command.

BOWES REED, *Secretar*..

COMMONWEALTH OF PENNSYLVANIA.

AN ACT appointing Deputies to the Convention intended to be held in the city of Philadelphia, for the purpose of revising the Federal Constitution.

SECTION 1. Whereas the General Assembly of this Commonwealth, taking into their serious consideration the representations heretofore made to the legislatures of the several States in the Union, by the United States in Congress assembled, and also weighing the difficulties under which the confederated States now labor, are fully convinced of the necessity of revising the Federal Constitution, for the purpose of making such alterations and amendments as the exigencies of our public affairs require. And whereas the Legislature of the State of Virginia have already passed an act of that Commonwealth, empowering certain commissioners to meet at the city of Philadelphia, in May next, a convention of commissioners or deputies from the different States; and the Legislature of this State are fully sensible of the important advantages which may be derived to the United States, and every of them, from co-operating with the Commonwealth of Virginia, and the other States of the Confederation, in the said design.

SEC. 2. *Be it enacted, and it is hereby enacted* by the representatives of the freemen of the Commonwealth of Pennsylvania, in General Assembly met, and by the authority of the same, that Thomas Mifflin, Robert Morris, George Clymer, Jared Ingersoll, Thomas Fitzsimons, James Wilson, and Gouverneur Morris, esqrs., are hereby appointed deputies from this State, to meet in the convention of the deputies of the respective States of North America, to be held at the city of Philadelphia on the second day of the month of May next; and the said Thomas Mifflin, Robert Morris, George Clymer, Jared Ingersoll, Thomas Fitzsimons, James Wilson, and Gouverneur Morris, esqrs., or any four of them, are hereby constituted and appointed deputies from this State, with powers to meet such deputies as may be appointed and authorized by the other States, to assemble in the said convention, at the city aforesaid, and to join with them in devising, deliberating on, and discussing all such alterations, and further provisions, as may be necessary to render the Federal Constitution fully adequate to the exigencies of the Union, and in reporting such act or acts, for that purpose, to the United States in Congress assembled, as, when agreed to by them, and duly confirmed by the several States, will effectually provide for the same.

SEC. 3. *And be it further enacted by the authority aforesaid,* That in case any of the said deputies hereby nominated shall happen to die, or to resign his or their said appointment or appointments, the supreme executive council shall be, and hereby are, empowered and required to nominate and appoint other person or persons in lieu of him or them so deceased, or who has or have so resigned, which person or persons, from and after such nomination and appointment, shall be, and hereby are declared to be, vested with the same powers respectively, as any of the deputies nominated and appointed by this act is vested with by the same: *Provided always,* That the council are not hereby authorized, nor shall they make any such nomination or appointment, except in vacation, and during the recess of the General Assembly of this State.

[L. S.] Signed by order of the House.

THOMAS MIFFLIN, *Speaker.*

Enacted into a law at Philadelphia, on Saturday, December the 30th in the year of our Lord 1786. PETER ZACHARY LLOYD,

Clerk of the General Assembly.

I, Mathew Irwine, esq., master of the rolls for the State of Pennsylvania, do certify the preceding writing to be a true copy (or exemplification) of a certain act of Assembly lodged in my office.

In witness whereof, I have hereunto set my hand and seal of office, the [L. S.] 15th May, A. D. 1787.

MATHEW IRWINE *M R.*

A supplement to the act entitled "An act appointing deputies to the convention intended to be held in the city of Philadelphia, for the purpose of revising the Federal Constitution."

SEC. 1st. Whereas by the act to which this act is a supplement, certain persons were appointed as deputies from this State to sit in the said convention: And whereas it is the desire of the General Assembly, that his excellency Benjamin Franklin, esq., president of this State, should also sit in the said convention as a deputy from this state: Therefore,

SEC. 2d. *Be it enacted, and it is hereby enacted* by the representatives of the freemen of the Commonwealth of Pennsylvania, in General Assembly met, and by the authority of the same, that his excellency Benjamin Franklin, esq., be, and he is hereby appointed and authorized to sit in the said convention as a deputy from this State, in addition to the persons heretofore appointed; and that he be, and he hereby is invested with like powers and authorities as are invested in the said deputies or any of them.

Signed by order of the House.

THOMAS MIFFLIN, *Speaker*.

Enacted into a law at Philadelphia, on Wednesday, the 28th day of March, in the year of our Lord 1787.

PETER ZACHARY LLOYD,
Clerk of the General Assembly.

I, Mathew Irwine, esq., master of the rolls for the State of Pennsylvania, do certify the above to be a true copy (or exemplification) of a supplement to a certain act of Assembly, which supplement is lodged in my office.

In witness whereof, I have hereunto set my hand and seal of office, [L. S.] the 15th May, A. D. 1787.

MATHEW IRWINE, *M. R.*

THE STATE OF NORTH CAROLINA.

To the honorable Alexander Martin, esq., greeting:

Whereas our General Assembly, in their late session, holden at Fayetteville, by adjournment, in the month of January last, did, by joint ballot of the Senate and House of Commons, elect Richard Caswell, Alexander Martin, William Richardson Davie, Richard Dobbs Spaight, and Willie Jones, esqrs., deputies to attend a convention of delegates from the several United States of America, proposed to be held at the city of Philadelphia in May next, for the purpose of revising the Federal Constitution,

We do, therefore, by these presents, nominate, commissionate, and appoint you, the said Alexander Martin, one of the deputies for and in our behalf, to meet with our other deputies at Philadelphia, on the first day of May next, and with them, or any two of them, to confer with such deputies as may have been, or shall be appointed by the other States, for the purposes aforesaid: To hold, exercise, and enjoy the appointment aforesaid, with all powers, authorities, and emoluments to the same belonging, or in any wise appertaining, you conforming, in every instance, to the act of our said Assembly, under which you are appointed.

Witness Richard Caswell, esq., our Governor, captain general and commander-in-chief, under his hand and our great seal, at Kingston, the 24th day of February, in the eleventh year of our independence, A. D. 1787.

[L. S.] RICH. CASWELL.

By his excellency's command.

WINSTON CASWELL, *P. Secretary.*

A commission, precisely similar to the above, was given "to the honorable William Richardson Davie, esq.," on the 24th February, 1787.

And also another, "to the honorable Richard Dobbs Spaight, esq., on the 14th of April, 1787.

STATE OF NORTH CAROLINA.

His excellency Richard Caswell, esq., Governor, captain general and commander-in-chief, in and over the State aforesaid.

To all to whom these presents shall come, greeting:

Whereas, by an act of the General Assembly of the said State, passed the sixth day of January last, entitled "An act for appointing deputies from this State to a convention proposed to be held in the city of Philadelphia, in May next, for the purpose of revising the Federal Constitution," among other things it is enacted, "That five commissioners be appointed by joint ballot of both Houses of Assembly, who, or any three of them, are hereby authorized as deputies from this State, to meet at Philadelphia, on the first day of May next, then and there to meet and confer with such deputies as may be appointed by the other States for similar purposes, and with them to discuss and decide upon the most effectual means to remove the defects of our Federal Union, and to procure the enlarged purposes which it was intended to effect; and that they report such an act to the General Assembly of this State, as, when agreed to by them, will effectually provide for the same." And it is by the said act further enacted, "That in case of the death or resignation of any of the deputies, or of their declining their appointments, his excellency the Governor, for the time being, is hereby authorized to supply such vacancies." And whereas, in consequence of the said act, Richard Caswell, Alexander Martin, William Richardson Davie, Richard Dobbs Spaight, and Willie Jones, esqrs., were, by joint ballot of the two Houses of Assembly, elected deputies for the purposes aforesaid: And whereas the said Richard Caswell has resigned his said appointment as one of the deputies aforesaid:

Now, know ye, that I have appointed, and by these presents do appoint, the honorable William Blount, esq., one of the deputies to represent this State in the convention aforesaid, in the room and stead of the aforesaid Richard Caswell, hereby giving and granting to the said William Blount, the same powers, privileges, and emoluments, which the said Richard Caswell would have been vested with, or entitled to, had he continued in the appointment aforesaid.

Given under my hand, and the great seal of the State, at Kingston, the 23d day of April, A. D. 1787, and in the eleventh year of [L. S.] American independence.

RICH. CASWELL.

By his excellency's command.

WINSTON CASWELL, *P. Secretary*.

STATE OF NORTH CAROLINA.

His excellency, Richard Caswell, esq., Governor, captain-general, and commander-in-chief, in and over the State aforesaid.

To all to whom these presents shall come, greeting:

Whereas, by an act of the General Assembly of the said State, passed the sixth day of January last, entitled "An act for appointing deputies from this State to a convention proposed to be held in the city of Philadelphia, in May next, for the purpose of revising the Federal Constitution," among other things it is enacted, "That five commissioners be appointed by joint ballot of both Houses of Assembly, who, or any three of them, are hereby authorized, as deputies from this State, to meet at Philadelphia on the first day of May next, then and there to meet and confer with such deputies as may be appointed by the other States for similar purposes, and with them to discuss and decide upon the most effectual means to remove the defects of our Federal Union, and to procure the enlarged purposes which it was intended to effect, and that they report such an act to the General Assembly of this State, as, when agreed to by them, will effectually provide for the same." And it is by the said act further enacted, "That in case of the death or resignation of any of the deputies, or their declining their appointments, his excellency the Governor, for the time being, is hereby authorized to supply such vacancies." And whereas, in consequence of the said act, Richard Caswell, Alexander Martin, William Richardson Davie, Richard Dobbs Spaight, and Willie Jones, esqrs., were, by joint ballot of the two Houses of Assembly, elected deputies for the purposes aforesaid. And whereas the said Willie Jones hath declined his appointment as one of the deputies aforesaid:

Now, know ye, that I have appointed, and by these presents do appoint, the honorable Hugh Williamson, esq., one of the deputies to represent this State in the convention aforesaid, in the room and stead of the aforesaid Willie Jones, hereby giving and granting to the said Hugh Williamson the same powers, privileges, and emoluments, which the said Willie Jones would have been vested with, and entitled to, had he acted under the appointment aforesaid.

Given under my hand, and the great seal of the State, at Kingston, the third day of April, A. D. 1787, and in the eleventh year of [L. S.] American Independence.

RICH. CASWELL.

By his excellency's command.

DALLAM CASWELL, *Pro Secretary.*

DELAWARE.

His excellency Thomas Collins, esq., President, captain-general and commander-in-chief of the Delaware State, to all to whom these presents shall come, greeting: Know ye, that among the [L. S.] laws of the said State, passed by the General Assembly of the same, on the 3d day of February, in the year of our Lord 1787, it is thus enrolled:

In the eleventh year of the independence of the Delaware State:

AN ACT appointing deputies from this State to the convention proposed to be held in the city of Philadelphia, for the purpose of revising the Federal Constitution.

Whereas the General Assembly of this State are fully convinced of the necessity of revising the Federal Constitution, and adding thereto such further provisions as may render the same more adequate to the exigencies of the Union: And whereas the Legislature of Virginia have already passed an act of that Commonwealth, appointing and authorizing certain commissioners to meet, at the city of Philadelphia, in May next, a convention of commissioners or deputies from the different States; and, this State being willing and desirous of co-operating with the Commonwealth of Virginia and the other States in the Confederation in so useful a design:

Be it therefore enacted by the General Assembly of Delaware, That George Read, Gunning Bedford, John Dickinson, Richard Bassett, and Jacob Broom, esqrs., are hereby appointed deputies from this State to meet in the convention of the deputies of other States, to be held at the city of Philadelphia, on the 2d day of May next: And the said George Read, Gunning Bedford, John Dickinson, Richard Bassett, and Jacob Broom, esqrs., or any three of them, are hereby constituted and appointed deputies from this State, with powers to meet such deputies as may be appointed and authorized by the other States to assemble in the said convention at the city aforesaid, and to join with them in devising, deliberating on, and discussing, such alterations and further provisions as may be necessary to render the Federal Constitution adequate to the exigencies of the Union, and in reporting such act or acts for that purpose to the United States in Congress assembled, as, when agreed to by them, and duly confirmed by the several States, may effectually provide for the same. So, always, and provided, that such alterations or further provisions, or any of them, do not extend to that part of the fifth article of the Confederation of the said States, finally ratified on the first day of March, in the year 1781, which declares that, "In determining questions in the United States in Congress assembled, each State shall have one vote."

And be it enacted, That, in case any of the said deputies hereby nominated shall happen to die, or to resign his or their appointment, the President or commander-in-chief, with the advice of the privy council, in the recess of the General Assembly, is hereby authorized to supply such vacancies.

Signed by order of the House of Assembly.

JOHN COOK, *Speaker*.

Passed at Dover, February 3, 1787.

Signed by order of the Council.

GEO. CRAGHED, *Speaker*.

All and singular which premises, by the tenor of these presents, I have caused to be exemplified. In testimony whereof, I have hereunto subscribed my name, and caused the great seal of the said State to be affixed to these presents, at New Castle, the second day of April, in the year of our Lord 1787, and in the eleventh year of the independence of the United States of America.

THOMAS COLLINS.

Attest: JAMES BOOTH, *Secretary*.

GEORGIA.

By the honorable George Mathews, esq., captain-general, Governor, and commander-in-chief, in and over the State aforesaid.

To all to whom these presents shall come, greeting:

Know ye, that John Milton, esq., who hath certified the annexed copy of an ordinance, entitled "An ordinance for the appointment of deputies from this State, for the purpose of revising the Federal Constitution," is secretary of the said State, in whose office the archives of the same are deposited; therefore, all due faith, credit, and authority, are, and ought to be, had and given the same.

In testimony whereof, I have hereunto set my hand, and caused the great seal of the State to be put and affixed, at Augusta, this 24th day of April, in the year of our Lord 1787, and of our sovereignty and independence the eleventh. [L. S.]

GEO. MATHEWS.

By his honor's command.

J. MILTON.

An ordinance for the appointment of deputies from this State, for the purpose of revising the Federal Constitution.

Be it ordained, by the representatives of the freemen of the State of Georgia, in General Assembly met, and by the authority of the same, that William Few, Abraham Baldwin, William Pierce, George Walton, William Houston, and Nathaniel Pendleton, esqrs., be, and they are hereby, appointed commissioners, who, or any two or more of them, are hereby authorized, as deputies from this State, to meet such deputies as may be appointed and authorized by other States, to assemble in convention at Philadelphia, and to join with them in devising and discussing all such alterations and farther provisions as may be necessary to render the Federal Constitution adequate to the exigencies of the Union, and in reporting such an act for that purpose to the United States in Congress assembled, as, when agreed to by them, and duly confirmed by the several States, will effectually provide for the same. In case of the death of any of the said deputies, or of their declining their appoint ments, the executive are hereby authorized to supply such vacancies.

By order of the House.

(Signed) WM. GIBBONS, *Speaker*

Augusta, the 10th February, 1787.

GEORGIA, Secretary's Office.

The above is a true copy from the original ordinance deposited in my office. J. MILTON, *Secretary*.

Augusta, 24th April, 1787.

The State of Georgia, by the grace of God, free, sovereign, and independent,

To the honorable William Few, esq.

Whereas you, the said William Few, are, in and by an ordinance of the General Assembly of our said State, nominated and appointed a deputy to represent the same in a convention of the United States, to be assembled at Philadelphia, for the purposes of devising and discussing all such alterations and farther provisions as may be necessary to render the Federal Constitution adequate to the exigencies of the Union:

You are therefore hereby commissioned to proceed on the duties required of you in virtue of the said ordinance.

[L. S.] Witness our trusty and well-beloved George Mathews, esq., our captain-general, Governor, and commander-in-chief, under his hand, and our great seal, at Augusta, this 17th day of April, in the year of our Lord 1787, and of our sovereignty and independence the eleventh.

GEO. MATHEWS.

By his honor's command.

J. MILTON, *Secretary*.

Commissions precisely similar to the above were given, on the said 17th April, 1787, to—

The honorable William Pierce, esq.

The honorable William Houston, esq.

STATE OF NEW YORK.

By his excellency George Clinton, esq., Governor of the State of New
[L. S.] York, general and commander-in-chief of all the militia, and admiral of the navy of the same:

To all to whom these presents shall come.

It is by these presents certified, that John M'Kesson, who has subscribed the annexed copies of resolutions, is clerk of the Assembly of this State.

In testimony whereof, I have caused the privy seal of the said State to be hereunto affixed, this ninth day of May, in the eleventh year of the independence of the said State.

GEO. CLINTON.

STATE OF NEW YORK, IN ASSEMBLY, FEBRUARY 28, 1787.

A copy of a resolution of the honorable the Senate, delivered by Mr. Williams, was read, and is in the words following, viz.:

Resolved, If the honorable the Assembly concur therein, that three delegates be appointed, on the part of this State, to meet such delegates as may be appointed on the part of the other States, respectively, on the second Monday in May next, at Philadelphia, for the sole and express purpose of revising the Articles of Confederation, and reporting to Congress, and to the several legislatures, such alterations and provisions therein as shall, when agreed to in Congress, and confirmed by the several States, render the Federal Constitution adequate to the exigencies of Government, and the preservation of the Union; and that, in case of such concurrence, the two Houses of the legislature will, on Tuesday next, proceed to nominate and appoint the said delegates, in like manner as is directed by the Constitution of this State for nominating and appointing delegates to Congress.

Resolved, That this House do concur with the honorable the Senate in the said resolution.

IN ASSEMBLY, MARCH 6, 1787.

Resolved, That the honorable Robert Yates, esq., and Alexander Hamilton and John Lansing, jun., esqrs., be, and they are hereby nominated by this House, delegates on the part of this State, to meet such delegates as may be appointed on the part of the other States, respectively, on the second Monday in May next, at Philadelphia, pursuant to concurrent resolutions of both Houses of the legislature on the 28th ultimo.

Resolved, That this House will meet the honorable the Senate immediately, at such place as they shall appoint, to compare the lists of persons nominated by the Senate and Assembly, respectively, as delegates on the part of this State, to meet such delegates as may be appointed on the part of the other States, respectively, on the second Monday in May next, at Philadelphia, pursuant to concurrent resolutions of both Houses of the legislature on the 28th ultimo.

Ordered, That Mr. N. Smith deliver a copy of the last preceding resolution to the honorable the Senate.

A copy of a resolution of the honorable the Senate was delivered by Mr. Vanderbelt, that the Senate will immediately meet this House in the Assembly chamber, to compare the lists of persons nominated by the Senate and Assembly, respectively, as delegates, pursuant to the resolution before mentioned.

The honorable the Senate accordingly attended in the Assembly chamber, to compare the lists of persons nominated for delegates, as above mentioned.

The list of persons nominated by the honorable the Senate, were the honorable Robert Yates, esq., and John Lansing, jun., and Alexander Hamilton, esqrs., and on comparing the lists of the persons nominated by the Senate and Assembly, respectively, it appeared that the same persons were nominated in both lists ; thereupon,

Resolved, That the honorable Robert Yates, John Lansing, jun., and Alexander Hamilton, esqrs., be, and they are hereby declared duly nominated and appointed delegates, on the part of this State, to meet such delegates as may be appointed on the part of the other States, respectively, on the second Monday in May next, at Philadelphia, for the sole and express purpose of revising the Articles of Confederation, and reporting to Congress, and to the several legislatures, such alterations and provisions therein as shall, when agreed to in Congress, and confirmed by the several States, render the Federal Constitution adequate to the exigencies of Government, and the preservation of the Union.

True extracts from the journals of the Assembly.

JOHN M'KESSON, *Clerk.*

STATE OF SOUTH CAROLINA.

By his excellency Thomas Pinckney, esq., Governor, and commander in-chief, in and over the State aforesaid.

To the honorable John Rutledge, esq., greeting:

By virtue of the power and authority in me vested by the legislature of this State, in their act passed the eighth day of March last, I do hereby commission you, the said John Rutledge, as one of the deputies appointed from this State, to meet such deputies or commissioners as may be appointed and authorized by other of the United States, to assemble in convention at the city of Philadelphia, in the month of May next, or as soon thereafter as may be, and to join with such deputies or commissioners (they being duly authorized and empowered) in devising and discussing all such alterations, clauses, articles, and provisions, as may be thought necessary to render the Federal Constitution entirely adequate to the actual situation and future good government of the confederated States; and that you, together with the said deputies or commissioners, or a majority of them who shall be present, (provided the State be not represented by less than two,) do join in reporting such an act to the United States in Congress assembled, as, when approved and agreed to by them, and duly ratified and confirmed by the several States, will effectually provide for the exigencies of the Union.

Given under my hand, and the great seal of the State, in the city of Charleston, this 10th day of April, in the year of our Lord 1787, [L. S.] and of the sovereignty and independence of the United States of America the eleventh.

THOMAS PINCKNEY.

By his excellency's command.

PETER FRENEAU, *Secretary*.

Commissions precisely similar to the above were given, on the said 10th April, 1787, to—

The honorable Charles Pinckney, esq.

The honorable Charles Cotesworth Pinckney, esq.

The honorable Pierce Butler, esq.

COMMONWEALTH OF MASSACHUSETTS.

By his excellency James Bowdoin, esq., Governor of the Commonwealth of Massachusetts.

To the honorable Francis Dana, Elbridge Gerry, Nathaniel Gorham, Rufus King, and Caleb Strong, esqrs., greeting:

Whereas Congress did, on the 21st day of February, A. D. 1787, resolve, "That, in the opinion of Congress, it is expedient that, on the second Monday in May next, a convention of delegates, who shall have been appointed by the several States, to be held at Philadelphia, for the sole and express purpose of revising the Articles of Confederation, and reporting to Congress, and the several legislatures, such alterations and provisions therein as shall, when agreed to in Congress, and confirmed by the States, render the Federal Constitution adequate to the exigencies of Government and the preservation of the Union." And whereas the general court have constituted and appointed you their delegates, to attend and represent this Commonwealth in the said proposed convention, and have, by a resolution of theirs of the tenth of March last, requested me to commission you for that purpose.

Now, therefore, know ye, that in pursuance of the resolutions aforesaid, I do, by these presents, commission you, the said Francis Dana, Elbridge Gerry, Nathaniel Gorham, Rufus King, and Caleb Strong, esqrs., or any three of you, to meet such delegates as may be appointed by the other, or any of the other States in the Union, to meet in convention at Philadelphia, at the time, and for the purposes aforesaid.

In testimony whereof, I have caused the public seal of the Commonwealth aforesaid to be hereunto affixed. Given at the council chamber, in Boston, the ninth day of April, A. D. 1787, and in the eleventh year of the independence of the United States of America.

[L. S.]

JAMES BOWDOIN.

By his excellency's command.

JOHN AVERY, JUN., *Secretary.*

STATE OF CONNECTICUT.

At a General Assembly of the State of Connecticut, in America, holden at Hartford, on the second Thursday of May, A. D. 1787.

[L. S.]

AN ACT for appointing delegates to meet in a convention of the States, to be held at the city of Philadelphia, on the second Monday of May instant.

Whereas the Congress of the United States, by their act of the 21st of February, 1787, have recommended that, on the second Monday of May instant, a convention of delegates, who shall have been appointed by the several States, be held at Philadelphia, for the sole and express purpose of revising the Articles of Confederation,

Be it enacted by the Governor, council, and representatives, in general court assembled, and by the authority of the same, That the honorable William Samuel Johnson, Roger Sherman, and Oliver Ellsworth, esqrs., be, and they hereby are, appointed delegates to attend the said convention, and are requested to proceed to the city of Philadelphia for that purpose, without delay; and the said delegates, and, in case of sickness or accident, such one or more of them as shall actually attend the said convention, is, and are hereby authorized and empowered to represent this State therein, and to confer with such delegates appointed by the several States, for the purposes mentioned in the said act of Congress, that may be present and duly empowered to act in said convention, and to discuss upon such alterations and provisions, agreeable to the general principles of republican government, as they shall think proper to render the Federal Constitution adequate to the exigencies of Government and the preservation of the Union; and they are further directed, pursuant to the said act of Congress, to report such alterations and provisions as may be agreed to by a majority of the United States represented in convention, to the Congress of the United States, and to the General Assembly of this State.

A true copy of record, examined by
GEORGE WYLLYS, *Sec'ry.*

STATE OF MARYLAND.

AN ACT for the appointment of, and conferring powers in, deputies from this State to the Federal Convention.

Be it enacted by the General Assembly of Maryland, That the honorable James M'Henry, Daniel of St. Thomas Jenifer, Daniel Carroll, John Francis Mercer, and Luther Martin, esqrs., be appointed and authorized, on behalf of this State, to meet such deputies as may be appointed and authorized by any other of the United States, to assemble in convention at Philadelphia, for the purpose of revising the Federal system, and to join with them in considering such alterations and further provisions as may be necessary to render the Federal Constitution adequate to the exigencies of the Union; and in reporting such an act for that purpose to the United States in Congress assembled, as, when agreed to by them and duly confirmed by the several States, will effectually provide for the same; and the said deputies, or such of them as shall attend the said convention, shall have full power to represent this State for the purposes aforesaid; and the said deputies are hereby directed to report the proceedings of the said convention, and any act agreed to therein, to the next session of the General Assembly of this State.

By the House of Delegates, May 26, 1787, read and assented to.

By order: WM. HARWOOD, *Clerk.*

True copy from the original. WM. HARWOOD, *Clerk H. D.*

By the Senate, May 26, 1787, read and assented to.

By order: J. DORSEY, *Clerk.*

True copy from the original. J. DORSEY, *Clerk Senate.*

W. SMALLWOOD.

STATE OF NEW HAMPSHIRE.

In the year of our Lord 1787.

AN ACT for appointing deputies from this State to the convention, proposed to be holden, in the city of Philadelphia, in May, 1787, for the purpose of revising the Federal Constitution.

Whereas, in the formation of the Federal compact, which frames the bond of union of the American States, it was not possible in the infant state of our republic to devise a system which, in the course of time and experience, would not manifest imperfections that it would be necessary to reform.

And whereas the limited powers, which by the Articles of Confederation are vested in the Congress of the United States, have been found far inadequate to the enlarged purposes which they were intended to produce. And whereas Congress hath, by repeated and most urgent representations, endeavored to awaken this and other States of the Union to a sense of the truly critical and alarming situation in which they may inevitably be involved, unless timely measures be taken to enlarge the powers of Congress, that they may be thereby enabled to avert the danger which threaten our existence as a free and independent people. And whereas this State hath been ever desirous to act upon the liberal system of the general good of the United States, without circumscribing its views to the narrow and selfish objects of partial convenience, and has been at all times ready to make every concession to the safety and happiness of the whole, which justice and sound policy could vindicate.

Be it therefore enacted, by the Senate and House of Representatives in general court convened, that John Langdon, John Pickering, Nicholas Gilman, and Benjamin West, esqrs., be, and hereby are appointed commissioners; they, or any two of them, are hereby authorized and empowered, as deputies from this State, to meet at Philadelphia said convention, or any other place to which the convention may be adjourned, for the purposes aforesaid, there to confer with such deputies as are, or may be, appointed by the other States for similar purposes, and with them to discuss and decide upon the most effectual means to remedy the defects of our Federal Union, and to procure and secure the enlarged purposes which it was intended to effect, and to report such an act to the United States in Congress, as, when agreed to by them, and duly confirmed by the several States, will effectually provide for the same.

STATE OF NEW HAMPSHIRE.

IN THE HOUSE OF REPRESENTATIVES, JUNE 27, 1787.

The foregoing bill having been read a third time—voted, that it pass to be enacted. Sent up for concurrence.

JOHN SPARHAWK, *Speaker.*

In Senate, the same day: The bill having been read a third time, voted, that the same be enacted.

JOHN SULLIVAN, *President.*

Copy examined, per

JOSEPH PEARSON, *Secretary.* [L. S.]

---

16. In pursuance of the foregoing powers, the Delegates met in Convention at Philadelphia on the 14th day, being the second Monday in May, A. D. 1787, and on the 17th of September, 1787, agreed to the Constitution as contained in the preceding part of this compilation, [from page 1 to 23,] which they transmitted to the United States in Congress assembled, together with the following resolutions and letter:

IN CONVENTION, MONDAY, SEPTEMBER 17, 1787.

Present: The States of New Hampshire, Massachusetts, Connecticut, Mr. Hamilton from New York, New Jersey, Pennsylvania, Delaware, Maryland, Virginia, North Carolina, South Carolina, and Georgia.

Resolved, That the preceding Constitution be laid before the United States in Congress assembled, and that it is the opinion of this convention that it should afterwards be submitted to a convention of delegates, chosen in each State by the people thereof, under the recommendation of its legislature, for their assent and ratification; and that each convention, assenting to and ratifying the same, should give notice thereof, to the United States in Congress assembled.

Resolved, That it is the opinion of this convention, that as soon as the conventions of nine States shall have ratified this Constitution, the United States in Congress assembled should fix a day on which electors should be appointed by the States which shall have ratified the same, and a day on which the electors should assemble to vote for the President, and the time and place for commencing proceedings under this Constitution. That after such publication the electors should be appointed, and the Senators and Representatives elected; that the electors should meet on the day fixed for the election of the President, and should transmit their votes certified, signed, sealed, and directed, as the Constitution requires to the Secretary of the United States in Congress assembled; that the Senators and Representatives should convene at the time and place assigned; that the Senators should appoint a president of the Senate, for the sole purpose of receiving, opening, and counting the votes for President; and that, after he shall be chosen, the Congress, together with the President, should without delay, proceed to execute this Constitution.

By the unanimous order of the convention.

GEORGE WASHINGTON, *President.*

WILLIAM JACKSON, *Secretary.*

IN CONVENTION, SEPTEMBER 17, 1787.

SIR: We have now the honor to submit to the consideration of the United States in Congress assembled, that Constitution which has appeared to us the most advisable.

The friends of our country have long seen and desired that the power of making war, peace, and treaties, that of levying money and regulating commerce, and the correspondent executive and judicial authorities, should be fully and effectually vested in the General Government of the Union; but the impropriety of delegating such extensive trust to one body of men is evident: hence results the necessity of a different organization.

It is obviously impracticable, in the Federal Government of these States, to secure all rights of independent sovereignty to each, and yet provide for the interest and safety of all. Individuals entering into society must give up a share of liberty to preserve the rest. The magnitude of the sacrifice must depend as well on situation and circumstance as on the object to be obtained. It is at all times difficult to draw with precision the line between those rights which must be surrendered and those which may be reserved; and on the present occasion this difficulty was increased by a difference among the several States as to their situation, extent, habits, and particular interests.

In all our deliberations on this subject, we kept steadily in our view that which appears to us the greatest interest of every true American—the consolidation of our Union—in which is involved our prosperity, felicity, safety, perhaps our national existence. This important consideration, seriously and deeply impressed on our minds, led each State in the convention to be less rigid on points of inferior magnitude than might have been otherwise expected; and thus the Constitution which we now present is the result of a spirit of amity, and of that mutual deference and concession which the peculiarity of our political situation rendered indispensable.

That it will meet the full and entire approbation of every State, is not, perhaps, to be expected; but each will doubtless consider that, had her interest been alone consulted, the consequences might have been particularly disagreeable or injurious to others; that it is liable to as few exceptions as could reasonably have been expected, we hope and be lieve; that it may promote the lasting welfare of that country so dear to us all, and secure her freedom and happiness, is our most ardent wish.

With great respect, we have the honor to be, sir, your excellency's most obedient humble servants.

By unanimous order of the convention.

GEORGE WASHINGTON, *President*.

His excellency the PRESIDENT OF CONGRESS.

17. Whereupon Congress passed the following resolution:

UNITED STATES IN CONGRESS ASSEMBLED.

FRIDAY, SEPTEMBER 28, 1787.

Present: New Hampshire, Massachusetts, Connecticut, New York, New Jersey, Pennsylvania, Delaware, Virginia, North Carolina, South Carolina, and Georgia, and from Maryland Mr. Ross.

Congress having received the report of the convention lately assembled in Philadelphia—

Resolved, unanimously, That the said report, with the resolutions and letter accompanying the same, be transmitted to the several legislatures, in order to be submitted to a convention of delegates chosen in each State by the people thereof, in conformity to the resolves of the convention made and provided in that case.

18. The States having accordingly passed acts for severally calling conventions, and the Constitution having been submitted to them, was ratified by the conventions of the several States, at the dates respectively as stated on page 24 of this compilation.

THE UNITED STATES IN CONGRESS ASSEMBLED.

SATURDAY, SEPTEMBER 13, 1788.

Congress assembled. Present: New Hampshire, Massachusetts, Con necticut, New York, New Jersey, Pennsylvania, Virginia, North Carolina, South Carolina, and Georgia; and from Rhode Island Mr. Arnold, and from Delaware Mr. Kearny.

On the question to agree to the proposition which was yesterday postponed by the State of Delaware, the yeas and nays being required by Mr. Gilman—

New Hampshire	Mr. Gilman,	ay	ay
	Wingate,	ay	
Massachusetts	Mr. Dana,	ay	ay
	Thatcher,	ay	
Connecticut	Mr. Huntington,	ay	ay
	Wadsworth,	ay	
New York	Mr. Hamilton,	ay	ay
	Gansevoort,	ay	
New Jersey	Mr. Clarke,	ay	ay
	Dayton,	ay	
Pennsylvania	Mr. Irwine,	ay	ay
	Meredith,	ay	
	Armstrong,	ay	
	Read,	ay	
Virginia	Mr. Griffin,	ay	ay
	Madison,	ay	
	Carrington,	ay	
	Lee,	ay	
South Carolina	Mr. Parker,	ay	ay
	Tucker,	ay	
Georgia	Mr. Few,	ay	ay
	Baldwin,	ay	

So it was resolved in the affirmative, as follows:

Whereas the convention assembled in Philadelphia, pursuant to the resolution of Congress of the 21st of February, 1787, did, on the 17th of September in the same year, report to the United States in Congress assembled a Constitution for the people of the United States; whereupon Congress, on the 28th of the same September, did resolve, unanimously, "That the said report, with the resolutions and letter accompanying the same, be transmitted to the several legislatures, in order to be submitted to a convention of delegates, chosen in each State by the people thereof, in conformity to the resolves of the convention made and provided in that case:" And whereas the Constitution so reported by the convention, and by Congress transmitted to the several legislatures, has been ratified in the manner therein declared to be sufficient for the establishment of the same, and such ratifications, duly authenticated, have been received by Congress, and are filed in the office of the Secretary; therefore—

Resolved, That the first Wednesday in January next be the day for appointing electors in the several States, which, before the said day, shall have ratified the said Constitution; that the first Wednesday in

February next be the day for the electors to assemble in their respective States, and vote for a President; and that the first Wednesday in March next be the time, and the present seat of Congress (New York) the place, for commencing the proceedings under the said Constitution.

19. The elections were held in the several states for Electors, in conformity with the above resolution, and the Electors so appointed met as therein required, and voted for President and Vice President, (the result of whose votes will be seen in the first table of electoral votes contained in this volume,) and the several states having, in conformity with the Constitution, elected the Senators and Representatives to which they were respectively entitled, proceedings commenced under the Constitution on the first Wednesday, being the 4th day of March, 1789, by the meeting of the Senators and Representatives in Congress on that day, from the eleven states which had then ratified the Constitution; but a quorum not appearing in either House, the House of Representatives adjourned from day to day until Wednesday, the 1st of April, when a quorum, consisting of a majority of the whole number, appearing, they elected a speaker and clerk and proceeded to business; the Senate in like manner adjourned from day to day, until Monday, the 6th of April, when a quorum, consisting of a majority of the whole number of Senators, appearing, "the Senate proceeded, by ballot, to the choice of a President, for the sole purpose of opening and counting the votes for President of the United States." The Electoral votes were accordingly opened and counted on the 6th of April, 1789, in the presence of the Senate and House of Representatives, and it appeared that George Washington was unanimously elected President, and that John Adams was duly elected Vice President of the United States, agreeably to the Constitution. The Senate then elected a President pro tempore, the Vice President not being present, and also a secretary, and proceeded to business; and having taken the proper measures to notify the individuals elected, John Adams, Vice President, appeared and assumed the chair as President of the Senate on Tuesday the 21st of April. George Washington was introduced into the Senate Chamber, by the committee appointed for the purpose, on Thursday, April 30,

1789, and was attended to the gallery in front of the Senate Chamber by the Vice President and Senators, the Speaker and Representatives and other public characters present. The oath required by the Constitution was then administered to him by the Chancellor of the State of New York, who proclaimed, "Long live George Washington, President of the United States," after which the President returned to the Senate Chamber and delivered his inaugural address to the Senate and House of Representatives.

Thus commenced the proceedings of the Constitutional Government of the United States of America. The Executive and Legislative branches so installed, possessed from that time, under the Constitution, the power to make laws and appoint all the officers necessary to constitute the Judiciary Branch, as well as all the Executive Departments and subordinate offices, both civil and military; all of which was effected in a convenient and proper time, and the whole system, then for the first time put in motion, has continued to operate, improve, and mature, until it has acquired a capacity, stability, and power adequate to its own security and preservation, and to the protection of the rights, the honor, and interest of its citizens over the entire surface of the globe, as well as to the preservation of the lives, the liberty, and happiness of its people at home; illustrating all the attributes of a good government, and proving incontestably the value and excellence of our own Constitution.

CHAPTER 3.

PROCEEDINGS IN THE CONGRESS OF THE UNITED COLONIES RESPECTING "A DECLARATION OF INDEPENDENCE, BY THE REPRESENTATIVES OF THE UNITED STATES OF AMERICA, IN CONGRESS ASSEMBLED."

IN THE CONGRESS OF THE UNITED COLONIES.

SATURDAY, JUNE 8, 1776.

Resolved, That the resolutions respecting independency be referred to a committee of the whole Congress.

The Congress then resolved itself into a committee of the whole; and, after some time, the President resumed the chair, and Mr. Harrison reported, that the committee have taken into consideration the matter to them referred, but not having come to any resolution thereon, directed him to move for leave to sit again on Monday.

Resolved, That this Congress will, on Monday next, at 10 o'clock, resolve itself into a committee of the whole, to take into their farther consideration the resolutions referred to them.

MONDAY, JUNE 10, 1776.

Agreeable to order, the Congress resolved itself into a committee of the whole, to take into their further consideration the resolutions to them referred; and, after some time spent thereon, the President resumed the chair, and Mr. Harrison reported, that the committee have had under consideration the matters referred to them, and have come to a resolution thereon, which they directed him to report.

The resolution agreed to in committee of the whole being read,

Resolved, That the consideration of the first resolution be postponed to Monday, the first day of July next; and in the meanwhile, that no time be lost, in case the Congress agree thereto, that a committee be appointed to prepare a declaration to the effect of the said first resolution, which is in these words: "That these United Colonies are, and of right ought to be, free and independent States; that they are absolved from all allegiance to the British crown: and that all political connexion between them and the State of Great Britain is, and ought to be, totally dissolved."

TUESDAY, JUNE 11, 1776.

Resolved, That the committee, for preparing the Declaration, consist of five:—The members chosen, Mr. Jefferson, Mr. John Adams, Mr. Franklin, Mr. Sherman, and Mr. R. R. Livingston.

TUESDAY, JUNE 25, 1776.

A declaration of the deputies of Pennsylvania, met in Provincial Conference, was laid before Congress, and read, expressing their willingness to concur in a vote of Congress, declaring the United Colonies free and independent States.

FRIDAY, JUNE 28, 1776.

"Francis Hopkinson, one of the delegates from New Jersey, attended, and produced the credentials of their appointment," containing the following instructions:—"If you shall judge it necessary or expedient for this purpose, we empower you to join in declaring the United Colonies independent of Great Britain, entering into a confederation for union and common defence," &c.

MONDAY, JULY 1, 1776.

'A resolution of the convention of Maryland, passed the 28th of June, was laid before Congress and read," containing the following instructions to their deputies in Congress:—"That the deputies of said colony, or any three or more of them, be authorized and empowered to concur with the other United Colonies, or a majority of them, in declaring the United Colonies free and independent States; in forming such further compact and confederation between them," &c.

The order of the day being read,

Resolved, That this Congress will resolve itself into a committee of the whole, to take into consideration the resolution respecting independency.

That the declaration be referred to said committee.

The Congress resolved itself into a committee of the whole. After some time the President resumed the chair, and Mr. Harrison reported, that the committee had come to a resolution, which they desired him to report, and to move for leave to sit again.

The resolution agreed to by the committee of the whole being read, the determination thereof was, at the request of a colony, postponed until to-morrow.

Resolved, That this Congress will, to-morrow, resolve itself into a committee of the whole, to take into consideration the declaration respecting independence.

TUESDAY, JULY 2, 1776.

The Congress resumed the consideration of the resolution reported from the committee of the whole; which was agreed to as follows:

Resolved, That these United Colonies are, and, of right, ought to be, Free and independent States; that they are absolved from all allegiance to the British crown, and that all political connexion between them, and the State of Great Britain, is, and ought to be, totally dissolved.

Agreeable to the order of the day, the Congress resolved itself into a committee of the whole; and, after some time, the President resumed the chair, and Mr. Harrison reported, that the committee have had under consideration the declaration to them referred; but, not having had time to go through the same, desired him to move for leave to sit again.

Resolved, That this Congress will, to-morrow, again resolve itself into a committee of the whole, to take into their further consideration the declaration respecting independence.

WEDNESDAY, JULY 3, 1776.

Agreeable to the order of the day, the Congress resolved itself into a committee of the whole, to take into their farther consideration the declaration; and, after some time, the President resumed the chair, and Mr. Harrison reported, that the committee, not having yet gone through it, desired leave to sit again.

Resolved, That this Congress will, to-morrow, again resolve itself into a committee of the whole, to take into their farther consideration the Declaration of Independence.

THURSDAY, JULY 4, 1776.

Agreeably to the order of the day, the Congress resolved itself into a committee of the whole, to take into their farther consideration the Declaration; and after some time the President resumed the chair, and Mr. Harrison reported that the committee had agreed to a declaration, which they desired him to report.

The Declaration being read, was agreed to as follows:

A Declaration by the Representatives of the United States of America, in Congress assembled.

When, in the course of human events, it becomes necessary for one people to dissolve the political bands which have connected them with another, and to assume, among the powers of the earth, the separate and equal station to which the laws of nature and of nature's God entitle them, a decent respect to the opinions of mankind requires that they should declare the causes which impel them to the separation.

We hold these truths to be self-evident, that all men are created equal; that they are endowed by their Creator with certain unalienable rights; that among these, are life, liberty, and the pursuit of happiness. That, to secure these rights, governments are instituted among men, deriving their just powers from the consent of the governed; that, whenever any form of government becomes destructive of these ends, it is the right of the people to alter or to abolish it, and to institute a new government, laying its foundation on such principles, and organizing its powers in such form, as to them shall seem most likely to effect their safety and happiness. Prudence, indeed, will dictate that governments long established, should not be changed for light and transient causes; and, accordingly, all experience hath shown, that mankind are more disposed to suffer, while evils are sufferable, than to right themselves by abolishing the forms to which they are accustomed. But, when a long train of abuses and usurpations, pursuing invariably the same object, evinces a design to reduce them under absolute despotism, it is their right, it is their duty, to throw off such government, and to provide new guards for their future security. Such has been the patient sufferance of these colonies, and such is now the necessity which constrains them to alter their former systems of government. The history of the present king of Great Britain is a history of repeated injuries and usurpations, all having, in direct object, the establishment of an absolute tyranny over these States. To prove this, let facts be submitted to a candid world:

He has refused his assent to laws the most wholesome and necessary for the public good.

He has forbidden his Governors to pass laws of immediate and pressing importance, unless suspended in their operation till his assent should be obtained; and, when so suspended, he has utterly neglected to attend to them.

He has refused to pass other laws for the accommodation of large districts of people, unless those people would relinquish the right of representation in the legislature; a right inestimable to them, and formidable to tyrants only.

He has called together legislative bodies at places unusual, uncomfortable, and distant from the depository of their public records, for the sole purpose of fatiguing them into compliance with his measures.

He has dissolved representative houses repeatedly, for opposing, with manly firmness, his invasions on the rights of the people.

He has refused, for a long time after such dissolutions, to cause others to be elected; whereby the legislative powers, incapable of annihilation, have returned to the people at large for their exercise; the State remaining, in the mean time, exposed to all the danger of invasion from without, and convulsions within.

He has endeavored to prevent the population of these States; for that purpose, obstructing the laws for naturalization of foreigners; refusing to pass others to encourage their migration hither, and raising the conditions of new appropriations of lands.

He has obstructed the administration of justice, by refusing his assent to laws for establishing judiciary powers.

He has made judges dependent on his will alone, for the tenure of their offices, and the amount and payment of their salaries.

He has erected a multitude of new offices, and sent hither swarms of officers to harass our people, and eat out their substance.

He has kept among us, in times of peace, standing armies, without the consent of our legislature.

He has affected to render the military independent of, and superior to, the civil power.

He has combined, with others, to subject us to a jurisdiction foreign to our constitution, and unacknowledged by our laws; giving his assent to their acts of pretended legislation:

For quartering large bodies of armed troops among us:

For protecting them, by a mock trial, from punishment, for any murders which they should commit on the inhabitants of these States:

For cutting off our trade with all parts of the world:

For imposing taxes on us without our consent:

For depriving us, in many cases, of the benefits of trial by jury:

For transporting us beyond seas to be tried for pretended offences:

For abolishing the free system of English laws in a neighboring province, establishing therein an arbitrary government, and enlarging its boundaries, so as to render it at once an example and fit instrument for introducing the same absolute rule into these colonies:

For taking away our charters, abolishing our most valuable laws, and altering, fundamentally, the powers of our governments:

For suspending our own legislatures, and declaring themselves invested with power to legislate for us in all cases whatsoever.

He has abdicated government here, by declaring us out of his protection, and waging war against us.

He has plundered our seas, ravaged our coasts, burnt our towns, and destroyed the lives of our people.

He is, at this time, transporting large armies of foreign mercenaries to complete the works of death, desolation, and tyranny, already begun, with circumstances of cruelty and perfidy scarcely paralleled in the most barbarous ages, and totally unworthy the head of a civilized nation.

He has constrained our fellow-citizens, taken captive on the high seas, to bear arms against their country, to become the executioners of their friends and brethren, or to fall themselves by their hands.

He has excited domestic insurrections amongst us, and has endeavored to bring on the inhabitants of our frontiers, the merciless Indian savages, whose known rule of warfare is an undistinguished destruction, of all ages, sexes, and conditions.

In every stage of these oppressions, we have petitioned for redress, in the most humble terms; our repeated petitions have been answered only by repeated injury. A prince, whose character is thus marked by every act which may define a tyrant, is unfit to be the ruler of a free people.

Nor have we been wanting in attention to our British brethren. We have warned them, from time to time, of attempts made by their legislature to extend an unwarrantable jurisdiction over us. We have reminded them of the circumstances of our emigration and settlement here. We have appealed to their native justice and magnanimity, and we have conjured them, by the ties of our common kindred, to disavow these usurpations, which would inevitably interrupt our connections and correspondence. They, too, have been deaf to the voice of justice and consanguinity. We must, therefore, acquiesce in the necessity, which denounces our separation, and hold them, as we hold the rest of mankind, enemies in war, in peace, friends.

We, therefore, the representatives of the UNITED STATES OF AMERICA, in GENERAL CONGRESS assembled, appealing to the Supreme Judge of the World for the rectitude of our intentions, do, in the name, and by the authority of the good people of these colonies, solemnly publish and declare, That these United Colonies are, and of right ought to be, **Free and Independent States**; that they are absolved from all allegiance to the British crown, and that all political connexion between them and the state of Great Britain, is, and ought to be, totally dissolved; and that, as *FREE AND INDEPENDENT STATES*, they have full power to levy war, conclude peace, contract alliances, establish commerce, and to do all other acts and things which INDEPENDENT STATES may of right do. And, for the support of this declaration, with a firm reliance on the protection of **DIVINE PROVIDENCE**, we mutually pledge to each other, our lives, our fortunes, and our sacred honor.

The foregoing declaration was, by order of Congress, engrossed, and signed by the following members:

JOHN HANCOCK.

New Hampshire.
Josiah Bartlett,
William Whipple,
Matthew Thornton.

Massachusetts Bay.
Samuel Adams,
John Adams,
Robert Treat Paine,
Elbridge Gerry.

Rhode Island.
Stephen Hopkins,
William Ellery.

Connecticut.
Roger Sherman,
Samuel Huntington,
William Williams,
Oliver Wolcott.

New York.
William Floyd,
Philip Livingston,
Francis Lewis,
Lewis Morris.

New Jersey.
Richard Stockton,
John Witherspoon,
Francis Hopkinson,
John Hart,
Abraham Clark.

Pennsylvania.
Robert Morris,
Benjamin Rush,
Benjamin Franklin,
John Morton,
George Clymer,
James Smith,
George Taylor,
James Wilson,
George Ross.

Delaware.
Cæsar Rodney,
George Read,
Thomas M'Kean.

Maryland.
Samuel Chase,
William Paca,
Thomas Stone,
Charles Carroll,of Carrollton

Virginia.
George Wythe,
Richard Henry Lee,
Thomas Jefferson,
Benjamin Harrison,
Thomas Nelson, jun.
Francis Lightfoot Lee,
Carter Braxton.

North Carolina.
William Hooper,
Joseph Hewes,
John Penn.

South Carolina.
Edward Rutledge,
Thomas Heyward, jun.
Thomas Lynch, jun.
Arthur Middleton.

Georgia.
Button Gwinnett,
Lyman Hall,
George Walton.

Resolved, That copies of the Declaration be sent to the several assemblies, conventions, and committees, or councils of safety, and to the several commanding officers of the continental troops; that it be proclaimed in each of the United States, and at the head the army.

CHAPTER 4.

PROMINENT POLITICAL ACTS OF

GEORGE WASHINGTON.

Appointment of George Washington to be commander-in-chief of the army, by the Congress of the Confederation, on the 15th June, 1775.

THURSDAY, JUNE 15, 1775.

Agreeable to order, the Congress resolved itself into a Committee of the Whole, and, after some time, the President resumed the chair, and Mr. Ward reported that the committee had come to some farther resolutions, which he was ordered to report.

The report of the committee being read and considered,

Resolved, That a general be appointed to command all the Continental forces raised, or to be raised, for the defence of American liberty.

That five hundred dollars per month be allowed for the pay and expenses of the general.

The Congress then proceeded to the choice of a general, by ballot, and George Washington, esq., was unanimously elected.

FRIDAY, JUNE 16, 1775.

Met according to adjournment. [The Delegates from the Colonies of New Hampshire, Massachusetts Bay, Connecticut, New York, New Jersey, Pennsylvania, Delaware counties, Maryland, Virginia, North Carolina, and South Carolina, being present.]

The President informed Colonel Washington that the Congress had yesterday unanimously made choice of him to be general and commander-in-chief of the American forces, and requested he would accept of that employment; to which Colonel Washington, standing in his place, answered:

"MR. PRESIDENT:

"Though I am truly sensible of the high honor done me, in this appointment, yet I feel great distress, from consciousness that my abilities and military experience may not be equal to the extensive and important trust: However, as the Congress desire it, I will enter upon the momentous duty, and exert every power I possess in tneir service, and for support of the glorious cause. I beg they will accept my most cordial thanks for this distinguished testimony of their approbation.

"But, lest some unlucky event should happen, unfavorable to my reputation, I beg it may be remembered, by every gentleman in the room, that I, this day, declare with the utmost sincerity, I do not think myself equal to the command I am honored with.

"As to pay, sir, I beg leave to assure the Congress, that, as no pecuniary consideration could have tempted me to accept this arduous employment, at the expense of my domestic ease and happiness, I do not wish to make any profit from it. I will keep an exact account of my expenses. Those, I doubt not, they will discharge, and that is all I desire."

Resolved, That a committee be appointed to draught a commission and instructions for the general.

The persons chosen to compose the committee, were Mr. Lee, Mr. E. Rutledge, and Mr. J. Adams.

SATURDAY, JUNE 17, 1775.

Met according to adjournment.

The committee appointed to draught a commission to the general reported the same, which, being read by paragraphs and debated, was agreed to as follows:

IN CONGRESS.

The delegates of the United Colonies of New Hampshire, Massachusetts Bay, Rhode Island, Connecticut, New York, New Jersey, Pennsylvania, the counties of Newcastle, Kent, and Sussex, on Delaware, Maryland, Virginia, North Carolina, and South Carolina:

TO GEORGE WASHINGTON, ESQ.

We, reposing special trust and confidence in your patriotism, valor, conduct, and fidelity, do, by these presents, constitute and appoint you to be general and commander-in-chief of the army of the United Colonies, and of all the forces now raised, or to be raised by them, and of all others who shall voluntarily offer their service, and join the said army for the defence of American liberty, and for repelling every hostile invasion thereof: And you are hereby vested with full power and authority to act as you shall think for the good and welfare of the service.

And we do hereby strictly charge and require all officers and soldiers, under your command, to be obedient to your orders, and diligent in the exercise of their several duties.

And we do also enjoin and require you, to be careful in executing the great trust reposed in you, by causing strict discipline and order to be observed in the army, and that the soldiers be duly exercised, and provided with all convenient necessaries.

And you are to regulate your conduct in every respect by the rules and discipline of war, (as herewith given you,) and punctually to observe and follow such orders and directions, from time to time, as you shall receive from this, or a future Congress of these United Colonies, or committee of Congress.

This commission to continue in force until revoked by this, or a future Congress.

By order of the Congress,

Ordered, That the same be fairly transcribed, signed by the President, attested by the secretary, and delivered to the general.

Resolved unanimously, Whereas, the delegates of all the Colonies, from Nova Scotia to Georgia, in Congress assembled, have unanimously chosen George Washington, esq., to be general and commander-in-chief of such forces as are, or shall be, raised for the maintenance and preservation of American liberty; this Congress doth now declare, that they will maintain and assist him, and adhere to him, the said George Washington, with their lives and fortunes in the same cause.

Address of the President of Congress to George Washington, and his reply, 26th August, 1783:

MONDAY, AUGUST 25, 1783.

Congress being informed of the arrival of the commander-in-chief in the neighborhood of Princeton:

Ordered, That he have an audience in Congress to-morrow at twelve o'clock.

TUESDAY, AUGUST 26, 1783.

According to order, General Washington attended, and being introduced by two members, the President addressed him as follows:

SIR: Congress feel particular pleasure in seeing your excellency, and in congratulating you on the success of a war, in which you have acted so conspicuous a part.

It has been the singular happiness of the United States, that during a war so long, so dangerous, and so important, Providence has been graciously pleased to preserve the life of a general, who has merited and possessed the uninterrupted confidence and affection of his fellow-citizens. In other nations many have performed services, for which they have deserved and received the thanks of the public. But to you, sir, peculiar praise is due. Your services have been essential in acquiring and establishing the freedom and independence of your country. They deserve the grateful acknowledgments of a free and independent nation. Those acknowledgments Congress have the satisfaction of expressing to your excellency.

Hostilities have now ceased, but your country still needs your services. She wishes to avail herself of your talents in forming the arrangements which will be necessary for her in the time of peace. For this reason your attendance at Congress has been requested. A committee is appointed to confer with your excellency, and to receive your assistance in preparing and digesting plans relative to those important objects.

To which his excellency made the following reply:

Mr. President: I am too sensible of the honorable reception I have now experienced, not to be penetrated with the deepest feelings of gratitude.

Notwithstanding Congress appear to estimate the value of my life beyond any services I have been able to render the United States, yet I must be permitted to consider the wisdom and unanimity of our national councils, the firmness of our citizens, and the patience and bravery of our troops, which have produced so happy a termination of the war, as the most conspicuous effect of the divine interposition and the surest presage of our future happiness.

Highly gratified by the favorable sentiments which Congress are pleased to express of my past conduct, and amply rewarded by the confidence and affection of my fellow-citizens, I cannot hesitate to contribute my best endeavors towards the establishment of the national security in whatever manner the sovereign power may think proper to direct, until the ratification of the definitive treaty of peace, or the final evacuation of our country by the British forces; after either of which events, I shall ask permission to retire to the peaceful shade of private life.

Perhaps, sir, no occasion may offer more suitable than the present to express my humble thanks to God, and my grateful acknowledgments to my country, for the great and uniform support I have received in every vicissitude of fortune, and for the many distinguished honors which Congress have been pleased to confer upon me in the course of the war.

Resignation, by George Washington, of the office of commander in-chief, to Congress, and answer of the President of Congress, 23d December, 1783.

SATURDAY, DECEMBER 20, 1783.

Congress assembled: Present, New Hampshire, Massachusetts, Rhode Island, Pennsylvania, Delaware, Maryland, Virginia, North Carolina, and South Carolina.

A letter, of this day, from the commander-in-chief, was read, informing Congress of his arrival in this city, with the intention of asking leave to resign the commission he has the honor of holding in their service, and desiring to know their pleasure in what manner it will be most proper to offer his resignation; whether in writing or at an audience. Whereupon,

Resolved, That his excellency, the commander-in-chief, be admitted to a public audience, on Tuesday next, at twelve o'clock.

Resolved, That a public entertainment be given to the commander-in-chief on Monday next.

TUESDAY, DECEMBER 23, 1783.

Congress assembled: Present as before.

According to order, his excellency the commander-in-chief was admitted to a public audience, and being seated, the President, after a pause, informed him, that the United States in Congress assembled were prepared to receive his communications: Whereupon he arose, and addressed as follows:

[To revive the recollection of this scene, and to renew, in the breasts of the American people, the emotions of gratitude, affection, and veneration, that swelled the hearts of Statesmen, Legislators, Warriors, and other citizens, on that ever-memorable occasion, much care has been taken to bring here to view the living Washington as he then appeared in the Congress Hall. Fortunately, the affectionate providence of his native state secured, in the best manner, the means of transmitting the semblance of those venerated features and form to posterity. The marble statue by Houdon, in the state-house at Richmond, is the most authentic likeness of George Washington extant; from this has been taken all that could be obtained from marble, the rest has been derived from the best paintings, and both combined by the artist who has produced this copy.

The sword is taken from the *original*, now in the Patent Office at Washington. Washington is here represented in the manner that he desired to be, as will be seen by the following memoranda and correspondence:

By the Legislature of Virginia, on Tuesday, the 22d June, 1784, it was

Resolved, That the executive be requested to take measures for procuring a statue of General Washington, to be of the finest marble and the best workmanship, with the following inscription on its pedestal:

THE GENERAL ASSEMBLY OF THE COMMONWEALTH OF VIRGINIA
HAVE CAUSED THIS STATUE TO BE ERECTED
AS A MONUMENT OF AFFECTION AND GRATITUDE TO
GEORGE WASHINGTON;
WHO,
UNITING TO THE ENDOWMENTS OF THE HERO THE VIRTUES OF THE PATRIOT,
AND EXERTING BOTH IN ESTABLISHING THE LIBERTIES OF HIS COUNTRY,
HAS RENDERED HIS NAME DEAR TO HIS FELLOW CITIZENS,
AND GIVEN THE WORLD AN IMMORTAL EXAMPLE
OF TRUE GLORY.

[Tradition says that this brief but noble tribute was penned by James Madison on his knee, in the midst of the legislature of Virginia, of which he was then a member.]

Accordingly Governor Harrison applied to Mr. Jefferson and Dr. Franklin, then in Paris, to engage a statuary. Mr. Houdon was engaged, and came to America, in 1785, in the same vessel with Dr. Franklin. He took from Mr. Jefferson a letter to Washington, from which the following is an extract:

FROM JEFFERSON TO WASHINGTON.

"*Paris*, 10 July, 1785

"Mr. Houdon would much sooner have had the honor of attending you, but for a spell of sickness, which long induced us to despair of his recovery, and from which he is but recently recovered. He comes now, for the purpose of lending the aid of his art to transmit you to posterity. He is without rivalship in it, being employed from all parts of Europe in whatever is capital. He has had a difficulty to withdraw himself from an order of the Empress of Russia; a difficulty, however, that arose from a desire to show her respect, but which never gave him a moment's hesitation about his present voyage, which he considers as promising the brightest chapter of his history. I have spoken of him as an artist only; but I can assure you also, that, as a man, he is disinterested, generous, candid, and panting for glory: in every circumstance meriting your good opinion. He will have need to see you much while he shall have the honor of being with you; which you can the more freely admit, as his eminence and merit give him admission into genteel societies here."

FROM WASHINGTON TO HOUDON

"*Mount Vernon*, 26 September, 1785.

"Sir,—By a letter, which I have lately had the honor to receive from Dr. Franklin, at Philadelphia, I am informed of your arrival at that place. Many letters from very respectable characters in France, as well as the Doctor's, inform me of the occasion; for which, though the cause is not of my seeking, I feel the most agreeable and grateful sensations. I wish the object of your mission had been more worthy of the masterly genius of the first statuary in Europe; for thus you are represented to me.

"It will give me pleasure, sir, to welcome you to this seat of my retirement; and whatever I have, or can procure, that is necessary to your purposes, or convenient and agreeable to your wishes, you must freely command, as inclination to oblige you will be among the last things in which I shall be found deficient, either on your arrival or during your stay.

"With sentiments of esteem, I am, sir," &c.

The artist reached Mount Vernon on the 3d of October, where he spent a fortnight, devoted to the purpose of his visit.

FROM JEFFERSON TO WASHINGTON.

"*Paris*, 4 January, 1786.

"I have been honored with your letter of September the 26th, which was delivered me by Mr. Houdon, who is safely returned. He has brought with him the mould of the face only, having left the other parts of his work with his workmen to come by some other conveyance. Dr. Franklin, who was joined with me in the superintendence of this just monument, having left us before what is calle the costume of the statue was decided on, I cannot so well satisfy myself, and I am persuaded I should not so well satisfy the world, as by consulting your own wish or inclination as to this article. Permit me, therefore, to ask you whether there is any particular dress, or any particular attitude, which you would rather wish to be adopted. I shall take a singular pleasure in having your own idea executed, if you will be so good as to make it known to me."

FROM WASHINGTON TO JEFFERSON.

"*Mount Vernon*, 1 August, 1786.

"In answer to your obliging inquiries respecting the dress and attitude, which I would wish to have given to the statue in question, I have only to observe, that, not having sufficient knowledge in the art of sculpture to oppose my judgment to the taste of connoisseurs, I do not desire to dictate in the matter. On the contrary, I shall be perfectly satisfied with whatever may be judged decent and proper. I should even scarcely have ventured to suggest, that perhaps a servile adherence to the garb of antiquity might not be altogether so expedient, as some little deviation *in favor of the modern costume*, if I had not learnt from Colonel Humphreys, that this was a circumstance hinted in conversation by Mr. West to Mr. Houdon. The taste, which has been introduced in painting by West, I understand is received with applause, and prevails extensively."

FROM JEFFERSON TO WASHINGTON.

"*Paris*, 14 August, 1787.

"I was happy to find, by the letter of August 1st, 1786, which you did me the honor to write to me, that *the modern dress for your statue would meet your approbation.* I found it strongly the sentiment of West, Copley, Trumbull, and Brown, in London; after which it would be ridiculous to add, that it was my own."

This work, therefore, purports to be an exact *portrait* statue of Washington,—an authentic historical monument,—*the costume being that in which he was accustomed to appear as Commander-in-chief.* No other statue was ever made from his person. This was modelled about two years after the close of his military career, in the fifty-fourth year of his age, a circumstance to be borne in mind in comparing it with later portraits. How well, in point of resemblance, it satisfied his contemporaries and associates, may be judged from the strong declaration of Judge Marshall to the person (Jared Sparks) to whom the world is indebted for the erection of Washington's *literary* monument,—that, to a spectator standing on the right hand of the statue, and taking a half-front view, "it represented the original as perfectly as a living man could be represented in marble."]

Mr. President: The great events on which my resignation depended having at length taken place, I have now the honor of offering my sincere congratulations to Congress, and of presenting myself before them, to surrender into their hands the trust committed to me, and to claim the indulgence of retiring from the service of my country.

Happy in the confirmation of our independence and sovereignty, and pleased with the opportunity afforded the United States of becoming a respectable nation, I resign with satisfaction the appointment I accepted, with diffidence; a diffidence in my abilities to accomplish so arduous a task; which however was superseded by a confidence in the rectitude of our cause, the support of the supreme power of the Union, and the patronage of Heaven.

The successful termination of the war has verified the most sanguine expectations; and my gratitude for the interposition of Providence, and the assistance I have received from my countrymen, increases with every review of the momentous contest.

While I repeat my obligations to the army in general, I should do injustice to my own feelings not to acknowledge, in this place, the peculiar services and distinguished merits of the gentlemen who have been attached to my person during the war. It was impossible the choice of confidential officers to compose my family should have been more fortunate. Permit me, sir, to recommend, in particular, those who have continued in the service to the present moment, as worthy of the favorable notice and patronage of Congress.

I consider it an indispensable duty to close this last act of my official life by commending the interests of our dearest country to the protection of Almighty God, and

Lith. by A. Hoen & Co. Balt.

those who have the superintendence of them to his holy keeping.

Having now finished the work assigned me, I retire from the great theatre of action, and bidding an affectionate farewell to this august body, under whose orders I have so long acted, I here offer my commission, and take my leave of all the employments of public life.

He then advanced and delivered to the President his commission, with a copy of his address, and having resumed his place, the President (THOMAS MIFFLIN) returned him the following answer:

SIR: The United States in Congress assembled receive, with emotions too affecting for utterance, the solemn resignation of the authorities under which you have led their troops with success through a perilous and doubtful war. Called upon by your country to defend its invaded rights, you accepted the sacred charge, before it had formed alliances, and whilst it was without funds or a government to support you. You have conducted the great military contest with wisdom and fortitude, invariably regarding the rights of the civil power through all disasters and changes. You have, by the love and confidence of your fellow-citizens, enabled them to display their martial genius, and transmit their fame to posterity. You have persevered till these United States, aided by a magnanimous king and nation, have been enabled, under a just Providence, to close the war in freedom, safety, and independence; on which happy event we sincerely join you in congratulations.

Having defended the standard of liberty in this new world; having taught a lesson useful to those who inflict and to those who feel oppression, you retire from the great theatre of action, with the blessings of your fellow-citizens; but the glory of your virtues will not terminate with your military command; it will continue to animate remotest ages.

We feel with you our obligations to the army in general, and will particularly charge ourselves with the interests of those confidential officers, who have attended your person to this affecting moment.

We join you in commending the interests of our dearest country to the protection of Almighty God, beseeching him to dispose the hearts and minds of its citizens to improve the opportunity afforded them of becoming a happy and respectable nation. And for you we address to him our earnest prayers, that a life so beloved may be fostered with all his care; that your days may be happy as they have been illustrious; and that he will finally give you that reward which this world cannot give

ELECTION OF GEORGE WASHINGTON AS PRESIDENT OF THE UNITED STATES, AND HIS INAUGURAL ADDRESS.

MONDAY, APRIL 6, 1789.

The President of the Senate, elected for the purpose of counting the votes, declared to the Senate, that the Senate and House of Representatives had met, and that he, in their presence, had opened and counted the votes of the Electors for President and Vice President of the United States; whereby it appears that

GEORGE WASHINGTON was unanimously elected President.

Whereupon the following certificate and letter, prepared by a committee, consisting of Messrs. Paterson, Johnson, Lee, and Ellsworth, were adopted by the Senate, and signed by their President.

Be it known, That the Senate and House of Representatives of the United States of America, being convened in the city and State of New York, the sixth day of April, in the Year of our Lord one thousand seven hundred and eighty-nine, the underwritten, appointed President of the Senate, for the sole purpose of receiving, opening, and counting the votes of the Electors, did, in the presence of the said Senate and House of Representatives, open all the certificates, and count all the votes of the Electors for a President and for a Vice President; by which it appears that GEORGE WASHINGTON, esq., was unanimously elected, agreeably to the Constitution, to the office of President of the United States of America.

In testimony whereof, I have hereunto set my hand and seal.

JOHN LANGDON.

NEW YORK, April 6, 1789.

SIR: I have the honor to transmit to your Excellency the information of your unanimous election to the office of President of the United States of America. Suffer me, sir, to indulge the hope, that so auspicious a mark of public confidence will meet your approbation, and be considered as a sure pledge of the affection and support you are to expect from a free and enlightened people.

I am, sir, with sentiments of respect, your obedient humble servant,

JOHN LANGDON.

To his Ex'cy GEORGE WASHINGTON, esq.

Thursday, April 30, 1789.

The oath of office having been administered by the Chancellor of the State of New York, in the presence of the Senate and House of Representatives, to George Washington, President of the United States, he then made the following Inaugural address:

Fellow-Citizens of the Senate, and
of the House of Representatives:

Among the vicissitudes incident to life, no event could have filled me with greater anxieties than that of which the notification was transmitted by your order, and received on the 14th day of the present month. On the one hand, I was summoned by my country, whose voice I can never hear but with veneration and love, from a retreat which I had chosen with the fondest predilection, and, in my flattering hopes, with an immutable decision, as the asylum of my declining years; a retreat which was rendered every day more necessary, as well as more dear to me, by the addition of habit to inclination, and of frequent interruptions in my health, to the gradual waste committed on it by time. On the other hand, the magnitude and difficulty of the trust to which the voice of my country called me, being sufficient to awaken in the wisest and most experienced of her citizens a distrustful scrutiny into his qualifications, could not but overwhelm with despondence one, who, inheriting inferior endowments from nature, and unpractised in the duties of civil administration, ought to be peculiarly conscious of his own deficiencies. In this conflict of emotions, all I dare aver, is, that it has been my faithful study to collect my duty from a just appreciation of every circumstance by which it might be affected. All I dare hope, is, that if, in executing this task, I have been too much swayed by a grateful remembrance of former instances, or by an affectionate sensibility to this transcendent proof of the confidence of my fellow-citizens, and have thence too little consulted my incapacity as well as disinclination for the weighty and untried cares before me, my error will be palliated by the motives which misled me, and its consequences be judged by my country, with some share of the partiality in which they originated.

Such being the impressions under which I have, in obedience to the public summons, repaired to the present station, it would be peculiarly improper to omit, in this first official act, my fervent supplications to that Almighty Being who rules over the universe—who presides in the councils of nations—and whose providential aids can supply every human defect, that his benediction may consecrate to the liberties and happiness of the people of the United States, a government instituted by themselves for these essential purposes: and may enable every instrument employed in its administration to execute with success the functions allotted to his charge. In tendering this homage to the Great Author of every public and private good, I assure myself that it expresses your sentiments not less than my own; nor those of my fellow-citizens at large, less than either. No people can be bound to acknowledge and adore the invisible hand which conducts the affairs of men, more than the people of the United States. Every step by which they have advanced to the character of an independent nation, seems to have been distinguished by some token of providential agency; and in the important revolution just accomplished in the system of their united government, the tranquil deliberations, and voluntary consent of so many distinct communities, from which the event has resulted, cannot be compared with the means by which most governments have been established, without some return of pious gratitude, along with an humble anticipation of the future blessings which the past seem to presage. These reflections, arising out of the present crisis, have forced themselves too strongly on my mind to be suppressed. You will join with me, I trust, in thinking that there are none, under the influence of which the proceedings of a new and free government can more auspiciously commence.

By the article establishing the executive department, it is made the duty of the President "to recommend to your consideration such measures as he shall judge necessary and expedient." The circumstances under which I now meet you will acquit me from entering into that subject, farther than to refer to the great constitutional charter under which you are assembled; and which, in defining your powers, designates the objects to which your attention is to be given. It will be more consistent with those circumstances, and far more congenial with the feelings which actuate me, to substitute, in place of a recommendation of particular measures, the tribute that is due to the talents, the rectitude, and the patriotism, which adorn the characters selected to devise and adopt them. In these honourable qualifications I behold the surest pledges that, as on one side, no local prejudices or attachments, no separate views, nor party animosities, will misdirect the comprehensive and equal eye which ought to watch over this great assemblage of communities and interests; so, on another, that the foundations of our national policy will be laid in the pure and immutable principles of private morality; and the pre-eminence of free government be exemplified by all the attributes which can win the affections of its citizens, and command the respect of the world. I dwell on this prospect with every satisfaction which an ardent love for my country can inspire: since there is no truth more thoroughly established, than that there exists in the economy and course of nature an indissoluble union between virtue and happiness—between duty and advantage—between the genuine maxims of an honest and magnanimous policy, and the solid rewards of public prosperity and felicity; since we ought to be no less persuaded that the propitious smiles of Heaven can never be expected on a nation that disregards the eternal rules of order and right, which Heaven itself has ordained; and since the preservation of the sacred fire of liberty, and the destiny of the republican model of government, are justly considered as deeply, perhaps as finally, staked, on the experiment entrusted to the hands of the American people.

Besides the ordinary objects submitted to your care, it will remain with your judgment to decide, how far an exercise of the occasional power delegated by the fifth article of the Constitution is rendered expedient at the present juncture, by the nature of objections which have been urged against the system, or by the degree of inquietude which has given birth to them. Instead of undertaking particular recommendations on this subject, in which I could be guided by no lights derived from official opportunities, I shall again give way to my entire confidence in your discernment and pursuit of the public good; for, I assure myself, that whilst you carefully avoid every alteration which might endanger the benefits of an united and effective government, or which ought to await the future lessons of experience, a reverence for the characteristic rights of freemen, and a regard for the public harmony, will sufficiently influence your deliberations on the question, how far the former can be more impregnably fortified, or the latter be safely and advantageously promoted.

To the preceding observations I have one to add, which will be most properly addressed to the House of Representatives. It concerns myself, and will, therefore, be as brief as possible. When I was first honored with a call into the service of my country, then on the eve of an arduous struggle for its liberties, the light in which I contemplated my duty, required that I should renounce every pecuniary compensation. From this resolution I have in no instance departed; and being still under the impressions which produced it, I must decline, as inapplicable to myself, any share in the personal emoluments which may be indispensably included in a permanent provision for the executive department; and must accordingly pray that the pecuniary estimates for the station in which I am placed, may, during my continuance in it, be limited to such actual expenditures as the public good may be thought to require.

Having thus imparted to you my sentiments, as they have been awakened by the occasion which brings us together, I shall take my present leave; but not without resorting once more to the benign Parent of the human race, in humble supplication, that, since he has been pleased to favor the American people with opportunities for deliberating in perfect tranquillity, and dispositions for deciding, with unparalleled unanimity, on a form of government for the security of their Union, and the advancement of their happiness, so his Divine blessing may be equally conspicuous in the enlarged views, the temperate consultations, and the wise measures, on which the success of this government must depend.

G. WASHINGTON.

April 30, 1789.

FAREWELL ADDRESS OF GEORGE WASHINGTON, PRESIDENT, TO THE PEOPLE OF THE UNITED STATES, SEPTEMBER 17, 1796.

Friends and Fellow-citizens:

The period for a new election of a citizen to administer the Executive Government of the United States being not far distant, and the time actually arrived when your thoughts must be employed in designating the person who is to be clothed with that important trust, it appears to me proper, especially as it may conduce to a more distinct expression of the public voice, that I should now apprize you of the resolution I have formed, to decline being considered among the number of those out of whom a choice is to be made.

I beg you, at the same time, to do me the justice to be assured that this resolution has not been taken without a strict regard to all the considerations appertaining to the relation which binds a dutiful citizen to his country; and that, in withdrawing the tender of service, which silence, in my situation, might imply, I am influenced by no diminution of zeal for your future interest; no deficiency of grateful respect for your past kindness; but am supported by a full conviction that the step is compatible with both.

The acceptance of, and continuance hitherto in, the office to which your suffrages have twice called me, have been a uniform sacrifice of inclination to the opinion of duty, and to a deference for what appeared to be your desire. I constantly hoped that it would have been much earlier in my power, consistently with motives which I was not at liberty to disregard, to return to that retirement from which I had been reluctantly drawn. The strength of my inclination to do this, previous to the last election, had even led to the preparation of an address to declare it to you; but mature reflection on the then perplexed and critical posture of our affairs with foreign nations, and the unanimous advice of persons entitled to my confidence, impelled me to abandon the idea.

I rejoice that the state of your concerns, external as well as internal, no longer renders the pursuit of inclination incompatible with the sentiment of duty or propriety ; and am persuaded, whatever partiality may be retained for my services, that, in the present circumstances of our country, you will not disapprove my determination to retire.

The impressions with which I first undertook the arduous trust were explained on the proper occasion. In the discharge of this trust, I will only say, that I have with good intentions contributed towards the organization and administration of the Government the best exertions of which a very fallible judgment was capable. Not unconscious in the outset of the inferiority of my qualifications, experience, in my own eyes—perhaps still more in the eyes of others—has strengthened the motives to diffidence of myself; and every day the increasing weight of years admonishes me, more and more, that the shade of retirement is as necessary to me as it will be welcome. Satisfied that if any circumstances have given peculiar value to my services, they were temporary, I have the consolation to believe that, while choice and prudence invite me to quit the political scene, patriotism does not forbid it.

In looking forward to the moment which is intended to terminate the career of my public life, my feelings do not permit me to suspend the deep acknowledgment of that debt of gratitude which I owe to my beloved country for the many honors it has conferred upon me; still more for the steadfast confidence with which it has supported me; and for the opportunities I have thence enjoyed of manifesting my inviolable attachment, by services faithful and persevering, though in usefulness unequal to my zeal. If benefits have resulted to our country from these services, let it always be remembered to your praise, and as an instructive example in our annals, that, under circumstances in which the passions, agitated in every direction, were liable to mislead; amidst appearances sometimes dubious, vicissitudes of fortune often discouraging; in situations in which, not unfrequently, want of success has countenanced the spirit of criticism,—the constancy of your support was the essential prop of the efforts, and a guarantee of the plans, by which they were effected. Profoundly penetrated with this idea,

I shall carry it with me to my grave, as a strong incitement to unceasing vows, that Heaven may continue to you the choicest tokens of its beneficence; that your union and brotherly affection may be perpetual; that the free Constitution, which is the work of your hands, may be sacredly maintained; that its administration, in every department, may be stamped with wisdom and virtue; that, in fine, the happiness of the people of these States, under the auspices of liberty, may be made complete, by so careful a preservation and so prudent a use of this blessing as will acquire to them the glory of recommending it to the applause, the affection, and the adoption of every nation which is yet a stranger to it.

Here, perhaps, I ought to stop; but a solicitude for your welfare, which cannot end but with my life, and the apprehension of danger natural to that solicitude, urge me, on an occasion like the present, to offer to your solemn contemplation, and to recommend to your frequent review, some sentiments, which are the result of much reflection, of no inconsiderable observation, and which appear to me all-important to the permanency of your felicity as a people. These will be afforded to you with the more freedom, as you can only see in them the disinterested warnings of a parting friend, who can possibly have no personal motive to bias his counsel; nor can I forget, as an encouragement to it, your indulgent reception of my sentiments on a former and not dissimilar occasion.

Interwoven as is the love of liberty with every ligament of your hearts, no recommendation of mine is necessary to fortify or confirm the attachment.

The unity of government, which constitutes you one people, is also now dear to you. It is justly so; for it is a main pillar in the edifice of your real independence—the support of your tranquillity at home, your peace abroad, of your safety, of your prosperity, of that very liberty which you so highly prize. But as it is easy to foresee that, from different causes and from different quarters, much pains will be taken, many artifices employed, to weaken in your minds the conviction of this truth; as this is the point in your political fortress against which the batteries of internal and external enemies will be most constantly and actively (though often covertly and insidiously) directed,—it is of infinite moment that you should properly estimate the immense value of your national union to your collective and individual happiness; that you should cherish a cordial, habitual, and immovable attachment to it; accustoming yourselves to think and speak of it as of the palladium of your political safety and prosperity; watching for its preservation with jealous anxiety; discountenancing whatever may suggest even a suspicion that it can, in any event, be abandoned; and indignantly frowning upon the first dawning of every attempt to alienate any portion of our country from the rest, or to enfeeble the sacred ties which now link together the various parts.

For this you have every inducement of sympathy and interest. Citizens by birth or choice, of a common country, that country has a right to concentrate your affections. The name of *American*, which belongs to you in your national capacity, must always exalt the just pride of patriotism, more than any appellation derived from local discriminations. With slight shades of difference, you have the same religion, manners, habits, and political principles. You have, in a common cause, fought and triumphed together; the independence and liberty you possess are the work of joint counsels and joint efforts, of common dangers, sufferings, and successes.

But these considerations, however powerfully they address themselves to your sensibility, are greatly outweighed by those which apply more immediately to your interest; here every portion of our country finds the most commanding motives for carefully guarding and preserving the union of the whole.

The North, in an unrestrained intercourse with the South, protected by the equal laws of a common government, finds, in the productions of the latter, great additional resources of maritime and commercial enterprise, and precious materials of manufacturing industry. The South, in the same intercourse, benefiting by the agency of the North, sees its agriculture grow, and its commerce expand. Turning partly into its own channels the seamen of the

North, it finds its particular navigation invigorated; and while it contributes, in different ways, to nourish and increase the general mass of the national navigation, it looks forward to the protection of a maritime strength to which itself is unequally adapted. The East, in like intercourse with the West, already finds, and in the progressive improvement of interior communication, by land and water, will more and more find, a valuable vent for the commodities which it brings from abroad, or manufactures at home. The West derives from the East supplies requisite to its growth and comfort; and what is perhaps of still greater consequence, it must, of necessity, owe the secure enjoyment of indispensable outlets for its own productions, to the weight, influence, and the future maritime strength of the Atlantic side of the Union, directed by an indissoluble community of interest as one nation. Any other tenure by which the West can hold this essential advantage, whether derived from its own separate strength, or from an apostate and unnatural connexion with any foreign power, must be intrinsically precarious.

While, then, every part of our country thus feels an immediate and particular interest in union, all the parts combined cannot fail to find, in the united mass of means and efforts, greater strength, greater resource, proportionably greater security from external danger, a less frequent interruption of their peace by foreign nations; and what is of inestimable value, they must derive from union an exemption from those broils and wars between themselves, which so frequently afflict neighboring countries, not tied together by the same government; which their own rivalships alone would be sufficient to produce, but which opposite foreign alliances, attachments, and intrigues, would stimulate and imbitter. Hence, likewise, they will avoid the necessity of those over-grown military establishments, which, under any form of government, are inaus picious to liberty, and which are to be regarded as particularly hostile to republican liberty; in this sense it is that your union ought to be considered as a main prop of your liberty, and that the love of the one ought to endear to you the preservation of the other.

These considerations speak a persuasive language to every reflecting and virtuous mind, and exhibit the continuance of the Union as a primary object of patriotic desire. Is there a doubt, whether a common government can embrace so large a sphere? Let experience solve it. To listen to mere speculation, in such a case, were criminal. We are authorized to hope, that a proper organization of the whole, with the auxiliary agency of governments for the respective subdivisions, will afford a happy issue to the experiment. It is well worth a fair and full experiment. With such powerful and obvious motives to Union, affecting all parts of our country, while experience shall not have demonstrated its impracticability, there will always be reason to distrust the patriotism of those, who, in any quarter, may endeavor to weaken its bands.

In contemplating the causes which may disturb our Union, it occurs, as a matter of serious concern, that any ground should have been furnished for characterizing parties by geographical discriminations—Northern and Southern—Atlantic and Western: whence designing men may endeavor to excite a belief that there is a real difference of local interests and views. One of the expedients of party to acquire influence within particular districts, is to misrepresent the opinions and aims of other districts. You cannot shield yourselves too much against the jealousies and heart-burnings which spring from these misrepresentations; they tend to render alien to each other those who ought to be bound together by fraternal affection. The inhabitants of our western country have lately had a useful lesson on this head; they have seen in the negotiation by the Executive, and in the unanimous ratification by the Senate, of the treaty with Spain, and in the universal satisfaction at that event throughout the United States, a decisive proof how unfounded were the suspicions propagated among them, of a policy in the General Government, and in the Atlantic States, unfriendly to their interests in regard to the Mississippi: they have been witnesses to the formation of two treaties—that with Great Britain, and that with Spain, which secure to them every thing they could desire in respect to our foreign relations, towards confirming their prosperity. Will it not be their wisdom to rely for the preservation of these advantages on the Union by which they were procured? Will they not henceforth be deaf to those advisers, if such there are, who would sever them from their brethren, and connect them with aliens?

To the efficacy and permanency of your Union, a Government for the whole is indispensable. No alliance, however strict between the parts, can be an adequate substitute; they must inevitably experience the infractions and interruptions which all alliances, in all time, have experienced. Sensible of this momentous truth, you have improved upon your first essay, by the adoption of a Constitution of Government better calculated than your former for an intimate Union, and for the efficacious management of your common concerns. This Government, the offspring of our own choice, uninfluenced and unawed, adopted upon full investigation and mature deliberation, completely free in its principles, in the distribution of its powers, uniting security with energy, and containing within itself a provision for its own amendment, has a just claim to your confidence and your support. Respect for its authority, compliance with its laws, acquiescence in its measures, are duties enjoined by the fundamental maxims of true liberty. The bases of our political systems, is the right of the people to make and to alter their constitutions of Government: but the Constitution which at any time exists, till changed by an explicit and authentic act of the whole people, is sacredly obligatory upon all. The very idea of the power, and the right of the people to establish Government, pre-supposes the duty of every individual to obey the established Government.

All obstructions to the execution of the laws, all combinations and associations, under whatever plausible character, with the real design to direct, control, counteract, or awe the regular deliberation and action of the constituted authorities, are destructive to this fundamental principle, and of fatal tendency. They serve to organize faction, to give it an artificial and extraordinary force, to put in the place of the delegated will of the nation, the will of a party, often a small but artful and enterprising minority of the community; and, according to the alternate triumphs of different parties, to make the public administration the mirror of the ill-concerted and incongruous projects of faction, rather than the organ of consistent and wholesome plans, digested by common counsels, and modified by mutual interests.

However combinations or associations of the above description may now and then answer popular ends, they are likely, in the course of time and things, to become potent engines, by which cunning, ambitious, and unprincipled men, will be enabled to subvert the power of the people, and to usurp for themselves the reins of Government; destroying, afterwards, the very engines which had lifted them to unjust dominion.

Towards the preservation of your Government, and the permanency of your present happy state, it is requisite, not only that you steadily discountenance irregular oppositions to its acknowledged authority, but also that you resist with care the spirit of innovation upon its principles, however specious the pretexts. One method of assault may be to effect, in the forms of the Constitution, alterations which will impair the energy of the system, and thus to undermine what cannot be directly overthrown. In all the changes to which you may be invited, remember that time and habit are at least as necessary to fix the true character of governments as of other human institutions; that experience is the surest standard by which to test the real tendency of the existing constitution of a country; that facility in changes, upon the credit of mere hypothesis and opinion, exposes to perpetual change, from the endless variety of hypothesis and opinion; and remember, especially, that for the efficient management of your common interests, in a country so extensive as ours, a Government of as much vigor as is consistent with the perfect security of liberty, is indispensable. Liberty itself will find in such a Government, with powers properly distributed and adjusted, its surest guardian. It is, indeed, little else than a name, where the Government is too feeble to withstand the enterprises of faction, to confine each member of the society within the limits prescribed by the laws, and to maintain all in the secure and tranquil enjoyment of the rights of person and property.

I have already intimated to you the danger of parties in the State, with particular reference to the founding of them on geographical discriminations. Let me now take a more comprehensive view, and warn you, in the most solemn manner, against the baneful effects of the spirit of party generally.

This spirit, unfortunately, is inseparable from our nature, having its root in the strongest passions of the human mind. It exists under different shapes, in all Governments, more or less stifled, controlled, or repressed; but in those of the popular form it is seen in its greatest rankness, and is truly their worst enemy.

The alternate domination of one faction over another, sharpened by the spirit of revenge, natural to party dissension, which, in different ages and countries, has perpetrated the most horrid enormities, is itself a frightful despotism. But this leads, at length, to a more formal and permanent despotism. The disorders and miseries which result, gradually incline the minds of men to seek security and repose in the absolute power of an individual; and, sooner or later, the chief of some prevailing faction, more able or more fortunate than his competitors, turns this disposition to the purposes of his own elevation on the ruins of public liberty.

Without looking forward to an extremity of this kind, (which, nevertheless, ought not to be entirely out of sight,) the common and continual mischiefs of the spirit of party are sufficient to make it the interest and duty of a wise people to discourage and restrain it.

It serves always to distract the public councils, and enfeeble the public administration. It agitates the community with ill-founded jealousies and false alarms; kindles the animosity of one part against another; foments, occasionally, riot and insurrection. It opens the door to foreign influence and corruption, which find a facilitated access to the Government itself, through the channels of party passions. Thus the policy and the will of one country are subjected to the policy and will of another.

There is an opinion that parties, in free countries, are useful checks upon the administration of the Government, and serve to keep alive the spirit of liberty. This, within certain limits, is probably true; and in Governments of a monarchical cast, patriotism may look with indulgence, if not with favor, upon the spirit of party. But in those of the popular character, in Governments purely elective, it is a spirit not to be encouraged. From their natural tendency, it is certain there will always be enough of that spirit for every salutary purpose. And there being constant danger of excess, the effort ought to be, by force of public opinion, to mitigate and assuage it. A fire not to be quenched, it demands a uniform vigilance to prevent its bursting into a flame, lest, instead of warming, it should consume.

It is important, likewise, that the habits of thinking, in a free country, should inspire caution in those intrusted with its administration, to confine themselves within their respective constitutional spheres, avoiding, in the exercise of the powers of one department, to encroach upon another. The spirit of encroachment tends to consolidate the powers of all the departments in one, and thus to create, whatever the form of Government, a real despotism. A just estimate of that love of power, and proneness to abuse it which predominates in the human heart, is sufficient to satisfy us of the truth of this position. The necessity of reciprocal checks in the exercise of political power, by dividing and distributing it into different depositories, and constituting each the guardian of the public weal, against invasions by the others, has been evinced by experiments, ancient and modern; some of them in our own country, and under our own eyes. To preserve them must be as necessary as to institute them. If, in the opinion of the people, the distribution or modification of the constitutional powers be, in any particular, wrong, let it be corrected by an amendment in the way which the Constitution designates. But let there be no change by usurpation; for though this, in one instance, may be the instrument of good, it is the customary weapon by which free Governments are destroyed. The precedent must always greatly overbalance, in permanent evil, any partial or transient benefit which the use can, at any time, yield.

Of all the dispositions and habits which lead to political prosperity, religion and morality are indispensable supports. In vain would that man claim the tribute of patriotism, who should labor to subvert these great pillars of human happiness, these firmest props of the duties of men and citizens. The mere politician, equally with the pious man, ought to respect and to cherish them. A volume could not trace all their connexions with private and public felicity. Let it simply be asked, where is the security for property, for reputation, for life, if the sense of religious obligation *desert* the oaths which are the instruments of investigation in courts of justice? And let us with caution indulge the supposition, that morality can be maintained without religion. Whatever may be conceded to the influence of refined education on minds of peculiar structure, reason and experience both forbid us to expect that national morality can prevail in exclusion of religious principles.

It is substantially true, that virtue or morality is a necessary spring of popular Government. The rule, indeed, extends with more or less force to every species of free Government. Who, that is a sincere friend to it, can look with indifference upon attempts to shake the foundation of the fabric?

Promote, then, as an object of primary importance, institutions for the general diffusion of knowledge. In proportion as the structure of a Government gives force to public opinion, it is essential that public opinion should be enlightened.

As a very important source of strength and security, cherish public credit. One method of preserving it is to use it as sparingly as possible; avoiding occasions of expense by cultivating peace, but remembering also that timely disbursements to prepare for danger, frequently prevent much greater disbursements to repel it; avoiding, likewise, the accumulation of debt, not only by shunning occasions of expense, but by vigorous exertions in time of peace to discharge the debts which unavoidable wars may have occasioned; not ungenerously throwing upon posterity the burden which we ourselves ought to bear. The execution of these maxims belongs to your representatives, but it is necessary that public opinion should co-operate. To facilitate to them the performance of their duty, it is essential that you should practically bear in mind, that towards the payment of debts there must be revenue; that to have revenue there must be taxes; that no taxes can be devised, which are not more or less inconvenient and unpleasant· that the intrinsic embarrassment inseparable from the selection of the proper objects, (which is always a choice of difficulties,) ought to be a decisive motive for a candid construction of the conduct of the Government in making it, and for a spirit of acquiescence in the measures for obtaining revenue, which the public exigencies may at any time dictate.

Observe good faith and justice towards all nations; cultivate peace and harmony with all; religion and morality enjoin this conduct; and can it be that good policy does not equally enjoin it? It will be worthy of a free, enlightened, and, at no distant period, a great nation, to give to mankind the magnanimous and too novel example of a people always guided by an exalted justice and benevolence. Who can doubt that, in the course of time and things, the fruits of such a plan would richly repay any temporary advantages which might be lost by a steady adherence to it? Can it be that Providence has not connected the permanent felicity of a nation with its virtue? The experiment, at least, is recommended by every sentiment which ennobles human nature. Alas! is it rendered impossible by its vices?

In the execution of such a plan, nothing is more essential than that permanent inveterate antipathies against particular nations, and passionate attachments for others, should be excluded; and that, in place of them, just and amicable feelings towards all should be cultivated. The nation which indulges towards another an habitual hatred, or an habitual fondness, is, in some degree, a slave. It is a slave to its animosity or to its affection; either of which is sufficient to lead it astray from its duty and its interest. Antipathy in one nation against another, disposes each more readily to offer insult and injury, to lay hold of slight causes of umbrage, and to be haughty and intractable, when accidental or trifling occasions of dispute occur. Hence frequent collisions, obstinate, envenomed, and bloody contests. The nation, prompted by ill will and resentment, sometimes impels to war the Government, contrary to the best calculations of policy. The Government sometimes participates in the national propensity, and adopts, through passion, what reason would reject; at other times it makes the animosity of the nation subservient to projects of hostility, instigated by pride, ambition, and other sinister and pernicious motives. The peace often, sometimes perhaps the liberty, of nations has been the victim.

So, likewise, a passionate attachment of one nation to another produces a variety of evils. Sympathy for the favorite nation, facilitating the illusion of an imaginary common interest, in cases where no real common interest exists, and infusing into one the enmities of the other, betrays the former into a participation in the quarrels and wars of the latter, without adequate inducement or justification. It leads also to concessions to the favorite nation of privileges denied to others, which is apt doubly to injure the nation making the concessions; by unnecessarily parting with what ought to have been retained, and by exciting jealousy, ill will, and a disposition to retaliate, in the parties from whom equal privileges are withheld; and it gives to ambitious, corrupted, or deluded citizens (who devote themselves to the favorite nation) facility to betray, or sacrifice the interest of their own country, without odium; sometimes even with popularity; gilding with the appearance of a virtuous sense of obligation, a commendable deference for public opinion, or a laudable zeal for public good, the base or foolish compliances of ambition, corruption, or infatuation.

As avenues to foreign influence in innumerable ways, such attachments are particularly alarming to the truly enlightened and independent patriot. How many opportunities do they afford to tamper with domestic factions, to practise the art of seduction, to mislead public opinion, to influence or awe the public councils! Such an attachment of a small or weak, towards a great and powerful nation, dooms the former to be the satellite of the latter.

Against the insidious wiles of foreign influence (I conjure you to believe me, fellow-citizens) the jealousy of a free people ought to be *constantly* awake; since history and experience prove that foreign influence is one of the most baneful foes of republican Government. But that jealousy, to be useful, must be impartial; else it becomes the instrument of the very influence to be avoided, instead of a defence against it. Excessive partiality for one foreign nation, and excessive dislike for another, cause those whom they actuate to see danger only on one side, and serve to veil, and even second, the arts of influence on the other. Real patriots, who may resist the intrigues of the favorite, are liable to become suspected and odious; while its tools and dupes usurp the applause and confidence of the people, to surrender their interests.

The great rule of conduct for us, in regard to foreign nations, is, in extending our commercial relations, to have with them as little political connexion as possible. So far as we have already formed engagements, let them be fulfilled with perfect good faith. Here let us stop.

Europe has a set of primary interests, which to us have none, or a very remote relation. Hence she must be engaged in frequent controversies, the causes of which are essentially foreign to our concerns. Hence, therefore, it must be unwise in us to implicate ourselves, by artificial ties, in the ordinary vicissitudes of her politics, or the ordinary combinations and collisions of her friendships or enmities.

Our detached and distant situation invites and enables us to pursue a different course. If we remain one people, under an efficient Government, the period is not far off when we may defy material injury from external annoyance; when we may take such an attitude as will cause the neutrality we may at any time resolve upon, to be scrupulously respected; when belligerent nations, under the impossibility of making acquisitions upon us, will not lightly hazard the giving us provocation; when we may choose peace or war, as our interest, guided by justice, shall counsel.

Why forego the advantages of so peculiar a situation? Why quit our own to stand upon foreign ground? Why, by interweaving our destiny with that of any part of Europe, entangle our peace and prosperity in the toils of European ambition, rivalship, interest, humor, or caprice?

It is our true policy to steer clear of permanent alliances with any portion of the foreign world; so far, I mean, as we are now at liberty to do it; for let me not be understood as capable of patronising infidelity to existing engagements. I hold the maxim no less applicable to public than to private affairs, that honesty is always the best policy. I repeat it, therefore, let those engagements be observed in their genuine sense. But, in my opinion, it is unnecessary, and would be unwise to extend them.

Taking care always to keep ourselves, by suitable establishments, on a respectable defensive posture, we may safely trust to temporary alliances for extraordinary emergencies.

Harmony, and a liberal intercourse with all nations, are recommended by policy, humanity, and interest. But even our commercial policy should hold an equal and impartial hand; neither seeking nor granting exclusive favors or preferences; consulting the natural course of things; diffusing and diversifying, by gentle means, the streams of commerce, but forcing nothing; establishing, with powers so disposed, in order to give trade a stable course, to define the rights of our merchants, and to enable the Government to support them, conventional rules of intercourse, the best that present circumstances and mutual opinions will permit, but temporary, and liable to be, from time to time, abandoned or varied, as experience and circumstances shall dictate; constantly keeping in view, that it is folly in one nation to look for disinterested favors from another; that it must pay, with a portion of its independence, for whatever it may accept under that character; that by such acceptance it may place itself in the condition of having given equivalents for nominal favors, and yet of being reproached with ingratitude for not giving more. There can be no greater error than to expect, or calculate upon, real favors from nation to nation. It is an illusion which experience must cure, which a just pride ought to discard.

In offering to you, my countrymen, these counsels of an old and affectionate friend, I dare not hope they will make the strong and lasting impression I could wish; that they will control the usual current of the passions, or prevent our nation from running the course which has hitherto marked the destiny of nations; but if I may even flatter myself that they may be productive of some partial benefit, some occasional good; that they may now and then recur to moderate the fury of party spirit, to warn against the mischiefs of foreign intrigues, to guard against the impostures of pretended patriotism; this hope will be a full recompense for the solicitude for your welfare by which they have been dictated.

How far, in the discharge of my official duties, I have been guided by the principles which have been delineated, the public records, and other evidences of my conduct, must witness to you and the world. To myself, the assurance of my own conscience is, that I have at least believed myself to be guided by them.

In relation to the still subsisting war in Europe, my proclama tion of the 22d of April, 1793, is the index to my plan. Sanctioned by your approving voice, and by that of your Representatives in both Houses of Congress, the spirit of that measure has continually governed me, uninfluenced by any attempts to deter or divert me from it.

After deliberate examination, with the aid of the best lights I could obtain, I was well satisfied that our country, under all the circumstances of the case, had a right to take, and was bound in duty and interest to take, a neutral position. Having taken it I determined, as far as should depend upon me, to maintain it with moderation, perseverance, and firmness.

The considerations which respect the right to hold this conduct, it is not necessary on this occasion to detail. I will only observe, that, according to my understanding of the matter, that right, so far from being denied by any of the belligerent powers, has been virtually admitted by all.

The duty of holding a neutral conduct may be inferred, without any thing more, from the obligation which justice and humanity impose on every nation, in cases in which it is free to act, to maintain inviolate the relations of peace and amity towards other nations.

The inducements of interest, for observing that conduct, will best be referred to your own reflections and experience. With me, a predominant motive has been to endeavor to gain time to our country to settle and mature its yet recent institutions, and to progress, without interruption, to that degree of strength and consistency which is necessary to give it, humanly speaking, the command of its own fortunes.

Though in reviewing the incidents of my administration, I am unconscious of intentional error; I am, nevertheless, too sensible of my defects not to think it probable that I may have committed many errors. Whatever they may be, I fervently beseech the Almighty to avert or mitigate the evils to which they may tend. I shall also carry with me the hope, that my country will never cease to view them with indulgence; and that, after forty-five years of my life dedicated to its service with an upright zeal, the faults of incompetent abilities will be consigned to oblivion, as myself must soon be to the mansions of rest.

Relying on its kindness in this, as in other things, and actuated by that fervent love towards it which is so natural to a man who views in it the native soil of himself and his progenitors for several generations, I anticipate, with pleasing expectation, that retreat in which I promise myself to realize, without alloy, the sweet enjoyment of partaking, in the midst of my fellow-citizens, the benign influence of good laws under a free Government—the ever favorite object of my heart—and the happy reward, as I trust, of our mutual cares, labors, and dangers.

GEORGE WASHINGTON.

United States, 17th September, 1796.

GEORGE WASHINGTON,

APPOINTED LIEUTENANT-GENERAL AND COMMANDER-IN-CHIEF OF ALL THE ARMIES RAISED OR TO BE RAISED IN THE UNITED STATES, BY AND WITH THE ADVICE AND CONSENT OF THE SENATE.—July 3, 1798.

THE calm and peaceful retreat which the great Washington promised himself beneath his own vine and fig-tree, in taking an affectionate leave of his fellow-citizens in his farewell address, was destined to be of short duration, for, difficulties having arisen with the then existing government of France, "the opinion was universally entertained, that Washington must be called on to take the command of the armies." The weight of his name and character was of the utmost importance to produce unanimity in the leaders, and to secure the confidence and support of the people. His extreme aversion to enter again into public life was known; but it was likewise well understood, that it was a principle with him, from which he had never deviated, that when his services were demanded by the general voice of his fellow-citizens, he never refused to bestow them; under this impression, therefore, the President, John Adams, had made up his mind to nominate him to the Senate in any event, both because he was the best man, and because the nation would not be satisfied with any other course, and he therefore declared to him in a letter of the 22d June, 1798, that "We must have your name, if you will in any case permit us to use it. There will be more efficacy in it than in many an army."

And the Secretary of War, James McHenry, on the 26th June, 1798, said to him—"You see how the storm thickens, and that our vessel will soon require its ancient pilot. Will you,—may we flatter ourselves, that, in a crisis so awful and important, you will accept the command of all our armies? I hope you will, because you alone can unite all hearts and all hands."—To the President, Washington replied on the 4th July, 1798, that "At the epoch of my retirement, an invasion of these States by any European power, or even the probability of such an event happening in my days, was so far from being contemplated by me, that I had no conception that that, or any other occurrence would arise in so short a period, which could turn my eyes from the shades of Mount Vernon. But this seems to be the age of wonders; and it is reserved for intoxicated and lawless France (for purposes of Providence far beyond the reach of human ken) to slaughter its own citizens, and to disturb the repose of all the world besides."

"From a view of the past and the present, and from the prospect of that which seems to be expected, it is not easy for me to decide, satisfactorily, on the part it might best become me to act. In case of *actual invasion* by a formidable force, I certainly should not intrench myself under the cover of age (67) and retirement, if my services should be required by my country to assist in repelling it."

To the Secretary of War, Washington replied also on the 4th July, 1798,—"The sentiments, which I mean to express to you in this letter on the subject of yours, shall be frank, undisguised and explicit; for I see, as you do, that clouds are gathering, and that a storm may ensue; and I find, too, from a variety of hints, that my quiet under these circumstances does not promise to be of long continuance.

"It cannot be necessary for me to premise to you, or to others, who know my sentiments as well, that, to quit the tranquil walks of retirement, and enter a boundless field of responsibility and trouble, would be productive of sensations, which a better pen than I possess would find it difficult to describe. Nevertheless, the principles by which my conduct has been actuated through life would not suffer me, in any great emergency, to withhold any services I could render, required by my country; especially in a case where its dearest rights are assailed by lawless ambition and intoxicated power, contrary to every principle of justice, and in violation of solemn compacts and laws, which govern all civilized nations; and this, too, with the obvious intent to sow 'hick the seeds of disunion, for the purpose of subjugating the government, and destroying our independence and happiness."

"In circumstances like these, accompanied by an actual invasion of our territorial rights, it would be difficult at any time for me to remain an idle spectator under the plea of age or retirement. With sorrow, it is true, I should quit the shades of my peaceful abode, and the ease and happiness I now enjoy, to encounter anew the turmoils of war, to which, possibly, my strength and powers might be found incompetent. These, however, should not be stumbling-blocks in *my own* way."

"As my whole life has been dedicated to my country in one shape or another, for the poor remains of it, it is not an object to contend for ease and quiet, when all that is valuable in it is at stake, further than to be satisfied that the sacrifice I should make of these is acceptable and desired by my country."

Before the reception of these communications from Washington, the following proceedings took place :—

IN EXECUTIVE SESSION, SENATE OF THE UNITED STATES.

MONDAY, JULY 2, 1798.

The following written message was received from the President of the United States, by Mr. Malcom his secretary :—

Gentlemen of the Senate :—

I nominate George Washington, of Mount Vernon, to be Lieutenant-general and Commander-in-chief of all the armies raised, or to be raised, in the United States.

JOHN ADAMS.

United States, July 2, 1798.

The message was read.

Ordered, That it lie for consideration.

TUESDAY, JULY 3, 1798.

The Senate took into consideration the message of the President of the United States, of the 2d instant, and the nomination contained therein, of George Washington, to office. Whereupon,

On the question to advise and consent to the appointment, it was determined in the affirmative: Yeas, 24.

The yeas and nays being required by one-fifth of the Senators present, Those who voted in the affirmative, are—Messrs. Anderson, Bingham, Brown, Chipman, Clayton, Foster, Goodhue, Greene, Hillhouse, Howard, Langdon, Latimer, Laurance, Livermore, Martin, Mason, North, Paine, Read, Rutherford, Sedgwick, Stockton, Tazewell and Tracy.

So it was,

Resolved, unanimously, That they do advise and consent to the appointment, agreeably to the nomination.

The following correspondence then ensued:—

Extract of a letter from John Adams, President of the United States, to James McHenry, Secretary of War:

"*Philadelphia*, July 6, 1798.

"DEAR SIR,—It is my desire, that you embrace the first opportunity to set out on your journey to Mount Vernon, and wait on General Washington with the commission of lieutenant-general and commander-in-chief of the armies of the United States, which, by the advice and consent of the Senate, has been signed by me.

"The reasons and motives, which prevailed with me to venture on such a step as the nomination of this great and illustrious character, whose voluntary resignation alone occasioned my introduction to the office I now hold, were too numerous to be detailed in this letter, and are too obvious and important to escape the observation of any part of America or Europe. But, as it is a movement of great delicacy, it will require all your address to communicate the subject in a manner that shall be in:f fensive to his feelings, and consistent with all the respect that is due from me to him.

"If the General should decline the appointment, all the world will be silent and respectfully acquiesce. If he should accept it, all the world, except the enemies of this country, will rejoice. If he should come to no decisive determination, but take the subject into consideration, I shall not appoint any other lieutenant-general till his conclusion is known."

"His advice in the formation of a list of officers would be extremely desirable to me." "Particularly I wish to have his opinion of the men most suitable for inspector-general, adjutant-general, and quartermaster-general."

"His opinion on all subjects would have great weight; and I wish you to obtain from him as much of his reflections upon the times and the service as you can."

Philadelphia, July 7, 1798.

DEAR SIR,—Mr. McHenry, the Secretary of War, will have the honor to wait on you, in my behalf, to impart to you a step I have ventured to take, and which I should have been happy to have communicated in person, if such a journey had been at this time in my power. As I said in a former letter, if it had been in my power to nominate you to be President of the United States, I should have done it with less hesitation and more pleasure. My reasons for this measure will be too well known to need any explanation to the public. Every friend and every enemy of America will comprehend them at first blush. To you, sir, I owe all the apologies I can make. The urgent necessity I am in of your advice and assistance, indeed of your conduct and direction of the war, is all I can urge, and that is a sufficient justification to myself and the world. I hope it will be so considered by yourself. Mr. McHenry will have the honor to consult you upon the organization of the army, and upon every thing relating to it.

With the highest respect, I have the honor to be, sir, your most obedient and most humble servant,

JOHN ADAMS.

Mount Vernon, July 13, 1798.

DEAR SIR,—I had the honor, on the evening of the 11th instant, to receive from the hands of the Secretary of War your favor of the 7th, announcing that you had, with the advice and consent of the Senate, appointed me lieutenant-general and commander-in-chief of all the armies raised or to be raised for the service of the United States.

I cannot express how greatly affected I am at this new proof of public confidence, and the highly flattering manner in which you have been pleased to make the communication; at the same time I must not conceal from you my earnest wish, that the choice had fallen on a man less declined in years, and better qualified to encounter the usual vicissitudes of war.

You know, sir, what calculations I had made relative to the probable course of events on my retiring from office, and the determination I had consoled myself with, of closing the remnant of my days in my present peaceful abode. You will, therefore, be at no loss to conceive and appreciate the sensations I must have experienced, to bring my mind to any conclusion that would pledge me, at so late a period of life, to leave scenes I sincerely love, to enter upon the boundless field of public action, incessant trouble, and high responsibility.

It was not possible for me to remain ignorant of, or indifferent to, recent transactions. The conduct of the Directory of France towards our country, their insidious hostilities to its government, their various practices to withdraw the affections of the people from it, the evident tendency of their arts and those of their agents to countenance and invigorate opposition, their disregard of solemn treaties and the laws of nations, their war upon our defenceless commerce, their treatment of our minister of peace, and their demands, amounting to tribute, could not fail to excite in me corresponding sentiments with those which my countrymen have so generally expressed in their affectionate addresses to you. Believe me, sir, no one can more cordially approve of the wise and prudent measures of your administration. They ought to inspire universal confidence, and will, no doubt, combined with the state of things, call from Congress such laws and means as will enable you to meet the full force and extent of the crisis.

Satisfied, therefore, that you have sincerely wished and endeavoured to avert war, and exhausted to the last drop the cup of reconciliation, we can with pure hearts appeal to Heaven for the justice of our cause, and may confidently trust the final result to that kind Providence, which has heretofore and so often signally favored the people of these United States.

Thinking in this manner, and feeling how incumbent it is upon every person of every description to contribute at all times to his country's welfare, and especially in a moment like the present, when every thing we hold dear is so seriously threatened, I have finally determined to accept the commission of commander-in-chief of the armies of the United States; with the reserve only, that I shall not be called into the field until the army is in a situation to require my presence, or it becomes indispensable by the urgency of circumstances.

In making this reservation, I beg to be understood, that I do not mean to withhold any assistance to arrange and organize the army, which you may think I can afford. I take the liberty also to mention, that I must decline having my acceptance considered as drawing after it any immediate charge upon the public, and that I cannot receive any emoluments annexed to the appointment, before entering into a situation to incur expense.

The Secretary of War being anxious to return to the seat of government, I have detained him no longer than was necessary to a full communication upon the several points he had in charge.

With very great respect and consideration, I have the honor to be, &c.

GEORGE WASHINGTON.

TO THE MEMORY OF

GEORGE WASHINGTON,

BORN FEBRUARY 22, 1732.—DIED AT MOUNT VERNON, DECEMBER 14, 1799.

THE illustrious Washington having filled the measure of his country's glory and exalted his own political and military fame and private character far above the standard of excellence attained by the greatest man of modern or ancient times; and having, on every occasion, performed his duty to his country, not only with that fidelity and devotion which became a good citizen, but with that wisdom, affection, and paternal solicitude which have obtained for him, by the unanimous voice of mankind, the title of "Father of his Country," was called, on the 14th December, 1799, by the ALMIGHTY FATHER OF HEAVEN, we hope, to the enjoyment of that rich reward which is reserved for those who *act well their part* on earth.

The universal gloom which pervaded the hearts of his countrymen on that solemn occasion, seems so far to have commingled with the veneration for his character which has been transmitted to posterity, as to inspire in the patriot's heart an indescribable awe in approaching the mementos of his glory, around which there is a halo so brilliant and penetrating as to reach the inmost intelligence of man, and to purify the moral and intellectual being, by the contemplation of every attribute that was excellent and noble in human nature. It is salutary to remember the outpourings of affection and sorrow on the departure of those whose virtues and goodness have endeared them to our hearts, it elevates the finer feelings of our nature, as the presence of innocence promotes the contemplation of that angelical virtue.

The sons and daughters of America mourned the loss their country had sustained in the death of their Washington, with a cause of sorrow which no other people, in any case, to the same extent could plead; their government, in unison with the feelings of the people, demonstrated that grief in measures of respect and veneration worthy of a nation's affection and a nation's gratitude, and *long—long*—may the remembrance of those deep and sincere effusions of affection and gratitude continue to warm the hearts of the American people. There let the memory of Washington be enshrined, and his private virtues and patriotic ardor will continue to animate this people to the remotest generation. It is proposed to conclude this chapter by consecrating the proceedings and measures of the Government on that memorable occasion

TO THE MEMORY OF

GEORGE WASHINGTON.

IN THE CONGRESS OF THE UNITED STATES OF AMERICA.

HOUSE OF REPRESENTATIVES,

THURSDAY, DECEMBER 19, 1799.

The House of Representatives of the United States, having received intelligence of the death of their highly valued fellow-citizen, George Washington, General of the armies of the United States, and sharing the universal grief this distressing event must produce,

Unanimously resolve:

1. That this House will wait on the President of the United States, in condolence of this national calamity.

2. That the Speaker's chair be shrouded with black, and that the members and officers of the House wear mourning, during the session.

3. That a joint committee of both Houses be appointed to report measures suitable to the occasion, and expressive of the profound sorrow with which Congress is penetrated on the loss of a citizen FIRST IN WAR, FIRST IN PEACE, AND FIRST IN THE HEARTS OF HIS COUNTRYMEN.*

4. That when this House adjourns, it will adjourn until Monday next.

Ordered, That Mr. Marshall and Mr. Smith be appointed a committee to wait on the President of the United States, to know when and where he will receive this House for the purpose expressed in the first resolution.

Ordered, That Mr. Marshall, Mr. Craik, Mr. Henry Lee, Mr. Eggleston, Mr. Smith, Mr. Stone, Mr. Rutledge, Mr. Abiel Foster, Mr. Muhlenberg, Mr. Van Cortlandt, Mr. Dwight Foster, Mr. Franklin Daven port, Mr. Claiborne, Mr. Morris, Mr. John Brown, and Mr. Taliaferro, be a committee, jointly with such committee as may be appointed on the part of the Senate, for the purpose expressed in the third resolution.

Ordered, That the clerk of this House do acquaint the Senate therewith.

A written message was received from the President of the United States, by Mr. Shaw, his secretary, which, together with the letter ac-

---

* The resolutions were drawn by Gen. Henry Lee and introduced by John Marshall, Representative from Virginia.

companying the same, was read, and referred to the committee last appointed, and is as follows:

Gentlemen of the Senate, and
Gentlemen of the House of Representatives:

The letter herewith transmitted will inform you that it has pleased Divine Providence to remove from this life our excellent fellow-citizen GEORGE WASHINGTON, by the purity of his character, and a long series of services to his country, rendered illustrious through the world. It remains for an affectionate and grateful people, in whose hearts he can never die, to pay suitable honors to his memory.

JOHN ADAMS.

United States, December 19, 1799.

"*Mount Vernon*, December 15, 1799.

"SIR: It is with inexpressible grief that I have to announce to you the death of the great and good General Washington. He died last evening, between ten and eleven o'clock, after a short illness of about twenty hours. His disorder was an inflammatory sore throat, which proceeded from a cold, of which he made but little complaint on Friday. On Saturday morning, about three o'clock, he became ill: Doctor Craik attended him in the morning, and Doctor Dick, of Alexandria, and Doctor Brown, of Port Tobacco, were soon after called in. Every medical assistance was offered, but without the desired effect. His last scene corresponded with the whole tenor of his life: not a groan nor a complaint escaped him in extreme distress. With perfect resignation, and in full possession of his reason, he closed his well-spent life.

"I have the honor to be, with the highest respect, sir, your most obedient and very humble servant,

"TOBIAS LEAR.

"The PRESIDENT OF THE UNITED STATES."

Mr. Marshall, from the committee appointed to wait on the President of the United States, to know when and where it will be convenient for him to receive this House, in condolence of the national calamity, reported that the committee had, according to order, performed that service, and that the President signified to them it would be convenient for him to receive this House at one o'clock this afternoon, at his own house.

A message from the Senate, by Mr. Otis, their secretary:

Mr. Speaker: The Senate have agreed to the resolution passed by the House of Representatives for the appointment of a joint committee of both Houses to report measures suitable to the occasion, and expressive of the profound sorrow with which Congress is penetrated on the loss of a citizen first in war, first in peace, and first in the hearts of his countrymen; and have appointed Mr. Dayton, Mr. Bingham, Mr. Dexter, Mr. Gunn, Mr. Lawrence, and Mr. Tracey, a committee on their part.

And then he withdrew.

The Speaker, attended by the House, then withdrew to the house of the President of the United States, when Mr. Speaker addressed the President as follows:

SIR: The House of Representatives, penetrated with a sense of the irreparable loss sustained by the nation in the death of that great and good man, the illustrious and beloved Washington, wait on you, sir, to express their condolence on this melancholy and distressing event.

To which the President replied as follows:

Gentlemen of the House of Representatives:

I receive, with great respect and affection, the condolence of the House of Representatives, on the melancholy and affecting event, in the death of the most illustrious and beloved personage which this country ever produced. I sympathize with you, with the nation, and with good men through the world, in this irreparable loss sustained by us all.

JOHN ADAMS.

United States, December 19, 1799.

MONDAY, DECEMBER 23, 1799.

Mr. Marshall, from the joint committee appointed to prepare and report measures suitable to the occasion, and expressive of the profound sorrow with which Congress is penetrated on the loss of their highly valued fellow-citizen, George Washington, General of the armies of the United States, made a report, in part; which he delivered in at the clerk's table, where the same was twice read and considered: Whereupon,—

It was resolved, that the House do unanimously agree to the following resolutions, to wit:

Resolved by the Senate and House of Representatives of the United States of America in Congress assembled, That a marble monument be erected by the United States, in the Capitol, at the city of Washington; and that the family of General Washington be requested to permit his body to be deposited under it; and that the monument be so designed as to commemorate the great events of his military and political life.

And be it further resolved, That there be a funeral procession from Congress Hall to the German Lutheran Church, in honor of the memory of General George Washington, on Thursday, the twenty-sixth instant, and that an oration be prepared at the request of Congress, to be delivered before both Houses, on that day; and that the President of the Senate and Speaker of the House of Representatives be desired to request one of the members of Congress to prepare and deliver the same.

And be it further resolved, That it be recommended to the people of the United States to wear crape on the left arm, as mourning, for thirty days.

And be it further resolved, That the President of the United States be requested to direct a copy of these resolutions to be transmitted to Mrs. Washington, assuring her of the profound respect Congress will ever bear to her person and character; of their condolence on the late afflicting dispensation of Providence, and entreating her assent to the interment of the remains of General George Washington in the manner expressed in the first resolution.

And be it further resolved, That the President of the United

States be requested to issue a proclamation, notifying to the people throughout the United States the recommendation contained in the third resolution.

Ordered, That the clerk of this House do carry the said resolutions to the Senate, and desire their concurrence.

A message from the Senate, by Mr. Otis, their secretary:

Mr. Speaker: The Senate have agreed to the resolutions passed by the House of Representatives, directing certain measures to be taken suitable to the occasion, and expressive of the profound sorrow with which Congress is penetrated on the loss of their highly valued fellow-citizen, George Washington, General of the armies of the United States.

TUESDAY, DECEMBER 24, 1799.

Mr. Gray, from the joint committee for enrolled bills, reported that the committee had examined the enrolled resolutions directing certain measures to be taken in honor of the memory of General George Washington, and had found the same to be truly enrolled: Whereupon,—

Mr. Speaker signed the said enrolled resolutions.

Ordered, That the clerk of this House do acquaint the Senate therewith.

Mr. Wadsworth, from the joint committee for enrolled bills, reported that the committee did, this day, present to the President of the United States, for his approbation, the enrolled resolutions directing certain measures to be taken in honor of the memory of General George Washington.

A message was received from the President of the United States, by Mr. Shaw, his secretary, notifying that the President did, this day, approve and sign the enrolled resolutions, which originated in this House, in honor of the memory of General George Washington.

The Speaker informed the House, that, conformably to the resolution of Congress, the President of the Senate and the Speaker of the House of Representatives had requested Major General Henry Lee, one of the Representatives from the State of Virginia, to prepare and deliver a funeral oration before both houses, on Thursday, the twenty-sixth instant, in honor of the memory of George Washington, late General of the armies of the United States; and that Mr. Lee had been pleased to accept of the appointment.

On motion, the House adjourned until Thursday morning, half-past ten o clock.

THURSDAY, DECEMBER 26, 1799.

This being the day appointed by the resolution of Congress for the funeral procession in honor of the memory of George Washington, late General of the armies of the United States, the House proceeded to the German Lutheran Church, where they attended the funeral oration prepared and delivered on the occasion by Major General Lee, one of the members of this House for the State of Virginia:

FUNERAL ORATION.

IN obedience to your will, I rise your humble organ, with the hope of executing a part of the system of public mourning which you have been pleased to adopt, commemorative of the death of the most illustrious and most beloved personage this country has ever produced; and which, while it transmits to posterity your sense of the awful event, faintly represents your knowledge of the consummate excellence you so cordially honor.

Desperate indeed is any attempt on earth to meet correspondingly this dispensation of Heaven; for, while with pious resignation we submit to the will of an all-gracious Providence, we can never cease lamenting, in our finite view of Omnipotent Wisdom, the heart-rending privation for which our nation weeps. When the civilized world shakes to its centre; when every moment gives birth to strange and momentous changes; when our peaceful quarter of the globe, exempt as it happily has been from any share in the slaughter of the human race, may yet be compelled to abandon her pacific policy, and to risk the doleful casualties of war: What limit is there to the extent of our loss?—None within the reach of my words to express; none which your feelings will not disavow.

The founder of our federate republic—our bulwark in war, our guide in peace, is no more! Oh that this were but questionable! Hope, the comforter of the wretched, would pour into our agonizing hearts its balmy dew. But, alas! there is no hope for us; our Washington is removed for ever! Possessing the stoutest frame, and purest mind, he had passed nearly to his sixty-eighth year, in the enjoyment of high health, when, habituated by his care of us to neglect himself, a slight cold, disregarded, became inconvenient on Friday, oppressive on Saturday, and, defying every medical interposition, before the morning of Sunday, put an end to the best of men. An end did I say?—his fame survives!—bounded only by the limits of the earth, and by the extent of the human mind. He survives in our hearts, in the growing knowledge of our children, in the affections of the good throughout the world; and when our monuments shall be done away; when nations now existing shall be no more; when even our young and far-spreading empire shall have perished, still will our Washington's glory unfaded shine, and die not, until love of virtue cease on earth, or earth itself sinks into chaos.

How, my fellow-citizens, shall I single to your grateful hearts his pre-eminent worth! Where shall I begin in opening to your view a character throughout sublime? Shall I speak of his warlike achievements, all springing from obedience to his country's will—all directed to his country's good?

Will you go with me to the banks of the Monongahela, to see your youthful Washington, supporting, in the dismal hour of Indian victory, the ill-fated Braddock, and saving, by his judgment and by his valor, the remains of a defeated army, pressed by the conquering savage foe? Or, when oppressed America, nobly resolving to risk her all in defence of her violated rights, he was elevated by the unanimous voice of Congress to the command of her armies:—Will you follow him to the high grounds of Boston, where to an undisciplined, courageous, and virtuous yeomanry, his presence gave the stability of system, and infused the invincibility of love of country; or shall I carry you to the painful scenes of Long Island, York Island and New Jersey, when, combating superior and gallant armies, aided by powerful fleets, and led by chiefs nigh in the roll of fame, he stood, the bulwark of our safety; undismayed by disaster; unchanged by change of fortune. Or will you view him in the precarious fields of Trenton, where deep gloom unnerving every arm, reigned triumphant through our thinned, worn down, unaided ranks; himself unmoved. Dreadful was the night. It was about this time of winter—the storm raged—the Delaware rolling furiously with floating ice, forbade the approach of man. Washington, self-collected, viewed the tremendous scene—his country called; unappalled by surrounding dangers, he passed to the hostile shore; he fought; he conquered. The morning sun cheered the American world. Our country rose on the event; and her dauntless chief, pursuing his blow, completed in the lawns of Princeton, what his vast soul had conceived on the shores of Delaware.

Thence to the strong grounds of Morristown he led his small but gallant band; and through an eventful winter, by the high efforts of his genius, whose matchless force was measurable only by the growth of difficulties, he held in check formidable hostile legions, conducted by a chief experienced in the art of war, and famed for his valor on the ever memorable heights of Abraham, where fell Wolfe, Montcalm, and since, our much lamented Montgomery—all covered with glory. In this fortunate interval, produced by his masterly conduct, our fathers, ourselves, animated by his resistless example, rallied around our country's standard, and continued to follow her beloved chief through the various and trying scenes to which the destinies of our Union led.

Who is there that has forgotten the vales of Brandywine—the fields of Germantown—or the plains of Monmouth? Everywhere present, wants of every kind obstructing, numerous and valiant armies encountering, himself a host, he assuaged our sufferings, limited our privations, and upheld our tottering republic. Shall I display to you the spread of the fire of his soul, by rehearsing the praises of the Hero of Saratoga, and his much loved compeer of the Carolinas? No; our Washington wears no borrowed glory: to Gates—to Greene, he gave without reserve the applause due to their eminent merit; and long may the chiefs of Saratoga, and of Eutaws, receive the grateful respect of a grateful people.

Moving in his own orbit, he imparted heat and light to his most distant satellites; and combining the physical and moral force of all within his sphere, with irresistible weight he took his course, commiserating folly, disdaining vice, dismaying treason, and invigorating despondency; until the auspicious hour arrived, when, united with the intrepid forces of a potent and magnanimous ally, he brought to submission the since conqueror of India; thus finishing his long career of military glory with a lustre corresponding to his great name, and in this his last act of war affixing the seal of fate to our nation's birth.

To the horrid din of battle sweet peace succeeded, and our virtuous chief, mindful only of the common good, in a moment tempting personal aggrandizement, hushed the discontents of growing sedition; and, surrendering his power into the hands from which he had received it, converted his sword into a ploughshare, teaching an admiring world that to be truly great, you must be truly good.

Was I to stop here, the picture would be incomplete, and the task imposed unfinished. Great as was our Washington in war, and as much as did that greatness contribute to produce the American Republic, it is not in war alone his pre-eminence stands conspicuous. His various talents combining all the capacities of a statesman with those of a soldier, fitted him alike to guide the councils and the armies of our nation. Scarcely had he rested from his martial toils, while his invaluable parental advice was still sounding in our ears, when he who had been our shield and our sword, was called forth to act a less splendid but more important part.

Possessing a clear and penetrating mind, a strong and sound judgment, calmness and temper for deliberation, with invincible firmness, and perseverance in resolutions maturely formed, drawing information from all, acting from himself, with incorruptible integrity and unvarying patriotism: his own superiority and the public confidence alike marked him as the man designed by Heaven to lead in the great political as well as military events which have distinguished the era of his life.

The finger of an overruling providence, pointing at Washington, was neither mistaken nor unobserved when, to realize the vast hopes to which our revolution had given birth, a change of political system became indispensable.

How novel, how grand the spectacle! Independent states stretched over an immense territory, and known only by common difficulty, clinging to their union as the rock of their safety, deciding by frank comparison of their relative condition, to rear on that rock, under the guidance of reason, a common government, through whose commanding protection, liberty and order, with their long train of blessings, should be safe to themselves, and the sure inheritance of their posterity.

This arduous task devolved on citizens selected by the people, from knowledge of their wisdom and confidence in their virtue. In this august assembly of sages and patriots, Washington of course was found; and, as if acknowledged to be most wise, where all were wise, with one voice he was declared their chief. How well he merited this rare distinction, how faithful were the labours of himself and his compatriots, the work of their hands and our union, strength and prosperity, the fruits of that work, best attest.

But to have essentially aided in presenting to his country this consummation of her hopes, neither satisfied the claims of his fellow-citizens on his talents, nor those duties which the possession of those talents imposed. Heaven had not infused into his mind such an uncommon share of its ethereal spirit to remain unemployed, nor bestowed on him his genius unaccompanied with the corresponding duty of devoting it to the common good. To have framed a Constitution, was showing only, without ealizing, the general happiness. This great work remained to be done; and America, steadfast in her preference, with one voice summoned her beloved Washington, unpractised as he was in the duties of civil administration, to execute this last act in the completion of the national felicity. Obedient to her call, he assumed the high office with that self-distrust peculiar to his innate modesty, the constant attendant of pre-eminent virtue. What was the burst of joy through our anxious land on this exhilarating event is known to us all. The aged, the young, the brave, the fair, rivaled each other in demonstrations of their gratitude; and this high-wrought, delightful scene was heightened in its effect, by the singular contest between the zeal of the bestowers and the avoidance of the receiver of the honors bestowed. Commencing his administration, what heart is not charmed with the recollection of the pure and wise principles announced by himself, as the basis of his political life. He best understood the indissoluble union between virtue and happiness, between duty and advantage, between the genuine maxims of an honest and magnanimous policy, and the solid rewards of public prosperity and individual felicity; watching with an equal and comprehensive eye over this great assemblage of communities and interests, he laid the foundations of our national policy in the unerring, immutable principles of morality, based on religion, exemplifying the pre-eminence of a free government; by all the attributes which win the affections of its citizens, or command the respect of the world.

"O fortunatos nimium, sua si bona norint!"

Leading through the complicated difficulties produced by previous obligations and conflicting interests, seconded by succeeding houses of Congress, enlightened and patriotic, he surmounted all original obstruction, and brightened the path of our national felicity.

The presidential term expiring, his solicitude to exchange exaltation for humility returned with a force increased with increase of age; and he had prepared his farewell address to his countrymen, proclaiming his intention, when the united interposition of all around him, enforced by the eventful prospects of the epoch, produced a further sacrifice of inclination to duty. The election of President followed, and Washington, by the unanimous vote of the nation, was called to resume the Chief Magistracy. What a wonderful fixture of confidence! Which attracts most our admiration, a people so correct, or a citizen combining an assemblage of talents forbidding rivalry, and stifling even envy itself? Such a nation ought to be happy, such a chief must be for ever revered.

War, long menaced by the Indian tribes, now broke out; and the terrible conflict, deluging Europe with blood, began to shed its baneful influence over our happy land. To the first, outstretching his invincible arm, under the orders of the gallant Wayne, the American eagle soared triumphant through distant forests. Peace followed victory; and the melioration of the condition of the enemy followed peace. Godlike virtue, which uplifts even the subdued savage.

To the second he opposed himself. New and delicate was the conjuncture, and great was the stake. Soon did his penetrating mind discern and seize the only course, continuing to us all the felicity enjoyed. He issued his proclamation of neutrality. This index to his whole subsequent conduct was sanctioned by the approbation of both houses of Congress, and by the approving voice of the people.

To this sublime policy he inviolably adhered, unmoved by foreign intrusion, unshaken by domestic turbulence.

> "Justum et tenacem propositi virum,
> Non civium ardor prava jubentium,
> Non vultus instantis tyranni,
> Mente quatit folida."

Maintaining his pacific system at the expense of no duty, America, faithful to herself, and sustained in her honor, continued to enjoy the delights of peace, while afflicted Europe mourns in every quarter under the accumulated miseries of an unexampled war; miseries in which our happy country must have shared, had not our pre-eminent Washington been as firm in council as he was brave in the field.

Pursuing steadfastly his course, he held safe the public happiness, preventing foreign war, and quelling internal discord, till the revolving period of a third election approached, when he executed his interrupted but inextinguishable desire of returning to the humble walks of private life.

The promulgation of his fixed resolution stopped the anxious wishes of an affectionate people, from adding a third unanimous testimonial of their unabated confidence in the man so long enthroned in their hearts. When before was affection like this exhibited on earth? Turn over the records of ancient Greece! Review the annals of mighty Rome! Examine the volumes of modern Europe; you search in vain. America and her Washington only afford the dignified exemplification. The illustrious personage called by the national voice in succession to the arduous office of guiding a free people, had new difficulties to encounter. The amicable effort of settling our difficulties with France, begun by Washington, and pursued by his successor in virtue as in station, proving abortive, America took measures of self-defence. No sooner was the public mind roused by a prospect of danger, than every eye was turned to the friend of all, though secluded from public view, and gray in public service. The virtuous veteran following his plough, received the unexpected summons with mingled emotions of indignation at the unmerited ill-treatment of his country, and of a determination once more to risk his all in her defence.

The annunciation of these feelings, in his affecting letter to the President, accepting the command of the army, concludes his official conduct.

First in war, first in peace, and first in the hearts of his countrymen, he was second to none in the humble and endearing scenes of private life: pious, just, humane, temperate, and sincere, uniform, dignified, and commanding, his example was as edifying to all around him as were the effects of that example lasting.

To his equals he was condescending; to his inferiors kind; and to the dear object of his affections exemplarily tender. Correct throughout, vice shuddered in his presence, and virtue always felt his fostering hand; the purity of his private character gave effulgence to his public virtues.

His last scene comported with the whole tenor of his life; although in extreme pain, not a sigh, not a groan escaped him; and with undisturbed serenity he closed his well-spent life. Such was the man America has lost. such was the man for whom our nation mourns! Methinks I see his august image, and hear, falling from his venerable lips, these deep-sinking words:

"Cease, sons of America, lamenting our separation: go on, and confirm by your wisdom the fruits of our joint councils, joint efforts, and common dangers. Reverence religion; diffuse knowledge throughout your land; patronize the arts and sciences; let liberty and order be inseparable companions; control party-spirit, the bane of free government; observe good faith to, and cultivate peace with all nations; shut up every avenue to foreign influence; contract rather than extend national connexion; rely on yourselves only; be American in thought and deed. Thus will you give immortality to that union, which was the constant object of my terrestrial labours. Thus will you preserve undisturbed to the latest posterity the felicity of a people to me most dear; and thus will you supply (if my happiness is now aught to you) the only vacancy in the round of pure bliss high Heaven bestows."

FRIDAY, DECEMBER 27, 1799.

On a motion made and seconded that the House do come to the following resolution, to wit:

The House of Representatives of the United States, highly gratified with the manner in which Mr. Lee has performed the service assigned to him, under the resolution desiring the President of the Senate and Speaker of the House of Representatives to request one of the members of Congress to prepare and deliver a funeral oration on the death of George Washington; and desirous of communicating to their fellow-citizens, through the medium of the press, those sentiments of respect for the character, of gratitude for the services, and of grief for the death, of that illustrious personage, which, felt by all, have, on this melancholy occasion, been so well expressed:

Resolved, That the Speaker present the thanks of this House to Mr. Lee, for the oration delivered by him to both Houses of Congress on Thursday, the twenty-sixth instant; and request that he will permit a copy thereof to be taken for publication:

The question was taken that the House do agree to the same,
And unanimously resolved in the affirmative.

MONDAY, DECEMBER 30, 1799.

The Speaker informed the House that, in pursuance of the resolution of Friday last, he had addressed to Major General Henry Lee, one of the members for the State of Virginia, the following letter:

"*Philadelphia*, December 27, 1799.

"DEAR SIR: The enclosed resolutions, which unanimously passed the House of Representatives this day, will make known to you how highly they have been gratified with the manner in which you have performed the service assigned to you, in preparing and delivering a funeral oration on the death of General Washington. That our constituents may participate in the gratification we have received from your having so well expressed those sentiments of respect for the character, of gratitude for the services, and of grief for the death, of that illustrious personage, I flatter myself you will not hesitate to comply with the request of the House, by furnishing a copy of your oration, to be taken for publication.

"Allow me, while performing this pleasing task of official duty in communicating an act of the representatives of the people, so just to you and so honorable to themselves, to embrace the opportunity to declare that

"I am, personally, with great esteem and sincere regard, dear sir, your friend and obedient servant,

"THEODORE SEDGWICK.

"The honorable Maj. Gen. LEE."

To which Mr. Lee had replied as follows:

"*Franklin Court*, December 28, 1799.

"DEAR SIR: I owe to the goodness of the House of Representatives the honor which their resolutions confer on my humble efforts to execute their wish.

"I can never disobey their will, and therefore will furnish a copy* of the oration delivered on the late afflicting occasion, much as I had flattered myself with a different disposition of it.

"Sincerely reciprocating the personal consideration with which you honor me, I am, very respectfully, sir, your friend and obedient servant,

"HENRY LEE.

"The SPEAKER of the House of Representatives."

Mr. Marshall, from the joint committee appointed to prepare and report measures in honor of the memory of General George Washington, made a further report, in part; which was read and considered: Whereupon,

It was unanimously resolved that the House do agree to the following resolutions:

Resolved by the Senate and House of Representatives of the United States of America in Congress assembled, That it be recommended to the people of the United States to assemble, on the twenty-second day of February next, in such numbers and manner as may be convenient, publicly to testify their grief for the death of General George Washington, by suitable eulogies, orations, and discourses, or by public prayers.†

And it is further resolved, That the President be requested to issue a proclamation, for the purpose of carrying the foregoing resolution into effect.

Ordered, That the clerk of this House do carry the said resolutions to the Senate, and desire their concurrence.

---

* Vide the Oration, page 217.

† In conformity with this recommendation, the people of every city, town, village, and hamlet, whose numbers were swelled by the neighboring country-people, assembled, and with deep devotion rendered their heartfelt tribute of affection for the memory of the Father of their Country. This outpouring of gratitude and affection of a nation of free citizens has never been equalled more nearly than by the spontaneous and universal demonstration of this NATIONAL VIRTUE on the occasion of the visit of General Lafayette to the United States, in 1824.

[These resolutions were agreed to by the Senate on the 31st December, 1799, and approved by the President of the United States on the 6th January, 1800.]

MONDAY, JANUARY 6, 1800.

A message was received from the President of the United States, by Mr. Adams, notifying that the President did, this day, approve and sign certain enrolled resolutions, which originated in this House, directing further measures in honor of the memory of General George Washington.

Ordered, That the clerk of this House do acquaint the Senate therewith.

WEDNESDAY, JANUARY 8, 1800.

A message, in writing, was received from the President of the United States, by Mr. Shaw, his secretary, as followeth:

Gentlemen of the Senate, and
Gentlemen of the House of Representatives:

In compliance with the request in one of the resolutions of Congress of the twenty-first of December last, I transmitted a copy of those resolutions, by my secretary, Mr. Shaw, to Mrs. Washington, assuring her of the profound respect Congress will ever bear to her person and character; of their condolence in the late afflicting dispensation of Providence; and entreating her assent to the interment of the remains of General George Washington, in the manner expressed in the first resolution. As the sentiments of that virtuous lady, not less beloved by this nation than she is at present greatly afflicted, can never be so well expressed as in her own words, I transmit to Congress her original letter.

It would be an attempt of too much delicacy to make any comments upon it; but there can be no doubt that the nation at large, as well as all the branches of the Government, will be highly gratified by any arrangement which may diminish the sacrifice she makes of her individual feelings.

JOHN ADAMS.

United States, January 6, 1800.

The letter referred to in the said message is as follows:

"*Mount Vernon*, December 31, 1799.

"SIR: While I feel, with keenest anguish, the late dispensation of Divine Providence, I cannot be insensible to the mournful tributes of respect and veneration which are paid to the memory of my dear deceased husband; and, as his best services and most anxious wishes were always devoted to the welfare and happiness of his country, to know that they were truly appreciated and gratefully remembered affords no inconsiderable consolation.

"Taught, by that great example which I have so long had before me, never to oppose my private wishes to the public will, I must consent to the request made by Congress, which you have had the goodness to transmit to me; and, in doing this, I need not, I cannot, say what a sacrifice of individual feeling I make to a sense of public duty.

"With grateful acknowledgments and unfeigned thanks for the personal respect and evidences of condolence expressed by Congress and yourself, I remain, very respectfully, sir, your most obedient humble servant,

"MARTHA WASHINGTON."

The said message, and letter accompanying the same, were read, and ordered to be referred to the joint committee appointed the nineteenth ultimo, on receipt of the intelligence of the death of General George Washington, to prepare and report measures suitable to the occasion.

FRIDAY, MARCH 28, 1800.

On motion,

Resolved, That all letters and packets to Mrs. Martha Washington, relict of the late General George Washington, shall be received and conveyed by post, free from postage, for and during her life.

Ordered, That a bill or bills be brought in pursuant to the said resolu tion; and that Mr. Henry Lee, Mr. Kittera and Mr. Dennis, do prepare and bring in the same.

Mr. Henry Lee, from the committee appointed, presented, according to order, a bill to extend the privilege of franking letters and packages to Martha Washington; which was received, and read the first time.

On motion, the said bill was read the second time, and ordered to be engrossed, and read the third time on Monday next.

MONDAY, MARCH 31, 1800.

An engrossed bill to extend the privilege of franking letters and packages to Martha Washington, was read the third time.

Resolved, That the said bill do pass :—

AN ACT to extend the privilege of franking letters and packages to Martha Washington.

Be it enacted by the Senate and House of Representatives of the United States of America in Congress assembled, That all letters and packages to and from Martha Washington, shall be received and conveyed by post free of postage, for and during her life.

[This act was passed by the Senate on the 1st of April, and approved by the President of the United States, on the 3d April, 1800.]

IN THE SENATE OF THE UNITED STATES.

THURSDAY, DECEMBER 19, 1799.

The following written message was received from the President of the United States, by Mr. Shaw, his secretary:

Gentlemen of the Senate, and
Gentlemen of the House of Representatives:

The letter herewith transmitted* will inform you that it has pleased Divine Providence to remove from this life

---

* See letter from Tobias Lear on page 243.

our excellent fellow-citizen George Washington; by the purity of his character, and a long series of services to his country rendered illustrious through the world. It remains for an affectionate and grateful people, in whose hearts he can never die, to pay suitable honors to his memory. JOHN ADAMS.

United States, December 19, 1799.

The message and letter were read.

Ordered, That they lie for consideration.

A message from the House of Representatives, by Mr. Oswald, in the absence of their clerk:

Mr. President: The House of Representatives having received intelligence of the death of their highly-valued fellow-citizen, General George Washington, and sharing the universal grief this distressing event must produce, have *Resolved*, That a joint committee be appointed, to report measures suitable to the occasion, and expressive of the profound sorrow with which Congress is penetrated on the loss of a citizen, first in war, first in peace, and first in the hearts of his countrymen; and having appointed a committee on their part, desire the concurrence of the Senate. And he withdrew.

The Senate proceeded to consider the foregoing resolution of the House of Representatives. Whereupon,

Resolved, That they do concur therein, and that Messrs. Dayton, Bingham, Dexter, Gunn, Laurance, Tracy, and Read, be the committee on the part of the Senate.

Ordered, That the Secretary acquaint the House of Representatives with the concurrence.

On motion,

Resolved, That the Senate will wait on the President of the United States, to condole with him on the distressing event of the death of General George Washington; and that a committee be appointed to prepare, for that occasion, an address to the President of the United States, expressive of the deep regret of the Senate; and that this committee consist of Messrs. Dexter, Ross, and Read.

On motion,

Resolved, That the chairs in the Senate chamber be covered, and the room hung with black, and that each member, and the officers of th

Senate go into mourning, by the usual mode of wearing a crape round the left arm, during the session.

The Senate adjourned to 11 o'clock on Monday morning.

MONDAY, DECEMBER 23, 1799.

Mr. Dexter, from the committee, appointed for the purpose on the 18th inst., reported the draught of an address to the President of the United States, on the death of General George Washington; which being read in paragraphs, was adopted, as follows:

To the President of the United States:

The Senate of the United States respectfully take leave, sir, to express to you their deep regret for the loss their country sustains in the death of General George Washington.

This event, so distressing to all our fellow-citizens, must be peculiarly heavy to you, who have long been associated with him in deeds of patriotism. Permit us, sir, to mingle our tears with yours; on this occasion it is manly to weep. To lose such a man, at such a crisis, is no common calamity to the world: our country mourns her Father. The Almighty Disposer of human events has taken from us our greatest benefactor and ornament. It becomes us to submit with reverence to him who "maketh darkness his pavilion."

With patriotic pride we review the life of our Washington, and compare him with those of other countries, who have been pre-eminent in fame. Ancient and modern names are diminished before him. Greatness and guilt have too often been allied; but his fame is whiter than it is brilliant. The destroyers of nations stood abashed at the majesty of his virtue. It reproved the intemperance of their ambition, and darkened the splendor of victory. The scene is closed, and we are no longer anxious lest misfortune should sully his glory; he has travelled to the end of his journey, and carried with him an increasing weight of honor; he has deposited it safely, where misfortune cannot tarnish it, where malice cannot blast it. Favored of Heaven, he departed without exhibiting the weakness of humanity. Magnanimous in death, the darkness of the grave could not obscure his brightness.

Such was the man whom we deplore. Thanks to God! his glory is consummated; Washington yet lives—on earth in his spotless example—his spirit is in heaven.

Let his countrymen consecrate the memory of the heroic general, the patriotic statesman, and the virtuous sage; let them teach their children never to forget that the fruit of his labors and his example are their inheritance.

SAMUEL LIVERMORE,
President of the Senate, pro tempore.

Ordered, That the committee who prepared the address, wait on the President of the United States, and desire him to acquaint the Senate at what time and place it will be most convenient for him that it should be presented.

Mr. Dexter reported, from the committee, that they had waited on the President of the United States, and that he had acquainted them that he would receive the address of the Senate immediately, at his own house.

Whereupon, the Senate waited on the President of the United States, and the President of the Senate, in their name, presented the address this day agreed to.

To which the President of the United States was pleased to make the following reply:—

Gentlemen of the Senate:

I receive, with the most respectful and affectionate sentiments, in this impressive address, the obliging expressions of your regard for the loss our country has sustained in the death of her most esteemed, beloved, and admired citizen.

In the multitude of my thoughts and recollections on this melancholy event, you will permit me only to say, that I have seen him in the days of adversity, in some of the scenes of his deepest distress and most trying perplexities: I have also attended him in his highest elevation, and most prosperous felicity, with uniform admiration of his wisdom, moderation, and constancy.

Among all our original associates in that memorable league of the continent in 1774, which first expressed the sovereign will of a free nation in America, he was the only one remaining in the general government.

Although, with a constitution more enfeebled than his, at an age when he thought it necessary to prepare for retirement, I feel myself alone, bereaved of my last brother; yet I derive a strong consolation from the unanimous disposition which appears, in all ages and classes, to mingle their sorrows with mine, on this common calamity to the world.

The life of our Washington cannot suffer by a comparison with those of other countries who have been most celebrated and exalted by fame. The attributes and decorations of royalty could have only served to eclipse the majesty of those virtues which made him, from being a modest citizen, a more resplendent luminary. Misfortune, had he lived, could hereafter have sullied his glory only with those superficial minds, who, believing that characters and actions are marked by success alone, rarely deserve to enjoy it. Malice could never blast his honor, and envy made him a singular exception to her universal rule. For himself, he had lived enough to life, and to glory.

For his fellow-citizens, if their prayers could have been answered, he would have been immortal. For me, his departure is at a most unfortunate moment. Trusting, however, in the wise and righteous dominion of Providence over the passions of men, and the results of their councils and actions, as well as over their lives, nothing remains for me but humble resignation.

His example is now complete, and it will teach wisdom and virtue to magistrates, citizens, and men, not only in the present age, but in future generations, as long as our history shall be read. If a Trajan found a Pliny, a Marcus Aurelius can never want biographers, eulogists, or historians. JOHN ADAMS.

United States, December 23, 1799.

The Senate returned to their own chamber.

A message from the House of Representatives, by Mr. Condy, their Clerk:

Mr. President: The joint committee appointed on the part of the House of Representatives, on the 19th instant, on the receipt of the intelligence of the death of General George Washington, having made report to that House, they have agreed to sundry resolutions thereupon, in which they desire the concurrence of the Senate. And he withdrew.

Mr. Dayton, from the joint committee, appointed the 19th instant, on the part of the Senate, on the receipt of the intelligence of the death of General George Washington, reported in past, and the report was agreed to. Whereupon,

Resolved, unanimously, That the Senate do concur in the aforesaid resolutions.

THURSDAY, DECEMBER 26, 1799.

In conformity to the resolve of the 23d instant, the Senate went in procession to the German Lutheran Church, where was delivered an oration* in honor of the memory of General George Washington. After which, they returned to their own chamber; and

Adjourned to 11 o'clock to-morrow morning.

---

* See oration of Henry Lee, p. 247

FRIDAY, DECEMBER 27, 1799.

On motion,

Resolved, That the thanks of the Senate be communicated, through their President, to General Henry Lee, for the eloquent and impressive oration to the memory of General George Washington, which he prepared and delivered at the request of Congress.

Resolved, That the Secretary be directed to apply to General Lee for a copy of the same.

CHAPTER 5.

INAUGURAL ADDRESSES OF THE PATRIOTS AND SAGES OF THE REVOLUTION, WHO WERE ELEVATED BY THE SUFFRAGES OF THEIR FELLOW-CITIZENS TO THE OFFICE OF PRESIDENT OF THE UNITED STATES.

1. In seeking, among the great mass of literary matter that has emanated from the able and intelligent minds and honest hearts of the statesmen of the Revolution, for compositions or productions which imbody more completely than any others, and within the smallest compass, the true principles, objects, and designs, duties and responsibilities, of the American Government under the Constitution, none can be found comparable to the inaugural addresses of those wise and true patriots who brought with them to the presidential office, not only the experience they had acquired in those times when the energies and resources of the stoutest hearts and ablest minds were constantly in requisition, but the advantages of the highest intelligence, resulting from that investigation of causes, and deliberation upon effects, constituting the prominent characteristics of truly great minds. These worthy spirits had witnessed and felt the oppression of the colonial system of bondage; the want of a general government for the United Colonies in the commencement and progress of the Revolution; the total inefficiency of the old form of government under the Confederation; and some had taken part in, while all had been eye-witnesses of, the efficient and paternal administration of government under the Constitution by the great and good Washington. The sentiments and principles emanating from such sources, upon a subject so momentous, cannot fail to be highly interesting and instructive to the young statesmen and patriots of our country; while, to every American citizen capable of reading and understanding, they will be an invaluable means of judging properly of the views and principles

of the public men who may be candidates for their suffrage and favor; for, if their declarations and sentiments contradict those contained in these inaugural addresses, doubts may well be entertained of their soundness or sincerity, and every man will be justified, in the exercise of his birthright as an American citizen, in supporting the Constitution as understood and executed by its framers and best friends.

2. THE INAUGURAL ADDRESS OF GEORGE WASHINGTON, PRESIDENT OF THE UNITED STATES,

April 30, 1789,

(Will be found with his political acts in Chapter 4, p. 211.)

3. INAUGURAL ADDRESS OF JOHN ADAMS, PRESIDENT OF THE UNITED STATES.

March 4, 1797.

When it was first perceived, in early times, that no middle course for America remained between unlimited submission to a foreign legislature and a total independence of its claims, men of reflection were less apprehensive of danger from the formidable power of fleets and armies they must determine to resist, than from those contests and dissensions which would certainly arise concerning the forms of government to be instituted over the whole and over the parts of this extensive country. Relying, however, on the purity of their intentions, the justice of their cause, and the integrity and intelligence of the people, under an overruling Providence, which had so signally protected this country from the first, the representatives of this nation, then consisting of little more than half its present number, not only broke to pieces the chains which were forging, and the rod of iron that was lifted up, but frankly cut asunder the ties which had bound them, and launched into an ocean of uncertainty.

The zeal and ardor of the people, during the revolutionary war, supplying the place of government, commanded a degree of order, sufficient at least for the temporary preservation of society. The Confederation, which was early felt to be necessary, was prepared from the models of the Batavian and Helvetic confederacies—the only examples which remain, with any detail and precision, in history, and certainly the only ones which the people at large had ever considered. But, reflecting on the striking difference, in so many particulars, between this country and those where a courier may go from the seat of government to the frontier in a single day, it was then certainly foreseen, by some who assisted in Congress at the formation of it, that it could not be durable.

Negligence of its regulations, inattention to its recommendations, if not disobedience to its authority, not only in individuals, but in States, soon appeared, with their melancholy consequences; universal languor; jealousies and rivalries of States; decline of navigation and commerce; discouragement of necessary manufactures; universal fall in the value of lands and their produce; contempt of public and private faith; loss of consideration and credit with foreign nations; and, at length, in discontents, animosities, combinations, partial conventions, and insurrection, threatening some great national calamity.

In this dangerous crisis, the people of America were not abandoned by their usual good sense, presence of mind, resolution, or integrity. Measures were pursued to concert a plan to form a more perfect union, establish justice, ensure domestic tranquillity, provide for the common defence, promote the general welfare, and secure the blessings of liberty. The public disquisitions, discussions, and deliberations, issued in the present happy constitution of government.

Employed in the service of my country abroad during the whole course of these transactions, I first saw the Constitution of the United States in a foreign country. Irritated by no literary altercation, animated by no public debate, heated by no party animosity, I read it with great satisfaction, as the result of good heads, prompted by good hearts—as an experiment, better adapted to the genius, character, situation, and relations, of this nation and country, than any which had ever been proposed or suggested. In its general principles and great outlines, it was conformable to such a system of government as I had ever most esteemed, and in some States, my own native State in particular, had contributed to establish. Claiming a right of suffrage, in common with my fellow-citizens, in the adoption or rejection of a Constitution which was to rule me and my posterity, as well as them and theirs, I did not hesitate to express my approbation of it, on all occasions, in public and in private. It was not then, nor has been since, any objection to it, in my mind, that the Executive and Senate were not more permanent. Nor have I ever entertained a thought of promoting any alteration in it, but such as the people themselves, in the course of their experience, should see and feel to be necessary or expedient, and, by their representatives in Congress and the State legislatures, according to the Constitution itself, adopt and ordain.

Returning to the bosom of my country, after a painful separation from it, for ten years, I had the honor to be elected to a station under the new order of things, and I have repeatedly laid myself under the most serious obligations to support the Constitution. The operation of it has equalled the most sanguine expectations of its friends; and, from an habitual attention to it, satisfaction in its administration, and delight in its effects upon the peace, order, prosperity and happiness of the nation, I have acquired an habitual attachment to it and veneration for it.

What other form of government, indeed, can so well deserve our esteem and love?

There may be little solidity in an ancient idea, that congregations of men into cities and nations are the most pleasing objects in the sight of superior intelligences; but this is very certain, that, to a benevolent human mind, there can be no spectacle presented by any nation more pleasing, more noble, majestic, or august, than an assembly like that which has so often been seen in this and the other chamber of Congress, of a government in which the executive authority, as well as that of all the branches of the legislature, are exercised by citizens selected, at regular periods, by their neighbors, to make and execute laws for the general good. Can any thing essential, any thing more than mere ornament and decoration, be added to this by robes and diamonds? Can authority be more amiable and respectable when it descends from accidents, or institutions established in remote antiquity, than when it springs fresh from the hearts and judgments of an honest and enlightened people? For it is the people only that are represented: it is their power and majesty that is reflected, and only for their good, in every legitimate government, under whatever form it may appear. The existence of such a government as ours, for any length of time, is a full proof of a general dissemination of knowledge and virtue throughout the whole body of the people. And what object or consideration more pleasing than this can be presented to the human mind? If national pride is ever justifiable, or excusable, it is when it springs, not from power or riches, grandeur or glory, but from conviction of national innocence, information, and benevolence.

In the midst of these pleasing ideas, we should be unfaithful to ourselves if we should ever lose sight of the danger to our liberties—if any thing partial or extraneous should infect the purity of our free, fair, virtuous, and independent elections. If an election is to be determined by a majority of a single vote, and that can be procured by a party, through artifice or corruption, the government may be the choice of a party, for its own ends—not of the nation, for the national good. If that solitary suffrage can be obtained by foreign nations by flattery or menaces, by fraud or violence, by terror, intrigue, or venality, the government may not be the choice of the American people, but of foreign nations. It may be foreign nations who govern us, and not we the people who govern ourselves. And candid men will acknowledge, that, in such cases, choice would have little advantage to boast of, over lot or chance.

Such is the amiable and interesting system of government (and such are some of the abuses to which it may be exposed) which the people of America have exhibited to the admiration and anxiety of the wise and virtuous of all nations, for eight years, under the administration of a citizen, who, by a long course of great actions, regulated by prudence, justice, temperance, and fortitude, conducting a people inspired with the same virtues, and animated with the same ardent patriotism and love of liberty, to independence and peace, to increasing wealth and unexampled prosperity, has merited the gratitude of his fellow-citizens, commanded the highest praises of foreign nations, and secured immortal glory with posterity.

In that retirement which is his voluntary choice, may he long live to enjoy the delicious recollection of his services, the gratitude of mankind, the happy fruits of them to himself and the world, which are daily increasing, and that splendid prospect of the future fortunes of this country which is opening from year to year. His name may be still a rampart, and the knowledge that he lives a bulwark, against all open or secret enemies of his country's peace. This example has been recommended to the imitation of his successors, by both houses of Congress, and by the voice of the legislatures and the people throughout the nation.

On this subject it might become me better to be silent, or to speak with diffidence; but, as something may be expected, the occasion, I hope, will be admitted as an apology, if I venture to say, That—

If a preference, upon principle, of a free republican government, formed upon long and serious reflection, after a diligent and impartial inquiry after truth; if an attachment to the Constitution of the United States, and a conscientious determination to support it, until it shall be altered by the judgments and wishes of the people, expressed in the mode prescribed in it; if a respectful attention to the constitutions of the individual States, and a constant caution and delicacy towards the State governments; if an equal and impartial regard to the rights, interest, honor, and happiness, of all the States in the Union, without preference or regard to a northern or southern, an eastern or western position, their various political opinions on unessential points, or their personal attachments; if a love of virtuous men, of all parties and denominations; if a love of science and letters, and a wish to patronize every rational effort to encourage schools, colleges, universities, academies, and every institution for propagating knowledge, virtue, and religion, among all classes of the people, not only for their benign influence on the happiness of life in all its stages and classes, and of society in all its forms, but as the only means of preserving our Constitution from its natural enemies, the spirit of sophistry, the spirit of party, the spirit of intrigue, the profligacy of corruption, and the pestilence of foreign influence, which is the angel of destruction to elective governments; if a love of equal laws, of justice, and humanity, in the interior administration; if an inclination to improve agriculture, commerce, and manufactures for necessity, convenience, and defence; if a spirit of equity and humanity towards the aboriginal nations of America, and a disposition to meliorate their condition, by inclining them to be more friendly to us, and our citizens to be more friendly to them; if an inflexible determination to maintain peace and inviolable faith with all nations, and that system of neutrality and impartiality among the belligerent powers of Europe which has been adopted by this government, and so solemnly sanctioned by both houses of Congress, and applauded by the legislatures of the States and the public opinion, until it shall be otherwise ordained by Congress; if a personal esteem for the French nation, formed in a residence of seven years chiefly among them, and a sincere desire to preserve the friendship which has been so much for the honor and interest of both nations; if, while the conscious honor and integrity of the people of America, and the internal sentiment of their own power and energies, must be preserved, an earnest endeavor to investigate every just cause, and remove every colorable pretence of complaint; if an intention to pursue, by amicable negotiation, a reparation for the injuries that have been committed on the commerce of our fellow-citizens, by whatever nation, and, if success cannot be obtained, to lay the facts before the legislature, that they may consider what further measures the honor and interest of the Government and its constituents demand; if a resolution to do justice, as far as may depend upon me, at all times and to all nations, and maintain peace, friendship, and benevolence, with all the world; if an unshaken confidence in the honor, spirit, and resources of the American people, on which I have so often hazarded my all, and never been deceived; if elevated ideas of the high destinies of this country, and of my own duties towards it, founded on a knowledge of the moral principles and intellectual improvements of the people, deeply engraven on my mind in early life, and not obscured, but exalted, by experience and age; and, with humble reverence, I feel it to be my duty to add, if a veneration for the religion of a people who profess and call themselves Christians, and a fixed resolution to consider a decent respect for Christianity among the best recommendations for the public service,—can enable me, in any degree, to comply with your wishes, it shall be my strenuous endeavor that this sagacious injunction of the two houses shall not be without effect.

With this great example before me—with the sense and spirit, the faith and honor, the duty and interest, of the same American people, pledged to support the Constitution of the United States, I entertain no doubt of its continuance in all its energy, and my mind is prepared, without hesitation, to lay myself under the most solemn obligations to support it to the utmost of my power.

And may that Being who is supreme over all, the Patron of order, the Fountain of justice, and the Protector, in all ages of the world, of virtuous liberty, continue His blessing upon this nation and its Government, and give it all possible success and duration; consistent with the ends of his Providence!

4. INAUGURAL ADDRESS OF THOMAS JEFFERSON, PRESIDENT OF THE UNITED STATES, AT HIS FIRST TERM OF OFFICE.

MARCH 4, 1801.

Friends and fellow-citizens:

Called upon to undertake the duties of the first executive office of our country, I avail myself of the presence of that portion of my fellow-citizens which is here assembled, to express my grateful thanks for the favor with which they have been pleased to look towards me, to declare a sincere consciousness that the task is above my talents, and that I approach it with those anxious and awful presentiments which the greatness of the charge and the weakness of my powers so justly inspire. A rising nation, spread over a wide and fruitful land; traversing all the seas with the rich productions of their industry; engaged in commerce with nations who feel power and forget right; advancing rapidly to destinies beyond the reach of mortal eye,—when I contemplate these transcendant objects, and see the honor, the happiness, and the hopes of this beloved country committed to the issue and the auspices of this day, I shrink from the contemplation, and humble myself before the magnitude of the undertaking. Utterly, indeed, should I despair, did not the presence of many whom I here see remind me that in the other high authorities provided by our Constitution I shall find resources of wisdom, of virtue, and of zeal, on which to rely under all difficulties. To you, then, gentlemen, who are charged with the sovereign functions of legislation, and to those associated with you, I look with encouragement for that guidance and support which may enable us to steer with safety the vessel in which we are all embarked, amidst the conflicting elements of a troubled world.

During the contest of opinion through which we have passed, the animation of discussions and of exertions has sometimes worn an aspect which might impose on strangers, unused to think freely, and to speak and to write what they think; but, this being now decided by the voice of the nation, announced, according to the rules of the Constitution, all will, of course, arrange themselves under the will of the law, and unite in common efforts for the common good. All, too, will bear in mind this sacred principle, that, though the will of the majority is in all cases to prevail, that will, to be rightful, must be reasonable; that the minority possess their equal rights, which equal laws must protect, and to violate would be oppression. Let us, then, fellow-citizens, unite with one heart and one mind; let us restore to social intercourse that harmony and affection without which liberty and even life itself are but dreary things. And let us reflect, that, having banished from our land that religious intolerance under which mankind so long bled and suffered, we have yet gained little, if we countenance a political intolerance as despotic, as wicked, and capable of as bitter and bloody persecutions. During the throes and convulsions of the ancient world; during the agonizing spasms of infuriated man, seeking, through blood and slaughter, his long-lost liberty, it was not wonderful that the agitation of the billows should reach even this distant and peaceful shore; that this should be more felt and feared by some, and less by others, and should divide opinions as to measures of safety: but every difference of opinion is not a difference of principle. We have called by different names brethren of the same principle. We are all republicans: we are all federalists. If there be any among us who would wish to dissolve this Union, or to change its republican form, let them stand, undisturbed, as monuments of the safety with which *error of opinion may be tolerated, where reason is left free to combat it.* I know, indeed, that some honest men fear that a republican government cannot be strong—that this Government is not strong enough. But would the honest patriot, in the full tide of successful experiment, abandon a Government which has so far kept us free and firm, on the theoretic and visionary fear that this Government, the world's best hope, may, by possibility, want energy to preserve itself? I trust not. I believe this, on the contrary, the strongest Government on earth. I believe it the only one where every man, at the call of the law, would fly to the standard of the law, and would meet invasions of the public order as his own personal concern. Sometimes it is said that man cannot be trusted with the government of himself. Can he then be trusted with the government of others? Or have we found angels, in the form of kings, to govern him? Let history answer this question.

Let us, then, with courage and confidence, pursue our own federal and republican principles—our attachment to union and representative government. Kindly separated by nature and a wide ocean from the exterminating havoc of one quarter of the globe;

too high-minded to endure the degradations of the others; possessing a chosen country, with room enough for our descendants to the thousandth and thousandth generation; entertaining a due sense of our equal right to the use of our own faculties, to the acquisitions of our own industry, to honor and confidence from our fellow-citizens, resulting, not from birth, but from our actions, and their sense of them; enlightened by a benign religion, professed, indeed, and practised, in various forms, yet all of them inculcating honesty, truth, temperance, gratitude, and the love of man; acknowledging and adoring an overruling Providence, which, by all its dispensations, proves that it delights in the happiness of man here, and his greater happiness hereafter,—with all these blessings, what more is necessary to make us a happy and prosperous people? Still one thing more, fellow-citizens: a wise and frugal Government, which shall restrain men from injuring one another, shall leave them otherwise free to regulate their own pursuits of industry and improvement, and shall not take from the mouth of labor the bread it has earned. This is the sum of good government, and this is necessary to close the circle of our felicities.

About to enter, fellow-citizens, on the exercise of duties which comprehend every thing dear and valuable to you, it is proper you should understand what I deem the essential principles of our Government, and, consequently, those which ought to shape its administration. I will compress them within the narrowest compass they will bear—stating the general principle, but not all its limitations. Equal and exact justice to all men, of whatever state or persuasion, religious or political; peace, commerce, and honest friendship with all nations, entangling alliances with none; the support of the State governments in all their rights, as the most competent administrations for our domestic concerns, and the surest bulwarks against anti-republican tendencies; the preservation of the General Government in its whole constitutional vigor, as the sheet-anchor of our peace at home and safety abroad; a jealous care of the right of election by the people; a mild and safe corrective of abuses which are lopped by the sword of revolution, where peaceable remedies are unprovided; absolute acquiescence in the decisions of the majority, the vital principle of republics, from which is no appeal but to force, the vital principle and immediate parent of despotism; a well-disciplined militia, our best reliance in peace, and for the first moments of war, till regulars may relieve them; the supremacy of the civil over the military authority; economy in the public expense, that labor may be lightly burdened; the honest payment of our debts, and sacred preservation of the public faith; encouragement of agriculture, and of commerce as its handmaid; the diffusion of information, and arraignment of all abuses at the bar of the public reason; freedom of religion, freedom of the press, and freedom of person, under the protection of the habeas corpus; and trial by juries impartially selected. These principles form the bright constellation which has gone before us, and guided our steps through an age of revolution and reformation. The wisdom of our sages and blood of our heroes have been devoted to their attainment. They should be the creed of our political faith, the text of civic instruction, the touchstone by which to try the services of those we trust; and should we wander from them in moments of error or of alarm, let us hasten to retrace our steps, and to regain the road which alone leads to peace, liberty, and safety.

I repair, then, fellow-citizens, to the post you have assigned me. With experience enough in subordinate offices to have seen the difficulties of this, the greatest of all, I have learnt to expect that it will rarely fall to the lot of imperfect man to retire from this station with the reputation and the favor which brought him into it. Without pretensions to that high confidence you reposed in our first and greatest revolutionary character, whose pre-eminent services had entitled him to the first place in his country's love, and destined for him the fairest page in the volume of faithful history, I ask so much confidence only as may give firmness and effect to the legal administration of your affairs. I shall often go wrong, through defect of judgment. When right, I shall often be thought wrong by those whose positions will not command a view of the whole ground. I ask your indulgence for my own errors, which will never be intentional, and your support against the errors of others, who may condemn what they would not if seen in all its parts. The approbation implied by your suffrage is a great consolation to me for the past; and my future solicitude will be, to retain the good opinion of those who have bestowed it in advance, to conciliate that of others by doing them all the good in my power, and to be instrumental to the happiness and freedom of all.

Relying, then, on the patronage of your good will, I advance with obedience to the work, ready to retire from it whenever you become sensible how much better choices it is in your power to make. And may that Infinite power which rules the destinies of the universe, lead our councils to what is best, and give them a favorable issue for your peace and prosperity.

5. INAUGURAL ADDRESS OF THOMAS JEFFERSON, PRESIDENT OF THE UNITED STATES, AT HIS SECOND TERM OF OFFICE.

March 4, 1805.

Proceeding, fellow-citizens, to that qualification which the Constitution requires before my entrance on the charge again conferred on me, it is my duty to express the deep sense I entertain of this new proof of confidence from my fellow-citizens at large, and the zeal with which it inspires me so to conduct myself as may best satisfy their just expectations.

On taking this station, on a former occasion, I declared the principles on which I believed it my duty to administer the affairs of our commonwealth. My conscience tells me I have, on every occasion, acted up to that declaration, according to its obvious import, and to the understanding of every candid mind.

In the transaction of your foreign affairs, we have endeavored to cultivate the friendship of all nations, and especially of those with which we have the most important relations. We have done them justice on all occasions, favor where favor was lawful, and cherished mutual interests and intercourse on fair and equal terms. We are firmly convinced, and we act on that conviction, that with nations, as with individuals, our interests, soundly calculated, will ever be found inseparable from our moral duties ; and history bears witness to the fact, that a just nation is trusted on its word, when recourse is had to armaments and wars to bridle others.

At home, fellow-citizens, you best know whether we have done well or ill. The suppression of unnecessary offices, of useless establishments and expenses, enabled us to discontinue our internal taxes. These, covering our land with officers, and opening our doors to their intrusions, had already begun that process of domiciliary vexation, which, once entered, is scarcely to be restrained from reaching, successively, every article of property and produce. If, among these taxes, some minor ones fell, which had not been inconvenient, it was because their amount would not have paid the officers who collected them, and because, if they had any merit, the State authorities might adopt them instead of others less approved.

The remaining revenue, on the consumption of foreign articles, is paid chiefly by those who can afford to add foreign luxuries to domestic comforts. Being collected on our seaboard and frontiers only, and incorporated with the transactions of our mercantile citizens, it may be the pleasure and the pride of an American to ask, what farmer, what mechanic, what laborer, ever sees a tax-gatherer of the United States ? These contributions enable us to support the current expenses of the Government ; to fulfil contracts with foreign nations; to extinguish the native right of soil within our limits; to extend those limits; and to apply such a surplus to our public debts as places at a short day their final redemption: and, that redemption once effected, the revenue thereby liberated may, by a just repartition of it among the States, and a corresponding amendment of the Constitution, be applied, *in time of peace*, to rivers, canals, roads, arts, manufactures, education, and other great objects, within each State. *In time of war*, if injustice by ourselves or others must sometimes produce war, increased, as the same revenue will be, by increased population and consumption, and aided by other resources reserved for that crisis, it may meet, within the year, all the expenses of the year, without encroaching on the rights of future generations, by burdening them with the debts of the past. War will then be but a suspension of useful works; and a return to a state of peace, a return to the progress of improvement.

I have said, fellow-citizens, that the income reserved had enabled us to extend our limits; but that extension may possibly pay for itself before we are called on, and, in the mean time, may keep down the accruing interest: in all events, it will replace the advances we shall have made. I know that the acquisition of Louisiana has been disapproved by some, from a candid apprehension that the enlargement of our territory would endanger its union. But who can limit the extent to which the federative principle may operate effectively? The larger our association, the less will it be shaken by local passions; and, in any view, is it not better that the opposite bank of the Mississippi should be settled by our own brethren and children, than by strangers of another family? With which should we be most likely to live in harmony and friendly intercourse?

In matters of religion, I have considered that its free exercise is placed by the Constitution independent of the powers of the General Government. I have therefore undertaken, on no occasion, to prescribe the religious exercises suited to it, but have left them, as the Constitution found them, under the direction and discipline of the church or State authorities acknowledged by the several religious societies.

The aboriginal inhabitants of these countries I have regarded with the commiseration their history inspires. Endowed with the faculties and the rights of men, breathing an ardent love of liberty and independence, and occupying a country which left them no desire but to be undisturbed, the stream of overflowing population from other regions directed itself on these shores. Without power to divert, or habits to contend against it, they have been overwhelmed by the current, or driven before it. Now reduced within limits too narrow for the hunter state, humanity enjoins us to teach them agriculture and the domestic arts, to encourage them to that industry which alone can enable them to maintain their place in existence, and to prepare them, in time, for that state of society which to bodily comforts adds the improvement of the mind and morals. We have, therefore, liberally furnished them with the implements of husbandry and household use: we have placed among them instructors in the arts of first necessity; and they are covered with the ægis of the law against aggressors from among ourselves.

But the endeavors to enlighten them on the fate which awaits their present course of life, to induce them to exercise their reason, follow its dictates, and change their pursuits with the change of circumstances, have powerful obstacles to encounter. They are combated by the habits of their bodies, prejudices of their minds, ignorance, pride, and the influence of interested and crafty individuals among them, who feel themselves something in the present order of things, and fear to become nothing in any other. These persons inculcate a sanctimonious reverence for the customs of their ancestors; that whatsoever they did must be done through all time; that reason is a false guide, and to advance under its counsel in their physical, moral, or political condition, is perilous innovation; that their duty is to remain as the Creator made them—ignorance being safety, and knowledge full of danger. In short, my friends, among them, also, is seen the action and counteraction of good sense and of bigotry. They, too, have their anti-philosophists, who find an interest in keeping things in their present state, who dread reformation, and exert all their faculties to maintain the ascendency of habit over the duty of improving our reason and obeying its mandates.

In giving these outlines, I do not mean, fellow-citizens, to arrogate to myself the merit of the measures: that is due, in the first place, to the reflecting character of our citizens at large, who, by the weight of public opinion, influence and strengthen the public measures. It is due to the sound discretion with which they select from among themselves those to whom they confide the legislative duties. It is due to the zeal and wisdom of the characters thus selected, who lay the foundations of public happiness in wholesome laws, the execution of which alone remains for others. And it is due to the able and faithful auxiliaries whose patriotism has associated them with me in the executive functions.

During this course of administration, and in order to disturb it, the artillery of the press has been levelled against us, charged with whatsoever its licentiousness could devise or dare. These abuses of an institution so important to freedom and science are deeply to be regretted, inasmuch as they tend to lessen its usefulness and to sap its safety. They might, indeed, have been corrected by the wholesome punishments reserved to and provided by the laws of the several States against falsehood and defamation; but public duties, more urgent, press on the time of public servants, and the offenders have therefore been left to find their punishment in the public indignation.

Nor was it uninteresting to the world, that an experiment should be fairly and fully made, whether freedom of discussion, unaided by power, is not sufficient for the propagation and protection of truth? Whether a government, conducting itself in the true spirit of its constitution, with zeal and purity, and doing no act which it would be unwilling the whole world should witness, can be written down by falsehood and defamation? The experiment has been tried. You have witnessed the scene. Our fellow-citizens looked on cool and collected. They saw the latent source from which these outrages proceeded. They gathered around their public functionaries; and, when the Constitution called them to the decision by suffrage, they pronounced their verdict honorable to those who had served them, and consolatory to the friend of man, who believes that he may be trusted with the control of his own affairs.

No inference is here intended that the laws provided by the States against false and defamatory publications should not be enforced. He who has time, renders a service to public morals and public tranquillity in reforming these abuses by the salutary coercions of the law. But the experiment is noted to prove that, since truth and reason have maintained their ground against false opinions, in league with false facts, the press, confined to truth, needs no other legal restraint. The public judgment will correct false reasonings and opinions, on a full hearing of all parties; and no other definite line can be drawn between the inestimable liberty of the press and its demoralizing licentiousness. If there be still improprieties which this rule would not restrain, its supplement must be sought in the censorship of public opinion.

Contemplating the union of sentiment now manifested so generally, as auguring harmony and happiness to our future course, I offer to our country sincere congratulations. With those, too, not yet rallied to the same point, the disposition to do so is gaining strength. Facts are piercing through the veil drawn over them; and our doubting brethren will at length see that the mass of their fellow-citizens, with whom they cannot yet resolve to act, as to principles and measures, think as they think, and desire what they desire; that our wish, as well as theirs, is, that the public efforts may be directed honestly to the public good, that peace be cultivated, civil and religious liberty unassailed, law and order preserved, equality of rights maintained, and that state of property, equal or unequal, which results to every man from his own industry or that of his father's. When satisfied of these views, it is not in human nature that they should not approve and support them. In the mean time, let us cherish them with patient affection; let us do them justice, and more than justice, in all competitions of interest,—and we need not doubt that truth, reason, and their own interests, will at length prevail—will gather them into the fold of their country, and will complete that entire union of opinion which gives to a nation the blessing of harmony, and the benefit of all its strength.

I shall now enter on the duties to which my fellow-citizens have again called me, and shall proceed in the spirit of those principles which they have approved. I fear not that any motives of interest may lead me astray. I am sensible of no passion which could seduce me, knowingly, from the path of justice; but the weaknesses of human nature, and the limits of my own understanding, will produce errors of judgment sometimes injurious to your interests. I shall need, therefore, all the indulgence which I have heretofore experienced from my constituents. The want of it will certainly not lessen with increasing years. I shall need, too, the favor of that Being in whose hands we are; who led our fathers, as Israel of old, from their native land, and planted them in a country flowing with all the necessaries and comforts of life; who has covered our infancy with His providence, and our riper years with His wisdom and power; and to whose goodness I ask you to join in supplications with me, that He will so enlighten the minds of your servants, guide their councils, and prosper their measures, that whatsoever they do shall result in your good, and shall secure to you the peace, friendship, and approbation of all nations.

6. INAUGURAL ADDRESS OF JAMES MADISON, PRESIDENT OF THE UNITED STATES, AT HIS FIRST TERM OF OFFICE.

MARCH 4, 1809.

Gentlemen of the Senate, and of the House of Representatives:

Unwilling to depart from examples of the most revered authority, I avail myself of the occasion now presented, to express the profound impression made on me, by the call of my country, to the station, to the duties of which I am about to pledge myself, by the most solemn of sanctions. So distinguished a mark of confidence, proceeding from the deliberate and tranquil suffrage of a free and virtuous nation, would, under any circumstances, have commanded my gratitude and devotion, as well as filled me with an awful sense of the trust to be assumed. Under the various circumstances which give peculiar solemnity to the existing period, I feel that both the honor and the responsibility allotted to me, are inexpressibly enhanced.

The present situation of the world is, indeed, without a parallel; and that of our country full of difficulties. The pressure of these two is the more severely felt, because they have fallen upon us at a moment when national prosperity, being at a height not before attained, the contrast resulting from this change has been rendered the more striking. Under the benign influence of our republican institutions, and the maintenance of peace with all nations, whilst so many of them were engaged in bloody and wasteful wars, the fruits of a just policy were enjoyed in an unrivalled growth of our faculties and resources. Proofs of this were seen in the improvements of agriculture; in the successful enterprises of commerce; in the progress of manufactures and useful arts; in the increase of the public revenue, and the use made of it in reducing the public debt; and in the valuable works and establishments everywhere multiplying over the face of our land.

It is a precious reflection, that the transition from this prosperous condition of our country, to the scene which has for some time been distressing us, is not chargeable on any unwarrantable views, nor, as I trust, on any involuntary errors in the public councils. Indulging no passions which trespass on the rights or the respose of other nations, it has been the true glory of the United States to cultivate peace, by observing justice, and to entitle themselves to the respect of the nations at war, by fulfilling their neutral obligations with the most scrupulous impartiality. If there be candor in the world, the truth of these assertions will not be questioned. Posterity, at least, will do justice to them.

This unexceptionable course could not avail against the injustice and violence of the belligerent powers. In their rage against each other, or impelled by more direct motives, principles of retaliation have been introduced, equally contrary to universal reason and acknowledged law. How long their arbitrary edicts will be continued, in spite of the demonstrations that not even a pretext for them has been given by the United States, and of the fair and liberal attempts to induce a revocation of them, cannot be anticipated. Assuring myself that, under every vicissitude, the determined spirit and united councils of the nation will be safeguards to its honor and its essential interests, I repair to the post assigned me, with no other discouragement than what springs from my own inadequacy to its high duties. If I do not sink under the weight of this deep conviction, it is because I find some support in a consciousness of the purposes, and a confidence in the principles which I bring with me into this arduous service.

To cherish peace and friendly intercourse with all nations, having correspondent dispositions; to maintain sincere neutrality towards belligerent nations; to prefer, in all cases, amicable discussion and reasonable accommodation of differences, to a decision of them by an appeal to arms; to exclude foreign intrigues and foreign partialities, so degrading to all countries, and so baneful to free ones; to foster a spirit of independence; too just to invade the rights of others; too proud to surrender our own; too liberal to indulge unworthy prejudices ourselves, and too elevated not to look down upon them in others; to hold the union of the States as the basis of their peace and happiness; to support the Constitution, which is the cement of the Union, as well in its limitations as in its authorities; to respect the rights and authorities reserved to the States and to the people, as equally incorporated with, and essential to the success of the general system; to avoid the slightest interference with the rights of conscience, or the functions of religion, so wisely exempted from civil jurisdiction; to preserve, to their full energy, the other salutary provisions in behalf of private and personal rights, and of the freedom of the press; to observe economy in public expenditures; to liberate the public resources by an honorable discharge of the public debts; to keep within the requisite limits a standing military force, always remembering, that an armed and trained militia is the firmest bulwark of republics; that without standing armies their liberty can never be in danger, nor, with large ones, safe; to promote, by authorized means, improvements friendly to agriculture, to manufactures, and to external as well as internal commerce; to favor, in like manner, the advancement of science and the diffusion of information, as the best aliment to true liberty; to carry on the benevolent plans which have been so meritoriously applied to the conversion of our aboriginal neighbors, from the degradation and wretchedness of savage life, to a participation of the improvements of which the human mind and manners are susceptible in a civilized state: As far as sentiments and intentions such as these can aid the fulfilment of my duty, they will be a resource which cannot fail me.

It is my good fortune, moreover, to have the path in which I am to tread, lighted by examples of illustrious services, successfully rendered in the most trying difficulties, by those who have marched before me. Of those of my immediate predecessor, it might least become me here to speak—I may, however, be pardoned for not suppressing the sympathy, with which my heart is full, in the rich reward he enjoys in the benedictions of a beloved country, gratefully bestowed for exalted talents, zealously devoted, through a long career, to the advancement of its highest interest and happiness. But the source to which I look for the aids, which alone can supply my deficiencies, is in the well-tried intelligence and virtue of my fellow-citizens, and in the councils of those representing them in the other departments associated in the care of the national interests. In these my confidence will, under every difficulty, be best placed; next to that which we have all been encouraged to feel in the guardianship and guidance of that Almighty Being, whose power regulates the destiny of nations, whose blessings have been so conspicuously dispensed to this rising Republic, and to whom we are bound to address our devcut gratitude for the past, as well as our fervent supplications and best hopes for the future.

CHAPTER 6.

GENERAL LAWS RELATING TO THE CONTINUED ORGANIZATION OF THE GOVERNMENT, AND PROVIDING THE AUTHORITIES AND MEANS OF EXECUTING THE CONSTITUTION, IN CERTAIN CONTINGENCIES, AND FOR OTHER PURPOSES.

These acts and parts of acts, forming a peculiar class of general import, being spread through the mass of laws, a copy of which is not always accessible, are inserted here for public convenience. They prescribe the forms of oaths to support the Constitution, &c.; authorize oaths to be administered by the presiding officers of the two Houses, and chairmen of the committees of Congress; relate to the election of President and Vice President; declare the officer who shall act as President in case of vacancies in offices, both of President and Vice President; provide compensation to the President and Vice President; to messengers to deliver electoral votes; apportion the Representatives in Congress according to the last census, and prescribe the district election of Representatives; establish a uniform time for holding elections for Electors, and prescribe the mode in which the public acts, records, and judicial proceedings, in each State, shall be authenticated so as to take effect in every other State; provide for the protection of Ambassadors and other public ministers; for the preservation of the neutrality of the United States, and establish Little & Brown's edition of the laws and treaties of the United States competent evidence in all the courts and offices of the United States and of the several States, &c.

1. AN ACT to regulate the time and manner of administering certain oaths.

SEC. 1. *Be it enacted by the Senate and House of Representatives of the United States of America in Congress assembled,* That the oath or affir mation required by the sixth article ot the Constitution of the United States, shall be administered in the form following, to wit: "*I, A. B., do solemnly swear or affirm* (as the case may be) *that I will support the Constitution of the United States.*" The said oath or affirmation shall be administered within three days after the passing of this act, by any one member of the Senate, to the President of the Senate, and by him to all the members, and to the Secretary; and by the speaker of the House of Representatives to all the members who have not taken a similar oath, by virtue of a particular resolution of the said House, and to the clerk: And in case of the absence of any member from the service of either House at the time prescribed for taking the said oath or affirmation, the same shall be administered to such member when he shall appear to take his seat.

SEC. 2. *And be it further enacted,* That at the first session of Congress after every general election of representatives, the oath or affirmation aforesaid shall be administered by any one member of the House of Representatives to the speaker; and by him to all the members present, and to the clerk, previous to entering on any other business; and to the members who shall afterwards appear, previous to taking their seats. The President of the Senate for the time being, shall also administer the said oath or affirmation to each Senator who shall hereafter be elected, previous to his taking his seat: And in any future case of a President of the Senate, who shall not have taken the said oath or affirmation, the same shall be administered to him by any one of the members of the Senate.

SEC. 3. *And be it further enacted,* That the members of the several State legislatures, at the next sessions of the said legislatures respectively, and all executive and judicial officers of the several States, who have been heretofore chosen or appointed, or who shall be chosen or appointed before the first day of August next, and who shall then be in office, shall, within one month thereafter, take the same oath or affirmation, except where they shall have taken it before; which may be administered by any person authorized by the law of the State, in which such office shall be holden, to administer oaths. And the members of the several State legislatures, and all executive and judicial officers of the several States, who shall be chosen or appointed after the said first day of August, shall, before they proceed to execute the duties of their respective offices, take the foregoing oath or affirmation, which shall be administered by the person or persons, who, by the law of the State, shall be authorized to administer the oath of office; and the person or persons so administering the oath hereby required to be taken, shall cause a record or certificate thereof to be made, in the same manner as, by the law of the State, he or they shall be directed to record or certify the oath of office.

SEC. 4. *And be it further enacted,* That all officers appointed, or hereafter to be appointed, under the authority of the United States, shall, before they act in their respective offices, take the same oath or affirmation, which shall be administered by the person or persons who shall be authorized by law to administer to such officers their respective oaths of office; and such officers shall incur the same penalties in case of failure, as shall be imposed by law in case of failure in taking their respective oaths of office.

SEC. 5. *And be it further enacted,* That the Secretary of the Senate, and the Clerk of the House of Representatives, for the time being, shall, at the time of taking the oath or affirmation aforesaid, each take an oath or affirmation in the words following, to wit: "*I, A. B., Secretary of the Senate, or Clerk of the House of Representatives* (as the case may be) *of the United States of America, do solemnly swear or affirm, that I will truly and faithfully discharge the duties of my said office, to the best of my knowledge and abilities.*"

Approved, June 1, 1789

2. AN ACT for the punishment of certain crimes against the United States.

SEC. 25. *And be it further enacted,* That if any writ or process shall at any time hereafter be sued forth or prosecuted by any person or persons, in any of the courts of the United States, or in any of the courts of a particular State, or by any judge or justice therein respectively, whereby the person of any ambassador or other public minister of any foreign prince or State, authorized and received as such by the President of the United States, or any domestic or domestic servant of any such ambassador or other public minister, may be arrested or imprisoned, or his or their goods or chattels be distrained, seized or attached, such writ or process shall be deemed and adjudged to be utterly null and void to all intents, construction and purposes whatsoever.

SEC. 26. *And be it further enacted,* That in case any person or persons shall sue forth or prosecute any such writ or process, such person or persons, and all attorneys or solicitors prosecuting or soliciting in such case, and all officers executing any such writ or process, being thereof convicted, shall be deemed violators of the laws of nations, and disturbers of the public repose, and imprisoned not exceeding three years, and fined at the discretion of the court.

SEC. 27. *Provided nevertheless,* That no citizen or inhabitant of the United States, who shall have contracted debts prior to his entering into the service of any ambassador or other public minister, which debts shall be still due and unpaid, shall have, take, or receive any benefit of this act, nor shall any person be proceeded against by virtue of this act, for having arrested or sued any other domestic servant of any ambassador or other public minister, unless the name of such servant be first registered in the office of the Secretary of State, and by such secretary transmitted to the marshal of the district in which Congress shall reside, who shall, upon receipt thereof, affix the same in some public place in his office, whereto all persons may resort and take copies without fee or reward.

SEC. 28. *And be it further enacted,* That if any person shall violate any safe-conduct or passport duly obtained and issued under the authority of the United States, or shall assault, strike, wound, imprison, or in any other manner infract the law of nations, by offering violence to the person of an ambassador or other public minister, such person so offending, on conviction, shall be imprisoned not exceeding three years, and fined at the discretion of the court.

Approved, April 30, 1790.

3. AN ACT to prescribe the mode in which the public acts, records, and judicial proceedings, in each State, shall be authenticated so as to take effect in every other State.

Be it enacted by the Senate and House of Representatives of the United States of America in Congress assembled, That the acts of the legislatures of the several States shall be authenticated by having the seal of their respective States affixed thereto:—That the records and judicial proceedings of the courts of any State shall be proved or admitted in any other court within the United States, by the attestation of the clerk, and the seal of the court annexed, if there be a seal, together with a certificate of the judge, chief justice, or presiding magistrate, as the case may be, that the said attestation is in due form. And the said records and judicial proceedings, authenticated as aforesaid, shall have such faith and credit given to them in every court within the United States, as they have by law or usage in the courts of the State from whence the said records are, or shall be taken.

Approved, May 26, 1790.

4. AN ACT supplemental to the act "establishing the Treasury Department," and for a farther compensation to certain officers.

SEC. 2. *And be it further enacted,* That each and every clerk, and other officer already appointed in any of the departments of the United States, and who have not, since their appointment, taken the oath or affirmation hereafter mentioned,) shall, within fifteen days after the passing of this act, and those who shall hereafter be appointed, shall, before they enter upon the duties of such appointment, take an oath or affirmation, before one of the justices of the Supreme Court, or one of the judges of a district court of the United States, to *support the Constitution of the United States*, and also an oath or affirmation, *well and faithfully to execute the trust committed to him*, which oaths or affirmations, subscribed by such clerk, and certified by the person administering the same, shall be filed in the office of the person employing such clerk.

Approved, 3 *March*, 1791.

5. AN ACT relative to the election of a President and Vice President of the United States, and declaring the officer who shall act as President in cases of vacancies in the offices both of President and Vice President.

SEC. 1. *Be it enacted by the Senate and House of Representatives of the United States of America in Congress assembled*, That except in case of an election of a President and Vice President of the United States, prior to the ordinary period, as hereinafter specified, electors shall be appointed in each State for the election of a President and Vice President of the United States, within thirty-four days preceding the first Wednesday in December, one thousand seven hundred and ninety-two, and within thirty-four days preceding the first Wednesday in December in every fourth year succeeding the last election, which electors shall be equal to the number of Senators and Representatives to which the several States may, by law, be entitled at the time when the President and Vice President, thus to be chosen, should come into office. *Provided always*, That where no apportionment of Representatives shall have been made after any enumeration, at the time of choosing electors, then the number of electors shall be according to the existing apportionment of Senators and Representatives.

SEC. 2. *And be it further enacted*, That the electors shall meet and give their votes on the said first Wednesday in December, at such place, in each State, as shall be directed by the legislature thereof; and the electors in each State shall make and sign three certificates of all the votes by them given, and shall seal up the same, certifying, on each, that a list of the votes of such State, for President and Vice President, is contained therein, and shall, by writing, under their hands, or under the hands of a majority of them, appoint a person to take charge of, and deliver to the President of the Senate, at the seat of Government, before the first Wednesday in January then next ensuing, one of the said certificates and the said electors shall forthwith forward, by the post-office, to the President of the Senate, at the seat of Government, one other of the said certificates; and shall, forthwith, cause the other of the said certificates to be delivered to the judge of that district in which the said electors shall assemble.

SEC. 3. *And be it further enacted,* That the executive authority of each State shall cause three lists of the names of the electors of such State to be made, and certified, and to be delivered to the electors on or before the said first Wednesday in December; and the said electors shall annex one of the said lists to each of the lists of their votes.

SEC. 4. *And be it further enacted,* That if a list of votes from any State shall not have been received at the seat of government, on the said first Wednesday in January, that then the Secretary of State shall send a special messenger to the district judge in whose custody such list shall have been lodged, who shall forthwith transmit the same to the seat of Government.

SEC. 5. *And be it further enacted,* That Congress shall be in session on the second Wednesday in February, one thousand seven hundred and ninety-three, and on the second Wednesday in February succeeding every meeting of the electors, and the said certificates, or so many of them as shall have been received, shall then be opened, the votes counted, and the persons who shall fill the offices of President and Vice President ascertained and declared, agreeably to the Constitution.

SEC. 6. *And be it further enacted,* That, in case there shall be no President of the Senate at the seat of Government on the arrival of the persons intrusted with the lists of the votes of the electors, then such persons shall deliver the lists of votes in their custody into the office of the Secretary of State, to be safely kept and delivered over, as soon as may be, to the President of the Senate.

SEC. 7. *And be it further enacted,* That the persons appointed by the electors to deliver the lists of votes to the President of the Senate, shall be allowed, on the delivery of the said lists, twenty-five cents for every mile of the estimated distance, by the most usual road, from the place of meeting of the electors to the seat of Government of the United States.

SEC. 8. *And be it further enacted,* That if any person, appointed to deliver the votes of the electors to the President of the Senate, shall, after accepting of his appointment, neglect to perform the services required of him by this act, he shall forfeit the sum of one thousand dollars.

SEC. 9. *And be it further enacted,* That in case of a removal, death, resignation, or inability, both of the President and Vice President of the

United States, the President of the Senate pro tempore, and, in case there shall be no President of the Senate, then the Speaker of the House of Representatives, for the time being, shall act as President of the United States, until the disability be removed, or a President shall be elected.

SEC. 10. *And be it further enacted,* That whenever the offices of President and Vice President shall both become vacant, the Secretary of State shall forthwith cause a notification thereof to be made to the executive of every State, and shall also cause the same to be published in, at least, one of the newspapers printed in each State, specifying that electors of the President of the United States shall be appointed or chosen, in the several States, within thirty-four days preceding the first Wednesday in December, then next ensuing: *Provided,* There shall be the space of two months between the date of such notification and the said first Wednesday in December; but if there shall not be the space of two months between the date of such notification and the first Wednesday in December, and if the term for which the President and Vice President last in office were elected shall not expire on the third day of March next ensuing, then the Secretary of State shall specify in the notification, that the electors shall be appointed or chosen within thirty-four days preceding the first Wednesday in December in the year next ensuing, within which time the electors shall accordingly be appointed or chosen, and the electors shall meet and give their votes on the said first Wednesday in December, and the proceedings and duties of the said electors, and others, shall be pursuant to the directions prescribed in this act.

SEC. 11. *And be it further enacted,* That the only evidence of a refusal to accept, or of a resignation of, the office of President or Vice President, shall be an instrument in writing, declaring the same, and subscribed by the person refusing to accept, or resigning, as the case may be, and delivered into the office of the Secretary of State.

SEC. 12. *And be it further enacted,* That the term of four years for which a President and Vice President shall be elected, shall, in all cases, commence on the fourth day of March next succeeding the day on which the votes of the electors shall have been given.

Approved, March 1, 1792.

6. AN ACT providing compensation to the President and Vice President of the United States.

SEC. 1. *Be it enacted by the Senate and House of Representatives of the United States of America in Congress assembled,* That from and after the third day of March, in the present year, the compensation of the President of the United States shall be at the rate of twenty-five thousand dollars per annum, with the use of the furniture and other effects belonging to the United States, and now in possession of the President: And that of the Vice President, at the rate of five thousand dollars per annum; in full for their respective services; to be paid quarter yearly, at the Treasury.

Approved, February 18, 1793.

7. AN ACT to authorize certain officers and other persons to administer oaths.

Be it enacted by the Senate and House of Representatives of the United States of America in Congress assembled, That the President of the Senate, the Speaker of the House of Representatives, a chairman of a committee of the whole, or a chairman of a select committee of either House, shall be empowered to administer oaths or affirmations to witnesses, in any case under their examination.

SEC. 2. *And be it further enacted,* That if any person shall wilfully, absolutely, and falsely swear or affirm, touching any matter or thing material to the point in question, whereto he or she shall be thus examined, every person so offending, and being thereof duly convicted, shall be subjected to the pains, penalties, and disabilities, which by law are prescribed for the punishment of the crime of wilful and corrupt perjury.

Approved, May 3, 1798.

8. AN ACT supplementary to the act, entitled "An Act to prescribe the mode in which the public acts, records, and judicial proceedings in each State shall be authenticated so as to take effect in every other State."

Be it enacted by the Senate and House of Representatives of the United States of America in Congress assembled, That from and after the passage of this act, all records and exemplifications of office books, which are or may be kept in any public office of any State, not appertaining to a court, shall be approved or admitted in any other court or office in any other State, by the attestation of the keeper of the said records or books, and the seal of his office thereto annexed, if there be a seal, together with a certificate of the presiding justice of the court of the county or district, as the case may be, in which such office is or may be kept; or of the Governor, the Secretary of State, the Chancellor or the keeper of the great seal of the State, that the said attestation is in due form and by the proper officer; and the said certificate, if given by the presiding justice of a court, shall be further authenticated by the clerk or prothonotary of the said court, who shall certify under his hand and the seal of his office, that the said presiding justice is duly commissioned and qualified; or if the said certificate be given by the Governor, the Secretary of State, the Chancellor or keeper of the great seal, it shall be under the great seal of the State in which the said certificate is made. And the said records and exemplifications, authenticated as aforesaid, shall have such faith and credit given to them in every court and office within the United States, as they have by law or usage in the courts or offices of the State from whence the same are or shall be taken.

SEC. 2. *And be it further enacted*, That all the provisions of this act, and the act to which this is a supplement, shall apply as well to the public acts, records, office books, judicial proceedings, courts and offices of the respective territories of the United States, and countries subject to the jurisdiction of the United States, as to the public acts, records, offices' books, judicial proceedings, courts and offices of the several States.

Approved, March 27, 1804.

9. AN ACT to extend the provisions of the act to authorize certain officers and other persons to administer oaths, approved May the 3d, 1798.

Be it enacted by the Senate and House of Representatives of the United States of America in Congress assembled, That the chairman of any standing committee, either of the House of Representatives, or of the Senate of the United States, shall be empowered to administer oaths or affirmations to witnesses in any case under their examination; and any person who shall be guilty of perjury before such committee shall be liable to the pains, penalties, and disabilities, prescribed for the punishment of the crime of wilful and corrupt perjury.

Approved, February 8, 1817.

10. AN ACT to provide for the Publication of the Laws of the United States, and for other purposes.

SEC. 2. *And be it further enacted*, That, whenever official notice shall have been received, at the Department of State, that any amendment which heretofore has been, or hereafter may be, proposed to the Constitution of the United States, has been adopted, according to the provisions of the Constitution, it shall be the duty of the said Secretary of State, forthwith to cause the said amendment to be published in the said newspapers authorized to promulgate the laws, with his certificate, spe cifying the States by which the same may have been adopted, and that the same has become valid, to all intents and purposes, as a part of the Constitution of the United States.

Approved, April 20, 1818.

11. AN ACT in addition to the "Act for the punishment of certain crimes against the United States," and to repeal the acts therein mentioned.

SEC. 1. *Be it enacted by the Senate and House of Representatives of the United States of America in Congress assembled,* That if any citizen of the United States shall, within the territory or jurisdiction thereof, accept and exercise a commission to serve a foreign prince, State, colony, district, or people, in war, by land or by sea, against any prince, State, colony, district, or people, with whom the United States are at peace, the person so offending shall be deemed guilty of a high misdemeanor, and shall be fined not more than two thousand dollars, and shall be imprisoned not exceeding three years.

SEC. 2. *And be it further enacted,* That if any person shall, within the territory or jurisdiction of the United States, enlist or enter himself, or hire or retain another person to enlist or enter himself, or to go beyond the limits or jurisdiction of the United States with intent to be enlisted or entered in the service of any foreign prince, State, colony, district, or people, as a soldier, or as a marine or seaman, on board of any vessel of war, letter of marque, or privateer, every person, so offending, shall be deemed guilty of a high misdemeanor, and shall be fined not exceeding one thousand dollars, and be imprisoned not exceeding three years: *Provided,* That this act shall not be construed to extend to any subject or citizen of any foreign prince, State, colony, district, or people, who shall transiently be within the United States, and shall, on board of any vessel of war, letter of marque, or privateer, which, at the time of its arrival within the United States, was fitted and equipped as such, enlist or enter himself, or hire or retain another subject or citizen of the same foreign prince, State, colony, district, or people, who is transiently within the United States, to enlist or enter himself to serve such foreign prince, State, colony, district, or people, on board such vessel of war, letter of marque, or privateer, if the United States shall then be at peace with such foreign prince, State, colony, district, or people.

SEC. 3. *And be it further enacted,* That if any person shall, within the limits of the United States, fit out and arm, or attempt to fit out and arm, or procure to be fitted out and armed, or shall knowingly be concerned in the furnishing, fitting out, or arming, of any ship or vessel, with intent that such ship or vessel shall be employed in the service of any foreign prince or State, or of any colony, district, or people, to cruise or commit hostilities against the subjects, citizens, or property, of any foreign prince or State, or of any colony, district, or people, with whom the United States are at peace, or shall issue or deliver a commission within the territory or jurisdiction of the United States, for any ship or vessel, to the intent that she may be employed as aforesaid, every person so offending shall be deemed guilty of a high misdemeanor, and shall be fined not more than ten thousand dollars, and imprisoned not more than three years; and every such ship or vessel, with her tackle, apparel, and furniture, together with all materials, arms, ammunition and stores, which may have been procured for the building and equipment thereof, shall be forfeited, one half to the use of the informer, and the other half to the use of the United States.

SEC. 4. *And be it further enacted,* That if any citizen or citizens of the United States shall, without the limits thereof, fit out and arm, or attempt to fit out and arm, or procure to be fitted out and armed, or shall knowingly aid or be concerned in the furnishing, fitting out, or arming, any private ship or vessel of war, or privateer, with intent that such ship or vessel shall be employed to cruise, or commit hostilities, upon the citizens of the United States, or their property, or shall take the command of, or enter on board of, any such ship or vessel, for the intent aforesaid, or shall purchase any interest in any such ship or vessel, with a view to share in the profits thereof, such person, so offending, shall be deemed guilty of a high misdemeanor, and fined not more than ten thousand dollars, and imprisoned not more than ten years; and the trial for such offence, if committed without the limits of the United States, shall be in the district in which the offender shall be apprehended or first brought.

SEC. 5. *And be it further enacted,* That if any person shall, within the territory or jurisdiction of the United States, increase or augment, or procure to be increased or augmented, or shall knowingly be concerned in increasing or augmenting, the force of any ship of war, cruiser, or other armed vessel, which, at the time of her arrival within the United States, was a ship of war, or cruiser, or armed vessel, in the service of any foreign prince or State, or of any colony, district, or people, or belonging to the subjects or citizens of any such prince or State, colony, district, or people, the same being at war with any foreign prince or state, or of any colony, district, or people, with whom the United States are at peace, by adding to the number of the guns of such vessel, or by changing those on board of her for guns of a larger calibre, or by the addition thereto of any equipment solely applicable to war, every person, so of fending, shall be deemed guilty of a high misdemeanor, shall be fined not more than one thousand dollars and be imprisoned not more tnan one year.

SEC. 6. *And be it further enacted,* That if any person shall, within the territory or jurisdiction of the United States, begin or set on foot, or provide or prepare the means for, any military expedition or enterprise, to be carried on from thence against the territory or dominions of any foreign prince or State, or of any colony, district, or people, with whom the United States are [at] peace, every person, so offending, shall be deemed guilty of a high misdemeanor, and shall be fined not exceeding three thousand dollars, and imprisoned not more than three years.

SEC. 7. *And be it further enacted,* That the district court shall take cognisance of complaints, by whomsoever instituted, in cases of captures made within the waters of the United States, or within a marine league of the coasts or shores thereof.

SEC. 8. *And be it further enacted,* That in every case in which a vessel shall be fitted out and armed, or attempted to be fitted out and armed, or in which the force of any vessel of war, cruiser, or other armed vessel, shall be increased or augmented, or in which any military expedition or enterprise shall be begun or set on foot, contrary to the provisions and prohibitions of this act; and in every case of the capture of a ship or vessel within the jurisdiction or protection of the United States as before defined, and in every case in which any process issuing out of any court of the United States shall be disobeyed or resisted by any person or persons having the custody of any vessel of war, cruiser, or other armed vessel, of any foreign prince or State, or of any colony, district, or people, or of any subjects or citizens of any foreign prince or State, or of any colony, district, or people, in every such case it shall be lawful for the President of the United States, or such other person as he shall have empowered for that purpose, to employ such part of the land or naval forces of the United States, or of the militia thereof, for the purpose of taking possession of and detaining any such ship or vessel, with her prize or prizes, if any, in order to the execution of the prohibitions and penalties of this act, and to the restoring the prize or prizes in the cases in which restoration shall have been adjudged, and also for the purpose of preventing the carrying on of any such expedition or enterprise from the territories or jurisdiction of the United States against the territories or dominions of any foreign prince or State, or of any colony, district, or people, with whom the United States are at peace.

SEC. 9. *And be it further enacted,* That it shall be lawful for the President of the United States, or such person as he shall empower for that purpose, to employ such part of the land or naval forces of the United States, or of the militia thereof, as shall be necessary to compel any foreign ship or vessel to depart the United States, in all cases in which, by the laws of nations or the treaties of the United States, they ought not to remain within the United States.

SEC. 10. *And be it further enacted,* That the owners or consignees of every armed ship or vessel sailing out of the ports of the United States, belonging wholly or in part to citizens thereof, shall enter into a bond to the United States with sufficient sureties, prior to clearing out the same, in double the amount of the value of the vessel and cargo on board, including her armament, that the said ship or vessel shall not be employed by such owners to cruise or commit hostilities against the subjects, citizens, or property, of any foreign prince or State, or of any colony, district, or people, with whom the United States are at peace.

SEC. 11. *And be it further enacted,* That the collectors of the customs be, and they are hereby, respectively authorized and required to detain any vessel manifestly built for warlike purposes, and about to depart the United States, of which the cargo shall principally consist of arms and munitions of war, when the number of men shipped on board, or other circumstances, shall render it probable that such vessel is intended to be employed by the owner or owners to cruise or commit hostilities upon the subjects, citizens, or property, of any foreign prince or State, or of any colony, district, or people, with whom the United States are at peace, until the decision of the President be had thereon, or until the owner or owners shall give such bond and security as is required of the owners of armed ships by the preceding section of this act.

SEC. 12. *And be it further enacted,* That the act passed on the fifth day of June, one thousand seven hundred and ninety-four, entitled "An act in addition to the act for the punishment of certain crimes against the United States," continued in force, for a limited time, by the act of the second of March, one thousand seven hundred and ninety-seven, and perpetuated by the act passed on the 24th of April, one thousand eight hundred, and the act, passed on the fourteenth day of June, one thousand seven hundred and ninety-seven, entitled "An act to prevent citizens of the United States from privateering against nations in amity with, or against the citizens of the United States," and the act, passed he third day of March, one thousand eight hundred and seventeen, entitled "An act more effectually to preserve the neutral relations of the United States," be, and the same are hereby, severally, repealed: *Provided nevertheless,* That persons having heretofore offended against any of the acts aforesaid, may be prosecuted, convicted, and punished, as if the same were not repealed; and no forfeiture heretofore incurred by a violation of any of the acts aforesaid shall be affected by such repeal.

SEC. 13. *And be it further enacted,* That nothing in the foregoing act shall be construed to prevent the prosecution or punishment of treason, or any piracy defined by the laws of the United States.

Approved, April 20, 1818.

12. AN ACT making compensation to the persons appointed by the Electors to deliver the votes for President and Vice President.

SEC. 1. *Be it enacted by the Senate and House of Representatives of the United States of America in Congress assembled,* That the person appointed by the electors to deliver to the President of the Senate a list of the votes for President and Vice President, shall be allowed, on delivery of said list, twenty-five cents for every mile of the estimated distance, by the most usual route, from the place of meeting of the electors to the seat of Government of the United States, going and returning.

SEC. 2. *And be it further enacted,* That this act shall take effect from the first of November, eighteen hundred and twenty-four.

Approved, February 11, 1825.

13. AN ACT for the apportionment of Representatives among the several States according to the Sixth Census.

SEC. 1. *Be it enacted by the Senate and House of Representatives of the United States of America in Congress assembled,* That from and after the third day of March, one thousand eight hundred and forty-three, the House of Representatives shall be composed of members elected agreeably to a ratio of one Representative for every seventy thousand six hundred and eighty persons in each State, and of one additional Representative for each State having a fraction greater than one moiety of the said ratio, computed according to the rule prescribed by the Constitution of the United States; that is to say: Within the State of Maine, seven; within the State of New Hampshire, four; within the State of Massachusetts, ten; within the State of Rhode Island, two; within the State of Connecticut, four; within the State of Vermont, four; within the State of New York, thirty-four; within the State of New Jersey, five; within the State of Pennsylvania, twenty-four; within the State of Delaware, one; within the State of Maryland, six; within the State of Virginia, fifteen; within the State of North Carolina, nine; within the State of South Carolina, seven; within the State of Georgia, eight; within the State of Alabama, seven; within the State of Louisiana, four; within the State of Mississippi, four; within the State of Tennessee, eleven; within the State of Kentucky, ten; within the State of Ohio, twenty-one; within the State of Indiana, ten; within the State of Illinois, seven; within the State of Missouri, five; within the State of Arkansas, one; and within the State of Michigan, three.

SEC. 2. *And be it further enacted,* That in every case where a State is entitled to more than one Representative, the number to which each State shall be entitled under this apportionment shall be elected by districts composed of contiguous territory equal in number to the number of Representatives to which said State may be entitled, no one district electing more than one Representative.

Approved, June 25, 1842.

14. AN ACT to provide further remedial justice in the courts of the United States.

SEC. 1. *Be it enacted by the Senate and House of Representatives of the United States of America in Congress assembled,* That either of the justices of the Supreme Court of the United States, or a judge of any district court of the United States, in which a prisoner is confined, in addition to the authority already conferred by law, shall have power to grant writs of habeas corpus in all cases of any prisoner or prisoners in jail or confinement, where he, she, or they, being subjects or citizens of a foreign State, and domiciled therein, shall be committed or confined, or in custody, under or by any authority or law, or process founded thereon, of the United States, or of any one of them, for or on account of any act done or committed under any alleged right, title, authority, privilege, protection, or exemption, set up or claimed under the commission, or order, or sanction, of any foreign State or Sovereignty the validity and effect whereof depend upon the law of nations, or under color thereof. And upon the return of the said writ, and due proof of the service of notice of the said proceedings to the Attorney-General or other officer prosecuting the pleas of the State, under whose authority the petitioner has been arrested, committed, or is held in custody, to be prescribed by the said justice or judge at the time of granting said writ, the said justice or judge shall proceed to hear the said cause; and if, upon hearing the same, it shall appear that the prisoner or prisoners is or are entitled to be discharged from such confinement, commitment, custody, or arrest, for or by reason of such alleged right, title, authority, privileges, protection or exemption, so set up and claimed, and the law of nations applicable thereto, and that the same exists in fact, and has been duly proved to the said justice or judge, then it shall be the duty of the said justice or judge forthwith to discharge such prisoner or prisoners accordingly. And if it shall appear to the said justice or judge that such judgment of discharge ought not to be rendered, then the said prisoner or prisoners shall be forthwith remanded: *Provided always*, That from any decision of such justice or judge an appeal may be taken to the Circuit Court of the United States for the district in which the said cause is heard; and from the judgment of the said Circuit Court to the Supreme Court of the United States, on such terms and under such regulations and orders as well for the custody and appearance of the prisoner or prisoners as for sending up to the appellate tribunal a transcript of the petition, writ of habeas corpus returned thereto, and other proceedings, as the judge hearing the said cause may prescribe; and pending such proceedings or appeal, and until final judgment be rendered therein, and after final judgment of discharge in the same, any proceeding against said prisoner or prisoners, in any State court, or by or under the authority of any State, for any matter or thing so heard and determined, or in process of being heard and determined, under and by virtue of such writ of habeas corpus, shall be deemed null and void.

Approved, August 29, 1842.

15. AN ACT to establish a uniform time for holding elections for electors of President and Vice President in all the States of the Union.

SEC. 1. *Be it enacted by the Senate and House of Representatives of the United States of America in Congress assembled*, That the electors of President and Vice President shall be appointed in each State on the Tuesday next after the first Monday in the month of November of the year in which they are to be appointed. *Provided*, That each state may by law provide for the filling of any vacancy or vacancies which may occur in its college of electors when such college meets to give its electoral vote. *And provided, also*, when any State shall have held an election for the purpose of choosing electors, and shall fail to make a choice on the day aforesaid, then the electors may be appointed on a subsequent day in such manner as the State shall by law provide.

Approved, January 23, 1845.

16. AN ACT to provide for the distribution of the edition of the laws and treaties of the United States, published by Little and Brown, under the provisions of the resolutions of Congress, approved March 3, 1845, and for other purposes.

SEC. 2. And whereas, said edition of the said Laws and Treaties of the United States has been carefully collated and compared with the original rolls in the archives of the government, under the inspection and supervision of the Attorney General of the United States, as duly certified by that officer; Therefore, *Be it further enacted,* That said edition of the Laws and Treaties of the United States, published by Little and Brown, is hereby declared to be competent evidence of the several public and private acts of Congress, and of the several treaties therein contained, in all the courts of law and equity, and of maritime jurisdiction, and in all the tribunals and public offices of the United States, and of the several States, without any further proof or authentication thereof.

Approved, August 8, 1846.

17. AN ACT for giving effect to certain treaty stipulations between this and foreign governments, for the apprehension and delivering up of certain offenders.

Be it enacted by the Senate and House of Representatives of the United States of America in Congress assembled, That in all cases in which there now exists, or hereafter may exist, any treaty or convention for extradition between the government of the United States and any foreign government, it shall and may be lawful for any of the justices of the supreme court or judges of the several district courts of the United States—and the judges of the several State courts, and the commissioners authorized so to do by any of the courts of the United States, are hereby severally vested with power, jurisdiction, and authority, upon complaint made under oath or affirmation, charging any person found within the limits of any state, district, or territory, with having committed within the jurisdiction of any such foreign government, any of the crimes enumerated or provided for by any such treaty or convention—to issue his warrant for the apprehension of the person so charged, that he may be brought before such judge or commissioner, to the end that the evidence of criminality may be heard and considered; and if, on such hearing, the evidence be deemed sufficient by him to sustain the charge under the provisions of the proper treaty or convention, it shall be his duty to certify the same, together with a copy of all the testimony taken before him, to the Secretary of State, that a warrant may issue upon the requisition of the proper authorities of such foreign government, for the surrender of such person, according to the stipulations of said treaty or convention; and it shall be the duty of the said judge or commissioner to issue his warrant for the commitment of the person so charged to the proper gaol, there to remain until such surrender shall be made.

SEC. 2. *And be it further enacted,* That in every case of complaint as aforesaid, and of a hearing upon the return of the warrant of arrest, copies of the depositions upon which an original warrant in any such foreign country may have been granted, certified under the hand of the person or persons issuing such warrant, and attested upon the oath of the party producing them to be true copies of the original depositions, may be received in evidence of the criminality of the person so apprehended.

SEC. 3. *And be it further enacted,* That it shall be lawful for the Secretary of State, under his hand and seal of office, to order the person so committed to be delivered to such person or persons as shall be authorized, in the name and on behalf of such foreign government, to be tried for the crime of which such person shall be so accused, and such person shall be delivered up accordingly; and it shall be lawful for the person or persons authorized, as aforesaid, to hold such person in custody, and to take him or her to the territories of such foreign government, pursuant to such treaty; and if the person so accused shall escape out of any custody to which he or she shall be committed, or to which he or she shall be delivered, as aforesaid, it shall be lawful to retake such person, in the same manner as any person, accused of any crime against the laws in force in that part of the United States to which he or she shall so escape, may be retaken on an escape.

SEC. 4. *And be it further enacted,* That when any person who shall have been committed under this act or any such treaty as aforesaid, to remain until delivered up in pursuance of a requisition as aforesaid, shall not be delivered up pursuant hereto and conveyed out of the United States within two calendar months after such commitment over and above the time actually required to convey the prisoner from the gaol to which he or she may have been committed by the readiest way out of the United States, it shall in every such case be lawful for any judge of the United States or of any State, upon application made to him by or on behalf of the person so committed, and upon proof made to him, that reasonable notice of the intention to make such application has been given to the Secretary of State, to order the person so committed to be discharged out of custody, unless sufficient cause shall be shown to such judge why such discharge ought not to be ordered.

SEC. 5. *And be it further enacted,* That this act shall continue in force during the existence of any treaty of extradition with any foreign government, and no longer.

SEC. 6. *And be it further enacted,* That it shall be lawful for the courts of the United States, or any of them, to authorize any person or persons to act as a commissioner or commissioners under the provisions of this act; and the doings of such person or persons so authorized, in pursuance of any of the provisions aforesaid, shall be good and available to all intents and purposes whatsoever. *Approved, August* 12, 1848.

18. AN ACT providing for the taking of the seventh and subsequent censuses of the United States, and to fix the number of members of the House of Representatives, and to provide for their future apportionment among the several States.

SEC. 23. *And be it further enacted,* That if no other law be passed providing for the taking of the eighth, or any subsequent census of the United States, on or before the first day of January, of any year, when, by the Constitution of the United States, any future enumeration of the inhabitants thereof is required to be taken, such census shall, in all things, be taken and completed according to the provisions of this act.

SEC. 24. *And be it further enacted,* That from and after the 3d day of March, 1853, the House of Representatives shall be composed of two hundred and thirty-three members, to be apportioned among the several States in the manner directed in the next section of this act.

SEC. 25. *And be it further enacted,* That so soon as the next and each subsequent enumeration of the inhabitants of the several States directed by the Constitution of the United States to be taken, shall be completed and returned to the office of the Department of the Interior, it shall be the duty of the Secretary of the Interior to ascertain the aggregate representative population of the United States, by adding to the whole number of free persons in all the States, including those bound to service for a term of years, and excluding Indians not taxed, three-fifths of all other persons; which aggregate population he shall divide by the number two hundred and thirty-three, and the product of such division, rejecting any fraction of an unit, if any such happen to remain, shall be the ratio, or rule of apportionment of Representatives among the several States under such enumeration: and the said Secretary of the Department of the Interioı shall then proceed, in the same manner, to ascertain the representative population of each State, and to divide the whole number of the representative population of each State, by the ratio already determined by him, as above directed; and the product of this last division shall be the number of Representatives apportioned to such State under the then last enumeration: *Provided,* That the loss in the number of members caused by the fractions remaining in the several States, on the division of the population thereof, shall be compensated for by assigning to so many States having the largest fractions, one additional member for each for its fraction, as may be necessary to make the whole number of Representatives two hundred and thirty-three. *And provided, also,* That if, after the apportionment of the Representatives under the next, or any subsequent census, a new State or States shall be admitted into the Union, the Representative or Representatives assigned to such new State or States, shall be in addition to the number of Representatives herein above limited; which excess of Representatives over two hundred and thirty-three shall only continue until the next succeeding apportionment of Representatives under the next succeeding census.

SEC. 26. *And be it further enacted,* That when the Department of the Interior shall have apportioned the Representatives in the manner above directed among the several States under the next, or any subsequent enumeration of the inhabitants of the United States, he shall, as soon as practicable, make out and transmit, under the seal of his office, to the House of Representatives, a certificate of the number of members apportioned to each State under the then last enumeration; and shall likewise make out and transmit without delay to the Executive of each State, a certificate under his seal of office, of the number of members apportioned to such State, under such last enumeration. *Approved,* 23 *May,* 1850.

[The preceding sections fall under the class of general Laws intended to be inserted in this compilation; the residue of this act, relating solely to the manner of taking and returning the census, will be found in the statutes of the United States.]

19. AN ACT to authorize Notaries Public to take and certify oaths, affirmations, and acknowledgments in certain cases.

Be it enacted by the Senate and House of Representatives of the United States of America in Congress assembled, That in all cases in which, under the laws of the United States, oaths or affirmations, or acknowledgments, may now be taken or made before any justice or justices of the peace of any State or Territory, such oaths, affirmations, or acknowledgments may be hereafter also taken or made by or before any Notary public duly appointed in any State or Territory, and, when certified under the hand and official seal of such Notary, shall have the same force and effect as if taken or made by or before such justice or justices of the peace. And all laws and parts of laws for punishing perjury, or subornation of perjury, committed in any such oaths or affirmations when taken or made before any such justice of the peace, shall apply to any such offence committed in any oaths or affirmations which may be taken under this act before a Notary public, or commissioner, as hereinafter named: *Provided always,* That on trial for either of these offences, the seal and signature of the Notary shall not be deemed sufficient in themselves to establish the official character of such Notary, but the same shall be shown by other and proper evidence.

SEC. 2. *And be it further enacted,* That all the powers and authority conferred in and by the preceding section of this act upon Notaries public, be, and the same are hereby vested in, and may be exercised by, any commissioner appointed, or hereafter to be appointed, by any Circuit Court of the United States, under any act of Congress authorizing the appointment of commissioners to take bail, affidavits, or depositions, in causes pending in the courts of the United States. *Approved,* 16 *September,* 1850.

20. A RESOLUTION relating to the publication of the Laws of the United States.

Resolved, by the Senate and House of Representatives of the United States of America in Congress assembled, That the Secretary of State be authorized and directed to contract with Little and Brown to furnish their annual statutes at large, printed in conformity with the plan adopted by Congress in eighteen hundred and forty-five, instead of the edition usually issued by his order, under the act of Congress of April 20, 1818, and which conforms to an edition of the Laws now out of use.

Approved, 26 *September,* 1850.

CHAPTER 7.

EXPLANATORY NOTES OF THE FOLLOWING TABLES.

1. The tables of Electoral votes for President and Vice President of the United States, commencing with page 315, present an historical synopsis of the leading political sentiments of the American people, from the adoption of the Constitution to the present time, as indicated by the votes given for the distinguished individuals whose opinions were supposed to imbody, from time to time, those sentiments, and a biographical notice of the individuals themselves; the statement of whose names alone will recall to memory their meritorious public services and exalted characters.

2. The table commencing with page 336, of the terms of office and length of service, in the Senate, of the Vice Presidents and Presidents pro tempore, may be supposed, generally, to show, from time to time, the leading political sentiments of the majority of that honorable body, as indicated by the choice of Senators to occupy the station of President pro tempore, whose political sentiments were, at the time, well known. This table also shows the commencement and termination of, as well as the number of days in, each Session of Congress and special

session of the Senate, from the 4th March, 1789, to the termination of the second session of the thirty-first Congress, being the 3d March, 1851.

3. The table commencing with page 346 shows the names, and the commencement and termination of the service, of every Senator of the United States, from the 4th March, 1789, to the 3d March, 1851, being the termination of the second session, thirty-first Congress. A geographical, rather than an alphabetical, arrangement was preferred, for the reason that a regular succession may be traced in the service of the several classes of Senators of each State, from the commencement of the Government, or the admission of such State into the Union, to the present time.

This table practically illustrates that provision of the Constitution which directs the arrangement of the Senators into three classes, whose terms of service expire alternately every two years, exhibiting the progressive application of the principle to the Senators from new States as they become qualified, by which the three classes are preserved equal in number, or as nearly so as practicable —one-third being elected biennially, and two-thirds being, at all times, prepared to attend the call of their country for the transaction of Legislative, Executive, or Judicial business; or, indeed, by a provident arrangement of the State Legislatures (as is the prevailing practice) in re-electing the Senators whose terms of service are about to expire, or electing others in anticipation of vacancies, the Senate may preserve a continued existence in full force.

4. The fourth table, page 385, contains the names and the commencement and termination of service of the secretaries of the Senate of the United States, there having been only four individuals in the occupancy of that responsible office from the commencement of the Government under the Constitution to the present time, a circumstance which has preserved to this Honorable Body the advantages of accumulated experience in the Officers in their service.

5. The table commencing with page 386, exhibits the names and terms of service of the Representatives in Congress who have been elected to, and have occupied, the distinguished station of Speaker of the House of Representatives of the United States, from the 4th March, 1789, to the 3d March, 1851, and the names of the States of which they were Representatives.

6. The sixth table, page 388, contains the names, and the commencement and termination of service of the Clerks of the House of Representatives of the United States, from which it appears that thirteen changes have taken place in the occupancy of this office since the 4th March, 1789; making an average of less than five years' service to each individual, a circumstance which has sometimes deprived that Honorable House of much of the advan-

tage of accumulated experience, which the business of legislation and the public interest so constantly require in the service of Legislative Bodies.

The second and fourth tables embrace the names of all those individuals who have occupied the stations of Vice President, President pro tempore, and Speaker of the House of Representatives; the occupants of which offices have been constituted a reserve corps by the provisions of the Constitution, and of the act of Congress of the 1st March, 1792, in the order in which they are here mentioned, to fill the office of President of the United States, in the event of its becoming vacant by any of the casualties enumerated in the Constitution. Hence has arisen the practice of the Vice President's retiring from the Chair of the Senate a short time previous to the adjournment of each session, with the view of affording the Senate an opportunity of choosing a President pro tempore, *who, according to the prevailing practice,* would hold that office until the reappearance of the Vice President in the Senate; and, should any casualty deprive the country of the services of the President and Vice President acting as President, during the recess of Congress, the President pro tempore so chosen, *according to the prevailing understanding,* would be prepared to occupy that office until a President could be elected; which office would otherwise, however, devolve on the Speaker of the House of Representatives, should the vacancy happen during the existence of a Congress; but should there be no President pro tempore, and the vacancy occur during a recess, after the expiration of one Congress and previous to the assembling of another, while there was no Speaker, there would then be no officer to fill that high and responsible station.

These tables may afford a useful suggestion of the importance of preserving the biography of distinguished citizens who may have been, or may be called to important public stations, with a view of extending the practical political history of the country, which, perhaps, could not be more effectually developed than by a faithful delineation of the characters, principles, and acts of the American statesmen, whose wisdom and patriotism have elevated the character of the Republic, and will continue to guide its destinies, as it is fervently hoped, through the long vista of ages to the consummation of time.

ELECTORAL VOTES FOR PRESIDENT AND VICE PRESIDENT OF THE UNITED STATES OF AMERICA.

Election for the First term, commencing 4th March, 1789, and terminating with 3d March, 1793.

No. of electors appointed by each State.	STATES.	G. Washington, of Virginia.	John Adams, of Massachusetts.	Sam'l Huntingdon, of Conn't.	John Jay, of N. York.	John Hancock, of Mass.	R. H. Harrison, of Maryland.	George Clinton, of New York.	John Rutledge, of S. Carolina.	John Milton, of Georgia.	Jas. Armstrong, of Georgia.	Edward Telfair, of Georgia.	Benj'n Lincoln, of Mass.
5	New Hampshire	5	5	..	..	..	..	..	..	..	..	..	..
10	Massachusetts	10	10	..	..	..	..	..	..	..	..	..	..
7	Connecticut	7	5	2	..	..	..	..	..	..	..	..	..
6	New Jersey	6	1	..	5	..	..	..	..	..	..	..	..
10	Pennsylvania	10	8	..	..	2	..	..	..	..	..	..	..
3	Delaware	3	..	..	3	..	..	..	..	..	..	..	..
6	Maryland	6	..	..	..	..	6	..	..	..	..	..	..
10	Virginia	10	5	..	1	1	..	3	..	..	..	..	..
7	South Carolina	7	..	..	..	1	..	..	6	..	..	..	..
5	Georgia	5	..	..	..	..	..	..	..	2	1	1	1
69	Whole No. of electors	69	34	2	9	4	6	3	6	2	1	1	1
	Majority 35												

George Washington, elected President, took the oath of office and entered upon its duties on 30th April, 1789.

John Adams, elected Vice President, entered upon his duties in Senate 21st April, 1789, and took the oath of office on 3d June, 1789.

Election for the Second term, commencing 4th March, 1793, *and terminating* 3*d March,* 1797.

No. of electors appointed by each State.	STATES.	G. Washington, of Virginia.	John Adams, of Massachusetts.	George Clinton, of New York.	Thos. Jefferson, of Virginia.	Aaron Burr, of New York.
6	New Hampshire	6	6	..	..	..
16	Massachusetts	16	16	..	..	..
4	Rhode Island	4	4	..	..	..
9	Connecticut	9	9	..	..	..
3	Vermont	3	3	..	..	..
12	New York	12	..	12	..	..
7	New Jersey	7	7	..	..	..
15	Pennsylvania	15	14	1	..	..
3	Delaware	3	3	..	..	..
8	Maryland	8	8	..	..	..
21	Virginia	21	..	21	..	..
4	Kentucky	4	..	..	4	..
12	North Carolina	12	..	12	..	..
8	South Carolina	8	7	..	..	1
4	Georgia	4	..	4	..	..
132	Whole No. of Electors Majority 67	132	77	50	4	1

George Washington, elected President, took the oath of office for a second term on 4th March, 1793.

John Adams, elected Vice President, took the oath of office and attended in Senate on 2d December, 1793.

Election for the Third term, commencing 4th March, 1797, *and terminating 3d March,* 1801.

Electors from each State.	STATES.	John Adams, of Mass.	Thos. Jefferson, of Va.	Thos. Pinckney, of S. C.	Aaron Burr, of N. York.	Sam. Adams, of Mass.	O. Ellsworth, of Conn.	John Jay, of N. York.	Geo. Clinton, of N. York.	S. Johnston, of N. C.	Jas. Iredell, of N. C.	G. Washington, of Va.	C. C. Pinckney, of S. C.	John Henry, of Md.
3	Tennessee	..	3	..	3	..	..	..	..	..	..	..	..	..
4	Kentucky	..	4	..	4	..	..	..	..	..	..	..	..	..
4	Georgia	..	4	..	..	..	..	..	4	..	..	..	..	..
8	South Carolina	..	8	8	..	..	..	..	..	..	..	..	..	..
12	North Carolina	1	11	1	6	..	..	..	..	..	3	1	1	..
21	Virginia	1	20	1	1	15	..	..	3	..	..	1	..	..
11	Maryland	7	4	4	3	..	..	..	..	..	..	..	..	2
3	Delaware	3	..	3	..	..	..	..	..	..	..	..	..	..
15	Pennsylvania	1	14	2	13	..	..	..	..	..	..	..	..	..
7	New Jersey	7	..	7	..	..	..	..	..	..	..	..	..	..
12	New York	12	..	12	..	..	..	..	..	..	..	..	..	..
9	Connecticut	9	..	4	..	..	..	5	..	..	..	..	..	..
4	Rhode Island	4	..	..	..	..	4	..	..	..	..	..	..	..
16	Massachusetts	16	..	13	..	..	1	..	..	2	..	..	..	..
4	Vermont	4	..	4	..	..	..	..	..	..	..	..	..	..
6	New Hampshire	6	..	..	..	..	6	..	..	..	..	..	..	..
139	Whole No. of electors	71	68	59	30	15	11	5	7	2	3	2	1	2
	Majority 70													

John Adams, elected President, took the oath of office, and entered upon its duties on 4th March, 1797.
Thomas Jefferson, elected Vice President, took the oath of office, and entered upon its duties on 4th March, 1797.

Election for the Fourth term, commencing 4th March, 1801, *and terminating 3d March,* 1805.

No. of electors appointed by each State.	STATES.	Thos. Jefferson, of Virginia.	Aaron Burr, of New York.	John Adams, of Massachusetts.	C. C. Pinckney, of S. Carolina.	John Jay, of New York.
6	New Hampshire	..	..	6	6	..
16	Massachusetts	..	..	16	16	..
4	Rhode Island	..	..	4	3	1
9	Connecticut	..	..	9	9	..
4	Vermont	..	..	4	4	..
12	New York	12	12	..	..	..
7	New Jersey	..	..	7	7	..
15	Pennsylvania	8	8	7	7	..
3	Delaware	..	..	3	3	..
10	Maryland	5	5	5	5	..
21	Virginia	21	21	..	..	..
4	Kentucky	4	4	..	..	..
12	North Carolina	8	8	4	4	..
3	Tennessee	3	3	..	..	..
8	South Carolina	8	8	..	..	..
4	Georgia	4	4	..	..	..
138	Whole No. of Electors	73	73	65	64	1
	Majority 70					

The electoral vote for Thomas Jefferson and Aaron Burr being equal, no choice was made by the people, and the House of Representatives proceeded on Wednesday, February 11, 1801, in the manner prescribed by the Constitution to the choice of *a President of the United States.* On the first ballot eight States voted for Thomas Jefferson, of Virginia, six States voted for Aaron Burr, of New York, and the votes of two States were divided. The balloting continued until Tuesday, 17th February, 1801, when the thirty-fifth ballot, as had all the previous ballots, resulted the same as the first. The House then proceeded to the thirty-sixth ballot, and it having been concluded, the Speaker declared that the votes of ten States had been given for Thomas Jefferson, of Virginia, the votes of four States for Aaron Burr, of New York, and the votes of two States in blank; and that, consequently, Thomas Jefferson, of Virginia, had been, agreeably to the Constitution, elected President of the United States, for the term of four years, commencing on the 4th day of March, 1801.

Thomas Jefferson, thus elected, took the oath of office, and entered upon his duties on 4th of March, 1801.

Aaron Burr, as Vice President, took the oath of office, and entered upon his duties on 4th of March, 1801.

Election for the Fifth term, commencing 4th March, 1805, and terminating 3d March, 1809.

No. of electors appointed by each State.	STATES.	PRESIDENT.		V. PRESIDENT.	
		Thos. Jefferson, of Virginia.	Charles Cotesworth Pinckney, of South Carolina.	George Clinton, of New York.	Rufus King, of New York.
7	New Hampshire	7	..	7	..
19	Massachusetts	19	..	19	..
4	Rhode Island	4	..	4	..
9	Connecticut	..	9	..	9
6	Vermont	6	..	6	..
19	New York	19	..	19	..
8	New Jersey	8	..	8	..
20	Pennsylvania	20	..	20	..
3	Delaware	..	3	..	3
11	Maryland	9	2	9	2
24	Virginia	24	..	24	..
14	North Carolina	14	..	14	..
10	South Carolina	10	..	10	..
6	Georgia	6	..	6	..
5	Tennessee	5	..	5	..
8	Kentucky	8	..	8	..
3	Ohio	3	..	3	..
176	Whole No. of electors Majority 89	162	14	162	14

Thomas Jefferson, elected President, took the oath of office for a second term on 4th March, 1805.

George Clinton, elected Vice President, took the oath of office in Senate Chamber on 4th March, 1805.

Election for the Sixth term, commencing 4th March, 1809, *and terminating 3d March,* 1813.

No. of electors appointed by each State.	STATES.	PRESIDENT.			VICE PRESIDENT.				
		James Madison, of Virginia.	George Clinton, of New York.	C. C. Pinckney, of S. Carolina.	George Clinton, of New York.	James Madison, of Virginia.	James Monroe, of Virginia.	John Langdon, of New Hampshire.	Rufus King, of New York.
7	New Hampshire .	..	..	7	..	..	..	..	7
19	Massachusetts ...	..	..	19	..	..	..	..	19
4	Rhode Island	..	..	4	..	..	..	..	4
9	Connecticut	..	..	9	..	..	..	..	9
6	Vermont	6	..	..	..	..	..	6	..
19	New York	13	6	..	13	3	3	..	..
8	New Jersey	8	..	..	8	..	..	..	..
20	Pennsylvania	20	..	..	20	..	..	..	..
3	Delaware	..	..	3	..	..	..	..	3
11	Maryland	9	..	2	9	..	..	..	2
24	Virginia	24	..	..	24	..	..	..	..
14	North Carolina ..	11	..	3	11	..	..	..	3
10	South Carolina ..	10	..	..	10	..	..	..	..
6	Georgia	6	..	..	6	..	..	..	..
7	Kentucky	7	..	..	7	..	..	..	..
5	Tennessee	5	..	..	5	..	..	..	..
3	Ohio	3	..	..	..	..	..	3	..
175	Whole No. of electors .... Majority 88	122	6	47	113	3	3	9	47

James Madison, elected President, took the oath of office, and entered upon its duties on 4th March, 1809.

George Clinton, elected Vice President, took the oath of office in Senate Chamber on 4th March, 1809.

Election for the Seventh term, commencing 4th March, 1813, *and terminating* 3*d March,* 1817.

No. of electors appointed by each State.	STATES.	PRESIDENT.		V. PRESIDENT.	
		James Madison, of Virginia.	De Witt Clinton, of New York.	Elbridge Gerry, of Massachusetts.	Jared Ingersoll, of Pennsylvania.
8	New Hampshire	..	8	1	7
22	Massachusetts	..	22	2	20
4	Rhode Island	..	4	..	4
9	Connecticut	..	9	..	9
8	Vermont	8	..	8	..
29	New York	..	29	..	29
8	New Jersey	..	8	..	8
25	Pennsylvania	25	..	25	..
4	Delaware	..	4	..	4
11	Maryland	6	5	6	5
25	Virginia	25	..	25	..
15	North Carolina	15	..	15	..
11	South Carolina	11	..	11	..
8	Georgia	8	..	8	..
12	Kentucky	12	..	12	..
8	Tennessee	8	..	8	..
7	Ohio	7	..	7	..
3	Louisiana	3	..	3	..
217	Whole No. of electors	128	89	131	86
	Majority 109				

James Madison, elected President for a second term. (There is no notice on the Journals of Congress of his having taken the oath.)

Elbridge Gerry, elected Vice President, attended in the Senate 24th May, 1813, and exhibited a certificate of his having taken the oath of office prescribed by law, which was read.

Election for the Eighth term, commencing 4th March, 1817, *and terminating 3d March,* 1821.

No. of electors appointed by each State.	STATES.	PRESIDENT.		VICE PRESIDENT.				
		James Monroe, of Virginia.	Rufus King, of New York.	Daniel D. Tompkins, of N. York.	John E. Howard, of Maryland.	James Ross, of Pennsylvania.	John Marshall, of Virginia.	Robert G. Harper, of Maryland.
8	New Hampshire	8	..	8	..	..	..	..
22	Massachusetts	..	22	..	22	..	..	..
4	Rhode Island	4	..	4	..	..	..	..
9	Connecticut	..	9	..	..	5	4	..
8	Vermont	8	..	8	..	..	..	..
29	New York	29	..	29	..	..	..	..
8	New Jersey	8	..	8	..	..	..	..
25	Pennsylvania	25	..	25	..	..	..	..
3	Delaware	..	3	..	..	..	..	3
8	Maryland	8	..	8	..	..	..	..
25	Virginia	25	..	25	..	..	..	..
15	North Carolina	15	..	15	..	..	..	..
11	South Carolina	11	..	11	..	..	..	..
8	Georgia	8	..	8	..	..	..	..
12	Kentucky	12	..	12	..	..	..	..
8	Tennessee	8	..	8	..	..	..	..
8	Ohio	8	..	8	..	..	..	..
3	Louisiana	3	..	3	..	..	..	..
3	Indiana	3	..	3	..	..	..	..
217	Whole No. of Electors. Majority 109	183	34	183	22	5	4	3

James Monroe, elected President, took the oath of office, and entered upon its duties on 4th March, 1817.

Daniel D. Tompkins, elected Vice President, took the oath of office, and attended in Senate on 4th March, 1817.

Election for the Ninth term, commencing 4th March, 1821, and terminating 3d March, 1825.

No. of votes to which each State is entitled.	STATES.	PRESIDENT.		VICE PRESIDENT.				
		James Monroe, of Virginia.	John Q. Adams, of Massachusetts.	Daniel D. Tompkins, of N. York.	Richard Stockton, of New Jersey.	Robert G. Harper, of Maryland.	Richard Rush, of Pennsylvania.	Daniel Rodney, of Delaware.
8	New Hampshire	7	1	7	..	..	1	..
15	Massachusetts	15	..	7	8	..	..	..
4	Rhode Island	4	..	4	..	..	..	..
9	Connecticut	9	..	9	..	..	..	..
8	Vermont	8	..	8	..	..	..	..
29	New York	29	..	29	..	..	..	..
8	New Jersey	8	..	8	..	..	..	..
25	Pennsylvania	24	..	24	..	..	..	..
4	Delaware	4	..	..	..	..	..	4
11	Maryland	11	..	10	..	1	..	..
25	Virginia	25	..	25	..	..	..	..
15	North Carolina	15	..	15	..	..	..	..
11	South Carolina	11	..	11	..	..	..	..
8	Georgia	8	..	8	..	..	..	..
12	Kentucky	12	..	12	..	..	..	..
8	Tennessee	7	..	7	..	..	..	..
8	Ohio	8	..	8	..	..	..	..
3	Louisiana	3	..	3	..	..	..	..
3	Indiana	3	..	3	..	..	..	..
3	Mississippi	2	..	2	..	..	..	..
3	Illinois	3	..	3	..	..	..	..
3	Alabama	3	..	3	..	..	..	..
9	Maine	9	..	9	..	..	..	..
3	Missouri	3	..	3	..	..	..	..
235	Whole No. of Electors. Majority 118	231	1	218	8	1	1	4

James Monroe, elected President for a second term. (There is no notice on the Journals of Congress of his having taken the oath.)

Daniel D. Tompkins, elected Vice President for a second term. (There is no notice on the Journals of Congress of his having taken the oath.)

Election for the Tenth term, commencing 4th March, 1825, and terminating 3d March, 1829

No. of electors appointed by each State.	STATES.	PRESIDENT.				VICE PRESIDENT.					
		Andrew Jackson, of Tennessee.	John Q. Adams, of Massachusetts.	William H. Crawford, of Georgia.	Henry Clay, of Kentucky.	John C. Calhoun, of South Carolina.	Nathan Sanford, of New York.	Nathaniel Macon, of North Carolina.	Andrew Jackson, of Tennessee.	Martin Van Buren, of New York.	Henry Clay, of Kentucky.
8	New Hampshire	..	8	..	..	7	..	..	1	..	..
15	Massachusetts	..	15	..	..	15	..	..	..	..	..
4	Rhode Island	..	4	..	..	3	..	..	..	..	..
8	Connecticut	..	8	..	..	..	..	..	8	..	..
7	Vermont	..	7	..	..	7	..	..	..	..	..
36	New York	1	26	5	4	29	7	..	..	..	..
8	New Jersey	8	..	..	..	8	..	..	..	..	..
28	Pennsylvania	28	..	..	..	28	..	..	..	..	..
3	Delaware	..	1	2	..	1	..	..	..	..	2
11	Maryland	7	3	1	..	10	..	..	1	..	..
24	Virginia	..	..	24	..	..	..	24	..	..	..
15	North Carolina	15	..	..	..	15	..	..	..	..	..
11	South Carolina	11	..	..	..	11	..	..	..	..	..
9	Georgia	..	..	9	..	..	..	..	..	9	..
14	Kentucky	..	..	..	14	7	7	..	..	..	..

11	Tennessee	11	..	..	..	11	..	..	..	..	..
16	Ohio	..	..	..	16	..	16	..	..	..	..
5	Louisiana	3	2	..	..	5	..	..	..	..	..
5	Indiana	5	..	..	..	5	..	..	..	..	..
3	Mississippi	3	..	..	..	3	..	..	..	..	..
3	Illinois	2	1	..	..	3	..	..	..	..	..
5	Alabama	5	..	..	..	5	..	..	..	..	..
9	Maine	..	9	..	..	9	..	..	..	..	..
3	Missouri	..	..	..	3	..	..	..	3	..	..
261	Whole No. of electors	99	84	41	37	182	30	24	13	9	2
	Majority 131										

John C. Calhoun, having been elected Vice President, took the oath of office, and attended in Senate on 4th of March, 1825.

Neither of the persons voted for as President having received a majority of the votes of the electors, it devolved on the House of Representatives of the United States to choose a President from the three highest on the list of those voted for by the electors for President, which three were, Andrew Jackson, John Quincy Adams, and William H. Crawford. A member from each State, making twenty-four, were appointed tellers, who having examined the ballots, announced that the votes of thirteen States had been given for John Quincy Adams; the votes of seven States for Andrew Jackson, and the votes of four States for William H. Crawford. The Speaker then declared that John Quincy Adams, having received a majority of the votes of all the States of this Union, was duly elected President of the United States for four years, to commence on the 4th of March, 1825.

John Quincy Adams, thus elected President, took the oath of office, and entered upon its duties on the 4th of March, 1825.

Election for the Eleventh term, commencing 4th March, 1829, *and terminating 3d March,* 1833.

No. of electors appointed by each State.	STATES.	PRESIDENT.		VICE PRESIDENT.		
		Andrew Jackson, of Tennessee.	John Q. Adams, of Massachusetts.	John C. Calhoun, of S. Carolina.	Richard Rush, of Pennsylvania.	William Smith, of South Carolina.
9	Maine	1	8	1	8	..
8	New Hampshire	..	8	..	8	..
15	Massachusetts	..	15	..	15	..
4	Rhode Island	..	4	..	4	..
8	Connecticut	..	8	..	8	..
7	Vermont	..	7	..	7	..
36	New York	20	16	20	16	..
8	New Jersey	..	8	..	8	..
28	Pennsylvania	28	..	28	..	..
3	Delaware	..	3	..	3	..
11	Maryland	5	6	5	6	..
24	Virginia	24	..	24	..	..
15	North Carolina	15	..	15	..	..
11	South Carolina	11	..	11	..	..
9	Georgia	9	..	2	..	7
14	Kentucky	14	..	14	..	..
11	Tennessee	11	..	11	..	..
16	Ohio	16	..	16	..	..
5	Louisiana	5	..	5	..	..
3	Mississippi	3	..	3	..	..
5	Indiana	5	..	5	..	..
3	Illinois	3	..	3	..	..
5	Alabama	5	..	5	..	..
3	Missouri	3	..	3	..	..
261	Whole No. of Electors	178	83	171	83	7
	Majority 131					

Andrew Jackson, elected President, took the oath of office, and entered upon its duties the 4th of March, 1829.

John C. Calhoun, elected Vice President, took the oath of office, and attended in Senate the 4th of March, 1829.

Election for the Twelfth term, commencing 4th March, 1833, *and terminating 3d March,* 1837.

No. of electors appointed by each State.	STATES.	PRESIDENT.				VICE PRESIDENT.				
		Andrew Jackson, of Tennessee.	Henry Clay, of Kentucky.	John Floyd, of Virginia.	Wm. Wirt, of Maryland.	M. Van Buren, of New York.	John Sergeant, of Pennsylvania.	William Wilkins, of Pennsylvania.	Henry Lee, of Massachusetts.	Amos Ellmaker, of Pennsylvania.
10	Maine	10	..	..	..	10	..	..	..	..
7	N. Hampshire	7	..	..	..	7	..	..	..	..
14	Massachusetts	..	14	..	..	..	14	..	..	..
4	Rhode Island	..	4	..	..	..	4	..	..	..
8	Connecticut	..	8	..	..	..	8	..	..	..
7	Vermont	..	..	..	7	..	..	..	..	7
42	New York	42	..	..	..	42	..	..	..	..
8	New Jersey	8	..	..	..	8	..	..	..	..
30	Pennsylvania	30	..	..	..	..	..	30	..	..
3	Delaware	..	3	..	..	..	3	..	..	..
10	Maryland	3	5	..	..	3	5	..	..	..
23	Virginia	23	..	..	..	23	..	..	..	..
15	North Carolina	15	..	..	..	15	..	..	..	..
11	South Carolina	..	..	11	..	..	..	..	11	..
11	Georgia	11	..	..	..	11	..	..	..	..
15	Kentucky	..	15	..	..	..	15	..	..	..
15	Tennessee	15	..	..	..	15	..	..	..	..
21	Ohio	21	..	..	..	21	..	..	..	..
5	Louisiana	5	..	..	..	5	..	..	..	.
4	Mississippi	4	..	..	..	4	..	..	..	..
9	Indiana	9	..	..	..	9	..	..	..	..
5	Illinois	5	..	..	..	5	..	..	..	..
7	Alabama	7	..	..	..	7	..	..	..	..
4	Missouri	4	..	..	..	4	..	..	..	..
288	No. of electors. Majority .. 145	219	49	11	7	189	49	30	11	7

Andrew Jackson, elected President, took the oath of office, and continued the duties 4th March, 1833.

Martin Van Buren, elected Vice President, took the oath of office and entered upon its duties 4th March, 1833.

Election for the Thirteenth term, commencing 4th March, 1837, *and terminating 3d March,* 1841.

No. of electors appointed by each State.	STATES.	PRESIDENT.					VICE PRESIDENT.			
		M. Van Buren, of New York.	Wm. H. Harrison, of Ohio.	Hugh L. White, of Tenn.	Daniel Webster, of Mass.	W. P. Mangum, of N. Carolina.	R. M. Johnson, of Kentucky.	Francis Granger, of New York.	John Tyler, of Virginia.	William Smith, of Alabama.
10	Maine.........	10	..	..	..	..	10	..	..	..
7	N. Hampshire..	7	..	..	..	..	7	..	..	..
14	Massachusetts .	..	..	..	14	..	..	14	..	..
4	Rhode Island ..	4	..	..	..	..	4	..	..	..
8	Connecticut....	8	..	..	..	..	8	..	..	..
7	Vermont	..	7	..	..	..	..	7	..	..
42	New York	42	..	..	..	..	42	..	..	..
8	New Jersey ...	..	8	..	..	..	..	8	..	..
30	Pennsylvania ..	30	..	..	..	..	30	..	..	..
3	Delaware......	..	3	..	..	..	..	3	..	..
10	Maryland......	..	10	..	..	..	..	..	10	..
23	Virginia.......	23	..	..	..	..	..	..	..	23
15	North Carolina	15	..	..	..	..	15	..	..	..
11	South Carolina.	..	..	..	..	11	..	..	11	..
11	Georgia	..	..	11	..	..	..	..	11	..
15	Kentucky......	..	15	..	..	..	..	15	..	..
15	Tennessee.....	..	..	15	..	..	..	..	15	..
21	Ohio..........	..	21	..	..	..	..	21	..	..
5	Louisiana......	5	..	..	..	..	5	..	..	..
4	Mississippi.....	4	..	..	..	..	4	..	..	..
9	Indiana........	..	9	..	..	..	..	9	..	..
5	Illinois	5	..	..	..	..	5	..	..	..
7	Alabama	7	..	..	..	..	7	..	..	..
4	Missouri.......	4	..	..	..	..	4	..	..	..
3	Arkansas......	3	..	..	..	..	3	..	..	..
3	Michigan......	3	..	..	..	..	3	..	..	..
294	No. of electors. Majority .. 148	170	73	26	14	11	147*	77	47	23

Martin Van Buren, elected President, took the oath of office, and entered upon its duties 4th March, 1837.

Richard M. Johnson, elected Vice President, took the oath of office, and attended in Senate 4th March, 1837. * Elected by the Senate.

Election for the Fourteenth term, commencing 4th March, 1841, *and terminating 3d March,* 1845.

No. of electoral votes.	STATES.	PRESIDENT.		VICE PRESIDENT.			
		Wm. H. Harrison, of Ohio.	M. Van Buren, of New York.	John Tyler, of Virginia.	R. M. Johnson, of Kentucky.	L. W. Tazewell, of Virginia.	James K. Polk, of Tennessee.
10	Maine	10	..	10	..	..	.
7	New Hampshire	..	7	..	7	..	..
14	Massachusetts	14	..	14	..	..	..
4	Rhode Island	4	..	4	..	..	..
8	Connecticut	8	..	8	..	..	..
7	Vermont	7	..	7	..	..	..
42	New York	42	..	42	..	..	..
8	New Jersey	8	..	8	..	..	..
30	Pennsylvania	30	..	30	..	..	..
3	Delaware	3	..	3	..	..	..
10	Maryland	10	..	10	..	..	..
23	Virginia	..	23	..	22	..	1
15	North Carolina	15	..	15	..	..	..
11	South Carolina	..	11	..	..	11	..
11	Georgia	11	..	11	..	..	..
15	Kentucky	15	..	15	..	..	..
15	Tennessee	15	..	15	..	..	..
21	Ohio	21	..	21	..	..	..
5	Louisiana	5	..	5	..	..	..
4	Mississippi	4	..	4	..	..	..
9	Indiana	9	..	9	..	..	..
5	Illinois	..	5	..	5	..	..
7	Alabama	..	7	..	7	..	..
4	Missouri	..	4	..	4	..	..
3	Arkansas	..	3	..	3	..	..
3	Michigan	3	..	3	..	..	..
294	Whole No. of electors Majority 148	234	60	234	48	11	1

William H. Harrison, elected President, took the oath of office, and entered upon its duties on 4th March, 1841.

John Tyler, elected Vice President, took the oath of office, and entered upon its duties on 4th March, 1841.

Y

TUESDAY, *April* 6, 1841.

Immediate.,' after the decease of the President, Mr. Webster, jr., Chief Clerk in tne Department of State, accompanied by Mr. Beall, an officer of the Senate, set out for the residence of the Vice President, in Virginia, bearing to him the following letter:

WASHINGTON, *April* 4, 1841.

To JOHN TYLER,
Vice President of the United States.

SIR: It has become our most painful duty to inform you that William Henry Harrison, late President of the United States, has departed this life.

This distressing event took place this day, at the President's Mansion in this city, at thirty minutes before one in the morning.

We lose no time in despatching the Chief Clerk in the State Department, as a special messenger, to bear you these melancholy tidings.

We have the honor to be, with the highest regard, your obedient servants,

DANIEL WEBSTER,
Secretary of State.

THOMAS EWING,
Secretary of the Treasury.

JOHN BELL,
Secretary of War.

JOHN J. CRITTENDEN,
Attorney General.

FRANCIS GRANGER,
Postmaster General.

CITY OF WASHINGTON, D. C.
Wednesday April 7, 1841.

By the extraordinary despatch used in sending the official intelligence to the Vice President, at Williamsburg, and similar despatch by him in repairing to the seat of Government, John Tyler, now President of the United States, arrived in this city yesterday morning, at 5 o'clock, and took lodgings at Brown's Hotel.

At 12 o'clock, all the Heads of Departments, except the Secretary of the Navy, (who has not yet returned to the city from his visit to his family,) waited upon him, to pay him their official and personal respects. They were received with all the politeness and kindness which characterize the new President. He signified his deep feeling of the public calamity sustained by the death of President Harrison, and expressed his profound sensibility to the heavy responsibilities so suddenly devolved upon himself. He spoke of the present state of things with great concern and seriousness, and made known his wishes that the several Heads of Departments would continue to fill the places which they now respectively occupy, and his confidence that they would afford all the aid in their power to enable him to carry on the administration of the Government successfully.

The President then took and subscribed the following oath of office:

I do solemnly swear, that I will faithfully execute the office of President of the United States, and will, to the best of my ability, preserve, protect, and defend the Constitution of the United States.

JOHN TYLER.

APRIL 6, 1841.

DISTRICT OF COLUMBIA,
City and County of Washington, ss.

I, William Cranch, Chief Judge of the Circuit Court of the District of Columbia, certify, that the above-named John Tyler personally appeared before me this day, and, although he deems himself qualified to perform the duties, and exercise the powers and office of President on the death of William Henry Harrison, late President of the United States, without any other oath than that which he has taken as Vice President, yet, as doubts may arise, and for greater caution, took and subscribed the foregoing oath before me.

W. CRANCH.

APRIL 6, 1841.

Election for the Fifteenth term, commencing 4th March, 1845, and terminating 3d March, 1849.

No. of electors appointed.	STATES.	PRESIDENT.		V. PRESIDENT.	
		James K. Polk, of Tennessee.	Henry Clay, of Kentucky.	George M. Dallas, of Pennsylvania.	T. Frelinghuysen, of New York.
9	Maine	9	..	9	..
6	New Hampshire	6	..	6	..
12	Massachusetts	..	12	..	12
4	Rhode Island and P. Plantations	..	4	..	4
6	Connecticut	..	6	..	6
6	Vermont	..	6	..	6
36	New York	36	..	36	..
7	New Jersey	..	7	..	7
26	Pennsylvania	26	..	26	..
3	Delaware	..	3	..	3
8	Maryland	..	8	..	8
17	Virginia	17	..	17	..
11	North Carolina	..	11	..	11
9	South Carolina	9	..	9	..
10	Georgia	10	..	10	..
12	Kentucky	..	12	..	12
13	Tennessee	..	13	..	13
23	Ohio	..	23	..	23
6	Louisiana	6	..	6	..
6	Mississippi	6	..	6	..
12	Indiana	12	..	12	..
9	Illinois	9	..	9	..
9	Alabama	9	..	9	..
7	Missouri	7	..	7	..
3	Arkansas	3	..	3	..
5	Michigan	5	..	5	..
275	Whole No. of electors	170	105	170	105
	Majority 138				

James K. Polk, elected President, took the oath of office, and entered upon its duties on 4th March, 1845.

George Mifflin Dallas, elected Vice President, attended in Senate, and took the oath of office on 4th March, 1845.

Election for the Sixteenth Term, commencing 4th March, 1849, *and terminating 3d March,* 1853.

No. of electors appointed by each State.	STATES.	PRESIDENT.		V. PRESIDENT.	
		Z. Taylor, of Louisiana.	Lewis Cass, of Michigan.	M. Fillmore, of New York.	W. O. Butler, of Kentucky.
9	Maine	...	9	...	9
6	New Hampshire	...	6	...	6
12	Massachusetts	12	...	12	...
4	Rhode Island	4	...	4	...
6	Connecticut	6	...	6	...
6	Vermont	6	...	6	...
36	New York	36	...	36	...
7	New Jersey	7	...	7	...
26	Pennsylvania	26	...	26	...
3	Delaware	3	...	3	...
8	Maryland	8	...	8	...
17	Virginia	...	17	...	17
11	North Carolina	11	...	11	...
9	South Carolina	...	9	...	9
10	Georgia	10	...	10	...
12	Kentucky	12	...	12	...
13	Tennessee	13	...	13	...
23	Ohio	...	23	...	23
6	Louisiana	6	...	6	...
6	Mississippi	...	6	...	6
12	Indiana	...	12	...	12
9	Illinois	...	9	...	9
9	Alabama	...	9	...	9
7	Missouri	...	7	...	7
3	Arkansas	...	3	...	3
5	Michigan	...	5	...	5
3	Florida	3	...	3	...
4	Texas	...	4	...	4
4	Iowa	...	4	...	4
4	Wisconsin	...	4	...	4
290	Whole number of electors	163	127	163	127

Zachary Taylor, elected President, took the oath of office, and entered upon its duties, 4th March, 1849.

Millard Fillmore, elected Vice President, took the oath of office, and entered upon its duties, 4th March, 1849.

Zachary Taylor, President of the United States, having deceased on Tuesday the 9th July, 1850; and Congress being then in session:—

IN SENATE OF THE UNITED STATES.
WEDNESDAY, *July* 10, 1850.

The following communication, received by the Secretary of the Senate, was read:

To the Senate of the United States:—

In consequence of the lamented death of Zachary Taylor, late President of the United States, I shall no longer occupy the chair of the Senate; and I have thought that a formal communication to the Senate, to that effect, through your Secretary, might enable you the more promptly to proceed to the choice of a presiding officer. MILLARD FILLMORE.

WASHINGTON, *July* 10, 1850.

The following message was received from the President of the United States, by Mr. Fisher:—

Fellow-citizens of the Senate and House of Representatives:—

I have to perform the melancholy duty of announcing to you that it has pleased Almighty God to remove from this life Zachary Taylor, late President of the United States. He deceased last evening, at the hour of half past ten o'clock, in the midst of his family and surrounded by affectionate friends, calmly and in the full possession of all his faculties. Among his last words were these, which he uttered with emphatic distinctness: "I have always done my duty—I am ready to die—my only regret is for the friends I leave behind me."

Having announced to you, fellow-citizens, this most afflicting bereavement, and assuring you that it has penetrated no heart with deeper grief than mine, it remains for me to say, that I propose this day, at 12 o'clock, in the Hall of the House of Representatives, in the presence of both Houses of Congress, to take the oath prescribed by the Constitution, to enable me to enter on the execution of the office which this event has devolved on me.

WASHINGTON, *July* 10, 1850. MILLARD FILLMORE.

A similar message having been communicated to the House of Representatives and the necessary arrangements made between the two Houses:—

At 12 o'clock meridian—

The President of the United States, the Heads of Departments, the Chief Judge of the Circuit Court of the District of Columbia, and the Senate of the United States, having entered the Hall of the House of Representatives—

The oath of office was administered to the President by the Honourable William Cranch, Chief Judge of the Circuit Court of the United States for the District of Columbia.

Synoptical table of terms of office, and length of service, in the Senate, and of the Presidents pro

Congress.	Session.	Commencement of Session.	Termination of Session.	Number of days in each Session.	Names of Vice Presidents of the United States.	
1	1	. .	. .	.	. . . . . .	1
		4 Mar. 1789	29 Sept. 1789	210	John Adams . .	2
		. .	. .	.	. . . . . .	3
		. .	. .	.	John Adams . .	4
1	2	4 Jan. 1790	12 Aug. 1790	221	John Adams . .	5
1	3	6 Dec. 1790	3 Mar. 1791	88	John Adams . .	6
Special	Ses. Sen.	4 Mar. 1791	4 Mar. 1791	1	John Adams . .	7
2	1	24 Oct. 1791	8 May 1792	198	John Adams . .	8
		. .	. .	.	. . . . . .	9
2	2	5 Nov. 1792	2 Mar. 1793	118	. . . . . .	10
		. .	. .	.	John Adams . .	11
		. .	. .	.	. . . . .	12
Special	Ses. Sen.	4 Mar. 1793	4 Mar. 1793	1	. . . . . .	13
3	1	2 Dec. 1793	9 June 1794	190	John Adams . .	14
		. .	. .	.	. . . . . .	15
3	2	3 Nov. 1794	3 Mar. 1795	121	. . . . . .	16
		. .	. .	.	John Adams . .	17
		. .	. .	.	. . . . . .	18
Special	Ses. Sen.	8 June 1795	26 June 1795	19	John Adams . .	19
4	1	7 Dec. 1795	1 June 1796	178	. . . . . .	20
		. .	. .	.	John Adams . .	21
		. .	. .	.	. . . . . .	22
4	2	5 Dec. 1796	3 Mar. 1797	89	John Adams . .	23
		. .	. .	.	. . . . .	24
Special	Ses. Sen.	4 Mar. 1797	4 Mar. 1797	1	Thomas Jefferson .	25
5	1	15 May 1797	10 July 1797	57	Thomas Jefferson .	26
		. .	. .	.	. . . . . .	27
5	2	13 Nov. 1797	16 July 1798	246	. . . . . .	28
		. .	. .	.	Thomas Jefferson .	29
		. .	. .	.	. . . . . .	30
Special	Ses. Sen.	17 July 1798	19 July 1798	3	. . . . . .	31
5	3	3 Dec. 1798	3 Mar. 1799	91	. . . . . .	32
		. .	. .	.	Thomas Jefferson .	33
		. .	. .	.	. . . . . .	34
6	1	2 Dec. 1799	14 May 1800	165	. . . . . .	35
		. .	. .	.	Thomas Jefferson .	36
		. .	. .	.	. . . . . .	37
6	2	17 Nov. 1800	3 Mar. 1801	107	. . . . . .	38
		. .	. .	.	Thomas Jefferson .	39
		. .	. .	.	. . . . .	40

of the Vice Presidents of the United States and Presidents of the Senate, tempore of the Senate, viz:

	TERMS OF OFFICE.		Names of Presidents pro tempore of the Senate.	SERVICE IN SENATE U. S.	
	Commenced.	Expired.		Attended.	Retired.
1	. .	. .	John Langdon . .	6 April 1789	21 April 1789
2	4 Mar. 1789	3 Mar. 1793	. . . . .	21 April 1789	6 Aug. 1789
3	. .	. .	John Langdon . .	7 Aug. 1789	19 Aug. 1789
4	. .	. .	. . . . .	20 Aug. 1789	29 Sept. 1789
5	. .	. .	. . . .	4 Jan. 1790	12 Aug. 1790
6	. .	. .	. . . . . .	6 Dec. 1790	3 Mar. 1791
7	. .	. .	. . . .	4 Mar. 1791	4 Mar. 1791
8	. .	. .	. . . . .	24 Oct. 1791	17 April 1792
9	. .	. .	Richard Henry Lee .	18 April 1792	8 May 1792
10	. .	. .	John Langdon .	5 Nov. 1792	4 Dec. 1792
11	. .	. .	. . . .	5 Dec. 1792	28 Feb. 1793
12	. .	. .	John Langdon .	1 Mar. 1793	3 Mar. 1793
13	. .	. .	John Langdon . .	4 Mar. 1793	4 Mar. 1793
14	4 Mar. 1793	3 Mar. 1797	. . . . .	2 Dec. 1793	30 May 1794
15	. .	. .	Ralph Izard . .	31 May 1794	9 June 1794
16	. .	. .	Ralph Izard . .	3 Nov. 1794	9 Nov. 1794
17	. .	. .	. . . .	10 Nov. 1794	19 Feb. 1795
18	. .	. .	Henry Tazewell .	20 Feb. 1795	3 Mar. 1795
19	. .	. .	. . . .	8 June 1795	26 June 1795
20	. .	. .	Henry Tazewell .	7 Dec. 1795	8 Dec. 1795
21	. .	. .	. . . .	9 Dec. 1795	5 May 1796
22	. .	. .	Samuel Livermore.	6 May 1796	1 June 1796
23	. .	. .	. . . .	5 Dec. 1796	15 Feb. 1797
24	. .	. .	William Bingham.	16 Feb. 1797	3 Mar. 1797
25	4 Mar. 1797	3 Mar. 1801	. . . . .	4 Mar. 1797	4 Mar. 1797
26	. .	. .	. . . .	15 May 1797	5 July 1797
27	. .	. .	William Bradford .	6 July 1797	10 July 1797
28	. .	. .	Jacob Read . .	22 Nov. 1797	12 Dec. 1797
29	. .	. .	. . . . . .	13 Dec. 1797	26 June 1798
30	. .	. .	Theodore Sedgwick .	27 June 1798	16 July 1798
31	. .	. .	Theodore Sedgwick	17 July 1798	17 July 1798
32	. .	. .	John Lawrence. .	6 Dec. 1798	26 Dec. 1798
33	.	. .	. . . . .	27 Dec. 1798	28 Feb. 1799
34	. .	. .	James Ross . .	1 Mar. 1799	3 Mar. 1799
35	. .	. .	Samuel Livermore.	2 Dec. 1799	29 Dec. 1799
36	. .	. .	. . . .	30 Dec. 1799	13 May 1800
37	. .	. .	Uriah Tracy . .	14 May 1800	14 May 1800
38	. .	. .	John Eager Howard.	21 Nov. 1800	27 Nov. 1800
39	. .	. .	. . . . .	28 Nov. 1800	28 Feb. 1801
40	. .	. .	James Hillhouse .	28 Feb. 1801	3 Mar. 1801

Congress.	Session.	Commencement of Session.	Termination of Session.	Number of days in each Session.	Names of Vice Presidents of the United States.	
Special	Ses. Sen.	4 Mar. 1801	5 Mar. 1801	2	Aaron Burr . . .	1
7	1	7 Dec. 1801	3 May 1802	148	. . . . . .	2
		. .	. .	.	Aaron Burr . . .	3
		. .	. .	.	. . . . . .	4
7	2	6 Dec. 1802	3 Mar. 1803	88	. . . . . .	5
		. .	. .	.	Aaron Burr . .	6
		. .	. .	.	. . . . . .	7
		. .	. .	.	Aaron Burr . .	8
		. .	. .	.	. . . . . .	9
8	1	17 Oct. 1803	27 Mar. 1804	163	. . . . . .	10
		. .	. .	.	Aaron Burr . . .	11
		.	. .	.	. . . . . .	12
		. .	. .	.	. . . . . .	13
8	2	5 Nov. 1804	3 Mar. 1805	119	Aaron Burr . . .	14
		. .	. .	.	. . . . . .	15
		. .	. .	.	Aaron Burr . . .	16
		. .	. .	.	. . . . . .	17
		.	. .	.	Aaron Burr . . .	18
		.	. .	.	. . . . . .	19
9	1	2 Dec. 1805	21 April 1806	141	. . . . . .	20
		. .	. .	.	George Clinton .	21
		. .	. .	.	. . . . . .	22
9	2	1 Dec. 1806	3 Mar. 1807	93	George Clinton .	23
		. .	. .	.	. . . . . .	24
10	1	26 Oct. 1807	25 April 1808	183	George Clinton .	25
		. .	. .	.	. . . . . .	26
10	2	7 Nov. 1808	3 Mar. 1809	117	George Clinton .	27
		. .	. .	.	. . . . . .	28
		. .	. .	.	George Clinton .	29
		.	. .	.	. . . . . .	30
Special	Ses. Sen.	4 Mar. 1809	7 Mar. 1809	4	. . . . . .	31
11	1	22 May 1809	28 June 1809	38	George Clinton . .	32
		. .	. .	.	. . . . . .	33
11	2	27 Nov. 1809	1 May 1810	156	. . . . . .	34
		. .	. .	.	George Clinton .	35
		. .	. .	.	. . . . . .	36
		. .	. .	.	George Clinton .	37
		. .	. .	.	. . . . . .	38
11	3	3 Dec. 1810	3 Mar. 1811	91	. . . . . .	39

TABLE—Continued.

	TERMS OF OFFICE.		Names of Presidents pro tempore of the Senate.	SERVICE IN SENATE U. S.	
	Commenced.	Expired.		Attended.	Retired.
1	4 Mar. 1801	3 Mar. 1805	. . . . . .	4 Mar. 1801	5 Mar. 1801
2	. .	. .	Abraham Baldwin .	7 Dec. 1801	14 Jan. 1802
3	. .	. .	. . . . . .	15 Jan. 1802	16 April 1802
4	. .	. .	Abraham Baldwin .	17 April 1802	3 May 1802
5	. .	. .	Stephen R. Bradley .	14 Dec. 1802	18 Jan. 18[illegible]
6	. .	. .	. . . . . .	19 Jan. 1803	24 Feb. 1803
7	. .	. .	Stephen R. Bradley .	25 Feb. 1803	25 Feb. 1803
8	. .	. .	. . . . . .	26 Feb. 1803	1 Mar. 1803
9	. .	. .	Stephen R. Bradley .	2 Mar. 1803	3 Mar. 1803
10	. .	. .	John Brown . .	17 Oct. 1803	6 Dec. 1803
11	. .	. .	. . . . . .	7 Dec. 1803	22 Jan. 1804
12	. .	. .	John Brown . .	23 Jan. 1804	9 Mar. 1804
13	. .	. .	Jesse Franklin .	10 Mar. 1804	27 Mar. 1804
14	. .	. .	. . . . . .	5 Nov. 1804	14 Jan. 1805
15	. .	. .	Joseph Anderson .	15 Jan. 1805	
16	. .	. .	. . . . . .	. .	27 Feb. 1805
17	. .	. .	Joseph Anderson .	28 Feb. 1805	2 Mar. 1805
18	. .	. .	. . . . . .	2 Mar. 1805	"
19	. .	. .	Joseph Anderson .	2 Mar. 1805	3 Mar. 1805
20	. .	. .	Samuel Smith . .	2 Dec. 1805	15 Dec. 1805
21	4 Mar. 1805	3 Mar. 1809	. . . . . .	16 Dec. 1805	17 Mar. 1806
22	. .	. .	Samuel Smith . .	18 Mar. 1806	21 April 1806
23	. .	. .	. . . . . .	1 Dec. 1806	2 Mar. 1807
24	. .	. .	Samuel Smith . .	2 Mar. 1807	3 "
25	. .	. .	. . . . . .	26 Oct. 1807	16 April 1808
26	. .	. .	Samuel Smith . .	16 April 1808	25 "
27	. .	. .	. . . . . .	7 Nov. 1808	27 Dec. 1808
28	. .	. .	Stephen R. Bradley .	28 Dec. 1808	
29	. .	. .	. . . . . .	. .	30 Jan. 1809
30	. .	. .	John Milledge . .	30 Jan. 1809	3 Mar. 1809
31	. .	. .	John Milledge . .	4 Mar. 1809	7 "
32	4 Mar. 1809	3 Mar. 1813	. . . . . .	22 May 1809	25 June 1809
33	. .	. .	Andrew Gregg .	26 June 1809	28 "
34	. .	. .	Andrew Gregg . .	27 Nov. 1809	18 Dec. 1809
35	. .	. .	. . . . . .	19 Dec. 1809	27 Feb. 1810
36	. .	. .	John Gaillard . .	28 Feb. 1810	
37	. .	. .	. . . . . .	. .	16 April 181
38	. .	. .	John Gaillard . .	17 April 1810	1 May 1810
39	. .	. .	John Gaillard . .	3 Dec. 1810	11 Dec. 1810

Congress.	Session.	Commencement of Session.	Termination of Session.	Number of days in each Session.	Names of Vice Presidents of the United States.	
		. .	. .	.	George Clinton . .	1
		. .	. .	.	. . . . . .	2
12	1	4 Nov. 1811	6 July 1812	245	George Clinton . .	3
		. .	. .	.	. . . . . .	4
12	2	2 Nov. 1812	3 Mar. 1813	122	. . . . . .	5
13	1	24 May 1813	2 Aug. 1813	71	Elbridge Gerry .	6
13	2	6 Dec. 1813	18 April 1814	134	. . . . . .	7
		. .	. .	.	Elbridge Gerry .	8
		. .	. .	.	. . . . . .	9
13	3	19 Sept. 1814	3 Mar. 1815	166	. . . . . .	10
		. .	. .		. . . . . .	11
14	1	4 Dec. 1815	30 April 1816	149	. . . . . .	12
14	2	2 Dec. 1816	3 Mar. 1817	92	. . . . . .	13
Special	Ses. Sen.	4 Mar. 1817	6 Mar. 1817	3	. . . . . .	14
15	1	1 Dec. 1817	20 April 1818	141	. . . . . .	15
		. .	. .	.	Daniel D. Tompkins	16
		. .	. .	.	. . . . . .	17
15	2	16 Nov. 1818	3 Mar. 1819	108	. . . . . .	18
		. .	. .	.	Daniel D. Tompkins	19
		. .	. .	.	. . . . . .	20
16	1	6 Dec. 1819	15 May 1820	162	. . . . . .	21
		. .	. .	.	Daniel D. Tompkins	22
		. .	. .	.	. . . . . .	23
16	2	13 Nov. 1820	3 Mar. 1821	111	. . . . . .	24
17	1	3 Dec. 1821	8 May 1822	157	. . . . . .	25
		. .	. .	.	Daniel D. Tompkins	26
		. .	. .	.	. . . . . .	27
17	2	2 Dec. 1822	3 Mar. 1823	92	. . . . . .	28
		. .	. .	.	Daniel D. Tompkins	29
		. .	. .	.	. . . . . .	30
18	1	1 Dec. 1823	27 May 1824	179	. . . . . .	31
		. .	. .	.	Daniel D. Tompkins .	32
		. .	. .	.	. . . . . .	33
18	2	6 Dec. 1824	3 Mar. 1825	88	. . . . . .	34
Special	Ses. Sen.	4 Mar. 1825	9 "	5	John C. Calhoun .	35
		. .	. .	.	. . . . . .	36

TABLE—Continued.

	TERMS OF OFFICE.		Names of Presidents pro tempore of the Senate.	SERVICE IN SENATE U. S.	
	Commenced.	Expired.		Attended.	Retired.
1	. .	. .	. . . . . .	12 Dec. 1810	22 Feb. 1811
2	. .	. .	John Pope . .	23 Feb. 1811	3 Mar. 1811
3	Died April,	1812.	. . . . . .	4 Nov. 1811	23 Mar. 1812
4	. .	. .	William H. Crawford	24 Mar. 1812	6 July 1812
5	. .	. .	William H. Crawford	2 Nov. 1812	3 Mar. 1813
6	4 Mar. 1813	3 Mar. 1817	. . . . . .	24 May 1813	2 Aug. 1813
7	. .	. .	Joseph B. Varnum .	6 Dec. 1813	3 Feb. 1814
8	Died Nov.	1814.	. . . . . .	4 Feb. 1814	17 April 1814
9	. .	. .	John Gaillard . .	18 April 1814	18 "
10	. .	. .	John Gaillard . .	19 Sept. 1814	24 Nov. 1814
11	. .	. .	John Gaillard . .	*24 Nov. 1814	2 Mar. 1815
12	. .	. .	John Gaillard . .	4 Dec. 1815	30 April 1815
13	. .	. .	John Gaillard . .	2 Dec. 1816	3 Mar. 1817
14	. .	. .	John Gaillard . .	4 Mar. 1817	6 "
15	. .	. .	John Gaillard . .	1 Dec. 1817	18 Feb. 1818
16	4 Mar. 1817	3 Mar. 1821	. . . . . .	19 Feb. 1818	30 Mar. 1818
17	. .	. .	John Gaillard . .	31 Mar. 1818	20 April 1818
18	. .	. .	John Gaillard . .	16 Nov. 1818	5 Jan. 1819
19	. .	. .	. . . . . .	6 Jan. 1819	14 Feb. 1819
20	. .	. .	James Barbour .	15 Feb. 1819	3 Mar. 1819
21	. .	. .	James Barbour . .	6 Dec. 1819	26 Dec. 1819
22	. .	. .	. . . . . .	27 Dec. 1819	24 Jan. 1820
23	. .	. .	John Gaillard . .	25 Jan. 1820	15 May 1820
24	. .	. .	John Gaillard . .	13 Nov. 1820	3 Mar. 1821
25	. .	. .	John Gaillard . .	3 Dec. 1821	27 Dec. 1821
26	4 Mar. 1821	3 Mar. 1825	. . . . . .	28 "	31 Jan. 1822
27	. .	. .	John Gaillard . .	1 Feb. 1822	8 May 1822
28	. .	. .	John Gaillard . .	2 Dec. 1822	2 Dec. 1822
29	. .	. .	. . . . . .	3 "	18 Feb. 1823
30	. .	. .	John Gaillard . .	19 Feb. 1823	3 Mar. 1823
31	. .	. .	John Gaillard . .	1 Dec. 1823	20 Jan. 1824
32	. .	. .	. . . . . .	21 Jan. 1824	20 May 1824
33	. .	. .	John Gaillard . .	21 May 1824	27 "
34	. .	. .	John Gaillard . .	6 Dec. 1824	3 Mar. 1825
35	4 Mar. 1825	3 Mar. 1829	. . . . . .	4 Mar. 1825	9 "
36	. .	. .	John Gaillard . .	9 "	9 "

* Re-election considered necessary on death of Vice President.

Congress.	Session.	Commencement of Session.	Termination of Session.	Number of days in each Session.	Names of Vice Presidents of the United States.	
19	1	5 Dec. 1825	22 May 1826	169	John C. Calhoun. .	1
		. .	. .	.	. . . . . .	2
19	2	4 Dec. 1826	3 Mar. 1827	90	John C. Calhoun. .	3
		. .	. .	.	. . . . . .	4
		. .	. .	.	John C. Calhoun. .	5
		. .	. .	.	. . . . . .	6
20	1	3 Dec. 1827	26 May 1828	176	John C. Calhoun. .	7
		. .	. .	.	. . . . . .	8
20	2	1 Dec. 1828	3 Mar. 1829	93	. . . . . .	9
		. .	. .	.	John C. Calhoun .	10
Special	Ses. Sen.	4 Mar. 1829	17 "	14	John C. Calhoun. .	11
		. .	. .	.	. . . . . .	12
21	1	7 Dec. 1829	31 May 1830	176	. . . . . .	13
		. .	. .	.	John C. Calhoun .	14
		. .	. .	.	. . . . . .	15
21	2	6 Dec. 1830	3 Mar. 1831	88	. . . . . .	16
		. .	. .	.	John C. Calhoun. .	17
		. .	. .	.	. . . . . .	18
22	1	5 Dec. 1831	16 July 1832	225	. . . . . .	19
		. .	. .	.	John C. Calhoun .	20
		. .	. .	.	. . . . . .	21
22	2	3 Dec. 1832	2 Mar. 1833	90	. . . . . .	22
23	1	2 Dec. 1833	30 June 1834	211	. . . . . .	23
		. .	. .	.	Martin Van Buren .	24
		. .	. .	.	. . . . . .	25
23	2	1 Dec. 1834	3 Mar. 1835	93	Martin Van Buren .	26
		. .	. .	.	. . . . . .	27
24	1	7 Dec. 1835	4 July 1836	211	Martin Van Buren .	28
		. .	. .	.	. . . . . .	29
24	2	5 Dec. 1836	3 Mar. 1837	89	Martin Van Buren .	30
		. .	. .	.	. . . . . .	31
Special	Ses. Sen.	4 Mar. 1837	10 "	7	Richard M. Johnson .	32
		. .	. .	.	Richard M. Johnson	33
25	1	4 Sept. 1837	16 Oct. 1837	44	Richard M. Johnson	34
		. .	. .	.	. . . . . .	35
25	2	4 Dec. 1837	9 July 1838	218	Richard M. Johnson .	36
		. .	. .	.	. . . . . .	37
25	3	3 Dec. 1838	3 Mar. 1839	91	. . . . . .	38

TABLE—Continued.

	TERMS OF OFFICE.		Names of Presidents pro tempore of the Senate.	SERVICE IN SENATE U. S.	
	Commenced.	Expired.		Attended.	Retired.
1	. .	. .	. . . . . .	5 Dec. 1825	20 May 1826
2	. .	. .	Nathaniel Macon .	20 May 1826	20 "
3	. .	. .	. . . . . .	4 Dec. 1826	29 Dec. 1826
4	. .	. .	Nathaniel Macon .	2 Jan. 1827	13 Feb. 1827
5	. .	. .	. . . . . .	14 Feb. 1827	2 Mar. 1827
6	. .	. .	Nathaniel Macon .	2 Mar. 1827	3 "
7	. .	. .	. . . . . .	3 Dec. 1827	14 May 1828
8	. .	. .	Samuel Smith .	15 May 1828	26 "
9	. .	. .	Samuel Smith . .	1 Dec. 1828	21 Dec. 1828
10	. .	. .	. . . . . .	22 "	3 Mar. 1829
11	4 Mar. 1829	3 Mar. 1833	. . . . . .	4 Mar. 1829	12 "
12	. .	. .	Samuel Smith .	13 "	17 "
13	. .	. .	Samuel Smith . .	7 Dec. 1829	13 Dec. 1829
14	. .	. .	. . . . . .	14 "	29 May 1830
15	. .	. .	Samuel Smith . .	29 May 1830	31 "
16	. .	. .	Samuel Smith .	6 Dec. 1830	2 Jan. 1831
17	. .	. .	. . . . . .	3 Jan. 1831	1 Mar. 1831
18	. .	. .	Samuel Smith .	1 Mar. 1831	3 "
19	. .	. .	Samuel Smith . .	5 Dec. 1831	11 Dec. 1831
20	Resigned 28	Dec. 1832.	. . . . . .	12 "	8 July 1832
21	. .	. .	Littleton W. Tazewell	9 July 1832	16 "
22	. .	. .	Hugh Lawson White .	3 Dec. 1832	2 Mar. 1833
23	. .	. .	Hugh Lawson White .	2 Dec. 1833	15 Dec. 1833
24	4 Mar. 1833	3 Mar. 1837	. . . . . .	16 "	27 June 1834
25	. .	. .	George Poindexter .	28 June 1834	30 "
26	. .	. .	. . . . . .	1 Dec. 1834	3 Mar. 1835
27	. .	. .	John Tyler . . .	3 Mar. 1835	3 "
28	. .	. .	. . . . . .	7 Dec. 1835	30 June 1836
29	. .	. .	William R. King .	1 July 1836	4 July 1836
30	. .	. .	. . . . . .	5 Dec. 1836	28 Jan. 1837
31	. .	. .	William R. King .	28 Jan. 1837	3 Mar. 1837
32	4 Mar. 1837	3 Mar. 1841	. . . . . .	4 Mar. 1837	6 "
33	. .	. .	William R. King .	7 "	10 "
34	. .	. .	. . . . . .	4 Sept. 1837	12 Sept. 1837
35	. .	. .	William R. King .	13 "	16 Oct. 1837
36	. .	. .	. . . . . .	4 Dec. 1837	1 July 1838
37	. .	. .	William R. King .	2 July 1838	9 "
38	. .	. .	William R. King .	3 Dec. 1838	18 Dec. 1838

Congress.	Session.	Commencement of Session.	Termination of Session.	Number of days in each Session.	Names of Vice Presidents of the United States.	
		. .	. .	.	Richard M. Johnson .	1
		. .	. .	.	. . . . . .	2
26	1	2 Dec. 1839	21 July 1840	233	. . . . . .	3
		. .	. .	.	Richard M. Johnson	4
		. .	. .	.	. . . . . .	5
26	2	7 Dec. 1840	3 Mar. 1841	87	. . . . . .	6
		. .	. .	.	Richard M. Johnson .	7
		. .	. .	.	. . . . . .	8
Special	Ses. Sen.	4 Mar. 1841	15 "	12	. . . . . .	9
		. .	. .	.	John Tyler . .	10
		. .	. .	.	. . . . . .	11
27	1	31 May 1841	13 Sept. 1841	106	. . . . . .	12
27	2	6 Dec. 1841	31 Aug. 1842	269	. . . . . .	13
		. .	. .	.	. . . . . .	14
27	3	5 Dec. 1842	3 Mar. 1843	89	. . . . . .	15
28	1	4 Dec. 1843	17 June 1844	197	. . . . . .	16
28	2	2 Dec. 1844	3 Mar. 1845	92	. . . . . .	17
Special	Ses. Sen.	4 Mar. 1845	20 "	17	. . . . . .	18
		. .	. .	.	George M. Dallas .	19
29	1	1 Dec. 1845	10 Aug. 1846	253	George M. Dallas .	20
		. .	. .	.	. . . . . .	21
29	2	7 Dec. 1846	3 Mar. 1847	87	George M. Dallas .	22
		. .	. .	.	. . . . . .	23
		. .	. .	.	George M. Dallas .	24
		. .	. .	.	. . . . . .	25
30	1	6 Dec. 1847	14 Aug. 1848	253	George M. Dallas .	26
		. .	. .	.	. . . . . .	27
		. .	. .	.	George M. Dallas .	28
		. .	. .	.	. . . . . .	29
		. .	. .	.	George M. Dallas .	30
		. .	. .	.	. . . . . .	31
		. .	. .	.	George M. Dallas .	32
		. .	. .	.	. . . . . .	33
30	2	4 Dec. 1848	3 Mar. 1849	90	. . . . . .	34
		. .	. .	.	George M. Dallas .	35
		. .	. .	.	. . . . . .	36
		. .	. .	.	George M. Dallas .	37
		. .	. .	.	. . . . . .	38
Special	Ses. Sen.	5 Mar. 1849	23 Mar. 1849	19	. . . . . .	39
31	1	3 Dec. 1849	30 Sept. 1850	302	Millard Fillmore .	40
		. .	. .	.	. . . . . .	41
		. .	. .	.	*Millard Fillmore .	42
		. .	. .	.	. . . . . .	43
		. .	. .	.	. . . . . .	44
31	2	2 Dec. 1850	3 Mar. 1851	92	. . . . . .	45
32	1	1 Dec. 1851	31 Aug. 1852	275	. . . . . .	46
32	2	6 Dec. 1852	3 Mar. 1853	88	. . . . . .	47

*The President having died on 9th July, Millard Fillmore succeeded to the Presidency.

TABLE—Continued.

	TERMS OF OFFICE.		Names of Presidents pro tempore of the Senate.	SERVICE IN SENATE U. S.	
	Commenced.	Expired.		Attended.	Retired.
1	. .	. .	. . . . . .	19 Dec. 1838	24 Feb. 1839
2	. .	. .	William R. King .	25 Feb. 1839	3 Mar. 1839
3	. .	. .	William R. King .	2 Dec. 1839	26 Dec. 1839
4	. .	. .	. . . . .	27 "	2 July 1840
5	. .	. .	William R. King .	3 July 1840	21 "
6	. .	. .	William R. King .	7 Dec. 1840	15 Dec. 1840
7	. .	. .	. . . . . .	16 "	2 Mar. 1841
8	. .	. .	William R. King .	2 Mar. 1841	3 "
9	. .	. .	William R. King .	4 "	4 "
10	4 Mar. 1841	*3 Mar. 1845	. . . . .	4 "	11 "
11	. .	. .	Samuel L. Southard.	11 "	15 "
12	. .	. .	Samuel L. Southard	31 May 1841	13 Sept. 1841
13	. .	. .	Samuel L. Southard.	6 Dec. 1841	30 May 1842
14	. .	. .	Willie P. Mangum.	31 May 1842	31 Aug. 1842
15	. .	. .	Willie P. Mangum .	5 Dec. 1842	3 Mar. 1843
16	. .	. .	Willie P. Mangum.	4 Dec. 1843	17 June 1844
17	. .	. .	Willie P. Mangum	2 Dec. 1844	3 Mar. 1845
18	. .	. .	Willie P. Mangum.	4 Mar. 1845	4 "
19	4 Mar. 1845	3 Mar. 1849	. . . . . .	4 "	20 "
20	. .	. .	. . . . .	1 Dec. 1845	8 Aug. 1846
21	. .	. .	David R. Atchison .	8 Aug. 1846	10 Aug. 1846
22	. .	. .	. . . . .	7 Dec. 1846	11 Jan. 1847
23	. .	. .	David R. Atchison .	11 Jan. 1847	14 Jan. 1847
24	. .	. .	. . . . .	14 Jan. 1847	3 Mar. 1847
25	. .	. .	David R. Atchison .	3 Mar. 1847	3 Mar. 1847
26	. .	. .	. . . . .	6 Dec. 1847	1 Feb. 1848
27	. .	. .	David R. Atchison .	2 Feb. 1848	8 Feb. 1848
28	. .	. .	. . . . .	9 Feb. 1848	31 May 1848
29	. .	. .	David R. Atchison .	1 June 1848	14 June 1848
30	. .	. .	. . . . .	15 June 1848	26 June 1848
31	. .	. .	David R. Atchison .	26 June 1848	29 June 1848
32	. .	. .	. . . . .	30 June 1848	28 July 1848
33	. .	. .	David R. Atchison .	29 July 1848	14 Aug. 1848
34	. .	. .	David R. Atchison.	4 Dec. 1848	4 Dec. 1848
35	. .	. .	. . . . . .	5 Dec. 1848	25 Dec. 1848
36	. .	. .	David R. Atchison.	26 Dec. 1848	1 Jan. 1849
37	. .	. .	. . . . . .	2 Jan. 1849	2 Mar. 1849
38	. .	. .	David R. Atchison.	2 Mar. 1849	3 Mar. 1849
39	. .	. .	David R. Atchison .	5 Mar. 1849	23 Mar. 1849
40	4 Mar. 1849	3 Mar. 1853	. . . . . .	3 Dec. 1849	5 May 1850
41	. .	. .	William R. King .	6 May 1850	19 May 1850
42	. .	. .	. . . . . .	20 May 1850	9 July 1850
43	. .	. .	† . . .	10 July 1850	10 July 1850
44	. .	. .	William R. King .	11 July 1850	30 Sept. 1850
45	. .	. .	William R. King .	2 Dec. 1850	3 Mar. 1851
46	. .	. .	William R. King.	1 Dec. 1851	31 Aug. 1852
47	. .	. .	William R. King.	1 Dec. 1852	20 Dec. 1852
			David R. Atchison.	20 Dec. 1852	3 Mar. 1853

* The President having died on 1st April, John Tyler succeeded to the Presidency.
† The Secretary called the Senate to order, and by consent put all questions.

Table of the Senators of the United States, from the commencement of the Government under the Constitution, (4th March, 1789,) to the termination of the 2d session of the 29th Congress, (3d March, 1847;) exhibiting their names, the commencement and termination of their service, respectively; the States represented by them, and the three classes into which they are divided, under the 2d clause, 3d section, 1st article, of the Constitution of the United States. The regular succession in each class, for each State, being shown from the commencement*

* Continued to include 31st Congress, 3 March, 1851. See page 382.

Class.	Names of Senators.	States represented by Senators.	Commencement of service.	Termination of service.	Remarks.
2	Paine Wingate	N. Hampshire	Mar. 4, 1789	Mar. 3, 1793	
2	Samuel Livermore	"	Mar. 4, 1793	Mar. 3, 1799	
2	Samuel Livermore	"	Mar. 4, 1799	Resigned	Successor appointed June 17, 1801.
2	Simeon Olcott	"	June 17, 1801	Mar. 3, 1805	By Legislature, in room of S. Livermore, resigned.
2	Nicholas Gilman	"	Mar. 4, 1805	Mar. 3, 1811	
2	Nicholas Gilman	"	Mar. 4, 1811	Died	Successor appointed June 24, 1814.
2	Thomas W. Thompson	"	June 24, 1814	Mar. 3, 1817	By Legislature, in place of N. Gilman, deceased.
2	David L. Morrill	"	Mar. 4, 1817	Mar. 3, 1823	
2	Samuel Bell	"	Mar. 4, 1823	Mar. 3, 1829	
2	Samuel Bell	"	Mar. 4, 1829	Mar. 3, 1835	
2	Henry Hubbard	"	Mar. 4, 1835	Mar. 3, 1841	
2	Levi Woodbury	"	Mar. 4, 1841	Resigned	Successor appointed November 12, 1845.
2	Benning W. Jenness	"	Nov. 12, 1845		By Governor, in room of L. Woodbury, resigned.
2	Joseph Cilley	"	June 13, 1846	Mar. 3, 1847	By Legislature, in room of L. Woodbury, resigned.
3	John Langdon	N. Hampshire	Mar. 4, 1789	Mar. 3, 1795	
3	John Langdon	"	Mar. 4, 1795	Mar. 3, 1801	
3	James Sheafe	"	Mar. 4, 1801	Resigned	Successor appointed June 17, 1802.

3	William Plumer	"	June 17, 1802	Mar. 3, 1807	By Legislature, in room of James Sheafe, resigned.
3	Nahum Parker	"	Mar. 4, 1807	Resigned	Successor appointed June 21, 1810.
3	Charles Cutts	"	June 21, 1810	Mar. 3, 1813	
3	Charles Cutts	"	April 2, 1813	June 10, 1813	By the Governor; superseded by appointment of Legislature.
3	Jeremiah Mason	"	June 10, 1813	Resigned	By Legislature; successor appointed June 27, 1817.
3	Clement Storer	"	June 27, 1817	Mar. 3, 1819	By Legislature, in room of J. Mason, resigned.
3	John F. Parrott	"	Mar. 4, 1819	Mar. 3, 1825	
3	Levi Woodbury	"	Mar. 4, 1825	Mar. 3, 1831	
3	Isaac Hill	"	Mar. 4, 1831	Resigned	Successor appointed June 8, 1836.
3	John Page	"	June 8, 1836	Mar. 3, 1837	By Legislature, in room of Isaac Hill, resigned.
3	Franklin Pierce	"	Mar. 4, 1837	Resigned	Successor appointed March 1, 1842.
3	Leonard Wilcox	"	Mar. 1, 1842	June 9, 1842	By Governor, in room of F. Pierce, resigned.
3	Leonard Wilcox	"	June 9, 1842	Mar. 3, 1843	By Legislature, in room of F. Pierce, resigned.
3	Charles G. Atherton	"	Mar. 4, 1843	Mar. 3, 1849	
1	Tristam Dalton	Massachusetts	Mar. 4, 1789	Mar. 3, 1791	
1	George Cabot	"	Mar. 4, 1791	Resigned	Successor appointed July 7, 1796.
1	Benjamin Goodhue	"	July 7, 1796	Mar. 3, 1797	By Legislature, in place of G. Cabot, resigned.
1	Benjamin Goodhue	"	Mar. 4, 1797	Resigned	Successor appointed Nov. 14, 1800.
1	Jonathan Mason	"	Nov. 14, 1800	Mar. 3, 1803	By Legislature, in room of B. Goodhue, resigned.
1	John Quincy Adams	"	Mar. 4, 1803	Resigned	Successor appointed June 9, 1808.
1	James Lloyd, jun.	"	June 9, 1808	Mar. 3, 1809	By Legislature, in room of John Q. Adams, resigned.
1	James Lloyd, jun.	"	Mar. 4, 1809	Resigned	Successor appointed May 5, 1813.

TABLE OF SENATORS– Continued.

Class.	Names of Senators.	States represented by Senators.	Commencement of service.	Termination of service.	Remarks.
1	Christopher Gore	"	May 5, 1813	May 29, 1813	By Governor, in place of J. Lloyd, jun., resigned.
1	Christopher Gore	"	May 29, 1813	Mar. 3, 1815	By Legislature in room of J. Lloyd, jun., resigned.
1	Christopher Gore	"	Mar. 4, 1815	Resigned	Successor appointed June 12, 1816.
1	Eli P. Ashmun	"	June 12, 1816	Resigned	By Legislature, in room C. Gore, resigned; succ'or app'd June 5, 1818.
1	Prentiss Mellen	"	June 5, 1818	Resigned	By Legislature, in room of E. P. Ashmun, resigned; successor appointed June 12, 1820.
1	Elijah H. Mills	"	June 12, 1820	Mar. 3, 1821	By Legislature, in room of P. Mellen, resigned.
1	Elijah H. Mills	"	Mar. 4, 1821	Mar. 3, 1827	
1	Daniel Webster	"	Mar. 4, 1827	Mar. 3, 1833	
1	Daniel Webster	"	Mar. 4, 1833	Mar. 3, 1839	
1	Daniel Webster	"	Mar. 4, 1839	Resigned	Successor appointed Feb. 23, 1841.
1	Rufus Choate	"	Feb. 23, 1841	Mar. 3, 1845	By Legislature, in room of D. Webster, resigned.
1	Daniel Webster	"	Mar. 4, 1845	Mar. 3, 1851	Resigned; succ'r app'd 22 July, 1850.
2	Caleb Strong	Massachusetts	Mar. 4, 1789	Mar. 3, 1793	
2	Caleb Strong	"	Mar. 4, 1793	Resigned	Successor appointed June 11, 1796.
2	Theodore Sedgwick	"	June 11, 1796	Mar. 3, 1799	By Legislature, in place of C. Strong, resigned.
2	Samuel Dexter	"	Mar. 4, 1799	Resigned	Successor appointed June 6, 1800.
2	Dwight Foster	"	June 6, 1800	Resigned	By Legislature, in room of S. Dexter, resigned; successor appointed March 2, 1803.

2	Timothy Pickering	"	Mar. 2, 1803	Mar. 3, 1805	By Legislature, appointed in room of D. Foster, resigned.
2	Timothy Pickering	"	Mar. 4, 1805	Mar. 3, 1811	
2	Joseph B. Varnum	"	June 8, 1811	Mar. 3, 1817	
2	Harrison Gray Otis	"	Mar. 4, 1817	Resigned	Successor appointed June 5, 1822.
2	James Lloyd	"	June 5, 1822	Mar. 3, 1823	By Legislature, in room of H. G. Otis, resigned.
2	James Lloyd	"	Mar. 4, 1823	Resigned	Successor appointed May 31, 1826.
2	Nathaniel Silsbee	"	May 31, 1826	Mar. 3, 1829	By Legislature, in room of J. Lloyd, resigned.
2	Nathaniel Silsbee	"	Mar. 4, 1829	Mar. 3, 1835	
2	John Davis	"	Mar. 4, 1835	Resigned	Successor appointed Jan. 13, 1841.
2	Isaac C. Bates	"	Jan. 13, 1841	Mar. 3, 1841	
2	Isaac C. Bates	"	Mar. 4, 1841	Died	Successor appointed March 24, 1845.
2	John Davis	"	Mar. 24, 1845	Mar. 3, 1847	By Legislature, in room of I. C. Bates, deceased.
1	Theodore Foster	Rhode Island	June 7, 1790	Mar. 3, 1791	
1	Theodore Foster	"	Mar. 4, 1791	Mar. 3, 1797	
1	Theodore Foster	"	Mar. 4, 1797	Mar. 3, 1803	
1	Samuel I. Potter	"	Mar. 4, 1803	Died	Successor appointed last Monday in October, 1804.
1	Benjamin Howland	"	Last Monday Oct., 1804	Mar. 3, 1809	By Legislature, in room of S. I. Potter, deceased.
1	Francis Malbone	"	Mar. 4, 1809	Died	Successor appointed 4th Monday in June, 1809.
1	Christopher G. Champlin	"	4th Monday in June, 1809	Resigned	By Legislature, in room of F. Malbone, deceased; successor appointed last Monday in October, 1811.
1	William Hunter	"	Last Monday Oct., 1811	Mar. 3, 1815	By Legislature, in room of C. G. Champlin, resigned.
1	William Hunter	"	Mar. 4, 1815	Mar. 3, 1821	

TABLE OF SENATORS—Continued.

Class.	Names of Senators.	States represented by Senators.	Commencement of service.	Termination of service.	Remarks.
1	James D'Wolf	"	Mar. 4, 1821	Resigned	Successor appointed last Monday in October, 1825.
1	Asher Robbins	"	Last Monday Oct., 1825	Mar. 3, 1827	By Legislature, in room of James D'Wolf, resigned.
1	Asher Robbins	"	Mar. 4, 1827	Mar. 3, 1833	
1	Asher Robbins	"	Mar. 4, 1833	Mar. 3, 1839	
1	Nathan F. Dixon	"	Mar. 4, 1839	Died	Successor appointed February 5, 1842.
1	William Sprague	"	Feb. 5, 1842	Resigned	Successor appointed Jan. 25, 1844.
1	John Brown Francis	"	Jan. 25, 1844	Mar. 3, 1845	By Legislature, in room of William Sprague, resigned.
1	Albert C. Greene	"	Mar. 4, 1845	Mar. 3, 1851	
2	Joseph Stanton	Rhode Island	June 7, 1790	Mar. 3, 1793	
2	William Bradford	"	Mar. 4, 1793	Resigned	Successor appointed on last Wednesday in October, 1797.
2	Ray Green	"	Last Wednes'y Oct., 1797	Mar. 3, 1799	By Legislature, in room of William Bradford, resigned.
2	Ray Green	"	Mar. 4, 1799	Resigned	Successor appointed first Wednesday in May, 1801.
2	Christopher Ellery	"	1st Wednes'y May, 1801	Mar. 3, 1805	By Legislature, in place of Ray Green, resigned.
2	James Fenner	"	Mar. 4, 1805	Resigned	Successor appointed last Monday in October, 1807.
2	Elisha Matthewson	"	Last Monday Oct., 1807	Mar. 3, 1811	By Legislature, in room of James Fenner, resigned.
2	Jeremiah B. Howell	"	Mar. 4, 1811	Mar. 3, 1817	
2	James Burrill	"	Mar. 4, 1817	Died	Successor appointed Jan. 9, 1821.

2	Nehemiah R. Knight....	..... "	Jan. 9, 1821	Mar. 3, 1823	By Legislature, in place of J. Burrill, deceased.
2	Nehemiah R. Knight....	..... "	Mar. 4, 1823	Mar. 3, 1829	
2	Nehemiah R. Knight....	..... "	Mar. 4, 1829	Mar. 3, 1835	
2	Nehemiah R. Knight....	..... "	Mar. 4, 1835	Mar. 3, 1841	
2	James F. Simmons	..... "	Mar. 4, 1841	Mar. 3, 1847	
1	Oliver Ellsworth	Connecticut ..	Mar. 4, 1789	Mar. 3, 1791	
1	Oliver Ellsworth	..... "	Mar. 4, 1791	Resigned.....	Successor appointed 2d Thursday in May, 1796.
1	James Hillhouse.........	..... "	2d Thursday May, 1796	Mar. 3, 1797	By Legislature, in room of O. Ellsworth, resigned.
1	James Hillhouse.........	..... "	Mar. 4, 1797	Mar. 3, 1803	
1	James Hillhouse.........	..... "	Mar. 4, 1803	Mar. 3, 1809	
1	James Hillhouse.........	..... "	Mar. 4, 1809	Resigned.....	Successor appointed 2d Thursday in May, 1810.
1	Samuel Whittlesey Dana	..... "	2d Thursday May, 1810	Mar. 3, 1815	By Legislature, in room of J. Hillhouse, resigned.
1	Samuel Whittlesey Dana	..... "	Mar. 4, 1815	Mar. 3, 1821	
1	Elijah Boardman.........	..... "	Mar. 4, 1821	Died.........	Successor appointed Oct. 8, 1823.
1	Henry W. Edwards.....	..... "	Oct. 8, 1823	....	By Governor, in room of E. Boardman, deceased.
1	Henry W. Edwards.....	..... "	1st Wednes'y May, 1824	Mar. 3, 1827	By Legislature, do.
1	Samuel A. Foot	..... "	Mar. 4, 1827	Mar. 3, 1833	
1	Nathan Smith...........	..... "	Mar. 4, 1833	Died.........	Successor appointed Dec. 14, 1835.
1	John M. Niles...........	..... "	Dec. 14, 1835	In May, 1836	By Governor, in room of N. Smith, deceased.
1	John M. Niles...........	..... "	1st Wednes'y May, 1836	Mar. 3, 1839	By Legislature, in room of N. Smith, deceased.
1	Thaddeus Betts.........	..... "	Mar. 4, 1839	Died.........	April 7, 1840.
1	Iabez W. Huntington...	..... "	1st Wednes'y May, 1840	Mar. 3, 1845	

TABLE OF SENATORS—Continued.

Class.	Names of Senators.	States represented by Senators.	Commencement of service.	Termination of service.	Remarks.
1	Jabez W. Huntington	"	Mar. 4, 1845	Mar. 3, 1851	Died; successor app'd 11 Nov., 1847.
3	Wm. Samuel Johnson	Connecticut	Mar. 4, 1789	Resigned	Successor appointed June 13, 1791.
3	Roger Sherman	"	June 13, 1791	Mar. 3, 1793	By Legislature, in room of W. S. Johnson, resigned.
3	Stephen M. Mitchell	"	Mar. 4, 1793	Mar. 3, 1795	
3	Jonathan Trumbull	"	Mar. 4, 1795	Resigned	Successor appointed 2d Thursday in October, 1796.
3	Uriah Tracy	"	2d Thursday Oct., 1796	Mar. 3, 1801	By Legislature, in room of J. Trumbull, resigned.
3	Uriah Tracy	"	Mar. 4, 1801	In May, 1801	By Governor, in recess Legislature.
3	Uriah Tracy	"	In May, 1801	Mar. 3, 1807	By Legislature.
3	Uriah Tracy	"	Mar. 4, 1807	Died	Successor appointed Oct. 25, 1807.
3	Chauncey Goodrich	"	Oct. 25, 1807	Mar. 3, 1813	By Legislature, in room of U. Tracy, deceased.
3	Chauncey Goodrich	"	Mar. 4, 1813	Resigned	Successor appointed 2d Thursday in May, 1813.
3	David Daggett	"	2d Thursday May, 1813	Mar. 3, 1819	By Legislature, in room of C. Goodrich, resigned.
3	James Lanman	"	Mar. 4, 1819	Mar. 3, 1825	
3	James Lanman	"	Mar. 4, 1825	....	Appointed by Governor in recess of Legislature, before vacancy occurred. Decided by Senate U. S., that Mr. Lanman was not entitled to a seat.
3	Calvin Willey	"	1st Wednes'y May, 1825	Mar. 3, 1831	Chosen by the Legislature.
3	Gideon Tomlinson	"	Mar. 4, 1831	Mar. 3, 1837	

3	Perry Smith	"	Mar. 4, 1837	Mar. 3, 1843	
3	John M. Niles	"	Mar. 4, 1843	Mar. 3, 1849	
1	Moses Robinson	Vermont	Oct. 17, 1791	Resigned	Successor appointed Oct. 18, 1796.
1	Isaac Tichenor	"	Oct. 18, 1796	Mar. 3, 1797	By Legislature, in room of M. Robinson, resigned.
1	Isaac Tichenor	"	Mar. 4, 1797	Resigned	Successor appointed Oct. 17, 1797.
1	Nathaniel Chipman	"	Oct. 17, 1797	Mar. 3, 1803	By Legislature, in room of I. Tichenor, resigned.
1	Israel Smith	"	Mar. 4, 1803	Resigned	Successor appointed Oct. 10, 1807.
1	Jonathan Robinson	"	Oct. 10, 1807	Mar. 3, 1809	By Legislature, in room of I. Smith, resigned.
1	Jonathan Robinson	"	Mar. 4, 1809	Mar. 3, 1815	
1	Isaac Tichenor	"	Mar. 4, 1815	Mar. 3, 1821	
1	Horatio Seymour	"	Mar. 4, 1821	Mar. 3, 1827	
1	Horatio Seymour	"	Mar. 4, 1827	Mar. 3, 1833	
1	Benjamin Swift	"	Mar. 4, 1833	Mar. 3, 1839	
1	Samuel S. Phelps	"	Mar. 4, 1839	Mar. 3, 1845	
1	Samuel S. Phelps	"	Mar. 4, 1845	Mar. 3, 1851	
3	Stephen R. Bradley	Vermont	Oct. 17, 1791	Mar. 3, 1795	
3	Elijah Paine	"	Mar. 4, 1795	Mar. 3, 1801	
3	Stephen R. Bradley	"	Oct. 15, 1801	Mar. 3, 1807	
3	Stephen R. Bradley	"	Mar. 4, 1807	Mar. 3, 1813	
3	Dudley Chase	"	Mar. 4, 1813	Resigned	Successor appointed Nov. 4, 1817.
3	James Fisk	"	Nov. 4, 1817	Resigned	By Legislature, in room of D. Chase, resigned; successor app'd Oct. 20, 1818.
3	William A. Palmer	"	Oct. 20, 1818	Mar. 3, 1819	By Legislature, in room of J. Fisk, resigned.
3	William A. Palmer	"	Mar. 4, 1819	Mar. 3, 1825	
3	Dudley Chase	"	Mar. 4, 1825	Mar. 3, 1831	
3	Samuel Prentiss	"	Mar. 4, 1831	Mar. 3, 1837	
3	Samuel Prentiss	"	Mar. 4, 1837	Resigned	Successor appointed April 23, 1842.

TABLE OF SENATORS—Continued.

Class.	Names of Senators.	States represented by Senators.	Commencement of service.	Termination of service.	Remarks.
3	Samuel C. Crafts	"	April 23, 1842	Oct. 26, 1842	By Governor, in room of S. Prentiss, resigned.
3	Samuel C. Crafts	"	Oct. 26, 1842	Mar. 3, 1843	By Legislature, do.
3	William Upham	"	Mar. 4, 1843	Mar. 3, 1849	
1	Philip Schuyler	New York	July 15, 1789	Mar. 3, 1791	
1	Aaron Burr	"	Mar. 4, 1791	Mar. 3, 1797	
1	Philip Schuyler	"	Did not take	his seat in Sen.	Having declined accepting the appointment.
1	John Sloss Hobart	"	Jan. 11, 1798	Resigned	By Legislature, in room of P. Schuyler, declined; successor appointed May 5, 1798.
1	William North	"	May 5, 1798		By Governor, in room of J. S. Hobart, resigned.
1	James Watson	"	Aug. 17, 1798	Resigned	By Legislature, in room of J. S. Hobart, resigned; successor appointed April 3, 1800.
1	Gouverneur Morris	"	April 3, 1800	Mar. 3, 1803	By Legislature, in place of J. Watson, resigned.
1	Theodorus Bailey	"	Mar. 4, 1803	Resigned	Successor appointed Feb. 4, 1804.
1	John Armstrong	"	Feb. 4, 1804	Resigned	By Legislature, in room of T. Bailey, resigned; successor appointed Nov. 9, 1804.
1	Samuel L. Mitchill	"	Nov. 9, 1804	Mar. 3, 1809	By Legislature, in room of J. Armstrong, resigned.
1	Obadiah German	"	Mar. 4, 1809	Mar. 3, 1815	
1	Nathan Sanford	"	Mar. 4, 1815	Mar. 3, 1821	

1	Martin Van Buren......	..... "	Mar. 4, 1821	Mar. 3, 1827	
1	Martin Van Buren......	..... "	Mar. 4, 1827	Resigned.....	Successor appointed Jan. 15, 1829.
1	Charles E. Dudley......	..... "	Jan. 15, 1829	Mar. 3, 1833	By Legislature, in room of M. Van Buren, resigned.
1	Nathaniel P. Tallmadge.	..... "	Mar. 4, 1833	Mar. 3, 1839	
1	Nathaniel P. Tallmadge.	..... "	Mar. 4, 1839	Resigned.....	Successor appointed Nov. 30, 1844.
1	Daniel S. Dickinson.....	..... "	Nov. 30, 1844	....	By Governor, in room of N. P. Tallmadge, resigned.
1	Daniel S. Dickinson.....	..... "	Jan. 18, 1845	Mar. 3, 1845	By Legislature, do.
1	Daniel S. Dickinson.....	..... "	Mar. 4, 1845	Mar. 3, 1851	
3	Rufus King............	New York ...	July 16, 1789	Mar. 3, 1795	
3	Rufus King............	..... "	Mar. 4, 1795	Resigned.....	Successor appointed Nov. 9, 1796.
3	John Laurance	..... "	Nov. 9, 1796	Resigned.....	By Legislature, in room of R. King, resigned; successor app'd Nov. 6, 1800.
3	John Armstrong........	..... "	Nov. 6, 1800	Mar. 3, 1801	By Legislature, in room of J. Laurance, resigned.
3	John Armstrong........	..... "	Mar. 4, 1801	Resigned.....	Successor appointed Feb. 9, 1802.
3	De Witt Clinton........	..... "	Feb. 9, 1802	Resigned.....	By Legislature, in room of J. Armstrong, resigned; successor appointed Nov. 10, 1803.
3	John Armstrong........	..... "	Nov. 10, 1803	Feb. 4, 1804	By Governor, in room of De Witt Clinton, resigned.
3	John Smith	..... "	Feb. 4, 1804	Mar. 3, 1807	By Legislature, in room of De Witt Clinton, resigned.
3	John Smith	..... "	Mar. 4, 1807	Mar. 3, 1813	
3	Rufus King............	..... "	Mar. 4, 1813	Mar. 3, 1819	
3	Rufus King............	..... "	Jan. 8, 1820	Mar. 3, 1825	
3	Nathan Sanford.........	..... "	Mar. 4, 1825	Mar. 3, 1831	
3	William L. Marcy	..... "	Mar. 4, 1831	Resigned.....	Successor appointed Jan. 4, 1833.
3	Silas Wright, jr........	..... "	Jan. 4, 1833	Mar. 3, 1837	
3	Silas Wright, jr........	..... "	Mar. 4, 1837	Mar. 3, 1843	
3	Silas Wright, jr........	..... "	Mar. 4, 1843	Resigned.....	Successor appointed Nov. 30, 1844.

TABLE OF SENATORS—Continued.

Class.	Names of Senators.	States represented by Senators.	Commencement of service.	Termination of service.	Remarks.
3	Henry A. Foster	"	Nov. 30, 1844	Jan. 18, 1845	By Governor, in room of S. Wright, jr., resigned.
3	John A. Dix	"	Jan. 18, 1845	Mar. 3, 1849	By Legislature, in room of Silas Wright, jr., resigned.
1	Jonathan Elmer	New Jersey	Mar. 4, 1789	Mar. 3, 1791	
1	John Rutherford	"	Mar. 4, 1791	Mar. 3, 1797	
1	John Rutherford	"	Mar. 4, 1797	Resigned	Successor appointed Dec. 5, 1798.
1	Franklin Davenport	"	Dec. 5, 1798	Feb. 14, 1799	By Governor, in room of J. Rutherford, resigned.
1	James Schureman	"	Feb. 14, 1799	Resigned	By Legislature, in room of J. Rutherford, resigned; successor appointed Feb. 26, 1801.
1	Aaron Ogden	"	Feb. 26, 1801	Mar. 3, 1803	By Legislature, in room J. Schureman, resigned.
1	John Condit	"	Sept. 1, 1803	Nov. 3, 1803	By Gov'r, in recess of Legislature.
1	John Condit	"	Nov. 3, 1803	Mar. 3, 1809	By the Legislature.
1	John Lambert	"	Mar. 4, 1809	Mar. 3, 1815	
1	Jas. Jefferson Wilson	"	Mar. 4, 1815	Resigned	Successor appointed Jan. 26, 1821.
1	Samuel L. Southard	"	Jan. 26, 1821	Mar. 3, 1821	By Governor, in room of J. J. Wilson, resigned.
1	Samuel L. Southard	"	Mar. 4, 1821	Resigned	Successor appointed Nov. 12, 1823.
1	Joseph McIlvaine	"	Nov. 12, 1823	Died	By Legislature, in room of S. L. Southard, resigned; successor appointed Nov. 10, 1826.
1	Ephraim Bateman	"	Nov. 10, 1826	Mar. 3, 1827	By Legislature, in room of J. McIlvaine, deceased.

1	Ephraim Bateman	"	Mar. 4, 1827	Resigned	Successor appointed Jan. 30, 1829.
1	Mahlon Dickerson	"	Jan. 30, 1829	Mar. 3, 1833	
1	Samuel L. Southard	"	Mar. 4, 1833	Mar. 3, 1839	
1	Samuel L. Southard	"	Mar. 4, 1839	Died	Successor appointed July 2, 1842.
1	William L. Dayton	"	July 2, 1842	Oct. 28, 1842	By Governor, in room of Samuel L. Southard, deceased.
1	William L. Dayton	"	Oct. 28, 1842	Mar. 3, 1845	By Legislature, do.
1	William L. Dayton	"	Mar. 4, 1845	Mar. 3, 1851	
2	William Paterson	New Jersey	Mar. 4, 1789	Resigned	Successor appointed Nov. 23, 1790.
2	Philemon Dickerson	"	Nov. 23, 1790	Mar. 3, 1793	By Legislature, in room of W. Paterson, resigned.
2	Frederick Frelinghuysen	"	Mar. 4, 1793	Resigned	Successor appointed Nov. 12, 1796.
2	Richard Stockton	"	Nov. 12, 1796	Mar. 3, 1799	By Legislature, in room of F. Frelinghuysen, resigned.
2	Jonathan Dayton	"	Mar. 4, 1799	Mar. 3, 1805	
2	Aaron Kitchell	"	Mar. 4, 1805	Resigned	Successor appointed Mar. 21, 1809.
2	John Condit	"	Mar. 21, 1809	Nov. 2, 1809	By Governor, in place of A. Kitchell, resigned.
2	John Condit	"	Nov. 2, 1809	Mar. 3, 1811	By Legislature, in place of A. Kitchell, resigned.
2	John Condit	"	Mar. 4, 1811	Mar. 3, 1817	
2	Mahlon Dickerson	"	Mar. 4, 1817	Mar. 3, 1823	
2	Mahlon Dickerson	"	Mar. 4, 1823	Mar. 3, 1829	
2	Theodore Frelinghuysen	"	Mar. 4, 1829	Mar. 3, 1835	
2	Garret D. Wall	"	Mar. 4, 1835	Mar. 3, 1841	
2	Jacob W. Miller	"	Mar. 4, 1841	Mar. 3, 1847	Re-elected by Legislature for 6 [years.
1	William Maclay	Pennsylvania	Mar. 4, 1789	Mar. 3, 1791	
1	Albert Gallatin	"	Feb. 28, 1793	Feb. 28, 1794	Seat vacated by resolution of Senate, he not being a citizen of the U. S. the term of years (9) required for a Senator by the Constitution U. S.

TABLE OF SENATORS—Continued.

Class.	Names of Senators.	States represented by Senators.	Commencement of service.	Termination of service.	Remarks.
1	James Ross	"	April 1, 1794	Mar. 3, 1797	
1	James Ross	"	Mar. 4, 1797	Mar. 3, 1803	
1	Samuel Maclay	"	Mar. 4, 1803	Resigned	Successor appointed Dec. 13, 1808.
1	Michael Leib	"	Dec. 13, 1808	Mar. 3, 1809	By Legislature, in room of Samuel Maclay, resigned.
1	Michael Leib	"	Mar. 4, 1809	Resigned	Successor appointed Feb. 24, 1814.
1	Jonathan Roberts	"	Feb. 24, 1814	Mar. 3, 1815	By Legislature, in room of M. Leib, resigned.
1	Jonathan Roberts	"	Mar. 4, 1815	Mar. 3, 1821	
1	William Findlay	"	Mar. 4, 1821	Mar. 3, 1827	
1	Isaac D. Barnard	"	Mar. 4, 1827	Resigned	Successor appointed Dec. 13, 1831.
1	George M. Dallas	"	Dec. 13, 1831	Mar. 3, 1833	Appointed by Legislature, in room of I. D. Barnard, resigned.
1	Samuel McKean	"	Mar. 4, 1833	Mar. 3, 1839	
1	Daniel Sturgeon	"	Mar. 4, 1839	Mar. 3, 1845	
1	Daniel Sturgeon	"	Mar. 4, 1845	Mar. 3, 1851	
3	Robert Morris	Pennsylvania	Mar. 4, 1789	Mar. 3, 1795	
3	William Bingham	"	Mar. 4, 1795	Mar. 3, 1801	
3	Peter Muhlenberg	"	Mar. 4, 1801	Resigned	Successor appointed July 13, 1801.
3	George Logan	"	July 13, 1801	....	By Governor, in room of P. Muhlenberg, resigned.
3	George Logan	"	Dec. 16, 1801	Mar. 3, 1807	By Legislature, in room of P. Muhlenberg, resigned.
3	Andrew Gregg	"	Mar. 4, 1807	Mar. 3, 1813	
3	Abner Lacock	"	Mar. 4, 1813	Mar. 3, 1819	
3	Walter Lowrie	"	Mar. 4, 1819	Mar. 3, 1825	
3	William Marks	"	Mar. 4, 1825	Mar. 3, 1831	

3	William Wilkins	"	Mar. 4, 1831	Resigned	Successor appointed Dec. 6, 1834.
3	James Buchanan	"	Dec. 6, 1834	Mar. 3, 1837	By Legislature, in room of W. Wilkins, resigned.
3	James Buchanan	"	Mar. 4, 1837	Mar. 3, 1843	
3	James Buchanan	"	Mar. 4, 1843	Resigned	Successor appointed Mar. 13, 1845.
3	Simon Cameron	"	Mar. 13, 1845	Mar. 3, 1849	By Legislature, in room of James Buchanan, resigned.
1	George Read	Delaware	Mar. 4, 1789	Mar. 3, 1791	
1	George Read	"	Mar. 4, 1791	Resigned	Successor appointed Mar. 19, 1794.
1	Kensey Johns	"	Mar. 19, 1794	Feb. 7, 1795	By Governor, in room of G. Read, resigned.
1	Henry Latimer	"	Feb. 7, 1795	Mar. 3, 1797	By Legislature, in room of G. Read, resigned.
1	Henry Latimer	"	Mar. 4, 1797	Resigned	Successor appointed Feb. 28, 1801.
1	Samuel White	"	Feb. 28, 1801	Jan. 14, 1802	By Governor, in room of H. Latimer, resigned.
1	Samuel White	"	Jan. 14, 1802	Mar. 3, 1803	By Legislature, in room of H. Latimer, resigned.
1	Samuel White	"	Mar. 4, 1803	Mar. 3, 1809	
1	Samuel White	"	Mar. 4, 1809	Died	Successor appointed Jan. 12, 1810.
1	Outerbridge Horsey	"	Jan. 12, 1810	Mar. 3, 1815	By Legislature in room of S. White, deceased.
1	Outerbridge Horsey	"	Mar. 4, 1815	Mar. 3, 1821	
1	Cæsar A. Rodney	"	Jan. 10, 1822	Resigned	Successor appointed Jan. 8, 1824.
1	Thomas Clayton	"	Jan. 8, 1824	Mar. 3, 1827	By Legislature, in room of C. A. Rodney, resigned.
1	Louis McLane	"	Mar. 4, 1827	Resigned	Successor appointed Jan. 7, 1830.
1	Arnold Naudain	"	Jan. 7, 1830	Mar. 3, 1833	In room of Louis McLane.
1	Arnold Naudain	"	Mar. 4, 1833	Resigned	Successor appointed June 17, 1836.
1	Richard H. Bayard	"	June 17, 1836	Mar. 3, 1839	By Legislature, in room of A. Naudain, resigned.
1	Richard H. Bayard	"	Mar. 4, 1839	Mar. 3, 1845	

TABLE OF SENATORS—Continued.

Class.	Names of Senators.	States represented by Senators.	Commencement of service.	Termination of service.	Remarks.
1	John M. Clayton	"	Mar. 4, 1845	Mar. 3, 1851	Resigned; succ'r app'd 23 Feb., 1849.
2	Richard Bassett	Delaware	Mar. 4, 1789	Mar. 3, 1793	
2	John Vining	"	Mar. 4, 1793	Resigned	Successor appointed Jan. 19, 1798.
2	Joshua Clayton	"	Jan. 19, 1798	Died	By Legislature, in room of J. Vining, resigned; successor appointed Jan. 17, 1799.
2	William Hill Wells	"	Jan. 17, 1799	Resigned	By Legislature, in room of J. Clayton, deceased; successor appointed Nov. 13, 1804.
2	James A. Bayard	"	Nov. 13, 1804	Mar. 3, 1805	By Legislature, in room of W. H. Wells, resigned.
2	James A. Bayard	"	Mar. 4, 1805	Mar. 3, 1811	
2	James A. Bayard	"	Mar. 4, 1811	Resigned	Successor appointed May 28, 1813.
2	William H. Wells	"	May 28, 1813	Mar. 3, 1817	By Legislature, in room of J. A. Bayard, resigned.
2	Nicholas Van Dyke	"	Mar. 4, 1817	Mar. 3, 1823	
2	Nicholas Van Dyke	"	Mar. 4, 1823	Died	Successor appointed Nov. 8, 1826.
2	Daniel Rodney	"	Nov. 8, 1826	Jan. 12, 1827	By Governor, in room of N. Van Dyke, deceased.
2	Henry M. Ridgely	"	Jan. 12, 1827	Mar. 3, 1829	By Legislature, in room of N. Van Dyke, deceased.
2	John M. Clayton	"	Mar. 4, 1829	Mar. 3, 1835	
2	John M. Clayton	"	Mar. 4, 1835	Resigned	Successor appointed January 9, 1837.
2	Thomas Clayton	"	Jan. 9, 1837	Mar. 3, 1841	By Legislature, in room of J. M. Clayton, resigned.
2	Thomas Clayton	"	Mar. 4, 1841	Mar. 3, 1847	

1	C. Carroll, of Carrollton.	Maryland	Mar. 4, 1789	Mar. 3, 1791	
1	C. Carroll, of Carrollton.	..... "	Mar. 4, 1791	Resigned.....	Successor appointed Jan. 10, 1793.
1	Richard Potts	..... "	Jan. 10, 1793	Resigned.....	By Legislature, in room of C. Carroll, resigned; successor appointed Nov. 30, 1796.
1	John Eager Howard	..... "	Nov. 30, 1796	Mar. 3, 1797	By Legislature, in room of R. Potts, resigned.
1	John Eager Howard	..... "	Mar. 4, 1797	Mar. 3, 1803	
1	Samuel Smith	..... "	Mar. 4, 1803	Mar. 3, 1809	
1	Samuel Smith	..... "	Mar. 4, 1809	Nov. 16, 1809	By Governor, in the recess of the Legislature.
1	Samuel Smith..........	..... "	Nov. 16, 1809	Mar. 3, 1815	By Legislature.
1	Robert G. Harper.......	..... "	Jan. 29, 1816	Resigned.....	Successor appointed Dec. 20, 1816.
1	Alex'r Contee Hanson ..	..... "	Dec. 20, 1816	Died.........	By Legislature, in room of R. G. Harper, resigned; successor appointed Dec. 21, 1819.
1	William Pinkney	..... "	Dec. 21, 1819	Mar. 3, 1821	By Legislature, in room of A. C. Hanson, deceased.
1	William Pinkney	..... "	Mar. 4, 1821	Died.........	Successor appointed Dec. 16, 1822.
1	Samuel Smith	..... "	Dec. 15, 1822	Mar. 3, 1827	By Legislature, in room of Wm. Pinkney, deceased.
1	Samuel Smith	..... "	Mar. 4, 1827	Mar. 3, 1833	
1	Joseph Kent............	..... "	Mar. 4, 1833	Died.........	Successor appointed Jan. 4, 1838.
1	William D. Merrick.....	..... "	Jan. 4, 1838	Mar. 3, 1839	By Legislature, in room of J. Kent, deceased.
1	William D. Merrick.....	..... "	Mar. 4, 1839	Mar. 3, 1845	
1	Reverdy Johnson.......	..... "	Mar. 4, 1845	Mar. 3, 1851	Resigned; succ'r app'd 6 Dec., 1849.
3	John Henry	Maryland	Mar. 4, 1789	Mar. 3, 1795	
3	John Henry	..... "	Mar. 4, 1795	Resigned.....	Successor appointed December 11, 1797.
3	James Lloyd	..... "	Dec. 11, 1797	Resigned.....	By Legislature, in room of J. Henry, resigned; successor appointed Dec. 12, 1800.

TABLE OF SENATORS—Continued.

Class.	Names of Senators.	States represented by Senators.	Commencement of service.	Termination of service.	Remarks.
3	William Hindman	"	Dec. 12, 1800	Mar. 3, 1801	By Legislature, in room of J. Lloyd, resigned.
3	William Hindman	"	Mar. 4, 1801	Nov. 19, 1801	By Governor, in recess of Legislature.
3	Robert Wright	"	Nov. 19, 1801	Resigned	By Legislature; successor appointed Nov. 25, 1806.
3	Philip Reed	"	Nov. 25, 1806	Mar. 3, 1807	By Legislature, in room of Robert Wright, resigned.
3	Philip Reed	"	Mar. 4, 1807	Mar. 3, 1813	
3	Rt. Hy. Goldsborough	"	May 21, 1813	Mar. 3, 1819	
3	Edward Lloyd	"	Dec. 21, 1819	Mar. 3, 1825	
3	Edward Lloyd	"	Mar. 4, 1825	Resigned	Successor appointed Jan. 24, 1826.
3	Ezekiel F. Chambers	"	Jan. 24, 1826	Mar. 3, 1831	By Legislature, in room of E. Lloyd, resigned.
3	Ezekiel F. Chambers	"	Mar. 4, 1831	Resigned	Successor appointed Jan. 13, 1835.
3	Rt. Hy. Goldsborough	"	Jan. 13, 1835	Died	By Legislature, in room of E. F. Chambers, resigned; successor appointed Dec. 31, 1836.
3	John S. Spence	"	Dec. 31, 1836	Mar. 3, 1837	
3	John S. Spence	"	Mar. 4, 1837	Died	Successor appointed Jan. 5, 1841.
3	John Leeds Ker	"	Jan. 5, 1841	Mar. 3, 1843	By Legislature, in room of J. S. Spence, deceased.
3	James Alfred Pearce	"	Mar. 4, 1843	Mar. 3, 1849	[See page 382]
1	William Grayson	Virginia	Mar. 4, 1789	Died	Successor appointed March 31, 1790.
1	John Walker	"	Mar. 31, 1790	Nov. 9, 1790	By Governor, in room of W. Grayson, deceased.

1	James Monroe..........	..... "	Nov. 9, 1790	Mar. 3, 1791	By Legislature, in room of W. Grayson, deceased.
1	James Monroe..........	..... "	Mar. 4, 1791	Resigned.....	Successor appointed Nov. 18, 1794.
1	Stevens T. Mason	..... "	Nov. 18, 1794	Mar. 3, 1797	By Legislature, in room of J. Monroe, resigned.
1	Stevens T. Mason	..... "	Mar. 4, 1797	Died	Successor appointed June 4, 1803.
1	John Taylor.............	..... "	June 4, 1803	Dec. 7, 1803	By Governor, in room of S. T. Mason, deceased.
1	Abraham B. Venable ...	..... "	Dec. 7, 1803	Resigned.....	By Legislature, in room of S. T. Mason, deceased; successor appointed Aug. 11, 1804.
1	William B. Giles.......	..... "	Aug. 11, 1804	Dec. 4, 1804	By Governor, in room of A. B. Venable, resigned; appointed Dec. 4, 1801.
1	Andrew Moore..........	..... "	Dec. 4, 1804	Mar. 3, 1809	By Legislature, in room of A. B. Venable, resigned.
1	Richard Brent...........	..... "	Mar. 4, 1809	Died	Successor appointed Jan. 2, 1815.
1	James Barbour	..... "	Jan. 2, 1815	Mar. 3, 1815	By Legislature, in room of R. Brent, deceased.
1	James Barbour	..... "	Mar. 4, 1815	Mar. 3, 1821	
1	James Barbour	..... "	Mar. 4, 1821	Resigned.....	Successor appointed Dec. 9, 1825.
1	John Randolph	..... "	Dec. 9, 1825	Mar. 3, 1827	By Legislature, in room of J. Barbour, resigned.
1	John Tyler...............	..... "	Mar. 4, 1827	Mar. 3, 1833	
1	John Tyler...............	..... "	Mar. 4, 1833	Resigned.....	Successor appointed Mar. 3, 1836.
1	William C. Rives.......	..... "	Mar. 3, 1836	Mar. 3, 1839	By Legislature, in room of John Tyler, resigned.
1	William C. Rives.......	..... "	Mar. 4, 1839	Mar. 3, 1845	
1	Isaac S. Pennybacker...	..... "	Mar. 4, 1845	Died	Successor appointed.
1	James M. Mason........	..... "	Jan. 21, 1847	Mar. 3, 1851	By Legislature, in room of Isaac S. Pennybacker, deceased.
	[By Legisla	ture for 6 years	from 3 March	1851.]	
2	Richard Henry Lee	Virginia......	Mar. 4, 1789	Resigned.....	Successor appointed October 18, 1792.

TABLE OF SENATORS—Continued.

Class.	Names of Senators.	States represented by Senators.	Commencement of service.	Termination of service.	Remarks.
2	John Taylor	"	Oct. 18, 1792	Mar. 3, 1793	By Legislature, in room of R. H. Lee, resigned.
2	John Taylor	"	Mar. 4, 1793	Resigned	Successor appointed Nov. 18, 1794.
2	Henry Tazewell	"	Nov. 18, 1794	Died	By Legislature, in room of John Taylor, resigned; successor appointed Dec. 5, 1799.
2	Wilson Cary Nicholas	"	Dec. 5, 1799	Resigned	By Legislature, in room of Henry Tazewell, deceased; successor appointed Aug. 11, 1804.
2	Andrew Moore	"	Aug. 11, 1804	Dec. 4, 1804	By Governor, in room of W. C. Nicholas, resigned.
2	William B. Giles	"	Dec. 4, 1804	Mar. 3, 1805	By Legislature, in room of W. C. Nicholas, resigned.
2	William B. Giles	"	Mar. 4, 1805	Mar. 3, 1811	
2	William B. Giles	"	Mar. 4, 1811	Resigned	Successor appointed Jan. 3, 1816.
2	Armistead T. Mason	"	Jan. 3, 1816	Mar. 3, 1817	By Legislature, in room of W. B. Giles, resigned.
2	John W. Eppes	"	Mar. 4, 1817	Resigned	Successor appointed Dec. 10, 1819.
2	James Pleasants	"	Dec. 10, 1819	Resigned	By Legislature, in room of John W. Eppes, resigned; successor appointed Dec. 18, 1822.
2	John Taylor	"	Dec. 18, 1822	Mar. 3, 1823	By Legislature, in room of James Pleasants, resigned.
2	John Taylor	"	Mar. 4, 1823	Died	Successor appointed Dec. 7, 1824.
2	Littleton W. Tazewell	"	Dec. 7, 1824	Mar. 3, 1829	By Legislature, in room of John Taylor, deceased.
2	Littleton W. Tazewell	"	Mar. 4, 1829	Resigned	Successor appointed Dec. 11, 1832.

2	W. C. Rives	"	Dec. 11, 1832	Resigned	In room L. W. Tazewell, resigned; successor appointed Feb. 27, 1834.
2	Benjamin W. Leigh	"	Feb. 27, 1834	Mar. 3, 1835	By Legislature, in room of Wm. C. Rives, resigned.
2	Benjamin W. Leigh	"	Mar. 4, 1835	Resigned	Successor appointed Dec. 12, 1836.
2	Richard E. Parker	"	Dec. 12, 1836	Resigned	By Legislature, in room of B. W. Leigh, resigned; successor appointed March 14, 1837.
2	William H. Roane	"	Mar. 14, 1837	Mar. 3, 1841	By Legislature, in room of R. E. Parker, resigned.
2	William S. Archer	"	Mar. 4, 1841	Mar. 3, 1847	
2	Samuel Johnston	North Carolina	Nov. 27, 1789	Mar. 3, 1793	
2	Alexander Martin	"	Mar. 4, 1793	Mar. 3, 1799	
2	Jesse Franklin	"	Mar. 4, 1799	Mar. 3, 1805	
2	James Turner	"	Mar. 4, 1805	Mar. 3, 1811	
2	James Turner	"	Mar. 4, 1811	Resigned	Successor appointed Dec. 4, 1816.
2	Montfort Stokes	"	Dec. 4, 1816	Mar. 3, 1817	By Legislature, in room of J. Turner, resigned.
2	Montfort Stokes	"	Mar. 4, 1817	Mar. 3, 1823	
2	John Branch	"	Mar. 4, 1823	Mar. 3, 1829	
2	John Branch	"	Mar. 4, 1829	Resigned	Successor appointed Dec. 9, 1829.
2	Bedford Brown	"	Dec. 9, 1829	Mar. 3, 1835	By Legislature, in room of John Branch, resigned.
2	Bedford Brown	"	Mar. 4, 1835	Resigned	Successor appointed Nov. 25, 1840.
2	Willie P. Mangum	"	Nov. 25, 1840	Mar. 3, 1841	By Legislature, in room of Bedford Brown, resigned.
2	Willie P. Mangum	"	Mar. 4, 1841	Mar. 3, 1847	
3	Benjamin Hawkins	North Carolina	Nov. 27, 1789	Mar. 3, 1795	
3	Timothy Bloodworth	"	Mar. 4, 1795	Mar. 3, 1801	
3	David Stone	"	Mar. 4, 1801	Mar. 3, 1807	
3	Jesse Franklin	"	Mar. 4, 1807	Mar. 3, 1813	
3	David Stone	"	Mar. 4, 1813		Successor appointed.

TABLE OF SENATORS—Continued.

Class.	Names of Senators.	States represented by Senators.	Commencement of service.	Termination of service.	Remarks.
3	Francis Locke	"	....	....	Does not appear to have accepted or taken his seat in Senate.
3	Nathaniel Macon	"	Dec. 5, 1815	Mar. 3, 1819	By Legislature, in room of F. Locke.
3	Nathaniel Macon	"	Mar. 4, 1819	Mar. 3, 1825	
3	Nathaniel Macon	"	Mar. 4, 1825	Resigned	Successor appointed Dec. 15, 1828.
3	James Iredell	"	Dec. 15, 1828	Mar. 3, 1831	By Legislature, in room of Nathaniel Macon, resigned.
3	Willie P. Mangum	"	Mar. 4, 1831	Resigned	Successor appointed Dec. 5, 1836.
3	Robert Strange	"	Dec. 5, 1836	Mar. 3, 1837	By Legislature, in room of W. P. Mangum, resigned.
3	Robert Strange	"	Mar. 4, 1837	Resigned	Successor appointed Nov. 25, 1840.
3	William A. Graham	"	Nov. 25, 1840	Mar. 3, 1843	By Legislature, in room of Robert Strange, resigned.
3	William H. Haywood	"	Mar. 4, 1843	Resigned	Successor appointed Nov. 25, 1846.
3	George E. Badger	"	Dec. 14, 1846	Mar. 3, 1849	By Legislature, in room of W. H. Haywood, resigned. [See page 382]
2	Pierce Butler	South Carolina	Mar. 4, 1789	Mar. 3, 1793	
2	Pierce Butler	"	Mar. 4, 1793	Resigned	Successor appointed Dec. 8, 1796.
2	John Hunter	"	Dec. 8, 1796	Resigned	By Legislature, in room of P. Butler, resigned; successor appointed Dec. 4, 1798.
2	Charles Pinckney	"	Dec. 4, 1798	Mar. 3, 1799	By Legislature, in room of John Hunter, resigned.
2	Charles Pinckney	"	Mar. 4, 1799	....	Successor appointed Dec. 3, 1801.
2	Thomas Sumpter	"	Dec. 3, 1801	Mar. 3, 1805	By Legislature, in room of Charles Pinckney, resigned.
2	Thomas Sumpter	"	Mar. 4, 1805	Resigned	Successor appointed Dec. 19, 1810.

2	John Taylor	"	Dec. 19, 1810	Mar. 3, 1811	By Legislature, in room of Thomas Sumpter, resigned.
2	John Taylor	"	Mar. 4, 1811	Resigned	Successor appointed Dec. 4, 1816.
2	William Smith	"	Dec. 4, 1816	Mar. 3, 1817	By Legislature, in room of John Taylor, resigned.
2	William Smith	"	Mar. 4, 1817	Mar. 3, 1823	
2	Robert Young Hayne	"	Mar. 4, 1823	Mar. 3, 1829	
2	Robert Young Hayne	"	Mar. 4, 1829	Resigned	Successor appointed Dec. 12, 1832.
2	John C. Calhoun	"	Dec. 12, 1832	Mar. 3, 1835	By Legislature, in room of R. Y. Hayne.
2	John C. Calhoun	"	Mar. 4, 1835	Mar. 3, 1841	
2	John C. Calhoun	"	Mar. 4, 1841	Resigned	Successor appointed Dec. 15, 1842.
2	Daniel Elliott Huger	"	Dec. 15, 1842	Resigned	By Legislature, in room of J. C. Calhoun, resigned; successor appointed Nov. 26, 1845.
2	John C. Calhoun	"	Dec. 26, 1845	Mar. 3, 1847	By Legislature, in room of D. E. Huger, resigned.
3	Ralph Izard	South Carolina	Mar. 4, 1789	Mar. 3, 1795	
3	Jacob Read	"	Mar. 4, 1795	Mar. 3, 1801	
3	John Ewing Colhoun	"	Mar. 4, 1801	Died	Successor appointed Nov., 1802.
3	Pierce Butler	"	Nov., 1802	Resigned	By Legislature, in room of J. E. Colhoun, deceased; successor appointed Dec. 6, 1804.
3	John Gaillard	"	Dec. 6, 1804	Mar. 3, 1807	By Legislature, in room of P. Butler, resigned.
3	John Gaillard	"	Mar. 4, 1807	Mar. 3, 1813	
3	John Gaillard	"	Mar. 4, 1813	Mar. 3, 1819	
3	John Gaillard	"	Mar. 4, 1819	Mar. 3, 1825	
3	John Gaillard	"	Mar. 4, 1825	Died	February 26, 1826.
3	William Harper	"	Mar. 8, 1826	Nov. 29, 1826	By Governor, in room of John Gaillard, deceased.
3	William Smith	"	Nov. 29, 1826	Mar. 3, 1831	By Legislature, in room of John Gaillard, deceased.

TABLE OF SENATORS—Continued.

Class.	Names of Senators.	States represented by Senators.	Commencement of service.	Termination of service.	Remarks.
3	Stephen D. Miller	"	Mar. 4, 1831	Resigned	Successor appointed Nov. 26, 1833.
3	William C. Preston	"	Nov. 26, 1833	Mar. 3, 1837	
3	William C. Preston	"	Mar. 4, 1837	Resigned	Successor appointed Dec., 1842.
3	George McDuffie	"	Dec., 1842	Mar. 3, 1843	By Legislature, in room of W. C. Preston, resigned.
3	George McDuffie	"	Mar. 4, 1843	Resigned	Successor appointed.
3	Andrew P. Butler	"	Dec. 21, 1846	Mar. 3, 1849	By Legislature, in room of George McDuffie, resigned.
2	William Few	Georgia	Mar. 4, 1789	Mar. 3, 1793	
2	James Jackson	"	Mar. 4, 1793	Resigned	Successor appointed November 16, 1795.
2	George Walton	"	Nov. 16, 1795	Feb. 20, 1796	By Governor, in room of James Jackson, resigned.
2	Josiah Tatnall	"	Feb. 20, 1796	Mar. 3, 1799	By Legislature, in room of James Jackson, resigned
2	Abraham Baldwin	"	Mar. 4, 1799	Mar. 3, 1805	
2	Abraham Baldwin	"	Mar. 4, 1805	Died	Successor appointed Aug. 27, 1807.
2	George Jones	"	Aug. 27, 1807	Nov. 7, 1807	By Governor, in room of Abraham Baldwin, deceased.
2	William H. Crawford	"	Nov. 7, 1807	Mar. 3, 1811	By Legislature, in room of Abraham Baldwin, deceased.
2	William H. Crawford	"	Mar. 4, 1811	Resigned	Successor appointed April 8, 1813.
2	Wm. Bellinger Bullock	"	April 8, 1813	Nov. 6, 1813	By Governor, in room of William H. Crawford, resigned.
2	William Wyatt Bibb	"	Nov. 6, 1813	Resigned	By Legislature, in room of W. H. Crawford, resigned; successor appointed Nov. 13, 1816.

2	George M. Troup	"	Nov. 13, 1816	Mar. 3, 1817	By Legislature, in room of William W. Bibb, resigned.
2	George M. Troup	"	Mar. 4, 1817	Resigned	Successor appointed Nov. 7, 1818.
2	John Forsyth	"	Nov. 7, 1818	Resigned	By Legislature, in room of G. M. Troup, resigned; successor appointed Nov. 6, 1819.
2	Freeman Walker	"	Nov. 6, 1819	Resigned	By Legislature, in room of J. Forsyth, resigned; successor appointed Nov. 10, 1821.
2	Nicholas Ware	"	Nov. 10, 1821	Mar. 3, 1823	By Legislature, in room of Freeman Walker, resigned.
2	Nicholas Ware	"	Mar. 4, 1823	Died	Successor appointed Nov. 4, 1824.
2	Thomas W. Cobb	"	Nov. 4, 1824	Resigned	By Legislature, in room of N. Ware, deceased; successor appointed Nov. 7, 1828.
2	Oliver H. Prince	"	Nov. 7, 1828	Mar. 3, 1829	
2	George M. Troup	"	Mar. 4, 1829	Resigned	Successor appointed Nov. 21, 1833.
2	John P. King	"	Nov. 21, 1833	Mar. 3, 1835	
2	John P. King	"	Mar. 4, 1835	Resigned	Successor appointed Nov. 22, 1837.
2	Wilson Lumpkin	"	Nov. 22, 1837	Mar. 3, 1841	By Legislature, in room of John P. King, resigned.
2	J. Macpherson Berrien	"	Mar. 4, 1841	Resigned	Reappointed.
2	J. Macpherson Berrien	"	Nov. 14, 1845	Mar. 3, 1847	Re-elected by the Legislature.
3	James Gunn	Georgia	Mar. 4, 1789	Mar. 3, 1795	
3	James Gunn	"	Mar. 4, 1795	Mar. 3, 1801	
3	James Jackson	"	Mar. 4, 1801	Died	Successor appointed June 19, 1806.
3	John Milledge	"	June 19, 1806	Mar. 3, 1807	By Legislature, in room of James Jackson, deceased.
3	John Milledge	"	Mar. 4, 1807	Resigned	Successor appointed Nov. 27, 1809.
3	Charles Tait	"	Nov. 27, 1809	Mar. 3, 1813	By Legislature, in room of John Milledge, resigned.
3	Charles Tait	"	Mar. 4, 1813	Mar. 3, 1819	
3	John Elliott	"	Mar. 4, 1819	Mar. 3, 1825	

TABLE OF SENATORS—Continued.

Class.	Names of Senators.	States represented by Senators.	Commencement of service.	Termination of service.	Remarks.
3	J. Macpherson Berrien	"	Mar. 4, 1825	Resigned	Successor appointed Nov. 9, 1829.
3	John Forsyth	"	Nov. 9, 1829	Mar. 3, 1831	By Legislature, in room of John Macpherson Berrien, resigned.
3	John Forsyth	"	Mar. 4, 1831	Mar. 3, 1837	
3	Alfred Cuthbert	"	Mar. 4, 1837	Mar. 3, 1843	
3	Walter T. Colquitt	"	Mar. 4, 1843	Mar. 3, 1849	Resigned; succ'r app'd 4 Feb., 1848.
2	John Brown	Kentucky	June 18, 1792	Mar. 3, 1793	
2	John Brown	"	Mar. 4, 1793	Mar. 3, 1799	
2	John Brown	"	Mar. 4, 1799	Mar. 3, 1805	
2	Buckner Thruston	"	Mar. 4, 1805	Resigned	Successor appointed Jan. 4, 1810.
2	Henry Clay	"	Jan. 4, 1810	Mar. 3, 1811	By Legislature, in room of Buckner Thruston, resigned.
2	George M. Bibb	"	Mar. 4, 1811	Resigned	Successor appointed Aug. 30, 1814.
2	George Walker	"	Aug. 30, 1814	Dec. 16, 1814	By Governor, in room of George M. Bibb, resigned.
2	William T. Barry	"	Dec. 16, 1814	Resigned	By Legislature, in room of George M. Bibb, resigned; successor appointed Nov. 13, 1816.
2	Martin D. Hardin	"	Nov. 13, 1816	Dec. 5, 1816	By Governor, in room of William T. Barry, resigned.
2	Martin D. Hardin	"	Dec. 5, 1816	Mar. 3, 1817	By Legislature, in room of William T. Barry, resigned.
2	John J. Crittenden	"	Mar. 4, 1817	Resigned	Successor appointed Dec. 10, 1819.
2	Richard M. Johnson	"	Dec. 10, 1819	Mar. 3, 1823	By Legislature, in room of J. J. Crittenden, resigned.
2	Richard M. Johnson	"	Mar. 4, 1823	Mar. 3, 1829	

2	George M. Bibb	"	Mar. 4, 1829	Mar. 3, 1835	
2	John J. Crittenden	"	Mar. 4, 1835	Mar. 3, 1841	
2	John J. Crittenden	"	Mar. 4, 1841	Resigned	Successor appointed Feb. 20, 1841.
2	James T. Morehead	"	Feb. 20, 1841	Mar. 3, 1847	
3	John Edwards	Kentucky	June 18, 1792	Mar. 3, 1795	
3	Humphrey Marshall	"	Mar. 4, 1795	Mar. 3, 1801	
3	John Breckenridge	"	Mar. 4, 1801	Resigned	Successor appointed Nov. 8, 1805.
3	John Adair	"	Nov. 8, 1805	Resigned	By Legislature, in room of John Breckenridge, resigned; successor appointed Nov. 19, 1806.
3	Henry Clay	"	Nov. 19, 1806	Mar. 3, 1807	By Legislature, in room of John Adair, resigned.
3	John Pope	"	Mar. 4, 1807	Mar. 3, 1813	
3	Jesse Bledsoe	"	Mar. 4, 1813	Resigned	Successor appointed Jan. 3, 1815.
3	Isham Talbot	"	Jan. 3, 1815	Mar. 3, 1819	By Legislature, in room of Jesse Bledsoe, resigned.
3	William Logan	"	Mar. 4, 1819	Resigned	Successor appointed Oct. 19, 1820.
3	Isham Talbot	"	Oct. 19, 1820	Mar. 3, 1825	By Legislature, in room of William Logan, resigned.
3	John Rowan	"	Mar. 4, 1825	Mar. 3, 1831	
3	Henry Clay	"	Mar. 4, 1831	Mar. 3, 1837	
3	Henry Clay	"	Mar. 4, 1837	Resigned	Successor appointed Feb. 25, 1842.
3	John J. Crittenden	"	Feb. 25, 1842	Mar. 3, 1843	By Legislature, in room of Henry Clay, resigned.
3	John J. Crittenden	"	Mar. 4, 1843	Mar. 3, 1849	Resigned; succ'r app'd 23 June, 1848.
1	William Cocke	Tennessee	Aug. 2, 1796	Mar. 3, 1797	
1	Andrew Jackson	"	Sept. 26, 1797	Resigned	Successor appointed Oct. 6, 1798.
1	Daniel Smith	"	Oct. 6, 1798	Dec. 12, 1798	By Governor, in room of Andrew Jackson, resigned.
1	Joseph Anderson	"	Dec. 12, 1798	Mar. 3, 1803	By Legislature, in room of Andrew Jackson, resigned.
1	Joseph Anderson	"	Mar. 4, 1803	Mar. 3, 1809	

TABLE OF SENATORS—Continued.

Class.	Names of Senators.	States represented by Senators.	Commencement of service.	Termination of service.	Remarks.
1	Joseph Anderson	"	Mar. 4, 1809	April 11, 1809	Appointed by the Governor.
1	Joseph Anderson	"	April 11, 1809	Mar. 3, 1815	By the Legislature.
1	George W. Campbell	"	Oct. 10, 1815	Resigned	Successor appointed Sept. 5, 1818.
1	John Henry Eaton	"	Sept. 5, 1818	Oct. 9, 1819	By Governor, in room of George W. Campbell, resigned.
1	John Henry Eaton	"	Oct. 9, 1819	Mar. 3, 1821	By Legislature, in room of George W. Campbell, resigned.
1	John Henry Eaton	"	Sept. 27, 1821	Mar. 3, 1827	
1	John Henry Eaton	"	Mar. 4, 1827	Resigned	Successor appointed Oct. 19, 1829.
1	Felix Grundy	"	Oct. 19, 1829	Mar. 3, 1833	By Legislature, in room of J. H. Eaton, resigned.
1	Felix Grundy	"	Mar. 4, 1833	Resigned	Successor appointed Sept. 17, 1838.
1	Ephraim H. Foster	"	Sept. 17, 1838	Mar. 3, 1839	By Governor, in room of Felix Grundy, resigned.
1	Felix Grundy	"	Mar. 4, 1839	Died	Successor appointed Dec. 25, 1840.
1	Alfred O. P. Nicholson	"	Dec. 25, 1840	Oct. 17, 1843	By Governor, in room of Felix Grundy, deceased.
1	Ephraim H. Foster	"	Oct. 17, 1843	Mar. 3, 1845	By Legislature, in room of Felix Grundy, deceased.
1	Hopkins L. Turney	"	Mar. 4, 1845	Mar. 3, 1851	
2	William Blount	Tennessee	Aug. 2, 1796	July 8, 1797	Expelled from Senate.
2	Joseph Anderson	"	Sept. 26, 1797	Dec. 12, 1798	By Legislature, in room of William Blount, expelled; (appointed in room A. Jackson, belonging to other class, resigned.)
2	William Cocke	"	Mar. 4, 1799	Mar. 3, 1805	
2	Daniel Smith	"	Mar. 4, 1805	Resigned	Successor appointed April 11, 1809.

2	Jenkin Whiteside	"	April 11, 1809	Mar. 3, 1811	By Legislature, in room of Daniel Smith, resigned.
2	Jenkin Whiteside	"	Mar. 4, 1811	Resigned	Successor appointed Oct. 8, 1811.
2	George W. Campbell	"	Oct. 8, 1811	Resigned	By Legislature, in room of Jenkin Whiteside, resigned; successor appointed March 17, 1814.
2	Jesse Wharton	"	Mar. 17, 1814	Oct. 10, 1815	By Governor, in room of George W. Campbell, resigned.
2	John Williams	"	Oct. 10, 1815	Mar. 3, 1817	By Legislature, in room of G. W. Campbell, resigned.
2	John Williams	"	Mar. 4, 1817	Oct. 2, 1817	By the Governor.
2	John Williams	"	Oct. 2, 1817	Mar. 3, 1823	By Legislature.
2	Andrew Jackson	"	Mar. 4, 1823	Resigned	Successor appointed Oct. 28, 1825.
2	Hugh Lawson White	"	Oct. 28, 1825	Mar. 3, 1829	By Legislature, in room of Andrew Jackson, resigned.
2	Hugh Lawson White	"	Mar. 4, 1829	Mar. 3, 1835	
2	Hugh Lawson White	"	Mar. 4, 1835	Resigned	Successor appointed Jan. 27, 1840.
2	Alexander Anderson	"	Jan. 27, 1840	Mar. 3, 1841	By Legislature, in room of H. L. White, resigned.
2	Spencer Jarnagin	"	Mar. 4, 1841	Mar. 3, 1847	
1	John Smith	Ohio	April 1, 1803	Resigned	Successor appointed Dec. 12, 1808.
1	Return J. Meigs, jr.	"	Dec. 12, 1808	Mar. 3, 1809	By Legislature, in room of John Smith, resigned.
1	Return J. Meigs, jr.	"	Mar. 4, 1809	Resigned	Successor appointed Dec. 15, 1810.
1	Thomas Worthington	"	Dec. 15, 1810	Resigned	By Legislature, in room of R. J. Meigs, jr., resigned; successor appointed Dec. 10, 1814.
1	Joseph Kerr	"	Dec. 10, 1814	Mar. 3, 1815	By Legislature, in room of Thomas Worthington, resigned.
1	Benjamin Ruggles	"	Mar. 4, 1815	Mar. 3, 1821	
1	Benjamin Ruggles	"	Mar. 4, 1821	Mar. 3, 1827	
1	Benjamin Ruggles	"	Mar. 4, 1827	Mar. 3, 1833	

TABLE OF SENATORS—Continued.

Class.	Names of Senators.	States represented by Senators.	Commencement of service.	Termination of service.	Remarks.
1	Thomas Morris	"	Mar. 4, 1833	Mar. 3, 1839	
1	Benjamin Tappan	"	Mar. 4, 1839	Mar. 3, 1845	
1	Thomas Corwin	"	Mar. 4, 1845	Mar. 3, 1851	Resigned; succ'r app'd 20 July, 1850.
3	Thomas Worthington	Ohio	April 1, 1803	Mar. 3, 1807	
3	Edward Tiffin	"	Mar. 4, 1807	Resigned	Successor appointed May 18, 1809.
3	Stanley Griswold	"	May 18, 1809	Dec. 11, 1809	By Governor, in room of Edward Tiffin, resigned.
3	Alexander Campbell	"	Dec. 11, 1809	Mar. 3, 1813	By Legislature, in room of Edward Tiffin, resigned.
3	Jeremiah Morrow	"	Mar. 4, 1813	Mar. 3, 1819	
3	William A. Trimble	"	Mar. 4, 1819	Died	Successor appointed Jan. 3, 1822.
3	Ethan Allen Brown	"	Jan. 3, 1822	Mar. 3, 1825	By Legislature, in room of W. A. Trimble, deceased.
	William H. Harrison	"	Mar. 4, 1825	Resigned	Successor appointed Dec. 10, 1828.
3	Jacob Burnet	"	Dec. 10, 1828	Mar. 3, 1831	
3	Thomas Ewing	"	Mar. 4, 1831	Mar. 3, 1837	
3	William Allen	"	Mar. 4, 1837	Mar. 3, 1843	
3	William Allen	"	Mar. 4, 1843	Mar. 3, 1849	
2	John Noel Destréhan	Louisiana	Sept. 3, 1812	Resigned	Successor appointed Oct. 8, 1812.
2	Thomas Posey	"	Oct. 8, 1812	Dec. 1, 1812	By Governor, in room of John N. Destréhan, resigned.
2	James Brown	"	Dec. 1, 1812	Mar. 3, 1817	By Legislature, in room of John N. Destréhan, resigned.
2	W. C. C. Claiborne	"	Mar. 4, 1817	Died	Not having taken his seat in Senate; successor appointed Jan. 12, 1818.

2	Henry Johnson	"	Jan. 12, 1818	Mar. 3, 1823	By Legislature, in room of W. C. C. Claiborne, deceased.
2	Henry Johnson	"	Mar. 4, 1823	Resigned	Successor appointed November 19, 1824.
2	Dominique Bouligny	"	Nov. 19, 1824	Mar. 3, 1829	By Legislature, in room of Henry Johnson, resigned.
2	Edward Livingston	"	Mar. 3, 1829	Resigned	Successor appointed November 19, 1831.
2	George A. Waggaman	"	Nov. 19, 1831	Mar. 3, 1835	In room of Edward Livingston, resigned.
2	Robert Carter Nicholas	"	Mar. 4, 1835	Mar. 3, 1841	
2	Alexander Barrow	"	Mar. 4, 1841	Died	Successor appointed.
2	Pierre Soulé	"	Feb. 3, 1847	Mar. 3, 1847	By Legislature, in room of Alexander Barrow, deceased.
3	Allan B. Magruder	Louisiana	Sept. 3, 1812	Mar. 3, 1813	
3	Eligius Fromentin	"	Mar. 4, 1813	Mar. 3, 1819	
3	James Brown	"	Mar. 4, 1819	Resigned	Successor appointed Jan. 15, 1824.
3	Josiah S. Johnston	"	Jan. 15, 1824	Mar. 3, 1825	By Legislature, in room of James Brown, resigned.
3	Josiah S. Johnston	"	Mar. 4, 1825	Mar. 3, 1831	
3	Josiah S. Johnston	"	Mar. 4, 1831	Died	Successor appointed Dec. 19, 1833.
3	Alexander Porter	"	Dec. 19, 1833	Resigned	By Legislature, in room of J. S. Johnston, deceased; successor appointed Jan. 12, 1837.
3	Alexander Mouton	"	Jan. 12, 1837	Mar. 3, 1837	By Legislature, in room of A. Porter, resigned.
3	Alexander Mouton	"	Mar. 4, 1837	Resigned	Successor took his seat April 14, 1842.
3	Charles M. Conrad	"	April 14, 1842	Mar. 3, 1843	By Legislature, in room of Alexander Mouton, resigned.
3	Henry Johnson	"	Mar. 4, 1843	Mar. 3, 1849	Elected February 12, 1844.
1	James Noble	Indiana	Nov. 8, 1816	Mar. 3, 1821	

TABLE OF SENATORS—Continued.

Class.	Names of Senators.	States represented by Senators.	Commencement of service.	Termination of service.	Remarks.
1	James Noble	"	Mar. 4, 1821	Mar. 3, 1827	
1	James Noble	"	Mar. 4, 1827	Died	Successor appointed Aug. 19, 1831.
1	Robert Hanna	"	Aug. 19, 1831	Dec. 9, 1831	By Governor, in room of James Noble, deceased.
1	John Tipton	"	Dec. 9, 1831	Mar. 3, 1833	By Legislature, in room of James Noble, deceased.
1	John Tipton	"	Mar. 4, 1833	Mar. 3, 1839	
1	Albert S. White	"	Mar. 4, 1839	Mar. 3, 1845	
1	Jesse D. Bright	"	Mar. 4, 1845	Mar. 3, 1851	
3	Waller Taylor	Indiana	Nov. 8, 1816	Mar. 3, 1819	
3	Waller Taylor	"	Mar. 4, 1819	Mar. 3, 1825	
3	William Hendricks	"	Mar. 4, 1825	Mar. 3, 1831	
3	William Hendricks	"	Mar. 4, 1831	Mar. 3, 1837	
3	Oliver H. Smith	"	Mar. 4, 1837	Mar. 3, 1843	
3	Edward A. Hannegan	"	Mar. 4, 1843	Mar. 3, 1849	
1	Walter Leake	Mississippi	Oct. 9, 1817	Resigned	Successor appointed Aug. 30, 1820.
1	David Holmes	"	Aug. 30, 1820	Mar. 3, 1821	By Legislature, in room of Walter Leake, resigned.
1	David Holmes	"	Mar. 4, 1821	Resigned	Successor appointed Sept. 28, 1825.
1	Powhatan Ellis	"	Sept. 28, 1825	Jan. 28, 1826	By Governor, in room of David Holmes, resigned.
1	Thomas B. Reed	"	Jan. 28, 1826	Mar. 3, 1827	By Legislature, in room of David Holmes, resigned.
1	Powhatan Ellis	"	Mar. 4, 1827	....	Vacated his seat, by acceptance of office of judge of United States court.

1	John Black	"	Nov. 12, 1832	Mar. 3, 1833	By Governor, in room of P. Ellis.
1	John Black	"	Mar. 4, 1833	Resigned	Successor appointed Jan. 22, 1838.
1	James F. Trotter	"	Jan. 22, 1838	Resigned	By Legislature, in room of John Black, resigned; successor appointed Nov. 12, 1838.
1	Thomas H. Williams	"	Nov. 12, 1838	Jan. 30, 1839	By Governor, in room of James F. Trotter, resigned.
1	Thomas H. Williams	"	Jan. 30, 1839	Mar. 3, 1839	By Legislature, do.
1	John Henderson	"	Mar. 4, 1839	Mar. 3, 1845	
1	Jesse Speight	"	Mar. 4, 1845	Mar. 3, 1851	Died; succes'r app'd 10 Aug., 1847.
2	Thomas H. Williams	Mississippi	Oct. 9, 1817	Mar. 3, 1823	
2	Thomas H. Williams	"	Mar. 4, 1823	Mar. 3, 1829	
2	Thomas B. Reed	"	Mar. 4, 1829	Died	Successor appointed Jan. 6, 1830.
2	Robert H. Adams	"	Jan. 6, 1830	Died	By Legislature, in room of Thomas B. Reed, deceased; successor appointed Oct. 15, 1830.
2	George Poindexter	"	Oct. 15, 1830	Nov. 18, 1830	By Governor, in room of Robert H. Adams, deceased.
2	George Poindexter	"	Nov. 18, 1830	Mar. 3, 1835	By Legislature, in room of Robert H. Adams, deceased.
2	Robert J. Walker	"	Mar. 4, 1835	Mar. 3, 1841	
2	Robert J. Walker	"	Mar. 4, 1841	Resigned	Successor appointed November 3, 1845.
2	Joseph W. Chalmers	"	Nov. 3, 1845	Jan. 10, 1846	By Governor, in room of Robert J. Walker, resigned.
2	Joseph W. Chalmers	"	Jan. 10, 1846	Mar. 3, 1847	By Legislature, do.
2	Jesse B. Thomas	Illinois	Oct. 7, 1818	Mar. 3, 1823	
2	Jesse B. Thomas	"	Mar. 4, 1823	Mar. 3, 1829	
2	John McLean	"	Mar. 4, 1829	Died	Successor appointed November 12, 1830.
2	David J. Baker	"	Nov. 12, 1830	Dec. 11, 1830	By Governor, in room of John McLean, deceased.

TABLE OF SENATORS—Continued.

Class.	Names of Senators.	States represented by Senators.	Commencement of service.	Termination of service.	Remarks.
2	John M. Robinson	"	Dec. 11, 1830	Mar. 3, 1835	By Legislature, in room of John McLean, deceased.
2	John M. Robinson	"	Mar. 4, 1835	Mar. 3, 1841	
2	Samuel McRoberts	"	Mar. 4, 1841	Died	Successor appointed April 16, 1843.
2	James Semple	"	Aug. 16, 1843	Dec. 11, 1844	By Governor, in room of Samuel McRoberts, deceased.
2	James Semple	"	Dec. 11, 1844	Mar. 3, 1847	By Legislature, in room of Samuel McRoberts, deceased.
3	Ninian Edwards	Illinois	Oct. 7, 1818	Mar. 3, 1819	
3	Ninian Edwards	"	Mar. 4, 1819	Resigned	Successor appointed Nov. 23, 1824.
3	John McLean	"	Nov. 23, 1824	Mar. 3, 1825	By Legislature, in room of Ninian Edwards, resigned.
3	Elias K. Kane	"	Mar. 4, 1825	Mar. 3, 1831	
3	Elias K. Kane	"	Mar. 4, 1831	Died	Successor appointed December 30, 1835.
3	William Lee D. Ewing	"	Dec. 30, 1835	Mar. 3, 1837	By Legislature, in room of Elias K. Kane, deceased.
3	Richard M. Young	"	Mar. 4, 1837	Mar. 3, 1843	
3	Sidney Breese	"	Mar. 4, 1843	Mar. 3, 1849	
2	William R. King	Alabama	Oct. 28, 1819	Mar. 3, 1823	
2	William R. King	"	Mar. 4, 1823	Mar. 3, 1829	
2	William R. King	"	Mar. 4, 1829	Mar. 3, 1835	
2	William R. King	"	Mar. 4, 1835	Mar. 3, 1841	
2	William R. King	"	Mar. 4, 1841	Resigned	Successor appointed April 22, 1844.
2	Dixon H. Lewis	"	April 22, 1844	Dec. 10, 1845	By Governor, in room of William R. King, resigned.

2	Dixon H. Lewis	"	Dec. 10, 1845	Mar. 3, 1847	By Legislature, in room of W. R. King, resigned.
3	John W. Walker	Alabama	Oct. 28, 1819	Resigned	Successor appointed December 12, 1822.
3	William Kelly	"	Dec. 12, 1822	Mar. 3, 1825	By Legislature, in room of J. W. Walker, resigned.
3	Henry Chambers	"	Mar. 4, 1825	Died	Successor appointed Feb. 17, 1826.
3	Israel Pickens	"	Feb. 17, 1826	Nov. 27, 1826	By Governor, in room of Henry Chambers, deceased.
3	John McKinley	"	Nov. 27, 1826	Mar. 3, 1831	By Legislature, in room of Henry Chambers, deceased.
3	Gabriel Moore	"	Mar. 4, 1831	Mar. 3, 1837	
3	John McKinley	"	Mar. 4, 1837	Resigned	Appointed an associate judge Supreme Court United States.
3	Clement C. Clay	"	Mar. 4, 1837	Resigned	Successor appointed Nov. 24, 1841.
3	Arthur P. Bagby	"	Nov. 24, 1841	Mar. 3, 1843	By Legislature, in room of C. C. Clay, resigned.
3	Arthur P. Bagby	"	Mar. 4, 1843	Mar. 3, 1849	Resigned; succ'r app'd 1 July, 1848.
1	John Holmes	Maine	June 13, 1820	Mar. 3, 1821	
1	John Holmes	"	Mar. 4, 1821	Mar. 3, 1827	
1	Albion K. Parris	"	Mar. 4, 1827	Resigned	Successor appointed Jan. 15, 1829.
1	John Holmes	"	Jan. 15, 1829	Mar. 3, 1833	
1	Ether Shepley	"	Mar. 4, 1833	Resigned	Successor appointed December 7, 1836.
1	Judah Dana	"	Dec. 7, 1836	Mar. 3, 1837	By Governor, in room of Ether Shepley, resigned.
1	Ruel Williams	"	Feb. 22, 1837 Mar. 4, 1837	Mar. 3, 1839	By Legislature, in room of Ether Shepley, resigned.
1	Ruel Williams	"	Mar. 4, 1839	Resigned	Successor appointed March 3, 1843.
1	John Fairfield	"	Mar. 3, 1843	Mar. 3, 1845	By Legislature, in room of Ruel Williams, resigned.
1	John Fairfield	"	Mar. 3, 1845	Mar. 3, 1851	Died; successor app'd 5 Jan., 1848.

TABLE OF SENATORS—Continued.

Class.	Names of Senators.	States represented by Senators.	Commencement of service.	Termination of service.	Remarks.
2	John Chandler	Maine	June 14, 1820	Mar. 3, 1823	
2	John Chandler	"	Mar. 4, 1823	Mar. 3, 1829	
2	Peleg Sprague	"	Mar. 4, 1829	Resigned	Successor appointed Jan. 20, 1835.
2	John Ruggles	"	Jan. 20, 1835	Mar. 3, 1835	By Legislature, in room of Peleg Sprague.
2	John Ruggles	"	Mar. 4, 1835	Mar. 3, 1841	
2	George Evans	"	Mar. 4, 1841	Mar. 3, 1847	
1	Thomas H. Benton	Missouri	Oct. 2, 1820	Mar. 3, 1827	
1	Thomas H. Benton	"	Mar. 4, 1827	Mar. 3, 1833	
1	Thomas H. Benton	"	Mar. 4, 1833	Mar. 3, 1839	
1	Thomas H. Benton	"	Mar. 4, 1839	Mar. 3, 1845	
1	Thomas H. Benton	"	Mar. 4, 1845	Mar. 3, 1851	
3	David Barton	Missouri	Oct. 2, 1820	Mar. 3, 1825	
3	David Barton	"	Mar. 4, 1825	Mar. 3, 1831	
3	Alexander Buckner	"	Mar. 4, 1831	Died	Successor appointed Oct. 25, 1833.
3	Lewis F. Linn	"	Oct. 25, 1833	....	By Governor, in room of Alexander Buckner, deceased.
3	Lewis F. Linn	"	Nov. 20, 1834	Mar. 3, 1837	By Legislature, in room of Alexander Buckner, deceased.
3	Lewis F. Linn	"	Mar. 4, 1837	Mar. 3, 1843	
3	Lewis F. Linn	"	Mar. 4, 1843	Died	Successor appointed October 14, 1843.
3	David R. Atchison	"	Oct. 14, 1843	Nov. 20, 1844	By Governor, in room of L. F. Linn, deceased.
3	David R. Atchison	"	Nov. 20, 1844	Mar. 3, 1849	By Legislature, in room of L. F. Linn, deceased.

2	William S. Fulton......	Arkansas.....	Sept. 18, 1836	Mar. 3, 1841	
2	William S. Fulton......	..... "	Mar. 4, 1841	Died.........	Successor appointed November 8, 1844.
2	Chester Ashley.........	..... "	Nov. 8, 1844	Mar. 3, 1847	Died; successor app'd 12 May, 1848.
3	Ambrose H. Sevier	Arkansas.....	Sept. 18, 1836	Mar. 3, 1837	
3	Ambrose H. Sevier	..... "	Mar. 4, 1837	Mar. 3, 1843	
3	Ambrose H. Sevier	..... "	Mar. 4, 1843	Mar. 3, 1849	Resigned; succ'r app'd 30 Mar., 1848.
1	Lucius Lyon	Michigan.....	Nov. 10, 1835	Mar. 3, 1839	Attended January 26, 1837.
1	Augustus S. Porter	..... "	Mar. 4, 1839	Mar. 3, 1845	
1	Lewis Cass.............	..... "	Mar. 4, 1845	Mar. 3, 1851	Resigned; succ'r app'd 8 June, 1848.
2	John Norvell...........	Michigan.....	Nov. 10, 1835	Mar. 3, 1841	Attended January 26, 1837.
2	William Woodbridge ...	..... "	Mar. 4, 1841	Mar. 3, 1847	
1	David Levy Yulee	Florida.......	July 1, 1845	Mar. 3, 1851	
2	James D. Westcott, jr...	Florida.......	July 1, 1845	Mar. 3, 1849	
1	Thomas F. Rusk	Texas........	Feb. 21, 1846	Mar. 3, 1851	Re-elected for 6 years.
2	Sam Houston...........	Texas........	Feb. 21, 1846	Mar. 3, 1847	

Table, Supplementary to the preceding, of the Senators of the United States, from the 3d of March, 1847, *to the termination of the Second Session,* 32d *Congress, on the* 3d *March,* 1853.

Class.	Names of Senators.	States represented by Senators.	Commencement of service.	Termination of service.	Remarks.
2	John P. Hale..................	New Hampshire	Mar. 4, 1847	Mar. 3, 1853	Charles G. Atherton, elected for 6 years from 3d March, 1853.
3	Moses Norris, Jr..............	.... "	Mar. 4, 1849	Mar. 3, 1855	
1	Robert C. Winthrop.........	Massachusetts..	July 27, 1850	Feb. 1, 1851	By the Governor, in room of Daniel Webster, who resigned 22d July, 1850.
1	Robert Rantoul...............	.... "	Feb. 1, 1851	Mar. 3, 1851	By Legislature, in place of Daniel Webster.
1	Charles Sumner...............	.... "	Mar. 4, 1851	Mar. 3, 1857	
2	John Davis......................	Massachusetts..	Mar. 4, 1847	Mar. 3, 1853	(Edward Everett, elected for 6 years, from 3d March, 1853.)
2	John H. Clarke................	Rhode Island...	Mar. 4, 1847	Mar. 3, 1853	
1	Charles T. James.............	Rhode Island...	Mar. 4, 1851	Mar. 3, 1857	
1	Roger S. Baldwin............	Connecticut.....	Nov. 11, 1847	....	By the Governor, in room of Jabez W. Huntington, deceased.
1	Roger S. Baldwin............	.... "	May, 1848	Mar. 3, 1851	By the Legislature, in room of Jabez W. Huntington, deceased.
1	Isaac Toucey...................	.... "	May 12, 1852	Mar. 3, 1857	
3	Trueman Smith..............	Connecticut......	Mar. 4, 1849	Mar. 3, 1855	
3	William Upham..............	Vermont.........	Mar. 4, 1849	....	Deceased.
3	Samuel S. Phelps............	.... "	Jan. 17, 1853	....	By the Governor, in room of William Upham, deceased.
1	Solomon Foot.................	Vermont.........	Mar. 4, 1851	Mar. 3, 1857	
3	William H. Seward..........	New York........	Mar. 4, 1849	Mar. 3, 1855	
1	Hamilton Fish................	New York........	Mar. 4, 1851	Mar. 3, 1857	
2	Jacob W. Miller...............	New Jersey......	Mar. 4, 1847	Mar. 3, 1853	
1	Robert F. Stockton..........	New Jersey......	Mar. 4, 1851	Mar. 3, 1857	

3	James Cooper.................	Pennsylvania...	Mar. 4, 1849	Mar. 3, 1855	
1	Richard Brodhead..........	Pennsylvania...	Mar. 4, 1851	Mar. 3, 1857	
1	John Wales....................	Delaware	Feb. 23, 1849	Mar. 3, 1851	By the Legislature, in room of John M. Clayton, resigned.
1	James A. Bayard	.... "	Mar. 4, 1851	Mar. 3, 1857	
2	Presley Spruance............	Delaware	Mar. 4, 1847	Mar. 3, 1853	(John M. Clayton, elected for 6 years, from 4th March, 1853.)
1	David Stewart................	Maryland........	Dec. 6, 1849	Jan. 12, 1850	By the Governor, in room of Reverdy Johnson, resigned.
1	Thomas G. Pratt............	.... "	Jan. 12, 1850	Mar. 3, 1851	By the Legislature, in room of Reverdy Johnson, resigned.
1	Thomas G. Pratt............	Maryland	Mar. 4, 1851	Mar. 3, 1857	
3	James Alfred Pearce........	Maryland........	Mar. 4, 1849	Mar. 3, 1855	
2	Robert M. T. Hunter........	Virginia..........	Mar. 4. 1847	Mar. 3, 1853	Re-elected for 6 years.
1	James M. Mason............	Virginia..........	Mar. 4, 1851	Mar. 3, 1857	
2	Willie P. Mangum..........	North Carolina..	Mar. 4, 1847	Mar. 3, 1853	
3	George E. Badger............	North Carolina..	Mar. 4, 1849	Mar. 3, 1855	
2	John C. Calhoun.............	South Carolina..	Mar. 4, 1847	Died.	March 31, 1850.
2	Franklin H. Elmore.........	.... "	April 11, 1850	Died.	By the Governor, in room of John C. Calhoun, deceased.
2	Robert W. Barnwell.........	.... "	June 4, 1850	....	By the Governor, in room of John C. Calhoun, deceased.
2	R. Barnwell Rhett...........	.... "	Dec. 18, 1850	Resigned.	By the Legislature, in room of John C. Calhoun, deceased.
2	Wm. F. Desaussure..........	.... "	May 10, 1850	....	By the Governor, in room of R. Barnwell Rhett, resigned.
2	Wm. F. Desaussure..........	.... "	Nov. 29, 1852	Mar. 3, 1853	By the Legislature, in place of R. Barnwell Rhett, resigned.
3	Andrew P. Butler............	South Carolina..	Mar. 4, 1849	Mar. 3, 1855	
2	John Macpherson Berrien..	Georgia...........	Mar. 4, 1847	Resigned.	
2	Robert M. Charlton.........	.... "	May 31, 1852	Mar. 3, 1853	By the Governor, in room of John M. Berrien, resigned.

TABLE OF SENATORS—Continued.

Class.	Names of Senators.	States represented by Senators.	Commencement of service.	Termination of service.	Remarks.
3	Herschell V. Johnson.......	Georgia..........	Feb. 4, 1848	Mar. 3, 1849	By the Governor, in room of Walter T. Colquitt, resigned.
3	William C. Dawson..........	.... "	Mar. 4, 1849	Mar. 3, 1855	
2	Joseph R. Underwood......	Kentucky	Mar. 4, 1847	Mar. 3, 1853	(John B. Thompson, elected for 6 years, from 3d March, 1853.)
3	Thomas Metcalf.............	Kentucky	June 23, 1848	Jan. 3, 1849	By the Governor, in room of John J. Crittenden, resigned.
3	Thomas Metcalf.............	Kentucky	Jan. 3, 1849	Mar. 3, 1849	By the Legislature, ditto, ditto.
3	Henry Clay....................	Kentucky	Mar. 4, 1849	....	
3	David Meriwether...........	.... "	July 6, 1852	Sept. 1, 1852	By Gov'r, in room of H. Clay, dec.
3	Archibald Dixon..............	.... "	Sept. 1, 1852	Mar. 3, 1855	By the Legislature, in room of H. Clay, resigned.
2	John Bell......................	Tennessee.......	Mar. 4, 1847	Mar. 3, 1853	
1	James C. Jones...............	Tennessee.......	Mar. 4, 1851	Mar. 3, 1857	
1	Thomas Ewing...............	Ohio	July 20, 1850	Mar. 3, 1851	By the Governor, in room of T. Corwin, resigned.
1	Benjamin F. Wade...........	.... "	Mar. 4, 1851	Mar. 3, 1857	
3	Salmon P. Chase............	Ohio	Mar. 4, 1849	Mar. 3, 1855	
2	Solomon W. Downs..........	Louisiana	Mar. 4, 1847	Mar. 3, 1853	(Hon. Mr. Benjamin, elected for 6 years, from 3d March, 1853.
3	Pierre Soulé..................	.... "	Mar. 4, 1849	Mar. 3, 1855	
3	James Whitcomb............	Indiana..........	Mar. 4, 1849	Deceased.	
3	Charles W. Cathcart.........	.... "	Nov. 23, 1852	....	By the Governor, in place of James Whitcomb, deceased.
3	John Pettit.....................	.... "	Jan. 11, 1853	Mar. 3, 1855	By the Legislature, ditto, ditto.
1	Jesse D. Bright...............	Indiana	Mar. 4, 1851	Mar. 3, 1857	
1	Jefferson Davis..............	Mississippi	Aug. 10, 1847	Jan. 11, 1848	By the Governor, in room of Jesse Speight, deceased.

1	Jefferson Davis	Mississippi	Jan. 11, 1848	Mar. 3, 1851	By the Legislature, in room of Jesse Speight, deceased.
1	Jefferson Davis	"	Mar. 4, 1851	Resigned.	
1	John J. McRae	"	Dec. 1, 1851	....	By the Governor, in room of J. Davis, resigned.
1	Stephen Adams	"	Feb. 19, 1852	....	By the Legislature, ditto, ditto.
2	Henry Stuart Foote	Mississippi	Mar. 4, 1847	Resigned.	
2	Walker Brooke	"	Feb. 18, 1852	Mar. 3, 1853	By the Legislature, in room of H. S. Foote, resigned.
2	Stephen A. Douglass	Illinois	Mar. 4, 1847	Mar. 3, 1853	Re-elected for 6 years.
3	James Shields	Illinois	Mar. 4, 1849	Mar. 3, 1855	Elected by the Legislature, 13th January, 1849, and also on 27th October, 1849.
2	Dixon H. Lewis	Alabama	Mar. 4, 1847	Died.	
2	Benjamin Fitzpatrick	"	Nov. 25, 1848	Nov. 30, 1849	By the Governor, in room of D. H. Lewis, deceased.
2	Jeremiah Clemens	"	Nov. 30, 1849	Mar. 3, 1853	By the Legislature, ditto, ditto.
3	William R. King	Alabama	July 1, 1848	Mar. 3, 1849	By the Governor, in room of Arthur P. Bagley, resigned.
3	William R. King	"	Mar. 4, 1849	Resigned.	
3	Benjamin Fitzpatrick	"	Jan. 14, 1853	....	By the Governor, in room of W. R. King, resigned.
1	Wyman B. S. Moor	Maine	Jan. 5, 1848	May 26, 1848	By the Governor, in room of John Fairfield, deceased.
1	Hannibal Hamlin	"	May 26, 1848	Mar. 3, 1851	By the Legislature, ditto, ditto.
1	Hannibal Hamlin	"	Mar. 4, 1851	Mar. 3, 1857	
2	James W. Bradbury	Maine	Mar. 4, 1847	Mar. 3, 1853	
3	David R. Atchison	Missouri	Mar. 4, 1849	Mar. 3, 1855	
1	Henry S. Geyer	Missouri	Mar. 4, 1851	Mar. 3, 1857	
2	Chester Ashley	Arkansas	Mar. 4, 1847	Died.	
2	William K. Sebastian	"	May 12, 1848	Nov. 17, 1848	By the Governor, in room of Chester Ashley, deceased.
2	William K. Sebastian	"	Nov. 17, 1848	Mar. 3, 1853	By the Legislature, ditto, ditto.

TABLE OF SENATORS—Continued.

Class.	Names of Senators.	States represented by Senators.	Commencement of service.	Termination of service.	Remarks.
2	William K. Sebastian......	Arkansas	Nov. 17, 1848	Mar. 3, 1853	(Re-elected for 6 years, from 3d March, 1853.)
3	Solon Borland.................	Arkansas	Mar. 30, 1848	Nov. 17, 1848	By the Governor, in room of A. H. Sevier, resigned.
3	Solon Borland.................	.... "	Nov. 17, 1848	Mar. 3, 1849	By the Legislature, ditto, ditto.
3	Solon Borland.................	.... "	Mar. 4, 1849	Mar. 3, 1855	
1	Thomas Fitzgerald...........	Michigan	June 8, 1848	Jan. 20, 1849	By the Governor, in room of L. Cass, resigned.
1	Lewis Cass......................	.... "	Jan. 20, 1849	Mar. 3, 1851	By the Legislature, ditto, ditto.
1	Lewis Cass......................	.... "	Mar. 4, 1851	Mar. 3, 1857	
2	Alpheus Felch.................	Michigan	Mar. 4, 1847	Mar. 3, 1853	
3	Jackson Morton...............	Florida...........	Mar. 4, 1849	Mar. 3, 1855	
1	Stephen R. Mallory.........	Florida...........	Mar. 4, 1851	Mar. 3, 1857	
1	Thomas F. Rusk.............	Texas.............	Mar. 4, 1851	Mar. 3, 1857	
2	Samuel Houston..............	Texas.............	Mar. 4, 1847	Mar. 3, 1853	(Re-elected for 6 years, from 3d March, 1853.)
1	Henry Dodge...................	Wisconsin	June 8, 1848	Mar. 3, 1851	
1	Henry Dodge...................	.... "	Mar. 3, 1851	Mar. 3, 1857	
3	Isaac P. Walker..............	Wisconsin	June 8, 1848	Mar. 3, 1849	
3	Isaac P. Walker..............	.... "	Mar. 4, 1849	Mar. 3, 1855	
2	George W. Jones.............	Iowa..............	Dec. 7, 1848	Mar. 3, 1853	(Re-elected for 6 years, from 3d March, 1853.)
3	Augustus C. Dodge..........	Iowa..............	Dec. 7, 1848	Mar. 3, 1849	
3	Augustus C. Dodge..........	.... "	Mar. 4, 1849	Mar. 3, 1855	
1	John C. Fremont.............	California	Dec. 20, 1849	Mar. 3, 1851	
1	John B. Weller................	.... "	Mar. 4, 1851	Mar. 3, 1857	
3	William M. Gwin.............	California........	Dec. 20, 1849	Mar. 3, 1855	

4. *Table of the Names, Place of Nativity or Residence when Appointed, Time of Appointment, and Expiration of Service of the Secretaries of the Senate of the United States.*

Names.	States.	Time of appointment.	Expiration of service.	Remarks.
Samuel Alyne Otis	Massachusetts	8 April 1789	18 April 1814*	The Senate met 4th March; formed a quorum 6th April; and did not elect a Secretary until the 8th; messages to the House having been previously communicated by a member of the Senate. Served upwards of 25 years.
Charles Cutts	N. Hampshire	11 Oct. 1814	12 Dec. 1825	The Chief Clerk acted as Secretary from decease of Mr. Otis until the election of Mr. Cutts.
Walter Lowrie	Pennsylvania .	12 Dec. 1825	5 Dec. 1836	Resigned. The Chief Clerk acted as Secretary from the resignation of W. Lowrie to the appointment of his successor.
Asbury Dickins.............	North Carolina	12 Dec. 1836	Present incumbent.	

* The records do not show the time of Mr. Otis's death more particularly than by the following resolution, which was adopted on the 7th October, 1814:—

Resolved, unanimously, That the Senate, from a sincere desire of testifying their respect for the long and faithful services of their late Secretary, Samuel A. Otis, esquire, who performed the duties of that office with punctuality and exactness, from the commencement of this government until the close of the last session of Congress, will go into mourning for one month, in the usual method of wearing crape round the left arm.

5. *Table of the Names of the Representatives in Congress who have been elected Speakers of the House of Representatives from the 4th March, 1789, to the Termination of the Second Session, 31st Congress, 3d March, 1851; showing the Commencement and Termination of their Service as such, and the States of which they were Representatives, respectively.*

Congress.	Session.	Names of Speakers.	Election, or commencement of service.	Termination of service.	States of which they were representatives.	Remarks.
1	1	Fred. A. Muhlenberg	April 1, 1789	Mar. 3, 1791	Pennsylvania.	
2	1	Jonathan Trumbull .	Oct. 24, 1791	Mar. 2, 1793	Connecticut.	
3	1	Fred. A. Muhlenberg	Dec. 2, 1793	Mar. 3, 1795	Pennsylvania.	
4	1	Jonathan Dayton....	Dec. 7, 1795	Mar. 3, 1797	New Jersey.	
5	1	Jonathan Dayton....	May 15, 1797	Mar. 3, 1799	do.	
		George Dent	April 20, 1798	April 23, 1798	Maryland	Pro tempore during sickness of Speaker.
		George Dent	May 28, 1798	May 29, 1798	.....do.......	
6	1	Theodore Sedgwick.	Dec. 2, 1799	Mar. 3, 1801	Massachusetts.	
7	1	Nathaniel Macon ...	Dec. 7, 1801	Mar. 3, 1803	N. Carolina.	
8	1	Nathaniel Macon ...	Oct. 17, 1803	Mar. 3, 1805	do.	
9	1	Nathaniel Macon ...	Dec. 2, 1805	Mar. 3, 1807	do.	
10	1	Joseph B. Varnum..	Oct. 26, 1807	Mar. 3, 1809	Massachusetts.	
11	1	Joseph B. Varnum..	May 22, 1809	Mar. 3, 1811	do.	
12	1	Henry Clay	Nov. 4, 1811	Mar. 3, 1813	Kentucky	Indisposed 19th and 20th May, 1812, and House adjourned.
13	1	Henry Clay	May 24, 1813	Jan. 19, 1814	.....do.......	Absent Dec. 27, 1813, House adjourned. Resigned Jan. 19, 1814.
	2	Langdon Cheves....	Jan. 19, 1814	Mar. 2, 1815	S. Carolina.	
14	1	Henry Clay	Dec. 4, 1815	Mar. 3, 1817	Kentucky	Absent Dec. 10, 1816. House adjourned.
15		Henry Clay	Dec. 1, 1817	Mar. 3, 1819	do.	
16	1	Henry Clay	Dec. 6, 1819	Nov. 13, 1820	.....do.......	Resigned, by letter, 20th Oct. 1820.
	2	John W. Taylor....	Nov. 15, 1820	Mar. 3, 1821	New York.	

17		Philip P. Barbour......	Dec. 3, 1821	Mar. 3, 1823	Virginia.	
18		Henry Clay..............	Dec. 1, 1823	Mar. 3, 1825	Kentucky........	Asked permission to vote, 22d Dec. 1824.
19		John W. Taylor.........	Dec. 5, 1825	Mar. 3, 1827	New York.	
20		Andrew Stevenson.....	Dec. 3, 1827	Mar. 3, 1829	Virginia.	
21		Andrew Stevenson.....	Dec. 7, 1829	Mar. 3, 1831	......do..........	Absent from sickness, Dec. 6, 1830. House adjourned.
22		Andrew Stevenson.....	Dec. 5, 1831	Mar. 2, 1833	do.	
23	1	Andrew Stevenson.....	Dec. 2, 1833	June 2, 1834	......do...........	Resigned 2d June, 1834.
		Henry Hubbard.........	May 19, 1834	May 19, 1834	N. Hampshire.	The Speaker having withdrawn, Henry Hubbard was substituted as Speaker, and acted that day.
24		John Bell.................	June 2, 1834	Mar. 3, 1835	Tennessee.	
25		James K. Polk..........	Dec. 7, 1835	Mar. 3, 1837	do.	
26		James K. Polk..........	Sept. 4, 1837	Mar. 3, 1839	do.	
27		Robert M. T. Hunter..	Dec. 16, 1839	Mar. 3, 1841	Virginia.	
28		John White.............	May 31, 1841	Mar. 3, 1843	Kentucky.	
		John W. Jones..........	Dec. 4, 1843	Mar. 3, 1845	Virginia.	
		George W. Hopkins...	Feb. 28, 1845	Feb. 28, 1845	......do...........	The Speaker having withdrawn, George W. Hopkins was substituted, and acted that day.
29		John W. Davis.........	Dec. 1, 1845	Mar. 3, 1847	Indiana.	
30		Robert C. Winthrop....	Dec. 6, 1847	Mar. 3, 1849	Massachusetts.	
		Armistead Burt.........	June 19, 1848	June 19, 1848	South Carolina..	The Speaker being absent, Mr. Burt was substituted for this day.
		Armistead Burt.........	June 20, 1848	June 22, 1848	......do...........	The Speaker being still sick, Mr. Burt was appointed Speaker pro. tem. for this week, &c.
31		Howell Cobb...........	Dec. 22, 1849	Mar. 3, 1851	Georgia.	
32		Linn Boyd..............	Dec. 1, 1351	Mar. 3, 1851	Kentucky.	

6. *Table of the Names, Residence when Appointed, Time of Appointment, and Expiration of Service of the Clerks of the House of Representatives of the United States.*

Names.	States.	Time of appointment.	Expiration of service.	Remarks.
John Beckley	Virginia	1 April 1789	15 May 1797	The House of Representatives met 4th March; formed a quorum on 1st April, and then elected a clerk.
Jonathan Williams Condy	Pennsylvania	15 May 1797	9 Dec. 1800	Resigned.
John Holt Oswald	Pennsylvania	9 Dec. 1800	7 Dec. 1801	
John Beckley	Virginia	7 Dec. 1801	26 Oct. 1807	
Patrick Magruder	Maryland	26 Oct. 1807	28 Jan. 1815	Resigned.
Thomas Dougherty	Kentucky	30 Jan. 1815	1822	Died during recess.
Matthew St. Clair Clarke	Pennsylvania	3 Dec. 1822	2 Dec. 1833	
Walter S. Franklin	Pennsylvania	2 Dec. 1833	20 Sept. 1838	Died.
Hugh A. Garland	Virginia	3 Dec. 1838	31 May 1841	
Matthew St. Clair Clarke	Pennsylvania	31 May 1841	6 Dec. 1843	
Caleb J. McNulty	Ohio	6 Dec. 1843	18 Jan. 1845	Dismissed.
Benjamin B. French	N. Hampshire	18 Jan. 1845	7 Dec. 1847	
Thomas Jefferson Campbell	Tennessee	7 Dec. 1847	13 April 1850	Died.
Richard M. Young	Illinois	17 April 1850	1 Dec. 1851	
John W. Forney	Pennsylvania	1 Dec. 1851	Present incumbent.	

CHAPTER 8.

THIS CHAPTER IS DEDICATED TO

THE EMINENT JURISTS

WHO HAVE OCCUPIED AND CONTINUE TO OCCUPY THE

BENCH OF THAT AUGUST TRIBUNAL,

THE SUPREME COURT OF THE UNITED STATES,

From the 4th March, 1789, *to the 3d March*, 1851.

CHIEF JUSTICES

OF THE SUPREME COURT OF THE UNITED STATES.

JOHN JAY, of New York, appointed by the President with the advice and consent of the Senate, 26th September, 1789. Nominated 16th, and confirmed 19th April, 1794, Envoy Extraordinary to England. Resigned as Chief Justice. Successor appointed 1st July, 1795.

JOHN RUTLEDGE, of South Carolina, appointed 1st July, 1795, in recess of Senate, in place of John Jay resigned, and presided on the Bench at August term, 1795. Nominated 10th, and rejected by the Senate 15th December, 1795.

WILLIAM CUSHING, of Massachusetts. Nomination confirmed and appointed, &c., 27th January, 1796, in place of John Jay, resigned. Declined the appointment. He was then an Associate Justice.

OLIVER ELLSWORTH, of Connecticut. Nomination confirmed and appointed, &c., 4th March, 1796, in place of W. Cushing, declined. Appointed Envoy Extraordinary and Minister Plenipotentiary to France, 27th February, 1799. He presided on the Bench at the August term, 1799. Proceeded on his mission to

France, 3d November, 1799. Resigned as Chief Justice. Successor appointed 19th December, 1800.

JOHN JAY, Governor of New York. Nomination confirmed and appointed, &c., 19th December, 1800, in place of Oliver Ellsworth, resigned. Declined the appointment.

JOHN MARSHALL, Secretary of State.* Nomination confirmed 27th, and appointed, &c., 31st January, 1801, in place of John Jay, declined. Died in 1835.

ROGER B. TANEY, of Maryland. Nomination confirmed and appointed, &c., 15th March, 1836, in the place of John Marshall, deceased.

ASSOCIATE JUSTICES

OF THE SUPREME COURT OF THE UNITED STATES.

JOHN RUTLEDGE, of South Carolina. Nomination confirmed and appointed 26th September, 1789. Resigned, and Thomas Johnson appointed.

WILLIAM CUSHING, of Massachusetts. Nomination confirmed 26th, and appointed 27th September, 1789. Died, and Levi Lincoln appointed.

JAMES WILSON, of Pennsylvania. Nomination confirmed 26th, and appointed 29th September, 1789. Died, and Bushrod Washington appointed.

JOHN BLAIR, of Virginia. Nomination confirmed 26th, and appointed 30th September, 1789. Resigned, and Samuel Chase appointed.

ROBERT H. HARRISON, of Maryland. Nomination confirmed 26th September, 1789. Resigned, and James Iredell appointed.

JAMES IREDELL, of North Carolina. Appointed in recess of Senate,

* John Marshall, Secretary of State, was nominated to the Senate as Chief Justice the 20th January, 1801, was confirmed on the 27th, commissioned 31st January, and presided on the Bench of the Supreme Court from the 4th to the 9th February, or during February term, 1801. From a message of the President to Congress, accompanied by a report from John Marshall, Secretary of State, dated 27th February, 1801, it appears that he also continued to act in the latter capacity until that day, and from other circumstances that he continued to act as such until the 3d March, 1801, on which day the then administration terminated.

in place of Robert H. Harrison, resigned. Nomination confirmed and appointed 10th February, 1790. Died, and Alfred Moore appointed.

THOMAS JOHNSON, of Maryland. Appointed 5th August, 1791, in recess of Senate, in place of John Rutledge, resigned. Nomination confirmed and appointed 7th November, 1791. Resigned, and William Paterson appointed.

WILLIAM PATERSON, Governor of New Jersey. Nomination confirmed and appointed 4th March, 1793, in place of Thomas Johnson, resigned. Died, and Brockholst Livingston appointed.

SAMUEL CHASE, of Maryland. Nomination confirmed and appointed 27th January, 1796, in place of John Blair, resigned. Died, and Gabriel Duval appointed.

BUSHROD WASHINGTON, of Virginia. Appointed 29th September, 1798, in recess of Senate, in place of James Wilson, deceased. Nomination confirmed and appointed 20th December, 1798. Died, and Henry Baldwin appointed.

ALFRED MOORE, of North Carolina. Nomination confirmed and appointed 10th December, 1799, in place of James Iredell, deceased. Resigned, and William Johnson appointed.

WILLIAM JOHNSON, of South Carolina. Nomination confirmed and appointed 26th March, 1804, in place of Alfred Moore, resigned. (Confirmed and appointed Collector of the Customs 22d Feb. 1819, and declined the appointment.) Died in 1834, and James M. Wayne appointed.

THOMAS TODD, of Kentucky. Nomination confirmed 2d, and appointed 3d March, 1807.

BROCKHOLST LIVINGSTON, of New York. Appointed 10th November, 1806, in recess of Senate, in place of William Paterson, deceased. Nomination confirmed and appointed 17th December, 1806. Died, and Smith Thompson appointed.

LEVI LINCOLN, of Massachusetts. Nomination confirmed and appointed 3d January, 1811, in place of William Cushing, deceased. Declined the appointment, and John Quincy Adams appointed.

JOHN QUINCY ADAMS, of Massachusetts. Nomination confirmed and appointed 22d February, 1811, in place of Levi Lincoln, declined. Declined the appointment, and Joseph Story appointed.

GABRIEL DUVAL, of Maryland. Nomination confirmed and appointed 18th November, 1811, in the place of Samuel Chase, deceased. Resigned, and Philip P. Barbour appointed.

JOSEPH STORY, of Massachusetts. Nomination confirmed and appointed 18th November, 1811, in place of John Quincy Adams, declined. Died and Levi Woodbury appointed.

SMITH THOMPSON, of New York. Appointed 1st September, 1823, in recess of the Senate, in place of Brockholst Livingston, deceased. Nomination confirmed and appointed 9th December, 1823. Died, and Samuel Nelson appointed.

ROBERT TRIMBLE, of Kentucky. Nomination confirmed and appointed 9th May, 1826, in the place of Thomas Todd, deceased. Died, and John McLean appointed.

JOHN McLEAN, of Ohio. Nomination confirmed and appointed 7th March, 1829, in the place of Robert Trimble, deceased.

HENRY BALDWIN, of Pennsylvania. Nomination confirmed and appointed 6th January, 1830, in place of Bushrod Washington, deceased. Died, and R. C. Grier appointed.

JAMES M. WAYNE, of Georgia. Nomination confirmed and appointed 9th January, 1835, in place of William Johnson, deceased.

PHILIP P. BARBOUR, of Virginia. Nomination confirmed and appointed 15th March, 1836, in place of Gabriel Duval, resigned. Died, and P. V. Daniel appointed.

JOHN CATRON, of Tennessee. Nomination confirmed and appointed 8th March, 1837.

WILLIAM SMITH, of Alabama. Nomination confirmed and appointed 8th March, 1837. Declined the appointment, and John McKinley appointed.

JOHN McKINLEY, of Alabama. Appointed 22d April, 1837, in recess of the Senate, in place of William Smith, declined. Nominationed confirmed and appointed 25th September, 1837.

PETER V. DANIEL, of Virginia. Nomination confirmed and appointed 3d March, 1841, in place of Philip P. Barbour, deceased.

SAMUEL NELSON, of New York. Nomination confirmed and appointed, 14th February, 1845, in place of Smith Thompson, de ceased.

LEVI WOODBURY, of New Hampshire. Appointed 20th Septem ber, 1845, in recess of the Senate, in place of Joseph Story, de ceased. Nomination confirmed and appointed 3d January, 1846.

ROBERT C. GRIER, of Pennsylvania. Nomination confirmed and appointed 4th August, 1846, in place of Henry Baldwin, deceased.

BENJAMIN ROBBINS CURTIS, of Massachusetts. Appointed during the recess of the Senate, in place of Levi Woodbury, deceased. Nomination confirmed and appointed 20th December, 1851.

CLERKS OF THE SUPREME COURT OF THE UNITED STATES.

John Tucker, of Massachusetts,	appointed	Feb. 3, 1790.	Resigned.
Samuel Bayard, of Delaware,	do.	Aug. 1, 1791.	Resigned.
Elias B. Caldwell, of N. J.	do.	Aug. 15, 1800.	Died.
William Griffith, of N. J.	do.	Feb. 9, 1826.	Died.
William T. Carroll, of D. C.	do.	Jan. 20, 1827.	Pres't inc't.

REPORTERS OF DECISIONS OF SUPREME COURT UNITED STATES.

Alexander J. Dallas,	reported	from	1789 to 1800, inclusive.
William Cranch,	do.	"	1801 to 1815, "
Henry Wheaton,	do.	"	1816 to 1827, "
Richard Peters, jun'r,	do.	"	1828 to 1842, "
Benjamin C. Howard,	do.	"	1843. Present incumbent.

MARSHALS OF THE UNITED STATES ATTENDANT ON THE SUPREME COURT OF THE UNITED STATES.

Under the construction of the judiciary act of 1789, the Marshals of all the *Districts* were required to attend the sessions of the Supreme Court, until, by the act of 9th June, 1794, the Marshal of the district alone in which the court shall sit was required to attend its sessions.

David Lenox,	Marshal Dist. of Pa.,	attended	Jan. 28, 1794 to Feb. 1801.
Daniel Carroll Brent,	Mar. D. C.,	"	Aug. 3, 1801, to Aug. 1808.
Washington Boyd,	do.	"	Feb. 1, 1808, to Aug. 1818.
Tench Ringgold,	do.	"	Nov. 30, 1818, to Aug. 1831.
Henry Ashton,	do.	"	Feb. 4, 1831, to Feb. 1834.
Alexander Hunter,	do.	"	March 6, 1834, to Dec. 1848.
Robert Wallace,	do.	"	Dec. 5, 1848, to Dec. 1849.
Richard Wallach,	do.	"	Dec. 4, 1849. Present incu't.

CHAPTER 9.

THIS CHAPTER IS APPROPRIATED TO THE

DISTINGUISHED INDIVIDUALS

WHO HAVE FILLED AND CONTINUE TO OCCUPY THE

SEVERAL HIGH EXECUTIVE DEPARTMENTS OR OFFICES OF THE GOVERNMENT,

From the 4th March, 1789, *to the 3d March,* 1851.

SECRETARIES OF STATE.

THOMAS JEFFERSON, of Virginia. Nomination confirmed and appointed 26th September, 1789. Resigned.

EDMUND RANDOLPH, of Virginia. Nomination confirmed and appointed 2d January, 1794. Resigned.

TIMOTHY PICKERING, of Pennsylvania. Nomination confirmed and appointed 10th December, 1795. Removed.

JOHN MARSHALL, of Virginia. Nomination confirmed and appointed 13th May, 1800. Appointed Chief Justice Supreme Court 31st January, 1801. Presided as such at February term, 1801. Continued to act as Secretary of State to 3d March, 1801.

JAMES MADISON, of Virginia. Nomination confirmed and appointed 5th March, 1801. Became President 4th March, 1809.

ROBERT SMITH, of Maryland. (Secretary of the Navy.) Nomination confirmed and appointed 6th March, 1809. Resigned, and James Monroe appointed.

JAMES MONROE, of Virginia. Appointed 2d April, 1811, in recess of Senate. Nomination confirmed and appointed 25th November, 1811. Appointed Secretary of War, 27th September, 1814.

JAMES MONROE, of Virginia. (Secretary of War.) Nomination confirmed and appointed 28th February, 1815. Became President of the United States 4th March, 1817.

JOHN QUINCY ADAMS, of Massachusetts. Nomination confirmed and appointed 5th March, 1817. Became President of the United States 4th March, 1825.

HENRY CLAY, of Kentucky. Nomination confirmed and appointed 7th March, 1825. Resigned.

MARTIN VAN BUREN, of New York. Nomination confirmed and appointed 6th March, 1829. Resigned, and Edward Livingston appointed.

EDWARD LIVINGSTON, of Louisiana, appointed 24th May, 1831, in recess of Senate. Nomination confirmed and appointed 12th January, 1832.

LOUIS McLANE, of Delaware. Appointed 29th May, 1833, in recess of Senate. Resigned.

JOHN FORSYTH, of Georgia. Nomination confirmed and appointed 27th June, 1834, in place of Louis McLane, resigned.

DANIEL WEBSTER, of Massachusetts. Nomination confirmed and appointed 5th March, 1841. Resigned.

ABEL P. UPSHUR, of Virginia, appointed 24th July, 1843, in recess of the Senate, in place of Daniel Webster, resigned. Nomination confirmed and appointed 2d January, 1844. (Abel P. Upshur was killed on 28th February, 1844, by the bursting of a large cannon on board of the United States steam frigate the Princeton.)

JOHN C. CALHOUN, of South Carolina. Nomination confirmed and appointed 6th March, 1844, in room of Abel P. Upshur, deceased.

JAMES BUCHANAN, of Pennsylvania. Nomination confirmed and appointed 5th March, 1845.

[*Continued on page* 403]

SECRETARIES OF THE TREASURY.

ALEXANDER HAMILTON, of New York. Nomination confirmed and appointed 11th September, 1789. Resigned.

OLIVER WOLCOTT, jun'r, of Connecticut. Nomination confirmed and appointed 3d February, 1795. Resigned, to take effect 31st December, 1800.

SAMUEL DEXTER, of Massachusetts. (Secretary of War.) Nomination confirmed and appointed 31st December 1800.

ALBERT GALLATIN, of Pennsylvania. Appointed 14th May, 1801, in recess of Senate. Nomination confirmed and appointed 26th January, 1802. Superseded by appointment of George W. Campbell, owing to his protracted absence in Europe as Public Minister of the United States.

GEORGE W. CAMPBELL, of Tennessee. Nomination confirmed and appointed 9th February, 1814. Resigned, and Alexander James Dallas appointed.

ALEXANDER JAMES DALLAS, of Pennsylvania. Nomination confirmed and appointed 6th October, 1814.

WILLIAM H. CRAWFORD, of Georgia. Appointed 22d October, 1816, in recess of the Senate. Nomination confirmed and appointed 5th March, 1817.

RICHARD RUSH, of Pennsylvania. Nomination confirmed and appointed 7th March, 1825.

SAMUEL D. INGHAM, of Pennsylvania. Nomination confirmed and appointed 6th March, 1829. Resigned, and Louis McLane appointed.

LOUIS McLANE, of Delaware. Appointed August 8th, 1831, in recess of the Senate. Nomination confirmed and appointed 13th January, 1832.

WILLIAM J. DUANE, of Pennsylvania. Appointed 29th May, 1833, in recess of the Senate. Superseded by appointment of Roger B. Taney.

ROGER B. TANEY, of Maryland, appointed 23d September, 1833, in recess of Senate, and continued until 24th June, 1834.

LEVI WOODBURY, of New Hampshire. Nomination confirmed and appointed 27th June, 1834.

THOMAS EWING, of Ohio. Nomination confirmed and appointed 5th March, 1841. Resigned, and W. Forward appointed.

WALTER FORWARD, of Pennsylvania. Nomination confirmed and appointed 13th September, 1841, in place of Thomas Ewing, resigned.

JOHN C. SPENCER, of New York. Nomination confirmed and appointed 3d March, 1843, in place of Walter Forward, resigned.

GEORGE M. BIBB, of Kentucky. Nomination confirmed and appointed 15th June, 1844, in place of John C. Spencer, resigned.

ROBERT J. WALKER, of Mississippi. Nomination confirmed and appointed 5th March, 1845.

[*Continued on page 403*]

SECRETARIES OF WAR.

HENRY KNOX, of Massachusetts. Nomination confirmed and appointed 12th September, 1789. Resigned.

TIMOTHY PICKERING, of Pennsylvania. Nomination confirmed and appointed, 2d January, 1795. Appointed Secretary of State 10th December, 1795.

JOHN McHENRY, of Maryland. Nomination confirmed and appointed 27th January, 1796. Resigned, to take effect 1st June, 1800.

JOHN MARSHALL, of Virginia. Nominated 7th May, 1800. Postponed 9th May, 1800. Appointed 13th May, 1800, Secretary of State.

SAMUEL DEXTER, of Massachusetts. Nomination confirmed and appointed 13th May, 1800. Appointed Secretary of the Treasury 31st December, 1800.

ROGER GRISWOLD, Member of House of Representatives from Connecticut. Nomination confirmed and appointed 3d February, 1801. Vacated.

HENRY DEARBORN, of Massachusetts. Nomination confirmed and appointed 5th March, 1801.

WILLIAM EUSTIS, of Massachusetts. Nomination confirmed and appointed 7th March, 1809. Resigned, and John Armstrong appointed.

JOHN ARMSTRONG, of New York. Nomination confirmed and appointed 13th January, 1813. Resigned, and James Monroe appointed.

JAMES MONROE, of Virginia. (Secretary of State.) Nomination confirmed and appointed 27th September, 1814. Appointed Secretary of State 28th February, 1815.

WILLIAM H. CRAWFORD, of Georgia. Nomination confirmed and appointed 3d March, 1815. Appointed Secretary of the Treasury 22d October, 1816.

GEORGE GRAHAM, of Virginia. Appointed 7th April, 1817, in recess of the Senate.

ISAAC SHELBY, of Kentucky. Nomination confirmed and appointed 5th March, 1817. Declined the appointment.

JOHN C. CALHOUN, of South Carolina. Appointed 8th October, 1817, in recess of the Senate. Nomination confirmed and appointed 15th December, 1817.

JAMES BARBOUR, of Virginia. Nomination confirmed and appointed 7th March, 1825.

PETER B. PORTER, of New York. Nomination confirmed and appointed 26th May, 1828.

JOHN H. EATON, of Tennessee. Nomination confirmed and appointed 9th March, 1829. Resigned, and Lewis Cass appointed.

LEWIS CASS, of Ohio. Appointed 1st August, 1831, in recess of the Senate. Nomination confirmed and appointed 30th December, 1831. Appointed Minister to France.

BENJAMIN F. BUTLER, of New York. Nomination confirmed and appointed 3d March, 1837.

JOEL R. POINSETT, of South Carolina. Nomination confirmed and appointed 7th March, 1837.

JOHN BELL, of Tennessee. Nomination confirmed and appointed 5th March, 1841. Resigned.

JOHN McLEAN, of Ohio. Nomination confirmed and appointed 13th September, 1841, in place of John Bell, resigned. Declined the appointment.

JOHN C. SPENCER, of New York. Appointed 12th October, 1841, in the recess of the Senate, in place of John McLean, declined. Nomination confirmed and appointed 20th December, 1841.

JAMES M. PORTER, of Pennsylvania. Appointed 8th March, 1843, in recess of the Senate, in place of John C. Spencer, resigned, and continued to serve until 30th January, 1844.

WILLIAM WILKINS, of Pennsylvania. Nomination confirmed and appointed 15th February, 1844.

WILLIAM L. MARCY, of New York. Nomination confirmed and appointed 5th March, 1845.

[*Continued on page* 404]

SECRETARIES OF THE NAVY.

GEORGE CABOT, of Massachusetts. Nomination confirmed and appointed 3d May, 1798.

BENJAMIN STODDERT, of Maryland. Nomination confirmed and appointed 21st May, 1798. Resigned.

ROBERT SMITH, of Maryland. Appointed 15th July, 1801, in recess of the Senate. Nomination confirmed and appointed 26th January, 1802. Appointed Attorney General 2d March, 1805.

JACOB CROWNINSHIELD, of Massachusetts. Nomination confirmed and appointed 2d March, 1805.

PAUL HAMILTON, of South Carolina. Nomination confirmed and appointed 7th March, 1809. Resigned, and William Jones appointed.

WILLIAM JONES, of Pennsylvania. Nomination confirmed and appointed 12th January, 1813. Resigned, and Benjamin W. Crowninshield appointed.

BENJAMIN W. CROWNINSHIELD, of Massachusetts. Nomination confirmed and appointed 17th December, 1814.

SMITH THOMPSON, of New York. Appointed 9th November, 1818, in recess of the Senate. Nomination confirmed and appointed 30th November, 1818. Resigned.

JOHN RODGERS. (President of the Board of Navy Commissioners.) Appointed 1st September, 1823, in recess of the Senate.

SAMUEL L. SOUTHARD, of New Jersey. Appointed 16th September, 1823, in recess of the Senate. Nomination confirmed and appointed 9th December, 1823.

JOHN BRANCH, of North Carolina. Nomination confirmed and appointed 9th March, 1829. Resigned.

LEVI WOODBURY, of New Hampshire, appointed 23d May, 1831, in recess of the Senate. Nomination confirmed and appointed 27th December, 1831. Resigned, to take effect after 30th June, 1834.

MAHLON DICKERSON, of New Jersey. Nomination confirmed and appointed 30th June, 1834. Resigned.

JAMES K. PAULDING, of New York. Nomination confirmed and appointed 20th June 1838, to take effect from 30th June, 1838, when M. Dickerson's resignation took effect.

GEORGE E. BADGER, of North Carolina. Nomination confirmed and appointed 5th March, 1841. Resigned.

ABEL P. UPSHUR, of Virginia. Nomination confirmed and appointed 13th September, 1841.

DAVID HENSHAW, of Massachusetts. Appointed 24th July, 1843, in recess of Senate, and served until 15th January, 1844.

THOMAS W. GILMER, of Virginia. Nomination confirmed and appointed 15th February, 1844, in the place of David Henshaw, rejected by the Senate. (Thomas W. Gilmer, killed 28th February, 1844, by the bursting of a large cannon on board the United States steam-frigate Princeton.)

JOHN Y. MASON, of Virginia. Nomination confirmed and appointed 14th March, 1844, in place of T. W. Gilmer, deceased. Appointed Attorney General 5th March, 1845.

GEORGE BANCROFT, of Massachusetts. Nomination confirmed and appointed 10th March, 1845. Resigned.

OHN Y. MASON, of Virginia. Appointed 9th September, 1846, in recess of the Senate, in the place of George Bancroft, resigned. Nomination confirmed and appointed 17th December, 1846.

[*Continued on page* 404]

POSTMASTER GENERALS.

SAMUEL OSGOOD, of Massachusetts. Nomination confirmed and appointed 26th September, 1789. Resigned.

TIMOTHY PICKERING, of Pennsylvania. Appointed 12th August, 1791, in the recess of the Senate. Nomination confirmed and appointed 7th November, 1791. Appointed 1st June, 1794, in the recess of the Senate, under the act of 8th May, 1794. Nomination confirmed and appointed 11th December, 1794. [Appointed (ex officio) Commissioner to settle affairs with the Indians, 1st March, 1793.] Appointed Secretary of War 2d January, 1795.

JOSEPH HABERSHAM, of Georgia. Nomination confirmed and appointed 25th February, 1795. Resigned.

GIDEON GRANGER, of Connecticut. Appointed 28th November, 1801, in recess of the Senate, in place of J. Habersham, resigned. Nomination confirmed and appointed 26th January, 1802.

RETURN JONATHAN MEIGS, jun'r. (Governor of Ohio.) Nomination confirmed and appointed 17th March, 1814. Resigned.

JOHN McLEAN, of Ohio. Appointed 26th June, 1823, in recess of the Senate. Nomination confirmed and appointed 9th December 1823.

WILLIAM T. BARRY, of Kentucky. Nomination confirmed and appointed 9th March, 1829.

AMOS KENDALL, of Kentucky. Appointed 1st May, 1835, in the recess of the Senate. Nomination confirmed and appointed 15th March, 1836.

JOHN M. NILES, of Connecticut. Nomination confirmed and appointed on 18th, to take effect from 25th May, 1840.

FRANCIS GRANGER, of New York. Nomination confirmed and appointed 6th March, 1841. Resigned.

CHARLES A. WICKLIFFE, of Kentucky. Nomination confirmed and appointed 13th September, 1841. Resigned.

CAVE JOHNSON, of Tennessee. Nomination confirmed and appointed 5th March, 1845.

[*Continued on page* 404.]

ATTORNEY GENERALS.

EDMUND RANDOLPH, of Virginia. Nomination confirmed and appointed 26th September, 1789. Appointed Secretary of State 2d January, 1794.

WILLIAM BRADFORD, of Pennsylvania. Nomination confirmed 27th January, and appointed 28th January, 1794. Died.

CHARLES LEE, of Virginia. Nomination confirmed and appointed 10th December, 1795. Appointed (ex officio) Commissioner to adjust claims of Georgia, 12th February, 1800. Appointed Chief Judge of the Fourth Circuit, &c., 20th February, 1801.

THEOPHILUS PARSONS, of Massachusetts. Nomination confirmed and appointed 20th February, 1801. Declined the appoint ment.

LEVI LINCOLN, of Massachusetts. Nomination confirmed and appointed 5th March, 1801. Resigned in 1805.

ROBERT SMITH, of Maryland. Nomination confirmed and appointed 2d March, 1805.

JOHN BRECKENRIDGE, of Kentucky. Nomination confirmed and appointed 23d December, 1805.

CÆSAR A. RODNEY, of Pennsylvania. Nomination confirmed and appointed 20th January, 1807. Resigned.

WILLIAM PINKNEY, of Maryland. Nomination confirmed and appointed 11th December, 1811.

RICHARD RUSH, of Pennsylvania. Nomination confirmed and appointed 10th February, 1814.

WILLIAM WIRT, of Virginia. Appointed 13th November, 1817, in recess of the Senate. Nomination confirmed and appointed 15th December, 1817.

JOHN MACPHERSON BERRIEN, of Georgia. Nomination confirmed and appointed 9th March, 1829. Resigned.

ROGER BROOKE TANEY, of Maryland. Appointed 20th July, 1831, in the recess of the Senate. Nomination confirmed and appointed 27th December, 1831.

BENJAMIN F. BUTLER, of New York. Appointed 15th November, 1833, in the recess of the Senate. Nomination confirmed and appointed 24th June, 1834. Resigned.

FELIX GRUNDY, of Tennessee. Nomination confirmed and appointed 7th July, 1838, to take effect 1st September, 1838, when resignation of B. F. Butler took effect. Resigned.

HENRY D. GILPIN, of Pennsylvania. Nomination confirmed and appointed 10th January, 1840.

JOHN J. CRITTENDEN, of Kentucky. Nomination confirmed and appointed 5th March, 1841. Resigned.

HUGH S. LEGARE, of South Carolina. Nomination confirmed and appointed 13th September, 1841. Died.

JOHN NELSON, of Maryland. Appointed 1st July, 1843, in the recess of the Senate. Nomination confirmed and appointed 2d January, 1844. Resigned.

JOHN Y. MASON, of Virginia. Nomination confirmed and appointed 5th March, 1845. Resigned. Appointed Secretary of the Navy 9th September, 1846.

NATHAN CLIFFORD, of Maine. Appointed 17th October, 1846, in the recess of the Senate. Nomination confirmed and appointed 23d December, 1846. Resigned.

ISAAC TOUCEY, of Connecticut. Nomination confirmed and appointed 21st June, 1848.

[*Continued on page* 404.]

SECRETARIES OF STATE.

JOHN M. CLAYTON, of Delaware. Nomination confirmed and appointed 7th March, 1849. Resigned.

DANIEL WEBSTER, of Massachusetts. Nomination confirmed and appointed 20th July, 1850. Died.

EDWARD EVERETT, of Massachusetts. Nomination confirmed and appointed 9th December, 1852.

SECRETARIES OF THE TREASURY.

WILLIAM MORRIS MEREDITH, of Pennsylvania. Nomination confirmed and appointed 7th March, 1849. Resigned.

THOMAS CORWIN, of Ohio. Nomination confirmed and appointed 20th June, 1850.

SECRETARIES OF THE INTERIOR.

THOMAS EWING, of Ohio. Nominated and confirmed 7th March, 1849. Resigned.

JAMES A. PEARCE, of Maryland. Nomination confirmed and appointed 20th July, 1850. Declined accepting.

THOMAS M. T. McKENNAN, of Pennsylvania. Nomination confirmed and appointed 15th August, 1850. Resigned.

ALEXANDER H. H. STUART, of Virginia. Nomination confirmed and appointed 12th September, 1850.

SECRETARIES OF WAR.

GEORGE W. CRAWFORD, of Georgia. Nomination confirmed and appointed 7th March, 1849. Resigned.

EDWARD BATES, of Missouri. Nomination confirmed and appointed 20th July, 1850. Declined accepting.

CHARLES M. CONRAD, of Louisiana. Nomination confirmed and appointed 15th August, 1850.

SECRETARIES OF THE NAVY.

WILLIAM BALLARD PRESTON, of Virginia. Nomination confirmed 7th March, 1849. Resigned.

WILLIAM A. GRAHAM, of North Carolina. Nomination confirmed and appointed 20th July, 1850. Resigned.

JOHN P. KENNEDY, of Maryland. Nomination confirmed and appointed 22d July, 1852.

ATTORNEY GENERALS.

REVERDY JOHNSON, of Maryland. Nominated and confirmed 7th March, 1849. Resigned.

JOHN J. CRITTENDEN, of Kentucky. Nomination confirmed and appointed 20th July, 1850.

POSTMASTER GENERALS.

JACOB COLLAMER, of Vermont. Nominated and confirmed 7th March. 1849. Resigned.

NATHAN K. HALL, of New York. Nomination confirmed and appointed 20th July, 1850. Resigned.

SAMUEL D. HUBBARD, of Connecticut. Nomination confirmed and appointed 31st August, 1852.

CHAPTER 10.

THE UNITED STATES OF AMERICA.

CHRONOLOGICAL statement of the formation of the governments of the several STATES; of their becoming members of the Union by their adoption or ratification of the Constitution of the United States, or by their admission as States since the establishment of the Constitution; with a particular account of the progress of each of the latter, either from the condition of territorial dependencies, or independent governments, to the rank of STATES.

MONDAY, SEPTEMBER 5, 1774.

A number of Delegates, chosen and appointed by the several Colonies and Provinces in North America, met to hold a Congress at Philadelphia, and assembled in Carpenter's Hall.

TUESDAY, SEPTEMBER 6, 1774.

Resolved, That in determining questions in this Congress, each Colony or Province shall have one vote—The Congress not being possessed of, or at present able to procure proper materials for ascertaining the importance of each Colony.

[This principle was confirmed by the Articles of Confederation which declared that, "In determining questions in the United States, in Congress assembled, each State shall have one vote." And they further declared that certain enumerated powers should never be determined by Congress, "unless nine States assent to the same: nor shall a question on any other point, except for adjourning from day to day, be determined, unless by the votes of a majority of the United States in Congress assembled."—These extracts show the relative authority or importance of the several States in the exercise of the sovereign power under the Confederation.]

TUESDAY, JULY 2, 1776.

Resolved, That these United Colonies are, and, of right, ought to be, Free and Independent States; that they are absolved from all allegiance to the British crown, and that all political connexion between them, and the State of Great Britain, is, and ought to be, totally dissolved.

THURSDAY, JULY 4, 1776.

The Congress agreed to A DECLARATION OF INDEPENDENCE BY THE REPRESENTATIVES OF THE UNITED STATES OF AMERICA, IN CONGRESS ASSEMBLED, to be signed by the members from the several States, which will be found in this volume.

MONDAY, SEPTEMBER 9, 1776.

Resolved, That in all continental commissions, and other instruments, where, heretofore, the words "United Colonies" have been used, the style be altered, for the future, to the UNITED STATES.

SATURDAY, NOVEMBER 15, 1777.

The Articles of Confederation and perpetual Union of the United States of America were agreed to by the Delegates of the thirteen original States in Congress assembled, subject to the ratification of the Legislatures of the several States.

These articles were ratified by 8 States on the 9th July, 1778.
Ditto. . . . . . . 1 State . . 21st July, 1778.
Ditto. . . . . . . 1 State . . . 24th July, 1778.
Ditto. . . . . . . 1 State . . 26th Nov. 1778.
Ditto. . . . . . . 1 State . . . 22d Feb., 1779.
Ditto. . . . . . . 1 State . . 1st March, 1781.

The ratification was therefore completed on the 1st March, 1781,* the articles being dated the 9th July, 1778, and this completed the *bond of union* of the thirteen original States, whose delegates assembled in Congress continued to legislate and execute the powers of the United States under the Articles of Confederation until the 4th March, 1789, when, by their resolution of the 13th September, 1788, the Constitution of the United States, also adopted and ratified by the people of the said original States, went into operation,

* Vide the notes under "Ohio" for the cause of the delay on the part of Maryland to ratify the Articles of Confederation until March 1, 1781.

forming thereby a more perfect UNION OF THE PEOPLE FOR THE GOVERNMENT OF THE UNITED STATES OF AMERICA.

The thirteen original States that formed and confirmed the Union by the adoption of the Constitution, are as follows :—

NEW HAMPSHIRE.

Embraced under the charters of Massachusetts, and continued under the same jurisdiction until September 18, 1679, when a separate charter and government was granted. A Constitution was formed on January 5, 1776, which was altered in 1784, and was further altered and amended on February 13, 1792.

This State ratified the Constitution of the United States, June 21, 1788.

MASSACHUSETTS.

Settled under compacts of the emigrants of November 3, 1620, and chartered on March 4, 1629; also chartered January 13, 1630; an explanatory charter granted August 20, 1726, and more completely chartered on October 7, 1731; formed a Constitution on March 2, 1780, which was altered and amended on November 3, 1820.

Ratified the Constitution of the United States, February 6, 1788.

RHODE ISLAND.

Embraced under the charters of Massachusetts, and continued under the same jurisdiction until July 8, 1662, when a separate charter was granted, which continued in force until a Constitution was formed in September, 1842.

Ratified the Constitution of the United States, May 29, 1790.

CONNECTICUT.

Embraced under the charters of Massachusetts, and continued under the same jurisdiction until April 23, 1662, when a separate charter was granted, which continued in force until a Constitution was formed on September 15, 1818.

Ratified the Constitution of the United States, January 9, 1788.

NEW YORK.

Granted to Duke of York, March 20, 1664; April 26, 1664; June 24, 1664. Newly patented on February 9, 1674; formed a Constitution on April 20, 1777, which was amended on October 27, 1801, and further amended November 10, 1821. A new Constitution was formed in 1846.

Ratified the Constitution of the United States, July 26, 1788.

NEW JERSEY.

Held under same grants as New York; separated into East and West Jersey on March 3, 1677. The government surrendered to the Crown in 1702, and so continued until the formation of a Constitution on July 2, 1776.

Ratified the Constitution of the United States, December 18, 1787.

PENNSYLVANIA.

Chartered on February 28, 1681; formed a Constitution on September 28, 1776; amended, &c., on September 2, 1790.

Ratified the Constitution of the United States, December 12, 1787.

DELAWARE.

Embraced in the charter, and continued under the government of Pennsylvania until the formation of a Constitution on September 20, 1776; a new Constitution formed on June 12, 1792.

Ratified the Constitution of the United States, December 7, 1787.

MARYLAND.

Chartered on June 20, 1632; formed a Constitution August 14, 1776, which was amended in 1795 and 1799, and further amended in November, 1812.

Ratified the Constitution of the United States, April 28, 1788.

VIRGINIA.

Chartered April 10, 1606, May 23, 1609, and March 12, 1312; formed a Constitution on July 5, 1776; amended January 15, 1830.

Ratified the Constitution of the United States, June 26, 1788.

NORTH CAROLINA.

Chartered in March 20, 1663, and June 30, 1665; formed a Constitution, December 18, 1776, which was amended in 1835.

Ratified the Constitution of the United States, November 21, 1789.

SOUTH CAROLINA.

Embraced in the charters of Carolina or North Carolina, from which it was separated in 1729; formed a Constitution March 26, 1776, which was amended on March 19, 1778, and June 3, 1790.

Ratified the Constitution of the United States, May 23, 1788.

GEORGIA.

Chartered on June 9, 1732; formed a Constitution on February 5, 1777, a second in 1785, and a third on May 30. 1798.

Ratified the Constitution of the United States, January 2, 1788.

The privilege of becoming members of the American Union by the mere ratification of the Constitution, was reserved to those States alone that were parties to the previous confederation and the compact or convention by which the Constitution was formed. The ratification of nine States being sufficient for the establishment of the Constitution; and, it having been ratified by eleven States, it was determined by Congress, on the 13th September,

1788, under the resolutions of the convention, that the Constitution had been established, and that it should go into operation on the first Wednesday (4th day) of March, 1789.—It therefore appears that two of the States did not ratify the Constitution until after its establishment, yet they were not treated as new States, requiring particular forms of admission, but their Senators and Representatives, as provided for in the 2d sect. 1st art. of the Constitution, were admitted in Congress upon the presentation of their authenticated forms of ratification. It was considered necessary, however, that the laws of the United States passed previous to their accession should be extended to them by special acts.

The Union having been thus completed, and its Constitution and government established, the United States under the 3d section of the 4th article of the Constitution reserved to themselves, in Congress assembled, the right and the power to admit new States, by declaring that "New States *may* be admitted by the Congress into this Union;" and, as the 4th section of the same article requires, that "The United States shall guarantee to every State in this Union a Republican form of government," it has in practice been deemed a pre-requisite that the people proposing to form a new State be authorized by law to form a Constitution, to be submitted to Congress, to enable that body to judge of its Republican character, before proceeding to exercise that high and sovereign power of admitting a distinct community of people to the inestimable rights, privileges, and immunities, secured by the organization of a State government,—and upon an equal footing, in all respects whatsoever, with those States that jointly achieved the independence of the country, and which, together with those that have become members of the Union since that eventful period, have borne the hardships, trials, and difficulties, both internal and external, through which the nation has passed, and which have secured the stability, power, and happiness of the country.

The Constitution of the United States declares, that "new States may be admitted by the Congress into this Union; but no new State shall be formed or erected within the jurisdiction of any other State, nor any State be formed by the junction of two or more

States, or parts of States, without the consent of the legislatures of the States concerned as well as of the Congress."

Upon this clause, James Madison, in the "Federalist," makes the following remarks:—

"In the articles of Confederation, no provision is found on this important subject. Canada was to be admitted of right, on her joining in the measures of the United States; and the other *colonies*, by which were evidently meant, the other British Colonies, at the discretion of nine States. The eventual establishment of new States seems to have been overlooked by the compilers of that instrument. We have seen the inconvenience of this omission, and the assumption of power into which Congress have been led by it. With great propriety, therefore, has the new system supplied the defect. The general precaution, that no new State shall be formed without the concurrence of the Federal authority, and that of the States concerned, is consonant to the principles which ought to govern such transactions. The particular precaution against the erection of new States, by the partition of a State without its consent, quiets the jealousy of the larger States; as that of the smaller is quieted by a like precaution, against a junction of States without their consent."

The Constitution also declares that "the Congress shall have power to dispose of, and make all needful rules and regulations respecting the territory or other property belonging to the United States; and nothing in this Constitution shall be so construed as to prejudice any claims of the United States, or of any particular State."

Under this clause, Congress exercises the power of creating territorial governments, which in process of time, by the increase of population and other concurrent causes, apply, on behalf of the people, for authority to form constitutions and state governments, with a view to admission into the Union, at a future period, and it is for the Congress of the United States in the exercise of their high constitutional powers, and under the solemn responsibilities imposed upon them as guardians of the rights and the welfare of the whole Union, to judge of the expediency and the time of admitting the *people* who may have become inhabitants of such territories, to all the peculiar and inestimable rights, privileges, and immunities of the *citizens* of one of the United States of America. Mr. Madison remarks upon this point that,

"This is a power of very great importance, and required by considerations similar to those which show the propriety of the former. The proviso annexed is very proper in itself, and was probably rendered absolutely necessary by jealousies and questions concerning the western territory sufficiently known to the public."

But the Constitution requires that "The United States shall guarantee to every State in this Union a Republican Form of Government, and shall protect each of them against Invasion; and on Application of the Legislature, or of the Executive, (when the Legislature cannot be convened,) against domestic Violence." And, upon this clause, Mr. Madison has expressed in the "Federalist" the following wise and just sentiments:

"In a Confederacy founded on republican principles, and composed of republican members, the superintending government ought clearly to possess authority to defend the system against aristocratic or monarchical innovations. The more intimate the nature of such a Union may be, the greater interest have the members in the political institutions of each other; and the greater right to insist, that the forms of government under which the compact was entered into, should be *substantially* maintained.

"But a right implies a remedy; and where else could the remedy be deposited, than where it is deposited by the Constitution? Governments of dissimilar principles and forms have been found less adapted to a federal coalition of any sort than those of a kindred nature. 'As the confederate republic of Germany,' says Montesquieu, 'consists of free cities and petty States, subject to different princes, experience shows us, that it is more imperfect than that of Holland and Switzerland.' 'Greece was undone,' he adds, 'as soon as the king of Macedon obtained a seat among the Amphictyons.' In the latter case, no doubt, the disproportionate force, as well as the monarchical form of the new confederate, had its share of influence on the events.

"It may possibly be asked, what need there could be of such a precaution, and whether it may not become a pretext for alterations in the State governments, without the concurrence of the States themselves. These questions admit of ready answers. If the interposition of the General Government should not be needed, the provision for such an event will be a harmless superfluity only in the Constitution. But who can say what experiments may be produced by the caprice of particular

States, by the ambition of enterprising leaders, or by the intrigues and influence of foreign powers?

"To the second question it may be answered, that if the General Government should interpose by virtue of this Constitutional authority, it will be of course bound to pursue the authority. But the authority extends no farther than to a *guarantee* of a republican form of government, which supposes a pre-existing government of the form which is to be guarantied. As long therefore as the existing republican forms are continued by the States, they are guarantied by the Federal Constitution. Whenever the States may choose to substitute other republican forms, they have a right to do so, and to claim the Federal guarantee for the latter. The only restriction imposed on them is, that they shall not exchange republican for anti-republican constitutions; a restriction which, it is presumed, will hardly be considered as a grievance."

THE "NEW STATES,"

ADMITTED INTO THE UNION SINCE THE ADOPTION OF THE CONSTITUTION OF THE UNITED STATES, ARE AS FOLLOWS:—

VERMONT,

Formed from part of the territory of New York, with the consent of its Legislature, by act of March 6, 1790. (Vide Journal Senate of the United States, Feb. 9, 1791, and appendix to Journal House of Representatives, vol. 1, p. 412.) Application of the Commissioners of Vermont to Congress for admission into the Union was received at Philadelphia, Feb. 9, 1791, a constitution having been formed Dec. 25, 1777. Vermont admitted by act of Congress approved Feb. 18, 1791, to take effect, i. e., "shall be received and admitted," on **March 4, 1791.**

Entitled to two Representatives by act of Congress Feb. 25, 1791.

An act giving effect to laws of the United States in Vermont, after March 3, 1791, approved March 2, 1791.

A constitution adopted by Vermont, July 9, 1793.

KENTUCKY,

Formed from the territory of Virginia with the consent of its Legislature by act of Dec. 18, 1789. (Vide Journal Senate of the United States, Dec. 9, 1790, and Bioren & Duane's edition Laws of the United States, vol. 1, page 673; and message or speech of President to Congress, Dec. 8, 1790.) Application of the convention of Kentucky received, Dec. 9, 1790. (See Journal House of Representatives, vol. 1, p. 411, appendix.) (Its constitution not then formed.) Act of Congress for its reception and admission on **June 1, 1792,** approved on Feb. 4, 1791.

Entitled to two Representatives, by act of Congress Feb. 25, 1791.

(No act giving effect to laws of the United States in Kentucky.)

A copy of the constitution formed for the State of Kentucky laid before Congress by the President of the United States, on November 7, 1792. A new constitution was adopted on August 17, 1799.

TENNESSEE,

Formed of territory ceded to the United States by the State of North Carolina, by act of December, 1789, conveyed to the United States by the Senators from North Carolina, Feb. 25, 1790, and accepted by act of Congress of April 2, 1790. An act for the government of the territory of the United States south of the river Ohio, was approved 26 May, 1790. See also act of 8 May, 1792. The people of that territory formed a convention, adopted a constitution on Feb. 6, 1796, and applied for admission, (vide Journal House of Representatives, April 8, and Senate Journal, April 11, 1796, and folio State Papers, "Miscellaneous," vol. 1, pp. 146—7, 150,) upon which "an act for the admission of the State of Tennessee into the Union was passed and approved, **June 1, 1796,** by which the laws of the United States were extended to that State, and it was allowed one Representative in Congress.

The said laws were again extended to the State of Tennessee by an act approved January 31, 1797, and by an act approved February 19, 1799. (This last act divided the State into Eastern and Western Districts.)

OHIO,

Formed out of a part of the territory north-west of the river Ohio, which was ceded to the United States by the General Assembly of Virginia, at their sessions begun October 20, 1783, and accepted by the Congress of the United States, March 1, 1784. The act of Virginia was modified by act of Assembly of December 30, 1788, consenting that the territory be divided into not more than five, nor less than three, States. An act to provide for the government of the territory north-west of the river Ohio, was approved on August 7, 1789. This territory was divided into two separate governments by act of Congress of May 7, 1800.

The census of the territory, and petitions from the people thereof, referred to committee of the House of Representatives. (See Journal, January 29, 1802. See report March 4, 1802, folio State Papers, "Miscellaneous," vol. 1, p. 325.) An act to enable the people of the eastern division of said territory to form a constitution and State government was passed and approved April 30, 1802, by which that State was allowed one Representative in Congress. A constitution was accordingly formed on November 1, 1802, and presented to Congress. (See Journal Senate, January 7, 1803.)

The said people having, on **November 29, 1802,** complied with the act of Congress, of April 30, 1802, whereby the said State became one of the United States, an act was passed and approved on February 19, 1803, for the due execution of the laws of the United States, &c., within that State.

An act in addition to, and in modification of, the propositions contained in the act of April 30, 1802, was passed and approved on March 3d, 1803.

NORTH-WESTERN AND WESTERN TERRITORY.

OHIO being the first State formed out of the territory north-west of the river Ohio, and admitted into the Union, it is deemed proper to insert here the circumstances and facts which led to the cession of that territory, and the principles agreed upon and established for the rule of its future government, which will apply equally to the other States formed out of this territory.

Preliminary to the "Ordinance for the government of the Territory of the United States north-west of the river Ohio, it may be proper to refer to the acts and proceedings which led to the cession of this and other territory to the United States by individual States; to the acts of cession themselves, and to other acts having a direct bearing upon this interesting subject.

The attention of the whole country appears to have been first drawn to the subject, in a forcible manner, by the decided stand taken by the State of Maryland, during the discussion in the Congress upon the objections of certain States to the articles of Confederation, in June, 1778. That State proposed, on the 22d June, 1778, and afterwards insisted, that the boundaries of each of the States, as claimed to extend to the river Mississippi, or South Sea, should be ascertained and restricted, and that the property in the soil of the western territories be held for the common benefit of all the States. From that time until 2d February, 1781, the State of Maryland refused to accede to the articles of Confederation, in consequence of having failed to obtain an amendment upon that point, against which course Virginia had remonstrated.

On the 25th November, 1778, the act of New Jersey for ratifying the articles of Confederation was presented, in which this and other difficulties were referred to; but their delegates were directed to sign those articles, "in the firm reliance that the candour and justice of the several States will, in due time, remove as far as possible the inequality which now subsists."

The delegate from Delaware having signed the articles of Confederation on the 22d February, 1779, presented on the 23d sundry resolutions passed by the Legislature of that State, among which were the following:

"*Resolved*, That this State thinks it necessary, for the peace and safety of the States to be included in the Union, that a moderate extent of limits should be assigned for such of those States as claim to the Mississippi or South Sea; and that the United States in Congress assembled, should, and ought to have the power of fixing their western limits."

"*Resolved*, That this State consider themselves justly entitled to a right, in common with the members of the Union, to that extensive tract of country which lies westward of the frontiers of the United States, the property of which was not vested in, or granted to, individuals at the commencement of the present war:—That the same hath been, or may be, gained from the King of Great Britain, or the native Indians, by the blood and treasure of all, and ought therefore to be a common estate, to be granted out on terms beneficial to the United States."

Upon which Congress passed the following resolution on the said 23d February, 1779, eight States voting in favor, and three against the same, viz.:

"*Resolved*, That the paper laid before Congress by the delegate from Delaware, and read, be filed; provided, that it shall never be considered as admitting any claim by the same set up or intended to be set up."

On the 21st May, 1779, the delegates from Maryland laid before Congress the following instructions received by them:

Instructions of the General Assembly of Maryland, to George Plater, William Paca, William Carmichael, John Henry, James Forbes, and Daniel of St. Thomas Jenifer, esquires.

Gentlemen:

Having conferred upon you a trust of the highest nature, it is evident we place great confidence in your integrity, abilities, and zeal to promote the general welfare of the United States, and the particular interest of this State, where the latter is not incompatible with the former; but, to add greater weight to your proceedings in Congress, and take away all suspicion that the opinions you there deliver, and the votes you give, may be the mere opinions of individuals, and not resulting from your knowledge of the sense and deliberate judgment of the State you represent, we think it our duty to instruct as followeth on the subject of the Confederation—a subject in which, unfortunately, a supposed difference of interest has produced an almost equal division of sentiments among the several States composing the Union. We say a supposed difference of interests; for if local attachments and prejudices, and the avarice and ambition of individuals, would give way to the dictates of a sound policy, founded on the principles of justice, (and no other policy but what is founded on those immutable principles deserves to be called sound,) we flatter ourselves this apparent diversity of interests would soon vanish, and all the States would confederate on terms mutually advantageous to all; for they would then perceive that no other confederation than one so formed can be lasting, Although the pressure of immediate calamities, the dread of their continuance from the appearance of disunion, and some other peculiar circumstances, may have induced some States to accede to the present Confederation, contrary to their own interests and judgments, it requires no great share of foresight to predict, that, when those causes cease to operate, the States which have thus acceded to the Confederation will consider it as no longer binding, and will eagerly embrace the first occasion of asserting their just rights, and securing their independence. Is it possible that those States who are ambitiously grasping at territories to which, in our judgment, they have not the least shadow of exclusive right, will use with greater moderation the increase of wealth and power derived from those territories, when acquired, than what they have displayed in their endeavors to acquire them? We think not. We are convinced the same spirit which hath prompted them to insist on a claim so extravagant, so repugnant to every principle of justice, so incompatible with the general welfare of all the States, will urge them on to add oppression to injustice. If they should not be incited by a superiority of wealth and strength to oppress by open force their less wealthy and less powerful neighbors, yet depopulation, and consequently the impoverishment of those States, will necessarily follow, which, by an unfair construction of the Confederation, may be stripped of a common interest, and the common benefits derivable from the western country. Suppose, for instance, Virginia indisputably possessed of the extensive and fertile country to which she has set up a claim: what would be the probable consequences to Maryland of such an undisturbed and undisputed possession? They cannot escape the least discerning.

Virginia, by selling on the most moderate terms a small proportion of the lands in question, would draw into her treasury vast sums of money and, in proportion to the sums arising from such sales, would be enabled to lessen her taxes. Lands comparatively cheap, and taxes comparatively low, with the lands and taxes of an adjacent State, would quickly drain the State thus disadvantageously circumstanced of its most useful inhabitants: its wealth, and its consequence in the scale of the confederated States, would sink, of course. A claim so injurious to more than one-half, if not to the whole of the United States, ought to be supported by the clearest evidence of the right. Yet what evidences of that right have been produced? What arguments alleged in support either of the evidence or the right? None that we have heard of deserving a serious refutation.

It has been said, that some of the delegates of a neighboring State have declared their opinion of the impracticability of governing the extensive dominion claimed by that State. Hence also the necessity was admitted of dividing its territory, and erecting a new State, under the auspices and direction of the elder, from whom, no doubt, it would receive its form of government, to whom it would be bound by some alliance or confederacy, and by whose councils it would be influenced. Such a measure, if ever attempted, would certainly be opposed by the other States as inconsistent with the letter and spirit of the proposed Confederation. Should it take place by establishing a sub-confederacy, imperium in imperio, the State possessed of this extensive dominion must then either submit to all the inconveniences of an overgrown and unwieldy government, or suffer the authority of Congress to interpose, at a future time, and to lop off a part of its territory, to be erected into a new and free State, and admitted into a confederation on such conditions as shall be settled by nine States. If it is necessary, for the happiness and tranquillity of a State thus overgrown, that Congress should hereafter interfere and divide its territory, why is the claim to that territory now made, and so pertinaciously insisted on? We can suggest to ourselves but two motives: either the declaration of relinquishing, at some future period, a proportion of the country now contended for, was made to lull suspicion asleep, and to cover the designs of a secret ambition, or, if the thought was seriously entertained, the lands are now claimed to reap an immediate profit from the sale. We are convinced, policy and justice require that a country unsettled at the commencement of this war, claimed by the British crown, and ceded to it by the treaty of Paris, if wrested from the common enemy by the blood and treasure of the thirteen States, should be considered as a common property, subject to be parcelled out by Congress into free, convenient, and independent governments, in such manner and at such times as the wisdom of that assembly shall hereafter direct.

Thus convinced, we should betray the trust reposed in us by our constituents, were we to authorize you to ratify on their behalf the Confederation, unless it be farther explained. We have coolly and dispassionately considered the subject; we have weighed probable inconveniences and hardships, against the sacrifice of just and essential rights; and do instruct you not to agree to the Confederation, unless an article or articles be added thereto in conformity with our declaration. Should we succeed in obtaining such article or articles, then you are hereby fully empowered to accede to the Confederation.

That these our sentiments respecting our Confederation may be more publicly known, and more explicitly and concisely declared, we have drawn up the annexed declaration, which we instruct you to lay before Congress, to have it printed, and to deliver to each of the delegates of the other States in Congress assembled, copies thereof, signed by yourselves, or by such of you as may be present at the time of delivery; to the intent and purpose that the copies aforesaid may be communicated to our brethren of the United States, and the contents of the said declaration taken into their serious and candid consideration.

Also we desire and instruct you to move, at a proper time, that these instructions be read to Congress by their secretary, and entered on the journals of Congress.

We have spoken with freedom, as becomes freemen; and we sincerely wish that these our representations may make such an impression on that assembly as to induce them to make such addition to the Articles of Confederation as may bring about a permanent union.

A true copy from the proceeding of December 15, 1778.

Test: T. DUCKETT, *C. H. D.*

On the 30th October, 1779, Congress, by a vote of eight States to three, and one being divided, passed the following:

Whereas the appropriation of vacant lands by the several States, during the continuance of the war, will, in the opinion of Congress, be attended with great mischiefs: therefore,

Resolved, That it be earnestly recommended to the State of Virginia to reconsider their late act of Assembly for opening their land office; and that it be recommended to the said State, and all other States similarly circumstanced, to forbear settling or issuing warrants for unappropriated lands, or granting the same during the continuance of the present war.

On the 7th March, 1780, the delegates from New York presented the following act, (which was fully carried into effect by said delegates in Congress on 1st March, 1781 :)

AN ACT to facilitate the completion of the Articles of Confederation and perpetual Union among the United States of America.

Whereas nothing under divine Providence can more effectually contribute to the tranquillity and safety of the United States of America than a federal alliance, on such liberal principles as will give satisfaction to its respective members: And whereas the Articles of Confederation and perpetual Union recommended by the honorable the Congress of the United States of America have not proved acceptable to all the States, it having been conceived that a portion of the waste and uncultivated territory within the limits or claims of certain States ought to be appropriated as a common fund for the expenses of the war: And the people of the State of New York being on all occasions disposed to manifest their regard for their sister States, and their earnest desire to promote the general interest and security, and more especially to accelerate the federal alliance, by removing, as far as it depends upon them, the beforementioned impediment to its final accomplishment:

Be it therefore enacted, by the people of the State of New York, represented in Senate and Assembly, and it is hereby enacted, by the authority of the same, That it shall and may be lawful to and for the delegates of this State in the honorable Congress of the United States of America, or the major part of such of them as shall be assembled in Congress, and they, the said delegates, or a major part of them, so assembled, are hereby fully authorized and empowered, for and on behalf of this State, and by proper and authentic acts or instruments, to limit and restrict the boundaries of this State, in the western parts thereof, by such line or lines, and in such manner and form, as they shall judge to be expedient, either with respect to the jurisdiction, as well as the right or pre-emption of soil, or reserving the jurisdiction in part, or in the whole, over the lands which may be ceded, or relinquished, with respect only to the right or pre-emption of the soil.

And be it further enacted by the authority aforesaid, That the territory which may be ceded or relinquished by virtue of this act, either with respect to the jurisdiction, as well as the right or pre-emption of soil, or the right or pre-emption of soil only, shall be and enure for the use and benefit of such of the United States as shall become members of the federal alliance of the said States, and for no other use or purpose whatever.

And be it further enacted by the authority aforesaid, That all the lands to be ceded and relinquished by virtue of this act, for the benefit of the United States, with respect to property, but which shall nevertheless remain under the jurisdiction of this State, shall be disposed of and appropriated in such manner only as the Congress of the said States shall direct; and that a warrant under the authority of Congress for surveying and laying out any part thereof, shall entitle the party in whose favor it shall issue to cause the same to be surveyed and laid out and returned, according to the directions of such warrant; and thereupon letters patent, under the great seal of this State, shall pass to the grantee for the estate specified in the said warrant; for which no other fee or reward shall be demanded or received than such as shall be allowed by Congress.

Provided always, and be it further enacted by the authority aforesaid, That the trust reposed by virtue of this act shall not be executed by the delegates of this State, unless at least three of the said delegates shall be present in Congress.

STATE OF NEW YORK, ss.

I do hereby certify that the aforegoing is a true copy of the original act passed the 19th of February, 1780, and lodged in the secretary's office.

ROBERT HARPUR, *Deputy Sec'y of State.*

In view of the premises, the following proceedings took place:

IN CONGRESS OF THE CONFEDERATION.

WEDNESDAY, SEPTEMBER 6, 1780.

Congress took into consideration the report of the committee to whom were referred the instructions of the General Assembly of Maryland to their delegates in Congress, respecting the Articles of Confederation, and the declaration therein referred to; the act of the Legislature of New York on the same subject, and the remonstrance of the General Assembly of Virginia; which report was agreed to, and is in the words following:

That having duly considered the several matters to them submitted, they conceive it unnecessary to examine into the merits or policy of the instructions or declarations of the General Assembly of Maryland, or of the remonstrance of the General Assembly of Virginia, as they involve questions, a discussion of which was declined, on mature consideration, when the Articles of Confederation were debated; nor in the opinion of the committee, can such questions be now revived with any prospect of conciliation; that it appears more advisable to press upon those states which can remove the embarrassments respecting the western country, a liberal surrender of a portion of their territorial claims, since they cannot be preserved entire without endangering the stability of the general confederacy; to remind them how indispensably necessary it is to establish the Federal Union on a fixed and permanent basis, and on principles acceptable to all its respective members; how essential to public credit and confidence, to the support of our army, to the vigor of our councils, and success of our measures; to our tranquillity at home, our reputation abroad, to our very existence as a free, sovereign, and independent people; that they are fully persuaded the wisdom of the respective legislatures will lead them to a full and impartial consideration of a subject so interesting to the United States, and so necessary to the happy establishment of the Federal Union; that they are confirmed in these expectations by a review of the before-mentioned act of the Legislature of New York, submitted to their consideration; that this act is expressly calculated to accelerate the Federal Alliance, by removing, as far as depends on that State, the impediment arising from the western country, and for that purpose to yield up a portion of territorial claim for the general benefit; Whereupon,

Resolved, That copies of the several papers referred to the committee be transmitted, with a copy of the report, to the legislatures of the several States, and that it be *earnestly recommended to those States, who have claims to the western country, to pass such laws, and give their delegates in Congress such powers as may effectually remove the only obstacle to a final ratification of the articles of Confederation;* and that the Legislature of Maryland be earnestly requested to authorize the delegates in Congress to subscribe the said articles.

IN CONGRESS OF THE CONFEDERATION.

TUESDAY, OCTOBER 10, 1780.

Resolved, That the unappropriated lands that may be ceded or relinquished to the United States, by any particular State, pursuant to the recommendation of Congress of the 6th day of September last, shall be disposed of for the common benefit of the United States, and be settled and formed into distinct republican States, which shall become members of the Federal Union, and have the same rights of sovereignty, freedom, and independence, as the other States: that each State which shall be so formed shall contain a suitable extent of territory, not less than one hundred nor more than one hundred and fifty miles square, or as near thereto as circumstances will admit: that the necessary and reasonable expenses which any particular State shall have incurred since the commencement of the present war, in subduing any British posts, or in maintaining forts or garrisons within and for the defence, or in acquiring any part of the territory that may be ceded or relinquished to the United States, shall be reimbursed.

That the said lands shall be granted or settled at such times, and under such regulations, as shall hereafter be agreed on by the United States, in Congress assembled, or any nine or more of them.

In pursuance of the recommendation contained in the resolution of Congress of the 6th September, 1780, the following States made cessions of territory to the United States at the dates respectively stated:—

The State of New York, on March 1, 1781.
" Virginia " March 1, 1784.
" do. " Dec. 30, 1788. By this act Virginia agreed to change the conditions of the act of cession of 1784 only so far as to ratify the 5th article of the compact or ordinance of 1787, on page 420.
" Massachusetts, on April 19, 1785.
" Connecticut " September 14, 1786, confirmed May 30, 1800.
" South Carolina " August 9, 1787.
" North Carolina " February 25, 1790.
" Georgia " April 24, 1802.

For these cessions, &c., and for the convention between South Carolina and Georgia, of 28th April, 1787, see Bioren and Duane's edition of the Laws of the United States, Vol. 1.

In relation to the government of the territory thus acquired by the United States, it may be sufficient to say, that the territory ceded by each state, except Virginia, was the subject of separate legislation by Congress, (as mentioned under the head of each of said States,) first as a dependent territory, and afterwards by being admitted into the Union as an independent member thereof.

The North-western Territory, ceded by the Commonwealth of Virginia, was the subject of special legislation by the Congress of the Confederation; first, by the passage of a resolution for its government, on the 23d April, 1784, and then by the adoption of an ordinance, whose importance renders its insertion here necessary:—

AN ORDINANCE for the Government of the Territory of the United States, north-west of the river Ohio.

Be it ordained by the United States in Congress assembled, That the said territory, for the purposes of temporary government, be one district; subject, however, to be divided into two districts, as future circumstances may, in the opinion of Congress, make it expedient.

Be it ordained by the authority aforesaid, That the estates both of resident and non-resident proprietors in the said territory, dying intestate, shall descend to and be distributed among their children and the descendants of a deceased child in equal parts; the descendants of a deceased child or grandchild to take the share of their deceased parent in equal parts among them; and where there shall be no children or descendants, then in equal parts to the next of kin, in equal degree; and among collaterals, the children of a deceased brother or sister of the intestate shall have in equal parts among them their deceased parent's share; and there shall in no case be a distinction between kindred of the whole and half blood; saving in all cases to the widow of the intestate her third part of the real estate for life, and one-third part of the personal estate; and this law relative to descents and dower shall remain in full force until altered by the legislature of the district. And until the governor and judges shall adopt laws as hereinafter mentioned, estates in the said territory may be devised or bequeathed by wills in writing, signed and sealed by him or her in whom the estate may be, (being of full age,) and attested by three witnesses; and real estates may be conveyed by lease and release, or bargain and sale, signed, sealed, and delivered by the person, being of full age, in whom the estate may be, and attested by two witnesses, provided such wills be duly proved, and such conveyances be acknowledged, or the execution thereof duly proved, and be recorded within one year after proper magistrates, courts, and registers shall be appointed for that purpose; and personal property may be transferred by delivery, saving, however, to the French and Canadian inhabitants, and other settlers of the Kaskaskies, Saint Vincent's, and the neighboring villages, who have heretofore professed themselves citizens of Virginia, their laws and customs now in force among them relative to the descent and conveyance of property.

Be it ordained by the authority aforesaid, That there shall be appointed from time to time, by Congress, a governor, whose commission shall continue in force for the term of three years, unless sooner revoked by Congress; he shall reside in the district, and have a freehold estate therein, in one thousand acres of land, while in the exercise of his office.

There shall be appointed from time to time, by Congress, a secretary, whose commission shall continue in force for four years, unless sooner revoked; he shall reside in the district, and have a freehold estate therein, in five hundred acres of land, while in the exercise of his office. It shall be his duty to keep and preserve the acts and laws passed by the legislature, and the public records of the district, and the proceedings of the governor in his executive department, and transmit authentic copies of such acts and proceedings every six months to the secretary of Congress. There shall also be appointed a court, to consist of three judges, any two of whom to form a court, who shall have a common-law jurisdiction, and reside in the district, and have each therein a freehold estate in five hundred acres of land, while in the exercise of their offices; and their commissions shall continue in force during good behavior.

The governor and judges, or a majority of them, shall adopt and publish in the district such laws of the original States, criminal and civil, as may be necessary and best suited to the circumstances of the district, and report them to Congress from time to time, which laws shall be in force in the district until the organization of the General Assembly therein, unless disapproved of by Congress; but afterwards, the legislature shall have authority to alter them as they shall think fit.

The governor, for the time being, shall be commander-in-chief of the militia, appoint and commission all officers in the same below the rank of general officers; all general officers shall be appointed and commissioned by Congress.

Previous to the organization of the General Assembly, the governor shall appoint such magistrates and other civil officers, in each county or township, as he shall find necessary for the preservation of the peace and good order in the same. After the General Assembly shall be organized, the powers and duties of magistrates and other civil officers shall be regulated and defined by the said Assembly; but all magistrates and other civil officers, not herein otherwise directed, shall, during the continuance of this temporary government, be appointed by the governor.

For the prevention of crimes and injuries, the laws to be adopted or made shall have force in all parts of the district, and for the execution of process, criminal and civil, the governor shall make proper divisions thereof; and he shall proceed from time to time, as circumstances may require, to lay out the parts of the district in which the Indian titles shall have been extinguished into counties and townships, subject, however, to such alterations as may thereafter be made by the legislature.

So soon as there shall be five thousand free male inhabitants, of full age, in the district, upon giving proof thereof to the governor, they shall receive authority, with time and place, to elect representatives from their counties or townships, to represent them in the General Assembly; provided that, for every five hundred free male inhabitants, there shall be one representative, and so on progressively with the number of free male inhabitants shall the right of representation increase, until the number of representatives shall amount to twenty-five, after which the number and proportion of representatives shall be regulated by the legislature; provided that no person be eligible or qualified to act as a representative unless he shall have been a citizen of one of the United States three years, and be a resident in the district, or unless he shall have resided in the district three years, and in either case shall likewise hold in his own right, in fee-simple, two hundred acres of land within the same: Provided also, that a freehold in fifty acres of land in the district, having been a citizen of one of the States, and being resident in the district, or the like freehold and two years' residence in the district, shall be necessary to qualify a man as an elector of a representative.

The representatives thus elected shall serve for the term of two years, and, in case of the death of a representative, or removal from office, the governor shall issue a writ to the county or township for which he was a member to elect another in his stead, to serve for the residue of the term.

The General Assembly, or Legislature, shall consist of the governor, legislative council, and a house of representatives. The legislative council shall consist of five members, to continue in office five years, unless sooner removed by Congress, any three of whom to be a quorum, and the members of the council shall be nominated and appointed in the following manner, to wit: As soon as representatives shall be elected, the governor shall appoint a time and place for them to meet together, and, when met, they shall nominate ten persons, residents in the district, and each possessed of a freehold in five hundred acres of land, and return their names to Congress; five of whom Congress shall appoint and commission to serve as aforesaid; and whenever a vacancy shall happen in the council, by death or removal from office, the house of representatives shall nominate two persons, qualified as aforesaid, for each vacancy, and return their names to Congress; one of whom Congress shall appoint and commission for the residue of the term; and every five years, four months at least before the expiration of the time of service of the members of council, the said house shall nominate ten persons, qualified as aforesaid, and return their names to Congress, five of whom Congress shall appoint and commission to serve as members of the council five years, unless sooner removed. And the governor, legislative council, and house of representatives, shall have authority to make laws, in all cases, for the good government of the district, not repugnant to the principles and articles in this ordinance established and declared. And all bills, having passed by a majority in the house, and by a majority in the council, shall be referred to the governor for his assent: but no bill or legislative act whatever, shall be of any force without his assent. The governor shall have power to convene, prorogue, and dissolve the General Assembly, when in his opinion it shall be expedient.

The governor, judges, legislative council, secretary, and such other officers as Congress shall appoint in the district, shall take an oath or affirmation of fidelity, and of office; the governor before the president of Congress, and all other officers before the governor. As soon as a legislature shall be formed in the district, the council and house assembled, in one room, shall have authority, by joint ballot, to elect a delegate to Congress, who shall have a seat in Congress, with a right of debating, but not of voting during this temporary government.

And for extending the fundamental principles of civil and religious liberty, which form the basis whereon these republics, their laws, and constitutions are erected; to fix and establish those principles as the basis of all laws, constitutions, and governments, which for ever hereafter shall be formed in the said territory; to provide, also, for the establishment of States, and permanent government therein, and for their admission to a share in the federal councils on an equal footing with the original States, at as early periods as may be consistent with the general interest:

It is hereby ordained and declared, by the authority aforesaid, That the following articles shall be considered as articles of compact, between the original States and the people and States in the said territory, and for ever remain unalterable, unless by common consent, to wit:

ART. 1. No person, demeaning himself in a peaceable and orderly manner, shall ever be molested on account of his mode of worship or religious sentiments, in the said territory.

ART. 2. The inhabitants of the said territory shall always be entitled to the benefits of the writ of habeas corpus, and of the trial by jury; of a proportionate representation of the people in the legislature, and of judicial proceedings according to the course of the common law. All persons shall be bailable, unless for capital offences, where the proof shall be evident, or the presumption great. All fines shall be moderate, and no cruel or unusual punishments shall be inflicted. No man shall be deprived of his liberty or property, but by the judgment of his peers, or the law of the land, and should the public exigencies make it necessary, for the common preservation, to take any person's property, or to demand his particular services, full compensation shall be made for the same. And, in the just preservation of rights and property, it is understood and declared, that no law ought ever to be made, or have force in the said territory, that shall, in any manner whatever, interfere with, or affect private contracts or engagements, bona fide, and without fraud previously formed.

ART. 3. Religion, morality, and knowledge, being necessary to good government, and the happiness of mankind, schools and the means of education shall for ever be encouraged. The utmost good faith shall always be observed towards the Indians; their lands and property shall never be taken from them without their consent; and in their property, rights, and liberty, they never shall be invaded or disturbed, unless in just and lawful wars authorized by Congress; but laws founded in justice and humanity shall, from time to time, be made, for preventing wrongs being done to them, and for preserving peace and friendship with them.

ART. 4. The said territory, and the States which may be formed therein, shall for ever remain a part of this confederacy of the United States of America, subject to the Articles of Confederation, and to such alterations therein as shall be constitutionally made; and to all the acts and ordinances of the United States, in Congress assembled, conformable thereto. The inhabitants and settlers in the said territory shall be subject to pay a part of the federal debts, contracted or to be contracted, and a proportional part of the expenses of government, to be apportioned on them by Congress, according to the same common rule and measure by which apportionments thereof shall be made on the other States; and the taxes for paying their proportion shall be laid and levied by the authority and direction of the legislatures of the district or districts, or new States, as in the original States, within the time agreed upon by the United States, in Congress assembled. The legislatures of those districts, or new States, shall never interfere with the primary disposal of the soil by the United States, in Congress assembled, nor with any regulations Congress may find necessary, for securing the title in such soil, to the bona fide purchasers. No tax shall be imposed on lands, the property of the United States; and in no case shall non-resident proprietors be taxed higher than residents. The navigable waters leading into the Mississippi and St. Lawrence, and the carrying places between the same, shall be common highways, and for ever free, as well to the inhabitants of the said territory as to the citizens of the United States, and those of any other States that may be admitted into the Confederacy, without any tax, impost, or duty therefor.

ART. 5. There shall be formed in the said territory, not less than three, nor more than five States; and the boundaries of the States, as soon as Virginia shall alter her act of cession, and consent to the same, shall become fixed and established as follows, to wit: the western State in the said territory, shall be bounded by the Mississippi, the Ohio, and Wabash rivers; a direct line drawn from the Wabash and Post Vincents, due north, to the territorial line between the United States and Canada; and by the said territorial line to the Lake of the Woods and Mississippi. The middle States shall be bounded by the said direct line, the Wabash, from Post Vincents to the Ohio, by the Ohio, by a direct line drawn due north from the mouth of the Great Miami to the said territorial line, and by the said territorial line. The eastern State shall be bounded by the last-mentioned direct line, the Ohio, Pennsylvania, and the said territorial line: provided, however, and it is further understood and declared, that the boundaries of these three States shall be subject so far to be altered, that, if Congress shall hereafter find it expedient, they shall have authority to form one or two States in that part of the said territory which lies north of an east and west line drawn through the southerly bend or extreme of Lake Michigan. And whenever any of the said States shall have sixty thousand free inhabitants therein, such State shall be admitted, by its delegates, into the Congress of the United States, on an equal footing with the original States, in all respects whatever; and shall be at liberty to form a permanent constitution and State government; provided the constitution and government, so to be formed, shall be republican, and in conformity to the principles contained in these articles · and, so far as can be consistent with the general interest of the Confederacy, such admission shall be allowed at an earlier period, and when there may be a less number of free inhabitants in the State than sixty thousand.

ART. 6. There shall be neither slavery nor involuntary servitude in the said territory, otherwise than in the punishment of crimes, whereof the party shall have been duly convicted; provided, always, that any person escaping into the same, from whom labor or service is lawfully claimed in any one of the original States, such fugitive may be lawfully reclaimed, and conveyed to the person claiming his or her labor or service as aforesaid.

Be it ordained by the authority aforesaid, That the resolutions of the 23d of April, 1784, relative to the subject of this ordinance, be, and the same are hereby, repealed, and declared null and void.

Done by the United States, in Congress assembled, the 13th day of July, in the year of our Lord 1787, and of their sovereignty and independence the 12th. CHARLES THOMSON, *Sec'y.*

For a history of this ordinance by Peter Force, see Nat. Intelligencer, Aug. 26, 1847.

LOUISIANA,

Formed out of part of the territory ceded to the United States by France, by treaty of April 30, 1803.

On October 31, 1803, an act to enable the President of the United States to take possession of the territories ceded by France to the United States, by the treaty concluded at Paris on the 30th of April last, and for the temporary government thereof, was passed and approved.

Louisiana was erected into two territories by act of Congress, approved March 26, 1804; one called the Territory of Orleans, and the other called the District of Louisiana.

An act further providing for the government of the Orleans territory, was approved March 2, 1805, which authorized the people to form a constitution and State government when their number should amount to 60,000.

A memorial of the Legislature of the territory of Orleans on behalf of the inhabitants, (see folio State Papers, "Miscellaneous," vol. 2, p. 51,) was presented in Senate United States. (See Journal, March 12, 1810.)

An act to enable the people of the territory of Orleans to form a constitution and State government, &c., by which that State was allowed one Representative until the next census, was passed and approved February 20, 1811. The said people having, on January 22, 1812, formed a constitution and State government, and given the State the name of Louisiana, in pursuance of the said act, an act for the admission of the State of Louisiana into the Union, and to extend the laws of the United States to the said State, was passed and approved, **April 8, 1812.**

On May 22, 1812, an act supplemental to the act of April 8, 1812, was approved.

INDIANA,

Formed out of a part of the North-western Territory which was ceded to the United States by Virginia. (See remarks under "Ohio.")

The territory established by act of May 7, 1800.

The territory divided into two separate governments, and that of Michigan created by act of January 11, 1805.

The territory again divided into two separate governments, and that of Illinois created by act of February 3, 1809.

The Legislature of the territory, on behalf of the people, applied to be enabled to form a constitution, &c. (See Journal of House of Representatives, December 28, 1815, and January 5, 1816; also folio State Papers, "Miscellaneous," vol. 2, p. 277.)

An act to enable the people of the Indiana territory to form a constitution and State government, &c., by which that State was allowed one Representative, was passed April 19, 1816.

The said people having, on June 29, 1816, formed a constitution, &c., a joint resolution for admitting the State of Indiana into the Union was passed and approved, **December 11, 1816.**

The laws of the United States extended to the State of Indiana, by act of March 3, 1817.

MISSISSIPPI,

Formed out of a part of the territory ceded to the United States by the commissioners of the State of South Carolina, on August 9, 1787, under the act of South Carolina of March 8, 1787, and by those of the State of Georgia, April 24, 1802, which was ratified by the Legislature of Georgia, on June 16, 1802. (For these cessions, &c., and for the convention between South Carolina and Georgia of April 28, 1787, see Bioren and Duane's edit. Laws, vol. 1, pp. 466, 467, 486 to 491.)

The government of the territory established by act of Congress of April 7, 1798.

Limits settled and government established by act of Congress of May 10, 1800.

Territory on the north added to the Mississippi territory, by act of Congress of March 27, 1804.

The boundaries enlarged on the south, by act of Congress of May 14, 1812.

A joint resolution of Congress "requesting the State of Georgia to assent to the formation of two States of the Mississippi territory," was passed and approved, June 17, 1812.

A motion was made in House of Representatives of the United States to inquire into the expediency of admitting Mississippi into the Union, December 28, 1810. Reported on by committee, January 9, 1811. (Vide folio State Papers, "Miscellaneous," vol. 2, p. 129.)

A petition from the inhabitants of Mississippi, that it be made a State, &c., presented in House of Representatives, November 13, 1811. Reported on by committee of House of Representatives, December 17, 1811. (Vide folio State Papers, "Miscellaneous," vol. 2, p. 163.)

Bill passed House of Representatives. Report adverse in Senate, April 17, 1812, and bill postponed. (Vide same book, p. 182.)

A memorial presented in House of Representatives, January 21, 1815. Reported on February 23, 1815. (Vide same book, p. 274.)

A memorial presented in House of Representatives, December 6, 1815. Reported on December 29, 1815. (Vide same book, p. 276.)

A memorial presented in House of Representatives, December 9, 1816. Reported on December 23, 1816. (Vide same book, p. 407.) Reported on January 17, 1817. (Vide same book, p. 416.)

An act to enable the people of the western part of the Mississippi territory to form a constitution and State government, &c., was passed and approved on March 1, 1817, by which the State was to have one Representative until the next census.

The said people having, on August 15, 1817, formed a constitution, &c., a joint resolution for the admission of the State of Mississippi into the Union was passed and approved, **December 10, 1817.**

On April 3, 1818, an act to provide for the due execution of the laws of the United States within the State of Mississippi, was approved.

ILLINOIS,

Formed out of a part of the North-western Territory which was ceded to the United States by the State of Virginia. (See remarks under "Ohio.") (For proclamation of General Gage respecting the country of Illinois, made December 30, 1764, see Bioren and Duane's edit. Laws, vol. 1, p. 506.)

An act for dividing the Indiana territory into two separate governments, and organizing the Illinois territory, was passed and approved February 3, 1809.

An act to amend the act of April 16, 1814, extending the western boundary of Illinois to the middle of the Mississippi, to include the islands between the middle and eastern margin of that river, was passed and approved, February 27, 1815.

A memorial of the legislative council, to be allowed to form a State government, &c., presented in House of Representatives, January 16, 1818.

An act to enable the people of the Illinois territory to form a constitution and State government, and authorizing one Representative in Congress, &c., was passed and approved April 18, 1818. (By this act a part of the territory of Illinois was attached to the territory of Michigan.)

The said people having, on August 26, 1818, formed a constitution, &c., a joint resolution declaring the admission of the State of Illinois into the Union was passed and approved, **December 3, 1818.**

An act to provide for the due execution of the laws of the United States within the State of Illinois, was passed and approved March 3, 1819.

ALABAMA,

Formed out of a part of the territory ceded to the United States by the States of South Carolina and Georgia. (See remarks under the head "Mississippi.")

The eastern part of Mississippi territory made a separate territory, and called "Alabama," by act of Congress, approved March 3, 1817.

A petition of the legislative council of Alabama on behalf of the people, praying to be allowed to form a constitution, &c., presented in the House of Representatives, December 7, 1818.

An act to enable the people of the Alabama territory to form a constitution and

State government, &c., authorizing one Representative in Congress, was passed and approved, March 2, 1819.

The said people having, on August 2, 1819, formed a constitution, &c., a joint resolution declaring the admission of the State of Alabama into the Union was passed and approved, **December 14, 1819.**

The laws of the United States were extended to the State of Alabama by act of April 21, 1820, to establish a District Court, &c.

MAINE,

Formed out of a part of the territory of Massachusetts.

A petition of a Convention on behalf of the people of the district of Maine, praying to be permitted to form a separate State, was presented in the House of Representatives of the United States, December 8, 1819.

A constitution adopted in Convention, October 29, 1819.

An act for the admission of the State of Maine into the Union, was passed and ...oved March 3, 1820, in the following words:—

"Whereas, by an act of the State of Massachusetts, passed on the 19th day of June, in the year 1819, entitled, 'An act relating to the separation of the district of Maine from Massachusetts proper, and forming the same into a separate and independent State,' the people of that part of Massachusetts heretofore known as the district of Maine, did, with the consent of the Legislature of said State of Massachusetts, form themselves into an independent State, and did establish a constitution for the government of the same, agreeably to the provisions of the said act: Therefore,

"*Be it enacted by the Senate and House of Representatives of the United States of America in Congress assembled*, That, from and after the **15th day of March, in the year 1820,** the State of Maine is hereby declared to be one of the United States of America, and admitted into the Union on an equal footing with the original States, in all respects whatever."

On the 7th April, 1820, the following act was passed and approved:

"AN ACT for apportioning the Representatives in the seventeenth Congress, to be elected in the State of Massachusetts and Maine, and for other purposes.

"*Be it enacted by the Senate and House of Representatives of the United States of America in Congress assembled*, That, in the election of Representatives in the seventeenth Congress, the State of Massachusetts shall be entitled to choose thirteen Representatives only; and the State of Maine shall be entitled to choose seven Representatives, according to the consent of the Legislature of said State of Massachusetts, for this purpose given, by their resolve passed on the 25th day of January last, and prior to the admission of the State of Maine into the Union.

"SEC. 2. *And be it further enacted*, That, if the seat of any of the Representatives in the present Congress, who were elected in and under the authority of the State of Massachusetts, and who are now inhabitants of the State of Maine, shall be vacated by death, resignation, or otherwise, such vacancy shall be supplied by a successor who shall, at the time of his election, be an inhabitant of the State of Maine."

MISSOURI,

Was formed out of part of the territory ceded by France by treaty of April 30 1803. It was created under the name of the district of Louisiana by the "Act erecting Louisiana into two territories, and providing for the temporary government thereof," which was approved March 26, 1804. By this act the government of this district was placed under the direction of the Governor and judges of the Indiana territory.

On the 3d March, 1805, an act further providing for the government of the district of Louisiana was approved. By this act a separate government was formed, under the title of the territory of Louisiana.

An act providing for the government of the territory of Missouri was passed and approved June 4, 1812, by which it was provided "That the territory heretofore called Louisiana shall hereafter be called Missouri," &c.

An act to alter certain parts of the act providing for the government of the territory of Missouri was passed and approved April 29, 1816.

An act establishing a separate territorial government in the southern part of the territory of Missouri, to be called Arkansas territory, was passed the 2d March, 1819.

A memorial of the legislative council and House of Representatives of the territory of Missouri, in the name and on behalf of the people, for admission into the Union as a State, was presented in the Senate on December 29, 1819.

An act to authorize the people of the Missouri territory to form a constitution and State government, and for the admission of such State into the Union on an equal footing with the original States, and to prohibit slavery in certain territories, was passed March 6, 1820.

The people having, on July 19, 1820, formed a constitution in pursuance of said act, the same was laid before Congress on November 16, 1820. Mr. Lowndes, from the committee to which it was referred, made a report to the House of Representatives, November 23, 1820, accompanied by a "Resolution declaring the admission of the State of Missouri into the Union." (Vide folio State Papers, "Miscellaneous," vol. 2, p. 625.)

The Senate passed a joint "Resolution declaring the admission of the State of Missouri into the Union," on December 12, 1820, which was referred to a select committee in the House of Representatives, and on February 10, 1821, Mr. Clay made a report. (Vide folio State Papers as above, p. 655.) The House rejected the resolution of the Senate, on February 14, 1821. On February 22, on motion of Mr. Clay, a committee on the part of the House was appointed, to join a committee on the part of the Senate, on the subject of the admission of Missouri.

On February 26, Mr. Clay, from the joint committee, reported a "Resolution providing for the admission of the State of Missouri into the Union, on a certain condition," which resolution was passed and approved March 2, 1821. The said condition was accepted by the Legislature of Missouri by "A solemn public act, declaring the assent of this State" to "the fundamental condition" contained in a resolution passed by the Congress of the United States, providing for the admission of the State of Missouri into the Union, on a certain condition, which was approved by the Governor on June 26, 1821.

On **August 10, 1821,** the President of the United States issued his proclamation declaring the admission of Missouri complete according to law. (See Little & Brown's edit. Laws, vol. 3, appendix 2.)

On March 16, 1822, an act to provide for the due execution of the laws of the United States within the State of Missouri, &c., was passed and approved.

ARKANSAS,

Formed out of part of the territory ceded to the United States by France, by treaty of April 30, 1803. (See remarks under the head of Missouri.)

An act establishing a separate territorial government in the southern part of the territory of Missouri, was passed March 2, 1819, by which it was named Arkansas

An act relative to the Arkansas territory, declaring that the act of June 4, 1812, for the government of Missouri, as modified by the act of April 29, 1816, should be in force in Arkansas, was passed April 21, 1820.

An act to fix the western boundary line of the territory of Arkansas, and for other purposes, was passed May 26, 1824.

An act to run and mark a line dividing Arkansas from Louisiana was passed and approved May 19, 1828.

A memorial of the inhabitants, by a convention, praying that Arkansas may be admitted into the Union, accompanied by a constitution formed by said convention, was presented in the House of Representatives on March 1, 1836. (See printed documents, House of Representatives, 1st session, 24th Congress, vol. 4, Nos. 133, 144–5.) The proceedings of said convention were also communicated to the House of Representatives through the President of the United States on March 10, 1836. (See said printed documents, vol. 4, No. 164.)

"An act for the admission of the State of Arkansas into the Union, and to provide for the due execution of the laws of the United States within the same, and for other purposes," was passed **June 15, 1836,** containing the following preamble, viz.:

"Whereas, the people of the territory of Arkansas did, on the 30th day of January, in the present year, by a convention of delegates called and assembled for that purpose, form for themselves a constitution and state government, which constitution and state government, so formed, is republican: And whereas, the number of inhabitants within the said territory exceeds forty-seven thousand seven hundred persons, computed according to the rule prescribed by the Constitution of the United States; and the said convention have, in their behalf, asked the Congress of the United States to admit the said territory into the Union as a State, on an equal footing with the original States."

By this act Arkansas was allowed one Representative until the next census, and the laws of the United States were extended over the same.

On June 23, 1836, an act supplemental to the foregoing act was passed and approved.

MICHIGAN,

Formed out of part of the territory ceded to the United States by the State of Virginia. (See remarks under "Ohio.")

An act to divide the Indiana territory into two separate governments, and establishing that of the territory of Michigan, was passed and approved January 11, 1805.

An act to authorize the President of the United States to ascertain and designate certain boundaries, was passed and approved May 20, 1812, by which the boundary between Ohio and Michigan was directed to be ascertained and marked.

By the act of April 18, 1818, to enable the people of Illinois to form a constitution and State government, &c., a part of that territory was attached to the territory of Michigan.

An act to amend the ordinance and acts of Congress for the government of the territory of Michigan, and for other purposes, was passed and approved March 3, 1823.

An act in addition to the above act, passed and approved February 5, 1825.

An act to provide for the taking of certain observations preparatory to the adjustment of the northern boundary line of the State of Ohio, was passed and approved July 14, 1832.

A memorial of the legislative council, praying that Michigan be admitted into the Union, was presented in Senate, January 25, 1833. (See Senate documents, 2d session, 22d Congress, vol. 1, No. 54.) A bill for that object was reported in the House of Representatives, on February 26, 1833.

A memorial for admission was presented in House of Representatives, December 11, 1833, and in Senate, February 28, 1834. (See documents House of Representatives, 1st session, 23d Congress, vol. 3, No. 168, vol. 4, Nos. 245, 302.)

A report was made by a select committee of the House of Representatives on the subject of boundary, &c., on March 11, 1834. (See reports of committees of House of Representatives, 1st session, 23d Congress, vol. 3, No. 334.) This report was accompanied by a bill to provide for taking a census or enumeration of the inhabitants of the eastern division of the territory of Michigan, and of the territory of Arkansas.

And on April 12, 1834, the same committee reported a bill establishing the territorial government of Huron.

An act to attach the territory of the United States west of the Mississippi river, and north of the State of Missouri, to the territory of Michigan, was passed and approved June 28, 1834.

A memorial was presented in the Senate, December 23d, and House of Representatives, December 29, 1834, for the erection of "Wisconsin" into a separate government. (See documents House of Representatives, 2d session, 23d Congress, vol. 2, Nos. 34, 47.)

Resolutions of the legislative council of Michigan, relative to boundary with Ohio, presented in House of Representatives, January 3, 1835. (See said vol. 2, No. 53.)

A memorial of legislative council of Michigan, relative to southern boundary thereof, presented in House of Representatives, March 2, 1835. (See saia documents, vol. 5, No. 183.)

Two maps prepared under resolution House of Representatives of June 11, 1834. (See said documents, vol. 5, No. 199.)

Two messages to Congress by the President of the United States, with docu ments relating to the boundaries and the admission of Michigan into the Union, were received on December 10, 1835. (See Senate documents, 1st session, 24th Congress, vol. 1, Nos. 5 and 6.)

A message from the President to Congress with documents and map relating to the boundary between Ohio and Michigan, was received January 12, 1836. (See Senate documents as above, vol. 2, No. 51.)

A report was made by a committee of the Senate on the subject of the boundary line, accompanied by a map, on March 1, 1836. (See Senate documents as above, vol. 3, No. 211.)

A report was made by a committee of the House of Representatives, on March 2, 1836, on the subject of admission, boundary, &c., (communicating a large collection of documents relating to the entire subject.) (See Reports of committees, House of Representatives, 1st session, 24th Congress, vol. 2, No. 380.)

"An act to establish the northern boundary line of the State of Ohio, and to provide for the admission of the State of Michigan into the Union, upon the conditions therein expressed," was passed June 15, 1836. By this act Michigan was authorized to send one Representative to Congress, until the next census. An act supplementary to the said act was passed June 23, 1836.

An act to provide for the due execution of the laws of the United States within the State of Michigan, was passed July 1, 1836.

An act to admit the State of Michigan into the Union, upon an equal footing with the original States, was passed **January 26, 1837,** containing the following preamble, viz.:

"Whereas, in pursuance of the act of Congress of June 15, 1836, entitled, 'An act to establish the northern boundary of the State of Ohio, and to provide for the admission of the State of Michigan into the Union upon the conditions therein expressed,' a convention of Delegates, elected by the people of the said State of Michigan, for the sole purpose of giving their assent to the boundaries of the said State of Michigan as described, declared, and established, in and by the said act, did, on December 15, 1836, assent to the provisions of said act, Therefore,

"*Be it enacted*, &c., That the State of Michigan shall be one, and is hereby declared to be one, of the United States of America, and admitted into the Union on an equal footing with the original States, in all respects whatever."

An act to ascertain and designate the boundary line between the State of Michigan and the territory of Wisconsin, was passed and approved June 12, 1838.

FLORIDA,

Formed out of the territory ceded by Spain to the United States, by treaty of February 22, 1819.

The boundaries of East and West Florida in the hands of the British government, October 7, 1763. (See vol. 1, Laws United States, Bioren and Duane's edit., p. 444.)

The boundaries of West Florida, as changed by the British government, June 6, 1764. (See said volume, p. 450.)

A resolution and several acts of Congress were passed to enable the President of the United States to take possession of the Floridas under certain contingencies, at the following dates, viz.:

A resolution,	January 15, 1811,	Laws United States,	vol. 6,	p. 592.
An act,	do.	do.	do.	592.
An act,	March 3, 1811.	do.	do.	593.
An act,	February 12, 1813,	do.	do.	593.

An act to authorize the President of the United States to take possession of East and West Florida, and establish a temporary government therein, was passed March 3, 1819.

An act for carrying into execution the treaty between the United States and Spain, concluded at Washington, on February 22, 1819, was passed March 3, 1821.

Ratification of the treaty and exchange of ratifications, February 22, 1821. (Laws United States, vol. 6, p. 631.)

Copies of grants of lands annulled by said treaty. (Same vol. p. 632—37.)

Articles of surrender of East Florida to the United States on July 10, 1821. (Same vol. p. 638.)

Article of surrender of West Florida to the United States on July 17, 1821. (Same vol. p. 639.)

Proclamation of General Jackson as governor, assuming authority over the said territories in the name of the United States, July 17, 1821. (Same vol. p. 641.)

An act for the establishment of a territorial government in Florida was passed March 30, 1822.

An act to amend "An act for the establishment of a territorial government in Florida," and for other purposes, was passed March 3, 1823. By this act East and West Florida were constituted one territory.

An act to amend the act of March 3, 1823, was passed and approved May 26, 1824.

An act to authorize the President of the United States to run and mark a line dividing the territory of Florida from the State of Georgia, was passed and approved May 4, 1826.

An act to amend the several acts for the establishment of the territorial government in Florida, was passed and approved May 15, 1826.

An act relating to the territorial government of Florida, passed and approved April 28, 1828.

An act to ascertain and mark the line between the State of Alabama and the territory of Florida, and the northern boundary of the State of Illinois, and for other purposes, was passed March 2, 1831.

A memorial of the people of Florida, proceedings of a convention, constitution, &c., presented to House of Representatives, February 20, 1839. (See documents House of Representatives, 3d session, 25th Congress, vol. 4, No. 208.)

A memorial of the inhabitants of St. Augustine, in Florida, that a law be passed to organize a separate territorial government for that part of Florida east of the Sawanee river, was presented in Senate, January 10, 1840. (See Senate documents, 1st session, 26th Congress, vol. 3, No. 67.)

A memorial of the people of Florida praying admission into the Union, was presented in Senate, February 12, 1840.

A bill to authorize the people of Middle and West Florida to form a constitution and State government, and to provide for the admission of said State into the Union, was reported in House of Representatives, March 5, 1840.

Resolutions by the Senate of Florida adverse to the division of that territory, were presented in the Senate of the United States, on March 6, 1840.

Resolutions of the Legislature of Florida for admission and against division, were presented in Senate of United States, March 11, and in House of Representatives, March 16, 1840.

A bill for the admission of Florida into the Union on certain conditions, and a bill for the division of Florida, and the future admission of the States of East and West Florida, on certain conditions, were reported in Senate, July 2, 1840.

The memorial for admission and the constitution again presented in House of Representatives, May 9, 1842. (See documents House of Representatives, 2d session, 27th Congress, vol. 4, No. 206.)

Memorials of citizens of Florida for the admission of that territory into the Union, presented in the Senate, July 15 and 21, August 10, 13, 15, 17, and 30, 1842.

Resolutions of the legislative council of Florida for a division of that Territory and the formation of two territorial governments, were presented to Congress March 26, 1844.

On June 17, 1844, the following resolution was reported in the Senate: Resolved, That the prayer of the memorialists ought not to be granted.

On same day, a report adverse to a division of the Territory was made. (See reports of committee, House of Representatives, 1st session, 28th Congress, vol. 3, p. 577.)

Resolutions of the legislative council for dividing the Territory again presented in House of Representatives, December 30, 1844.

A bill for the admission of the States of Iowa and Florida into the Union was reported January 7, 1845.

Resolutions of the legislative council of Florida, for the admission of Florida at the same time with Iowa, were presented in House of Representatives, February 11, 1845. (See documents House of Representatives, 2d session, 28th Congress, vol. 3, No. 111.)

An act for the admission of the States of Iowa and Florida into the Union was passed on **March 3, 1845,** containing the following preamble, viz.:

Whereas the people of the Territory of Iowa did, on the seventh day of October, 1844, by a convention of delegates called and assembled for that purpose, form for themselves a constitution and State government; and whereas the people of the Territory of Florida did, in like manner, by their delegates on the 11th day of January, 1839, form for themselves a constitution and State government, both of which said constitutions are republican; and said conventions having asked the admission of their respective Territories into the Union as States, on equal footing with the original States:

Be it enacted, &c., That the States of Iowa and Florida be, and the same are hereby, declared to be States of the United States of America, and are hereby admitted into the Union on equal footing with the original States, in all respects whatsoever, &c.

"Sec. 5. *And be it further enacted*, That the said State of Florida shall embrace the territories of East and West Florida which, by the treaty of amity, settlement, and limits, between the United States and Spain, on the 22d day of February, 1819, were ceded to the United States."

One Representative in Congress allowed to Florida until the next census.

An act supplemental to the act for the admission of Florida and Iowa into the Union, and for other purposes, was passed March 3, 1845.

By this act grants of land were made to Florida, and the laws of the United States were extended to that State

Resolutions of the Legislature of Florida, in relation to the disputed boundaries between that State and Georgia and Alabama, were presented in the Senate, February 2, 1846. (See Senate documents, 1st session, 29th Congress, vol. 4, Nos. 96 and 133.)

On March 4, 1846, a bill respecting the settlement of the boundary line between the State of Florida and the State of Georgia, was reported from the committee.

TEXAS,

An independent republic, admitted into the Union by the following joint resolutions and act of Congress:

A joint resolution for annexing Texas to the United States, approved March 1, 1845.

JOINT RESOLUTION for annexing Texas to the United States.

Resolved by the Senate and House of Representatives of the United States of America in Congress assembled, That Congress doth consent that the territory properly included within and rightfully belonging to the Republic of Texas may be erected into a new State, to be called the State of Texas, with a republican form of government, to be adopted by the people of said republic, by deputies in convention assembled, with the consent of the existing government, in order that the same may be admitted as one of the States of this Union.

SEC. 2. *And be it further resolved*, That the foregoing consent of Congress is given upon the following conditions, and with the following guarantees, to wit:

FIRST. Said State to be formed, subject to the adjustment by this Government of all questions of boundary that may arise with other governments; and the constitution thereof, with the proper evidence of its adoption by the people of said Republic of Texas, shall be transmitted to the President of the United States, to be laid before Congress for its final action, on or before the first day of January, one thousand eight hundred and forty-six.

SECOND. Said State, when admitted into the Union, after ceding to the United States all public edifices, fortifications, barracks, ports, and harbors, navy and navy-yards, docks, magazines, arms, armaments, and all other property and means pertaining to the public defence belonging to said Republic of Texas, shall retain all the public funds, debts, taxes, and dues of every kind, which may belong to or be due and owing said republic; and shall also retain all the vacant and unappropriated lands lying within its limits, to be applied to the payment of the debts and liabilities of said Republic of Texas; and the residue of said lands, after discharging said debts and liabilities, to be disposed of as said State may direct; but in no event are said debts and liabilities to become a charge upon the Government of the United States.

THIRD. New States, of convenient size, not exceeding four in number, in addition to said State of Texas, and having sufficient population, may hereafter, the consent of said State, be formed out of the territory thereof, which shall be entitled to admission under the provisions of the Federal Constitution. And such States as may be formed out of that portion of said territory lying south of thirty-six degrees thirty minutes north latitude, commonly known as the Missouri compromise line, shall be admitted into the Union with or without slavery, as the people of each State asking admission may desire. And in such State or States as shall be formed out of said territory north of said Missouri compromise line, slavery, or involuntary servitude, (except for crimes,) shall be prohibited.

SEC. 3. *And be it further resolved*, That if the President of the United States shall, in his judgment and discretion, deem it most advisable, instead of proceeding to submit the foregoing resolution to the Republic of Texas, as an overture on the part of the United States, for admission, to negotiate with that republic; then,

Be it resolved, That a State, to be formed out of the present Republic of Texas, with suitable extent and boundaries, and with two Representatives in Congress, until the next apportionment of representation, shall be admitted into the Union, by virtue of this act, on an equal footing with the existing States, as soon as the terms and conditions of such admission, and the cession of the remaining Texan territory to the United States, shall be agreed upon by the Governments of Texas and the United States: That the sum of one hundred thousand dollars be, and the same is hereby, appropriated to defray the expenses of missions and negotiations, to agree upon the terms of said admission and cession, either by treaty to be submitted to the Senate, or by articles to be submitted to the two Houses of Congress, as the President may direct.

Approved March 1, 1845.

A joint resolution for the admission of the State of Texas into the Union, approved December 29, 1845.

JOINT RESOLUTION for the admission of the State of Texas into the Union.

Whereas the Congress of the United States, by a joint resolution approved March the first, eighteen hundred and forty-five, did consent that the territory properly included within and rightfully belonging to the Republic of Texas might be erected into a new State, to be called the State of Texas, with a republican form of government, to be adopted by the people of said republic, by deputies in convention assembled, with the consent of the existing government, in order that the same might be admitted as one of the States of the Union; which consent of Congress was given upon certain conditions specified in the first and second sections of said joint resolution: and whereas the people of the said Republic of Texas, by deputies in convention assembled, with the consent of the existing government, did adopt a constitution, and erect a new State, with a republican form of government, and, in the name of the people of Texas, and by their authority, did ordain and declare that they assented to and accepted the proposals, conditions, and guarantees contained in said first and second sections of said resolution: and whereas the said constitution, and the proper evidence of its adoption by the people of the Republic of Texas, have been transmitted to the President of the United States, and laid before Congress, in conformity to the provisions of said joint resolution: Therefore,

Resolved by the Senate and House of Representatives of the United States of America

in Congress assembled, That the State of Texas shall be one, and is hereby declared to be one, of the United States of America, and admitted into the Union on an equal footing with the original States in all respects whatever.

SEC. 2. *And be it further resolved*, That until the Representatives in Congress shall be apportioned according to an actual enumeration of the inhabitants of the United States, the State of Texas shall be entitled to choose two Representatives.

Approved **December 29, 1845.**

An act to extend the laws of the United States over the State of Texas, and for other purposes, approved December 29, 1845, viz.:

AN ACT to extend the laws of the United States over the State of Texas, and for other purposes.

Be it enacted by the Senate and House of Representatives of the United States of America in Congress assembled, That all the laws of the United States are hereby declared to extend to and over, and to have full force and effect within, the State of Texas, admitted at the present session of Congress into the Confederacy and Union of the United States. *Approved December* 29, 1845.

WISCONSIN.

[By act **29th May, 1848,** the state of Wisconsin was admitted into the Union. Entitled to three Representatives in Congress after 3d March, 1849.]

On December 12, 1832, a resolution passed in House of Representatives directing a committee to inquire into the expediency of creating a territorial government for Wisconsin out of part of Michigan.

On December 6, 1832, the committee made a report accompanied by a bill. (See reports of committees House of Representatives, 1st session, 22d Congress, vol. 1. No. 145.)

A memorial of the legislative council of Michigan for the division of that territory, and that the territory of Wisconsin be established, was presented in Senate of the United States, December 23, 1834. (See Senate documents 2d session, 23d Congress, vol. 2, No. 24.)

On February 11, 1836, a bill establishing the territorial government of Wisconsin, reported in House of Representatives.

On March 1, 1836, a memorial of legislative council of Michigan for same, presented in House of Representatives. (See documents House of Representatives, 1st session 24th Congress, vol. 4, No. 153.)

On April 20, 1836, an act establishing the territorial government of Wisconsin was passed and approved.

On March 5, 1838, a resolution directing a committee to inquire into the expediency of authorizing the territory of Wisconsin to take a census and adopt a constitution, preparatory to being admitted into the Union, was passed.

On May 11, 1838, the said committee reported a bill to enable the people of East Wisconsin to form a constitution and State government, and for the admission of such State into the Union.

On June 12, 1838, an act to divide the territory of Wisconsin, and to establish the territorial government of Iowa, was passed and approved.

On June 12, 1838, an act to ascertain and designate the boundary line between the State of Michigan and the territory of Wisconsin, was passed and approved.

On January 28, 1839, a memorial of the Legislative Assembly of Wisconsin, praying an alteration in the southern boundary of that territory, was presented in the Senate. (See Senate documents, 3d session, 25th Congress, vol. 3, No. 149.)

On March 3, 1839, an act to alter and amend the organic law of the territories of Wisconsin and Iowa, was passed and approved.

On May 25, 1840, the proceedings of a public meeting at Galena in relation to the southern boundary of Wisconsin territory, was presented in the House of Representatives. (See documents House of Representatives, 1st session, 26th Congress, vol. 6, No. 226.) (For, "An Ordinance for the government of the Territory of the United States, north-west of the river Ohio," passed by the Congress of the Confederation, July 13, 1787. (See the same, under the head "Ohio.")

On February 3, 1841, a message was received in Senate from the President, communicating the reports, maps, &c., relating to boundary line between Michigan and Wisconsin. (See Senate documents, 2d session, 26th Congress, vol. 4, No. 151.)

On February 8, 1841, a memorial of the Legislative Assembly of Wisconsin, that a law defining the western boundary line of said territory be passed, was presented in Senate. (See Senate documents as above, vol. 4, No. 171.)

On February 15, 1841, resolutions of the General Assembly of Michigan in relation to the boundary line between that State and the territory of Wisconsin, were presented in the Senate. (See Senate documents, 2d session, 26th Congress, vol. 4, No. 186.)

On March 19, 1841, resolutions of the Legislative Assembly of Wisconsin territory in relation to the boundary between Michigan and Wisconsin, were presented in House of Representatives. (See documents House of Representatives, 2d session, 27th Congress, vol. 3, No. 147.)

On March 20, 1845, a resolution of the legislative council of Wisconsin asking that provision be made for taking a census and holding a convention to form a State constitution, was presented in the Senate.

On January 13, 1846, a bill to enable the people of Wisconsin to form a constitution and State government, was introduced on leave in House of Representatives.

On August 6, 1846, an act to enable the people of Wisconsin territory to form a constitution and State government, and for the admission of such State into the Union, was passed and approved. To be entitled to two Representatives until the next census, and the laws of the United States extended to the same when admitted.

On January 21, 1847, the constitution adopted by the people of Wisconsin, the census and other documents, were presented in House of Representatives. (See documents House of Representatives, 2d session, 29th Congress, vol. 3, No. 49.)

On March 3, 1847, an act for the admission of the State of Wisconsin into the Union, was passed and approved. To be admitted on condition that the constitution adopted on December 16, 1846, shall be assented to by the qualified electors of the State, and as soon as such assent shall be given, the President of the United States shall announce the same by proclamation, and therefrom the admission of Wisconsin shall be considered as complete.

IOWA.

On December 19, 1836, a resolution directing the committee on territories to inquire into the expediency of establishing the Iowa territory out of part of Wisconsin, passed the House of Representatives.

On December 14, 1837, a resolution of same tenor passed House of Representatives.

On December 13 and 20, 1837, memorials of the people of Iowa for a division or separation from Wisconsin, was presented in the Senate.

On December 14, 1837, same presented in House of Representatives.

On December 13, 1837, a memorial of the people of Iowa for settlement of boundary with Missouri, was presented in the Senate.

On January 2, 1838, proceedings of Legislature of Wisconsin relative to boundary line between Iowa and Missouri, were presented in the Senate. (See Senate documents, 2d session, 25th Congress, vol. 1, No. 63.)

On February 6, 1838, a report was made by committee of House of Representatives on expediency of establishing a separate territorial government for Iowa, accompanied by a bill.

On June 12, 1838, an act to divide the territory of Wisconsin, and to establish the territorial government of Iowa, was passed and approved.

On June 18, 1838, an act to authorize the President of the United States to cause the southern boundary line of the territory of Iowa to be ascertained and marked. was passed and approved.

On January 30, 1839, a report of the Secretary of State with maps, made in compliance with resolutions of the Senate and House of Representatives, in relation to the southern boundary of the territory of Iowa, were received. (See documents House of Representatives, 3d session, 25th Congress, vol. 4, No. 128.)

On March 3, 1839, an appropriation was made for the survey of the southern boundary of the territory of Iowa, of $969 05.

On March 3, 1839, an act to define and establish the eastern boundary line of the territory of Iowa, was passed and approved.

On March 3, 1839, an act to alter and amend the organic law of the territories of Wisconsin and Iowa, was passed and approved.

On December 24, 1839, a message from the President, with documents relating to the disputed boundary between Missouri and Iowa, was received in Senate, and in the House of Representatives on December 27. (See Senate documents, 1st session, 26th Congress, vol. 1, No. 4. House of Representatives, vol. 1, No. 5.)

On December 30, 1839, additional documents on same subject communicated to House of Representatives, and to the Senate on January 3, 1840. (See Senate documents, 1st session, 26th Congress, vol. 2, No. 35. House of Representatives, vol. 2, No. 36.)

On January 9, 1840, additional documents on same subject, communicated to the Senate.

On January 31, 1840, additional documents on same subject were communicated to the Senate, in compliance with two resolutions of the Senate of December 30. 1839. (See Senate documents, 1st session, 26th Congress, vol. 4, No. 138.)

On January 8, 1840, a memorial of the legislative council of Iowa, praying the settlement of the disputed boundary with Missouri, was presented in Senate. (See Sen. docs., 1st ses., 26th Cong., vol. 2. No. 53.)

On January 9, 1840, a doc. relating to same subject, presented in Senate by Mr. Benton.

On January 10, 1840, a representation by delegate from Iowa on same subject presented in Senate.

On February 4, 1840, report made in Ho. of Reps., by a committee on boundary between Missouri and Iowa, with a bill to establish and define the northern boundary line of the State of Missouri. (See reps. of comms. of Ho. of Reps., 1st ses., 26th Cong., vol. 1, No. 2.)

On February 12, 1840, a message from the President, with additional documents relating to disputed boundary between Missouri and Iowa. (See docs. Ho. of Reps., 1st ses., 26th Cong., vol. 3, No. 97.)

On March 5, 1840, a bill reported by the committee on territories of the Ho. of Reps., "to enable the people of Iowa to form a constitution and State government, and for the admission of such State into the Union."

On February 11, 1841, a bill for ascertaining and settling the southern boundary line of the territory of Iowa, reported in Senate.

On March 9, 1841, a resolution of legislative council of Iowa relative to southern boundary line of said territory, was presented in Ho. of Reps.

On March 19, 1841, a message from the President, relative to boundary line between Missouri and Iowa, received in Ho. of Reps. (See docs. Ho. of Reps., 2d ses., 27th Cong., vol. 3, No. 141.)

On May 26, 1841, the committee on territories of the Ho. of Reps. made a report, with a bill, fixing the boundary line between Missouri and Iowa, which passed the Ho. of Reps. only. (For report, see reports Ho. of Reps., 2d ses., 27th Cong., vol. 4, No. 791.)

On January 21, 1843, a report made in Ho. of Reps. from committee on territories, accompanied by a bill fixing the boundary between Missouri and Iowa. (For report, see Reps. Committees, Ho. of Reps., 3d ses., 27th Cong., vol. 1, No. 86.)

On December 31, 1842, a resolution, that report of Albert M. Lea, in reference to the northern boundary of Missouri; the report of Capt. Guion and Lieut. Fremont, in reference to the Des Moines river, and the evidence in reference to the northern boundary of Missouri, be referred and printed, was passed. (See docs. Ho. of Reps., 3d ses., 27th Cong., vol. 3, No. 38.)

On December 22, 1843, an act of the Legislature of Missouri respecting the boundary line with Iowa territory, was presented in Ho. of Reps. (See docs. Ho. of Reps., 1st ses., 28th Cong., vol. 1, No. 26.)

On February 12, 1844, a message from the President, with a memorial from the Legislative Assembly of Iowa for admission into the Union, was received in Senate.

On April 2, 1844, the committee on territories of Ho. of Reps. reported a bill to enable the people of Iowa to form a constitution and State government, and for the admission of such State into the Union.

On December 9, 1844, a memorial of a convention, with copy of a constitution adopted for the people of Iowa, asking admission into the Union, was received in Senate, and on 12th December in Ho. of Reps. (See Senate docs., 2d ses., 28th Cong., vol. 1, No. 3, and docs. Ho. of Reps., vol. 1, No. 5, and vol. 3, No. 77.)

On January 7, 1845, a bill for the admission of the States of Iowa and Florida into the Union, was reported in Ho. of Reps.

On February 19, 1845, a memorial of the General Assembly of Missouri, praying that the southern boundary line of Iowa be made to conform to the northern boundary line of Missouri, &c., was presented in Senate. (See Senate docs., 2d ses., 28th Cong., vol. 7, No. 110.)

On June 17, 1844, an act respecting the northern boundary of the State of Missouri, was passed and approved.

On March 3, 1845, an act for the admission of the States of Iowa and Florida into the Union, was passed and approved. To this act the assent of the people of Iowa is to be given, to be announced by proclamation by the President, and the State then admitted without further proceedings on the part of Congress. The State to be entitled to one Representative until the next census.

On March 3, 1845, an act supplemental to the act for the admission of the States of Iowa and Florida into the Union, was passed and approved. This act extends the laws of the U. S. to the State of Iowa.

On December 19, 1845, a bill to define the boundaries of the State of Iowa, and to repeal so much of the act of March 3d, 1845, as relates to the boundaries of said State, was introduced on leave in Ho. of Reps., and referred to a com. on territories.

On March 27, 1846, an amendatory bill reported by said committee.

On January 9, 1846, a joint resolution of the legislative council of the territory of Iowa, relative to boundaries of the future State of Iowa, was presented in Ho. of Reps.

On February 5, 1846, a memorial of a Convention of the people of Missouri on subject of the northern boundary of that State, and the admission of Iowa into the Union, was presented in Ho. of Reps. (See docs. Ho. of Reps., 1st ses., 29th Cong., vol. 4, No. 104.)

On February 17, 1846, a memorial of the Legislature of the territory of Iowa relative to boundary between Iowa and Missouri, was presented in Ho. of Reps. (See same docs., vol. 4, No. 126.)

On June 10, in Senate, and July 6, 1846, in Ho. of Reps., copies of the constitution of Iowa were presented. (See docs. Ho. of Reps., 1st ses., 29th Cong., vol. 7, No. 217, and docs. of Senate, vol. 8, No. 384.)

On August 4, 1846, an act to define the boundaries of the State of Iowa, and to repeal so much of the act of March 3, 1845, as relates to boundaries of Iowa, was passed and approved.

On December 15, 1846, a copy of the constitution adopted by the people of Iowa, with a proclamation of the governor, &c., were presented in Ho. of Reps. (See docs. Ho. of Reps., 2d ses., 29th Cong., vol. 2, No. 16.)

On **December 28, 1846,** an act for the admission of the State of Iowa into the Union, was passed and approved.

CALIFORNIA.

Formed out of part of the territory ceded to the United States by the Mexican Republic by Treaty, concluded at Guadalupe Hidalgo, the 2d February, 1848.

Bill (S. 324) reported in Senate by Hon. John M. Clayton from select committee "to establish the territorial governments of Oregon, California, and New Mexico," 1[illegible] July,

1848; vide Senate Journal, 1 Sess. 30 Congress, pages 477, 490, 492, 495, 498—passed Senate 503—26 July. Laid on the table House of Representatives, 28 July, 1848.

Bill (S. 350) introduced by Hon. Stephen A. Douglass, "for the admission of California into the Union as a state," 11 Dec., 1848, and referred. Reported from committee and not again taken up.

Bill (H. R. 685) reported in House of Representatives by Hon. Caleb B. Smith, "to establish the territorial government of Upper California," 20 Dec. 1848, passed 27 Feb. 1849. In Senate referred 28 Feb.: committee discharged 3 March, 1849, and Senate refused to consider the bill.

The "Bill (H. R. 692) making appropriations for the civil and diplomatic expenses of the government for the year ending the 30 June, 1850, and for other purposes," being under consideration in the Senate, the Hon. Isaac P. Walker of Wisconsin, on 21 Feb. 1849, submitted an amendment for the regulation and government of all the territory acquired from the Mexican Republic by the treaty of 2d Feb. 1848; for proceedings on which, vide Senate Journal, 2 Sess. 30 Congress, pages 241, 255, 257, 262, 264, 277; agreed to in Senate 28 Feb., 1849. The House of Representatives agreed to said amendment with an amendment. The Senate disagreed to said amendment of the House of Representatives, and receded from said amendment submitted by Mr. Walker, 3 March, 1849, page 331. For proceedings of House of Representatives on this amendment, vide Journal House of Representatives, 2d Sess. 30 Congress, pages 600, 601, 637—647, and 670.

The "Bill (S. 55) to provide for the organization of the territorial governments of California, Deseret, and New Mexico, and to enable the people of Jacinto, with the consent of the State of Texas, to form a constitution and state government, and for the admission of such state into the Union upon an equal footing with the original States in all respects whatever," was introduced on leave, by Hon. Henry S. Foote, 16 Jan., and on 22 Jan., 1850, referred to the Committee on Territories. Not reported.

Resolutions submitted by Hon. Henry Clay, relative to California, &c., 29 Jan., 1850, vide Senate Journal, pages 118, 299.

Resolutions submitted by Hon. John Bell, relative to California, &c., 28 Feb. 1850, vide Senate Journal, pages 184, 299.

Resolutions submitted by Hon. Thomas H. Benton, relative to California, &c., 18 April, 1850, vide Senate Journal, pages 293, 299.

"A Bill (S. 225) to admit California as a state into the Union, to establish territorial governments for Utah and New Mexico, and making proposals to Texas for the establishment of her western and northern boundaries," together with a special report from the select committee, was submitted by Hon. Henry Clay, 8th May, 1850, vide Senate Journal, 1 Sess. 31 Congress, pages 327, 374, 379, 382, 392, 396, 405, 408, 410, 414, 428, 449, 455, 460, 462, 468, 471, 474, 479, 485, 491, 494, (Amendment of Mr. Pearce, 495,) 518; passed Senate as amended, **1 August, 1850**, being reduced to "An act to establish a territorial government for Utah." (See Utah.)

"A Bill (S. 169) for the admission of the State of California into the Union," was reported by Hon. Stephen A. Douglass from Committee on Territories, 25 March, 1850, vide Senate Journal, 1 Sess. 31 Congress, pages 234, 292, 301, 517, 520, 522, 530, 533, 546, 553, 557, which bill passed Senate 14 August, 1850; considered in House of Representatives, vide Journal, 1 Sess. 31 Congress, pages 1415 to 1424; passed House of Representatives 7 Sept., and became a law, **9 September, 1850.**

OREGON TERRITORY.

The boundaries of this territory have been determined by the following treaties with foreign powers, viz.:—

1. Treaty with France, ceding Louisiana to the United States, of April 30, 1803.
2. Treaty of amity, settlement and limits with Spain, of February 22, 1819.
3. Treaty of limits westward of the Rocky Mountains, with Great Britain, of June 15, 1846.

A Bill (H. R. 533) "to establish a territorial government in Oregon," was reported by Hon. Stephen A. Douglass, House of Representatives, 6 Aug., 1846; passed that House same day. In Senate referred 7 Aug., reported 8 Aug., 1846, with special report, but not further acted on.

A Bill (S. 41) "to organize a territorial government in the Oregon Territory, and for other purposes," was introduced on leave in Senate by Hon. Sidney Breese, 23 Dec., 1846, and referred to Committee on the Judiciary, but not reported therefrom.

A Bill (H. R. 571) "to establish the territorial government of Oregon," was reported by Hon. Stephen A. Douglass, House of Representatives, 23 Dec., 1846, passed that House the 16th Jan., 1847. In Senate referred to Committee of Judiciary, 18 Jan.; reported with amendments 25 Jan.; re-committed 29 Jan.; reported with amendments 10 Feb.; ordered, That it lie on the table, 3d March, 1847.

A Bill (S. 59) "to establish the territorial government of Oregon," was introduced on leave in Senate by Hon. Stephen A. Douglass, on 10 Jan., 1848, and after consideration by the Senate until 13 July, 1848, was, on motion of Hon. John M. Clayton, referred to a select committee. On 18 July, Mr. Clayton from said committee reported it without amendment, and reported Bill (S. 324) "to establish the territorial governments of Oregon, California and New Mexico," which bill passed the Senate 26 July, 1848, and was laid on the table in the House of Representatives 28 July, 1848. Not further acted upon.

A Bill (H. R. 201) "to establish the territorial government of Oregon," was reported from Committee on Territories, House of Representatives, 8 Feb., 1848, by Hon. Caleb B. Smith, passed the House of Representatives 2d Aug.; passed the Senate with amendments 10 Aug., 1848, and became a law on the **14th August, 1848.**

TERRITORY OF MINESOTA.

Formed out of part of territory ceded to the United States by France by Treaty of April 30, 1803.

A Bill (H. R. 568) "establishing the territorial government of Minesota," was passed by the House of Representatives 17 Feb., and laid upon the table in the Senate 3d March, 1847.

A Bill (S. 152) "to establish the territorial government of Minesota," was introduced on leave by Hon. Stephen A. Douglass, 23 Feb., 1848. Reported and recommitted, and, on 8 Aug., 1848, reported with amendments. Not further acted on at 1 Sess. 30 Congress.

Resumed 20 Dec., 1848, 2 Sess. 30 Congress; passed the Senate 19 Jan., 1849; passed House of Representatives with amendments, 28 Feb., and became a law, **3d March, 1849.**

TERRITORY OF NEW MEXICO.

Formed out of part of the territory ceded to the United States by the Mexican Republic by Treaty, concluded at Guadalupe Hidalgo, the 2d February, 1848.

[For statement of propositions for forming a territorial government for New Mexico, see under head of "California."]

A Bill (S. 170) "to establish the governments of Utah and New Mexico, and for other purposes," was reported by Hon. Stephen A. Douglass, 25 March, and passed the Senate 15 Aug., 1850, amended to "An act to establish a territorial government for New Mexico." [This bill, with the addition of a new section, was engrafted on Bill (S. 307) in House of Representatives. See following statement.]

In House of Representatives, 28 Aug., 1850, the Bill (S. 307) entitled "An act proposing to the State of Texas the establishment of her northern and western boundaries, the relinquishment by the said state of all territory claimed by her exterior to said boundaries, and of all her claims upon the United States," having been under consideration until 5th Sept., 1850, was then amended by providing a territorial government for New Mexico, and on the 6 Sept. was passed, and the title amended by adding—*And to establish a territorial government for New Mexico.* The Senate concurred in the amendments, and the bill became a law on the **9th September, 1850.**

TERRITORY OF UTAH.

Formed out of part of the territory ceded to the United States by the Mexican Republic by Treaty, concluded at Guadalupe Hidalgo, the 2d Feb., 1848.

[For statement of propositions for forming a territorial government for Utah, see under head of California and New Mexico.]

The Bill (S. 225) "to admit California as a state into the Union, to establish territorial governments for Utah and New Mexico, and making proposals to Texas for the establishment of her western and northern boundaries," was reported by Hon. Henry Clay, 8 May, and was amended and passed the Senate 1 August; being reduced to a provision for, and the title having been amended to, "An act to establish a territorial government for Utah," which bill passed the House of Representatives 7 Sept., and became a law on the **9th September, 1850.**

TERRITORY OF NEBRASKA.

Formed out of part of the territory ceded to United States by France by Treaty of 30 April, 1803.

A Bill (H. R. 444) "to establish the territory of Nebraska," was introduced on leave by Hon. Stephen A. Douglass, 17 Dec., 1844, and referred. An amendatory bill reported 7 Jan., 1845, but no further action thereon.

A Bill (S. 170) "to establish the territory of Nebraska," was introduced on leave by Hon. Stephen A. Douglass, 15 March, and referred. Reported without amendment 20 April, 1848. Recommitted 20 Dec., 1848. Not reported.

DISTRICT OF COLUMBIA.

Established under the 17th clause, 8th section, 1st article of the Constitution of the United States: "Congress shall have power to exercise exclusive legislation in all cases whatsoever, over such district (not exceeding ten miles square) as may, by cession of particular States, and the acceptance of Congress, become the seat of the Government of the United States," &c. In pursuance of which provision the State of Maryland, on December 23, 1788, passed "An act to cede to Congress a district of ten miles square in this state, for the seat of the Government of the United States."

And the State of Virginia, on December 3, 1789, passed "An act for the cession of ten miles square, or any lesser quantity of territory within this state, to the United States in Congress assembled, for the permanent seat of the General Government."

These cessions were accepted by Congress as required by the Constitution, and the permanent seat of government established by the "Act for establishing the temporary and permanent seat of the government of the United States," approved July 16, 1790; and the act to amend the same, approved March 3, 1791.

The district of ten miles square was accordingly located, and its lines and boundaries particularly established by a proclamation of George Washington, President of the United States, on March 30, 1791, and by the "Act concerning the District of Columbia," approved February 27, 1801, Congress assumed complete jurisdiction over the said district, as contemplated by the framers of the Constitution.

CHAPTER 11.

SOURCES OF HISTORICAL, POLITICAL, STATISTICAL, AND OTHER INFORMATION, REGARDING THE LEGISLATIVE, EXECUTIVE, AND JUDICIAL ACTION OF THE GOVERNMENT OF THE UNITED STATES OF AMERICA, IN POSSESSION OF THE PUBLIC OFFICES AT THE SEAT OF GOVERNMENT.

In the course of experience in public business, it has been found that great embarrassment arises to persons entering into public life in obtaining a practical knowledge of the operations of the Government from its foundation to the period of their entering upon the arena—which knowledge cannot well be dispensed with by unbelievers in the doctrine that *statesmanship comes by intuition or inspiration.* They modestly approach the highly important and responsible stations in the legislative or executive branches of the Government to which the partiality of their fellow-citizens has called them, and prepare with diligence, however well acquainted with the general history of the country, to qualify themselves for a consistent, intelligent, and faithful discharge of duty, by a revision of the acts and proceedings of their predecessors tending to or terminating in measures of state policy, which have either been confirmed by repeated legislation, or remain open questions for investigation and discussion, and by an examination of the foreign and domestic relations, the matter and form of legislative business generally, and the facts and minutiæ of cases requiring, by appointment and a proper discharge of duty, particular attention.

It may, therefore, not be unacceptable to citizens entering into public life, or to those who may expect at some future period to take part in public affairs, or to those who may desire to extend their information concerning the measures, policy, and business concerns of the government, to be furnished with references to *some of the sources* and means of acquiring such information.

To the uninitiated, the accumulated mass of books, records, and documents, contained in the public archives, is calculated to dampen the ardor, if not to repulse the ordinary scholar or man of business from the attempt to fathom the depths of the arcana; and the present effort of the author and compiler to aid in this undertaking is more with the view of essaying a treatise which by extension and improvement may hereafter become a *vade mecum* to the statesman and legislator, and subserving the public interest and convenience, than with the hope of effecting such object in the present edition.

The design of this undertaking is simply to refer to and briefly describe the books, records, and documents of a public character, to be found in the public archives at the Seat of Government, constituting the principal sources of political and statistical information. With a view of preserving perspicuity in the system, the whole will be arranged into classes and sections, as follows, viz.:

CLASS No. 1.

THE COLONIAL HISTORY OF THE UNITED STATES, AND DOCUMENTARY AND OTHER HISTORY OF THE REVOLUTION.

Sec. 1. COLONEL PETER FORCE'S AMERICAN ARCHIVES: Consisting of a collection of authentic records, state papers, debates, and letters and other notices of public affairs: the whole forming A DOCUMENTARY HISTORY of the origin and progress of the North American Colonies; of the causes and accomplishment of the American Revolution; and of the Constitution of Government for the United States, to the final ratification thereof.

IN SIX SERIES.

First Series. From the discovery and settlement of the North American Colonies to the revolution in England, in 1688.

Second Series. From the revolution in England, in 1688, to the cession of Canada to Great Britain, by treaty at Paris, in 1763.

Third Series. From the cession of Canada, in 1763, to the king's message to Parliament, of March 7, 1774, on the proceedings in North America.

Fourth Series. From the king's message of March 7, 1774, to the Declaration of Independence by the United States, in 1776.

Fifth Series. From the Declaration of Independence, in 1776, to the definitive treaty of peace with Great Britain, in 1783.

Sixth Series. From the treaty of peace, in 1783, to the final ratification of the

Constitution of Government for the United States, proposed by the convention held at Philadelphia in 1787.

[Of this work, the fourth series only, in six volumes, has been completed, the other parts being in progress of execution.]

This work was authorized by the "Act making provision for the publication of the Documentary History of the American Revolution," approved March 2, 1833, which directs that it be distributed in the same manner as the American State Papers, under the resolution of July 10, 1832. It was further distributed by the general appropriation act of March 3, 1839.

CLASS No. 2.

LEGISLATIVE PROCEEDINGS AND ACTS OF THE CONGRESS OF THE CONFEDERATION, FROM THE COMMENCEMENT OF THE REVOLUTION TO THE COMMENCEMENT OF THE GOVERNMENT UNDER THE CONSTITUTION.

Sec. 1. THE PUBLIC JOURNAL OF CONGRESS, contained in 4 volumes octavo:

Vol. 1. From September 5, 1774, to December 31, 1776.

Vol. 2. From January 1, 1777, to July 31, 1778.

Vol. 3. From August 1, 1778, to March 31, 1782.

Vol. 4. From April 1, 1782, to March 3, 1789.

This edition was published by Way & Gideon, in 1823; each volume having a separate index. The addresses to the king, Parliament, and people of Great Britain, and other documents preceding and succeeding the commencement of hostilities and the Declaration of Independence, are contained in vol. 1. The Articles of Confederation are contained in vol. 2. And the Journal of the Committee of the States empowered to act for Congress in the recess from June 4 to August 19, 1784; the powers to the Board of Treasury to contract for the sale of the western territory; contracts for moneys borrowed in Europe; credentials of deputies from the States to the convention that formed the Constitution; the Constitution; the ratifications of the Constitution by the conventions of the several States,—are contained in vol. 4.

Sec. 2. THE SECRET JOURNALS OF THE CONGRESS OF THE CONFEDERATION, in four volumes:

Vol. 1. On Domestic Affairs, from 1774 to 1788; History of the Confederation.

Vol. 2. On Foreign Affairs, from 1774 to August 16, 1781.

Vol. 3. On Foreign Affairs, from July, 1781, to May 15, 1786.

Vol. 4. On Foreign Affairs, from May 17, 1786, to September 16, 1788.

CLASS No. 3.

Sec. 1. THE JOURNAL, ACTS, AND PROCEEDINGS OF THE CONVENTION WHICH FORMED THE CONSTITUTION OF THE UNITED STATES, FROM MAY 14 TO SEPTEMBER 17, 1787: In one volume, published under a resolution of Congress of March 27, 1818.

This volume contains the credentials of the deputies to the Convention, the Constitution, the ratifications by the State conventions, &c.

Sec. 2. THE CONSTITUTION OF THE UNITED STATES: a critically correct copy of which, together with an analytical index, are the prominent objects of this book. The former will be found at page 1, and the latter at page 37, of this volume.

Sec. 3. THE DEBATES IN THE CONVENTION WHICH FORMED THE CONSTITUTION, AND IN THE STATE CONVENTIONS FOR THE RATIFICATION OF THE SAME: In four volumes, published by Jonathan Elliott:

Vol. 1 contains the Debates in Massachusetts and New York

Vol. 2 contains the Debates in Virginia.

Vol. 3 contains the Debates in North Carolina and Pennsylvania.

Vol. 4 contains

1. Index to Journal of Federal Convention.
2. Index to Secret Debates of, Ditto.
3. Index to Congressional Opinions on Constitutional questions, from 1789 to 1830.
4. Articles of Confederation.
5. Memoranda relative to drafts and plans in convention that formed the Constitution—names of the Members—their Credentials—Journal of the Convention, &c. &c.—Edmund Randolph's proposition—Charles Pinckney's draft—William Patterson's proposition—David Brereley's draft—Alexander Hamilton's plan—James Madison's minutes of the proceedings.
6. Ratifications of the Constitution by the States, &c.
7. Digest of decisions in the courts of the Union involving Constitutional principles.
8. Secret proceedings of the Federal Convention; Luther Martin's information to Legislature of Maryland; Robert Yates' minutes and notes of debates, &c.
9. Reasons of Robert Yates, John Lansing, jun., and Edmund Randolph for not signing the Constitution.
10. Opinions selected from debates in Congress involving Constitutional principles from 1789 to 1830.
11. James Madison's letters on the Constitutionality of the Tariff, in September and October, 1828.
12. Opinions of Washington, Jefferson, and Madison on the subject.
13. Chart of State constitutions in 1830.

Sec 4. THE FEDERALIST: Being a collection of able essays in explanation of the prominent articles of the Constitution, and in vindication of its principles, by Alexander Hamilton, John Jay, and James Madison, all over the signature of "Publius," and considered of high authority in explanation and in elucidation of that paramount law.

CLASS No. 4.

THE JOURNAL OF THE HOUSE OF REPRESENTATIVES OF THE UNITED STATES, FROM MARCH 4, 1789, TO MARCH 3, 1851.

This Journal as re-printed by order of the House of Representatives, from the commencement to March 3, 1815, is contained in 9 volumes octavo; each having one index.

Sec. 1. Vol. 1. From March 4, 1789, to March 2, 1793.
Vol. 2. From December 2, 1793, to March 3, 1797.
Vol. 3. From May 15, 1797, to March 3, 1801.
Vol. 4. From December 7, 1801, to March 27, 1804.
Vol. 5. From November 5, 1804, to March 3, 1807.
Vol. 6. From October 26, 1807, to March 3, 1809.
Vol. 7. From May 22, 1809, to March 3, 1811.
Vol. 8. From November 4, 1811, to March 3, 1813.
Vol. 9. From May 24, 1813, to March 2, 1815.

Sec. 2. This Journal from March 3, 1815, to March 3, 1851, is contained in 38 volumes, octavo, being one for each session. Each volume having an index.

CLASS No. 5.

THE LEGISLATIVE JOURNAL OF THE SENATE OF THE UNITED STATES, FROM MARCH 4, 1789, TO MARCH 3, 1851.

This Journal as re-printed by order of the Senate, from the commencement to March 3, 1815, is contained in 5 volumes octavo :—

Sec. 1. Vol. 1. From March 4, 1789, to March 2, 1793, containing 5 separate indexes to its contents.
Vol. 2. From March 4, 1793, to March 3, 1799. do. 7 do.
Vol. 3. From March 4, 1799, to March 3, 1805. do. 6 do.
Vol. 4. From March 4, 1805, to March 3, 1811. do. 7 do.
Vol. 5. From March 4, 1811, to March 3, 1815. do. 5 do.

Sec. 2. This Journal, from March 4, 1815, to March 3, 1851, is contained in 38 volumes octavo, being one for each Legislative session. Each volume having an index

CLASS No. 6.

THE EXECUTIVE JOURNAL OF THE SENATE, FROM MARCH 4, 1789, TO MARCH 3, 1851.

This Journal, from the commencement to March 3, 1829, from all of which the injunction of secrecy has been removed, has been printed in 3 volumes octavo, by order of the Senate. Each volume having an index.

Sec. 1. Vol. 1. From March 4, 1789, to March 3, 1805.
Vol. 2. From March 4, 1805, to March 3, 1815.
Vol. 3. From March 4, 1815, to March 3, 1829.

Sec. 2. Those parts of the Executive Journal from which the injunction of secrecy has been removed, from March 4, 1829, to March 3, 1851, will be found printed as an appendix to the Legislative Journal of the session when the injunction was removed.

Sec. 3. The Executive Journal of the Senate from March 4, 1829, to March 3, 1851, from which the injunction of secrecy has not been removed, is contained alone in manuscript record-books, and is accessible only to the President, to the Members, the Secretary and certain officers of the Senate. No extract from this record can be furnished, except by special order of the Senate.

CLASS No. 7.

THE JOURNAL OR RECORD OF THE SENATE ON TRIALS OF IMPEACHMENT, FROM MARCH 4, 1789, TO MARCH 3, 1851.

Sec. 1. On the trial of William Blount, a Senator of the United States, from December 17, 1798, to January 14, 1799.

Sec. 2. On the trial of John Pickering, Judge of the New Hampshire District, from March 3, 1803, to March 12, 1803.

Sec. 3. On the trial of Samuel Chase, one of the Associate Justices of the Supreme Court of the United States, from November 30, 1804, to March 1, 1805.

The preceding cases will be found as an appendix to the third volume of the Legislative Journal of the Senate.

Sec. 4. On the trial of James H. Peck, Judge of the Missouri District, from May 11, 1830, to May 25, 1830; and from December, 13, 1830, to January 31, 1831.

The proceedings in this case will be found as an appendix to the Legislative Journal of the Senate of 1830, 1831.

The Legislative Journals of the Senate and House of Representatives, exhibit the action of Congress from the establishment of the Government under the Constitution, in the introduction, progress and enactment of the Laws of the United States; they contain a record of the introduction by individual members of petitions, motions or resolutions, and bills; notices of the reports of all committees, the names of the members voting on all subjects where the yeas and nays are demanded; all the messages from the President of the United States to either House of Congress, and the inaugural addresses, from the commencement of the Government, will be found at length upon the journals; a brief statement of the subject of every report or communication from the several Executive Departments and Bureaus is entered upon the Journal of the House to which it may be directed; acts and resolutions of the State Legislatures are entered upon the Journals; schedules of the electoral votes for President and Vice President are placed upon the Journals of both Houses, and the names of the members with those of the States which they represent are entered on the Journals of the respective Houses on the days of their first attendance at each session.

The volumes of Journals have indexes referring to the names of petitioners, members, States, Executive Departments, Presidents' messages, committees, motions, resolutions and bills with references to all the proceedings thereon, and generally to all the subjects treated of in the body of the Journal.

But with the exception of the cases above stated, the reasons for or grounds of Legislation, from their voluminous nature and their number, could not be embodied within the narrow compass of the Journals.

These are contained in the manuscript files and records, the printed documents, and the reported speeches of the members of the two Houses to be sought for from various sources.

The manuscript files and records are preserved in the office of the House in which they may have been presented, or to which they may have been communicated. The printed documents and speeches, however, require a more particular description and reference, which will be given as concisely as practicable.

CLASS No. 8.

EMBRACING THE DOCUMENTS ORDERED TO BE PRINTED BY THE TWO HOUSES OF CONGRESS SINCE MARCH 4, 1789.

These consist of messages from the President, reports from the several Executive Departments and Bureaus, reports of committees of the two Houses, with documents and tables communicated therewith, as well as memorials, petitions, resolutions of State Legislatures, and all other papers printed under the order of either House. These will be arranged into sections :—

SEC. 1. THE FOLIO EDITION OF STATE PAPERS PUBLISHED UNDER JOINT RESOLUTIONS OF CONGRESS, AND PRINTED BY MESSRS. GALES & SEATON, CONSISTS OF 21 VOLUMES.

These documents were selected with much care from the mass of manuscript and printed documents, papers and books in the offices of the two Houses, from all sources, and upon all subjects, having deficiencies supplied from the archives and records of the Executive Departments. These were divided into ten different classes, according to their nature or subject, viz.:—

4 vols. Foreign Relations. Vol. 1, from March 4, 1789, to Feb. 28, 1797.
Vol. 2, from Feb. 28, 1797, to Feb. 19, 1807.
Vol. 3, from Feb. 19, 1807, to March 3, 1815.
Vol. 4, from March 3, 1815, to May 3, 1822

2 vols. Indian Affairs. Vol. 1, from March 4, 1789, to Nov. 18, 1814.
Vol. 2, from Nov. 18, 1814, to March 1, 1827.

3 vols. Finances. Vol. 1, from March 4, 1789, to April 29, 1802.
Vol. 2, from April 29, 1802, to March 2, 1815.
Vol. 3, from March 2, 1815, to March 12, 1822.

2 vols. Commerce and Navigation. Vol. 1, from March 4, 1789, to Feb. 9, 1815
Vol. 2, from Feb. 9, 1815, to Feb. 25, 1823.

2 vols. Military Affairs. Vol. 1, from March 4, 1789, to Feb. 25, 1819.
Vol. 2, from Feb. 25, 1819, to Feb. 28, 1825.

1 vol. Naval Affairs. Vol. 1, from March 4, 1789, to March 5, 1825.

1 vol. Post-Office. Vol. 1, from March 4, 1789, to March 2, 1833.

3 vols. Public Lands. Vol. 1, from March 4, 1789, to Feb. 27, 1809.
Vol. 2, from Feb. 27, 1809, to Feb. 14, 1815.
Vol. 3, from Feb. 14, 1815. to May 26, 1824.

1 vol. Claims. Vol. 1, from March 4, 1789, to March 3, 1823.

2 vols. Miscellaneous. Vol. 1, from March 4, 1789, to Feb. 16 1809
Vol. 2, from Feb 16, 1809, to March 3, 1823.

There will also be included in this section the two additional volumes on Public Lands that were printed by Duff Green, by order of the Senate, viz. :—

2 vols. on Public Lands. Vol. 4, from May 26, 1824, to Jan. 2, 1828.
Vol. 5, from Jan. 2, 1828, to Jan. 21, 1834.

In the compilation of these state papers, care was taken to render each class as complete as practicable. The authority for the publication, and the manner of proceeding in the execution of the work, will be found stated at the beginning of the first volume on Foreign Relations. As it purports to be a *selection* of those documents and papers, it will not, of course, be expected to embrace *every* document and paper presented in or communicated to either House of Congress, as these can alone be found in the archives of Congress; but it was intended that they should embrace *every important document* of the classes to which they respectively belong, considered valuable as precedents for the future action of the Government, or material in its political and statistical history, or as establishing principles in the allowance or rejection of private pecuniary claims against the Government, or in the settlement of private land claims.

These state papers were printed under the authority of the act of Congress "making provision for a subscription to a compilation of congressional documents," approved March 2, 1831, and continued under the joint resolution of March 2, 1833, which limited the continuation to eight volumes, and which, with those previously authorized, made twenty-one volumes. These were disposed of by a joint "resolution directing the distribution of a compilation of congressional documents, and for other purposes," approved July 10, 1832.

CLASS No. 9.

Sec. 1 WILL EMBRACE THE DOCUMENTS PRINTED IN OCTAVO FORM BY ORDER OF THE SENATE, during each session, from March 4, 1789, to March 3, 1851. These are numbered as they are sent to the printer; loose copies are furnished to the members of both Houses of Congress and other public functionaries, and sometimes extra copies for distribution, as they are printed; and other copies are retained and bound, in as many volumes as necessary, with copious indexes, for preservation, when the printing of each session is completed. The more important of these printed documents will be found reprinted, under their appropriate heads, in the folio state papers, where they will be found more conveniently, in connection with kindred subjects which had accumulated from March 4, 1789, to the time to which the class they belong to was reprinted, as stated in the preceding section; from which time, recourse must be had to these bound documents of each session—every session having a separate index.

In addition to these documents, the bills and resolutions of the Senate are printed in folio form, and distributed nearly as the octavo documents. Several copies of these have been bound into volumes, with indexes, since 1824–5.

CLASS No. 10.

Sec. 1 WILL EMBRACE THE DOCUMENTS PRINTED IN OCTAVO FORM BY ORDER OF THE HOUSE OF REPRESENTATIVES, from March

4, 1789, to March 3, 1851. These are divided into several series, each being numbered as sent to the printer. One series consists of the reports of committees of the House of Representatives, with their accompanying documents; and the other series consists of messages, reports, and documents, from the Executive Departments, and all other documents ordered to be printed by that House. Loose copies are furnished to members of both Houses of Congress, and other public functionaries, and sometimes extra copies for distribution, as they are printed; and other copies are retained and bound, each series separately, (in as many volumes as necessary, with separate indexes,) for preservation, when the printing of each session is completed. The more important of these documents, of both series, will be found reprinted, under their appropriate heads, in the folio state papers, as mentioned in the preceding section, as far as they extend; from which time, recourse must be had to these bound documents of each session—every session having a separate index for each series of these documents.

In addition to these documents, the bills and joint resolutions of the House of Representatives have been printed in folio form, and distributed as the octavo documents. Several copies of these have been bound, with indexes, since 1825.

CLASS No. 11.

DEBATES IN CONGRESS:

Embracing the speeches made in the two Houses of Congress, from March 4, 1789, to March 3, 1851.

When it is desired to find the discussion in either House upon any particular subject, it is necessary first to ascertain from the journal of the House in which the discussion has taken place, when, or on what days, such subject was under consideration in the House, and then seek for the publication of the proceedings of those days in the public newspapers that published such debates, or in the various compilations of debates, as either may be found to embrace the time at which the discussion may have taken place.

Sec. 1. The compilation of Joseph Gales, senior, in 2 volumes, contains the debates in the first Congress, 1789 to 1791.*

Sec. 2. The Congressional Register, or History of the Proceedings and Debates of the first House of Representatives, by Thomas Lloyd, 1789-91.

Sec. 3. History of Congress, exhibiting a classification of the proceedings of the Senate and House of Representatives, from March 4, 1789, to March 3, 1793.

Sec. 4. Debates in the Congress of the United States on the bill for repealing the law "for the more convenient organization of the courts of the United States:" Albany, 1802. (State Department.)

Sec. 5. Debates in the House of Representatives of the United States on questions involved in the British treaty of 1794, (Jay's treaty:) Philadelphia, 1808. (State Department.)

---

* This compilation has been continued by Gales & Seaton, under the patronage of Congress.

Sec. 6. Debates in the House of Representatives of the United States on the Seminole war, in January and February, 1819. (State Department.)

Sec. 7. Dunlap's American Daily Advertiser, from 1791 to 1793. (Congress Library.)

Sec. 8. Dunlap & Claypole's Advertiser, from 1794 to 1795. (Cong. Lib.)

Sec. 9. Brown's Philadelphia Gazette, from 1794 to 1800. (Cong. Lib.)

Sec. 10. Bache's General Advertiser, from 1795 to 1797. (Cong. Lib.)

Sec. 11. Bache & Duane's Aurora, from 1798 to 1814. (Cong. Lib.)

Sec. 12. Carey's United States Recorder, from 1798 to 1800. (Cong. Lib.)

Sec. 13. Delaware Gazette, Political Mirror, from 1798 to 1800. (Cong. Lib.)

Sec. 14. Dennison's Republican Watch Tower, from 1800 to 1809. (Cong.Lib.)

Sec. 15. Duane's Weekly Aurora, from 1810 to 1821. (Cong. Lib.)

Sec. 16. Fenno's Gazette of the United States, from 1789 to 1798. (Cong. Lib.)

Sec. 17. National Intelligencer, (tri-weekly,) from 1800 to 1813. (Cong. Lib.)
National Intelligencer, (daily,) from 1814 to 1851. (Cong. Lib.)

Sec. 18. Universal Gazette, (by Samuel Harrison Smith,) from 1798 to 1808.

Sec. 19. Philadelphia Gazette, from 1795 to 1797. (Cong. Lib.)

Sec. 20. Virginia Argus, from 1797 to 1803. (Cong. Lib.)

Sec. 21. Virginia Argus and Enquirer, (bound together,) from 1804 to 1808 (Cong. Lib.)

Sec. 22. Richmond Enquirer, from 1809 to 1814. (Cong. Lib.)

Sec. 23. Washington City Gazette, from 1815 to 1826. (Cong. Lib.)

Sec. 24. National Journal, from 1826 to 1831. (Cong. Lib.)

Sec. 25. United States Telegraph, from 1828 to 1837. (Cong. Lib.)

Sec. 26. Globe, from 1832 to 1845. (Cong. Lib.)

Sec. 27. Madisonian, from 1837 to 1838. (Cong. Lib.)

Sec. 28. Register of Debates in Congress, comprising the leading debates and incidents of each session, with an appendix containing important state papers and public documents, and the laws of a public nature enacted during each session, with an index to the subject of debate and to the names of the speakers in each House of Congress for each session, viz.:

2d	Session,	18th	Congress,	1824–5, in 1st volume.
1st	"	19th	"	1825–6, in 2d volume, in 2 parts.
2d	"	19th	"	1826–7, in 3d volume.
1st	"	20th	"	1827–8, in 4th volume, in 2 parts
2d	"	20th	"	1828–9, in 5th volume.
1st	"	21st	"	1829–30, in 6th volume, in 2 parts.
2d	"	21st	"	1830–31, in 7th volume.
1st	"	22d	"	1831–2, in 8th volume, in 3 parts.
2d	"	22d	"	1832–3, in 9th volume, in 2 parts.
1st	"	23d	"	1833–4, in 10th volume, in 4 parts.
2d	"	23d	"	1834–5, in 11th volume in 2 parts.
1st	"	24th	"	1835–6, in 12th volume in 4 parts.
2d	"	24th	"	1836–7, in 13th volume, in 2 parts.
1st	"	25th	"	1837, 14th volume, in 2 parts.

Sec. 29. The Congressional Globe and Appendix, containing sketches of the proceedings and incidental debates, and also the debates at large in the two

Houses of Congress, with an index of the subject of debate, and names of the speakers in each House for each session, viz:—

1st and 2d Sessions, 23d Congress, 1833-4-5, 1st and 2d volumes in 1.
1st Sess. 24th Cong. 1835-6, 3d vol.
2d " 24th " 1386-7, 4th vol.
1st " 25th " 1837, 5th vol.
2d " 25th " 1837-8, 6th vol.
3d " 25th " 1838-9, 7th vol.
1st " 26th " 1839-40, 8th vol.
2d " 26th " 1840-1, 9th vol.
1st " 27th " 1841, 10th vol.
2d " 27th " 1841-2, 11th vol.
3d Sess. 27th Cong. 1842-3, 12th vol.
1st " 28th " 1843-4, 13th vol.
2d " 28th " 1844-5, 14th vol.
1st " 29th " 1845-6, New Series, 1 vol. in 2 parts.
2d " 29th " 1846-7, "
1st " 30th " 1847-8, "
2d " 30th " 1848-9, "
1st " 31st " 1849-50, "
2d " 31st " 1850-51, "

CLASS No. 12.

LAWS OF THE UNITED STATES.

THIS CLASS WILL EMBRACE THE SEVERAL EDITIONS OR SERIES OF THE LAWS OF THE UNITED STATES AND INDEXES TO THE LAWS.

Sec. 1. The series containing in separate volumes the laws usually published in pamphlet form at the termination of each session of Congress. In this series the laws are published *in extenso*, none being omitted.

The first of this series was published in 1797, in 3 volumes, by Richard Folwell, embracing the laws, resolutions, and treaties, from March 4, 1789, to March 3, 1797. These were continued by Matthew Carey, to include the 4th volume, to March 3, 1799; by William Duane to include the 5th and 6th volumes, to March 3, 1803; by Roger C. Weightman, to include the 7th, 8th, 9th, and 10th volumes, to March 3, 1811; and were continued by various individuals, "By authority," in pamphlet form at the termination of every session of Congress, down to March 3, 1851.

Sec. 2. An edition of the laws was published in 1815 by Bioren & Duane and R. C. Weightman. This edition was compiled by J. B. Colvin, upon the basis of a plan prepared by Richard Rush, then Attorney-General of the United States, and adopted by James Monroe, Secretary of State, in conformity with the act of Congress of the 18th April, 1814. It consists of five volumes, and embraces the laws of the United States from March 4, 1789, to March 3, 1815, with the exception of "the local judiciary acts, and all acts confiding power to corporate bodies in the District of Columbia, or which have been otherwise passed by Congress in their character of Legislature for the District," which were excluded.

Vol. 1 contains—The Declaration of Independence, Articles of Confederation.
The Constitution, and proceedings which led to its adoption.
Treaties with foreign nations and Indian tribes, from 1778 to 1814.
Grants, treaties, and cessions, by which lands have been acquired by the United States, from 1783 to 1814.

Old proclamations and grants of lands, and treaties between foreign governments relating to titles to lands, and boundaries of territories now included within the United States.

Grant to the Hudson's Bay Company.

Cessions of land by several States to the United States.

Title of the United States to Louisiana.—Grant to Crozat.

Evidence respecting Yazoo and other land claims.

Treaty of Paris, of 10th February, 1763, between Great Britain, France, and Spain.

Titles to, and boundaries of the Floridas.

Explanatory notes of the acquisition, surveys, sales, donations, and other disposition of, and regulations concerning, the public lands in the early periods of the Government.

Important claims to land, either rejected or requiring a critical examination.

Extracts from early English charters conveying territory.

Ordinance for the government of the territory north-west of the river Ohio.

Boundaries of South Carolina and Georgia established.

Ohio company's claims to land.

Illinois company's claims to land.

Wabash company's claims to land.

Wilkins' grant and Governor St. Clair's confirmation.

Spanish regulations for the allotment of lands.

Grand Maison's claim on Washita.

Houma's claim on New Orleans Island.

Bastrop's, St. Vrain, now John Smith, T.

Renaut's, Dubuque's, and Chouteau's claims to lands and lead mines.

An ordinance for ascertaining the mode of disposing of lands in the western territory.

Boundary lines between Virginia and Kentucky ascertained.

Location of Virginia military bounty land.

Powers of the board of Treasury to contract for the sale of western territory.

Relinquishment of a tract of land to Pennsylvania.

Bounties to foreign deserters.

Provision for refugees from Canada and Nova Scotia.

Resolutions of old Congress relative to military bounty land.

Donation to Arnold Henry Dohrman.

Donation to the Society of the United Brethren.

Claims and donations in territories of Indiana, Illinois, and Michigan.

ORIGIN, &c., OF THE DEPARTMENT OF STATE for the United States.

ORIGIN, &c., OF THE DEPARTMENT OF WAR.

Commencement and progress of Indian affairs.

ORIGIN, &c., OF THE NAVAL ESTABLISHMENT of the United States.

ORIGIN, &c., OF THE TREASURY DEPARTMENT.

ORIGIN, &c., OF THE MINT of the United States.

ORIGIN, &c., OF THE GENERAL POST-OFFICE of the United States.

An ordinance for settling the accounts between the United States and the individual States.

Light-houses, beacons, buoys, and public piers, and cessions of land for same from the States to the United States.

Military establishment of the United States in 1787, and lands held for military purposes.

Concerning the seat of the general Government.—FLAG of the United States.—Device for a GREAT SEAL.—Device for copper coinage.

Half pay.—Commutation.—Invalids.—Pensions.—Acts of limitation.

Vol. 2 contains the Laws of the United States, from March 4, 1789 to March 3, 1797.

Vol. 3 contains do. from March 3, 1797, to March 3, 1805.

Vol. 4 contains do. from March 3, 1805, to March 3, 1815.

Vol. 5 contains, 1. A list of all acts and resolutions from 1789 to 1815.
2. A General Index to private acts from 1789 to 1815.
3. Statement of Receipts and Expenditures from 1789 to 1815.
4. A General Index Laws United States from 1789 to 1815.

The series of Laws contained in the preceding volumes of the edition of Bioren and Duane, have been continued to March 3, 1845, by a 6th, 7th, 8th, 9th, and 10th volumes:

Vol. 6, Printed by Davis & Force in 1822, contains Laws of the United States including Treaties, from March 3, 1815, to March 3, 1821, with an Index thereto.

Vol. 7. Printed by P. Force in 1827. Ditto March 3, 1821, to March 3, 1827, do. With this volume there was printed a general index of all the Acts, Resolutions, Treaties, and other matter contained in the seven preceding volumes. It was prepared by Samuel Burch, under a resolution of the House of Representatives, and is one of the best, most full and systematic Indexes of the Laws of the United States extant, for the time it embraces, viz., March 4, 1789, to March 3, 1827. It has been separately bound.

Vol. 8. Printed by W. A. Davis in 1835, and contains the Acts, Resolutions and Treaties from March 3, 1827, to March 3, 1833.

Vol. 9. Printed by order of Congress in 1839, and contains the Acts, Resolutions and Treaties from March 3, 1833, to March 3, 1839.

Vol. 10. Printed by J. and G. S. Gideon in 1845, and contains the Acts, Resolutions and Treaties, from March 3, 1839, to March 3, 1845. From March 3, 1845, to March 3, 1851, the Laws and Treaties will be found in pamphlet form.

Sec. 3. The Public and General Statutes of the United States, from 1789 to 1827 inclusive, whether expired, repealed, or in force: arranged in chronological order, with marginal references, and a copious index: to which is added the Constitution and an Appendix: published under the inspection of Judge Story. Boston, 1827.

Sec. 4. An edition of the Statutes at large was edited by Richard Peters, and published by Little & Brown, in 1845.*

* This edition of the Statutes has been continued in pamphlet form for each session of Congress.

Vol. 1 contains, 1. The Declaration of Independence.
2. The Articles of Confederation.
3. The Constitution of the United States.
4. The Public acts of Congress from March 4, 1789, to March 3, 1799.

Vol. 2 contains the Public Acts of Congress from March 3, 1799, to March 3, 1813.

Vol. 3 contains do. do. from March 3, 1813, to March 3, 1823.

Vol. 4 contains do. do. from March 3, 1823, to March 3, 1835.
Also Acts of Virginia, Pennsylvania, and Maryland.
Proceedings and Charter of Potomac Company relating to Chesapeake and Ohio canal.
Act of Alabama to incorporate the Cahawba Navigation Company.
Proclamations by the President of the United States on Commercial Affairs with Foreign Nations.

Vol. 5 contains the Public Acts of Congress from March 3, 1835, to March 3, 1845.
Also a Proclamation of the President on extinguishment of Indian title to land in Missouri.
An act of Virginia relating to Chesapeake and Ohio Canal Company, February 27, 1829.

Vol. 6 contains Private Statutes at large, from March 4, 1789, to March 3, 1845.

Vol. 7 contains Treaties with Indian tribes, from September 17, 1778, to March 3, 1845.

Vol. 8 contains the Treaties with Foreign Nations, from February 6, 1778, to March 3, 1845.

Each of the preceding volumes contains an index to the matter therein; this 8th volume also contains:—

1. Table showing relative chapters of this and other editions of the Laws.
2. Tables of Acts of Congress, from 1789, to 1845 inclusive, relating to the Judiciary.
3. Table of Acts of do. relating to Imports and Tonnage.
4. Table of Acts of do. relating to Public Lands.
5. Table of Acts of do. relating to the Post-Office.
6. Index to the five volumes of Public Statutes.
7. A General Index to the matter contained in the 8 volumes above mentioned.

Sec. 4. The Acts of Congress in relation to the District of Columbia from July 16, 1790, to March 4, 1831 inclusive, and of the Legislatures of Virginia and Maryland, passed especially in regard to that District, or to persons or property within the same, with preliminary notes of the proceedings of the Congress, under the Confederation, as well as under the present Constitution, in regard to the permanent seat of the Government of the United States. Printed by William A. Davis, 1831.

CLASS No. 13.

ABRIDGMENTS AND DIGESTS OF THE LAWS OF THE UNITED STATES.

Sec. 1. DIGEST of all such Acts of Congress as concern the United States at large; all existing Treaties, &c., by William Graydon, in 1813.

Sec. 2. DIGEST of the Laws of the United States, including an abstract of the Judicial Decisions relating to the Constitutional and Statutory Law, with Notes explanatory and historical, by Thomas F. Gordon. Printed in 1827.

Sec. 3. AN ABRIDGMENT of the Acts of Congress now in force, excepting those of a private and local application, with notes of Decisions, giving construction to the same, in the Supreme Court of the United States, by Edward Ingersoll. Printed in 1825.

Sec. 4. DIGEST of the Laws of the United States including the Treaties with Foreign Powers, and an abstract of the Judicial Decisions relating to the Constitutional and Statutory Law. By Thomas F. Gordon, printed in 1844.

CLASS No. 14.

INDEXES PREPARED IN CONFORMITY WITH ORDERS OR RESOLUTIONS OF THE SENATE AND HOUSE OF REPRESENTATIVES OF THE UNITED STATES, RESPECTIVELY.

Sec. 1. GENERAL INDEX to the Laws of the United States of America, from March 4, 1789, to March 3, 1827, including all Treaties entered into between those periods; in which the principles involved in acts for the relief of individuals, or of a private or local nature, are arranged under general heads, to which such principles appropriately belong: arranged to the edition commenced by Bioren, Duane & Weightman, in 1815, and subsequently continued by Davis & Force, and William A. Davis. [This is the most complete and useful index of the laws, up to March 3, 1827, extant; and it would add to the public convenience if a similar one were made of the laws from that period up to the present time.]

Sec. 2. INDEX to the Executive Communications made to the House of Representatives, from March 4, 1789, to March 3, 1817: *first*, by a reference, in alphabetical order, to the printed and also to the manuscript reports, according to the subject-matter; *second*, by a reference to the same matter, arranged under the head of the department whence it came. Also, an

Sec. 3. INDEX to all the printed Reports of Committees, alphabetically arranged, from March 4, 1789, to March 3, 1817: printed in 1824.

Sec. 4. INDEX to the Executive Communications and Reports of Committees made to the House of Representatives, from December 3, 1817, to March 3, 1823: printed in 1823.

Sec. 5. A DIGESTED INDEX to the Executive Documents (that is, all documents ordered to be printed) and Reports of Committees of the House of Representatives, from March 3, 1823, to March 3, 1831, inclusive: printed in 1832.

Sec. 6. A DIGESTED INDEX to the Executive Documents and Reports of Committees of the House of Representatives, from March 4, 1831, to March 3 1839, inclusive.

Sec. 7. INDEX, or alphabetical list of Private Claims which have been before the SENATE, from December 4, 1815, to March 3, 1849, with the proceedings of the Senate thereon: showing the names of the claimants; the nature or object of each claim; at what session, and in what manner, it was brought before the Senate; to what committee it was referred; the nature of the report, and (where special reports were made) the number of the report, if printed, and, if not, the date of the report; the number of the bill, distinguishing between Senate and House bills; the manner in which the claim was disposed of by the Senate; and, in cases where it passed both Houses, the date of the act of Congress: the whole compiled from the journals of the Senate, and by reference, when necessary, to the journals of the House of Representatives, the reports of committees, the bills of the two Houses, and the laws of the United States. Prepared by orders of the Senate of April 9, 1840, February 27, 1841, and February 8, 1849.

CLASS No. 15.

REPORTS OF THE DECISIONS OF THE SUPREME COURT OF THE UNITED STATES.

1. By ALEXANDER JAMES DALLAS, from February term, 1790, to August term, 1800, inclusive.
2. By WILLIAM CRANCH, from August term, 1801, to February term, 1815, inclusive.
3. By HENRY WHEATON, from February term, 1816, to January term, 1827, inclusive.
4. By RICHARD PETERS, jun., from January term, 1828, to January term, 1842, inclusive.
5. By BENJAMIN C. HOWARD, from January term, 1843, to January term, 1851, inclusive.
6. Condensed Reports of cases in the Supreme Court of the United States, containing the whole series of the decisions of the court from its organization to the commencement of Peters' Reports, at January term, 1827, with copious notes and parallel cases in the Supreme and Circuit Courts of the United States.

CLASS No. 16.

PUBLICATIONS ON THE SUBJECT OF THE PUBLIC LANDS AND PRIVATE LAND CLAIMS UNDER THE AUTHORITY OF THE UNITED STATES.

1. LAWS OF THE UNITED STATES, Resolutions of Congress under the Confederation, Treaties, Proclamations, and other documents, having operation and respect to the Public Lands: collected, digested, and arranged, pursuant to the act of Congress, approved April 27, 1810, by Albert Gallatin, Secretary of the Treasury: revised, completed, and printed, under the act of January 20, 1817.

[This is a valuable treatise and compilation of charters, treaties, grants, cessions, compacts, resolutions, acts relating to the early history, acquisition, regulation, and disposition of the public lands, and evidence of the nature and exten. of private land claims.]

2. LAWS OF THE UNITED STATES, Resolutions of Congress under the Confederation, Treaties, Proclamations, Spanish Regulations, and other documents, respecting the Public Lands: compiled, in obedience to a resolution of the House of Representatives of the United States of March 1, 1826, by M. St. C. Clarke, and printed by order of the House of Representatives of February 19, 1827: in one volume.

3. LAWS OF THE UNITED STATES, Treaties, Regulations, and other documents, respecting the Public Lands; with the Opinions of the Courts of the United States in relation thereto, from 1826 to 1833: by M. St. C. Clarke, under a resolution of the House of Representatives of March 1, 1833.

4. DOCUMENTS, LEGISLATIVE AND EXECUTIVE, of the Congress of the United States, in relation to the Public Lands, from March 4, 1789, to June 15, 1824, in five volumes: compiled under the resolutions of the Senate of February 26, 1833, and January 3, 1834. Printed by Duff Green.

5. GENERAL PUBLIC ACTS OF CONGRESS respecting the sale and disposition of the Public Lands; with Instructions issued from time to time by the Secretary of the Treasury and Commissioner of the General Land Office, and Official Opinions of the Attorney-General on questions arising under the land laws; in two parts, or volumes:

Part 1 contains the laws from March 4, 1789, to July 9, 1838.

Part 2 contains the instructions and opinions, from March 4, 1789, to August 17, 1838.

Prepared and printed under the resolution of the Senate of February 28, 1837.

CLASS No. 17.

REVENUE LAWS, COMMERCIAL REGULATIONS, DIGESTS OF TARIFF LAWS, &c.

1. A SELECTION OF ALL THE LAWS OF THE UNITED STATES in force, relative to commercial subjects, with marginal notes and references, classed under separate heads, viz.: Acts for collection of duties on imports and tonnage; Table of tonnage duty and fees of office; Registering, recording, enrolling, and licensing of ships or vessels; Mediterranean passports; Quarantine and health; Remission of fines, penalties, and forfeitures; Fisheries; Naturalization; Restriction of trade with an enemy; Letters of marque and reprisal; Salvage; Slave trade; Consuls and vice-consuls; Seamen in the merchants' service; Sea letters; British licenses; and for regulating foreign coins, &c.: by John Brice: 1814.

2. COMMERCIAL REGULATIONS OF THE FOREIGN COUNTRIES with which the United States have commercial intercourse: collected, digested, and printed, under the direction of the President of the United States, conformably to a resolution of the Senate of March 3, 1817.

3. A DIGEST OF THE COMMERCIAL REGULATIONS OF THE DIFFERENT FOREIGN NATIONS with which the United States have intercourse: in compliance with a resolution of the House of Representatives of January 21, 1823.

4. JONES'S DIGEST: being a particular and detailed account of the duties

performed by the various officers belonging to the custom-house departments of the United States; together with a description of some of the principal books and documents in general use in the several offices of the custom-house, with the usual routine through which merchants and captains must pass on entering vessels and merchandise, &c.: by Andrew A. Jones, in 1835.

5. REPORT OF THE SECRETARY OF STATE ON THE COMMERCIAL RELATIONS OF THE UNITED STATES WITH FOREIGN NATIONS: comparative tariffs of the United States and other nations; tabular statements of the domestic exports of the United States; duties on importation of the staple or principal productions of the United States into foreign countries; navigation; and British tariff, corn-laws, &c.: prepared in compliance with the resolutions of the House of Representatives of Sept. 3, 1841, and January 31, 1842.

6. TARIFFS, from 1789 to 1833, with the votes in each House of Congress thereon, arranged according to States.

7. A COLLECTION OF THE LAWS OF THE UNITED STATES relating to revenue, navigation, and commerce and light-houses, including treaties with foreign powers, up to March 4, 1843: compiled for the Treasury Department of the United States, by Thomas F. Gordon: 1844.

8. A DIGEST of the existing commercial regulations of foreign countries with which the United States have intercourse: prepared under the direction of the Secretary of the Treasury, in compliance with a resolution of the House of Representatives of March 3, 1831. Printed in 1833, in 3 volumes octavo.

9. A STATISTICAL VIEW OF THE COMMERCE OF THE UNITED STATES: its connection with agriculture and manufactures; and an account of the public debt, revenues, and expenditures of the United States; with a brief review of the trade, agriculture, and manufactures of the Colonies, previous to their independence; and a table illustrative of the principles and objects of the work: by Timothy Pitkin; 1817.

10. A DICTIONARY, practical, theoretical, and historical, of commerce and commercial navigation; in 2 volumes: by J. R. McCulloch: 1840.

CLASS No. 18.

MISCELLANEOUS BOOKS PRINTED OR FURNISHED UNDER THE AUTHORITY OR PATRONAGE OF THE UNITED STATES, AND NOT NOTICED UNDER PARTICULAR HEADS.

1. THE "BLUE BOOK," or Biennial Register of all officers and agents, civil, military and naval, in the service of the United States. Compiled by the Secretary of State, as required by the resolution of Congress, approved April 27, 1816.

The printers of the Laws, printers to Congress, the allowances to each, allowances to contractors for carrying the mail, were directed to be included in the Biennial Register by the resolution of July 14, 1832.

2. WAIT'S STATE PAPERS and public documents of the United States, from March 4, 1789, to August 1, 1818. [These are believed to have been included in folio State Papers in the series on Foreign Relations.]

3. CONTESTED ELECTIONS in Congress of Senators and Representatives,

from 1789 to 1834, inclusive, compiled by M. St. Clair Clarke and David A. Hall, and printed by order of the House of Representatives.

4. REPORT OF THE TRIAL OF JAMES H. PECK, Judge of the United States Court for the District of Missouri, on an impeachment. 1833.

5. LEGISLATIVE AND DOCUMENTARY HISTORY OF THE BANK OF THE UNITED STATES, including the original Bank of North America. By M. St. Clair Clarke and David A. Hall.

6. REPORT OF COMMITTEE of the House of Representatives, with documents relative to the conduct of GENERAL JAMES WILKINSON, February 26, 1811.

7. TREATIES WITH THE SEVERAL INDIAN TRIBES, from 1778 to 1837, compiled under the direction of the Commissioner of Indian Affairs, 1837.

8. REPORTS ON THE FINANCES of the United States from 1790 to 1836; with the reports of Alexander Hamilton on Public Credit, a National Bank, Manufactures and the Mint. In 3 volumes octavo.

9. THE PENSION LAWS OF THE UNITED STATES, including sundry resolutions of Congress, from 1776 to 1833, executed at the War Department, with the opinions of the Attorneys General of the United States, and the rules and regulations adopted by the Secretary of War, relative to the execution of those Laws: 1833.

10. LAWS OF THE UNITED STATES RELATIVE TO THE NAVY AND MARINE CORPS to March 3, 1841; with acts and resolutions, granting medals, swords, and votes of thanks, &c., private acts, a table of appropriations and expenditures for the Naval Service from 1791 to 1840 inclusive; also a synopsis of Legislation of Congress on Naval Affairs during the Revolutionary war: 1841.

11. RESOLUTIONS, LAWS AND ORDINANCES RELATING TO THE PAY, HALF-PAY, COMMUTATION OF HALF-PAY, BOUNTY LANDS AND OTHER PROMISES made by Congress to the officers and soldiers of the Revolution; to the settlement of accounts between the United States and the several States, and to the funding of the revolutionary Debt: 1838. Compiled by W. S. Franklin, Clerk, under resolution of the House of Representatives of April 11, 1836.

12. STATEMENT OF THE ARTS AND MANUFACTURES OF THE UNITED STATES for 1810, by Tench Coxe, under direction of Albert Gallatin, Secretary of the Treasury, in obedience to a resolution of Congress of March 19, 1812.

13. TABLES OF THE CENSUS of the United States for 1790, 1800, 1810, 1820, 1830, 1840.

14. COMPENDIUM OF THE 6th CENSUS for 1840, exhibiting the population, wealth, and resources of the country, the aggregate value and produce, and number of persons employed in Mines, Agriculture, Commerce, Manufactures, &c., with an abstract of each preceding census, and the apportionment of Representatives under the same: 1841.

15. STATISTICAL VIEW OF THE POPULATION OF THE UNITED STATES, FROM 1790 TO 1830, inclusive, published in accordance with the resolutions of the Senate of the United States of February 26, 1833, and March 31, 1834.

16. A CENSUS OF PENSIONERS for Revolutionary or Military services; with their names, ages, and places of residence as returned by the Marshals: 1841.

17. MILITARY LAWS OF THE UNITED STATES, including those relating to the Marine Corps, by Trueman Cross. 1838.

18. A SYSTEM OF PENAL LAWS FOR THE UNITED STATES of America, consisting of a code of Crimes and Punishments; a code of Proceedings in criminal cases; a code of Prison Discipline; and a book of Definitions. Prepared and presented to the House of Representatives of the United States, by Edward Livingston: 1828.

19. THE DIPLOMATIC CORRESPONDENCE OF THE AMERICAN REVOLUTION, being letters of Benjamin Franklin, Silas Dean, John Adams, John Jay, Arthur Lee, William Lee, Ralph Izard, Francis Dana, William Carmichael, Henry Laurens, John Laurens, M. Dumas and others, concerning the Foreign Relations of the United States during the whole Revolution; with replies from the Secret Committee of Congress, and the Secretary of Foreign Affairs; also correspondence with the French Ministers Gerard and Luzerne. By Jared Sparks, under resolution of Congress of March 27, 1818, in 12 volumes, from March 3 1776 to 1784.

20. THE DIPLOMATIC CORRESPONDENCE of the United States, from the Treaty of Peace of 1783 to March 4, 1789; being letters of the Presidents of Congress, Secretary of Foreign Affairs, American Ministers of foreign courts, foreign Ministers near Congress, Reports of Committees of Congress, Reports of Secretary for Foreign Affairs, and from individuals on Public Affairs. By Jared Sparks, under direction of the Secretary of State, conformably to act of Congress of May 5, 1832, in 7 volumes.

21. STATE PAPERS AND PUBLIC DOCUMENTS OF THE UNITED STATES, FROM MARCH 4, 1789, TO 1819; including Confidential Documents first published, Inaugural Speeches, Messages from the President, and Documents on Foreign Relations, &c. &c. By Thomas B. Wait & Sons, in 12 volumes, under the patronage of Congress.

22. RECEIPTS AND EXPENDITURES OF THE UNITED STATES, published annually by the Treasury Department in obedience to the 7th clause, 9th section, 1st article of the Constitution of the United States, and conformably to a standing order of the House of Representatives of December 30, 1791.

23. THE MADISON PAPERS; being James Madison's correspondence and reports of debates during the Congress of the Confederation, and his reports of debates in the Federal Convention, from the original manuscripts purchased by order of Congress. Published in 3 volumes by direction of the Joint Library Committee of Congress, under the superintendence of Henry D. Gilpin: 1841.

24. TABLE OF POST-OFFICES IN THE UNITED STATES, arranged in alphabetical order. Exhibiting the States, Territories and Counties; Names of Postmasters; the Distances from Washington city to the Capitals of the several States and Territories; and the post-offices arranged by States and counties. Published under authority of the Postmaster-General from time to time.

25. OFFICIAL ARMY REGISTER OF THE UNITED STATES. Published annually by order of the Secretary of War, in compliance with a resolution of

the Senate, of December 13, 1815, and of the House of Representatives of February 1, 1830.

26. OFFICIAL REGISTER OF THE OFFICERS AND CADETS OF THE UNITED STATES MILITARY ACADEMY, WEST POINT. Published annually by order.

27. OFFICIAL NAVY REGISTER OF THE UNITED STATES. Printed by order of the Secretary of the Navy, in compliance with a resolution of the Senate of the United States of December 13, 1815.

CLASS No. 19.

MISCELLANEOUS PUBLICATIONS, CONTAINING USEFUL POLITICAL, STATISTICAL, AND OTHER INFORMATION.

1. NILES' WEEKLY REGISTER: containing political, historical, geographical, scientifical, astronomical, statistical, biographical documents, essays, and facts, together with notices of the arts and manufactures, and a record of the events of the times, from September, 1811, to March, 1847.

2. HAZARD'S "Register of Pennsylvania: devoted to the preservation of facts and documents, and every other kind of useful information, respecting the State of Pennsylvania," from January, 1828, to January, 1836, in 16 volumes.

3. HAZARD'S UNITED STATES COMMERCIAL AND STATISTICAL REGISTER: containing documents, facts, and other useful information, illustrative of the history and resources of the American Union, and of each State; embracing commerce, manufactures, agriculture, internal improvements, banks, currency, finances, education, &c., &c.; from July, 1839, to July, 1842; in 6 volumes.

4. A CONNECTED VIEW OF THE WHOLE INTERNAL NAVIGATION OF THE UNITED STATES, natural and artificial, present and prospective, with maps: Carey & Lea: 1826.

5. THE TRIAL OF COL. AARON BURR, on an indictment for treason, before the Circuit Court of the United States, at Richmond, Virginia, 1807, including the arguments and decisions; in three volumes: by T. Carpenter.

6. REPORT OF THE TRIAL BY IMPEACHMENT OF JAMES PRESTCOTT, Judge of the Probate of Wills, before the Senate of Massachusetts, in 1821; with an account of former impeachments in that State: 1821.

7. HISTORICAL REGISTER OF THE UNITED STATES, FROM THE DECLARATION OF WAR, in 1812, to January 1, 1814; in 4 volumes: 1816. Review of the political institutions of the United States; official documents of the war, &c., &c.

8. THE NATIONAL REGISTER: containing a series of public documents, proceedings in Congress, statistical tables, reports, and essays, upon agriculture, manufactures, commerce, finance, science, literature, and the arts; with biographical sketches and political events: by Joel K. Mead: 1816.

9. STATISTICAL ANNALS: embracing views of the population, commerce, navigation, fisheries, public lands, post-office establishment, revenues, mint, military and naval establishments, expenditures, public debt, and sinking fund of the

United States of America, founded on official documents, commencing March 4, 1789, and ending April 20, 1818: by Adam Seybert.

CLASS No. 20.

THE LIBRARY OF CONGRESS.

The library provided for Congress, after the removal of the Government to Washington, having been destroyed in the burning of the Capitol by the enemy, in 1814, the valuable library of Thomas Jefferson, which, with the best opportunities and his well-known ability, it had taken that eminent statesman a long series of years to accumulate, was purchased for Congress, under a joint resolution of October 21, 1814, and an act of January 30, 1815, and now constitutes the basis of the Congressional or National Library. Upon this foundation Congress have, by a moderate but regular process, been adding to the volume of literature, science, and the fine arts, which, in the acquisition of the library of that republican patriarch, had already adorned the Capitol of the republic; and by the operation of this regular annual provision, managed, as it has been, and will continue to be, by the united judgment of the joint committee of the two Houses of Congress, aided in their active measures by their literary agents, and by the zeal and experience of the worthy librarian and his assistants, is destined to become an ample source of useful knowledge, which, through the able minds and eloquent voices of the distinguished representatives of the States and of the people, as well as of those of other citizens who have free access to this perennial source, will be diffused through the country for the public benefit, elevating its literary taste and character, purifying its moral sentiment, and increasing its power; for true knowledge, communicated through pure channels, is the solid source of these and other national blessings.

The limited space to which we are here necessarily confined will only admit of a reference to the general heads or chapters embraced in this collection, and to a few particulars which the political history and public transactions of our own country may render more immediately interesting.

TABLE OF CHAPTERS.

1. Ancient History.
2. Modern History:
   - Southern Europe.
   - Northern Europe.
   - Turkey.
   - Asia.
   - Africa, &c., &c.
3. Modern History:
   - England.
   - Scotland.
   - Ireland.
4. Modern History:
   - America.
   - American Newspapers.

5. Ecclesiastical History.
6. Natural Philosophy.
7. Agriculture.
8. Chemistry.
9. Surgery.
10. Medicine.
11. Anatomy.
12. Zoology.
13. Botany.
14. Mineralogy and Conchology.
15. Occupations of Man—Technical Arts.
16. Ethics:
    1. Moral Philosophy.
    2. Law of Nature and Nations.
17. Religion.
18. Common Law:
    1. Commentaries, Treatises, Entries, Conveyancing, &c.
    2. Criminal Law and Trials.
    3. Military Law, Courts-Martial, &c.
19. Common Law:
    British Reports
    American Reports, viz.:
    Supreme Court United States.
    Circuit Courts United States.
    General Digests of Reports.
    Courts of Maine.
    New Hampshire.
    Vermont.
    Massachusetts.
    Connecticut.
    New York.
    New Jersey.
    Pennsylvania.
    Delaware.
    Maryland.
    Virginia.
    North Carolina.
    South Carolina.
    Georgia.
    Alabama
    Tennessee.
    Kentucky.
    Ohio.
    Indiana.
19. Common Law:
    American Reports, viz.:
    Courts of Illinois.
    Louisiana.
    Mississippi.
20. Equity—Treatises and Reports.
21. Law, Ecclesiastical—Treatises and Reports.
22. Law, Merchant and Maritime—Treatises and Reports.
23. Law:
    1. Civil Law, Codes, &c.
    2. British Statutes.
    3. Laws of the U. S. and of the several States, &c., viz.:
    The United States.
    State of Maine.
    New Hampshire.
    Vermont.
    Massachusetts.
    Rhode Island.
    Connecticut.
    New York.
    New Jersey.
    Pennsylvania.
    Delaware.
    Maryland.
    Virginia.
    North Carolina.
    South Carolina.
    Georgia.
    Alabama.
    Arkansas.
    Kentucky.
    Tennessee
    Ohio.
    Indiana.
    Illinois.
    Michigan.
    Missouri.
    Louisiana.
    Mississippi.
    Florida.
    District of Columbia.
24. Politics.
25. Mathematics, Pure—Arithmetic
26. Mathematics, Pure—Geometry.

27. Physico-Mathematics:
    Mechanics, Statics, Dynamics, Pneumatics, Phonics, Optics.
28. Astronomy.
29 Geography:
    Section 1. General.
    2. Europe.
    3. Asia.
    4. Africa.
    5. America.
    Maps.
30. Fine Arts—Architecture.
31. Fine Arts—Gardening, Painting, Sculpture, &c.
32. Fine Arts—Music.
33. Poetry, Epic.
34. Romance—Tales, Fables, &c.
35. Poetry—Pastorals, Odes, Elegies &c.
36. Poetry, Didactic.
37. Tragedy.
38. Comedy.
39. Dialogue, Epistolary.
40. Logic; Rhetoric; Orations.
41. Criticism—Theory.
42. Criticism—Bibliography
43. Criticism—Languages.
44. Polygraphical.

AMERICAN HISTORY.

Allen, Paul. History of the American Revolution. Printed in 1822.

Bancroft, Aaron. Life of George Washington: 1826.

Bancroft, George. History of the United States from discovery of the American Continent to 1837.

Blount, Joseph. Historical Sketch of the formation of the Confederacy, Provincial Limits, and the Jurisdiction of the General Government over Indian Tribes and Public Territory: 1825.

Carpenter, T. C. Memoirs of Thomas Jefferson: 1809.

Davis, Paris M. Authentic History of the late War between the United States and Great Britain; with a full Account of every Battle by Sea and by Land. 1836.

Hamilton, John C. Life of Alexander Hamilton: 1834.

Jefferson. Memoir, Correspondence, and Miscellanies, from the Papers of Thomas Jefferson, in 4 volumes. By Thomas Jefferson Randolph: 1830.

Madison. The Madison Papers; being James Madison's Correspondence and Reports of Debates during the Congress of the Confederation, and his Reports of Debates in the Federal Convention from the Original Manuscript purchased by order of Congress. Published by direction of the Joint Library Committee, under the superintendence of Henry D. Gilpin, in three volumes: 1841.

Marshal, John. Life of George Washington; with an Atlas: 1832.

Tucker, George. Life of Thomas Jefferson; with parts of his Correspondence never before published, and Notices of his Opinions on Questions of Civil Government, National Policy, and Constitutional Law: 1837.

Washington. Writings of George Washington; being his Correspondence, Addresses, Messages, and Papers, Official and Private, selected and published from the Original Manuscripts; with a Life of the Author, by Jared Sparks: 1837.

NEWSPAPERS.

Bache's General Advertiser, 1795–6–7.

Bache & Duane's Aurora, from 1798 to 1814

Brown's Philadelphia Gazette, from 1794 to 1800.
Carey's United States Recorder, from 1798 to 1800.
Delaware Gazette, Political Mirror, &c., from 1798 to 1800.
Denniston's Republican Watch Tower, from 1800 to 1809.
Duane's Weekly Aurora, from 1810 to 1821.
Dunlap's American Daily Advertiser, from 1791 to 1793.
Dunlap & Claypole's American Daily Advertiser, 1794–5.
Dunlap & Claypole's Pennsylvania Packet, &c., from 1785 to 1789.
Fenno's Gazette of the United States, from 1789 to 1798.
Globe, Daily, City of Washington, from 1832 to 1845.
Madisonian, do. 1837–8.
National Intelligencer, do. from 1800 to 1813.
Do. Daily, from 1814 to 1847.
National Journal, Daily, from 1826 to 1831.
Philadelphia Gazette, &c., 1795 to 1797.
Richmond Enquirer, 1809 to 1814.
United States Telegraph, Daily, 1828 to 1837.
Universal Gazette, by Samuel Harrison Smith, Philadelphia and Washington City, 1798 to 1808.
Virginia Argus and Enquirer, (bound together,) 1804 to 1808
Do. do. do. 1797 to 1803, and 1809 to 1813.
Washington City Gazette, from 1815 to 1826.

POLITICS.

ADAMS, JOHN. Defence of the Constitutions of Government of the United States: 1787.
ADAMS, JOHN. History of the Dispute with America, from its Origin in 1754, to 1784.
ADAMS, JOHN QUINCY. Duplicate Letters; The Fisheries and the Mississippi; Documents relating to the transactions at the Negotiations of Ghent: 1822.
ADAMS & SEWALL. Novanglus and Massachusettensis, or Political Essays: 1774–5.
AMERICAN REMEMBRANCER; or, an Impartial Collection of Essays, Resolves, Speeches, &c., relative to "Jay's Treaty" with Great Britain: 1795.
AMERICAN GUIDE. Constitutions of the several States: 1833.
AMES, FISHER. Works; with his Life and Character: 1809.
ARISTOTLE. Treatise on Government. Translated from the Greek. Lond. 1778.
BECCARIA, B. C., Marquis. Meditazioni sulla Economia Politica. Genoa, 1771.
CARPENTER, THOMAS. American Senator; or, Report of the Debates in the Congress of the United States in 1796–7.
DEBATES in first House of Representatives of the United States from 1789 to 1791; by Thomas Lloyd.
DEBATES and Proceedings in Congress of the United States, from March 4, 1789, to March 3, 1791: by Joseph Gales, sen.
DEBATES in the House of Representatives of the United States, on "Jay's Treaty" with Great Britain: 1796

DEBATES in Congress of the United States on the bill for repealing the law "for the more convenient organization of the Courts of the United States:" 1802.

DEBATE in House of Representatives on the Seminole War, in 1819.

DEBATES in Congress on passage of Bill for removal of the Indians in 1830.

DICKINSON, JOHN. Political Writings: 1801.

DIPLOMATIC CORRESPONDENCE of the United States from September 10, 1783, to March 4, 1789; by Jared Sparks: 1834.

DUER, WILLIAM A. Outlines of the Constitutional Jurisprudence of the United States: 1833.

DU PONCEAU, PETER S. Brief View of the Constitution of the United States: 1834.

FEDERALIST, on the New Constitution, written in the year 1788, by Hamilton, Madison, and Jay; with the Letters of Pacificus and Helvidius, on the Pro clamation of Neutrality of 1793: 1818.

FRANKLIN, BENJAMIN. Political, Miscellaneous, and Philosophical Pieces: 1779.

GALES & SEATON. Register of Debates in Congress from 1824 to 1837.

GALLATIN, ALBERT. Considerations on the Currency and Banking System of the United States: 1831.

GALLATIN, ALBERT. Sketch of the Finances of the United States: 1796.

HAMILTON, ALEXANDER. Works; comprising his most important Official Reports; The Federalist; Pacificus, &c.: 1810.

HATSELL, JOHN. Precedents of Proceedings in the House of Commons; with observations. New edition; with additions: 1818.

JACKSON, ANDREW. Annual Messages, Veto Messages, Proclamations, &c., from 1829 to 1834.

JEFFERSON, THOMAS. Manual of Parliamentary Practice, for the use of the Senate of the United States, with the Rules of the Senate and of the House of Representatives; Constitution of the United States, &c.: 1828.

JOURNAL of Convention that formed the Constitution of the United States: 1787.

JOURNAL of Convention of Virginia for ratifying same: 1788.

JOURNAL of the House of Burgesses of Virginia from 1740 to 1774.

JOURNAL of the House of Delegates of Virginia from 1774 to 1790.

JOURNAL of the Convention of Massachusetts for framing a Constitution, in 1779–1780.

JOURNAL of the Convention of the people of South Carolina in 1832–3.

JOURNAL of the Convention of New York in 1821.

JOURNAL of the House of Representatives of Pennsylvania from 1806 to 1816.

JOURNAL of the Senate and Assembly of New York from 1820 to 1838.

JOURNALS of the American Congress from 1774 to 1788.

JOURNALS of the House of Representatives of the United States, from 1789 to 1847.

JOURNALS of the Senate of the United States, from 1789 to 1847.

KEY to both Houses of Parliament; consisting of Alphabetical Notices of the Lords and Commons; the Regulations and Standing Orders of both Houses; with every other species of Information respecting the Constitution, History, and Usages of Parliament. London: 1832.

LOCKE, JOHN. Two Treatises on Government. London: 1821.

LOUISIANA. Debates in the Senate of the United States on the *Mississippi Question*, February, 1803. Remarks on the Violation of the Treaty relative to the Mississippi River, by Coriolanus and Camillus. Addresses on the late cession of Louisiana to the United States.

LOUISIANA. Message from the President communicating Discoveries in Exploring the Missouri, Red River, and Washita, by Lewis, Clark, Sibley, and Dunbar; with a Statistical Account of the Countries adjacent: 1806.

McCULLOCH, J. R. Dictionary, Practical, Theoretical, and Historical, of Commerce and Commercial Navigation; illustrated with Maps, with Supplement thereto to 1835.

MADISON, JAMES. Letters to Mr. Monroe on Impressment, Colonial trade, &c., extracts from and enclosures in the letters of Mr. Monroe. 1808.

MADISON, JAMES. Letters to Messrs. Monroe and Pinckney, with their communications to the Secretary of State, relative to the treaty of 1806. 1808.

MAGNA CHARTA. MS. copy.

MALTHUS, T. R. Definitions in Political Economy. London, 1828.
Essay on the Principles of Population. Lond. 1806.
Additions thereto. Lond. 1831.
Inquiry into the Nature and Progress of Rent. Lond. 1815.
Principles of Political Economy considered, with a view to their practical application. Lond. 1836.

MANUAL of the Practice of Parliament, in passing Public and Private Bills, with Standing Orders of both Houses, from 1685 to 1829. Lond. 1829.

MARYLAND. Proceedings of the Conventions of the Province of Maryland, held at Annapolis in 1774, 1775, 1776.

MONROE, JAMES. View of the conduct of the Executive in the Foreign Affairs of the United States, as connected with the mission to the French Republic in 1794.

MONROE, JAMES. Correspondence relative to the British Treaty of 1806.

MONTESQUIEU, C. de Secondat, Baron de. Œuvres; 1767.
Spirit of Laws, translated by Thomas Nugent: 1823.

MOSES, MYER. Commercial Directory and a Digest of the Laws of the United States relating to Commerce; including a Tariff, or Rates of Duties and Tables of Calculation, applicable to all manufactures of wool or cotton imported into the United States: 1830.

NEW JERSEY. Journal of Provincial Congress; of the Convention; Committee of Safety; Ordinance for regulating the Militia, in 1775.

NEW YORK. Journals and Documents of the Senate and Assembly of the State of New York, from 1820 to 1838.

NORTH CAROLINA. Declaration of Independence by the citizens of Mecklenburg county, on May 20, 1775, with accompanying documents and proceedings of the Cumberland Association, and proceedings of the Provincial Congress of North Carolina at Halifax, April 4, 1776.

NORTH CAROLINA. Proceedings and Debates of the Convention to amend the Constitution in 1835.

ORDERS. Essential and fundamental Rules, &c., of the House of Commons, relating to their Forms of Proceedings, Privileges, &c.: 1756.

ORDERS on Controverted Elections and Returns: 1741.

PAMPHLETS, POLITICAL, in relation to the Revolutionary war of the United States of America, from 1765 to 1781.

PAMPHLETS, POLITICAL. The same by A. Hamilton, J. Madison and others; also, Plea for the poor soldiers who really and actually supported the burden of the war.—[With a large collection made by Mr. Jefferson of Political Pamphlets on various exciting and interesting subjects, which in turn agitated the public mind, from 1798 to 1812, several of which were written by himself, J. Madison, A. Hamilton, E. Randolph, A. Gallatin, R. G. Harper, De Witt Clinton, W. C. Nichols, C. Pinckney, R. H. Lee, Oliver Wolcott, John Adams, Samuel Adams, T. Pickering, S. Smith, W. Giles, Earl of Buchan, Mr. Leigh, of Dinwiddie, James Monroe, and many other distinguished statesmen, as well as other political writers and Editors of public Journals.]

PITKIN, TIMOTHY. Statistical view of the Commerce of the United States; Banks, Manufactures, and Internal Trade and Improvements; also Revenue and Expenditures of the General Government: 1835.

POLITICAL CLASSICS, viz.: Algernon Sidney's Discourses on Government, with his letters and memoirs of his life, &c.: 1795.

PRESIDENTS' ADDRESSES and Messages, from 1789 to 1837.

RAWLE, WILLIAM. View of the Constitution of the United States: 1829.

REGISTER OF OFFICERS and Agents, Civil, Military and Naval, in the service of the United States in 1802, the same from 1816 to 1845.

REPORTS of the Secretary of the Treasury on the Finances, from 1790 to 1836.

SAY, J. B. Catechism of Political Economy, letters to Malthus, Traité d'Economie Politique, Treatise on Political Economy; translated from the French, with notes: 1821.

SECRET JOURNALS of the Acts and Proceedings of Congress, from the first meeting in 1774, to the dissolution of the Confederation, in 1789.

SEYBERT, ADAM. Statistical Annals; embracing views of the Population, Commerce, Fisheries, Public Lands, Revenues, Mint, &c.: 1818.

STORY, JOSEPH. Commentaries on the Constitution of the United States, with a Preliminary Review of the Constitutional History of the Colonies and States, before the adoption of the Constitution: 1833.

STORY, JOSEPH. Constitutional Class Book, being a brief exposition of the Constitution: 1834.

TEXAS. Constitution of the Republic of Mexico and of the State of Coahuila and Texas: 1832.

TENNESSEE. Description of this State and its constitution: 1796.

TRACTS. Considerations on the Society or Order of Cincinnati: 1783.

VINDICATION of Edmund Randolph's Resignation: 1795.

VIRGINIA and Kentucky resolutions of 1798 and 1799, with T. Jefferson's original draught thereof; also Madison's report; Calhoun's address: 1832.

VIRGINIA. Proceedings of the Convention of Delegates for the Counties and Corporations in the Colony of Virginia, held in Richmond, March 20, 1775: 1816.

WAIT'S State Papers and Public Documents of the United States, from 1789 to 1818.

WATTERSTON AND VAN ZANDT. Tabular Statistical Views of the Commerce, &c., of the United States: 1829.—Continuation of the same: 1833.

YATES, ROBERT. Secret Proceedings and Debates of the Convention which formed the Constitution of the United States: 1821.

CLASS No. 21.

DEPARTMENT OF STATE.

The eminent statesmen who have from time to time occupied the highly important and responsible station of Secretary of State, have not been unmindful of the utility of providing for themselves and their successors in office, a choice and valuable collection of books, maps, charts, and atlases appropriate to the peculiar business of the Department, and indispensable in the performance of their extensive and varied duties, as well as others in various branches of the liberal arts, literature and science. The limited design of this volume will not admit of the insertion of more than the general heads, and a reference to a few volumes of general public utility of this collection:—

GENERAL HEADS.

Ancient history—Modern history, Foreign, British and American—Biography and Memoirs—Natural history—Botany—Mineralogy and Geology—Natural philosophy—Agriculture and Horticulture—Chemistry—Anatomy and Surgery—Medicine—Occupations of Man, Technical Arts, Education, Roads and Canals, Military Tactics—Mental Philosophy and Ethics—Religion—Law of Nature and Nations—Laws of the United States—Laws of the several States and Territories—JURISPRUDENCE; comprehending, Law in general, the Civil Law, the Law of Equity, the Common Law, Constitutional Law, the Law Merchant and Maritime, the Law Military and the Law Ecclesiastical—JURISPRUDENCE; comprehending, English and American Reports of Cases—Foreign Law—POLITICS; comprehending, Diplomacy, Treaties, Negotiations, Constitutions or forms of Government, Statistics, Commerce, Finance, Political Economy, Journals and histories of Legislative Bodies, Foreign State Papers, Political Pamphlets and General Treatises—POLITICS; comprehending American State Papers and Political Pamphlets—Mathematics—Arts and Sciences—GEOGRAPHY; comprehending, General Geography, Voyages and Travels—GEOGRAPHY; comprehending, Atlases, Maps and Charts—PHILOLOGY; comprehending, Dictionaries, Lexicons, Grammars and Elementary works—Oratory and Rhetoric—Magazines, Reviews and Political Journals—Miscellaneous.

Of these, particular reference will be made only to the following:—

LAW OF NATURE AND OF NATIONS.

ARNOULD. Systême Maritime et Politique des Européens, pendent le dix-huitiême siècle, fondé sur leurs Traités de Paix, de Commerce, et Navigation: 1797.

BOUCHER. Consulat de la Mer, ou Pandectes du Droit Commercial et Maritime: 1494. Printed, 1808.

BOUCHER. Institution au Droit Maritime: 1803.

BURLAMAQUI. Principes du Droit de la Nature et des Gens. The same translated into English, by Nugent: 1823.

BURLAMAQUI. Elémens du Droit Naturel, par Burlamaqui; et Devoirs de L'Homme et du Citoyen, tels qu'ils lui sont prescrits par la Loi Naturelle, traduits du Latin de Pufendorf par Barbeyrac, avec les Notes du Traducteur et le judgement de Leibnitz: 1820.

CORNELII Van Bynkershoek, Opera: 1752.

CODIGO de las Costumbres Maritimas de Barcelona, hasta aqui vulgarmente Llamado Libro del Consulado: por D. Antonio de Capmany, y de Monpalan. Madrid: 1791.

GROTIUS'S rights of War and Peace, including the Law of Nature and Nations. translated from the original Latin, with Notes and illustrations from the best political and legal writers.—[In French, 1724, and English, 1814.]

HEINECCIUS, Scriptores de Jure Maritimo: 1740.

JACOBSEN'S Laws of the Sea, with reference to Maritime Commerce during peace and war: 1818.—[In German and English.]

LE BRUN. Libertad de los Mares: 1820.

LE NOUVEAU VALIN, ou Code Commercial Maritime par Sanfourche-Laporte: 1809.

MABLY. Le Droit public de L'Europe fondé sur les Traites: 1764.

MARTENS'S Summary of the Law of Nations, with a list of the principal Treaties concluded since 1748 down to the present time, indicating the works in which they are to be found; translated from the French by William Cobbett: 1795.

MARTENS. Guide Diplomatique ou traité des droits, des immunités et des devoirs, des Ministres publics, des agens diplomatiques et consulaires, dans toute l'etendue de leurs fonctions, précédé de considérations générales sur l'étude de la diplomatie; suivi d'un traité du style des compositions diplomatique, d'une bibliographie diplomatique choisie, etc. etc. Paris: 1837.

PEUCHET, Du Commerce des Neutres en temps de Guerre, traduit de L'Italien de Lampredi: 1802.

PUFENDORFII de Jure Naturæ et Gentium. Libri octo: 1698.

RUTHERFORD'S Institutes of Natural Law: 1799.

SYSTEME Universel des principes de Droit Maritime de L'Europe, par D. A. Azuni, traduit d'Italien par M. Digeon: 1798.

TRATADO JURIDICO-POLITICO, sobre Pressas de Mar, y calidades que deben concurrir para hacerse legitimamente el Corso: su Autor Don Felix Joseph de Abreu, y Bertoduno. Cadiz: 1746.

VALIN. Nouveau Commentaire sur L'Ordonnance de la Marine: 1681.

VATTEL'S Law of Nations; or principles of the Law of Nature, applied to the conduct and affairs of Nations and Sovereigns.—[In French, 1775, and English, 1820.]

WARD'S Inquiry into the foundations and history of the Law of Nations in Europe, from the time of the Greeks and Romans, to the age of Grotius: 1795.

WENCKII Codex Jurisgentium.

WHEATON'S Digest of the Law of Maritime Captures and Prizes: 1815.

Elements of International Law: 1846.

WICQUEFORT'S Ambassador and his functions: to which is added an historical Discourse concerning the election of the Emperor, and the Electors. translated into English by Mr. Digby.

MISCELLANEOUS BOOKS.

ELLIOT'S Diplomatic Code of the United States of America: embracing a collection of Treaties and Conventions between the United States and Foreign Powers, from 1778 to 1827.

HALL'S Observations on the Warehousing System and Navigation Laws, &c.: 1821.

HAMILTON'S (Alexander) Works, printed in 1810.

HATSELL'S Precedents of Proceedings in the House of Commons; with observations: 1786.

LORD'S Principles of Currency and Banking. New York: 1829.

McARTHUR'S Financial and Political Facts of the 18th Century: 1801.

MALTHUS'S Principles of Political Economy: 1821.

Essay on the Principle of Population: 1809.

PHILLIPS'S Manual of Political Economy: 1828.

RAYMOND'S Elements of Political Economy: 1823.

SAY'S Treatise on Political Economy, translated from the French: 1827.

Catechism of Political Economy, do.: 1816.

SKIDMORE'S Rights of Man to Property: 1829.

SMITH'S Inquiry into the Nature and Causes of the Wealth of Nations, with Notes and Supplementary Chapters, by William Playfair: 1818.

TAYLOR'S Construction Construed, and Constitutions Vindicated: 1820.

THE DIPLOMACY of the United States: being an account of the Foreign Relations of the country, from 1778 to 1814. Printed in 1826.

A DIGEST of the Commercial Regulations of the different Foreign Nations with which the United States have intercourse: 1824.

A GENERAL Outline of the United States of North America, her Resources and Prospects, with a Statistical Comparison, showing the advances made in National Opulence in thirty years: 1823.

NOVANGLUS AND MASSACHUSETTENSIS, or Political Essays, published in 1774 and 1775, on the principal points of controversy between Great Britain and her colonies: the former by John Adams, the latter by Jonathan Sewall: 1819.

PITKIN'S Statistical View of the Commerce of the United States of America, its connection with Agriculture and Manufactures: 1817.

POLITICAL MISCELLANIES, compiled by W. B. Giles: 1829.

SELECT PAMPHLETS, consisting of an exposition of the causes and character of the war; and an examination of the British Doctrine which subjects to capture a Neutral Trade not open in time of peace: 1815.

SEYBERT'S Statistical Annals of the United States of America: 1818.

THE AMERICAN REMEMBRANCER, or an Impartial collection of Essays, Resolves, Speeches, &c., relative to the Treaty (Jay's) with Great Britain: 1795.

THE DIPLOMATIC Correspondence of the American Revolution. By Jared Sparks: 1829.

THE DUPLICATE LETTERS; the Fisheries, and the Mississippi: documents relating to transactions at the negotiations of Ghent, collected and published by John Quincy Adams: 1822.

WAIT'S State Papers, and public documents of the United States: 1819.

WATTERSTON AND VAN ZANDT'S Tabular Statistical Views of the United States: 1829.

BLOUNT'S Historical Sketch of the formation of the Confederation, particularly with reference to the Provincial Limits and the Jurisdiction of the General Government over Indian tribes and the public territory: 1825.

DEBATES and other Proceedings of the Convention of Virginia, convened in June, 1788, for the purpose of deliberating on the Constitution of the United States: 1805.

CHAPTER 12.

ARTICLES OF CONFEDERATION AND PERPETUAL UNION BETWEEN THE STATES.

(See remarks, Chapter 2, pages 129 to 131, and residue of that Chapter, " Chapter 10, pages 397, 398, and 406 to 421.)

The following have been critically compared with the original Articles of Confederation in the Department of State, and found to conform minutely to them in text, letter, and punctuation. It may therefore be relied upon as a true copy.

TO ALL TO WHOM THESE PRESENTS SHALL COME, WE THE UNDERSIGNED DELEGATES OF THE STATES AFFIXED TO OUR NAMES, SEND GREETING.—Whereas the Delegates of the United States of America in Congress assembled did on the 15th day of November in the Year of our Lord 1777, and in the Second Year of the Independence of America agree to certain articles of Confederation and perpetual Union between the States of New Hampshire, Massachusetts-bay, Rhode-island and Providence Plantations, Connecticut, New-York, New-Jersey, Pennsylvania, Delaware, Maryland, Virginia, North-Carolina, South-Carolina, and Georgia, in the words following, viz.

"ARTICLES OF CONFEDERATION AND PERPETUAL UNION BETWEEN THE STATES OF NEW-HAMPSHIRE, MASSACHUSETTS-BAY, RHODE-ISLAND AND PROVIDENCE PLANTATIONS, CONNECTICUT, NEW-YORK, NEW-JERSEY, PENNSYLVANIA, DELAWARE, MARYLAND, VIRGINIA, NORTH-CAROLINA, SOUTH-CAROLINA, AND GEORGIA.

ARTICLE I. The Stile of this confederacy shall be "The United States of America."

ARTICLE II. Each state retains its sovereignty, freedom and independence, and every Power, Jurisdiction and right, which is not by this confederation expressly delegated to the united states, in congress assembled.

ARTICLE III. The said states hereby severally enter into a firm league of friendship with each other, for their common defence, the security of their Liberties, and their mutual and general welfare, binding themselves to assist each other, against all force offered to, or attacks made upon them, or any of them, on account of religion, sovereignty, trade, or any other pretence whatever.

ARTICLE IV. The better to secure and perpetuate mutual friendship and intercourse among the people of the different states in this union, the free inhabitants of each of these states, paupers, vagabonds, and fugitives from Justice excepted, shall be entitled to all privileges and immunities of free citizens in the several states; and the people of each state shall have free ingress and regress to and from any other state, and shall enjoy therein all the privileges of trade and commerce, subject to the same duties, impositions and restrictions as the inhabitants thereof respectively, provided that such restriction shall not extend so far as to prevent the removal of property imported into any state, to any other state of which the Owner is an inhabitant; provided also that no imposition, duties or restriction shall be laid by any state, on the property of the united states, or either of them.

If any person guilty of, or charged with treason, felony, or other high misdemeanor in any state, shall flee from Justice, and be found in any of the united states, he shall upon demand of the Governor or executive power, of the state from which he fled, be delivered up and removed to the state having jurisdiction of his offence.

Full faith and credit shall be given in each of these states to the records, acts and judicial proceedings of the courts and magistrates of every other state.

ARTICLE V. For the more convenient management of the general interest of the united states, delegates shall be annually appointed in such manner as the legislature of each state shall direct, to meet in congress on the first Monday in November, in every year, with a power reserved to each state, to recal its delegates, or any of them, at any time within the year, and to send others in their stead, for the remainder of the Year.

No state shall be represented in congress by less than two, nor by more than seven members; and no person shall be capable of being a delegate for more than three years in any term of six years; nor shall any person, being a delegate, be capable of holding any office under the united states, for which he, or another for his benefit receives any salary, fees or emolument of any kind.

Each state shall maintain its own delegates in any meeting of the states, and while they act as members of the committee of the states.

In determining questions in the united states, in congress assembled, each state shall have one vote.

Freedom of speech and debate in congress shall not be impeached or questioned in any Court, or place out of congress, and the members of congress shall be protected in their persons from arrests and imprisonments, during the time of their going to and from, and attendance on congress, except for treason, felony, or breach of the peace.

ARTICLE VI. No state without the Consent of the united states in congress assembled, shall send any embassy to, or receive any embassy from, or enter into any conference, agreement, alliance or treaty with any King prince or state; nor shall any person holding any office of profit or trust under the united states, or any of them, accept of any present, emolument, office or title of any kind whatever from any king, prince or foreign state; nor shall the united states in congress assembled, or any of them, grant any title of nobility.

No two or more states shall enter into any treaty, confederation or alliance whatever between them, without the consent of the united states in congress assembled, specifying accurately the purposes for which the same is to be entered into, and how long it shall continue.

No state shall lay any imposts or duties, which may interfere with any stipulations in treaties, entered into by the united states in congress assembled, with any king, prince or state, in pursuance of any treaties already proposed by congress, to the courts of France and Spain.

No vessels of war shall be kept up in time of peace by any state, except such number only, as shall be deemed necessary by the united states in congress assembled, for the defence of such state, or its trade; nor shall any body of forces be kept up by any state, in time of peace, except such number only, as in the judgment of the united states, in congress assembled, shall be deemed requisite to garrison the forts necessary for the defence of such state; but every state shall always keep up a well regulated and disciplined militia, sufficiently armed and accoutred, and shall provide and have constantly ready for use, in public stores, a due number of field pieces and tents, and a proper quantity of arms, ammunition and camp equipage.

No state shall engage in any war without the consent of the united states in congress assembled, unless such state be actually invaded by enemies, or shall have received certain advice of a resolution being formed by some nation of Indians to invade such state, and the danger is so imminent as not to admit of a delay, till the united states in congress assembled can be consulted: nor shall any state grant commissions to any ships or vessels of war, nor letters of marque or reprisal, except it be after a declaration of war by the united states in congress assembled, and then only against the kingdom or state and the subjects thereof, against which war has been so declared, and under such regulations as shall be established by the united states in congress assembled, unless such state be infested by pirates, in which case vessels of war may be fitted out for that occasion, and kept so long as the danger shall continue, or until the united states in congress assembled shall determine otherwise.

ARTICLE VII. When land-forces are raised by any state for the common defence, all officers of or under the rank of colonel, shall be appointed by the legislature of each state respectively by whom such forces shall be raised, or in such manner as such state shall direct, and all vacancies shall be filled up by the state which first made the appointment.

ARTICLE VIII. All charges of war, and all other expenses that shall be incurred for the common defence or general welfare, and allowed by the united states in congress assembled, shall be defrayed out of a common treasury, which shall be supplied by the several states, in proportion to the value of all land within each state, granted to or surveyed for any Person, as such land and the buildings and improvements thereon shall be estimated according to such mode as the united states in congress assembled, shall from time to time, direct and appoint. The taxes for paying that proportion shall be laid and levied by the authority and direction of the legislatures of the several states within the time agreed upon by the united states in congress assembled.

ARTICLE IX. The united states in congress assembled, shall have the sole and exclusive right and power of determining on peace and war, except in the cases mentioned in the 6th article—of sending and receiving ambassadors—entering into treaties and alliances, provided that no treaty of commerce shall be made whereby the legislative power of the respective states shall be restrained from imposing such imposts and duties on foreigners, as their own people are subjected to, or from prohibiting the exportation or importation of any species of goods or commodities whatsoever—of establishing rules for deciding in all cases, what captures on land or water shall be legal, and in what manner prizes taken by land or naval forces in the service of the united states shall be divided or appropriated—of granting letters of marque and reprisal in times of peace—appointing courts for the trial of piracies and felonies committed on the high seas and establishing courts for receiving and determining finally appeals in all cases of captures, provided that no member of congress shall be appointed a judge of any of the said courts.

The united states in congress assembled shall also be the last resort on appeal in all disputes and differences now subsisting or that hereafter may arise between two or more states concerning boundary, jurisdiction or any other cause whatever; which authority shall always be exercised in the manner following. Whenever the legislative or executive authority or lawful agent of any state in controversy with another shall present a petition to congress, stating the matter in question and praying for a hearing, notice thereof shall be given by order of congress to the legislative or executive authority of the other state in controversy, and a day assigned for the appearance of the parties by their lawful agents, who shall then be directed to appoint by joint consent, commissioners or judges to constitute a court for hearing and determining the matter in question: but if they cannot agree, congress shall name three persons out of each of the united states, and from the list of such persons each party shall alternately strike out one, the petitioners beginning, until the number shall be reduced to thirteen; and from that number not less than seven, nor more than nine names as congress shall direct, shall in the presence of congress be drawn out by lot, and the persons whose names shall be so drawn or any five of them, shall be commissioners or judges, to hear and finally determine the controversy, so always as a major part of the judges who shall hear the cause shall agree in the determination: and if either party shall neglect to attend at the day appointed, without showing reasons, which congress shall judge sufficient, or being present shall refuse to strike, the congress shall proceed to nominate three persons out of each state, and the secretary of congress shall strike in behalf of such party absent or refusing; and the judgment and sentence of the court to be appointed, in the manner before prescribed, shall be final and conclusive; and if any of the parties shall refuse to submit to the authority of such court, or to appear or defend their claim or cause, the court shall nevertheless proceed to pronounce sentence, or judgment, which shall in like manner be final and decisive, the judgment or sentence and other proceedings being in either case transmitted to congress, a d lodged among the acts of congress for the security of the parties concerned: provided that every commissioner, before he sits in judgment, shall take an oath to be administered by one of the judges of the supreme or superior court of the state, where the cause shall be tried, "well and truly to hear and determine the matter in question, according to the best of his judgment, without favour, affection or hope of reward:" provided also that no state shall be deprived of territory for the benefit of the united states.

All controversies concerning the private right of soil claimed under different grants of two or more states, whose jurisdictions as they may respect such lands, and the states which passed such grants are adjusted, the said grants or either of them being at the same time claimed to have originated antecedent to such settlement of jurisdiction, shall on the petition of either party to the congress of the united states, be finally determined as near as may be in the same manner as is before prescribed for deciding disputes respecting territorial jurisdiction between different states.

The united states in congress assembled shall also have the sole and exclusive right and power of regulating the alloy and value of coin struck by their own authority, or by that of the respective states—fixing the standard of weights and measures throughout the United States—regulating the trade and managing all affairs with the Indians, not members of any of the states, provided that the legislative right of any state within its own limits be not infringed or violated—establishing or regulating post-offices from one state to another, throughout all the united states, and exacting such postage on the papers passing thro' the same as may be requisite to defray the expenses of the said office—appointing all officers of the land forces, in the service of the united states, excepting regimental officers—appointing all the officers of the naval forces, and commissioning all officers whatever in the service of the united states—making rules for the government and regulation of the said land and naval forces, and directing their operations.

The united states in congress assembled shall have authority to appoint a committee, to sit in the recess of congress, to be denominated "A Committee of the States," and to consist of one delegate from each state; and to appoint such other committees and civil officers as may be necessary for managing the general affairs of the united states under their direction—to appoint one of their number to preside, provided that no person be allowed to serve in the office of president more than one year in any term of three years; to ascertain the necessary sums of Money to be raised for the service of the united states, and to appropriate and apply the same for defraying the public expenses—to borrow money, or emit bills on the credit of the united states, transmitting every half year to the respective states an account of the sums of money so borrowed or emitted,—to build and equip a navy—to agree upon the number of land forces, and to make requisitions from each state for its quota, in proportion to the number of white inhabitants in such state; which requisition shall be binding, and thereupon the legislature of each state shall appoint the regimental officers, raise the men and cloath, arm and equip them in a soldier like manner, at the expense of the united states; and the officers and men so cloathed, armed and equipped shall march to the place appointed, and within the time agreed on by the united states in congress assembled: But if the united states in congress assembled shall, on consideration of circumstances judge proper that any state should not raise men, or should raise a smaller number than its quota, and that any other state should raise a greater number of men than the quota thereof, such extra number shall be raised, officered, cloathed, armed and equipped in the same manner as the quota of such state, unless the legislature of such state shall judge that such extra number cannot be safely spared out of the same, in which case they shall raise officer, cloath, arm and equip as many of such extra number as they judge can be safely spared. And the officers and men so cloathed, armed and equipped, shall march to the place appointed, and within the time agreed on by the united states in congress assembled.

The united states in congress assembled shall never engage in a war, nor grant letters of marque and reprisal in time of peace, nor enter into any treaties or alliances, nor coin money, nor regulate the value thereof, nor ascertain the sums and expenses necessary for the defence and welfare of the united states, or any of them, nor emit bills, nor borrow money on the credit of the united states, nor approrpiate money, nor agree upon the number of vessels of war, to be built or purchased, or the number of land or sea forces to be raised, nor appoint a commander in chief of the army or navy, unless nine states assent to the same: nor shall a question on any other point, except for adjourning from day to day be determined, unless by the votes of a majority of the united states in congress assembled.

The Congress of the united states shall have power to adjourn to any time within the year, and to any place within the united states, so that no period of adjournment be for a longer duration than the space of six months, and shall publish the Journal of their proceedings monthly, except such parts thereof relating to treaties, alliances or military operations, as in their judgment require secrecy; and the yeas and nays of the delegates of each state on any question shall be entered on the Journal, when it is desired by any delegate; and the delegates of a state, or any of them, at his or their request shall be furnished with a transcript of the said Journal, except such parts as are above excepted, to lay before the legislatures of the several states.

ARTICLE X. The committee of the states, or any nine of them, shall be authorized to execute, in the recess of congress, such of the powers of congress as the united states in congress assembled, by the consent of nine states, shall from time to time think expedient to vest them with; provided that no power be delegated to the said committee, for the exercise of which, by the articles of confederation, the voice of nine states in the congress of the united states assembled is requisite.

ARTICLE XI. Canada acceding to this confederation, and joining in the measures of the united states, shall be admitted into, and entitled to all the advantages of this union: but no other colony shall be admitted into the same, unless such admission be agreed to by nine states.

ARTICLE XII. All bills of credit emitted, monies borrowed and debts contracted by, or under the authority of congress, before the assembling of the united states, in pursuance of the present confederation, shall be deemed and considered as a charge against the united states, for payment and satisfaction whereof the said united states, and the public faith are hereby solemnly pledged.

ARTICLE XIII. Every state shall abide by the determinations of the united states in congress assembled, on all questions which by this confederation is submitted to them. And the Articles of this confederation shall be inviolably observed by every state, and the union shall be perpetual; nor shall any alteration at any time hereafter be made in any of them; unless such alteration be agreed to in a congress of the united states, and be afterwards confirmed by the legislatures of every state.

And Whereas it hath pleased the Great Governor of the World to incline the hearts of the legislatures we respectively represent in congress, to approve of, and to authorize us to ratify the said articles of confederation and perpetual union. Know Ye that we the undersigned delegates, by virtue of the power and authority to us given for that purpose, do by these presents, in the name and in behalf of our respective constituents, fully and entirely ratify and confirm each and every of the said articles of confederation and perpetual union, and all and singular the matters and things therein contained: And we do further solemnly plight and engage the faith of our respective constituents, that they shall abide by the determinations of the united states in congress assembled, on all questions, which by the said confederation are submitted to them. And that the articles thereof shall be inviolably observed by the states we respectively represent, and that the union shall be perpetual. In witness whereof we have hereunto set our hands in Congress. Done at

Philadelphia in the state of Pennsylvania the 9th Day of July in the Year of our Lord, 1778, and in the 3d year of the Independence of America.

Josiah Bartlett,	John Wentworth, jun. August 8th, 1778,	On the part and behalf of the state of New Hampshire.
John Hancock, Samuel Adams, Elbridge Gerry,	Francis Dana, James Lovell, Samuel Holten,	On the part and behalf of the state of Massachusetts-Bay.
William Ellery, Henry Marchant,	John Collins,	On the part and behalf of the state of Rhode-Island and Providence Plantations.
Roger Sherman, Samuel Huntington, Oliver Wolcott,	Titus Hosmer, Andrew Adam,	On the part and behalf of the state of Connecticut.
Jas Duane, Fras Lewis,	William Duer, Gouvr Morris,	On the part and behalf of the state of New-York.
Jno Witherspoon,	Nathl Scudder,	On the part and behalf of the state of New-Jersey, November 26th, 1778.
Robt Morris, Daniel Roberdeau, Jona Bayard Smith,	William Clingan, Joseph Reed, 22d July, 1778,	On the part and behalf of the state of Pennsylvania.
Tho. M'Kean, Feb. 12, 1779, John Dickinson, May 5, 1779,	Nicholas Van Dyke,	On the part and behalf of the state of Delaware.
John Hanson, March 1st, 1781,	Daniel Carroll, March 1st, 1781,	On the part and behalf of the state of Maryland.
Richard Henry Lee, John Banister, Thomas Adams,	Jno Harvie, Francis Lightfoot Lee,	On the part and behalf of the state of Virginia.
John Penn, July 21st, 1778,	Corns Harnett, Jno Williams,	On the part and behalf of the state of North-Carolina.
Henry Laurens, William Henry Drayton, Jno Matthews,	Richd Hutson, Thos. Heyward, jun.	On the part and behalf of the state of South-Carolina.
Jno Walton, 24th July, 1778,	Edwd Telfair, Edwd Langworthy,	On the part and behalf of the state of Georgia.

THE THIRTY-THIRD CONGRESS OF THE UNITED STATES.

THE SENATE.

David R. Atchison, President pro tempore.
Asbury Dickens, Secretary of the Senate.

SENATORS FROM THE SEVERAL STATES, WITH THEIR PLACES OF RESIDENCE OR POST OFFICES, RESPECTIVELY.

New Hampshire.

Moses Norris, Manchester. Jared W. Williams, Lancaster.

Massachusetts.

Charles Sumner, Boston. Julius Rockwell, Pittsfield.

Rhode Island.

Charles T. James, Providence. Philip Allen, Providence.

Connecticut.

Isaac Toucey, Hartford. Francis Gillette, Hartford.

	Vermont.	
Solomon Foot, Ruttland.		
	New York.	
Hamilton Fish, New York		William H. Seward, Auburn, Cayuga co.
	New Jersey.	
John R. Thomson, Princeton.		William Wright, Newark.
	Pennsylvania.	
James Cooper, Pottsville.		Richard Brodhead, Easton.
	Delaware.	
James A. Bayard, Wilmington.		John M. Clayton, Chippewa.
	Maryland.	
James A. Pearce, Chestertown.		Thomas G. Pratt, Annapolis.
	Virginia.	
James M. Mason, Winchester.		Robert M. T. Hunter, Lloyd's, Essex co.
	North Carolina.	
George E. Badger, Raleigh.		
	South Carolina.	
Andrew P. Butler, Edgefield C. H.		J. I. Evans, Society Hill.
	Georgia.	
William C. Dawson, Greensborough.		Robert Toombs, Washington.
	Kentucky.	
John B. Thompson, Harrodsburg.		A. Dixon, Henderson.
	Tennessee.	
John Bell, Nashville.		J. C. Jones, Memphis.
	Ohio.	
Salmon P. Chase, Cincinnati.		Benjamin Wade, Jefferson.
	Louisiana.	
J. P. Benjamin, New Orleans.		John Slidell, New Orleans.
	Indiana.	
Jesse D. Bright, Madison.		John Pettit, Lafayette.
	Mississippi.	
Stephen Adams, Aberdeen.		Albert G. Brown, Newtown, Hinds co.
	Illinois.	
Stephen A. Douglas, Chicago.		James Shields, Belleville.
	Alabama.	
Benjamin Fitzpatrick, Wetumpka.		C. C. Clay, Jr., Huntsville.
	Maine.	
Hannibal Hamlin, Hampden.		William Pitt Fessenden, Portland.
	Missouri.	
David R. Atchison, Platt City.		H. S. Geyer, St. Louis.
	Arkansas.	
William K. Sebastian, Helena.		Robert W. Johnson, Little Rock.
	Michigan.	
Lewis Cass, Detroit.		Charles E. Stuart, Kalamazoo.
	Florida.	
Jackson Morton, Pensacola.		S. R. Mallory, Jacksonville.
	Texas.	
Sam. Houston, Huntsville.		Thomas J. Rusk, Nacogdoches.
	Wisconsin.	
Henry Dodge, Dodgeville.		Isaac P. Walker, Milwaukie.
	Iowa.	
Augustus C. Dodge, Burlington.		George W. Jones, Dubuque.
	California.	
William M. Gwin, San Francisco.		John B. Weller, San Francisco.

HOUSE OF REPRESENTATIVES.

LINN BOYD, of Kentucky, Speaker.

John W. Forney, of Pennsylvania, Clerk.

REPRESENTATIVES from the several States for the Districts as numbered, and Delegates from the several Territories, with their places of residence, or Post Offices, respectively.

New Hampshire.

1. George W. Kittredge, New Market.
2. George W. Morrison, Manchester.
3. Harry Hibbard, Bath.

Massachusetts.

1. Jonathan D. Eliot, New Bedford.
2. Samuel L. Crocker, Taunton.
3. J. Wiley Edmands, Newton Corner.
4. Samuel H. Walley, Roxbury.
5. William Appleton, Boston.
6. Charles W. Upham, Salem.
7. Nathaniel P. Banks, Jr., Waltham.
8. Tappan Wentworth, Lowell.
9. Alexander De Witt, Oxford.
10. Edward Dickinson, Amherst.
11. John Z. Goodrich, Stockbridge.

Rhode Island.

1. Thomas Davis, Providence.
2. Benjamin B. Thurston, Hopkinton.

Connecticut.

1. James T. Pratt, Rocky Hill.
2. Colin M. Ingersoll, New Haven.
3. Nathan Belcher, New London.
4. Origen S. Seymour, Litchfield.

Vermont.

1. James Meacham, Middlebury.
2. Andrew Tracy, Woodstock.
3. Alvah Sabin, Georgia.

New York.

1. James Maurice, Maspeth.
2. Thomas W. Cumming, Brooklyn.
3. Hiram Walbridge, New York.
4. Mike Walsh, New York.
5. William M. Tweed, New York.
6. John Wheeler, New York.
7. William A. Walker, New York.
8. Francis B. Cutting, New York.
9. Jared V. Peck, Portchester.
10. William Murray, Goshen.
11. Theodk. R. Westbrook, Kingston.
12. Gilbert Dean, Poughkeepsie.
13. Russell Sage, Troy.
14. Rufus W. Peckham, Albany.
15. Charles Hughes, Sandy Hill.
16. George A. Simmons, Keeseville.
17. Bishop Perkins, Ogdensburg.
18. Peter Rowe, Schenectady.
19. George W. Chase, Schenevers.
20. Orsamus B. Matteson, Utica.
21. Henry Bennett, New Berlin.
22. Gerrit Smith, Petersborough.
23. Caleb Lyon, of Lyonsdale.
24. Daniel T. Jones, Baldwinsville.
25. Edwin B. Morgan, Aurora, Cayuga co.
26. Andrew Oliver, Pen Yan.
27. John J. Taylor, Owego.
28. George Hastings, Mount Morris.
29. Davis Carpenter, Brockport.
30. Benjamin Pringle, Batavia, Genesee co.
31. Thomas T. Flagler, Lockport.
32. Solomon G. Haven, Buffalo.
33. Reuben E. Fenton, Frewsburg.

New Jersey.

1. Nathan T. Stratton, Mullica Hill.
2. Charles Skelton, Trenton.
3. Samuel Lilly, Lambertville.
4. George Vail, Morristown.
5. Alexander C. M. Pennington, Newark.

Pennsylvania.

1. Thomas B. Florence, Philadelphia.
2. Joseph R. Chandler, Philadelphia.
3. John Robbins, Jr., Kensington.
4. William H. Witte, Richmond.
5. John McNair, Norristown.
6. William Everhart, West Chester.
7. Samuel A. Bridges, Allentown.
8. J. Glancy Jones, Reading.
9. Isaac E. Hiester, Lancaster.
10. Ner Middleswarth, Beavertown.
11. Christian M. Straub, Pottsville.
12. Hendrick B. Wright, Wilkesbarre.
13. Asa Packer, Mauch Chunk.
14. Galusha A. Grow, Glenwood.
15. James Gamble, Jersey Shore.
16. William H. Kurtz, York.
17. Samuel L. Russell, Bedford.
18. John McCulloch, Shaver's Creek.
19. Augustus Drum, Indiana.
20. John L. Dawson, Brownsville.
21. David Ritchie, Pittsburg.
22. Thomas M. Howe, Alleghany City.
23. Michael C. Trout, Sharon.
24. Carlton B. Curtis, Warren.
25. John Dick, Meadville.

Delaware.

1. George Read Riddle, Wilmington.

Maryland.

1. John R. Franklin, Snow Hill.
2. Jacob Shover, Manchester.
3. Joshua Vansant, Baltimore.
4. Henry May, Baltimore.
5. William T. Hamilton, Hagerstown.
6. Augustus R. Sollers, Prince Fredericks-[town, Calvert co.

Virginia.

1. Thomas H. Bayly, Accomac C. H.
2. John S. Millson, Norfork.
3. John S. Caskie, Richmond.
4. William O. Goode, Boydton.
5. Thomas S. Bocock, Appomattox C. H.
6. Paulus Powell, Amherst C. H.
7. William Smith, Warrenton.
8. Charles J. Faulkner, Martinsburg.
9. John Letcher, Lexington.
10. Zedekiah Kidwell, Fairmont.
11. John F. Snodgrass, Parkersburg, (de-[ceased.)
12. Henry A. Edmundson, Salem, Roanoke [co.
13. Fayette McMullen, Rye Cove.

North Carolina.

1. Henry M. Shaw, Indiantown.
2. Thomas Ruffin, Goldsborough
3. William S. Ashe, Wilmington.
4. Sion H. Rogers, Raleigh.
5. John Kerr, Yanceyville.
6. Richard C. Puryear, Huntsville.
7. Burton Craige, Salisbury.
8. Thomas L. Clingman, Asheville.

South Carolina.

1. John McQueen, Marlborough C. H.
2. William Aiken, Charleston.
3. Lawrence M. Keitt, Orangeburgh C. H.
4. Preston S. Brooks, Ninety-six.
5. James L. Orr, Anderson.
6. William W. Boyce, Winnsborough.

Georgia.

1. James L. Seward, Thomasville.
2. Alfred H. Colquitt, Newton.
3. David J. Bailey, Jackson.
4. William B. W. Dent, Newnan.
5. Elijah W. Chastain, Tacoah.
6. Junius Hillyer, Monroe, Walton co.
7. David A. Reese, Monticello.
8. Alexander H. Stephens, Crawfordsville.

Kentucky.

1. Linn Boyd, Paducah.
2. Ben. Edwards Grey, Hopkinsville.
3. Presley Ewing, Russellville.
4. James S. Chrisman, Monticello.
5. Clement S. Hill, Lebanon.
6. John M. Elliott, Prestonsburg.
7. William Preston, Louisville.
8. John C. Breckenbridge, Lexington.
9. Leander M. Cox, Flemingsburg.
10. Richard H. Stanton, Maysville.

Tennessee.

1. Nathaniel G. Taylor, Happy Valley.
2. Wm. M. Churchwell, Knoxwell.
3. Samuel A. Smith, Charleston.
4. William Cullom, Carthage.
5. Charles Ready, Murfreesborough.
6. George W. Jones, Fayetteville.
7. Robert M. Bugg, Lynnville.
8. Felix K. Tillicoffer, Nashville.
9. Emerson Etheridge, Dresden.
10. Frederick P. Stanton, Memphis.

Ohio.

1. David T. Disney, Cincinnati.
2. John Scott Harrison, Cleves, Hamilton [co.
3. Lewis D. Campbell, Hamilton.
4. Matthias H. Nichols, Lima.
5. Alfred P. Edgerton, Hicksville.
6. Andrew Ellison, Georgetown.
7. Aaron Harlan, Yellow Springs.
8. Moses B. Corwin, Urbana.
9. Frederick W. Green, Tiffin.
10. John L. Taylor, Chillicothe.
11. Thomas Ritchie, Somerset.
12. Edson B. Olds, Circleville.
13. William D. Lindsley, Sandusky City.
14. Harvey H. Johnson, Ashland.
15. William R. Sapp, Mount Vernon.
16. Edward Ball, Zanesville.
17. Wilson Shannon, St. Clairsville.
18. George Bliss, Akron.
19. Edward Wade, Cleveland.
20. Joshua R. Giddings, Jefferson.
21. Andrew Stuart, Steubenville.

Louisiana.

1. William Dnnbar, New Orleans.
2. Theodore G. Hunt, New Orleans.
3. John Perkins, Jr., Ashwood, Tensas [Parish.
4. Roland Jones, Shreveport.

Indiana.

1. Smith Miller, Patoka.
2. William H. English, Lexington.
3. Cyrus L. Dunham, Valley Farm.
4. James H. Lane. Lawrenceburg.
5. Samuel W. Parker, Connersville.
6. Thomas A. Hendricks, Shelbyville.

7. John G. Davis, Rockville.
8. Daniel Mace, Lafayette.
9. Norman Eddy, South Bend.
10. Ebr. M. Chamberland, Goshen.
11. Andrew J. Harlan, Marion.

Mississippi.

1. Daniel B. Wright, Salem.
2. William S. Barry, Greenwood.
3. O. R. Singleton, Canton.
4. Wiley P. Harris, Monticello, Lawrence [co.
5. William Barksdale, Columbus.

Ilinois.

1. Elihu B. Washburn, Galena.
2. John Wentworth, Chicago.
3. Jesse O. Norton, Joliet, Will co.
4. James Knox, Knoxville.
5. Wm. A. Richardson, Quincy.
6. Richard Yates, Jacksonville.
7. James C. Allen, Palestine.
8. William H. Bissell, Belleville.
9. Willis Allen, Marion.

Alabama.

1. Philip Philips, Mobile.
2. James Abercrombie, Girard.
3. Sampson W. Harris, Wetumpka.
4. William R. Smith, Fayette C. H.
5. George S. Houston, Athens.
6. Williamson R. W. Cobb, Bellefonte.
7. James F. Dowdell, Chambers C. H.

Maine.

1. Moses McDonald, Portland.
2. Samuel Mayall, Gray.
3. E. Wilder Farley, Newcastle.
4. Samuel P. Benson, Winthrop.
5. Israel Washburn, Jr., Orons.
6. Thomas J. D. Fuller, Calais.

Missouri.

1. Thomas H. Benton, St. Louis.
2. Alfred W. Lamb, Hannibal.
3. James J. Lindley, Monticello, Lewis co.
4. Mordecai Oliver, Richmond.
5. John G. Miller, Boonville.
6. John S. Phelps, Springfield.
7. Samuel Caruthers, Fredericktown.

Arkansas.

1. Alfred B. Greenwood, Bentonville.
2. Edward A. Warren, Camden.

Michigan.

1. David Stuart, Detroit.
2. David A. Noble, Monroe.
3. Samuel Clark, Kalamazoo.
4. Hestor L. Stevens, Pontiac.

Florida.

1. Augustus E. Maxwell, Tallahassee.

Texas.

1. George W. Smythe, Jasper.
2. P. H. Bell, Austin.

Iowa.

1. Bernhart Henn, Fairfield.
2. John P. Cook, Davenport.

Wisconsin.

1. Daniel Wells, Jr., Milwaukie.
2. Ben. C. Eastman, Platteville.
3. John B. Macey, Fond du Lac.

California.

1. James A. McDougal, San Francisco.
2. Milton S. Latham, Sacramento City.

Minnesota Territory.

1. Henry M. Rice, Delegate, St. Paul.

Oregon Territory.

1. Joseph Lane, Delegate, Winchester.

Territory of New Mexico.

1. José Manuel Gallegos, Delegate, Albuquerque.

Utah Territory.

1. John M. Bernhisel, Delegate, Salt Lake City.

Washington Territory.

1. Columbus Lancaster, Delegate, St. Helen's, Oregon Territory.

INDEX.

THE ANALYTICAL INDEX OF THE CONSTITUTION OF THE UNITED STATES WILL BE FOUND AT PAGE 38. THE FOLLOWING INDEX REFERS TO THE RESIDUE OF THE MATTER CONTAINED IN THIS VOLUME.

ABRIDGMENTS and Digests of the Laws of the U. S. Description of books of 465

ACTS, Records, and Judicial Proceedings of one State in every other State, Territory, &c. An act for the authentication of 290–294

ACTS of the several States for appointment of Deputies to Convention to form the Constitution of the U. S. 167

ADAMS, President of the U. S., March 4, 1797. Inaugural Address of John 270

ADAMS, Vice President of the U. S. First election of John 315

ADAMS, Vice President of the U. S. Second election of John 316

ADAMS, as President of the U. S. Election of John 317

ADAMS, as President of the U. S. Election of John Quincy 324, 325

ADAMS, Vice President, in Senate of the U. S. Attendance of John 336

ADDRESS of George Washington, accepting commission as commander-in-chief of the army, June 16, 1775 201

ADDRESS of the President of Congress to George Washington, August 26, 1783, on termination of the war 203

ADDRESS of George Washington in reply to the same 204

ADDRESS of George Washington to Congress, on resigning his commission as commander-in-chief of the army, December 23, 1783 208

ADDRESS of Thomas Mifflin, President of Congress, in answer to the same 209

ADDRESS of George Washington, as President of the U. S., April 30, 1789. Inaugural 211

ADDRESS of George Washington to the people of the U. S., September 17, 1796. Farewell 215

ALABAMA. Chronological statement of the formation of the government of 431

AMBASSADORS and their domestics. An act for the protection of foreign 289

AMENDMENTS of the Constitution of the U. S. 25

AMENDMENTS of the Constitution of the U. S. by the States. Dates of ratification of first ten 34

AMENDMENTS of the Constitution of the U. S. Same of the eleventh and twelfth 36

AMENDMENTS of the Constitution, when ratified by the States, to be published by the Secretary of State 295

ANALYTICAL Index of the Constitution and amendments. An 38

ANNAPOLIS, in 1796, recommending the Convention to form the Constitution. Proceedings of the commissioners at 161

APPOINTMENT of George Washington to be commander-in-chief of the army, June 15, 1775 201

APPOINTMENT of George Washington to be lieutenant-general and commander-in-chief of all the armies of the U. S., July 3, 1798 231–239

APPORTIONMENT of Representatives among the several States according to the Sixth Census 300

ARKANSAS. Chronological statement of the formation of the government of 434

ARMAMENTS being prepared in the U. S. against foreign powers with whom the U. S. are at peace. An act to prevent 296

ARMIES of the U. S. Appointment of George Washington to be lieutenant-general and commander-in-chief of the 231–239

ARMY of the United Colonies, June 15, 1775. George Washington elected commander-in-chief of the 201

ARMY of the United Colonies fixed at $500 per month. Pay and expenses of the General to command the 201

ARMY of the U. S., December 23, 1783. Resignation by George Washington of his commission as commander-in-chief of the 208

ATTORNEY GENERALS of the U. S., from 1789 to 1851. Names, States, service, &c., of the 402

AUDIENCE in Congress granted to George Washington, commander-in-chief, August 25, 1783 203

AUDIENCE in Congress, December 20, 1783. George Washington, commander-in-chief, admitted to a public 205

AUTHENTICATION of Acts, Records, and Judicial Proceedings of one State in every other State, Territory, &c. 290–294

BERRIEN, Senator of the U. S. Letter of approbation from John Macp... xvii

BOOKS and other sources of historical, political, statistical, and other information relative to the action of the Government, in possession of the public offices at the Seat of Government. Description of 451

BOOKS, published under the patronage of Congress and otherwise, containing useful political, statistical, and other information. Description of miscellaneous 468–471

BOOKS in Congress Library. Description of selection of certain 472

BOOKS in the State Department. Description of selection of certain 479

BREESE, Senator of the U. S. Letter of approbation from Sidney xii

BURR, as Vice President of the U. S. Election of Aaron 318

BURR, Vice President, in the Senate of the U. S. Attendance of Aaron 338

BURR, as Senator of the U. S. Term of service of Aaron 354

CALHOUN, Vice President of the U. S. First election of John C 324

CALHOUN, Vice President of the U. S. Second election of J. C 326

CALHOUN, Vice President, in Senate of the U. S. Attendance of J. C .. 340–342

CALHOUN resigned as Vice President, December 28, 1832. John C 342, 343

CALHOUN, as Senator of the U. S. Terms of service of John C 367

CASS, Senator of the U. S. Letter of approbation from Lewis xx

CLAY, Senator of the U. S. Letter of approbation from Henry xix

CALIFORNIA. Chronological statement of the formation of the government of 437
CEDE their Western lands to the U. S. Resolution of Congress recommending to the several States to ········ ································ 421
CEDED by the States, should be disposed of for the common benefit of the U. S., and formed into Republican States. Resolution of Congress that the lands·· 422
CEDED to the U. S., and dates of cession. Names of States by which Western lands were ··· 422
CENSUS. Apportionment of Representatives among the several States according to the Sixth ··· 300
CENSUSES U. S., and fix number of Representatives. Act for taking Seventh, and subsequent ··· 305
CESSION of the North-Western and Western Territory to the U. S. by certain States. Proceedings which led to the ·································· 414
CESSION of its Western or Vacant Lands to the U. S. Act of New York for the 419
CHAIRMAN of Committees of Congress authorized to administer Oaths···· 294, 295
CHAPTERS. General contents of. See Table of Contents················ xxxviii
CHARTERS of the original States. Chronological statement of the········407, 408
CHRONOLOGICAL statement of the Charters and formation of the Governments of the several States and Territories of the U. S.······ ················ 405–446
CITIZEN to understand the Constitution. Introductory remarks on duty of every ·· xxiii
CLERK of the House of Representatives of the U. S. Oaths to be taken by the ···22, 288, 289
CLERKS in all the Departments of Government. Oaths to be taken by the 290, 291
CLERKS of the House of Representatives of the U. S. from 1789 to 1851. Names, States, services, &c. of the ··· 388
CLERKS of the Supreme Court of the U. S. from 1789 to 1851. Names, &c. of the ··· 393
CLINTON, Vice President of the U. S. Election of George················319, 320
CLINTON, Vice President, in Senate of the U. S. Attendance of George·····338–340
COLLECTORS of the Customs authorized to detain vessels built for warlike purposes ··· 299
COLONIAL and Revolutionary Documentary History. Books relating to the·· 452
COLUMBIA established the permanent seat of Government. The District of····449
COMMERCE. Resolution of Virginia for a uniform system of trade, commerce, &c., January 21, 1786··· 160
COMMERCE. Proceedings of Convention at Annapolis appointed for said purpose, September 14, 1786··· 161
COMMERCE. Resolution of Congress, of February 21, 1787, calling the Convention which formed the Constitution····· ····························· 166
COMMERCE. Acts of the several States for the appointment of deputies to said Convention, to revise and report the means of enabling Congress to provide more effectually for the commercial interests of the U. S., and to remedy all the defects of the Federal system, &c.································· 167
COMMERCE. The Constitution declares that "The Congress shall have power to regulate commerce with foreign nations, and among the several States, and with the Indian tribes"······································· 15

COMMERCIAL Regulations. Description of books containing Tariff and Revenue Laws, &c. 467
COMMITTEES of Congress to administer Oaths. Authority for the Chairman of 294, 295
COMMUNICATIONS to the author and compiler in relation to this work ix–xxi
COMPENSATION to the President and Vice President of the U. S. An act making 293
COMPENSATION to persons appointed to deliver the Electoral votes of President, &c., 1792 292
COMPENSATION to do. do. do., 1825 300
CONFEDERATION, showing the inefficiency of that government, and leading to the adoption of the Constitution. Proceedings of the Congress of the 129
CONFEDERATION. The formation of a Convention to frame the Constitution, recommended in 1786, as a means to remedy the defects in the Articles of 166
CONFEDERATION. The Articles of 483
CONFEDERATION, until March 1, 1781. Dates of ratification by the States, and cause of the delay of Maryland to ratify the Articles of 406–415
CONGRESS of the Confederation, which led to the adoption of the Constitution. Proceedings of the 129
CONGRESS of the Confederation, and resolutions of that body, showing the impotency of the Government to provide a revenue for its wants and necessities, &c. Reports of committees of 131–139, 140–142–146–150, 151
CONGRESS of the Confederation appointing a Committee to represent the Financial and Commercial difficulties to the several States, May 22, 1782. Resolution of 154
CONGRESS of the Confederation in 1787, recommending the Convention which formed the Constitution. Proceedings of 164
CONGRESS of the Confederation, of September 28, 1787, transmitting the Constitution to the States, to be submitted to Conventions thereof. Resolution of 189
CONGRESS of the Confederation of September 13, 1788, providing for commencing proceedings under the Constitution of the U. S. Resolution of the 190
CONGRESS of July 2, 1776, that THE UNITED COLONIES ARE, AND OF RIGHT OUGHT TO BE FREE AND INDEPENDENT STATES. Resolution of 195
CONGRESS assembled, July 4, 1776. Declaration of Independence by the Representatives of the U. S. in 195
CONGRESS, for promulgating the Declaration of Independence. Resolution of 200
CONGRESS of the Confederation, of June 17, 1775, declaring that they would maintain and assist George Washington, and adhere to him for the maintenance and preservation of American liberty, with their lives and fortunes. Resolutions of the 203
CONGRESS, on August 26, 1783, to George Washington, on the termination of the war, and his reply. Address of the President of 203, 204
CONGRESS, of December 20, 1783, admitting George Washington, commander-in-chief, to a public audience. Resolution of 205

CONGRESS, of December 20, 1783, that a public entertainment be given to the commander-in-chief, on December 22. Resolution of 205
CONGRESS, December 23, 1783, and answer of Thomas Mifflin, President. Resignation, by George Washington, of his commission to 208
CONGRESS on the death of George Washington in 1799. Proceedings of 240–268
CONGRESS shall be in session on the second Wednesday in February, succeeding every meeting of Electors of President and Vice President of the U. S. 292
CONGRESS. Provision for dividing States into districts for the election of Representatives in 159–301
CONGRESS, from March 4, 1789, to March 3, 1851. Commencement and termination of, and number of days in each session of 336–345
CONGRESS, from 1789 to 1851. Names of Senators in 346–384
CONGRESS, elected Speaker of House of Representatives, from 1789 to 1851. Names of Representatives in 386
CONGRESS to admit "New States" into the Union. Remarks on the right and discretionary power of 408
CONGRESS of the Confederation. Books relating to the proceedings of the .. 453
CONGRESS from 1789 to 1851. Description of the Books, Newspapers, &c., containing the Debates in 459
CONGRESS Library. Description of selection of certain books in 472
CONNECTICUT, in 1787, appointing deputies to Convention to form the Constitution. Act of 184
CONNECTICUT. Chronological statement of the Charters and Constitutions of 407
CONNECTICUT ceded western lands to U. S., September 14, 1786, and May 30, 1800 422
CONSTITUTION. Introductory remarks, on duty of every citizen to understand the xxiii
CONSTITUTION of the United States of America. The 1
CONSTITUTION by the States. Dates of ratification of the 24
CONSTITUTION of the U. S. Articles in addition to, and amendments of, the 25
CONSTITUTION by the States. Dates of ratification of the first ten amendments of the 34
CONSTITUTION by the States. Dates of ratification of eleventh and twelfth amendments of the 36
CONSTITUTION and amendments. An analytical index of the 38
CONSTITUTION of the U. S. Official proceedings and proximate causes which led to the adoption and ratification of the 129
CONSTITUTION of the U S. Remarks relative to the States that were prominent in the proceedings which immediately led to the adoption of the .. 153
CONSTITUTION for the U. S. Resolutions of the General Assembly of New York, passed July 21, 1782, recommending a Convention to form a 155
CONSTITUTION of the U. S. was formed. Proceedings of Commissioners at Annapolis, in 1786, recommending the appointment of deputies to meet at Philadelphia, by whom the 161

CONSTITUTION. Recommendation of Congress of the Confederation, in 1787, for appointment of deputies to the Convention which formed the ... 165
CONSTITUTION of the U. S. Acts of the several States for the appointment of deputies to the Convention for forming a, viz. 167
Of Virginia, on October 16, 1786 167
Of New Jersey, on November 23, 1786 170
Of Pennsylvania, on December 30, 1786 172
Of North Carolina, on January 6, 1787 174
Of Delaware, on February 3, 1787 177
Of Georgia, on February 10, 1787 179
Of New York, on February 28, 1787 181
Of South Carolina, on March 8, 1787 182
Of Massachusetts, on March 10, 1787 183
Of Connecticut, May, 1787 184
Of Maryland, on May 26, 1787 185
Of New Hampshire, on 27th June, 1787 186
CONSTITUTION of the U. S. to Congress of the Confederation. Letter of George Washington, and resolutions of the Convention of September 17, 1787, transmitting the 187, 188
CONSTITUTION of the U. S. to the several States, to be submitted to Conventions thereof. Resolution of Congress of Confederation, September 28, 1787, transmitting the 189
CONSTITUTION of the U. S. Resolution of Congress of the Confederation, of September 13, 1788, for commencing proceedings under the 190
CONSTITUTION in certain contingencies, and for other purposes. General Laws providing the means of executing the 287
CONSTITUTION of the U. S. is to be taken. (See *Oath.*) By whom the oath to support the 15, 22, 288, 289
CONSTITUTION, when ratified by the States, to be published by the Secretary of State. Amendments to the 295
CONVENTION at Annapolis, September, 1786. Proceedings of the 161
CONVENTION at Philadelphia to form a Constitution, recommended by Convention at Annapolis, September 14, 1786 161
CONVENTION which formed the Constitution recommended by Congress, in 1787, as a means to remedy the defects in the Articles of Confederation 165
CONVENTION to form the Constitution. Acts of the several States for appointing deputies to the 167
CONVENTION, in 1787, transmitting the Constitution to Congress of the Confederation, and suggesting measures for commencing proceedings under the Constitution. Letter of George Washington, and resolutions of the 187
CONVENTIONS of the States. Resolution of Congress, of September 28, 1787, submitting the Constitution to 189
CONVENTION that formed the Constitution. Boooks relating to the proceedings of the 453
COURT. (See *Supreme Court of the U. S.*)
COURTS of the U. S., or State courts against a foreign Ambassador or his domestics to be utterly null and void, &c. All process or writs from the 289

COURTS of the U. S. An act to provide further remedial justice in the. [This act empowers the U. S. judges to grant the writ of habeas corpus, and to discharge foreigners confined in the prison of a State, in certain cases.] 301
COURTS of the U. S. and of the several States. Little & Brown's edition of the Laws of the U. S. declared to be evidence in all the tribunals, offices, and 302, 303
COURT of the U. S. from 1789 to 1851. Description of books of Reports of decisions of the Supreme 466
CRANCH, Chief Justice of the Circuit Court of the U. S. for the District of Columbia. Letter of approbation from William xiv
CRIMES against the U. S., providing for the protection of foreign Ambassadors and their domestics. An act for the punishment of certain 289
CRIMES against the U. S., &c., for preserving their neutrality. An act in addition to an act for the punishment of certain 296

DALLAS, Vice President of the U. S., and President of the Senate. Dedication to, and letter of approbation from George M. ix
DALLAS, as Vice President of the U. S. Election of George M. 330
DALLAS, Vice President, in the Senate of the U. S. Attendance of George M. 332
DALLAS, as Senator of the U. S. Term of service of George M. 358
DAVIS, Speaker of the House of Representatives of the U. S. Letter of approbation from John W. xi
DEATH of George Washington. Proceedings of the Government and funeral oration of Henry Lee on the 240–247
DEBATES in the two Houses of Congress from 1789 to 1851. Description of the books, newspapers, &c., containing the 459
DECLARATION of Independence, from June 8 to July 4, 1776. Proceedings in Congress of the United Colonies respecting the 193
DECLARATION of Independence, by the Representatives of the U. S. in Congress assembled, July 4, 1776 195
DECLARATION of Independence. Resolution of Congress for promulgating the 200
DECLARATION by the Congress, June 17, 1775, that, for the maintenance and preservation of American liberty, they would maintain, assist, and adhere to, George Washington, as commander-in-chief, with their lives and fortunes 203
DELAWARE, in 1787, appointing deputies to Convention to form the Constitution. Act of 177
DELAWARE. Chronological statement of the charters and constitutions of 408
DELAWARE, declaring the common right of all the States to the western territory, &c. Resolutions of the State of 415
DEPUTIES to the Convention who signed the Constitution. Names of 23
DEPUTIES to Convention to form the Constitution. Acts of the States for appointment of 167
DIGESTS of the Laws of the U. S. Description of the books of 465

DISTRICT of Columbia, established the permanent seat of the Government of the U. S. 449

DISTRICTS for election of Representatives in Congress. Provision for dividing the States into 301

DOCUMENTS, Journals, and other sources of historical, political, statistical, and other information regarding the legislative, executive, and judicial action of the Government, in the public offices at the Seat of Government. Description of 451

DOCUMENTS ordered to be printed by the Senate and House of Representatives of the U. S. from 1789 to 1851. Remarks descriptive of the regular 457–459

ELECTIONS under and by virtue of the Constitution, (analytical index) ... 61, 62

ELECTION of a President and Vice President of the U. S., &c., approved March 1, 1792. An act relative to the 291

ELECTION of Electors of a President and Vice President, in case of vacancies in those offices by casualty, &c. Provision for the 293

ELECTIONS for Electors of President and Vice President in all the States. An act to establish a uniform time for holding 302

ELECTORAL votes for President and Vice President of the U. S. Provisions of the Constitution regarding the 28

ELECTORAL votes for President and Vice President of the U. S. Regulations, by law, for the giving, making lists of, transmitting to the Seat of Government, opening, and counting the 291

ELECTORAL votes. Compensation to, and penalties of, persons appointed to deliver the 292

ELECTORAL votes. Compensation of persons appointed to deliver the 300

ELECTORAL votes for President and Vice President of the U. S., viz.:

- First term, George Washington and John Adams, commencing March 4, 1789 315
- Second term, George Washington and John Adams, commencing March 4, 1793 316
- Third term, John Adams and Thomas Jefferson, commencing March 4, 1797 317
- Fourth term, Thomas Jefferson and Aaron Burr, elected by the House of Representatives, commencing March 4, 1801 318
- Fifth term, Thomas Jefferson and George Clinton, commencing March 4, 1805 319
- Sixth term, James Madison and George Clinton, commencing March 4, 1809 320
- Seventh term, James Madison and Elbridge Gerry, commencing March 4, 1813 321
- Eighth term, James Monroe and Daniel D. Tompkins, commencing March 4, 1817 322
- Ninth term, James Monroe and Daniel D. Tompkins, commencing March 4, 1821 323
- Tenth term, John Quincy Adams and John C. Calhoun, commencing March 4, 1825 325

ELECTORAL votes for President and Vice President of the U. S.—*continued*
Eleventh term, Andrew Jackson and John C. Calhoun, commencing March 4, 1829 326
Twelfth term, Andrew Jackson and Martin Van Buren, commencing March 4, 1833 327
Thirteenth term, Martin Van Buren and R. M. Johnson, commencing March 4, 1837 328
Fourteenth term, Wm. H. Harrison and John Tyler, commencing March 4, 1841 329–331
Fifteenth term, James K. Polk and George M. Dallas, commencing March 4, 1845 332
Sixteenth term, Zachary Taylor and M. Fillmore, commencing March 4, 1849 333
ELECTORS of President and Vice President, equal to the number of Senators and Representatives in Congress from each State. Each State shall appoint a number of 13
ELECTORS shall be equal to the number of Senators and Representatives to which the States may be entitled at the time when the President and Vice President should come into office. The 291
ELECTORS of President and Vice President of the U. S. Enactments of the law for the government of the 291
ELECTORS of the President and Vice President in all the States. An act to establish a uniform time for holding elections of 302
ELECTORS. Each State may, by law, provide for filling vacancies in the college of 302
EVIDENCE in all tribunals and offices of the United States, and of the individual States. Little & Brown's edition of the Laws of the U. S. declared to be competent 302, 303
EXECUTIVE officers of the Government, from 1789 to 1851. Names, States, service, &c., of all the high 395
EXTRADITION Treaties. Act giving effect to 303

FAREWELL Address of George Washington, President of the U. S., September 17, 1796 215
"FIRST in War, First in Peace, and First in the hearts of his Countrymen," as applicable to George Washington. Origin of the words 242
FLORIDA. Chronological statement of the formation of the Government of 436
FOREIGN Ambassadors and their Domestics. An act for the protection of 289
FOREIGN Powers. An act to preserve the neutrality of the U. S., with 296
FOREIGN Nation with whom the U. S. are at peace. An act to prevent any armament by land or water being fitted out in the U. S. against any 296
FOREIGN State confined in any state prison in certain cases. The Judges of the U. S. Courts empowered to grant the writ of Habeas Corpus, and to discharge the citizens of any 301
FUNERAL Procession and Oration of Henry Lee, in honor of Gen. George Washington 245–247

GEORGIA, in 1787, appointing deputies to Convention to form the Constitution. Act of 179
GEORGIA. Chronological statement of the Charters and Constitutions of ... 408
GEORGIA ceded western lands to the U. S. April 24, 1802 422
GERRY, Vice President of the U. S. Election of Elbridge 321
GERRY, Vice President, in the Senate of the U. S. Attendance of Elbridge 340
GIBSON, Chief Justice of the Supreme Court of Pennsylvania. Letter of approbation from John B. xiii
GOVERNMENT of the Confederation to provide for its support, defence, &c. Reports of committees and Resolutions of Congress exhibiting the inefficiency of the 131–139, 140–142–146–150, 151
GOVERNMENT under the Constitution of the U. S. Resolutions of Congress of the Confederation of September 13, 1788, providing for the commencement of the 190
GOVERNMENT under the Constitution. Brief statement of the manner of commencing proceedings of the 191
GOVERNMENT. George Washington's opinions of the principles and policy of our 211–215
GOVERNMENT. John Adams' ..... do. ..... do. 270
GOVERNMENT. Thomas Jefferson's. .. do. ..... do. ..... xxxi. 275–279
GOVERNMENT. James Madison's ..... do. ..... do. ..... xxxii. 283
GOVERNMENT and providing the means of executing the Constitution, &c. General Laws relating to the continued organization of the 287
GOVERNMENTS of the several States and territories. Chronological statement of the Charters and formation of the 405–449
GOVERNMENT of the territory of the U. S. north-west of the river Ohio. An ordinance for the 423
GOVERNMENT of the U. S. in possession of the public offices. Description of the sources of information regarding the Legislative, Executive and Judicial action of the 451

HABEAS Corpus in all cases of foreigners confined in the U. S., &c. The judges of the U. S. Courts authorized to grant writs of 301
HARRISON, as President of the U. S Election of William Henry 329–331
HISTORICAL and other information in the public offices at the seat of Government. Description of the sources of 451
HOUDON'S statue of Washington at Richmond, Virginia. Remarks and correspondence relative to 205–206
HOUSE of Representatives of the U. S. Oaths of office to be taken by the Members and Clerk of the 22, 288–289
HOUSE of Representatives, from 1789 to 1851. Names of Speakers of the 386–387
HOUSE of Representatives of the U. S., from 1789 to 1851. Names, service, &c., of the Clerks of the 385
HOUSE of Representatives of the U. S. Description of the Journals of the 452–456
HOUSE of Representatives of the U. S., from 1789 to 1851. Remarks descriptive of the documents printed by order of the 457, 458, 459

ILLINOIS. Chronological statement of the formation of the Government of 431
IMPEACHMENTS from 1789 to 1851. Description of the Journal or record of the Senate on 456
IMPOST duties of April 18, 1783, was the cause of proceedings which ultimately led to the adoption of the Constitution. Report of Committee of the Congress of Confederation, showing that the failure of the States to carry the general system of 131–139, 140–142–146, 150, 151
IMPOST, &c., as provided by resolution of Congress, April 18, 1783. See *Commerce.*) Resolutions of Congress of February 15, 1786, recommending to the States to empower Congress to carry into effect a general system of 139, 141–149, 151–153
INAUGURAL address of George Washington, President of the U. S. April 30, 1789 211
INAUGURAL address of John Adams, President of the U. S. 270
INAUGURAL address of Thomas Jefferson, President of the U. S. 275
INAUGURAL address of Thomas Jefferson, President of the U. S. 279
INAUGURAL address of James Madison, President of the U. S. 283
INDEPENDENCE of mind. Importance to every citizen of preserving ... xxv
INDEPENDENCE. Proceedings in Congress of the United Colonies, from June 8, to July 4, 1776, respecting a declaration of 193
INDEPENDENCE by the Representatives of the United States in Congress assembled, July 4, 1776. The Declaration of 195
INDEPENDENCE. Resolution of Congress for promulgating the Declaration of 200
INDEPENDENT STATES. Resolution of Congress of July 2, 1776, that THE UNITED COLONIES ARE, AND OF RIGHT OUGHT TO BE, FREE AND 195
INDEX to the Constitution and amendments. An Analytical 38
INDEXES prepared by order of the two Houses of Congress. Description of 465
INDIANA. Chronological statement of the formation of the Government of .. 430
INTRODUCTORY remarks to the work and to the several chapters. (See *Remarks.*)
IOWA. Chronological statement of the formation of the Government of 443

JACKSON, as President of the U. S. First election of Andrew 326
JACKSON, as President of the U. S. Second election of Andrew 327
JEFFERSON'S declaration of the principles of our Government. Thomas xxxi, 275–279
JEFFERSON, President of the U. S., on March 4, 1801. First inaugural address of Thomas 275
JEFFERSON, President of the U. S., on March 4, 1805. Second inaugural address of Thomas 279
JEFFERSON, as Vice President of the U. S. Election of Thomas 317
JEFFERSON, as President of the U. S. First election by House of Representatives of Thomas 318
JEFFERSON, as President of the U. S. Second election by electors of Thomas 319

JEFFERSON, Vice President, in Senate of the U. S. Attendance of Thomas 336
JOHNSON, as Vice President of the U. S. Election by the Senate of Richard M. 328
(The number of electoral votes required for an election being 148, and R. M. Johnson having received only 147, the election then devolved upon the Senate, and R. M. Johnson was elected.)
JOHNSON, Vice President, in Senate of the U. S. Attendance of Richard M. 342–344
JOHNSON, as Senator of the U. S. Terms of service of Richard M. 370
JOURNALS of the Congress of the Confederation, 1774 to 1789. Description of the 453
JOURNAL of the Convention that formed the Constitution in 1787. Description of the 453
JOURNAL of the House of Representatives of the U. S. from 1789 to 1851. Description of 454–456
JOURNAL of the Senate of the U. S. from 1789 to 1851. Description of Legislative 455, 456
JOURNAL of the Senate of the U. S. from 1789 to 1851 (in part). Description of the Executive 455
JOURNAL or record of the Senate on impeachments, from 1789 to 1851. Description of 456
JOURNALS of the Senate and House of Representatives of the U. S. Remarks descriptive of the contents of the Legislative 456
JUDGES of Courts of the U. S. authorized to grant writs of Habeas Corpus in all cases of foreigners confined in the United States, and to discharge them. The 301
JUDGES of the Supreme Court of the U. S., from 1789 to 1851. Names, states, length of service, &c., of the 389
JUDICIAL proceedings of one State in every other State, territory, &c. Authentication of 290–294
JUSTICE in the Courts of the U. S. An act to provide further remedial 301

KANE, Judge of the District Court of the U. S. for the Eastern District of Pennsylvania. Letter of approbation from J. K. xiii
KENTUCKY. Chronological statement of the formation of the Government of 412
KNOWLEDGE. Remarks on the proper mode of acquiring and imparting xix

LAND in the north-western and western territory of the U. S. Proceedings which led to the cession by the States, of the 414
LANDS to the U. S. Act of New York for the cession of its western or vacant 419
LANDS to the U. S. Resolution of Congress recommending to the States to cede their western 421

LANDS ceded by the States should be disposed of for the common benefit of the U. S., and formed into Republican States. Resolution of Congress of October 10, 1780, that the 422
LANDS were ceded to the U. S., and dates of cession. Names of States by which the western 422
LANDS of the U. S., and private land claims to March 3, 1851. Description of the publications under the authority of the U. S. relating to the public .. 460
LAW. Definition and sanctity of the civil xxv
LAWS, relating to the continued organization of the Government, and providing the authorities and means of executing the Constitution, in certain contingencies, and for other purposes, &c. 287
LAWS of the U. S. declared competent evidence in all tribunals and offices of the U. S., and of the several States. Little and Brown's edition of the 302, 303
LAWS of the U. S., including the Treaties. Description of the books containing the 461
LAWS of the U. S. Description of Books of Abridgments and Digests of the 465–467
LEGISLATIVE Journals. (Vide *Journals.*)
LEE, on the death of George Washington. Funeral oration of Henry 247
LETTERS-OF-MARQUE being fitted out in the U. S. against foreign powers. An act to prevent Privateers or 296
LIBERTY. Definition of rational or civil xxii
LIBERTY and independence on July 4, 1776. Declaration of 195
LIBERTY, &c., on June 17, 1775. Declaration of Congress for the maintenance of American 203
LIBERTY consists. In what the enjoyment and even the support and preservation of xxix
LIBRARY of Congress. Description of selection of certain books in the 472
LIBRARY of the State Department. Description of selection of certain books in the 479
LIEUTENANT-GENERAL and commander-in-chief of the Armies of the U. S., July 3, 1798. Appointment of George Washington to be 231–239
LIGHT as regards the fundamental law. Remarks on necessity of the people's having xxxiii
LITTLE and Brown's editions of the Laws of the U. S., declared to be competent evidence in all tribunals and offices of the U. S., and of the several States 302, 303
LOUISIANA. Chronological statement of the formation of the Government of 429

MADISON'S declaration of the principles of our Government. James . xxxii. 283
MADISON, President of the U. S. on March 4, 1809. Inaugural Address of James 283
MADISON, President of the U. S. First election of James 420
MADISON, President of the U. S. Second election of James 421
MAINE. Chronological statement of the formation of the Government of ... 432

MARSHALS attendant on the Supreme Court of the U. S., from 1789 to 1851. Names, &c. of the 393
MARYLAND, in 1787, appointing deputies to convention to form the Constitution. Act of 183
MARYLAND to ratify the Articles of Confederation, until March 1, 1781. Dates of ratification by the States and cause of the delay of 406–414
MARYLAND. Chronological statement of the Charters and Constitutions of 408
MARYLAND to ratify the Articles of Confederation until the States possessing the North-Western and Western Territory should cede the same to the U. S. for the common benefit of all the States. Statement of the causes of delay by 414
MARYLAND on said subject. Instructions to the Delegates in Congress from 415
MARYLAND to ratify the Articles of Confederation. Resolution of Congress earnestly requesting 421
MASSACHUSETTS, in 1787, appointing deputies to Convention to form the Constitution. Act of 183
MASSACHUSETTS. Chronological statement of the Charters and Constitutions of 407
MASSACHUSETTS ceded Western lands to the U. S. April 19, 1785 422
MEMBERS of the Senate and House of Representatives to take an Oath to support the Constitution, and the manner and form thereof. An act prescribing the time for 22, 288
MESSENGERS or persons to deliver electoral votes. Compensation to, and penalties of 292
MESSENGERS or persons to deliver electoral votes. Compensation to 300
MICHIGAN. Chronological statement of the formation of the Government of 434
MIFFLIN, President of Congress, to George Washington, in answer to resignation of his commission. Address of Thomas 209
MINESOTA Territory. Proceedings in Congress relative to the 447
MINISTERS and their domestics. An act for the protection of Foreign 289
MISSISSIPPI. Chronological statement of the formation of the Government of 430
MISSOURI. Chronological statement of the formation of the Government of 433
MONROE, President of the U. S. First election of James 322
MONROE, President of the U. S. Second election of James 323
MONUMENT be erected to General Washington in the Capitol at Washington. Resolution of Congress that a marble 245
MOURNING of the Government on the Death of George Washington. Proceedings and 240–269

NAVY from 1789 to 1851. Names, States, services, &c., of Secretaries of the 399
NEBRASKA Territory. Proceedings in Congress relative to the 448
NEUTRALITY of the U. S. by prohibiting its citizens, within its limits, from preparing any offensive means against a foreign nation. An act to preserve the 296

NEW HAMPSHIRE, in 1787, appointing deputies to Convention to form the Constitution. Act of 186
NEW HAMPSHIRE. Chronological statement of the Charters and Constitutions of 407
NEW JERSEY, at the meeting at Annapolis, in 1786, having more enlarged powers than the Commissioners from other States, was stated as the ground for calling the Convention which formed the Constitution. The Commissioners of 162
NEW JERSEY, in 1786, appointing deputies to Convention to form the Constitution. Acts of 170
NEW JERSEY. Chronological statement of the Charters and Constitutions of 407
NEW JERSEY ratified the Articles of Confederation "in the firm reliance that the" Western Territory would be ceded by the States in possession to the U. S., &c. 414
NEW MEXICO TERRITORY. Proceedings in Congress relative to the 448
NEW YORK, July 21, 1782, on the critical state of the Confederation, and recommending a Convention to form a Constitution. Resolutions of the General Assembly of 155
NEW YORK, in 1787, appointing deputies to the Convention to form the Constitution. Act of 181
NEW YORK. Chronological statement of the Charters and Constitutions of ... 407
NEW YORK for the cession of its Western or vacant lands to the U. S., in order to conciliate the Union under the Confederation. Act of 419–422
NEW YORK. Special approbation of Congress for this act of 421
NORTH CAROLINA, in 1787, appointing deputies to Convention to form the Constitution. Act of 174
NORTH CAROLINA. Chronological statement of the Charters and Constitutions of 408
NORTH CAROLINA ceded Western lands to the U. S., February 25, 1790 422
NORTH-WESTERN and Western Territory to the U. S. Proceedings which led to the cession by the States of the 414
NORTH-WESTERN Territory ceded to the U. S. by Virginia, March 1, 1784 422
NORTH-WESTERN Territory. An ordinance for the Government of the 423

OATH of office, as President, administered to George Washington, by the Chancellor of the State of New York, April 30, 1789 211
OATH of John Tyler, Vice President, to qualify him as President of the U. S ... 331
OATHS to support the Constitution of the United States, and for performance of official duty, to be taken by the following officers and persons, viz.:
1. The President of the U. S. 15
2. The President of the Senate 288
3. The Senators of the U. S. 22, 288
4. The Secretary of the Senate 22, 288, 289
5. The Senators of the U. S. on trial of impeachment 4
6. The Speaker of the House of Representatives 288
7. The members of the House of Representatives of the U. S. 22, 288

OATHS to support the Constitution, &c.—*continued.*
8. The Clerk of the House of Representatives ····· 22, 288, 289
9. The members of the several State Legislatures ····· 22, 288
10. The executive and judicial officers both of the U. S. and of the several States ····· 22, 288
11. All officers appointed under the authority of the U. S. ····· 288
12. Each and every clerk and other officer in any of the departments of the U. S. ····· 288
"OATHS of office" are to be taken. By whom ····· 22, 288, 289, 290, 291
OATHS. The presiding officers of the two Houses, and chairmen of committees of Congress, authorized to administer ····· 294, 295
OATHS, prescribing the forms, &c. An act to regulate the time and manner of administering certain ····· 287
OFFICERS required to take an oath to support the Constitution of the United States ····· 22, 288, 289, 290, 291
OFFICE of President and Vice President to commence March 4, &c. The term of ····· 293
OFFICES of the U. S. and of the States. Little & Brown's edition of the Laws of the U. S. declared to be competent evidence in all courts, tribunals, and ····· 303
OHIO. Chronological statement of the formation of the government of ····· 413
ORATION by Henry Lee on the death of George Washington. Funeral ····· 247
ORDINANCE for the government of the territory of the U. S. north-west of the river Ohio. An ····· 423
OREGON Territory. Reference to treaties fixing the boundaries, and to proceedings in Congress relative to the ····· 447

PASSPORT issued under authority of the U. S. Penalty for violating a ····· 290
PAY and expenses of the General to command all the continental forces fixed at $500 per month, by resolution of Congress ····· 201
PENALTY for neglect to deliver the electoral votes by the messengers, &c. 292
PENALTY for violating the laws of neutrality in the U. S. against a foreign power at peace ····· 296
PENNSYLVANIA, in 1786, appointing deputies to Convention to form the Constitution. Act of ····· 172
PENNSYLVANIA. Chronological statement of the charters and constitutions of ····· 408
PEOPLE to support the Constitution. Responsibilities of the ····· xxiii
POLITICAL and other information in the public offices at the Seat of Government. Description of the sources of ····· 451
POLK as President of the U. S. Election of James K. ····· 332
POSTMASTER GENERALS, from 1789 to 1851. Names, States, service, &c., of the ····· 401
PREFACE to this edition, and to the chapters. (See *Remarks.*)
PRESIDENT of the U. S. Certificate of the election of George Washington as 210

PRESIDENT and Vice President of the U. S., and declaring the officer to act as President in case of vacancies in offices of President and Vice President, approved March 1, 1792. An act relative to election of 291
PRESIDENT and Vice President, in case of vacancies in those offices by casualty. Provision for the election of a 293
PRESIDENT or Vice President of the U. S. to be delivered into the office of Secretary of State. A resignation or refusal to accept office of 293
PRESIDENT and Vice President of the U. S. to commence March 4, &c. Term of office of the 293
PRESIDENT and Vice President of the U. S. An act providing compensation to the 293
PRESIDENT and Vice President of the U. S. Compensation to, and penalty of, persons appointed to deliver electoral votes for 292
PRESIDENT and Vice President of the U. S. Compensation to persons, &c., to deliver electoral votes for 300
PRESIDENT and Vice President of the U. S. An act to establish a uniform time for holding elections for electors of 302
PRESIDENT and Vice President of the U. S., from 1789 to 1849. (See *Electoral Votes.*) Electoral votes, &c., for 315–334
PRESIDENT of the U. S., on the death of Wm. H. Harrison, President. Proceedings introducing John Tyler to office as acting 330, 331
PRESIDENT of the Senate authorized to administer oaths. The........288, 294
PRESIDENT pro tempore of the Senate to act as President of the U. S. in case of vacancies in office of President and Vice President. The 293
PRESIDENTS pro tempore, from March 4, 1789, to March 3, 1851. Names and attendance in Senate of the Vice Presidents and.................336–345
PRINTED by order of the two Houses of Congress, from 1789 to 1851. Remarks descriptive of the documents 457, 458, 459
PRIVATEERS being fitted out in the U. S. against foreign powers at peace with the U. S. An act to prevent 296
PUBLICATION of amendments to the Constitution of the U. S. Provision for the 295

RATIFICATION of the Constitution by the States. Dates of the 24
RATIFICATION of first ten amendments of the Constitution by the States. Dates of the 34
RATIFICATION of the eleventh and twelfth amendments of the Constitution, &c. 36
RECORDS of one State in every other State, territory, &c. Authentication of the 290–294
REMARKS or preface to the second edition of this book..................... vii
REMARKS on the propriety of reading and understanding the Constitution xxiii
REMARKS on the authenticity of this edition of the Constitution xlv
REMARKS on the design of the Alphabetical Analysis of the Constitution... 37
REMARKS on the official proceedings, and the causes which led to the adoption and ratification of the Constitution of the U. S. *29

REMARKS on the causes which immediately led to the formation of the Constitution, and on the States having a leading agency in that important event 153
REMARKS on the manner of commencing proceedings of the Government under the Constitution of the U. S. 191
REMARKS on the picture of George Washington, as taken from Houdon's statue at Richmond, Virginia 205
REMARKS relative to the appointment of George Washington to be Lieutenant-General and Commander-in-Chief of the armies of the U. S. July 3, 1798 231
REMARKS in relation to the national mourning and solemnities on the death of George Washington 240
REMARKS relative to the inaugural addresses of the first four Presidents of the U. S. 269
REMARKS introductory to the General Laws, forming a peculiar class of general import inserted herein 287
REMARKS explanatory of the several tables contained in this volume 309
REMARKS on the ratification of the Constitution by the original States, and on the discretionary right and power of Congress to admit "New States" into the Union 408
REMARKS relative to the sources of historical, political, statistical, and other information regarding the Legislative, Executive, and Judicial action of the Government in possession of the public offices at the seat of Government 451
REMARKS descriptive of the contents of the Legislative Journals of the Senate and House of Representatives of the U. S. 456
REMARKS descriptive of the regular documents ordered to be printed by the Senate and House of Representatives, from 1789 to 1851 .... 457, 458, 459
REMARKS in relation to the books procured for the Congress or National Library, and the means employed for a regular increase of their number 472
REMARKS relative to the books in the Department of State 479
REMEDIAL justice in the Courts of the U. S. An act to provide further.... 301
REPORTERS of decisions of the Supreme Court of the U. S. from 1789 to 1851. Names, &c., of the 393
REPORTS of decisions of the Supreme Court of the U. S. from 1789 to 1851. Description of the books of 457
REPRESENTATIVES in Congress elected Speakers, from March 4, 1789, to March 3, 1851, showing the commencement and termination of their service, and the States represented by them 386, 387
REPRESENTATIVES in Congress among the several States, according to the sixth census. An act for the apportionment of. (See *States*.) 300
REPRESENTATIVES in Congress. Provision for dividing States into districts for election of 301
REPRESENTATIVES of the U. S. in Congress assembled, on July 4, 1776. Declaration of Independence by the 195
RESIGNATION or refusal to accept the office of President or Vice President of the U. S. to be delivered into the office of the Secretary of State........ 298

RESIGNATION to Congress, by George Washington, of his commission as Commander-in-Chief of the American army, on December 23, 1783 208
REVENUE from impost duties as recommended by Congress in 1783, was the cause of proceedings which led to the adoption of the Constitution. Report of Committee of Congress of Confederation, showing that the failure of the States to carry out the general system of..........131–139, 140–142–146–150, 151
REVENUE from impost, as provided by resolution of Congress of April 18, 1783. (See *Commerce.*) Resolutions of Congress of February 15, 1786, recommending to the States to empower Congress to carry into effect a general system of 139–141–149–151–153
REVENUE and Tariff laws, &c. Description of books relating to.............. 467
REVOLUTION. Books relating to the history of the American Colonies and the 452
RHODE ISLAND. Chronological statement of the charters and constitutions of 407

SAFE-CONDUCT issued under the authority of the U. S. Penalty for violating a 290
SEAT of Government of the U. S. The District of Columbia established the permanent.. 449
SECRETARIES of the Senate of the U. S., from 1789 to 1851. Table of the names, service, &c., of the.. 385
SECRETARY of the Senate of the U. S. Oaths to be taken by the......22, 288, 289
SENATE of the U. S. directing the purchase of copies of this Book. Resolutions of the v
SENATE of the U. S. Oaths of office to be taken by the members and Secretary of the.. ....22, 288, 289
SENATE, of the Vice Presidents and Presidents pro tempore, from March 4, 1789 to March 3, 1851. Names of and attendance in the................336–345
SENATE of the U. S. Table of the names, service, &c., of the Secretaries of the 385
SENATE of the U. S. Description of the Legislative and Executive Journals and Records of Impeachments of the 455, 456
SENATE of the U. S., from 1789 to 1851. Remarks descriptive of the Documents printed by order of the 457, 458, 459
SENATORS of the U. S. in office, from March 4, 1789 to March 3, 1851, showing their names, commencement and termination of their service, States represented by them, &c., viz.:

CLASSES:—				
	2	3	From New Hampshire	346
1	2	-	From Massachusetts..............................	347
1	2	-	From Rhode Island................................	349
1	-	3	From Connecticut.................................	351
1	-	3	From Vermont.....................................	353
1	-	3	From New York	354
1	2	-	From New Jersey	356
1	-	3	From Pennsylvania...............................	357
1	2	-	From Delaware....................................	359
1	-	3	From Maryland....................................	361

CLASSES:—				
1	2	-	From Virginia	362
-	2	3	From North Carolina	365
-	2	3	From South Carolina	366
-	2	3	From Georgia	368
-	2	3	From Kentucky	370
1	2	-	From Tennessee	371
1	-	3	From Ohio	373
-	2	3	From Louisiana	374
1	-	3	From Indiana	375
1	2	-	From Mississippi	376
-	2	3	From Illinois	377
-	2	3	From Alabama	378
1	2	-	From Maine	379
1	-	3	From Missouri	380
-	2	3	From Arkansas	381
1	2	-	From Michigan	381
1	-	3	From Florida	381
1	2	-	From Texas	381
1	-	3	From Wisconsin	384
-	2	3	From Iowa	384
1	-	3	From California	384
20	20	21		

[When Senators shall take their seats from States that have not yet appointed Senators, they shall be placed by lot in the foregoing classes, but in such a manner as shall keep the classes as nearly equal as may be in numbers. *Vide* resolution of the Senate, May 14, 1789. *The first class expire in* 1851; *the second in* 1847, *and the third in* 1849. *Vide* the Constitution, page 3.]

SESSION of Congress from March 4, 1789 to March 3, 1851. Commencement and termination of, and number of days in, each 336–345

SOUTH CAROLINA, in 1787, appointing deputies to Convention to form the Constitution. Act of 182

SOUTH CAROLINA. Chronological statement of the Charters and Constitutions of 408

SOUTH CAROLINA ceded Western lands to the U. S. August 9, 1787 422

SPEAKER of the House of Representatives shall act as President of the U. S. in case of vacancy, &c. Provisions that the 293

SPEAKER of the House of Representatives authorized to administer oaths. The 288–294

SPEAKERS of the House of Representatives of the U. S., from March 4, 1789 to March 3, 1851, showing the commencement and termination of their service, and States represented by them 386, 387

SPEECHES in the two Houses of Congress from 1789 to 1851. Description of the Books, Newspapers, &c., containing the 459

STATE to receive electoral votes in absence of the President of the Senate,

and to send a special messenger to district judge for electoral votes in case of failure to be received otherwise. The Secretary of ... 293
STATE, in case of vacancies in the office of President and Vice President of the U. S. Duties of the Secretary of ... 293
STATE. A resignation or refusal to accept of the office of President or Vice President to be delivered into the office of the Secretary of ... 293
STATE, regarding the publication of amendments to the Constitution of the U. S. Duties of the Secretary of ... 295
STATE from 1789 to 1851. Names, States, service, &c., of all the Secretaries of ... 395
STATE Department. Description of selection of certain books in the Library of the ... 479
STATE or Territory, &c. An act for the authentication of Acts, Records, and Judicial proceedings of one State or Territory in every other ... 290–294
STATE in certain cases—the proceedings in State Courts in such cases to be null and void. The U. S. Judges empowered to grant the writ of Habeas Corpus, and to discharge the citizens of any foreign State confined in the prison of any ... 301
STATES. Dates of ratification of the Constitution by the ... 24
STATES. Dates of ratification of first ten amendments of the Constitution by the ... 34
STATES. Ratification of the eleventh and twelfth amendments by the ... 36
STATES in providing revenue for the support of the Federal Government, as recommended by Congress on April 18, 1783. Reports of committees showing the failure of the several ... 131–139, 140–142–146–150, 151
STATES that were prominent in the proceedings which immediately led to the adoption of the Constitution of the U. S. Remarks in relation to the ... 153
STATES. Resolution of Congress of the Confederation of May 22, 1782, appointing a committee to represent the financial and commercial difficulties to the several ... 154
STATES to form a Constitution of the U. S. Resolutions of the General Assembly of New York, July 21, 1782, recommending a Convention of the ... 155
STATES to remedy the difficulties. Resolution of the Confederation of Virginia, of January 21, 1786, for a Convention of the ... 160
STATES, at Annapolis, in 1786, recommending the appointment of deputies to form the Constitution. Proceedings of commissioners from several of the ... 161
STATES, for the appointment of deputies to Convention to form the Constitution of the U. S. Acts of the several—viz.: ... 167
Of Virginia, passed October 16, 1786 ... 167
Of New Jersey, passed November 23, 1786 ... 170
Of Pennsylvania, passed December 30, 1786 ... 172
Of North Carolina, passed January 6, 1787 ... 174
Of Delaware, passed February 3, 1787 ... 177
Of Georgia, passed February 10, 1787 ... 179
Of New York, passed February 28, 1787 ... 181
Of South Carolina, passed March 8, 1787 ... 182

Of Massachusetts, passed March 10, 1787 ... 183
Of Connecticut, passed May, 1787 ... 184
Of Maryland, passed May 26, 1787 ... 185
Of New Hampshire, passed June 27, 1787 ... 186
STATES by which it was ratified. Resolution of Congress of September 28, 1787, submitting the Constitution to Conventions of the ... 189
STATES. Oaths to support the Constitution of the U. S. to be taken by the members of the Legislatures and by all Executive and Judicial officers of the several ... 22, 288
STATES, according to the sixth census. Appointment of Representatives among the several—viz. ... 300

N. Hamp.	4	South Carolina	7	Arkansas	1
Mass.	10	Georgia	8	Michigan	3
R. Island	2	Kentucky	10	[*Florida*	1
Connecticut	4	Tennessee	11	*Texas*	2
Vermont	4	Ohio	21	*Iowa*	2
New York	34	Louisiana	4	*Wisconsin*	3
New Jersey	5	Indiana	10	*California*	2
Penn.	24	Mississippi	4	Whole num.	233
Delaware	1	Illinois	7	*Oregon T. del.*	1
Maryland	6	Alabama	7	*Minesota T. del.*	1
Virginia	15	Maine	7	*New Mexico T. del.*	1
North Carolina	9	Missouri	5	*Utah T. del.*	1

STATES into districts for election of Representatives. Provision, by act of 1842, for dividing the ... 301
STATES of the Union. An act to establish a uniform time for holding elections for electors of President and Vice President in all of the ... 302
STATES may by law provide for filling vacancies in the College of Electors. Each of the ... 302
STATES and Territories of the U. S. Chronological statement of the Charters and formation of the Governments of the several ... 405–449
STATES. The time of ratification of the Articles of Confederation by the ... 406
STATES" into the Union. Remarks on the ratification of the Constitution by the original States, and the right and discretionary power of Congress to admit "New ... 408
STATES in possession thereof. Proceedings which led to the cession of the North-Western and Western Territory to the U. S. by the ... 414
STATES to cede their western lands to the U. S. Resolution of Congress of September 6, 1780, recommending to the ... 421
STATES should be disposed of for the common benefit of the U. S., and formed into Republican States. Resolution of Congress of October 10, 1780, that the Lands ceded by the ... 422
STATES by which the western lands were ceded to the U. S., and dates of cession. Names of the ... 422
STATES out of the North-Western Territory. Provision in the Ordinance of July 13, 1787, for forming ... 428
STATISTICAL and other information in the public offices at the seat of Government. Description of the sources of ... 451

STATUE of George Washington by Houdon. Description of the 205-207
SUPREME and other Courts of the U. S. empowered to grant writs of Habeas Corpus, and to discharge foreigners confined in the state prisons in certain cases. The Judges of the 301
SUPREME COURT of the U. S., from 1789 to 1851. Names, States, commencement and termination of service of the Chief and Associate Justices of the 389-392
SUPREME COURT of the U. S., from 1789 to 1851. Names, service, &c. of the Clerks, Reporters of decisions and Marshals of the 393
SUPREME COURT of the U. S., from 1789 to 1851. Description of Books of Reports of decisions of the 466

TABLES contained in this volume. Explanatory remarks on the several .. 309
TABLES of electoral votes for President and Vice President of the U. S., from March 4, 1789, to March 4, 1853 315-332
TABLE of terms of office and length of service in the Senate, of the Vice Presidents and Presidents pro tempore; and of the commencement, and termination, and number of days in each session of Congress, and special session of the Senate, from March 4, 1789, to March 3, 1851 336-345
TABLE of the names, classes, length of service of, and States represented by all the Senators of the U. S., from March 4, 1789, to March 3, 1851.... 346-384
TABLE of the names, places of nativity or residence, time of appointment, and expiration of service of the Secretaries of the Senate of the U. S.... 385
TABLE of the names, time of service of, and States represented by, the Speakers of the House of Representatives of the U. S. 386, 387
TABLE of the names, residence, when appointed, and time of service of, the Clerks of the House of Representatives of the U. S. 388
TANEY, Chief Justice of the Supreme Court of the U. S. Letter of approbation from Roger B. xi
TARIFF Laws, Revenue Laws, &c., description of books relating to 467
TENNESSEE. Chronological statement of the formation of the Government of 413
TERM of office of four years, of President and Vice President, to commence on March 4, &c. The 293
TERRITORIES. An act for the authentication of acts, records, and judicial proceedings of States and 290-294
TERRITORY to the U. S. Proceedings which led to the cession of the North-Western and Western 414
TERRITORY of the U. S. north-west of the river Ohio. An ordinance for the Government of the 423
TEXAS was admitted into the Union. Joint resolution and act of Congress by which 439
TOMPKINS, Vice President of the U. S. First election of Daniel D. 322
TOMPKINS, Vice President of the U. S. Second election of Daniel D. 323
TOMPKINS, Vice President, in Senate of the U. S. Attendance of Daniel D. 340

TRADE and commerce for the U. S. Resolution of Virginia, in 1786, to provide a general system of 160
TREASURY, from 1789 to 1851. Names, States, service, &c., of the Secretaries of the 396
TREATIES of the U. S. Description of the books containing the Laws and 461
TYLER, as Vice President of the U. S. Election of John 329–331
TYLER to office as acting President of the U. S., on the death of W. H. Harrison, President. Proceedings introducing John........ 330, 331
TYLER, as Vice President, in Senate of the U. S. Attendance of John 344

UNION of the people for the government of the U. S. of America. The Constitution adopted for the purpose of forming a more perfect 1
UNION supported by the Constitution. Brief remarks on the importance of the........ 129
UNION hazarded by the inefficiency of the Government under the old Confederation. The existence of the 149–155
UNION. Declaration in resolution of February 15, 1786, that the Congress of the Confederation were denied the means of satisfying engagements for the common benefit of the........ 149
UNION. Declaration by the convention at Annapolis, September 14, 1786, that further provisions were necessary to make the Government adequate to the exigencies of the 164
UNION. Declaration, by resolution of Congress, February 21, 1787, that such alterations were necessary in the articles of Confederation as to render the Federal Constitution adequate to the exigencies of the Government and preservation of the........ 166
UNION is involved our prosperity, felicity, safety, and perhaps our national existence. Opinion of George Washington, that in the consolidation of our 188
UNION. Remarks on the ratification of the Constitution by the original States, and on the right and discretionary power of Congress to admit "New States" into the 408
UTAH Territory. Proceedings in Congress relative to the........ 448

VACANCIES in representation of Congress—how filled........ 3
VACANCIES in seats of Senators in Congress—how filled 3
VACANCIES in offices of the U. S. that may happen during recess of the Senate—how filled 16
VACANCIES in the offices both of President and Vice President. An act declaring the officer who shall act as President in case of........ 291
VACANCIES in the college of electors, &c. Each State may provide by law for filling........ 302
VAN BUREN, as Vice President of the U. S. Election of Martin........ 327
VAN BUREN, as President of the U. S. Election of Martin 328
VAN BUREN, Vice President, in Senate of the U. S. Attendance of Martin 342
VAN BUREN, as Senator of the U. S. Terms of service of Martin 355

VESSELS being fitted out or armed, in whole or in part, in the U. S., against any foreign power with which the U. S. is at peace. An act to prevent.. 296
VERMONT. Chronological statement of the formation of the Government of 412
VICE PRESIDENT of the U. S. from 1789 to 1853. (See *Electoral Votes.*) Electoral votes for 315-332
VICE PRESIDENT of the U. S. by the Senate, he not having a majority of electoral votes. Richard M. Johnson elected 328
VICE PRESIDENTS and Presidents pro tempore from March 4, 1789, to March 3, 1851. Attendance in the Senate of the 336-345
VICE PRESIDENT. Act relative to election of President and Vice President, and declaring what officer shall act as President in case of vacancies in offices of President and 291
VICE PRESIDENT in case of vacancies in those offices. Provision for the election of a President and 293
VICE PRESIDENT to be delivered into the office of Secretary of State. A resignation or refusal to accept the office of 293
VICE PRESIDENT to commence on March 4, &c. Term of office of the... 293
VICE PRESIDENT of the U. S. An act providing compensation to the President and 293
VICE PRESIDENT in all the States. An act to establish a uniform time for elections of electors of President and 302
VICE PRESIDENT, to qualify him as President of the U. S. Oath of John Tyler 331
VIRGINIA, in 1786, appointing Commissioners to meet those of other States at Annapolis, to consider a general and uniform system of trade, &c., and commerce. Resolution of the commonwealth of 160
VIRGINIA, in 1786, for appointing deputies to Convention to revise Federal Constitution. Act of the Commonwealth of 167
VIRGINIA. Chronological statement of the charters and constitutions of ... 408
VIRGINIA, in relation to the North-Western Territory. Recommendation by Congress to 418
VIRGINIA, on March 1, 1784. North-Western Territory ceded to the U. S. by 422
VOTES for President and Vice President of the U. S. Provision of the Constitution relative to electoral 29
VOTES for President and Vice President of the U. S. from 1789 to 1853. Electoral 315-334
VOTES for President and Vice President of the U. S. Enactments of law regarding the electoral 291
VOTES. Compensation to, and penalties of, persons to deliver the electoral 292
VOTES. Compensation to the persons to deliver the electoral 300

WAR, from 1789 to 1847. Names, States, services, &c., of the Secretaries of 398
WASHINGTON to be General and commander-in-chief of the army of the United Colonies, June 17, 1775. Appointment by Congress of the Confederation of George 201

WASHINGTON to Congress, accepting the appointment. Address of George 201
WASHINGTON as General and commander in-chief. Commission to George 202
WASHINGTON, with their lives and fortunes, for the maintenance and preservation of American liberty. Resolution of Congress of June 17, 1775, that they will maintain, assist, and adhere to George 203
WASHINGTON, August 26, 1783, on the termination of the war. Address of the President of Congress to George 203
WASHINGTON to the same. Reply of George 204
WASHINGTON, commander-in-chief. Resolution of Congress of December 20, 1783, that a public audience be given to George 205
WASHINGTON, commander-in-chief. Resolution of Congress of December 20, 1783, that a public entertainment be given to George 205
WASHINGTON of his commission as commander-in-chief of the American army, December 23, 1783. Resignation by George 208
WASHINGTON, in answer to the same. Address of Thomas Mifflin, President of Congress, to George 209
WASHINGTON by Houdon. Remarks and correspondence relating to, and John Marshall's opinion of the accuracy of, the statuary likeness of George 205–207
WASHINGTON appointed a deputy from Virginia to the Convention which formed the Constitution. George 169
WASHINGTON, President of the Convention, in 1787, transmitting the Constitution to the Congress of the Confederation. Letter from George 188
WASHINGTON, President of the U. S. First election of George 315
WASHINGTON, as President of the U. S., dated April 6, 1789. Certificate of the election of George 210
WASHINGTON, as President of the U. S., by the Chancellor of the State of New York, April 30, 1789. The oath of office administered to George 211
WASHINGTON, as President of the U. S. April 30, 1789. Inaugural address of George 211
WASHINGTON, President of the U. S. Second election of George 316
WASHINGTON, President of the U. S., September 17, 1796. Farewell address of George 215
WASHINGTON, as Lieutenant-general and commander-in-chief of the armies of the U. S., July 3, 1798. Appointment of George 231–239
WASHINGTON. Proceedings of the Government and funeral oration of Henry Lee on the death of George 240–247
WASHINGTON. Origin of the words "First in war, first in peace, and first in the hearts of his countrymen," as applicable to George 242
WASHINGTON. Addresses of the Senate and House of Representatives, respectively, to the President of the U. S., and his replies thereto, on the death of George 244, 264
WASHINGTON in the Capitol at the city of Washington, and that his body be deposited under it. Resolution of Congress directing that a marble monument be erected by the U. S. to General 245

WASHINGTON, consenting that the body of her deceased husband, George Washington, be interred under a monument in the city of Washington. Letter from Martha 261
WASHINGTON. Act of Congress extending the privilege of franking letters and packages to Martha 262
WAYNE, an Associate Justice of the Supreme Court of the U. S. Letter of approbation from James M. xii
WEBSTER, Secretary of State of the United States, Letter of approbation from Daniel xxii
WISCONSIN. Chronological statement of the formation of the government of 441
WRIGHT, late Governor of New York, Senator of the U. S., &c. Letter of approbation from Silas xv

THE END.

www.ingramcontent.com/pod-product-compliance
Lightning Source LLC
LaVergne TN
LVHW021230110826
845150LV00002B/290

* 9 7 8 1 4 2 5 5 6 3 0 4 2 *